The Wh
Pub Gu
2005

WHICH? BOOKS

Which? Books is the book publishing arm of Consumers' Association, which was set up in 1957 to improve the standards of goods and services available to the public. Everything Which? publishes aims to help consumers, by giving them the independent information they need to make informed decisions. These publications, known throughout Britain for their quality, integrity and impartiality, have been held in high regard for four decades.

Independence does not come cheap: the guides carry no advertising, and no restaurant or pub can buy an entry in our guides, or treat our inspectors to free meals or accommodation. This policy, and our practice of rigorously re-researching our guides for each edition, helps us to provide our readers with information of a standard and quality that cannot be surpassed.

The Which?
Pub Guide
2005

**Edited by
Andrew Turvil**

CONSUMERS' ASSOCIATION

Which? Books are commissioned and researched by
Consumers' Association and published by Which? Ltd,
2 Marylebone Road, London NW1 4DF
Email address: whichpubguide@which.net

Distributed by The Penguin Group:
Penguin Books Ltd, 80 Strand, London WC2R 0RL

First edition 1993
Second edition 1995
Third edition 1997
Fourth edition 1999
Fifth edition 2001
Sixth edition 2003
Seventh edition 2004

Base mapping © European Map Graphics Ltd 2004
Map information © Which? Ltd 2004

British Library Cataloguing in Publication Data
A catalogue record for this book is available from the British Library

ISBN 0 85202 979 9

For a full list of Which? books, please write to:
Which? Books, Castlemead, Gascoyne Way,
Hertford X, SG14 1LH
or access our web site at www.which.net

Contributing writers and editors: Elizabeth Carter, Bill Evans,
David Kenning, David Mabey, Hugh Morgan, Richard John Wheelwright

Proofreading: Katharine Cowherd, Alison Williams

Cover design by Price Watkins
Cover photograph by James Duncan

Typeset by Saxon Graphics Ltd, Derby
Printed and bound by Clays Ltd, St Ives plc

Contents

How to use the Guide

The Guide is divided into two parts. At the front is the main section, which lists pubs throughout Britain selected for the quality of their food, drink and atmosphere; the selections are based on reports from the general public backed up by independent inspections. Towards the back you will find the 'Round-up' section, which features more than 350 additional pubs which are also well worth a visit. These have been selected less on the basis of the food they offer (some do not offer food at all; in other cases, we have had insufficient feedback to be able to assess cooking), but rather for other qualities that set them apart – perhaps for their superlative beers, hospitality, character, setting, history or other attribute.

Layout
Both parts of the Guide are further divided into the following sections: London (main section only), England, Scotland and Wales. Pubs are listed alphabetically by locality (by name of pub in the London Section); they are put in their true *geographical* location, rather than at their postal address. If a pub is difficult to find, directions are given (after the address and telephone number). It is always worth checking by telephone if you are unsure about the exact location of an out-of-the-way pub.

How to find a pub in a particular area
Go to the maps at the back of the book and choose the general area that you want. Cities, towns and villages where pubs in the Guide are located are marked with a tankard symbol; turn to that locality in the appropriate section of the book, where you will find details of the pub (or pubs) there.

Symbols and awards
✿ ✿ denotes a pub where the quality of the bar food is comparable to that of a 'serious' restaurant – i.e. ingredients are consistently first-class and imagination and style are hallmarks of the kitchen. See page 9 for a list of these pubs.

✿ signifies that the pub offers above-average bar food that shows ambition and good ideas, or simple pub fare prepared particularly well. See pages 10–11 for list.

NEW ENTRY appears after a pub's name if it did not feature in the last edition as a main entry. See pages 12–13 for list.

🍺 denotes a pub serving exceptional draught beers. See pages 472–3 for list.

🍷 indicates a pub serving better-than-average wines, imaginatively chosen and decently priced, with a good selection (usually six or more) by the glass. See pages 474–5 for list.

▲ indicates a pub which offers accommodation.

 'Flashes' These highlight a particular point of interest in selected main entries. For this edition we feature five: 'fish', 'waterside', 'vegetarian', 'brew pub' and 'Thai'.

Sample dishes

These are listed at the end of each main entry and are examples of typical dishes from the menu. Prices are based on figures provided by the pub licensee; in most cases, prices have been rounded up to the nearest 25 pence. Note that items listed may not always be available (particularly if they are 'specials').

Food and drink

Details of bar food mentioned in the entries are based on all the feedback we have received since the last edition of the Guide was published, including official inspections, notes from readers, and information provided by the licensees. Many pubs vary their menus from day to day, so specific items may no longer be in the kitchen's repertoire. If dishes are available in a separate restaurant and not in the bar, we mention that in the entry. Similarly, the range of draught beers may differ from time to time, especially if a pub has guest brews. Any real ciders are also listed. Information about wine is geared to what is generally available in the bar; in some pubs with a separate restaurant, you may need to request to see the full wine list (most pubs will oblige). The number of wines available by the glass is usually given in the text.

'Details'

The information given in the section at the end of each entry has been supplied by the pub and may be subject to change. If you are making a special journey, it is always worthwhile phoning beforehand to check opening and bar food times, and any other details that are important to you, such as restrictions on children or dogs, wheelchair access, the availability of no-smoking areas, etc.

- **Licensee:** the current licensee is given, followed by the name of the pub's owner (such as a brewery or pub group) in brackets; 'freehouse' is given if that is the case.
- **'Open' times:** these are the pub's full licensing hours. (Sunday hours are given separately if different.) Opening times may vary, especially in pubs that rely heavily on seasonal trade; days and times when a pub is closed are also listed.
- **Bar food (and restaurant) times:** these denote when food is served in the bar (and restaurant, if there is one).
- **Children:** often children are allowed in a family room or eating area of a pub, but not in the main bar area. Any restrictions on children are listed.
- **Car park:** if a pub has its own car park, this is noted.
- **Wheelchair access:** this means that the proprietor has confirmed that the entrance to the bar/dining-room is at least 80cm wide and passages at least 120cm across – the Royal Association for Disability and Rehabilitation (RADAR) recommendations. If 'also WC' is given, it means that the proprietor has told us that the toilet facilities are suitable for disabled people.
- **Garden/patio:** this is noted for pubs with outside seating areas. If a pub has a children's play area or another interesting feature – e.g. a boules pitch – this is mentioned in the text.
- **Smoking:** restrictions on smoking or special areas designated for non-smokers are noted.
- **Music:** if background or live music is ever played, or if a pub has a jukebox, this is stated.

○ Dogs: any restrictions on dogs *inside* the pub are listed. Most pubs will allow dogs in their gardens. Guide dogs are normally exempt from restrictions, although it is best to check beforehand if you have special requirements.

○ Cards: major credit and debit cards are listed if a pub accepts these as a means of payment. If a pub does not accept cards, we note this.

○ Accommodation: if a pub offers overnight accommodation, the number of bedrooms and a range of B&B prices – from the lowest you can expect to pay for a single room (or single occupancy of a twin/double) to the most you are likely to pay for a twin/double – are listed. Pub bedrooms have not been officially inspected for this guide.

Report forms

At the very back of the book are report forms which you may use to recount your pub-going experiences. The address is FREEPOST, so no stamp is necessary (full details are on the report forms; or email us at *whichpubguide@which.net*). Because *The Which? Pub Guide*, like its sister publication *The Good Food Guide*, relies to a great extent on unsolicited feedback from readers, your comments are invaluable to us and will form a major part of our research when we prepare future editions.

The top-rated pubs

 indicates a pub where the quality of the bar food is comparable to that of a serious restaurant – i.e. ingredients are consistently first-class, and imagination and skill are hallmarks of the kitchen.

LONDON
Anchor & Hope, SE1
Admiral Codrington, SW3
Cow Dining Room, W2

ENGLAND
Cambridgeshire
Old Bridge Hotel, Huntingdon
Pheasant Inn, Keyston
Three Horseshoes, Madingley

Cumbria
Punch Bowl Inn, Crosthwaite

Devon
Dartmoor Inn, Lydford

Dorset
Museum Inn, Farnham

East Sussex
Jolly Sportsman, East Chiltington

Gloucestershire
Bell at Sapperton, Sapperton
Falcon Inn, Poulton

Greater Manchester
White Hart, Lydgate

Hampshire
Greyhound, Stockbridge

Herefordshire
Lough Pool Inn, Sellack
Stagg Inn, Titley

Kent
Sportsman, Whitstable
White Horse, Bridge

Lancashire
Feilden's Arms, Mellor Brook

North Yorkshire
Angel Inn, Hetton
Blue Lion, East Witton
Star Inn, Harome

Oxfordshire
Boar's Head, Ardington
Sir Charles Napier, Chinnor

Shropshire
Sun Inn, Marton
Waterdine, Llanfair Waterdine

Wiltshire
Angel Inn, Upton Scudamore
Vine Tree, Norton

WALES
Monmouthshire
The Foxhunter, Nant-y-derry

☘ indicates a pub offering distinctly above-average bar food that shows ambition and good ideas, or simple pub dishes prepared particularly well.

LONDON
Anglesea Arms, W6
Cumberland Arms, W14
Drapers Arms, N1
Eagle, EC1
Ealing Park Tavern, W5
Fox Dining Room, EC2
Grand Union, W9
Havelock Tavern, W14
The House, N1
Lansdowne, NW1
St Johns, N19
Salisbury Tavern, SW6
Salisbury Pub and Dining Room, NW6
Sutton Arms, EC1
White Horse, SW6
William IV, NW10

ENGLAND
Bath & N.E. Somerset
Hop Pole, Bath

Berkshire
Dundas Arms, Kintbury
George & Dragon, Swallowfield
Red House, Marsh Benham
Royal Oak, Yattendon

Buckinghamshire
Crooked Billet, Newton Longville
Royal Oak, Bovingdon Green

Cambridgeshire
Anchor Inn, Sutton Gault

Co Durham
The County, Aycliffe
Oak Tree Inn, Hutton Magna
Rose and Crown, Romaldkirk

Cornwall
Rising Sun, St Mawes
Trengilly Wartha Inn, Constantine

Cumbria
Bay Horse Hotel, Ulverston
Drunken Duck Inn, Ambleside
Queens Head Hotel, Troutbeck

Derbyshire
Red Lion, Hognaston
Red Lion Inn, Hollington

Devon
Arundell Arms, Lifton
Drewe Arms, Broadhembury
Jack in the Green, Rockbeare
Kings Arms, Strete

Nobody Inn, Doddiscombsleigh
Peter Tavy Inn, Peter Tavy
White Hart, Dartington

Dorset
Fox Inn, Corscombe

East Riding of Yorkshire
Wellington Inn, Lund

East Sussex
Best Beech Inn, Wadhurst
Curlew, Bodiam
Griffin Inn, Fletching

Essex
Bell Inn, Horndon on the Hill
Sun Inn, Dedham
White Hart, Great Yeldham

Gloucestershire
Churchill Arms, Paxford
Fox Inn, Lower Oddington
Kings Arms, Stow-on-the-Wold
Old Passage Inn, Arlingham
Trouble House, Tetbury
Village Pub, Barnsley
White Horse, Frampton Mansell
Yew Tree, Clifford's Mesne

Hampshire
East End Arms, East End
Hampshire Arms, Crondall
Peat Spade, Longstock
Red House Inn, Whitchurch
Three Tuns, Romsey
Wykeham Arms, Winchester

Herefordshire
Roebuck Inn, Brimfield
Three Crowns Inn, Ullingswick

Isle of Wight
Seaview Hotel, Seaview

Kent
Dove, Dargate
Froggies at the Timber Batts, Bodsham
Green Cross Inn, Goudhurst
Spotted Dog Inn, Smart's Hill
Three Chimneys, Biddenden

Lancashire
Bay Horse Inn, Forton
Eagle & Child, Bispham Green
Mulberry Tree, Wrightington
Spread Eagle, Sawley

Leicestershire
Fox & Hounds, Knossington
Red Lion, Stathern

Lincolnshire
Wig & Mitre, Lincoln

Norfolk
Hoste Arms, Burnham Market
Three Horseshoes,
    Warham All Saints
White Horse, Brancaster Staithe
Wildebeest Arms, Stoke Holy Cross

North Lincolnshire
George, Winterton

North Yorkshire
Appletree, Marton
Crab & Lobster, Asenby
Durham Ox, Crayke
Fox and Hounds, Sinnington
Galphay Arms, Galphay
General Tarleton, Ferrensby
Golden Lion, Osmotherley
Sandpiper Inn, Leyburn
Sportsman's Arms,
    Wath-in-Nidderdale

Northamptonshire
Falcon Inn, Fotheringhay
Snooty Fox, Lowick

Northumberland
Cook and Barker Inn,
    Newton-on-the-Moor
Feathers Inn, Hedley on the Hill
General Havelock Inn, Haydon Bridge
Queens Head Inn, Great Whittington

Nottinghamshire
Caunton Beck, Caunton
Martins Arms, Colston Bassett

Oxfordshire
Fox & Hounds, Christmas Common
Lamb at Buckland, Buckland
Trout at Tadpole Bridge, Tadpole Bridge
White Hart, Wytham

Rutland
Finch's Arms, Upper Hambleton
Olive Branch, Clipsham

Shropshire
Malthouse, Ironbridge

Somerset
Three Horseshoes, Batcombe

Suffolk
Anchor Inn, Nayland
Cornwallis, Brome
St Peter's Hall and Brewery,
    St Peter South Elmham

Swan Inn, Monks Eleigh

Warwickshire
Inn at Farnborough, Farnborough
Kings Head, Aston Cantlow

West Sussex
King's Arms, Fernhurst
Lickfold Inn, Lickfold
Royal Oak, East Levant

West Yorkshire
Bay Horse, Kirk Deighton
Fleece, Addingham
Millbank, Millbank
Ring O' Bells, Thornton
Shibden Mill Inn, Halifax
Three Acres Inn, Roydhouse
Travellers Rest, Sowerby

Wiltshire
Angel Inn, Hindon
Forester, Donhead St Andrew
George & Dragon, Rowde
George Hotel, Codford
Linnet, Great Hinton
Pear Tree Inn, Whitley

Worcestershire
Bell and Cross, Holy Cross
Walter de Cantelupe Inn, Kempsey

SCOTLAND
Argyll & Bute
Crinan Hotel, Crinan

Glasgow
Ubiquitous Chip, Glasgow

WALES
Conwy
Queen's Head, Glanwydden

Denbighshire
White Horse Inn, Hendrerwydd

Gwynedd
Penhelig Arms Hotel, Aberdovey

Isle of Anglesey
Ye Olde Bulls Head Inn, Beaumaris

Monmouthshire
Bell at Skenfrith, Skenfrith
Clytha Arms, Clytha

Powys
Bear Hotel, Crickhowell
Felin Fach Griffin, Felinfach
Nantyffin Cider Mill Inn, Crickhowell
Wynnstay Hotel, Machynlleth

New entries

The following pubs are new to the main section of this edition, although some may have appeared in the Round-up section in the last edition.

LONDON
Alma, SW18
Anchor & Hope, SE1
Astons, NW10
Bedford, SW12
Bridge Pub and Dining Room, SW13
Coach & Horses, EC1
Cumberland Arms, W14
Earl Spencer, SW18
Endurance, W1
Gunmakers, EC1
Junction Tavern, NW5
Magdala, NW3
Queens, NW1
Seven Stars, WC2
Ship Inn, SW18
The Social, N1
Victoria, SW14

ENGLAND
Bedfordshire
Hare & Hounds, Old Warden

Berkshire
Royal Oak, Paley Street

Buckinghamshire
Royal Oak, Bovingdon Green
Woolpack, Stoke Mandeville

Cheshire
Hanging Gate, Higher Sutton
Legh Arms, Prestbury
Ship Inn, Wincle

Co Durham
Oak Tree Inn, Hutton Magna

Cornwall
Falcon Inn, St Mawgan
Mill House Inn, Trebarwith
Old Inn, St Breward
Springer Spaniel, Treburley

Cumbria
Pheasant, Bassenthwaite Lake
Yanwath Gate Inn, Yanwath

Derbyshire
Barrel, Bretton

Devon
Elizabethan Inn, Luton
Fox and Goose, Parracombe

Kings Arms, Strete
Rising Sun, Woodland
White Hart, Dartington

Dorset
Acorn Inn, Evershot
Brace of Pheasants, Plush
West Bay, West Bay

East Sussex
Basketmakers Arms, Brighton
Curlew, Bodiam
Greys, Brighton

Essex
Prince of Wales, Stow Maries
Sun Inn, Dedham

Gloucestershire
Beehive, Cheltenham
Eight Bells, Chipping Campden
Hare & Hounds, Foss Cross
Halfway Inn, Box
New Inn, Coln St Aldwyns

Greater Manchester
The Bridge, Manchester
Britons Protection Hotel, Manchester
Sinclair's, Manchester

Hampshire
American Bar, Portsmouth
Bush Inn, Ovington
Five Bells, Nether Wallop
Yew Tree, Highclere

Herefordshire
Verzons Country Inn, Trumpet

Isles of Scilly
Hell Bay Hotel, Bryher

Kent
Chapter Arms, Chartham Hatch
Froggies at the Timber Batts, Bodsham
Spotted Dog Inn, Smart's Hill
Swan on the Green, West Peckham
Tiger, Stowting
The Unicorn, Bekesbourne

Lancashire
Black Bull Inn, Chatburn
Black Bull, Rimington

Leicestershire
Fox & Hounds, Knossington

Lincolnshire
Chequers, Woolsthorpe
Farmers Arms, Welton Hill

Merseyside
The Monro, Liverpool

Norfolk
Crown, Colkirk
Lord Nelson, Burnham Thorpe
Wig and Pen, Norwich

North Yorkshire
Buck Inn, Buckden
Old Bell Tavern, Harrogate

Northamptonshire
Kings Arms, Farthingstone
Snooty Fox, Lowick
Star, Sulgrave

Northumberland
Lord Crewe Arms, Blanchland
Pheasant, Stannersburn

Nottinghamshire
Bell Inn, Nottingham
Waggon & Horses, Halam

Oxfordshire
Fleece, Witney
Fox & Hounds, Christmas Common
George & Dragon, Shutford

Rutland
Fox and Hounds, Exton

Somerset
Carew Arms, Crowcombe
Helyar Arms, East Coker
Rising Sun, West Bagborough

Staffordshire
Boat, Lichfield
Goats Head, Abbots Bromley

Suffolk
Anchor Inn, Nayland
St Peter's Hall and Brewery,
   St Peter South Elmham

Surrey
Hare & Hounds, Lingfield
Plough, Blackbrook
Running Horses, Mickleham
Withies Inn, Compton

Warwickshire
Inn at Farnborough, Farnborough
One Elm, Stratford-upon-Avon

West Sussex
Green Man, Partridge Green
Horse & Groom, East Ashling
Keeper's Arms, Trotton
White Horse Inn, Chilgrove

West Yorkshire
Bay Horse, Kirk Deighton
Boat, Allerton Bywater
King's Arms, South Crosland
Pack Horse Inn, Widdop

Wiltshire
Forester, Donhead St Andrew
George Hotel, Codford
Horseshoe Inn, Ebbesbourne Wake

Worcestershire
Admiral Rodney Inn, Berrow Green

SCOTLAND
Highland
Plockton Hotel, Plockton

Midlothian
Roslin Glen Hotel, Roslin

Stirling
Lade Inn, Kilmahog

WALES
Cardiff
Waterguard, Cardiff
Y Mochyn Du, Cardiff

Carmarthenshire
Brunant Arms, Caio

Denbighshire
Corn Mill, Llangollen
Druid Inn, Llanferres
White Horse Inn, Hendrerwydd

Monmouthshire
Raglan Arms, Llandenny

Pembrokeshire
Old Kings Arms Hotel, Pembroke
Swan Inn, Little Haven

Introduction

This guidebook will not change your life, but it may well lead you to some places that will enrich it. The following pages will reveal some truly exceptional pubs, many in beautiful locations, and all representing the very best that Britain has to offer.

For centuries the public house has been a part of British life, and at the beginning of the twenty-first century its role in society is still causing ructions. Over the past ten years or so the atmosphere has changed in towns and cities, and one of the main culprits is the rise of the super-pub. These vast places dominate the high streets and attract hordes of people, creating the social problems that have been so well documented. But that is only one side of the licensed-trade story, and the one that usually captures the headlines.

The other, far more positive side is represented by the examples listed in this guide. Our readers have told us about their favourite pubs, ones that are worth travelling to for high standards of hospitality and, most importantly of all, good drinking and eating. We have sent our researchers along to these recommended pubs, and the results of their endeavours are the 1,000 establishments featured in this guide.

There are some 60,000 pubs in the UK: about one for every thousand of the population. Plenty to go around then; but we've included only those that stand out from the crowd. According to the British Beer & Pub Association, 15 million people drink in a pub at least once a week, and I'm guessing that – seeing as you've got this guide in your hand – you're one of them.

Secret formula

Many large pub companies spend a lot of time and money on research to find the 'formula' that will create the ideal environment, the perfect look, the whatever it is that will draw in the customers: perhaps a bit of Irish charm; the expansion of the food operation; or resources thrown into going 'upmarket'. There is no end to the potential marketing of the pub. Some of the results of all these marketing meetings can look quite passable at first glance; but in the majority of cases the dull range of big brand beers, the loud music and, more often than not, staff who don't give a hoot soon give the game away.

Nevertheless the large pub-owning companies dominate the market and are likely to continue doing so. The big difference in recent years is that many of them have gone for diversification, adding to their mass-market boozing pubs a second string to their bows: more food-orientated pubs, where the atmosphere is a little more sedate and where women are more likely than men to be targeted as customers. Food pubs of this ilk could seem a positive antidote to the large drinking dens pushing cheap lager and Alco-pops, but they remain formulaic and, as in the case of fast-food restaurants, you know what to expect: not much.

So, what is the secret formula – the one that makes a pub stand out from the crowd?

Location isn't everything, but …
You can't move bricks and mortars (well, not easily), so we try not to be too harsh on pubs for not having a fantastic setting. For those with less salubrious locations, what makes all the difference, of course, is the quality of what they offer once the customer has come through the door. Take the Endurance (page 30) in the heart of London's Soho: from the outside, this pub in a dull 1960s block seems not to warrant a second glance from passers-by busying through the market on Berwick Street; inside, the story is quite different. It manages to retain the feel of a 'proper' pub, the food is of a high standard, and, to boot, there are a couple of real ales on draught.

But for pubs blessed with a great location, well, that is a huge natural advantage that goes a long way to pulling in customers. Too bad, however, that so many 'blow it': our researchers time after time have told us stories about having pitched up at beautiful pubs only to find shabby interiors, poor food and an absence of enthusiasm from the staff. That is especially galling when the journey there involved negotiating miles and miles of narrow country lanes. Fortunately, they also found many excellent examples of fine pubs that make the most of their beautiful locations: for example, the Byre Inn at Brig o'Turk (page 358), with its breathtaking views over the Trossachs, a stream and the hills acting as the perfect backdrop for the pretty garden where on fine days you can enjoy a drop of real ale and a bite to eat.

Other publicans have worked hard to create exceptional gardens: for example, the Rose & Crown in Perry Green, Kent (page 261). Here, a good play area provides entertainment (and distraction) for children while adults can indulge in the excellent range of real ales and the good honest bar food. There are many pubs in this guide that are very special as far as location is concerned – whether being part of a 1,000-acre estate incorporating 28 acres of amazing gardens (White Hart, Dartington, Devon; p134), or having distant views to Snowdonia (Groes Inn, Tyn-y-Groes, Conwy; p394).

A great location and a fantastic view, though wonderful assets, are not enough on their own to make a pub worth the effort to get to. Those that back up what nature has provided with good beer, decent wines and carefully prepared fresh food will be the ones that thrive – and give the greatest enjoyment to their customers.

Food: the proof is in the sourcing
I won't be telling you anything new by saying that pub food has had a bad reputation. Passing by in the car or on foot we see good food promised here, there and everywhere on large, glossy signs, or chalked on blackboards on the

doorstep: 'home-made', they hail, or 'good value'. The results are often far from convincing: yes, cheap perhaps but certainly not value for money when you bring quality into the equation.

The news is not all bad: in this edition we have awarded 173 food awards this year, which proves there are good food pubs out there if you know where to look. The term 'gastro-pub' is usually used by pub operators and journalists to describe pubs, often at the smarter end of the market, that really do put the focus on food. The best of these places still operate as pubs, and we have a fair share of them in this guide. The same attention to detail is required whether a pub is providing simple, straightforward food or more complicated, fancy stuff. The relaxed atmosphere in pubs is well suited to simple food, but the quality of the bread and cheese in a ploughman's is just as important as that of the beef in a posh pot-au-feu. More and more publicans are becoming passionate about using high-quality ingredients, whether organic, local, or the best they can find from further afield. The case for local produce is well founded – the benefits include freshness and seasonality – and an increasing number of pubs are beginning to appreciate that there are plenty of potential customers out there wanting to eat 'good stuff', not just commercially produced steak-and-kidney pie.

Pubs like the Boar's Head in Ardington, Oxfordshire (page 53) keep bar food simple and quality high with one-plate dishes like Toulouse sausage cassoulet, or lunchtime baguettes, alongside a more ambitious restaurant menu. The customer can have a fine, straightforward bar meal, or a smarter restaurant experience; there's also a dartboard in the corner and real ales at the pumps. In London the Anchor & Hope (page 20) is so successful in its food operation that eaters are likely to outnumber drinkers, but eating there is still a pub experience – unpretentious and relaxed – where the menu changes twice a day and table bookings are not taken.

A rosette – or double-rosette for exceptional cooking – appears in the entries of pubs with food awards: see the lists on pages 9–11. If you visit one of these, you can expect a pub that shows food the respect it deserves, buys quality produce and employs people who know how to cook it with care and skill. The numbers of fine food pubs are growing, but nationally these places still remain far too rare.

No place for stuffiness

Whether you're in a smart dining pub or a village local, the relative informality and lack of stuffiness is always part of the appeal. We expect to feel relaxed in a pub. The attitude of the staff, especially the head honcho, helps set the tone. The right balance of good hospitality, efficient service and friendliness is not always easy to maintain, and staffing problems are a genuine headache for the industry. So, a key to success is the licensee: the best are dedicated, demand high standards in all areas – and it helps if they enjoy what they do.

The atmosphere of any pub is generated by the customers. The large super-pubs attract a young, lively crowd with the lure of drink promotions, 'happy hours' and loud music. Not every city pub has to go down this route, and many offer food and eschew gimmicks. Pubs like the Old Harkers Arms in Chester (page 107) – owned by Brunning & Price pub company – offer an alternative to the high street chains, with good food and an excellent range of regional beers. In Liverpool the architecturally stunning Philharmonic (page 220) keeps food very simple, makes a feature of its range of real ales, and is lively but friendly.

Some dining pubs have, in the opinion of our readers and researchers, stepped over the line that defines them as pubs rather than restaurants. A few of the pubs listed in the guide in fact are positively skirting the edges of qualification for a pub guide, so do let us know if you think we should reconsider any current entries for inclusion next year. A pub should welcome customers wanting nothing more than a drink. Simple as that. Many have chosen to position themselves more as restaurants, but have maintained an informal atmosphere and seem willing to welcome drinkers, so we've kept the best of those in the guide. Drinkers often have more room to extend their elbows in the summer months when pub gardens increase the available space.

Drink and be merry

There are 121 pubs with beer awards in this edition, and 105 serve wine that is well above average in terms of quality and value for money. To impress our researchers, a pub has to offer a good choice of drinks. We keep banging on about real ale because that is the heart and soul of every pub. It is a fresh, living product that needs some looking after: real ale continues fermenting and maturing in the cask, unlike keg beers, which need to be revitalised by carbon dioxide gas when served to the customer. Keg beer and real ale have as much in common as a frozen lasagne made in a factory on an industrial estate has to a linguine alle vongole made by an Italian grandmother for her family.

Pubs like the Peter Tavy Inn in Peter Tavy (page 262) certainly know the difference and they intelligently look close by for interesting local beers from Devon: on tap you just might find Princetown's Jail Ale, or something called Tavy Tipple from nearby Blackawton. This gives the visitor a chance to get a real taste of the local area. Unhappily for their customers, far too many pubs look no further than the big brewers when such wonderful choice is out there. See our list of top beer pubs on page 472.

Wine in pubs was for decades considered a joke, and in many establishments today the range and quality are still lamentable. This continues even though, as a nation, our proven interest in wine (just look at those supermarket shelves) is resulting in some serious attention being paid to the grape. The Blue Ball in Triscombe (page 323) shows the way with a wine list of some 100 well-chosen wines, with prices that won't scare the horses, and a selection of eight by the glass for when a bottle is too much. And there is the Crooked Billet in Newton Longville, Buckinghamshire, where every one of the 300 or so wines on the list is available by the glass. See our list of top wine pubs on page 474.

The choice of non-alcoholic drinks (stay with me) is more often than not bitterly disappointing. Most of us have to take turn driving sometimes, and the range of soft drinks on offer is usually very predictable. Fresh juices are a rarity, home-made lemonade or ginger beer equally illusive. Even high-quality bought-in products are hard to find. Children have to choose from the usual suspects of sweet and sugary stuff – unless you go for the diet version of course. Let's see some imagination in this area, with freshly squeezed fruit juices, smoothies perhaps, or real lemonade and ginger beer.

So, the very best pubs have relaxed and inviting atmospheres, and offer something good by way of food and drink. That's what we have looked for when putting together the guide, and that's what you can expect to discover in the pages that follow. Some pubs have it all – the Star in Harome (page 177), for example – but every entry is worth a visit on its own merits, even though every entry can't excel equally in all areas. And the secret formula, by the way, is…avoid formulas.

Reports, please

I would like to thank all the readers who took the time to let us know about their experiences in pubs, and I hope that many of you will feel inspired to help us with the next edition. There are forms at the back of the book and an email address (*whichpubguide@which.net*), so please make use of them and let us know what you think of British pubs. We're on the look-out for great places in towns, cities, villages or in the middle of nowhere. There are many pubs in the UK that are failing to deliver acceptable standards of food, drink and hospitality, and it is vital we support those getting it right. The pub, potentially, has a great future as the guardian of relaxed and informal hospitality in this country, where people can gather to eat a meal with friends or family, or simply while away a few hours over a drink. There will always be many sides to the British pub, and those featured in this guide represent the very best.

Andrew Turvil
Editor

Admiral Codrington 🏆🏆

map 12

17 Mossop Street, SW3 2LY   TEL: (020) 7581 0005

Affectionately known as 'the Cod', this unassuming Victorian pub in a residential Chelsea backwater is still very much a locals' hangout, although it has a few additional aces up its sleeve. The pubby bar upfront – with banquettes and sofas around panelled walls – delivers a no-nonsense lunchtime menu running from eggs florentine and grilled chicken Caesar salad to ribeye burger with chips. On handpump are Wells Bombardier Premium Bitter and Old Speckled Hen. Out back, a long, bright and cheerful restaurant – with a sliding glass roof, some booth seating and apt piscatorial prints – cranks things up a culinary gear. True to its name, fish is a speciality, with potted shrimps, and crispy-fried squid with chilli dressing among the starters, and main courses ranging from organic salmon and smoked haddock fishcakes with Savoy cabbage and tomato butter to chargrilled tuna with aubergine caviar and red pepper vinaigrette. Meat eaters are not neglected, with full-blooded ideas such as braised belly pork with white bean purée and pancetta jus. As a finale, there are straightforward desserts including, perhaps, a trio of crème brûlées, or Baileys cheesecake. On Sundays, you can tuck into a full English breakfast, brunch or roast beef with Yorkshire pudding. Virtually every bottle on the list of around 30 wines is available by the glass from £3 (£12 a bottle), champagne drinkers are well served, and connoisseurs might want to dip into the fine wine list. SAMPLE DISHES: wild mushroom tartlet with a purée of baby shallots £6.75; roast breast of corn-fed chicken with home-made herb gnocchi £13; sticky toffee pudding with honeycomb ice cream £5.25.

Licensee Michael Bailey (Longshot plc)
Open 11.30 to 11, Sun 12 to 10.30; bar food Mon to Fri 12 to 2.30, Sat 11 to 3.30, Sun 12 to 4.30,
restaurant Mon to Fri 12 to 2.30, 7 to 11, Sat 11 to 3.30, 7 to 11, Sun 12 to 4.30, 7 to 10; closed 24 to 26 Dec
Details Children welcome   Wheelchair access (also WC)   Garden   Background music   No dogs   Amex,
Delta, MasterCard, Switch, Visa

Albert

map 12

11 Princess Road, NW1 8JR   TEL: (020) 7722 1886

Still undeniably recognisable as a pub, the food-orientated Albert, not far from London Zoo, maintains its all-round appeal to drinkers as well as eaters. The décor in the main bar features bare floorboards, prints of Prince Albert on the walls, and fittings including some 1950s dining room furniture and traditional cast-iron-framed tables. Towards the rear is a no-smoking conservatory extension and beyond that a leafy patio. The printed menu changes monthly, and there are usually some blackboard specials too. Winter starters might include parsnip and apple soup, or crispy-fried 'bashed' potatoes, while main courses take in hearty dishes like roast loin of pork with all the trimmings, smoked haddock florentine, and baked butternut squash filled with lemon and sage risotto. Ploughman's and burgers also feature, while desserts could range from white chocolate and macadamia nut brownie to Italian orange cake. Wells Bombardier Premium Bitter, Fuller's London Pride, and Greene King IPA are on handpump; there are also some Continental alternatives such as Hoegaarden and Pilsner Urquell. Eight wines are available by the glass from a short, good-value list of 15 bottles; prices start at £10.95. SAMPLE DISHES: smoked salmon pâté with melba toast £5.25; lamb rump with boulangère potatoes, vegetables and rosemary jus £11; apple pie with custard £4.25.

Licensees A.E.L. and M.L. Campbell (Simply Pubs)
Open 11 to 11, Sun 12 to 10.30; bar food Mon to Fri 12 to 2.30 (3 Fri), 6.30 to 10, Sat 12 to 10, Sun 12 to 9.30; open 12 to 2 25 Dec
Details Children welcome   Wheelchair access (not WC)   Patio   No smoking in conservatory   Background music   Dogs welcome on a lead   Delta, MasterCard, Switch, Visa

Alma   NEW ENTRY   map 3

499 Old York Road, SW18 1TF   TEL: (020) 8870 2537
WEBSITE: www.thealma.co.uk

'A self-confident institution that keeps itself up to date without being swayed by fashion' is how a reporter summed up this 'delightful' Art Nouveau-style pub in Wandsworth. The elegantly curved, green-tiled exterior is topped by a domed garret, and there's plenty of pavement space for summertime drinking. Inside is a large open-plan area with a bright, uncluttered feel, a colour scheme of olive green and orange, and mirrors embossed with Japanese-inspired images. Sit at wooden or marble-topped tables in the bar or make your way to the restaurant: one menu is served throughout. The repertoire is a mix of modern-sounding dishes and 'traditional boys' food', ranging from pumpkin and purple basil risotto balls with 'gooey' Taleggio, and sea bass on fennel mash with asparagus and crab hollandaise, to steak and frites with Heinz and HP sauces or a mighty helping of organic lamb's liver with crunchy Savoy cabbage, mash and onion gravy. If you have room, finish off with, say, damson and amaretti crumble or raspberry fool with red berries. Real ales are from the nearby Young's brewery, and the pub has a well-spread list of around two dozen wines including ten by the glass (£2.70 to £4). Charles Gotto also runs the Ship Inn (see entry). SAMPLE DISHES: caramelised fig and pancetta salad with warm Roquefort dressing £4.50; game pie with roasted winter vegetables £10.50; creamy rice pudding with mixed berry jam £4.

Licensee Charles Gotto (Young's)
Open 11 to 11, Sun 12 to 10.30; bar food and restaurant 12 to 4, 6 to 10.30
Details Children welcome in eating areas   Wheelchair access (also WC)   No music   Dogs welcome on a lead   Amex, MasterCard, Switch, Visa

Anchor & Hope ♥ ♥   NEW ENTRY   map 12

36 The Cut, SE1 8LP   TEL: (020) 7928 9898

'This is a kitchen that knows its business,' concluded an inspector after visiting this classic pub at the east end of The Cut close to cultural hot spots like the Young Vic, the South Bank and Tate Modern. It may seem more of a restaurant than a watering hole, although drinkers can still quaff pints of Wells Bombardier Premium Bitter and Eagle IPA or Luscombe Valley cider in the comfortable and homely 1960s-style bar, with its bare-boarded floor, deep-reddish-brown walls and ceiling, heavy cotton curtains, and big windows. Overall, it feels 'warm and uncluttered, without a trace of nostalgia'. The menu changes twice daily, and it reads like a litany of pub dishes for the twenty-first century, with daring ideas and uncompromising flavours very much the hallmarks of the cooking. You might find beetroot and horseradish salad, and duck hearts on toast alongside more substantial things like ham in hay with carrots and parsley sauce, or a mighty whole lamb neck hotpot for four or five people to share. Elsewhere, oxtail stew with mashed potato has been exactly that, no more, no less: 'utterly unctuous...gutsy, honest meat cookery of the highest order.' The balance is tilted towards carnivorous tastes, but others might like to consider smoked herring with lentils, salt-cod with borlotti beans and aïoli, or chicory tart with morels and Parmesan. Bread is 'outstanding', while side orders are likely to include duck fat potato cake, kale, lentils and so on. Desserts could be as simple as rhubarb with cream and shortbread or saffron ice cream, although a slab of rich chocolate cake ('tall, dark and handsome') dazzled one recipient with its deep, elemental flavours. The wine list sticks to the best sort of pub formula with restrained pricing and a dozen or so by the glass or small carafe from a flavoursome but unflashy range. And as befits a pub, the Anchor & Hope doesn't accept bookings. SAMPLE DISHES: potato soup and foie gras £8; calf's liver and semolina gnocchi £13; pear and almond tart £5.

Licensees Robert Shaw, Harry Lester and Jonathon Jones (Wells)
Open *Mon 5 to 11, Tue to Sat 11 to 11; bar food and restaurant Mon 6 to 10.30, Tue to Sat 12 to 2.30, 6 to 10.30*
Details *Children welcome   Wheelchair access (also WC)   Patio   Background music   Dogs welcome   Delta, MasterCard, Switch, Visa*

Anglesea Arms 🍴 🍷 map 3

35 Wingate Road, W6 0UR   TEL: (020) 8749 1291

The Anglesea Arms buzzes with a young frisky crowd and has the unmistakable air of 'le patron mange ici'. It's one of the old stagers of the London gastro-pub scene, a genuinely happy hostelry with a wood-panelled bar and a long counter that curves around into the brick-walled dining area. Eaters quickly pack the place, so 'grab whatever table is available', advises one reporter. The menu is chalked on boards, and French chef Jacky Lelièvre has stamped his mark on proceedings. The choice is quite limited, but each dish has a touch of intrigue: purple-sprouting broccoli with blood orange hollandaise is offered as a starter, and deep-fried courgette flowers are stuffed with goats' curd and basil. Main courses veer between 'perfectly rare' seared tuna on a copious mound of dressed rocket and peasant-style pot-roast chicken breast with white pudding, sage and Puy lentils. To conclude, you might try caramelised banana rum baba, or verbena buttermilk pudding with biscotti. Food comes quickly once ordered, although the start may take a while; even so, there's no fuss and the young waiting team do their job well. Beer drinkers perch on high stools at the bar and order pints of Adnams Broadside, Greene King IPA, and Shepherd Neame Spitfire Premium Ale, among others. The wine list of around 50 lives up to the gastro billing without forgetting it's in a pub. So there's house at £10.95, loads of good stuff under £15 (and all by the glass) and well-chosen bottles further up the range. SAMPLE DISHES: crab ravioli with bisque and tarragon £5.75; sautéed calf's liver with black treacle bacon, white beans, beetroot and horseradish £11; hot chocolate pudding with coffee ice cream £4.50.

Licensees Fiona Evans and Jamie Wood (freehouse)
Open 11 to 11, Sun 12 to 10.30; bar food 12.30 to 2.45 (3.30 Sun), 7 to 10.30 (10.15 Sun); closed 1 week Christmas, 1 Jan
Details Children welcome   Wheelchair access (not WC)   Patio   Occasional background music   Dogs welcome exc in eating areas   Delta, MasterCard, Switch, Visa

Astons   NEW ENTRY

map 3

2 Regent Street, NW10 5LG   TEL: (020) 8969 2184

The location, between Notting Hill and Kilburn, is not the most attractive – 'this is Kensal Green, which has yet to be gentrified' – and shows just how the gastro-pub phenomenon has spread throughout the capital. But the mix of casual, rough-and-ready and the rather grand is appealing: old bare floorboards and mix-and-match wooden chairs and tables are offset by crystal chandeliers, fake coal fires, gilt-framed mirrors, modern prints and large vases of flowers, attracting a young, vibrant crowd, especially at weekends when there are DJs and it can get noisy. During the week, noise levels are lower, and partitions give some feeling of intimacy. Blackboards, which are brought to your table, list well-made staples along the lines of leek and potato soup, or red peppers stuffed with tomatoes, cheese and pesto to start, and main courses of baked chicken with hummus and sweet potato, and 'good, plentiful' lamb steaks with garlic mash, mango and mint salsa, with almond and apricot sponge, or pears poached in red wine to finish. Courage Best is on handpump, and eight wines are sold by the glass. SAMPLE DISHES: tiger prawns with chilli, coriander and lime £6; meatballs with linguine and Parmesan £9; chocolate brownie with crème fraîche and raspberries £4.

Licensee Paul Rayner (freehouse)
Open 12 to 11; bar food Mon to Sat 12.30 to 3.30, 6.30 to 10.30, Sun 12 to 9
Details Children welcome in bar eating area   Wheelchair access (not WC)   Patio   Background music; jukebox   Dogs welcome on a lead   Delta, Diners, MasterCard, Switch, Visa

Atlas

map 12

16 Seagrave Road, SW6 1RX   TEL: (020) 7385 9129

The Atlas is a cheerful place filled with soft background music and friendly young staff. The revamped old pub, in a residential area near Earls Court Exhibition Centre, attracts both drinkers and diners, with both spilling out on to a small enclosed patio in warm weather. The deep, oblong-shaped room has a long bar with comfortable seating (banquettes and chairs) and old-fashioned wrought-iron pub tables, and to the rear is a dining area. The short menu goes in for hearty cooking, with around a dozen choices and no distinction between courses. But behind this seemingly casual approach lies a good degree of flair. A starter of pan-fried pigeon breast, for example, comes with sautéed potatoes, watercress, a soft-boiled egg and horseradish salsa. Among main courses, roast fillet of wild salmon is served with grilled fennel and courgette salad with basil and lemon and a fig and onion compote, while pheasant and merquez tagine is accompanied by quince and saffron couscous salad. Fuller's London Pride, Adnams Broadside and Caledonian Deuchars IPA are among the real ales. Wines are good value (outstanding value when you consider that this is Fulham), and the short, modern list is chosen with care and flair. Around a dozen come by the glass from £2.70. SAMPLE DISHES: Tuscan tomato and bread soup with basil £4; confit of duck leg with star anise, smashed parsnips, baked apple and aged balsamic £10.50; chocolate and almond cake with vanilla cream £4.

Licensees George and Richard Manners (freehouse)
Open *12 to 11 (10.30 Sun); bar food 12.30 to 3, 7 to 10.30 (10 Sun); closed Christmas, Easter*
Details *Children welcome before 7pm   Garden   Background music   Dogs welcome on a lead   Delta, MasterCard, Switch, Visa*

Barnsbury
map 12

209–211 Liverpool Road, N1 1LX   TEL: (020) 7607 5519
WEBSITE: www.thebarnsbury.co.uk

A more or less square room makes up the Barnsbury, and a simple, classic look is created by oak half-panelling with walls above painted a shade of eggshell blue-grey, a central bar also of oak with 'chandeliers' above made from inverted stemmed wine glasses, pine tables, church chairs and pews. Two coal-effect gas fires add warmth, and decoration and colour are provided by changing exhibitions of paintings, a gilt-framed mirror and bunches of flowers, and atmosphere by the satisfied clientele. The short, lively menu sticks largely within the Mediterranean sphere of influence: for instance, starters of Swiss chard, pancetta and red wine risotto, or beetroot and dill gravad lax with sorrel crème fraîche, with main courses of pan-fried fillet of sea bass with tapenade and coriander butter, or chump of English lamb with goats' cheese and salsa rossa. Good old chocolate truffle cake and pear tarte Tatin take their places with El Dovnajo cheese and quince jelly at dessert stage. Fuller's London Pride, Timothy Taylor Landlord and a guest beer are on draught. Around half the wines on the list of 20-plus bottles are organic, and eight or so are served by the glass. SAMPLE DISHES: curried parsnip soup with apple crisps £3.50; steak, kidney and mushroom pie £10.50; Bakewell tart with custard £4.

Licensee Jeremy Gough (freehouse)
Open *12 to 11 (10.30 Sun); bar food Mon to Sat 12 to 3 (4 Sat), 6.30 to 10, Sun 12 to 4, 6.30 to 9*
Details *Children welcome   Wheelchair access (also WC)   Garden and patio   Background music   Dogs welcome   Amex, Delta, MasterCard, Switch, Visa*

Bedford   NEW ENTRY
map 12

77 Bedford Hill, SW12 9HD   TEL: (020) 8682 8940
WEBSITE: www.thebedford.co.uk

In an up-and-coming area of Balham, the Bedford is sure to add to the desirability of this particular neighbourhood. The genuine pub atmosphere and real pub food (without the trimmings of a restaurant) draws in the crowds. It's a huge, imposing red-brick building, a long-established theatre pub with characteristic London Victorian architecture. Two entrances lead to large bars that are not connected inside, but theatrical oatmeal-gold drapes and many prints and sketches of Shakespearean characters are a running theme, reflecting the adjoining mini Globe Theatre. Two further floors both have live entertainment. The menu lists a few 'lite bites' and 16 dishes with no line between starters and main courses to encourage informal eating.

It's good cooking along the lines of plump, crispy sesame chicken strips with yakitori sauce, mayonnaise and sweet chilli dipping sauce, or crisp, pink honey-roast duck breast with fried sweet potatoes, crunchy fine green beans and a rich dark sauce, with things like chocolate nemesis or Ben and Jerry's ice cream for dessert. Fuller's London Pride, Wadworth 6X, Courage Best and Young's Bitter are on handpump, and 14 wines from the short, global list are available by the glass. SAMPLE DISHES: sticky pork salad £5; chicken and leek pie £9; panettone bread-and-butter pudding £4.

Licensee Christopher Scholey (Unique)
Open *Mon to Wed 11 to 11, Thur 11 to 12, Fri and Sat 11 to 2am, Sun 12 to 10.30; bar food 12 to 3 (3.30 Sat, 5 Sun), 7 to 10*
Details *Children welcome   Wheelchair access (also WC)   Garden   No-smoking area   Occasional live music Dogs welcome   Amex, Delta, MasterCard, Switch, Visa*

Bridge Pub and Dining Room   NEW ENTRY   map 3
204 Castelnau, SW13 9DW   TEL: (020) 8563 9811
WEBSITE: www.thebridgeinbarnes.co.uk

Proximity to Hammersmith Bridge gives meaning to the name, but the Bridge has moved on from being a traditional local boozer – major refurbishment has turned it into a dining pub. A series of high-ceilinged rooms delivers a clean, modern look, yet with a strong pubby feel, especially in the bar where highly polished wood, a long, red-upholstered banquette and leather pews create a comfortable feel, and Ruddles Best Bitter, Marston's Pedigree and Wells Bombardier Premium Bitter are on hand-pump. The lounge has a log fire, large leather sofas and a few tables for eating, and the restaurant has its own separate entrance from the street. The same menu is available wherever you choose to sit, and culinary influences come from the Mediterranean and beyond, which means an array of dishes from Cajun chicken ciabatta with avocado, rocket and chunky chips to tuna burger with a crusty roll, pickled cucumbers and dill dressing, and from a salad of warm oriental roast duck with paw-paw and Chinese dressing to grilled ribeye steak with chopped tomato, mozzarella, and basil salad. For dessert, think passion-fruit crème brûlée or mascarpone cheesecake with Cointreau-soaked orange segments. From a list of about 40 wines, 10 are offered by the large glass. SAMPLE DISHES: New England clam chowder £5.50; veal T-bone steak with couscous with dried figs and olives, wilted greens and harissa £13; baked almond and raspberry tart with Cassis cream £4.50.

Licensees Murray J. Harris and Harvey Simpson (Scottish Courage)
Open *11 to 11, Sun 12 to 10.30; bar food and restaurant 12 to 3.30, 5.30 to 10.30, Sun 12 to 9.30*
Details *Children welcome in eating areas   Wheelchair access (also WC)   Garden and patio   No smoking in restaurant   Background music   No dogs   Delta, Diners, MasterCard, Switch, Visa*

Chapel   map 12
48 Chapel Street, NW1 5DP   TEL: (020) 7402 9220

'Classy' and 'no nonsense' is the general view of this modern-day gastro-pub in a Victorian building on a corner set back off the Edgware Road. It's spacious too – open-plan, with stripped floorboards and cream walls – with the large, traditional bar painted dark green, while well-spaced wooden tables are accompanied by bentwood chairs. Beside the bar is an open-plan kitchen with a large charcoal grill. The menu, on blackboards, steps out on typically modern lines, perhaps featuring ragoût of sea bass, red snapper and oysters with baby corn and lime to start. That big chargrill comes into play for T-bone steak accompanied by pak choi and Portobello mushroom cream, while another main course could be roast chicken breast stuffed with salami and green pepper cheese. Finish with pineapple, ginger and coconut tart, or banana crème brûlée. Blackboards also display the globetrotting wine options (with nine by the glass), while handpumps deliver Adnams Bitter and Greene King IPA. SAMPLE DISHES: smoked chicken and vegetable terrine £5; baked monkfish with Serrano ham and aubergine, tomato and anchovy dressing £13; raspberry, strawberry and lemon parfait £3.50.

Licensee Lakis Hondrogiannis (Chapel Inns plc)
Open 12 to 11 (10.30 Sun); bar food 12 to 2.30 (12.30 to 3 Sun), 7 to 10
Details Children welcome   Wheelchair access (also WC)   Garden   Background music   Dogs welcome
Amex, Delta, Diners, MasterCard, Switch, Visa

Coach & Horses   NEW ENTRY   map 12

26–28 Ray Street, EC1R 3DJ   TEL: (020) 7278 8990

Set behind the *Guardian* building and surrounded by former factories and warehouses – some now loft-style apartments – the revamped Coach & Horses is nowadays more orientated towards eating than drinking, but it happily caters to all-comers. It has two entrances, one leading into the former public bar, the other into the lounge, the rooms separated by a wooden and glass arch. Both are heavily panelled and filled with closely spaced tables and light wooden dining chairs with seats of faux cream leather, the décor 'stark and businesslike, conveying a strong impression that food/eating is the preoccupation'. The cooking style shows a broad range of influences: a half-pint of prawns with mayonnaise, a warm salad of confit duck with pear and pecan nuts, and gado-gado salad are typical choices among starters. Confit belly of pork with sage and semolina gnocchi with raisins, or roast chump of lamb with minted flageolet beans are eye-catching contemporary creations, as are desserts: say, a double shot of butterscotch schnapps with vanilla ice cream, or orange and almond cake with blood orange curd and mascarpone cream. Fuller's London Pride and Adnams Bitter are the real ales on draught, and around ten wines are sold by the glass from a short, interesting list. SAMPLE DISHES: celeriac soup £4.25; roast cod with chorizo, chickpeas and saffron aïoli £10.75; rhubarb syllabub £5.

Licensee Giles Webster (Punch Pubs)
Open 11 to 11; bar food 12 to 3, 6 to 10
Details Children welcome in bar eating area   Garden   Background music   Dogs welcome   Delta,
MasterCard, Switch, Visa

Cow Dining Room 😊 😊   map 12

89 Westbourne Park Road, W2 5QH   TEL: (020) 7221 0021

The Cow certainly has style, a mix of carefully contrived grunge and shabby chic creating the look of a 'real boozer'. The bar has lots of dark wood, chairs and tables in various styles, and some leather-covered banquettes, all looking as though nothing has changed since the 1950s, and menus painted on mirrors add to the feeling of working man's pub meets French bistro. The ground-floor bar is loosely separated into two halves, with a sign at the entrance to the back half informing that this area is for eating (and people have been known to be asked to return to the drinking area 'pretty sharpish' once they've finished eating). Food is taken seriously here – both in the upstairs dining room and ground-floor bar – and materials are of good quality. Oysters and a seafood platter (for two) kick off the short printed menu, with other items written on a blackboard. Robustly flavoured dishes are what to expect: hearty vegetable, bacon and chorizo broth, then lamb's kidney with black pudding and mustard sauce, slow-roast belly of Old Spot pork with wild mushrooms, or whole roast partridge with braised red cabbage. Fuller's ESB, Jack Frost and London Pride are on draught, along with Guinness (to pair with those oysters) and various lagers, and around a dozen wines are served by the glass from a short, well-chosen list. SAMPLE DISHES: duck confit with black pudding and a poached egg £7.75; line-caught Cornish cod with spiced chickpeas and gremolata £13.75; crème brûlée £5.25.

Licensees Tom Conran and Bardi Berisha (freehouse)
Open *12 to 11, Sun 12 to 10.30; bar food 12 to 3.30, 6 to 10.30, restaurant Mon to Sat 7 to 11, Sun 12.30 to 3.30, 7 to 11; closed 25 Dec, 1 Jan*
Details *Children welcome Patio Background music No dogs Delta, MasterCard, Switch, Visa*

Crown 🍺

map 3

223 Grove Road, E3 5SN   TEL: (020) 8981 9998
WEBSITE: www.singhboulton.co.uk

As at its sister, the Duke of Cambridge in Islington (see entry), everything sold at this substantial end-of-terrace Victorian pub is organic, right down to the ketchup. The large open-plan main room has a simple unadorned look, with a few plants, mismatched wooden chairs and large tables. Food is listed on a blackboard by the bar, and like the décor it takes a straightforward approach, with dishes ranging from simple snacks to full-blown main courses and some items available in small or large portions. Roast tomato soup with tapenade might appear alongside home-smoked lamb fillet with potato, aubergine and feta gratin, or romesco fish stew (in a sauce of tomatoes, garlic and almonds). Wines are also listed on boards – about 20 of each colour, with five of each by the glass – and beers include Eco Warrior and Shoreditch Organic Stout. There is also a good choice of fruit juices and cordials. SAMPLE DISHES: roast peppers stuffed with rocket and olives £6.50; roast beef in a salt crust with beetroot, fennel and horseradish cream £14; rhubarb crumble with coconut anglaise £5.

Licensee Geetie Singh (freehouse)
Open *Mon 5 to 11 (bank hol Mons 10.30 to 11), Tue to Fri 12 to 11, Sat 10.30 to 11, Sun 10.30 to 10.30; bar food and restaurant Mon 7 to 10.30, Tue to Fri 12.30 to 3, 7 to 10.30, Sat and Sun 10.30 to 4, 7 to 10.30 (10 Sun); closed 25 and 26 Dec, 1 Jan*
Details *Children welcome Wheelchair access (also WC) Garden No-smoking area in bar, no smoking in restaurant No music Dogs welcome Delta, Diners, MasterCard, Switch, Visa*

Cumberland Arms ✿   NEW ENTRY

map 12

29 North End Road, W14 8SZ   TEL: (020) 7371 6806
WEBSITE: www.thecumberlandarmspub.co.uk

The corner-sited pub may look traditional from the outside, but, within, the wooden floor, mix-and-match furniture, modern prints on the walls, a basket of games, and large vases of flowers bear all the hallmarks of a modern-day gastro-pub. Indeed, the menu has a sophistication that's above the norm for a pub, with a style similar to its siblings (the Atlas – see entry – and the Fox & Hounds), encouraging casual dining, with some of the starters eminently suitable as a light meal. Antipasti may include chicken wings, artichoke, Parma ham, asparagus and tomato frittata, smoked salmon with new potatoes, red onions and mixed leaves, while porcini risotto is well made with 'a good nutty texture'. Main-course options may include rustic grilled Italian sausages with fennel, Puy lentils, thyme, red wine and tapenade, or 'beautifully grilled' whole sea bass on the bone with roasted fennel and orange and parsley salsa, while oxtail casserole is slowly cooked in a rich sauce so that it 'glides off the bone' and is accompanied by polenta creamed with mascarpone. From the limited range of desserts come chocolate and almond cake or a duo of Italian cheeses. Beers are Fuller's London Pride, Caledonian Deuchars IPA, and Wells Bombardier Premium Bitter. The wine list is a short, globetrotting selection with a dozen by the large or small glass from £2.70. SAMPLE DISHES: Tuscan bread and tomato soup £4; pan-fried skate wing with sautéed spinach, tomato, fennel and garlic £10; pear, apple and almond tart with strawberry coulis £4.

Licensees Richard Manners, George Manners and James Gill (freehouse)
Open 12 to 11 (10.30 Sun); bar food 12.30 to 3, 7 to 10.30 (10 Sun); closed 23 Dec to 2 Jan, Easter
Details Children welcome in bar eating area before 7pm   Wheelchair access (not WC)   Patio   Background music   Dogs welcome on a lead   Delta, MasterCard, Switch, Visa

Drapers Arms ✿   map 12
44 Barnsbury Street, N1 1ER   TEL: (020) 7619 0348

The setting is residential Islington, away from the frenetic goings-on of Upper Street, and this premier-league pub in a Georgian house puts on a homely face, with sofas, easy chairs and wooden tables on the ground floor and a rather plain-looking restaurant upstairs. Sandwiches, such as chicken BLT, are served in the bar at lunchtimes, alongside a full menu, also served in the restaurant in the evening, of intriguing, eclectic dishes, taking in starters like courgette fritters with smoked eel or foie gras parfait with quince jelly and sour-dough bread, before main courses of deep-fried plaice with pea purée, chips and tartare sauce, slow-cooked rabbit with olives and sherry vinegar, or maize-fed chicken with chanterelles, turnip dauphinois and a black pudding jus. To finish, take your pick from, say, nougat glace with mango and basil or bitter chocolate and ginger tart with Chantilly cream. You can enjoy a late breakfast on Sundays. Real ales are Old Speckled Hen, Courage Best and a guest brew; Dunkerton's organic cider and Belgian beers are available in bottles, and there is a list of around 60 superior-quality but good-value wines, of which 16 are served by the glass. SAMPLE DISHES: salad of chicken livers, pancetta, frisée and a soft poached egg £5.50; linguine with mussels, peppers, garlic and parsley £9.50; white chocolate and vanilla cheesecake with roast plums £5.50.

Licensees Paul McElhinney and Mark Emberton (freehouse)
Open 11 to 11, Sun 12 to 10.30; bar food all week 12 to 3, Mon to Sat 7 to 10.30, restaurant Mon to Sat 7 to 10, Sun 12 to 3; closed 4 days Christmas, 1 and 2 Jan
Details Children welcome   Wheelchair access (not WC)   Garden   Background music   Dogs welcome in bar and garden only   Amex, Delta, MasterCard, Switch, Visa

Duke of Cambridge 🍺

30 St Peter's Street, N1 8JT   TEL: (020) 7359 3066
WEBSITE: www.singhboulton.co.uk

map 12

Green credentials are evident right across the board at this totally organic gastro-pub. Beers, including own-label Singhboulton, are from London organic brewers Pitfield, plus Organic Best Bitter from St Peter's brewery and Freedom organic lager; there's also a list of around 40 organic wines with about 10 by the glass. The décor is basic and minimalist, with original features restored using reclaimed building materials, while the furniture is all second-hand. On the food front, the shortish menus offer modern-sounding dishes with a broad scope of influences (mostly French and Italian) that are less economical than the décor. Start perhaps with celeriac, chickpea and cabbage soup, then something like navarin of lamb with salsify, globe artichokes, broad beans and minted new potatoes, or pan-fried red mullet with linguine and lemon and chilli sauce, and finish with pear and honey polenta cake. The Crown (see entry) in E3 is under the same ownership. SAMPLE DISHES: asparagus and white-bean minestrone £4.50; boiled ham hock with mustard, mashed potato and Savoy cabbage £12.50; apple compote with cinnamon custard £4.50.

Licensee Geetie Singh (freehouse)
Open 12 to 11, Sun 12 to 10.30; bar food and restaurant 12.30 to 3 (3.30 Sat and Sun), 7 to 10.30 (10 Sun); closed 25 and 26 Dec, 1 Jan
Details Children welcome   Garden   No-smoking area in bar, no smoking in restaurant   No music   Dogs welcome   Delta, MasterCard, Switch, Visa

Eagle 🏵

159 Farringdon Road, EC1R 3AL   TEL: (020) 7837 1353

map 12

Widely regarded as the mother of all gastro-pubs, the Eagle is flying high after more than 13 years in business. It is still the same large, casual and bustling single room on Farringdon Road near the *Guardian*'s office. There is no division between drinking and eating areas, and no bookings are taken, which often means getting here early or fighting the crowds for a table. The menus change with the seasons, and dishes are listed on blackboards over the bar. There isn't a huge choice, but the untypical ingredients and inventive flavour combinations make a good impression. The style is hearty and modern, with Spanish and Italian influences in evidence: start with, say, gazpacho Andaluz or bruschetta with spiced aubergines, roast cherry tomatoes and buffalo mozzarella, then move on to grilled swordfish with peppers, mint, new potatoes and balsamic, or roast chicken with preserved lemons, potatoes, mustard leaves and aïoli. If you're not in the mood for a full meal, you can opt for bife ana (a marinated steak sandwich). Pastéis de nata, Portuguese custard tarts, are the only, unchanging dessert option; otherwise round things off with cheese. Wells Bombardier Premium Bitter and Eagle IPA are on draught, and all dozen or so reasonably priced wines (from £10.50 to £15) are served by the glass (£2.50 to £3.75). Michael Belben also runs the Fox Dining Room, EC2 (see entry). SAMPLE DISHES: courgette and saffron risotto £8; cuttlefish stewed with chilli, garlic, parsley, onions and broad beans £12.50; Wigmore cheese with rhubarb jam and toast £6.50.

Licensee Michael Belben (freehouse)

Open *12 to 11, Sun 12 to 5; bar food Mon to Sat 12.30 to 3 (3.30 Sat), 6.30 to 10.30, Sun 12.30 to 3.30;
closed 1 week Christmas, bank hols*
Details *Children welcome   Wheelchair access (not WC)   Background music   Dogs welcome   Delta,
MasterCard, Switch, Visa*

Ealing Park Tavern ♥   map 3
222 South Ealing Road, W5 4RL   TEL: (020) 8758 1879

Passers-by get a view of the goings-on in the high-ceilinged bar and dark-panelled
interior of this vast pub on a busy road a short drive from the M4. The sign 'Dining
Room' displayed outside announces its intentions, although there's still a pubby feel
to the place, with Fuller's London Pride, Timothy Taylor Landlord and Breton cider
on tap, plus the offer of tapas like charcuterie and cheese as bar snacks. The separate
dining room has an open-to-view kitchen in the larger of two areas, both set out with
chunky wooden tables and assorted wooden chairs; contemporary zinc lamps hang
from the ceiling, with its navy-blue-painted beams. The compact, modern British
menu, chalked on a blackboard, moves with the times. Portions are sizeable, ingredients are fresh, and dishes look good on the plate. To start, you could pick, say, seared
Cornish scallops and artichoke with orange and rosemary, or a salad of roast beetroot,
goats' cheese, French beans and walnuts. Main courses are mostly gutsy dishes like
double pork chop with sage jackets and apricot stuffing, peppered Scotch sirloin with
chips and watercress, or bourride with aïoli and croûtons, while desserts range from
Normandy apple tart with ice cream to spotted dick with custard. The predominantly
European wine list offers 12 by the glass. SAMPLE DISHES: warm caramelised onion
and pecorino tart £5; duck confit with parsnip rösti, apple compote and Calvados jus
£12.50; mango pannacotta with lime sauce £4.50.

Licensees *Nicholas Sharpe and V. Morse (V.A. Morse and N. Sharpe)*
Open *11 to 11, Sun 12 to 11; bar food 6 to 10.30 (9 Sun), restaurant Mon to Sat 12 to 3, 6 to 10.30,
Sun 12 to 4, 6 to 9; closed Mon lunchtimes, 25 and 26 Dec*
Details *Children welcome   Wheelchair access (not WC)   Garden and patio   Background music   Dogs
welcome   MasterCard, Switch, Visa*

Earl Spencer [NEW ENTRY]   map 3
260–262 Merton Road, SW18 5JL   TEL: (020) 8870 9244
WEBSITE: www.theearlofspencer.co.uk

The early twentieth-century building on a main road through a residential area looks
pretty unprepossessing from the outside, but inside you will find honest and interesting food and a real pub in terms of décor and atmosphere. It has been knocked into
one large room, a modern, airy and well-lit space, but retains some original features
such as splendid 'classic boozer-style brass chandeliers'. It is not at all pretentious, and
the beers are good: a substantial central wooden bar dispenses Fuller's London Pride,
Shepherd Neame Spitfire Premium Ale and Hook Norton Best Bitter. Daily-changing blackboards as well as a printed sheet offer a range of unfussy, modern-sounding
dishes that remain loyal to the pub ethos. On offer might be starters of Spanish
mountain pâté with mushrooms, apple, herbs and pickles alongside sautéed gnocchi
with field mushrooms, sprouting broccoli, Parmesan and truffle oil (described as 'a
classy dish'), and main courses of pork and beef meatballs with tomato sauce, chickpeas and spaghetti, or stuffed suckling pig with rosemary-roast potatoes. Treacle and

apple tart with custard, and sticky gingerbread pudding with vanilla ice cream and toffee sauce are typical desserts. Around ten wines are served by the glass from a list numbering about 30 bottles. SAMPLE DISHES: parsnip, apple and rosemary soup £4; confit chicken leg with dauphinois potatoes, green beans and onion gravy £10; rhubarb fool £3.50.

Licensee Jonathan Cox (Enterprise Inns)
Open 11 to 11, Sun 12 to 10.30; bar food 12.30 to 2.30, 7 to 10, Sun 12.30 to 3, 7 to 9.30
Details Children welcome   Wheelchair access (not WC)   Patio   No music   Dogs welcome   Amex, Delta, Diners, MasterCard, Switch, Visa

Endurance   NEW ENTRY
map 12

90 Berwick Street, W1F 0QB   TEL: (020) 7437 2944

The Endurance enjoys a central location in the heart of Soho, with Berwick Street Market right at the door. It may be set in a grim 1960s concrete shopping parade, but it all changes inside – you step into a stylish, spacious, airy pub with picture windows across the front allowing a good view of the street action. And there are lots of classic pubby characteristics too: a dark wood floor, deep-red flock wall panels, dark red paint, and black leather seats and banquettes, and on the walls a boar's head, a stuffed trout in a glass case and a pair of cow's horns – 'all in all a successful interpretation of traditional pub décor for a design-sophisticated clientele'. A short, monthly-changing menu offers a sensible range of above-average pub food: say, roast tomato soup with basil pesto to start, then 'juicy, flavoursome' rump of lamb with crushed potatoes, French beans, and rosemary-scented red wine sauce, with apple and cinnamon crumble to finish. Real ales include Fuller's London Pride and Deuchars IPA on handpump, and a handful of wines is served by the glass. SAMPLE DISHES: steamed mussels with white wine and parsley sauce £7; sirloin steak with chips, watercress and béarnaise sauce £12.50; orange pannacotta with winter berry compote £5.50.

Licensee Alan Drew (Courage)
Open 12.30 to 11, Sun 12.30 to 10.30; bar food all week 12.30 (1 Sun) to 4
Details Children welcome   Car park   Wheelchair access (also WC)   Patio   Jukebox   Dogs welcome exc at mealtimes   Delta, Diners, MasterCard, Switch, Visa

Engineer
map 12

65 Gloucester Avenue, NW1 8JH   TEL: (020) 7722 0950
WEBSITE: www.the-engineer.com

Within this white-painted corner building, closely spaced plain wooden tables laid up for eating immediately brand the Engineer as a gastro-pub. Although handpumps dispensing Fuller's London Pride and Adnams Bitter should hearten real ale fans, the space for drinking is relatively small. An array of dining areas exhibiting modern art, a walled garden for summer days, and a homely, laid-back, buzzy atmosphere are what to expect. The trendy, crowd-pleasing modern European menu, with Mediterranean and far-flung influences, shows its hand in eclectic dishes such as tequila-cured salmon with blinis, horseradish cream and cucumber, or a warm salad of chorizo, potato, baby onion, watercress, and a poached egg with chipotle aïoli, and main-course red-braised crisp belly pork with steamed baby gem lettuce, pickled vegetables and caramelised chilli sauce. The modern globetrotting wine list runs in tune with the cooking and offers a handful by the glass. SAMPLE DISHES: steamed mussels in Thai-spiced coconut broth £7.25; grilled swordfish with braised lemon-scented fennel and Bloody Mary sauce £14.50; vanilla bavarois with balsamic mixed berry compote £5.50.

Licensees Abigail Osborne and Tamsin Olivier (freehouse)
Open 11 to 11 (10.30 Sun); bar food and restaurant 12 to 3.30, 7 to 11 (10.30 Sun); bar snacks available all day, breakfast available from 9am; closed 25 and 26 Dec, 1 Jan
Details Children welcome   Wheelchair access (also WC)   Garden   Background music   Dogs welcome exc in restaurant   Delta, MasterCard, Switch, Visa

Fentiman Arms   map 12
64 Fentiman Road, SW8 1LA   TEL: (020) 7793 9796

The Fentiman has a relaxed feel and good food, plus a beer garden which makes it stand out from the crowd. The garden has an air of both fun and purpose about it, with vegetables rather than flower borders, and tall bamboo in galvanised pots, and the outside space also runs to tables on the front patio under large parasols. Inside, there's an informal feel, with large windows, plank flooring and mix-and-match tables and chairs. On one side of the U-shaped bar is a chill-out area with large cush-ions and chairs in oak and mahogany and a library-style ambience, while the other side of the bar is for drinking. The menus move with the times and could feature a ricotta and pesto cake to start, and main courses following the trend with the likes of crisp smoked cod and spring onion fishcake, and chocolate sponge pudding for dessert. Greene King IPA and Wadworth 6X are on handpump, while over half a dozen of the fairly priced wines are sold by the glass from £2.95. SAMPLE DISHES: crab, prawn and avocado pâté £6; grilled Cumberland sausage £10; raspberry crème brûlée £4.

Licensee Talufik Yahia (freehouse)
Open 11 to 11, Sun 12 to 10.30; bar food Mon to Sat 12 to 2.45, 7 to 9.45, Sun 12 to 4, 7 to 9
Details Children welcome   Garden   Background music   Dogs welcome   Delta, MasterCard, Switch, Visa

Fire Station   map 12
150 Waterloo Road, SE1 5SB   TEL: (020) 7620 2226
WEBSITE: www.wizardinns.co.uk

The former fire station has morphed into a unique pub. It's a great piece of industrial architecture with much of its original structure and features intact, emphasised by the huge red doors that open on to the street, often with crowds spilling out. The front part is for drinkers only, although bar snacks are available here, along with a decent selection of real ales, including Young's Bitter, Fuller's London Pride and Shepherd Neame Spitfire Premium Ale, plus a few interesting bottled Belgian beers. Beyond is the cavernous dining room, with its open kitchen running along the back wall adding to the sense of drama. The menus offer inventive global cooking, starters taking in everything from a fish platter to chargrilled pigeon breast, with main courses featur-ing bistro classics like calf's liver and bacon alongside such popular things as green Thai chicken curry. Desserts are conservative: plum bread-and-butter pudding, for example, or apple and pear crumble. Most bottles on the list of around 40 wines are under £20, and 10 are available by the glass. SAMPLE DISHES: mixed meze plate £6; bouillabaisse £15.50; crème brûlée £4.50.

Licensee Philippe Ha Yeung (Wizard Inns)
Open *11 to 11, Sun 12 to 10.30; bar food 11 to 10.30, Sun 12 to 9.30, restaurant Mon to Fri 12 to 3, 5.30 to 10.45, Sat 12 to 10.45, Sun 12 to 9.30; closed 25 and 26 Dec, 1 Jan, Easter Sun*
Details *Children welcome in eating areas   Wheelchair access (also WC)   Patio   Live or background music No dogs   Amex, Diners, MasterCard, Switch, Visa*

Fox Dining Room ☸   map 12
28 Paul Street, EC2A 4LB   TEL: (020) 7729 5708

On the corner of Scrutton Street and Paul Street stands the Fox, a pub with attitude and good food. Like its sibling, the Eagle on Farringdon Road (see entry), the décor demonstrates a no-frills, rough-and-ready approach, with bare floorboards, plain wooden tables and mismatched seating. The food shows considerable panache while still keeping things simple. Listed on a blackboard over the bar might be a daily-changing pie, home-made Scotch eggs, hot salt-beef sandwich, sausage rolls, and Neal's Yard cheese ploughman's, while the upstairs dining room has a fixed-price menu of more ambitious dishes (also served in the bar): perhaps pickled herring with beetroot, followed by veal chop with sage polenta, or lemon sole with purple-sprouting broccoli and anchovy dressing. To finish, there might be Seville orange marmalade pudding, or pannacotta with rhubarb. Wells Bombardier Premium Bitter is the only real ale offered, while wines run to a list of around 15 good-value bottles, the majority between £10.50 and £15, most of which are also available by the glass. SAMPLE DISHES: red onion soup with Parmesan; belly pork and lentils; pear and almond tart: 2 courses £15, 3 courses £19.75.

Licensee Michael Belben (Unique)
Open *Mon to Fri 12 to 11; bar food 12 to 3, restaurant 12 to 3, 6 to 10; closed 24 Dec to 4 Jan, bank hols*
Details *Children welcome   Wheelchair access (not WC)   Patio   Background music   Dogs welcome   Delta, MasterCard, Switch, Visa*

Grand Union ☸   map 12
45 Woodfield Road, W9 2BA   TEL: (020) 7286 1886

'Public Bar & Dining Rooms' is how this remodelled Victorian pub overlooking the Grand Union Canal defines itself. The location may not be as immediately attractive as the name suggests, with Westbourne Park's bus depot on the opposite bank and the concrete Westway more or less overhead. The décor is typically modern gastro-pub (bare floorboards, mix-and-match wooden furniture, a large red-leather sofa), while a wrought-iron spiral staircase leads to a basement dining room and a small terrace for fair-weather drinks. At heart, the Grand Union is still first and foremost a pub rather than a restaurant manqué, delivering food that is forthright, earthy and refreshingly honest. Pies are a house speciality, from beef with potato and horseradish to pumpkin, vegetable and cashew nut. Elsewhere, the kitchen dips into the modern pub repertoire for crispy fried squid with salad, lemon and sweet chilli mayonnaise, pan-fried liver and bacon with black pudding and bubble and squeak, or roast trout with sweet potatoes, caper berries, almonds and lemon butter (a contemporary take on a well-worn restaurant classic). Desserts are comforting and familiar: banoffi tart with chocolate sauce or pancakes with butterscotch sauce and vanilla ice cream, for example. Adnams Bitter and Broadside are on handpump, with Regatta putting in a seasonal appearance during the summer. The short list of around 20 wines offers 12 by the glass (including champagne); most bottles will leave change from a £20 note. SAMPLE DISHES: rocket, dried tomato and Parmesan salad £6; pheasant and wild boar sausages with apple mash and red wine gravy £9; bread-and-butter pudding £4.

Licensee Matthew Leitl (freehouse)
Open 12 to 11 (10.30 Sun); bar food 12 to 10 (9 Sun)
Details Children welcome   Wheelchair access (not WC)   Garden   Background music   Dogs welcome
Delta, MasterCard, Switch, Visa

Gunmakers   NEW ENTRY   map 12
13 Eyre Street Hill, EC1R 5ET   TEL: (020) 7278 1022

The façade of this tiny narrow building on a sloping, cobbled street off Clerkenwell Road looks as if it might have been an old-fashioned shopfront in a former life. Stripped floors, mid-green walls, red-leather banquettes, rather 'ironically tacky' fringed red shades on the wall lights, and small red glowing vases containing candles give a stylish edge to the one very small bar. Although the focus is on drinking (Greene King IPA and Fuller's London Pride), blackboards list 'perfect bar food', aimed at one-course satisfaction in the shape of perhaps two rounds of toasted cheese and tomato sarnie, steak sarnie with tomato, mustard mayonnaise, mixed leaves and chips, or fish and chips with tartare sauce. Otherwise there could be Gloucester Old Spot pork chop served with mustard mash and wilted winter greens that so impressed one reporter, and an excellent rhubarb and apple crumble 'topped off very nicely indeed' with fresh vanilla bean custard. Details such as home-made mayonnaise, whipped up on request to accompany a generous glassful of shell-on prawns, show a serious kitchen at work. Around ten wines are offered by the glass. SAMPLE DISHES: leek and potato soup £4.50; smoked haddock, squid and mussel stew with white beans and spicy sausage £8; a selection of British cheeses £6.50.

Licensee Nicholas Rouse (Kushti Ltd)
Open Mon to Fri 12 to 11, Sun 1 to 5; bar food Mon to Fri 12 to 3, 6 to 10, Sun 1 to 4
Details Children welcome   Patio   Background music   Dogs welcome   Amex, Delta, Diners, MasterCard,
Switch, Visa

Havelock Tavern ✿   map 3
57 Masbro Road, W14 0LS   TEL: (020) 7603 5374
WEBSITE: www.thehavelocktavern.co.uk

The Havelock's blue-tiled frontage is a splash of colour among the terraced houses of Brook Green. This is the urban neighbourhood pub as it should be: casual and relaxed, and aiming high with food and drink. It looks and feels every inch a pub, with a large open-plan space providing plenty of standing room by the bar. Wooden floorboards are well trodden, and mixed styles of wooden tables and chairs fill up quickly. Real ales include Brakspear Bitter, Marston's Pedigree and Fuller's London Pride, and the wine list, on blackboards as well as a printed sheet, offers a sensible range of food-friendly stuff, starting with house French at £10; around ten wines are available by the glass. At lunchtime the food is aimed at one-course satisfaction, with perhaps warm leek,

Gorgonzola and tomato salad, or skate with chips and lemon and herb mayonnaise. In the evening you might start with seared scallops with pea purée and a tomato and mint dressing, go on to roast chump of lamb with a stew of white beans, tomatoes and red peppers, and finish with orange ice cream with chocolate sauce, or a plate of Wealdway with toast and green tomato chutney. There's no pressure to eat more than one course, dishes disappear from the blackboard as the evening progresses, and credit and debit cards are not accepted. SAMPLE DISHES: chorizo, white-bean and cabbage soup £4; smoked haddock with horseradish mash, spinach and lemon £10.50; grilled banana bread with vanilla ice cream and butterscotch sauce £4.

Licensees Peter Richnell and Jonny Haughton (freehouse)
Open 11 to 11, Sun 12 to 10.30; bar food 12.30 to 2.30 (3 Sun), 7 to 10 (9.30 Sun); closed 22 to 26 Dec, Easter Sun, second Mon in Aug
Details Children welcome Wheelchair access (not WC) Garden and patio No music Dogs welcome No cards

The House ✿
63–69 Canonbury Road, N1 2DG TEL: (020) 7704 7410
WEBSITE: www.inthehouse.biz

                 map 12

The denizens of Islington seem to appreciate this particular House, judging by the happy buzz generated by the clientele. It is relaxed and modern in approach, and is some way from a traditional boozer. A drinking area around the entrance is furnished with deep armchairs and sofas, while the dining area has smartly laid tables with gleaming cutlery and glasses. The décor throughout is restful, with modern prints and mellow tones on the walls. The concise menu blends modern and traditional ideas, as in starters of carpaccio of tuna with croquant vegetables, or spinach and ricotta cannelloni in tomato sauce with gremolata. Main courses typically feature corn-fed chicken roasted with lemon and thyme served with artichoke risotto, and roast sea bass with pipérade, tapenade and langoustine oil. At weekends, the regular lunch menu is replaced by a brunch menu of things like salmon fishcake with a poached egg and sorrel sauce, shepherd's pie, and lamb masala. The wine list, grouped into somewhat whimsical headings, covers a good range of styles and countries. Prices start at £12.50, and there are eight wines by the glass. Adnams Bitter is the one real ale on offer. SAMPLE DISHES: tarte Tatin of red onion and grilled goats' cheese £6; confit of Barbary duck leg with bittersweet jus £13.50; coffee and orange parfait with white coffee ice cream £5.50.

Licensee Barnaby Meredith (Punch Pubs)
Open Mon 5 to 11, Tue to Sat 12 to 11, Sun 12 to 10.30; bar food and restaurant Mon 5.30 to 10.30, Tue to Sat 12 to 2.30 (3.30 Sat), 5.30 (6.30 Sat) to 10.30, Sun 12 to 3.30, 6.30 to 9.30; closed evening 24 to 27 Dec
Details Children welcome Wheelchair access (also WC) Garden No-smoking area in restaurant Live or background music Dogs welcome in bar only Delta, MasterCard, Switch, Visa

Ifield
59 Ifield Road, SW10 9AY TEL: (020) 7351 4900

                 map 12

The Ifield has made the successful move from old-fashioned boozer to gastro-pub and it gets the balance right. The food ranges from the quite ambitious to traditional favourites and the pubs caters for anyone looking for a good pint and some hearty yet sophisticated cooking. The long L-shaped room has a drinking area at one end and an eating area at the other, although there is no formal distinction, and a pleasant atmosphere prevails throughout. The menus are sensibly short and unfussy, but the cooking shows some panache: risotto with a quail's egg, truffles and Savoy cabbage, for example, to start, and among main courses, Calvados-glazed roast duck with pommes purée and mustard beans, or more traditional crispy fried cod and chips with minted peas and tartare sauce. Desserts might include sticky date pudding with toffee sauce. Beers include Fuller's London Pride and Adnams Bitter, and the short, well-balanced wine list keeps most prices under £20, with a handful of each colour by the glass. SAMPLE DISHES: French onion soup £3.75; grilled lamb steak with anchovy and rosemary butter and flageolet bean cassoulet £10.75; apple and rhubarb crumble £3.75.

Licensees Sam Freeman and Clark White (Punch Taverns)
Open Mon to Thur 5 to 12, Fri and Sat 11 to 12, Sun 11 to 11; bar food Mon to Thur 5 to 11, Fri to Sun 12 to 11
Details Children welcome Background music No dogs Amex, Delta, MasterCard, Switch, Visa

Junction Tavern   NEW ENTRY   map 12
101 Fortess Road, NW5 1AG   TEL: (020) 7485 9400

The entrance to this large street-corner pub is actually on Lady Somerset Road, but everyone seems to find their way in without problems. Drinkers head for the bar at the back, which has a couple of leather sofas around a coffee table, assorted furniture, dark panelling and pillars, plus handpumps dispensing Fuller's London Pride, Deuchars IPA and a guest such as Winter Tipple from the Wye Valley Brewery. Off the bar is a light, airy conservatory, but most of the foodie action takes place in the open-plan front bar, which features more panelling and pillars, globe wall lights and bare tables with paper napkins. One menu serves the whole pub, and it's a daily selection of eclectic dishes catering for today's palates. Prices are fair, and it's worth noting that from Monday to Friday all lunchtime main courses are pegged at £6.50. The kitchen delivers the goods, judging by recent favourable reports, which have singled out starters like feta salad with dates, dried cranberries and red cabbage, and goats' cheese and red onion tart, as well as main courses of 'crisp-skinned' grilled mackerel fillet on braised fennel with watercress and salsa verde. Finish with an 'accomplished' lemon cake with strawberry coulis, or perhaps poached plums with clotted cream ice cream. A youthful wine list keeps its prices in check and includes nine by the glass, with prices from £3.20. SAMPLE DISHES: celeriac soup with Parmesan croûtons £4; smoked haddock fishcake with slow-roast tomatoes and lemon butter £9.50; chocolate pot with whipped cream £4.50.

Licensees Jacky Kitching and Chris Leech (Unique Pub Co)
Open 12 to 11, Sun 12 to 10.30; bar food 12 to 3 (4 Sat), 6.30 to 10.30, Sun 12 to 4, 6.30 to 9.30; closed 24 to 26 Dec, 1 Jan
Details No children Wheelchair access (not WC) Patio Background music in bar Dogs welcome exc in eating area Delta, MasterCard, Switch, Visa

Lansdowne ✿   map 12
90 Gloucester Avenue, NW1 8HX   TEL: (020) 7483 0409

The Lansdowne is the perfect neighbourhood foodie pub, with its relaxed air yet underlying seriousness about food and drink. A well-worn look is testimony to its popularity and position as one of the first gastro-pubs in London, with the wood-floored ground-floor room filled with light from big windows and solid wooden furniture. Upstairs is a more relaxing restaurant, with table service, which accepts reservations. Downstairs, order at the bar, and advice from regulars is to order everything at once (getting the bill involves the same queuing). The modish blackboard menu changes regularly and could feature chicken liver parfait to start, followed by grilled Black Mountain ribeye with chips, watercress and tartare sauce, or roast organic chicken with braised chard and celeriac mash. Desserts follow the route of chocolate cake with hazelnut cream, or lemon tart. Woodforde's Wherry Best Bitter and Fuller's London Pride on handpump, plus around eight wines by the glass, help seal success for a well-run and friendly operation. SAMPLE DISHES: cauliflower and vanilla soup £4.25; coq au Beaujolais with Dijon mustard mash £10.50; pannacotta with strawberry coulis £4.50.

Licensee Amanda Pritchett (freehouse)
Open 12 to 11, Sun 12 to 10.30; bar food Tue to Sun 12.30 to 3 (3.30 Sun; pizza menu available every day to 7pm), all week 7 to 10, restaurant Tue to Sat 7 to 10.30, Sun 1 to 3
Details No children   Wheelchair access (also WC)   Patio   No music   Dogs welcome   Delta, MasterCard, Switch, Visa

Lock Tavern   map 12
35 Chalk Farm Road, NW1 8AJ   TEL: (020) 7482 7163

The corner site opposite Camden Lock Market means that the Lock Tavern heaves when the market is open. Five evenings a week DJs play splendidly eclectic music, but the volume does permit conversation – the young, fashionable and vaguely alternative will lap it up (along with Fuller's London Pride and Greene King IPA). There is a roof garden at the top, a garden at the bottom, and the two bars in between have a laid-back, fashionable but unpretentious feel and friendly, informal service to match. The menu is simple and good value: a handful of starters, a pudding or two, and hearty main dishes for vegetarians and meat eaters. These might well include Toulouse sausages with mash, peas and gravy, or pork belly with parsley mash, beans, broccoli and mustard and cider sauce, and roasted red pepper stuffed with leek, pumpkin and sunflower seed risotto. Meat pies are made by the Square Pie Company around the corner, old-fashioned chips are served with sweet chilli sauce and mayonnaise, and those wishing to graze will be happy with roast suckling ribs with hoisin garlic sauce. Around a dozen wines are listed, with eight available by the glass. If you're young enough (in mind or body) to enjoy it here, enjoy it you will. SAMPLE DISHES: chicken wings with yoghurt dip £4.50; chorizo and mixed-bean stew £7; passion cake £3.

Licensees Rebekkah Potter and Dan Crouch (Mitchell & Butler)
Open 12 to 11, Sun 12 to 10.30; bar food Mon to Fri 12 to 3, 5 to 9, Sat 12 to 4, 5 to 9, Sun 12 to 5.30, 7 to 9; closed 25 and 26 Dec, 1 Jan
Details No children   Garden and patio   Background music; live music Wed to Sun evenings; jukebox   No dogs   MasterCard, Switch, Visa

Lord Palmerston   map 3
33 Dartmouth Park Hill, NW5 1HU   TEL: (020) 7485 1578

On the corner of Dartmouth Park Hill and Chetwynd Road, the Lord Palmerston is a substantial Victorian pub that still fulfils its traditional role as a local watering hole. A large island bar dominates the interior, with plenty of high stools for drinkers. Bare-wood floors, tables and chairs – some with prayer-book ledges – and plain, unadorned walls create an unpretentious space with a neighbourhood atmosphere, while generous windows allow light to stream in. To the rear, one room has a glass roof and beyond it there's a small, if rather shady, garden for fine-weather drinking. Food is also on the agenda: dishes are chalked on a blackboard, and you order at the bar from a menu that has a modish Mediterranean slant. It's a well-balanced, quite ambitious repertoire, with the fruits of the sea represented by crispy spiced red snapper with tomato rice and a lime, coriander and sweet chilli dressing, or fillet of brill stuffed with crab, chilli and mixed herbs accompanied by field mushrooms, garlic, spinach and a prawn bisque sauce. Braised oxtail in a red wine and wild mushroom sauce with root vegetable mash might tempt carnivores, while vegetarian dishes could feature baked aubergine topped with roasted peppers, tomato, red onion and mozzarella. Young's Bitter and Special are on draught beside a guest brew, and the list of around 35 wines – chalked on boards – includes more than two dozen by the glass. SAMPLE DISHES: carrot and coriander soup £3.50; grilled chicken breast with chorizo, avocado and asparagus salad £10.25; pear and almond tart £3.50.

Licensees Simon Palmer and Adrian Zimmerman (freehouse)
Open 12 to 11 (10.30 Sun); bar food Mon to Sat 12.30 to 3, 7 to 10, Sun 1 to 4, 7 to 9
Details Children welcome Garden No music Dogs welcome Delta, MasterCard, Switch, Visa

Lots Road Pub & Dining Room map 12

114 Lots Road, SW10 0RJ TEL: (020) 7352 6645
WEBSITE: www.thespiritgroup.com

Lots Road is an appealing and unusual road abounding with large warehouses and artisanal buildings, with an old power station virtually next door to this erstwhile boozer – now a thoroughly modern gastro-pub. The décor is in contemporary minimalist style, with dark wood floors, a zinc-topped bar counter, and red textile wall hangings adding splashes of colour to the cream-painted walls. There is a small, separate dining area, but one menu is served throughout. Value is good for this part of the world, and the cooking is sophisticated and cosmopolitan while remaining loyal to the pub ethos. Thus, the daily-changing menu may well offer ribeye steak sandwich with big chips alongside tiger prawns with shrimp, chorizo, noodles, vegetables and Thai sauce. Other options might include baked cod with wild mushrooms, grilled vegetables, pappardelle and mascarpone sauce, and pan-fried duck breast on dauphinois potatoes with crisp onion rings and orange gravy, with chocolate mousse, or banana cake with banoffi ice cream to finish. Wadworth 6X, Adnams Bitter, and Fuller's London Pride will keep real ale fans happy, and wine drinkers should be equally pleased with a wide-ranging list that offers two dozen by the glass from £3 for the basic French white and Spanish red to £5.75 for a red Rioja. SAMPLE DISHES: sweet potato and coconut soup £4.50; slow-roast belly pork with crushed new potatoes, spinach and glazed carrots £10.50; crème brûlée with raspberries £4.

Licensees Letitia Creevy and Peter Myers (Spirit Group)
Open 11 to 11, Sun 12 to 10.30; bar food and restaurant Mon to Fri 12 to 3, 5.30 to 10 (10.30 Fri), Sat 12 to 10.30, Sun 12 to 10
Details Children welcome Wheelchair access (also WC) Background music Dogs welcome Amex, MasterCard, Switch, Visa

Magdala   NEW ENTRY

map 12

2A South Hill Park, NW3 2SB   TEL: (020) 7435 2503

Ruth Ellis (the last woman to be hanged in Britain) gunned down and killed her lover outside this pub on the edge of Hampstead Heath. Regulars still hang out in the original bar, but the main business now takes place in the light, high-ceilinged dining room, where narrow strips of stained glass frame its large windows, and doors open on to a small patio. Plants brighten up the windowsills, and some Art Deco-ish paintings hang on the walls. The atmosphere is pleasantly chatty and buzzy, thanks to a goodly mix of customers. At lunchtime, the focus is on jacket potatoes, salads, open sandwiches and 'hot stuff' ranging from stir-fried pork with noodles to promising specials like pan-fried quail with spinach and pine-nut salad. In the evening the kitchen aims higher and conjures up a few more upmarket dishes for an 'appreciative audience'. Expect eclectic ideas like marinated duck livers with mizuna leaf salad, and monkfish tail wrapped in prosciutto with lemon butter sauce as well as smoked gammon steak with bubble and squeak and shallot gravy. To finish, vanilla crème brûlée might share the billing with apple and cinnamon galette with toffee sauce. Familiar names like Greene King IPA, Fuller's London Pride and Young's Special are on the handpumps, and there's a short list of 20 fairly priced wines including six by the glass. SAMPLE DISHES: sweetcorn and Cheddar potato cakes with garlic mayonnaise £4.50; breast of guinea fowl with caramelised onion sauce £9.50; white chocolate and raspberry tart with vanilla ice cream £4.50.

Licensee Sandra Colling
Open 11 to 11, Sun 12 to 10.30; bar food Mon to Fri 12 to 2.30, 6 to 10, Sat 12 to 10, Sun 12 to 9.30; restaurant Thur to Sat 7 to 10, Sun 12 to 4
Details Children welcome in eating areas   Wheelchair access (not WC)   Patio   Background music   Dogs welcome   Delta, MasterCard, Switch, Visa

Peasant

map 12

240 St John Street, EC1V 4PH   TEL: (020) 7336 7726
WEBSITE: www.thepeasant.co.uk

This good example of a London pub is imposing, handsome and inviting, with large windows revealing the hustle and bustle inside. It makes the most of its original features, including an impressive mosaic floor and, in one corner, a tiled mural. The food is more contemporary. There's a bar menu of vegetarian meze (hummus, lentil purée, piquillo peppers, Tetilla cheese, aubergine salad, herb couscous and pickles), or charcuterie of chorizo, Serrano ham, lomo, pickled figs, chillies and red onion focaccia, as well as salmon and crab cakes, steak sandwich, slow-cooked belly pork, and roast cod with wok-fried beans, mange-tout and chilli sauce. It's ideal pub food, perfect to soak up the beer. For those after a full meal, the restaurant-like upstairs dining room offers a more substantial menu, typically featuring chicken liver parfait on parsley, cucumber and anchovy salad, followed by roast stuffed rabbit with spinach, sultanas and roast pine nuts, with spiced Yorkshire treacle tart with toffee bananas and whipped cream for dessert. Wells Bombardier Premium Bitter and Shepherd Neame Spitfire are the real ales on draught, and there are a few interesting bottled beers, including Leiffman's Kriek and Leffe. The wine list runs to 40 bottles, ranging from simple house wines at £11.50 to some fairly upmarket offerings for big spenders. Half a dozen of each colour are served by the glass. SAMPLE DISHES: artichoke ravioli with ricotta and walnut sauce £8.75; grilled sardines on sautéed lentils with coriander £7.25; steamed stem ginger and allspice pudding with warm custard and roasted rhubarb £4.50.

Licensees Gregory and Patrick Wright (freehouse)
Open 12 to 11, Sun 12 to 10; bar food Mon to Fri 12 to 3.30, Mon to Sat 6.30 to 10.30, Sun 12 to 4, 6.30 to 10, restaurant Tue to Fri 12 to 3.30, 6.30 to 10.30, Sat 6.30 to 10.30, Sun 12 to 4, 6.30 to 10
Details Children welcome in bar eating area   Wheelchair access (not WC)   Patio   Background music in bar   Dogs welcome in bar only   Delta, MasterCard, Switch, Visa

Perseverance   map 12

63 Lamb's Conduit Street, WC1N 3NB   TEL: (020) 7405 8278

Real flock wallpaper, faux crystal chandeliers, dark wooden floors, tables and chairs, and banquettes along dark red walls create an unmistakable retro mood in this unassuming pub on the corner of Great Ormond Street and Lamb's Conduit Street. Upstairs, the small restaurant offers quite a contrast. Painted pink, with a couple of mirrors and modern artwork by way of decoration, it's a small, bright room, with large windows overlooking the street, and with white tablecloths demonstrating a slightly more serious tone than the downstairs. The restaurant menu doesn't follow the retro theme but instead moves with the times to deliver appealing and ambitious dishes: starters of salt-cod potato cake with sauce gribiche or caponata with goats' cheese and rocket might be followed by roast mallard with sarladaise potato and cavolo nero, roast monkfish teamed up with squid, white-bean, saffron and almond stew with gremolata or – for vegetarians – wild mushroom and celeriac gratin with spinach, Parmesan and truffle oil. Cheeses and a few desserts such as white chocolate and Baileys pannacotta or bread-and-butter pudding with rhubarb complete the picture. A tapas/meze menu is available in the bar from 6.30 in the evening (apart from Sundays) and soup, pies and mash are dished up on cold winter nights for £5 or less. Courage Directors and Deuchars IPA are on handpump, and succinct tasting notes are a reliable guide through the well-spread modern wine list. Mark-ups are on the high side for a pub but nine come by the glass from £2.80. SAMPLE DISHES: smoked salmon with crème fraîche, grated egg and capers £7; Charolais sirloin steak with pommes dauphinois and caramelised endive £16; warm chocolate brownie with Chantilly cream £5.50.

Licensee Alan Lyndon Drew (Pub Estate Co)
Open 11 to 11, Sun 11.30 to 10.30; bar food Mon to Sat 6.30 to 10, restaurant all week 12 to 3 (4 Sun), Mon to Sat 7 to 10; closed 25 Dec, 1 Jan
Details Children welcome   Wheelchair access (not WC)   Jukebox   Dogs welcome in bar only after 3pm   Amex, Delta, MasterCard, Switch, Visa

Queens   NEW ENTRY   map 12

49 Regent's Park Road, NW1 8XD   TEL: (020) 7586 0408

'A good little local pub that very much fits its area,' was how one reporter described this end-of-terrace hostelry set among the smart shops of Regent's Park Road. It's a strangely shaped, narrow building with a small roof terrace attached to the restaurant upstairs giving great views over Primrose Hill. The narrow ground-floor bar, which has attempted to create a feeling of more space by making maximum use of mirrors, has quite subtle lighting, stripped floors, and old wooden tables and chairs. Upstairs, the restaurant is decked out in vivid red tones and has a large opening into the kitchen where chefs can be seen beavering away. The menu chalked up in the bar corresponds with the printed one offered in the restaurant, delivering a repertoire that gravitates towards the Mediterranean in a warm salad of figs, green beans, olives and a poached egg, and bruschetta provençale with Parma ham, roasted tomatoes, mozzarella, and basil, or main courses of wild mushroom risotto with rocket and truffle oil. Otherwise the kitchen adds a certain amount of dash to some essentially classic pub dishes, accompanying grilled Cumberland sausages and mash with roast garlic and shallots, for example. Desserts are resolutely old-fashioned, with apple and cinnamon crumble and bread-and-butter pudding typical choices. As part of the Geronimo Inns chain within Young's, beer drinkers can expect the latter's Bitter and Special. Around a dozen wines are served by the glass. SAMPLE DISHES: cream of spinach soup £4; roast lamb chump with ratatouille, dauphinois potatoes and red wine jus £13; baked chocolate tart with mango coulis £4.

Licensee Robert McGill (Young's)

Open *11 to 11, Sun 12 to 10.30; bar food and restaurant Mon to Sat 12 to 3, 7 to 10 (10.15 Fri and Sat), Sun 12.30 to 4, 7 to 9*

Details *Children welcome   Patio   No smoking in restaurant   Background music   Dogs welcome   Delta, MasterCard, Switch, Visa*

St Johns ✿   map 3
91 Junction Road, N19 5QU   TEL: (020) 7272 1587

The large Victorian pub is faced in glazed tiles and takes a whole space between two small side streets, but there's nothing to mark it out of the ordinary. Considering its location, on the humdrum main drag between Tufnell Park and Archway, the exceptional food is as much a find as the interior is a surprise. The large, buzzy bar has high ceilings and wooden floors filled with pine and oak tables, wooden chairs (some school-room style), leather sofas and a coal fire. A few designer touches run to large sprays of flowers and modern artworks, but overall there's an unpretentious, welcoming, almost old-fashioned appeal to the place. At the back is the dining room (though you can eat anywhere), a vast space with magnificent glass chandeliers, another coal fire and simply laid tables, and it's considerably quieter than the bar. The modish menu of sophisticated but hearty dishes, chalked on blackboards, could open with langoustine, dill and clotted cream tart, with, to follow, perhaps chargrilled sea bass with sautéed potatoes, green beans and tapenade, or lamb fillet with roast garlic mash, spinach, and redcurrant and rosemary jus. Beers, which change frequently, might include Fuller's London Pride and Adnams on handpump, while the compact wine list offers a dozen by the glass. SAMPLE DISHES: crab bisque £5; sautéed chicken and mussels with tarragon, new potatoes and kale £10.50; banana and butterscotch pavlova £4.50.

Licensee Nick Sharpe (Unique Pub Company)

Open *11 to 11, Sun 12 to 10.30; bar food and restaurant Mon to Fri 12 to 3, 6.30 to 11, Sat and Sun 12 to 4, 6.30 to 11*

Details *Children welcome   Wheelchair access (not WC)   Patio   Background music   Dogs welcome   Amex, Delta, MasterCard, Switch, Visa*

Salisbury Tavern ✿   map 12

21 Sherbrooke Road, SW6 7HX   TEL: (020) 7381 4005

On the corner of Dawes Road and Sherbrooke Road, the Salisbury looks pleasantly unpretentious and ordinary from the outside, belying its stylish, upmarket interior. The large open space has light pouring through big windows, bright and cheerful paintwork and board floors. Seating is in booths and banquettes, on sofas, armchairs or wooden chairs, and there's a real neighbourhood atmosphere, with TV screens installed above the bar. It draws an affluent crowd (it's under the same ownership as the Admirable Codrington; see entry) for straightforward, traditional pub fare offered at lunchtime only, from cocktail sausages with honey and whole-grain mustard dressing, and chicken Caesar salad, to ribeye burger with chips; in the evening the separate, upmarket dining room at the rear cranks up the culinary gears with more ambitious ideas such as wild mushroom tartlet with hollandaise, braised belly pork, or pan-fried fillet of sea bass with truffle velouté. Regular ales Fuller's London Pride and Wells Bombardier Premium Bitter on handpump are joined by a guest like Old Speckled Hen, and all the wines on the 27-bottle list are available by the glass. SAMPLE DISHES: risotto of crayfish and spring onion £7; braised lamb shank with carrot and swede purée £13.50; chocolate cheesecake £5.

Licensees Ty Simons and Kim Cottingham (Punch)
Open 11 to 11, Sun 12 to 10.30; bar food 12 to 2.30 (3.30 Sat, 4.30 Sun), restaurant 7 to 11
Details Children welcome   Wheelchair access (also WC)   Background music   Dogs welcome exc in restaurant   Amex, Delta, MasterCard, Switch, Visa

Salusbury Pub and Dining Room ✿ ❦   map 12

50–52 Salusbury Road, NW6 6NN   TEL: (020) 7328 3286

The minicab offices and takeaways clustered around Queen's Park tube station give way to smart delis, restaurants and upmarket estate agents as you head north on the busy Salusbury Road, and it is among these that you will find the Salusbury. At the left of the double-fronted building, the sign reads 'Pub', and it gets packed with a lively young crowd who can generate decibels aplenty; lubrication comes in the form of Adnams Bitter and Broadside. On the right, behind the sign saying 'Dining Room', are bare wooden floors, a few oriental-looking prints on the plain walls and a hotch-potch of tables, chairs and benches of various shapes and sizes. The cooking is rustic Italian, so expect pasta (in the shape of maybe ravioli of spinach and ricotta with sun-dried tomato pesto), risotto – red wine and Taleggio, for example – and plenty of gusto in main dishes like roast fillet of pork with balsamic, Savoy cabbage and mash, or seared tuna loin with red wine and sweet onions. Start a meal with, say, red onion soup with ewes' milk cheese, and round it off with pannacotta with oranges or Vin Santo with cantuccini. Sixty or so wines grouped by style are crammed into two hand-written pages, with a dozen by the glass from £2.60 to £4.45. The list ranges the world looking for great flavours, but not a lot of bottles will give you change out of £15. SAMPLE DISHES: prawns sautéed with chilli and garlic £7.50; broth of Welsh lamb leg with vegetables and pecorino £12; pear poached in red wine £4.50.

Licensees Robert Claassen and Nicholas Mash (freehouse)
Open Mon 5 to 12, Tue to Sat 12 to 12, Sun 12 to 10.30; bar food and restaurant Mon 7 to 10.15, Tue to Sun 12.30 to 3.30, 7 to 10.15 (10 Sun); closed 25 and 26 Dec, 1 Jan
Details Children welcome before 7pm   No cigars/pipes in restaurant   Background music   Dogs welcome on a lead   Delta, MasterCard, Switch, Visa

Seven Stars NEW ENTRY   map 12

53–54 Carey Street, WC2A 2JB   TEL: (020) 7242 8521

Built in 1602, the last full year of Elizabeth I's reign, and a rare survivor in these parts
of the great fire of 1666, the Seven Stars is considered to be one of London's oldest
inns. Now a small, traditional dining pub purveying 'basic, rustic old England', the
bar encompasses distinctive wooden beams and panelling. Custom comes from the
imposing Royal Courts of Justice opposite, with owner Roxy Beaujolais presiding
over bar and kitchen. About a dozen dishes are written on a blackboard; there are no
starters or puddings as such (although sometimes a soup is on offer), and dishes range
from mussel and scallop stew with crusty bread, via organic poached salmon with
mayonnaise and boiled potatoes, to 'well-presented' Napoli sausages with sliced belly
pork and cauliflower purée, or spicy corn-fed chicken breast on focaccia. Beers are
Adnams Bitter and Broadside, and Harveys Sussex Best Bitter, with occasional guests
from Young's or Fuller's, and six wines are available by the glass. SAMPLE DISHES:
bruschetta with tomatoes and rocket £6.75; chargrilled sirloin steak £9.50; Cheddar
cheese with oatcakes £7.

Licensee Roxy Beaujolais (freehouse)
Open Mon to Fri 11 to 11, Sat 12 to 11.30; bar food 12 to 9; closed 25 and 26 Dec, 1 Jan, Easter Sun and Mon
Details No children   No music   Dogs welcome   Amex, Delta, MasterCard, Switch, Visa

Ship Inn NEW ENTRY   map 3

Jews Row, SW18 1TB   TEL: (020) 8870 9667   WATERSIDE
WEBSITE: www.theship.co.uk

With extensive outdoor riverside seating, an outdoor bar, daily summer barbecues,
and the additional draw of a barge moored alongside, the Ship attracts crowds in
summer. Mind you, it's equally crowded in winter, when the action moves inside.
The old Victorian building has been opened up in typically modern style (a cosy dark-
toned front bar, a light conservatory, various dining rooms, a mishmash of wooden
and leather furniture, a wood-burner, and book-lined shelves), and the focus is
certainly on food. A short, lively menu sticks largely to modern and British sensibili-
ties: for instance, 'good, hearty' mushroom and coriander soup, game terrine with
plum salad, and main courses of a thick, rich Catalan-style seafood stew with garlic
bread, or Lincolnshire sausages with grain mustard mash and onion gravy. Good old
apple and rhubarb crumble stands alongside walnut tart with honeycomb ice cream at
dessert stage. The Ship is part of Charles and Linda Gotto's mini-empire within
Young's, and they take the sourcing of raw materials seriously: meat comes from the
Gottos' own farm, ice cream is from Devon, and the cheeseboard features
Godminster vintage Cheddar. Young's Bitter, Special and seasonal ales are on handpump, and 15 wines are available by the glass from a short, globetrotting list. SAMPLE
DISHES: sautéed prawns with red chard and lime oil £5.25; roast Barbary duck breast
with gratin dauphinois and red wine jus £13.50; cherry bread-and-butter pudding
£4.50.

Licensee Charles Gotto (Young's)
Open 11 to 11, Sun 12 to 10.30; bar food and restaurant 12 to 10.30 (10 Sun)
Details Children welcome   Wheelchair access (not WC)   Garden   No music   Dogs welcome   Amex, Delta,
MasterCard, Switch, Visa

The Social   NEW ENTRY   map 12

33 Linton Street, N1 7DU   TEL: (020) 7354 5809
WEBSITE: www.thesocial.com

The Social is a subtly modernised mid-twentieth-century pub (still with its original
name, the Hanbury Arms, on high), pubbily unpretentious, with a décor of panelling
and wooden floors, and a jukebox playing 'NME-approved pop music a touch above
background level'. The emphasis is firmly on food – 'the first thing you see on entering are the stoves' – but with an upstairs bar for sofa-sitting, drinking and pool. The
menu brings together some contemporary culinary notions while keeping faith with
pub tradition. After a starter of creamy courgette, spinach and nut soup, main courses
range from grilled tuna with spinach, roast new potatoes and pomegranate salad, to
beef and Guinness pie with creamy mash, or a vegetarian gratin of potatoes and
spinach with asparagus, roast tomatoes and basil, with warm chocolate brownie with
chocolate sauce for dessert. Bombardier is the only beer on handpump; otherwise
there's a bigger-than-usual choice of spirits and liqueurs, and eight or so wines by the
glass from a short, global list. SAMPLE DISHES: seared scallops with crispy bacon and
tomato and orange sauce £6.50; creamy chicken and leek pie £8.50; rhubarb and apple
crumble £4.

Licensee David Christopher Read (Charles Wells)
Open *Mon to Fri 5 to 11, Sat 12 to 11, Sun 12 to 10.30; bar food Mon to Fri 6 to 10.30, Sat 12.30 to 10.30,
Sun 12.30 to 9.30; closed 25 to 30 Dec*
Details *Children welcome   Wheelchair access (also WC)   Jukebox   No dogs   Amex, Delta, MasterCard,
Switch, Visa*

Sutton Arms ☺   map 12

6 Carthusian Street, EC1M 6EB   TEL: (020) 7253 0723

Georgian architecture and modern concrete live side by side in this area of ancient
byways between Smithfield Market and Charterhouse Square. Set among all this is
the Sutton Arms: on the ground floor it is an unreconstituted backstreet boozer with
an easygoing atmosphere (even the décor looks as if it hasn't been changed for generations), while upstairs is a dining room with an interesting menu (also available in the
pub) and a kitchen producing some well-thought-out and accomplished cooking.
With Ottis Reading rather than Garage playing on the jukebox ('the best jukebox in
the City (FREE!)', the pub tells us), friendly and efficient staff behind the bar, one
reporter rated the 'comfort factor' high. A large blackboard announces the daily bar
specials of, say, cream of parsnip soup, breaded cod fillet with chips and tartare sauce,
Cumberland sausage, and vegetable penne pasta; while a printed menu delivers
snacks like samosas, and spring rolls with a dip. Upstairs is a full restaurant menu
offering generously portioned starters of perfectly executed game terrine with
Cumberland sauce, or smoked haddock and chive fishcakes, while mains run to rack
of lamb with a leek and potato cake and mint and caper sauce, or seared scallops on a
bed of spinach with a creamy saffron sauce – with apple and calvados crème brûlée to
finish. Beer drinkers will find Fuller's London Pride on handpump, and eight or so
wines are available by the glass; wines can also be ordered from the restaurant list.
SAMPLE DISHES: home-cured gravadlax, dill and mustard sauce £7; roast breast of duck

with parsnip purée and caramelised onion sauce £16; croissant bread-and-butter pudding £4.50.

Licensee Christopher Johnson (Remarkable Restaurants)
Open Mon to Fri 12 to 11, Sat 7 to 11; bar food and restaurant Mon to Fri 12.30 to 3, 6 to 9.30; closed Christmas and New Year
Details No children   Wheelchair access (not WC)   Jukebox   Guide dogs only   Amex, Delta, MasterCard, Switch, Visa

Swag & Tails
map 12
10–11 Fairholt Street, SW7 1EG   TEL: (020) 7584 6926
WEBSITE: www.swagandtails.com

Impeccably turned out and unobtrusive in its pretty mews, this upmarket pub is just what one might expect of Knightsbridge. The interior doesn't disappoint, either. The informal but civilised bar is decked out with floorboards, wooden furniture and a fire, with cream walls packed with prints above the half-panelling. Behind it, the dining areas have a more contemporary edge, with mirrors, posters, prints and contemporary artwork on the walls, while the conservatory-style room beyond has a tiled floor. The menu brings together some contemporary ideas, from a starter of pan-fried squid with red onions, chorizo, baby chicken and a red pepper dressing, to main courses of balsamic-glazed chicken breast with pesto mash, sautéed Portobello mushrooms, roasted red peppers and Parmesan cream sauce, or confit duck leg with a cassoulet of white beans, Toulouse sausages, tomatoes, baby onions, spinach and black truffle, and desserts of perhaps crispy coconut rice pudding parcel with mango sorbet and kiwi fruit sauce. Those after something more traditional could opt for classic burgers, or chargrilled ribeye with fat chips. The wine list, arranged by grape variety, is a well-chosen selection, with nine, plus some dessert wines and a champagne, offered by the glass, including a white Menetou-Salon. Marston's Pedigree and Wells Bombardier Premium Bitter are on draught. SAMPLE DISHES: pan-seared foie gras with quince jam, spiced red wine reduction and sherry vinegar caramel £9.75; pork and ginger sausages with coriander mash, wok-fried choi sum and a chilli and lemongrass jus £11.50; date sponge pudding with caramel sauce £5.50.

Licensee Annemaria Boomer Davies (freehouse)
Open Mon to Fri 11 to 11; bar food and restaurant 12 to 3, 6 to 10; closed Christmas to New Year, bank hols
Details Children welcome in restaurant   Wheelchair access (not WC)   No cigars/pipes in restaurant
Background music   Dogs welcome in bar evenings only   Amex, Delta, MasterCard, Switch, Visa

▲ Victoria 🍇   NEW ENTRY
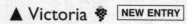
map 3
10 West Temple Sheen, SW14 7RT   TEL: (020) 8876 4238
WEBSITE: www.thevictoria.net

Some might say that this is a gastro-pub; others might define it as a bar/restaurant-with-rooms. Either way, it's a stylishly refurbished venue, with whitewashed floor-boards throughout and brown-leather armchairs in the lounge area – as well as a table football machine. There's also a delightful light conservatory restaurant on two levels with wooden chairs and white paper table covers over damask cloths. The menu is flexible, and several dishes (including a few desserts) can be ordered as small or large portions. A portion of bread and olives (£3.50) is 'a meal in itself', with lots of additional nibbles thrown in, and the all-day tapas plate is a good bet for grazing. Otherwise, the kitchen mines the modern European repertoire for some unusual combinations, including a take on the transport café cooked breakfast consisting of duck confit hash with a fried egg, bacon and home-made herb ketchup, or pan-fried cod with a casserole of Puy lentils and zampone with piquillo pepper relish. Eggs Benedict and chicken club sandwich with fries strike a more recognisable note for Sunday brunch, while capably handled desserts might include rhubarb crumble, or passion-fruit tart with mango sorbet. Deuchars IPA and Hoegaarden are on draught. A quality-conscious, if pricy, wine list completes the picture and includes eight by the glass. SAMPLE DISHES: Serrano ham with grilled chicory and sherry vinegar dressing £7; grilled black bream with couscous salad and pomegranate relish £13; chocolate and Seville orange tart with crème fraîche £6.

Licensees Mark Chester and Adele Stebbings (Unique Pub Company)
Open 11 to 11; bar food and restaurant 12 to 2.30 (3 Sat and Sun), 7 to 10
Details Children welcome Car park Wheelchair access (also WC) Garden and patio No cigars/pipes in restaurant Background music No dogs Amex, Delta, MasterCard, Switch, Visa Accommodation: 7 rooms, B&B £82.50 to £92.50

White Horse 🏵 🍺 map 3

1 Parsons Green, SW6 4UL TEL: (020) 7736 2115
WEBSITE: www.whitehorsesw6.com

The White Horse, on a corner by Parsons Green, is a considerably sized pub with an equally considerable reputation for its beer, food and sporting ambience. Inside, the décor comprises crimson walls, oak panels, a flagstone floor, church pews and large pine tables, which all add up to give the place a traditional feel, though large plants, mirrors and Venetian blinds give a touch of modernity, and as well as the main bar there is a restaurant upstairs. Not only does the printed menu come with suggested wines, but beers are recommended to match dishes: Oakham JHB to go with linguine with poached free-range chicken, chilli, rocket and lemon oil, for example. They really know their beers here, and the range on offer is seriously impressive. As well as top-quality British real ales like Harveys Sussex Best Bitter, Fuller's ESB, Rooster's Yankee, Adnams Broadside and the aforementioned Oakham JHB on draught, there are over 80 bottled beers from around the world. And there is an impressive list of over 120 wines, some with three-figure price tags; 20 come by the glass. Food, though not cheap, is also of a high standard. Old favourites like pork sausages and mash with beer onion gravy and steak sandwich are on the menu, but more unusual are king prawns, squid and mussels in a fragrant Thai laksa with noodles and coconut, and rump of lamb with roast sweet potatoes, couscous and a minted yoghurt dressing. Substantial starters (perfect for a light supper) might feature baked field mushrooms with Stinking Bishop and spinach, or chicken Caesar salad. SAMPLE DISHES: roast pumpkin salad with rocket, pine nuts and goats' cheese £6.75; salmon fishcake with fresh horseradish and a watercress and fennel salad £8.25; rum bread-and-butter pudding £4.50.

Licensee Mark Dorber (Mitchell & Butler)
Open 11 to 11, Sun 12 to 10.30; bar food and restaurant Mon to Fri 12 to 3, 6 to 10, Sat and Sun 12 to 10; closed 25 Dec
Details Children welcome in eating areas Wheelchair access (not WC) Garden and patio No smoking in restaurant Occasional live music Dogs welcome Amex, Delta, MasterCard, Switch, Visa

William IV ✿

map 3

786 Harrow Road, NW10 5JX   TEL: (020) 8969 5944
WEBSITE: www.william-iv.co.uk

It may be quite a hike from the nearest tube (and the traffic on the Harrow Road can be relentless), but this tastefully refurbished Victorian pub is quite a surprise – the kind of place you wish were your local. Bar and restaurant are separate entities, with a garden each for al fresco dining and drinks. The bar occupies a large, high-ceilinged room painted in rather gloomy shades of pale green and cream, dotted with wooden tables, chairs and well-worn sofas; although it may be cavernous, it feels comfortable. The menu runs on modern lines and might feature venison, pigeon and black pudding terrine with green tomato chutney, chargrilled sardines with braised Puy lentils and salsa verde, or roast duck breast with mash, spinach and confit garlic gravy. There's a good-value one-course lunch option for £8, and an early-evening special of two courses for £12. For beer drinkers there's Fuller's London Pride, Adnams Best Bitter plus a guest – perhaps Golden Arrow from the Cottage Brewing Company – while the wine list offers some dozen or so wines by the glass. SAMPLE DISHES: deep-fried skate cheeks with lemon and tartare sauce £5.25; slow-roast belly of pork with roasted celeriac, salsify and mustard sauce £11; chocolate and caramel tart £4.50.

Licensees Patrick Morcas, Nicholas Daniel and Carlos Horrillo (freehouse)
Open Mon to Wed 12 to 11, Thur to Sat 12 to 12, Sun 12 to 10.30; bar food and restaurant 12 to 3 (4 Sat and Sun), 6 to 11; closed 25 Dec, 1 Jan
Details Children welcome in eating areas   Garden   Occasional background music   Dogs welcome   Amex, Delta, Diners, MasterCard, Switch, Visa

England

ABBOTS BROMLEY   Staffordshire   map 5

Goats Head   NEW ENTRY
Abbots Bromley WS15 3BP   TEL: (01283) 840254

Abbots Bromley is an attractive village with a thirteenth-century Butter Cross and a small green at its heart. Overlooking all this is the Goats Head, a fine black and white timbered building dating from the sixteenth century (from the lawn at the back there's a view of the church). It's been modernised inside, but the ancient interior retains some character, notably in heavy Tudor beams and standing timbers within the carpeted main lounge bar and dining area. A few cushioned oak settles, two fire-places, plenty of brass and simple prints add up to a pleasant look. A short, hand-written snack menu lists sandwiches, jacket potatoes, and ploughman's, while an equally short selection of the day's specials is chalked on a board. It's sensible pub food, good home cooking that ranges from starters such as leek and potato soup and chicken liver pâté to main courses of pork loin steak with creamy apple sauce, perhaps, or sirloin steak, and braised lamb shank with mint and red wine gravy. Marston's Pedigree and Greene King Abbot Ale are on handpump, and a dozen wines are available by the glass. SAMPLE DISHES: sliced black pudding and apple pan-fried in garlic butter £4; pan-fried medallions of beef fillet in creamy grain mustard and mushroom sauce £14.50; bread-and-butter pudding £3.50.

Licensee Kristian Hine (Punch Taverns)
Open 12 to 3, 6 to 11; bar food Tue to Sun 12 to 2, Mon to Sat 6.30 to 9; closed lunchtime Mon
Details No children   Wheelchair access (also WC)   Garden and patio   No smoking   Background music
No dogs   Delta, MasterCard, Switch, Visa

ADDINGHAM   West Yorkshire   map 8

Fleece ☺
Main Street, Addingham LS29 0LY   TEL: (01943) 830491

Addingham is a small village sandwiched between Ilkley and Skipton, with the Fleece 'occupying a good spot' as you drive into the village. It attracts a mixed bunch of locals, diners and walkers, drawn as much by the atmosphere as by the food. Black-painted beams, stone walls, flagstone floors, and a lovely wood-burning stove and a log fire provide a comfortable environment, while there are plenty of things to look at, from a stag's head to copper kettles and pans hanging from the ceiling; in summer the front terrace is a draw. There are lots of things to choose from on the long, enterpris-ing menu boards, too. You could mix traditional pub staples with more up-to-date ideas, starting, perhaps, with curried parsnip soup, or a warm salad of chorizo and pear, then proceed to lamb hotpot, local bangers and mash with onion gravy, or roast Wigglesworth mallard with ginger and mandarin. Omelettes and sandwiches – among them honey-roast ham with excellent home-made piccalilli – are also possibilities, and a range of farmhouse cheeses is a good alternative to dessert. Black Sheep Best Bitter, Tetley Bitter and Timothy Taylor Landlord are on draught, and a dozen wines are sold by the glass, with the full, well-chosen selection approaching 50 bottles. SAMPLE DISHES: Yorkshire ham rarebit £4.50; charred Barnsley chop with slow-roast aubergine £10; selection of organic cheese £5.50.

Licensee Chris Monkman (Punch Group)
Open *12 to 11; bar food and restaurant Mon to Sat 12 to 2.15, 6 to 9.30, Sun 12 to 8*
Details *Children welcome   Car park   Wheelchair access (also WC)   Garden   No smoking in restaurant Occasional live music   Dogs welcome exc in restaurant   Delta, MasterCard, Switch, Visa*

ALDBURY   Hertfordshire   **map 3**

Valiant Trooper

Trooper Road, Aldbury HP23 5RW   TEL: (01442) 851203
off A41, 2½m E of Tring

A small, pinkwashed, cottagey building in a decidedly rural part of Hertfordshire, the Trooper has valiantly stood up for the virtues of good old-fashioned hospitality since the mid-eighteenth century. In the main bar there are enough low oak beams, open fires and antique-looking wooden furniture to keep even the most ardent traditionalist happy. Bar menus also have a simple, old-fashioned appeal, with jacket potatoes, ciabattas and open sandwiches, all with a wide choice of fillings, plus assorted ploughman's. The separate dining room to the rear has a blackboard menu listing more imaginative dishes such as pork fillet stuffed with red peppers and wrapped in bacon. Real ales on draught are Fuller's London Pride, Adnams Bitter and Morrells Oxford Blue, plus two guest beers, and a modest but well-priced list of 17 wines includes nine by the glass. SAMPLE DISHES: smoked salmon and Mediterranean prawn platter £5; herb chicken breast with a lime and cream cheese sauce £9.50; sticky toffee pudding £3.75.

Licensee Tim O'Gorman (freehouse)
Open *11.30 to 11, Sun 12 to 10.30; bar food and restaurant all week 12 to 2 (2.30 Sun), Tue to Sat 6.30 to 9.15; closed 25 Dec*
Details *Children welcome in eating areas   Car park   Wheelchair access (also WC)   Garden and patio No-smoking area in bar, no smoking in dining room   No music   Dogs welcome on lead   Diners, MasterCard, Switch, Visa*

ALDERMINSTER   Warwickshire   **map 5**

Bell

Shipston Road, Alderminster CV37 8NY   TEL: (01789) 450414
WEBSITE: www.thebellald.co.uk
on A3400, 4m S of Stratford-upon-Avon

This large, custard-coloured eighteenth-century coaching inn is situated a few miles south of Stratford-upon-Avon, and views over the Stour Valley can be appreciated either from the large garden or the conservatory. Inside, it has the civilised atmosphere of a family home, with classical music in the background and lots of plants. There's a comfortable lounge area with low sofas, but the rest of the place is given over to dining, with well-spaced tables. The menus take in a range of modern and traditional ideas – cheese-stuffed chicken fillet wrapped in Parma ham in a crème fraîche sauce on the one hand, and steak and kidney pie on the other. Alternatives run from spinach and ricotta tortellini to Thai-style chicken curry with sticky rice and mango and bean sprout salad. Greene King IPA and Abbot Ale are the real ales offered, and a generous number of wines are available by the small or large glass from a short, good-value list of bottles. SAMPLE DISHES: crab au gratin £6; liver on bubble and squeak with smoked bacon £10.25; passion-fruit and mango parfait £4.25.

Licensee Keith Brewer (freehouse)
Open 12 to 2.30, 7 to 11 (10.30 Sun); bar food and restaurant 12 to 2, 7 to 9.30 (8.30 Sun); closed evenings 24 to 30 Dec and 1 Jan
Details Children welcome   Car park   Wheelchair access (not WC)   Garden   No smoking exc in entrance bar   Occasional live or background music   Dogs welcome in bar only   Amex, Delta, Diners, MasterCard, Switch, Visa   Accommodation: 6 rooms, B&B £27 to £65

ALDFORD   **Cheshire**   map 7

Grosvenor Arms 🍺

Chester Road, Aldford CH3 6HJ   TEL: (01244) 620228
WEBSITE: www.grosvenorarms-aldford.co.uk
just off B5130, 5m S of Chester

Once the estate workers' beerhouse on the vast Grosvenor Estate, the imposing Victorian building commands a corner of the village centre, with views of rich pastureland and the River Dee. There's an immense beer garden to the rear, over-looked from a huge conservatory and a substantial patio. Several distinct areas surround the bar and servery at the heart of the building, each with a slightly different mood – one has the feel of a local's tap room with its splendid mosaic-tiled floor, and the 'snug' bar has a coal fire. Handpumps dispense Caledonian Deuchars IPA and beers from the local Robinson's and Weetwood breweries, among others – usually around six ales are on offer at a time. Around ten wines are available by the glass from a short but enthusiastic wine list. House wines are £10 and half the list is £15 or under. An enormous blackboard lists the food (admirably served all day), and the choice is extensive: from soups such as split pea, and sandwiches like egg and bacon mayonnaise with sun-dried tomato bread, to main courses of pork steak with Stilton rarebit topping and creamed cabbage and potatoes, finishing up along the lines of tiramisù terrine with a coffee and brandy syrup. Note that this pub is part of a small chain; see also Dysart Arms, Bunbury; the Hare, Langton Green; Old Harkers Arms, Chester; and the Pant-yr-Ochain, Gresford. SAMPLE DISHES: pan-fried duck livers with a hot hoisin noodle salad £5.75; whole grilled plaice with lemon, capers and tarragon butter £11; passion-fruit cheesecake £4.50.

Licensees R.G. Kidd and D.J. Brunning (Brunning & Price Ltd)
Open 11.30 to 11, Sun 12 to 10.30; bar food 12 to 10 (9 Sun)
Details Children welcome; no under-14s after 6pm   Car park   Wheelchair access (also WC)   Garden No-smoking area   No music   Dogs welcome in 1 bar   Amex, Delta, MasterCard, Switch, Visa

---

Food mentioned in the entries is available in the bar, although it may also be possible to eat in a dining room.

ALDWORTH Berkshire map 2

Bell Inn 🍺

Aldworth RG8 9SE TEL: (01635) 578272
on B4009, 3m W of Streatley

The red-brick frontage of this ancient building, with its pitched porch on the front incorporating a couple of seats, doesn't immediately smack of being a pub – despite being one for 400 years – but then the Bell is no ordinary hostelry. The first thing you notice on entering is the dark wooden and glass-panelled bar kiosk-cum-hatch ('rather like a Victorian cashier's office') instead of the more conventional bar counter. This sets the atmosphere: a 'timeless gem' that makes no real concessions to modernity, so expect simple hardwood furniture, a wood-burner, no music or games machines, and a trip to the gent's means a journey outside. Beer is the main focus, and the pub stocks a good selection of well-kept ales, among them West Berkshire Maggs, Magnificent Mild, Old Tyler Bitter, and Arkells 3B and Kingsdown Ale. Wine hardly counts, although Berry Bros and Rudd's Good Ordinary Claret, one of four house wines sold by the glass, is decent enough. Food in the bar (there is no restaurant) is limited to home-made soup – say, parsnip or artichoke – Aga-warmed rolls with generous, good-quality hot fillings ranging from Devon crab to ox tongue, ploughman's, and a dish of the day, which might be pasta, plus jam sponge. The Bell has been with the Macaulay family for over 200 years. SAMPLE DISHES: tomato soup £3; hot crusty filled roll £2.25; treacle sponge £2.50.

Licensee H.E. Macaulay (freehouse)
Open Tue to Sun and bank hol Mon 11 to 3, 6 to 11, Sun 12 to 3, 7 to 10.30; bar food 11 to 2.45, 6 to 10.35; closed 25 Dec
Details Children welcome in family room Car park Wheelchair access (not WC) Garden Occasional live music Dogs welcome on a lead No cards

ALFRISTON East Sussex map 3

▲ George Inn

High Street, Alfriston BN26 5SY TEL: (01323) 870319

Alfriston, a very pretty village, is the home of the Clergy House, the first property the National Trust ever bought, and lies in a valley cutting through the South Downs (great walking country). In the main street the George's frontage dominates an ancient brick-and-flint terrace, standing out because its upper storey is half-timbered. The 'smashing and spacious' interior has two huge bar areas and a large dining room. The former offer Greene King IPA and Abbott Ale, Morland Original and Old Speckled Hen in spare surroundings dominated by old, dark wood – floor, ceiling and stripped studwork partitions – and the flickering of a log fire. In the latter, where apricot-coloured walls give a softer, more domestic feel, the food is good, 'nice raw materials, all nicely timed'. Light meals at lunchtime – like grilled sardines with a tomato and red onion salsa, or garlic-sautéed flat mushrooms topped with smoked bacon and goats' cheese – are much cheaper than the evening menu: vodka-marinated salmon on hot beetroot with new potatoes, maybe, or pork loin with ginger and honey on braised fennel. Vegetarians are well catered for with, say, tomatoes stuffed with vegetable risotto served with watercress sauce, and desserts might include crème brûlée or chocolate fudge cake. Out of about 20 wines, starting from £10, eight or so are served by the glass. SAMPLE DISHES: salmon fishcakes £5; fillet of veal medallions on grilled vegetables and aïoli £15; apple crumble £4.

Licensees Roland and Cate Couch (Greene King)
Open 12 to 11, Sun 12 to 10.30; bar food 12 to 2.30, 7 to 9 (10 Fri and Sat); closed 25, 26 and 27 Dec
Details Children welcome in eating areas   Garden   No smoking in dining room   Occasional background music
Dogs welcome   Delta, MasterCard, Switch, Visa   Accommodation: 7 rooms, B&B £40 to £100

ALLERTON BYWATER   West Yorkshire   map 9

Boat 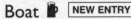 NEW ENTRY

Allerton Bywater WF10 2BX   TEL: (01977) 552216   **BREW PUB**
village off A656 just N of Castleford

This whitewashed canalside pub has an extensive outside eating area with swings for children and reputedly a ghost inside. Beer drinkers will be more interested in the pub's own microbrewery-produced Boat ales – including 'Man in the Boat' – which are served alongside guests such as Tetley Bitter. (There are also nine wines, all offered by the glass.) Off the bar are two dining areas full of dark wooden tables and chairs, with an open fire, and old photographs and a local artist's work on the walls. The menu is mostly familiar stuff, opening with the likes of good, home-made cauliflower soup, or a giant Yorkshire pudding. Most main courses come in two sizes, with the larger option 'enough for two', according to one reporter, and Cumberland sausage with onion gravy is a hefty sausage. Sunday roasts are popular, with well-cooked and tender roast lamb, served with cauliflower in a creamy mustard sauce, getting the thumbs up at inspection. Puddings are of the rich and creamy variety and are displayed in a cold cabinet. SAMPLE DISHES: chicken with a mushroom and Stilton cream sauce £6; steak and Boat ale pie £12; jam roly-poly with custard £2.25.

Licensee Lee Gwinnell (freehouse)
Open Mon to Thur 11 to 3, 5.30 to 11, Fri to Sun 11 to 9.30; bar food Mon to Fri 12 to 2, 6 to 9, Sat 12 to 9.30, Sun 12 to 7
Details Children welcome   Car park   Wheelchair access (also WC)   Garden and patio   No-smoking area in bar   Background music   No dogs   Amex, Delta, Diners, MasterCard, Switch, Visa

ALNMOUTH   Northumberland   map 10

▲ Saddle Hotel

24–25 Northumberland Street, Alnmouth NE66 2RA   TEL: (01665) 830476
from A1, take Alnwick turn-off, then Alnmouth exit at mini-roundabout

Billed as a 'Hotel and Grill', this old stone hostelry is handily situated on the main street of the village on an isthmus between the North Sea and the estuary of the River Aln, just minutes from the beach. Inside, all is homely and comfortable, with fires, a striped green carpet and busily patterned wallpaper setting the tone; a separate restaurant deals in set-price menus, although people just wanting one course can order from these in the bar. The bar menu itself is extensive enough to satisfy most tastes, with some North Country specialities like Craster kippers, Barnsley chops, and Northumbrian sausages in Yorkshire pudding sharing the stage with chicken pancakes topped with bolognese sauce, Hawaiian toast, and beef Elizabeth (in a mushroom, French mustard and red wine sauce). Sandwiches are made with Northumbrian stottie bread, and blackboard specials broaden the range, while desserts revolve around gâteaux, cheesecakes, and ice cream concoctions. Old Speckled Hen and Theakston Cool Cask are on draught, and three house wines are available by the glass. SAMPLE DISHES: egg and prawn cocktail £4.50; chicken and ham pie £6.50; banana split £4.25.

Licensees Mr and Mrs M. McMonagle (freehouse)
Open 11 to 11, Sun 12 to 10.30; bar food 12 to 2, 6 to 9 (8.30 Sun), restaurant 6 to 8.30
Details Children welcome in eating areas   Wheelchair access (not WC)   No smoking in restaurant   Occasional background music   Dogs welcome   Delta, MasterCard, Switch, Visa   Accommodation: 8 rooms, B&B £44 to £78

AMBLESIDE   Cumbria   map 8

▲ Drunken Duck Inn

Barngates, Ambleside LA22 0NG   TEL: (015394) 36347
WEBSITE: www.drunkenduckinn.co.uk
off B5286, between Ambleside and Hawkshead, 3m S of Ambleside

BREW PUB

This well-maintained stone pub stands in an isolated spot on the twisty, undulating back route from Ambleside to Coniston. It's understandably popular with passing walkers, but worth considering as a destination in its own right. Bar areas are elegantly styled with polished dark floorboards and plain-coloured walls covered with a mix of prints, watercolours and advertising posters. Lunch and dinner menus are wide-ranging, modern and inventive, and make good use of local produce. Start perhaps with liquorice-marinated pigeon breast on Agen prune and Parmesan risotto, or smoked trout with potato and green mustard salad, and follow with cocoa-marinated venison on chestnut polenta with caramelised figs and espresso pistachio nuts, or perhaps baked cod on smoked bacon and lentil cassoulet with sauce maltaise and field mushroom fritters. Gourmands might squeeze in a pannacotta with damson compote, or a selection of serious cheeses. For lubrication there are four first-class real ales from the on-site Barngates brewery, or something from the superior list of 80 wines, which has something for all pockets and no fewer than 20 by the glass, from a simple Sauvignon Blanc at £3 to a premier cru Chablis at £9. SAMPLE DISHES: dressed crab on garlic bruschetta with wild rocket and lemon dressing £7; rack of Cumbrian lamb with rosemary, beetroot, Cumbrian air-dried ham, roast potatoes and redcurrant lamb glaze £16.50; warm rhubarb and custard tart with crumble ice cream £5.75.

Licensee Stephanie Barton (freehouse)
Open 11.30 to 11, Sun 12 to 10.30; bar food and restaurant 12 to 2.30, 6 to 9; restaurant and guest accommodation closed 24 and 25 Dec
Details Children welcome   Car park   Wheelchair access (also WC)   Patio   No smoking in eating areas   Background music in restaurant   Dogs welcome in bar only   Amex, Delta, MasterCard, Switch, Visa   Accommodation: 16 rooms, B&B £56.25 to £165

ARDELEY   Hertfordshire   map 3

Jolly Waggoner

Ardeley SG2 7AH   TEL: (01438) 861350
off B1037 at Cromer, 5m E of Stevenage

The village is little more than a hamlet with the Jolly Waggoner at its heart, clearly a very old building. The interior is unpretentious, with beams, an open fire, and an old-fashioned look that runs to horse brasses, bunches of fake flowers, and pink walls. Several blackboards list the bar food, specials, and puddings, with the emphasis on English brasserie dishes with nods to the orient and Mediterranean. Omelette Arnold Bennett is served with a light béchamel sauce, steak is accompanied by Gorgonzola sauce, and liver and bacon with a Roquefort sauce – both the last proving to be 'vast platefuls' served with herby sautéed potatoes and a salad of leaves, carrot and tomato. Those looking for a snack can opt for an open toasted sandwich of ham and mature Cheddar, or stir-fried chicken and cashew nut salad, and to finish there could be bread-and-butter pudding with raspberry coulis. Next door, a slightly smarter, but still tiny, restaurant, Rose Cottage, seems almost like the dining room of a private house, and serves a more elaborate menu, from wild mushroom risotto to fillet of lamb wrapped in Parma ham, duxelles and puff pastry with rosemary gravy. Greene King IPA and Abbot Ale are on draught, and the wine list offers a compact selection, with four by the glass. SAMPLE DISHES: smoked salmon and warm goats' cheese croûton £6.50; fillet of chicken cooked in a cream, garlic, wine, mushroom and onion sauce £12; chocolate truffle torte £4.25.

Licensee D.J. Perkins (Greene King)
Open Tue to Sat and bank hol Mon 12 to 2.30 (3 Sat), 6.30 to 11, Sun 12 to 3, 7 to 10.30; bar food Tue to Sun and bank hol Mon 12 to 2, Tue to Sat and bank hol Mon 6.30 to 9/9.30; closed Tue after bank hol Mon
Details No children under 7 Car park Garden and patio No-smoking area No music No dogs Delta, MasterCard, Switch, Visa

---

ARDINGTON Oxfordshire map 2

▲ Boar's Head
Church Street, Ardington OX12 8QA TEL: (01235) 833254
off A417, 2m E of Wantage

In a typically old-world village with pub and church side by side, the well-maintained appearance of this half-timbered inn belies its age – it has in fact been a pub since the eighteenth century. The open-plan bar areas are simply decorated, and an informal mood is set by the crowd of drinkers congregating around the bar. This is very much a pub (including a dartboard in one corner), but one that has a serious restaurant and serves excellent bar meals. The restaurant menu (not available in the bar) goes in for an ambitious and inventive style: witness fillet of Aberdeen Angus beef with sweet-and-sour onions, wild mushrooms and foie gras sauce. By contrast, the philosophy when it comes to bar food is to keep everything simple. The succinct blackboard menu mostly consists of lunchtime baguettes plus one-dish meals: a generous poached egg salad with black pudding and bacon, for example, or Toulouse sausage cassoulet. Bread is a highlight, with several interesting varieties baked daily on the premises. Beer spotters will appreciate the rarely sighted Dr Hexter's Wedding Ale from the West Berkshire Brewery as well as Hook Norton Best Bitter. The wine list opens with an earnest selection of Burgundies and Bordeaux. If your heart sinks at the sight of high price tags, fear not: there are rich pickings under £20 from all over the world, including these classic French regions. Eight or so come by the glass. SAMPLE DISHES: Cornish mussels in wine and cream £6.50; Thai fishcakes with coconut salad £8.50; bread-and-butter pudding with prune and Armagnac ice cream £6.

Licensee Bruce Buchan (freehouse)
Open 12 to 3, 6 to 11 (10.30 Sun); bar food and restaurant 12 to 2, 7 to 9.30 (10 Fri and Sat)
Details Children welcome Car park Garden and patio No smoking in restaurant Occasional background music Dogs welcome in bar only Amex, Delta, MasterCard, Switch, Visa Accommodation: 3 rooms, B&B £65 to £120

ARKESDEN   Essex   map 3

Axe and Compasses

Arkesden CB11 4EX   TEL: (01799) 550272
off B1038, 1m N of Clavering

'The Axe', as it is known locally, is the heartbeat of this picture-postcard village of some 300 inhabitants. The core of the pub is a thatched building dating from 1650, but the right-hand extension, now the public bar, is from the early nineteenth century. The interior is traditional, with a profusion of oak beams, standing timbers, horse brasses and assorted farm accoutrements. The frequently changing bar menus might include lunchtime sandwiches, grilled sardines, steak and kidney pie, Barnsley chop with mint gravy, and battered cod fillet. The lengthy restaurant menu (not served in the bar) might take you from king prawns and green-lipped mussels grilled with garlic butter, or strips of duck breast pan-fried with spring onions and cucumber served with a pancake and plum sauce, to main courses of grilled medallions of monkfish with prawn and lemon parsley butter, or sirloin steak Diane. Portions are generous, but those wanting a pudding could go for something fruity like strawberries and cream. Drink Greene King IPA, Abbot or Old Speckled Hen or one of the guest beers. Around 16 wines are sold by the glass, with the full list approaching 40 bottles. SAMPLE DISHES: avocado pear baked with Parma ham and Stilton £7; whole grilled lemon sole £13; lemon meringue crunch £4.

Licensees Themis and Diane Christou (Greene King)
Open *11 to 2.30, 6 to 11, Sun 12 to 3, 7 to 10.30; bar food and restaurant 12 to 2, 6.45 to 9.30; restaurant closed Sun evening winter*
Details *Children welcome in restaurant   Car park   Garden and patio   No smoking in restaurant   No music No dogs   Delta, MasterCard, Switch, Visa*

ARLINGHAM   Gloucestershire   map 2

▲ Old Passage Inn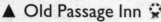

Passage Road, Arlingham GL2 7JR   TEL: (01452) 740547
WEBSITE: www.fishattheoldpassageinn.co.uk
off A38 and B4071, 13m SW of Gloucester

In a stunningly remote position on the bank of the Severn (beyond Arlingham village), this green-painted inn stands on the site of the ancient ford – or passage – that was once the river's lowest crossing point. 'Riverside Seafood Restaurant' says a note at the top of the menu, and the chic interior, with its eau-de-nil colour scheme, reinforces that impression; even so, the atmosphere is relaxed, and you are welcome to call in for just a drink. Seafood cookery, however, is the real draw, with oysters, lobsters and fruits de mer showing up as big players. Some dishes have a familiar ring – for example, deep-fried squid with chilli dip, moules marinière, or beer-battered Cornish day-boat cod with hand-cut chips – but more sophisticated options abound: seared Shetland salmon with an artichoke, olive oil and saffron-infused 'barigal', or fillet of wild sea bass with buttered spinach, pak choi and vanilla butter sauce. Those in search of something meaty might be offered, say, a salad of pan-fried foie gras with scallops and black pudding, followed by chargrilled steak from the Severn Vale with Oxford Blue cheese butter and salad. Desserts keep up the momentum with the likes of strawberry and saffron crème brûlée or warm fig and almond tart; alternatively, go for the selection of half a dozen prime West Country cheeses. To drink, there is draught Bass; otherwise consider the well-spread list of over 40 bins, which includes a fair number of half-bottles and four wines (plus 'sweeties') by the glass. Prices climb steeply from £10.50 a bottle. SAMPLE DISHES: warm salmon and dill sausage with creamed leeks and red wine sauce £8; poached turbot on spring onion mash with wild mushrooms and white truffle oil emulsion £19.50; blackberry sorbet with red berries £4.50.

Licensees Josephine Moore and Patrick Le Mesurier (freehouse)
Open *Tue to Sat 12 (11 summer) to 3, 6.30 (6 summer) to 11, Sun 12 to 2; bar food Tue to Sun 12 to 2, Tue to Sat 6.45 to 9; closed 24 to 30 Dec*
Details *Children welcome   Car park   Wheelchair access (also WC)   Garden and patio   No-smoking area in bar, no smoking in eating area   Occasional background music   Dogs welcome   Amex, Delta, MasterCard, Switch, Visa   Accommodation: 3 rooms, B&B £50 to £95*

ARMATHWAITE   Cumbria   map 10

Duke's Head Hotel

Armathwaite CA4 9PB   TEL: (016974) 72226
off A6, between Carlisle and Penrith

The Duke's Head Hotel is an unpretentious, down-to-earth pub on a corner on the main road through the village. You can't miss its pink-washed stucco façade, and inside are two bar areas, one a slightly austere room with table skittles, the other a comfortable, homely lounge with a log fire; beyond the lounge is the restaurant. One menu is served throughout, offering a generous range of mostly straightforwardly prepared but interesting pub food, such as locally smoked salmon and prawns, Cumberland sausage and black pudding with apple purée, and grilled venison steak with a wood mushroom, red wine and redcurrant sauce. The blackboard specials might deliver a starter of home-made smoked duck, duck liver and gin pâté, and then venison, pheasant and hare pie, or halibut grilled with Wabberthwaite ham and chervil butter, and puddings such as Cumberland rum nicky. Old Speckled Hen and Cumberland Ale from Jennings are on draught, and six wines are served by the glass. The surrounding Eden Valley is a paradise for bird-watchers and walkers. SAMPLE DISHES: cream of parsnip and apple soup £3.50; poached fillet of plaice with cheese and prawn sauce £8.25; lemon and gin mousse £3.50.

Licensee Henry Lynch (Pubmaster)
Open *11.30 to 3, 5.30 to 11; bar food and restaurant 12 to 1.45, 6.15 to 9; open all day Sat and Sun Easter to 1 Oct*
Details *Children welcome   Car park   Wheelchair access (also WC)   Garden   No smoking in restaurant Background music   Dogs welcome in 1 bar only   Delta, MasterCard, Switch, Visa   Accommodation: 6 rooms, B&B £32.50 to £55.50*

ASENBY   North Yorkshire   map 9

Crab & Lobster 🏵

Dishforth Road, Asenby YO7 3QL   TEL: (01845) 577286
WEBSITE: www.crabandlobster.co.uk
off A168, between A19 and A1

Even the rocking horse, the old advertising signs hanging on an outside wall, and the thatch-work crabs and lobsters scuttling across the roof of this creeper-covered pub do not quite prepare the uninitiated for the riot of bric-à-brac and memorabilia that fills almost every inch of the interior, from bar to pavilion (conservatory). Conversation is unlikely to dry up. The adjacent hotel (Crab Manor) continues the theme, with rooms designed to echo exotic locations around the world. True to its name, seafood is the main attraction on an equally exuberant and thoroughly modern global menu. Starters such as chunky British fish soup, stir-fried mussels with chilli, lemongrass, ginger and coconut cream, or deep-fried cod and haddock fishcakes could give way to posh fish and chips, roast garlic lobster with scallops and king prawns, or a Goan curry of fish and king prawns. There are plenty of meat dishes too – pan-fried calf's liver with bacon and Bury black pudding, for example – and for dessert there might be deep-fried apple strudel spring rolls with nutmeg ice cream and Calvados custard. Seven wines are available by the glass, and the choice of hand-pumped ales on offer includes Theakston XB and John Smith's Bitter. This is a popular place, so booking is advisable. SAMPLE DISHES: wild mushroom risotto £5.50; roast monkfish tail with leek and bacon mash and red wine and prawn sauce £15.50; warm chocolate tart with plum confit £5.75.

Licensee Mark Spenceley (freehouse)
Open 11.30 to 11, Sun 12 to 10.30; bar food and restaurant 12 to 2, 7 to 9; closed evening 25 Dec
Details Children welcome   Car park   Wheelchair access (also WC)   Garden   Background music   Dogs welcome   MasterCard, Switch, Visa   Accommodation: 12 rooms, B&B £150 to £200

ASHMORE GREEN   Berkshire
map 2

Sun in the Wood

Stoney Lane, Ashmore Green RG18 9HF   TEL: (01635) 42377
from roundabout junction of A339 and A4 in Newbury, take B4009 Shaw road, turn right at roundabout in Shaw on to Kiln road, then after ½m turn left into Stoney Lane; pub 1m on left

This cream-painted inn on a narrow country lane is a popular refuge for business people escaping from Newbury for lunch, and a large woodland garden with a children's play area makes it ideal for families too. There's a relaxed mood throughout the three interconnecting rooms, which have a mix of flagstones and polished floorboards, pots and pans hanging from the ceiling, and walls lined with food and wine prints. A long, diverse menu takes in everything from pork, apple and Calvados pâté to tempura prawns with garlic and chive dressing among starters, mains ranging from crispy roast duck breast on roast garlic and mushroom compote to fillet steak Rossini. Blackboard specials extend choice further, and there are hot and cold filled baguettes at lunchtime. This is a Wadworth pub serving 6X, JCB and Henry's IPA. The wine list opens with eight 'special selections' from £10.25 a bottle, £2.85/£3.85 a glass, and efficiently covers the world in around 30 good-value bottles including well-chosen French whites. SAMPLE DISHES: leek, cream cheese and tomato filo parcel with tomato and oregano sauce £4.75; braised lamb shoulder with sautéed Savoy and red cabbage in a merlot and rosemary sauce £14; warm pear and frangipane tart £4.50.

Licensee Philip Davison (Wadworth)
Open Tue to Sat 12 to 2.30, 6 to 11, Sun 12 to 2.30, 7 to 10.30; bar food and restaurant Tue to Sun 12 to 2 (3 Sun), Tue to Sat 6 to 9.30
Details Children welcome   Car park   Wheelchair access (also WC)   Garden   No-smoking area in bar, no smoking in restaurant   Background music   Guide dogs only   Amex, Delta, MasterCard, Switch, Visa

ASHURST   **West Sussex**   map 3

Fountain Inn

Ashurst BN44 3AP   TEL: (01403) 710219
on B2135, 4m N of Steyning

This brick and cream-painted sixteenth-century village pub 'attracts a range of customers from regulars seated by the inglenook, personal tankards in hand, who look as though they never move from the spot, to people from further afield coming specifically for the food', declares a reporter. A small entrance opens into a beamed bar decorated with horse brasses and the 'usual rural memorabilia' and with a general sense of balance between drinking and eating which changes in favour of the latter as you go deeper into the rambling, much-extended building. The food covers a lot of territory. As well as the usual pub offerings of lunchtime sandwiches and ploughman's, steak, mushroom and ale pie or deep-fried fillet of plaice, there could be Sussex smokie (smoked haddock and prawns in cheese sauce), chargrilled chicken breast with a sun-blush tomato and pesto dressing, and stuffed peppers with couscous. A few blackboard specials are added each day, and 'very good' puddings (someone in the kitchen clearly knows how to make pastry) could include a first-rate Bakewell tart with custard ('the real thing'), and apple pie with cream. The beers on handpump are all from southern breweries, including Horsham Best Bitter from King, Sussex Best Bitter from Harveys, and Fuller's London Pride, as well as guests such as Shepherd Neame Spitfire Premium Ale. Wines are stacked on shelves behind the bar, and a selection of six by the glass is chalked on a blackboard: prices are fair, starting at £10.95 a bottle. SAMPLE DISHES: caramelised onion, goats' cheese and cranberry tart £9; home-made burger with bacon, mozzarella and onion relish £10; hot chocolate fudge cake £4.25.

Licensee Craig Gillet (freehouse)
Open *11.30 to 2.30, 6 to 11, Sun 12 to 3, 7 to 10.30; bar food 11.30 to 2, 6 to 9.30*
Details *No children under 10   Car park   Garden and patio   No music   Dogs welcome in 2 rooms   Delta, Diners, MasterCard, Switch, Visa*

ASKRIGG   **North Yorkshire**   map 8

Kings Arms

Main Street, Askrigg DL8 3HQ   TEL: (01969) 650817
WEBSITE: www.kingsarmsaskrigg.com
off A684 Hawes to Leyburn road, 1½m NE of Bainbridge

Askrigg is a charming village, full of 'noble old houses' and cottages set by a stream above the River Ure, and its welcoming Georgian coaching inn oozes character. There's a large mounting block outside the door, and slab flooring leads inside to characterful, Georgian-feeling rooms that are beamed and panelled or decorated in cheerful yellowy-creamy tones. The two bars (with a huge log fire in the Herriot Bar – the pub was the Drovers in *All Creatures Great and Small*) serve Theakston Old Peculier and Best Bitter, John Smith's Bitter, Black Sheep Best Bitter, and McEwan 80/-, and a lunchtime menu of baguettes, sandwiches and other dishes. The Silks restaurant operates only on Friday and Saturday evenings, but the same menu appears on the bar blackboards every night. You might start with a trio of breaded and deep-fried Wensleydale cheeses with redcurrant jelly, or roast chicken and chorizo salad, before tucking in to roast breast of duckling with apricot relish, or chicken, mushroom and leek pie. From a short, mostly New World list, six wines are served by the glass. SAMPLE DISHES: pork, chicken liver and wild mushroom terrine £5.25; roast cod fillet with creamy mustard sauce £9.75; caramel and apple betty £4.

Licensee Stuart Gatty (freehouse)
Open Mon to Fri 11 to 3, 6 to 11, Sat 11 to 11, Sun 12 to 10.30; bar food 12 to 2, 6.30 to 9; restaurant Fri and Sat 6.30 to 9
Details Children welcome Patio No-smoking area in bar, no smoking in restaurant Background music Dogs welcome MasterCard, Switch, Visa

ASTON Cheshire map 7

Bhurtpore Inn 🍺 🍇

Wrenbury Road, Aston CW5 8DQ TEL: (01270) 780917
off A530, 5m S of Nantwich

'A gem', said one reporter of this traditional village local, 'subtly updated without losing its indefinable character'. Named after the city of Bharatpur, captured by local landowner Lord Combermere in 1826, it contains Indian-themed pieces, including etchings relating to the siege, rugs, carvings, wood, china and porcelain elephants, alongside local photographs and prints, and countless water jugs suspended from beams. The Indian connection extends to a blackboard menu that includes curries and baltis with traditional accompaniments. Expect also to find dishes as varied as black pudding in grain mustard and apple sauce, or mushrooms in creamy Stilton sauce among starters, with main courses running to grilled duck breast in damson and Belgian ale sauce, and sea bass fillets sautéed with spring onion, ginger, coriander and a lime and coconut sauce. There are sandwiches, jacket potatoes and good vegetarian choices too. The commendable range of real ales includes Hanby Drawwell Bitter and ten frequently changing guest brews (the pub gets through around a thousand a year). Then there are about 140 bottled beers, mostly Belgian, regularly changing bottled cider, and a long list of whiskies, mainly malts. Wine consists of a short, imaginative list of fruity everyday drinking from £8.50, plus a quirky fine wine selection priced from £15.50; there are blackboard specials too. SAMPLE DISHES: smoked haddock in a cheese and leek sauce wrapped in a herb pancake £4.75; Maynard's Redcastle sausages with root vegetable mash, ale gravy and caramelised red onions £9; apricot and almond tart £3.75.

Licensees Simon and Nicky George (freehouse)
Open 12 to 2.30, 6.30 to 11, Sun 12 to 10.30; bar food and restaurant 12 to 2, 6.45 to 9.30, Sun 12 to 9
Details Children welcome in eating areas exc after 8pm Car park Wheelchair access (also WC) Garden No-smoking area in bar, no smoking in restaurant Occasional live music Dogs welcome in games room Delta, Diners, MasterCard, Switch, Visa Accommodation: 2 rooms £30 to £40

ASTON CANTLOW Warwickshire map 5

Kings Head 🌼

Aston Cantlow B95 6HY TEL: (01789) 488242
village signposted off A3400 NW of Stratford or off A46 Stratford to Alcester road

A large, tidy garden filled with 'lots and lots' of trestle tables, and a 'positive wall of stacked logs', creates a favourable impression of this quirky, creeper-covered, black and white half-timbered building. The most striking feature inside is the quantity of original beams, conveying an impression of great antiquity; adding to the ambience are particularly low ceilings, varnished floorboards, and bare wooden furniture. To the back is a light and airy restaurant done out in blond and slate-grey, but the same brasserie-style menu, supplemented by daily specials, is served throughout and people tend to gravitate towards the main bar area. Fish, perhaps a smoked haddock rarebit, or roast cod suprême with champ, spicy tomato and basil sauce, and the Kings Head duck supper – confit of leg and slices of breast on a bed of sticky and sweet braised red cabbage – provide the main thrust of the specials. Otherwise, traditional-sounding dishes are given a modern twist: sautéed kidneys, black pudding, apple and mustard cream sauce, or pork, apple and leek sausages, olive oil mash and onion jus. Greene King Abbot Ale, M&B Brew XI and Black Sheep Best Bitter are on tap, while wine drinkers are offered a list of around 30 bottles, with eight sold by the glass. SAMPLE DISHES: aubergine, Gorgonzola and thyme tart £5.75; salmon, spring onion and coriander fishcakes £10; chocolate torte £4.75.

Licensees Miss Anelle Dessels and Mr H. Fentum (Furlong Leisure)
Open Mon to Fri 11 to 3, 5.30 to 11, Sat and Sun 12 to 10.30; bar food and restaurant Mon to Sat 12 to 2.30, 7 to 10, Sun 12.30 to 3, 7 to 9; closed evenings 25 Dec and 1 Jan
Details Children welcome   Car park   Wheelchair access (also WC)   Garden and patio   No smoking in 1 room   Background music   Dogs welcome in bar area   Amex, Delta, MasterCard, Switch, Visa

AWRE   Gloucestershire   map 2

Red Hart Inn
Awre GL14 1EW   TEL: (01594) 510220
off A48 Newnham to Chepstow road, 3m S of Newnham

Bright white plaster and black timbers give this fifteenth-century pub in a secluded Forest of Dean village a distinctively traditional look. The theme continues inside, where you will find black beams draped in hops and a stone well and pump in the middle of the bar, though warm, bright colours (yellow walls, red carpets) add a touch of Mediterranean to the already convivial atmosphere. Traditional dishes such as moules marinière or beef Wellington appear on the menu alongside more innovative options ranging from chicory, smoked salmon and pear salad to pan-fried venison steak with whisky sauce and horseradish mash. Though food-oriented, child-friendly and mostly smoke-free, the Red Hart still attracts a fair crowd of locals who come for the beer. As well as three Gloucestershire real ales – Freeminer Resolution, Goff's Jouster and Wickwar BOB – there's Fuller's London Pride and Stowford Press Cider, while an attractive and sensibly priced list of 34 wines includes six by the large or small glass. SAMPLE DISHES: smoked meat platter £4.50; chargrilled lamb steak in Chinese-style honey, ginger and coriander sauce £10; bread-and-butter pudding £3.75.

Licensee Jerry Bedwell (freehouse)
Open Tue to Sat (Mon to Sat summer) 12 to 3, 6 to 11, Sun 12 to 3, 7 to 10.30; bar food and restaurant Tue to Sat (Mon to Sat summer) 12 to 2, 6.30 to 9, Sun 12 to 2, 7 to 9; closed 25 Dec and 1 Jan
Details Children welcome in bar eating area before 8.30   Car park   Garden   No-smoking area in bar, no smoking in dining room   Occasional background music   No dogs   Amex, Delta, MasterCard, Switch, Visa

AYCLIFFE   Co Durham   map 10

The County ❀

13 The Green, Aycliffe DL5 6LX   TEL: (01325) 312273
WEBSITE: www.the-county.co.uk
from A1(M) junction 59, take A167 for Newton Aycliffe; turn half right at first roundabout, take second right then first right

A cream-painted nineteenth-century building overlooking the village green, the County has an open-plan interior with a fresh, minimalist feel, bare wooden floor, pale walls with a few pictures for decoration, and pine furniture. Blackboard bar menus offer plenty of traditional-sounding dishes, such as lamb's liver and bacon with mash and onion gravy, but chef-licensee Andrew Brown trained under Raymond Blanc, and the main dining room menu accordingly goes in for more upmarket dishes along the lines of pan-fried crisp-skinned duck breast with garlic and thyme rösti, turnip purée and orange glaze, or chargrilled tuna steak with vanilla and basil risotto and lemon samphire. Four real ales are on draught: regular Wells Bombardier Premium Bitter and Theakston Best plus two guests, perhaps from the local Northumberland brewery, while the list of around 25 mostly New World wines includes around half a dozen served by the large or small glass. SAMPLE DISHES: Greek salad £5; chicken casseroled in red wine with smoked bacon, mushrooms and baby onions £15; chocolate bread-and-butter pudding £5.

Licensee Andrew Brown (freehouse)
Open *Mon to Sat 12 to 2, 5.30 (6.45 Sat) to 11, Sun 12 to 3; bar food all week 12 to 2 (3 Sun), Mon to Sat 6 (6.30 Sat) to 9.15*
Details *Children welcome   Car park   No smoking in restaurant   Background music   Guide dogs only Amex, Delta, Diners, MasterCard, Switch, Visa*

AYMESTREY   Herefordshire   map 5

▲ Riverside Inn

Aymestrey HR6 9ST   TEL: (01568) 708440
on A4110, 6m NW of Leominster

The long, narrow, half-timbered inn runs parallel to the road and down sloping ground towards the River Lugg. As a result, the interior is on different levels, and the main restaurant, the Barn Restaurant, is at the lowest level down a steep flight of stairs; large patio doors open from the restaurant on to an inner courtyard. The bar and an ancillary dining area with spindle-back chairs and brightly patterned carpet are on the ground floor, and beams, bare wooden tables, garlands of dried hops and log fires contribute to the simple country atmosphere. The menu – both printed and displayed on blackboards – runs to Cornish crab cakes with a sweet chilli sauce and home-made smooth chicken liver terrine with toasted brioche to begin, while main courses might feature locally reared beef (sirloin steak with peppercorn sauce and red onion marmalade). Separate blackboards list vegetarian and fish dishes, perhaps respectively baked tomato and courgette with a trio of cheeses and lemon couscous, or fillet of gurnard with rocket and tapenade. The selection of English and Welsh cheeses from the Mousetrap in Leominster is not to be missed, and there might be traditional bread-and-butter pudding or prune and Cognac custard tart among desserts. The Wood Brewery's Shropshire Lad, and the Wye Valley Brewery's

Dorothy Goodbody's Golden Ale and Winter Tipple are on draught along with seasonal ales and Brook Farm cider (made in the next village). All seven house wines are served by the glass (175ml at £3, 250ml at £3.80), while the full list runs to over 30 bottles. SAMPLE DISHES: warm salad of Lugg trout with samphire and summer herb vinaigrette £5.25; herb-crusted local pork tenderloin with a sage jus £12.25; lemon tart with elderflower ice cream £4.25.

Licensee Richard Gresko (freehouse)
Open winter 11 to 3, 6 to 11, Sun 12 to 3, 6 to 10.30, summer 11 to 11, Sun 12 to 10.30; bar food and restaurant 12 to 2.15, 7 to 9.15; closed 25 Dec
Details Children welcome in bar eating area   Car park   Garden   No-smoking area in bar, no smoking in restaurant   Background music   Dogs welcome in bar only   Delta, MasterCard, Switch, Visa   Accommodation: 5 rooms, B&B £40 to £85

BADBY   Northamptonshire

map 5

Windmill

Main Street, Badby NN11 3AN   TEL: (01327) 702363
WEBSITE: www.windmillinn-badby.com
off A361, 2m S of Daventry

Dating back to the seventeenth century, this thatched, stone-built village inn has been sensitively updated over the years and now functions primarily as a small hotel within easy reach of tourist hot spots like Althorp Park and Canons Ashby House. Inside, it looks modern and understated, with scrubbed wooden furniture, red patterned rugs on the flagstone floor and plain coloured walls adorned with sporting memorabilia, although the friendly public bar still retains much of its original character. The menu offers generous helpings of familiar pub staples like home-made pâté, or chicken and ham pie, alongside more unusual offerings such as crostini of smoked salmon with cream cheese, avocado and prawns; wild boar steak with cider and apple sauce; or roast Gressingham duck breast with honey, ginger, mango, lime and chilli glaze. Bread-and-butter pudding with bananas and rum might make a final over-indulgence. Old Speckled Hen, Fuller's London Pride and Wadworth 6X are among the real ales on draught, and four wines are served by the glass from a world-spanning list of 20-odd bottles; house wines are from £9.50. SAMPLE DISHES: Badby Stilton mushrooms £5; baked cod with garlic, olive oil and herbs £12; vanilla cheesecake with raspberry coulis £3.50.

Licensees John Freestone and Carol Sutton (freehouse)
Open 11.30 to 3, 5.30 to 11, Sun 12 to 4, 6.30 to 10.30; bar food and restaurant 12 to 2, 7 to 9.30 (9 Sun)
Details Children welcome   Car park   Wheelchair access   Garden   No smoking in eating areas   Background music   Dogs welcome   Amex, Delta, Diners, MasterCard, Switch, Visa   Accommodation: 10 rooms, B&B £59.50 to £72.50

BALLINGER COMMON   Buckinghamshire

map 3

Pheasant

Ballinger Common HP16 9LF   TEL: (01494) 837236
WEBSITE: www.wimpennys.com
E of A413, 2m N of Great Missenden

The Pheasant is a true village pub overlooking the cricket pitch, a children's play-ground and the green. Outside there are flowers, picnic benches and parasols on the patio for summer eating and drinking, while inside are beams, a modern conservatory, and assorted prints, china plates, a stuffed pheasant and bric-à-brac creating a busy look. The printed menu runs to the likes of devilled whitebait, prawn fritters with a lime dip, calf's liver sautéed in garlic butter with bacon, home-made burgers, and steak, kidney and mushroom pie, but it's worth casting an eye over the list of blackboard specials, which change once or twice a week. If you've room, there might be treacle and walnut tart, or crème brûlée to finish. Adnams Best Bitter is on draught, as is Stowford Press cider, and a world wine list of 40 or so bottles ranges from £12.75 to £38. SAMPLE DISHES: Thai fishcakes with sweet chilli sauce £5; leek and ham hotpot £9; chocolate and raspberry roulade £4.50.

Licensee Nigel Wimpenny-Smith (freehouse)
Open Wed to Sun 12 to 3, 6.30 to 11; bar food Wed to Sun 12 to 2 (2.30 Sun), 7 to 9
Details No children under 7 Car park Wheelchair access (also WC) Patio No smoking in conservatory Occasional background music No dogs Amex, Delta, Diners, MasterCard, Switch, Visa

BANTHAM   Devon   map 1

▲ Sloop Inn

Bantham TQ7 3AJ   TEL: (01548) 560489
off A379, 4m W of Kingsbridge

Three miles of single-track road (with passing places) deliver you to this hugely popular coastal inn. Dating in part from the sixteenth century, it is just 300 yards from one of the finest sandy beaches along this stretch of coast. New owners have taken over since the last edition of the Guide, but nothing has changed. The interior retains its traditional feel (beams, flagstone floors and a wood-burning stove) and a nautical outlook lent by lots of seagoing memorabilia; the plainly furnished rear restaurant is designed in the shape of a ship's cabin, with sloping polished wooden walls, ship's windows, and an unusual curved bar counter made out of old boat timbers. The printed menu may list all the favourites, including basket meals of breaded scampi or roast chicken, steaks from the chargrill, and battered local cod (people come here just for the fish and chips), but add crab sandwiches, whole lemon or Dover sole, and daily blackboard specials offering more imaginative dishes such as smoked fish platter, or cumin-coated tuna with coriander, mango and red onion sauce, and the Sloop should not disappoint on the food front. On draught are Bass, **Copper Ale and IPA from Palmers Brewery**, with local Luscombe organic cider also available, as well as 20-plus malt whiskies. The West Country keeps its end up on the wine list, too, with a page devoted to Devon's Sharpham Estate. Ten wines are sold by the glass. SAMPLE DISHES: a pot of shrimps £5; grilled skate wing £9.50; treacle tart £3.75.

Licensee G. Gillard (freehouse)
Open 11 to 2.30, 6 to 11, Sun 12 to 2.30, 6.30 to 10.30; bar food and restaurant 12 to 2, 7 to 10
Details Children welcome Car park Garden and patio No cigars/pipes No music Dogs welcome Delta, Switch Accommodation: 5 rooms, B&B £35 to £72

After the main section of the Guide is the 'Round-up' section listing additional pubs where food may not be the main focus but which are well worth a visit for, perhaps, their inviting ambience, fine beers, a stunning setting, special history or other attribute. Reports on these entries are most welcome.

BARNSLEY Gloucestershire map 2

▲ Village Pub ♥

Barnsley GL7 5EF TEL: (01285) 740421
WEBSITE: www.thevillagepub.co.uk
on B4425, 4m NE of Cirencester

Tim Haigh and Rupert Pendered took over the late Rosemary Verey's Barnsley House and gardens, diagonally opposite the Village Pub, opening it as a hotel in 2003. The pub itself has no garden, but it does have a well-designed brick courtyard crammed with tables and chairs for outdoor eating, while the interior is an inviting mix of the trendy and the rustically traditional, with botanical prints and faux bookcases contributing to the genteel feel. No distinction is made between the various eating areas in a warren of little rooms, and the same short menu is offered throughout. Start, perhaps, with suckling pig and cabbage terrine with mustard celeriac, and follow it with pan-fried Barnsley chop with sautéed potatoes and rosemary-roasted carrots, or whole lemon sole with new potatoes, asparagus and morels. Finish with rice pudding with apple jelly, or pain d'épice crème brûlée. To drink are draught Stowford Press Scrumpy Supreme and Hook Norton Best Bitter and Wadworth 6X on tap. The enterprising wine list, arranged by style, includes a generous 13 by two sizes of glass. SAMPLE DISHES: pan-fried chicken livers with grilled polenta and mushrooms £5.50; grilled pork chop with caraway, black pudding and bubble and squeak £11; chocolate brownie with peanut butter ice cream £5.

Licensees Tim Haigh and Rupert Pendered (freehouse)
Open 11 to 3, 6 to 11, Sun 12 to 3, 7 to 10.30; bar food 12 to 2.30 (3 Sat and Sun), 7 to 9.30 (10 Fri and Sat); closed 25 Dec
Details Children welcome Car park Wheelchair access (not WC) Patio No music Dogs welcome
Delta, MasterCard, Switch, Visa Accommodation: 6 rooms, B&B £65 to £125

BARNSTON Merseyside map 7

Fox & Hounds

Barnston CH61 1BW TEL: (0151) 648 1323
WEBSITE: www.the-fox-hounds.co.uk
on A551, 2m NE of Heswall

The Fox & Hounds, an imposing whitewashed building rebuilt in 1911 on a site dating from 1754, stands beside a farm amid copious flowerpots and troughs, creepers and bushes. The surrounding mature trees keep the wind off in winter and offer shade in summer. It expanded into some barns in the 1980s – and the old farmyard behind now sports parasol-decked bench tables. The older part has a cosy old-style smoke room and snug, the newer section a largely open-plan lounge with solid wooden tables and walls decked with old photographs, paintings and an intriguing titfer collection (bowler, policeman's helmet, etc. – thereby must hang a tale or two). The regular ales are Theakston (Best, Cool Cask and Old Peculier) and Webster's Green Label, plus guests such as Everards Tiger Best, Marston's Pedigree, or Spooky Doo from Shropshire's experimental Hanby Ales, and there are over fifty whiskies as well as ten wines by the glass. Food is served only at lunchtime, with the bar menu offering sandwiches, soups, and platters of mixed meats, fish or seafood, but blackboard dishes expand the choices with perhaps lasagne or steak and kidney pie, with apple bread pudding for dessert. SAMPLE DISHES: potted shrimps £3.50; beef stroganoff £6; peach and caramel cheesecake £3.

Licensee Ralph Leech (freehouse)
Open 11 to 11, Sun 12 to 10.30; bar food 12 to 2
Details Children welcome in family room   Car park   Wheelchair access (not WC)   Garden   No music
Dogs welcome exc at food times   Amex, Delta, Diners, MasterCard, Switch, Visa

BARROWDEN   Rutland   map 6

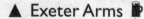 ▲ **Exeter Arms**

Main Street, Barrowden LE15 8EQ   TEL: (01572) 747247
WEBSITE: www.exeterarms.com
off A47, 9m W of A1

BREW PUB

The BBC (Blencowe Brewing Company) is housed in a stone barn adjacent to this old pub overlooking the village green and the duck pond. What it produces is an entire family of 'Boys' beers (Boys with Attitude clocks in at 6 per cent ABV, Bevin Boys at 4.5 per cent), which you can sample at the long, wood-panelled bar: smokers head for the Tap Room (decorated with framed beer mats), while others settle into another low-beamed area where food is the main order of the day. Menus are on a daily-changing blackboard, and local produce is used to good effect in dishes like pigeon breast with gooseberry sauce, or pot-roast pheasant. Fish could include anything from moules marinière to Arctic char with Pernod and mushrooms, or black halibut steak with garlic butter, while vegetarians might home in on potato, mushroom, chestnut and Stilton bake. Rounding things off are puddings such as spotted dick and banana split. Live music is a regular attraction, and there's an outdoor pétanque court for fine days. The wine list is a short, ever-changing slate with at least eight normally offered by the glass. SAMPLE DISHES: smoked salmon salad £4.75; lamb cutlets with redcurrant and juniper sauce £11; chocolate sponge with chocolate sauce £3.50.

Licensees Peter and Elizabeth Blencowe (freehouse)
Open Tue to Sat 12 to 2, Mon to Sat 6 to 11, Sun 12 to 3, 7 to 10.30; bar food Tue to Sun 12 to 2, Tue to Sat 6.45 to 9
Details Children welcome in eating area   Car park   Wheelchair access (also WC)   Garden and patio
No-smoking area in bar, no smoking in eating area   Live or background music   Dogs welcome exc at bar and in eating area   Delta, Diners, MasterCard, Switch, Visa   Accommodation: 3 rooms, B&B £30 to £60

BASSENTHWAITE LAKE   Cumbria   map 10

 ▲ **Pheasant**   NEW ENTRY

Bassenthwaite Lake, nr Cockermouth CA13 9YE   TEL: (017687) 76234
WEBSITE: www.the-pheasant.co.uk
signposted off A66, at NW end of lake

WATERSIDE

Centuries old and tucked away in the shadow of a pine-forested hill on the other side of the road from the lake, this old-fashioned hostelry is run in the grand manner of years gone by. The bar must rank as one of the best known in the Lake District, with its 'wonderful' atmosphere, antique furniture and dark burgundy-coloured walls hung with oil paintings; there's also a more spacious lounge overlooking the gardens. It is all very stylish, and service is as polished as the furniture. Bar food, available only at lunchtime, is mostly robust, honest stuff like 'excellent' carrot and orange soup with equally good home-made bread, potted Silloth shrimps, and steak, Guinness and mushroom pie with mash. Alternatively, there are all manner of upmarket open sandwiches (smoked salmon with smoked tomato and cream cheese, for example), plus desserts like poached pears with cinnamon ice cream. Separate fixed-price restaurant menus move into the realms of seared king scallops with lobster mayonnaise, and pan-fried Gressingham duck breast with sweet potato mash, baked apple and peach sauce. Jennings Cumberland Ale, Theakston Best and Bass are on handpump. The rather pricy wine list takes the modern route of listing by grape variety and gives New and Old Worlds an equal shout. A premium 'reserve selection' tops it off while plenty of half-bottles and a half-dozen by the glass (from £4.25) cater for more modest occasions. SAMPLE DISHES: Stilton, walnut and apricot pâté £5; seafood platter £8.75; Grand Marnier pannacotta £4.25.

Licensee Matthew Wylie (freehouse)

Open 11 to 2.30, 5.30 to 11, Sun 12 to 2.30, 6 to 10.30; bar food 12 to 2, restaurant 12 to 2, 7 to 9; closed 25 Dec

Details Children over 8 welcome Car park Wheelchair access (not WC) Garden No smoking in restaurant No music Dogs welcome Delta, MasterCard, Switch, Visa Accommodation: 15 rooms, B&B £65 to £170

BATCOMBE Somerset   map 2

Three Horseshoes ✿

Batcombe BA4 6HE TEL: (01749) 850359
off A359 between Bruton and Frome, 3m N of Bruton

Finding your way to Batcombe along country lanes requires a good map, but pinpointing the pub can present difficulties (especially in the dark); head for the church – the pub is next door. The long, low-ceilinged main bar, its warm terracotta walls hung with paintings (for sale), has an inglenook with a wood-burning stove. Beers are from Butcombe, or Mine Beer from Blindmans Brewery in nearby Leighton, and there's Thatcher's cider. The restaurant, a converted barn, has sporting paintings on exposed-stone walls, cream woodwork and exuberant artificial flora. The menu includes the day's specials, many involving fresh fish from Brixham. A tian of Cornish crab and prawns comes with dill crème fraîche, and crayfish tails are served as a salad with palm hearts and basil and lemon sauce. Fairly elaborate main courses could include pan-fried medallions of beef fillet glazed with Devon blue cheese served on rösti with a shallot jus, or perhaps grilled fillets of sea bass with a sun-blush tomato and herb salsa on crushed olive new potatoes. Golden syrup sponge has a comforting cold-weather appeal, or there could be banana and mango honey pancake with ice cream for dessert. An international selection of 60-odd wines includes a dozen by the glass (with house selections £11.40 per bottle and the bulk of the list between £15 and £20) and is supplemented by a dozen pricier 'celebration' wines, mostly from France. SAMPLE DISHES: butter-bean, carrot and coriander soup £3.75; pot-roast duck in garlic and herbs with apricot and walnut stuffing £14.75; white and dark chocolate rum cappuccino mousse £4.50.

Licensee David Benson (freehouse)

Open 12 to 3, 6.30 to 11, Sun 12 to 3, 7 to 10.30; bar food and restaurant 12 to 2 (2.30 Sat and Sun), 7 to 9.30 (10 Fri and Sat, 9 Sun); closed 25 Dec, evening 26 Dec

Details Children welcome Car park Wheelchair access (also WC) Garden and patio No smoking in restaurant No music Dogs welcome in bar only Delta, MasterCard, Switch, Visa

Hop Pole ✿ 🍺

7 Albion Buildings, Upper Bristol Road, Bath BA1 3AR   TEL: (01225) 446327
WEBSITE: www.bathales.co.uk

It's a measure of this pub's gastronomic success that its old skittle alley has been
turned into an extra dining room. The Hop Pole stands just outside the city centre
opposite Royal Victoria Park, and it bears all the designer hallmarks of premises
owned by Bath Ales. Everywhere there seems to be tongue-and-groove woodwork,
the atmosphere is charmingly relaxed, and the brewery's draught ales – including
Gem, SPA and Barnstormer – are dispensed in slender elegant glasses. The pub also
stocks bottles of Weston's organic cider and some Continental brews like Chimay and
Duval. Lunch is a simple affair, taking in run-of-the-mill sandwiches as well as salads
(feta and sun-dried tomato, for example), duck rillettes with pickles and toast, and
chargrilled ribeye steak with chips. In the evening, events take an even more serious
turn, when the kitchen gets to grips with the likes of seared Scottish scallops with
piquillo pepper filled with Cornish crab, parsley and garlic oil, or a carnivorous
extravaganza involving braised belly pork with a black pudding and bacon sausage, a
pork faggot and sage jus. Desserts are few in number, but they might include buttermilk pannacotta with blood orange sauce, or chocolate and caramel tart with crème
fraîche. The workmanlike list of two dozen reasonably priced wines includes six by
the glass. In summer, this is one of the few pubs in Bath where you can eat in the
garden. SAMPLE DISHES: pan-fried mackerel on beetroot and horseradish salad £5;
herb-roast breast of guinea fowl with goats' cheese and vegetable lasagne £11; crème
brûlée £5.

Licensee Elaine Dennehy (Bath Ales)
Open winter Mon to Thur 12 to 2.30, 5 to 11, Fri to Sun 12 to 11; summer 12 to 11 (10.30 Sun); bar food
and restaurant Tue to Sun 12 to 2 (4 Sun), Tue to Sat 7 to 10
Details Children welcome exc in bar after 9pm   Wheelchair access (not WC)   Garden   No-smoking area in
bar, no smoking in restaurant   Background music   No dogs   Delta, MasterCard, Switch, Visa   ·

Ring O' Bells

10 Widcombe Parade, Bath BA2 4JT   TEL: (01225) 448870
Widcombe Parade is just SE of railway station, on S side of River Avon

The Ring O' Bells is on the far side of the River Avon from Bath's city centre. In lieu
of a traditional pub sign it has a giant metal hoop with six large bells dangling from it,
and inside, things aren't so traditional either, for the small open-plan space has a
definite bistro bent. Bright and cheerful Mediterranean colours (yellow walls and a
blue tongue-and-groove bar counter lined with stools), pale pine furniture and jazz
music reinforce the contemporary feel. The short menu lists simple, fresh, well-
priced bistro fare: perhaps smoked haddock chowder, followed by venison sausage
with lentils and sweet and sour figs, or confit of duck with Puy lentils and pancetta.
A blackboard lists the fish of the day, and the set-price two-course lunch menu is
good value at £7.95. Beers change regularly but could include Gem Bitter from Bath
Ales, and Fuller's London Pride, and there are five wines by the glass plus decent
coffee. SAMPLE DISHES: chicken and pigeon terrine and apple chutney £4.75; breast of

pheasant with crisp bacon and garlic mash potato £10; Belgian waffles with vanilla ice cream and maple syrup £4.50.

Licensee Jo Lucas (Philip George)
Open Mon 5 to 11, Tue to Sat 12 to 11, Sun 12 to 6 (12 to 4 summer); bar food and restaurant Tue to Sun 12 to 2.30, Mon to Sat 6 to 10
Details Children welcome Background music No dogs MasterCard, Switch, Visa

Salamander ▮

3 John Street, Bath BA1 2JL   TEL: (01225) 428889
WEBSITE: www.bathales.co.uk

Still a relative newcomer, Bath Ales has already made a favourable impression with its distinctive, high-quality real ales (see also the Hop Pole above). Spa, Barnstormer and Gem from Bath Ales are dispensed, joined by up to three guest beers. There was a change of licensee here in summer 2004, so reports please. The pub itself is a pleasant environment, decorated in a timeless, traditional style, with orangey-terracotta walls, dark wood panelling, bare floorboards and various pubby artefacts. Bar food is interesting without being too ambitious. Alongside dishes of an old-fashioned nature such as Barnstormer bangers with mustard mash and onion gravy, or Gem ale, steak and mushroom pie, are more cosmopolitan options such as a salad of grilled artichokes, roast peppers and sun-dried tomatoes with basil dressing. More ambitious dishes appear on the separate restaurant menu: chargrilled lamb steak on mixed bean ragoût with red wine and rosemary, for example. Bottle prices on the short wine list start at £11.60, and six wines are available by the glass. SAMPLE DISHES: grilled goats' cheese crostini £4; chunky fish in beer and herb batter with chips £6.25; Spa ale cake £5.

Licensees Roger Jones and Deborah Campbell (Bath Ales)
Open 11.30 to 11, Sun 12 to 10.30; bar food Tue to Sun 12 to 2.30 (3 Sun), Tue to Sat 6.30 to 9.30, restaurant Tue to Sat 6.30 to 9.30, Sun 12 to 3
Details Children welcome in restaurant No-smoking area in bar, no smoking in restaurant Live or background music Guide dogs only Delta, MasterCard, Switch, Visa

BEETHAM Cumbria   map 8

▲ Wheatsheaf

Beetham LA7 7AL   TEL: (015395) 62123
WEBSITE: www.wheatsheafbeetham.com
just off A6, 5m N of Carnforth

Those travelling north or south on the A6 should consider stopping off at Beetham for refreshment at the Wheatsheaf. The sixteenth-century inn, by the river and the church, makes a striking impression with its tall stone chimneys, steeply pitched roof and half-timbered corner bay. The taproom has a traditional pub atmosphere generated by a lively crowd of locals enjoying the Jennings Bitter and Cumberland Ale, or whatever guest beer happens to be on. If candles, flowers and full table service are your thing, head for the 'lounge bar' – dark-coloured walls, curtained windows and fresh flowers give it a country-house drawing room feel – or one of the upstairs dining rooms. Light bar lunches give way in the evening to a full menu that offers a generous and varied choice of dishes, ranging from filo parcels of melting Cumbrian cheese to honey, soy and coriander marinated duck breast on bacon and chicory gratin, via staples such as salmon fishcakes, and chicken korma. Eight of the 30 wines are available by the glass. SAMPLE DISHES: minute steak club sandwich with salad and fries £8; suprême of chicken with pancetta and Italian cheese on Savoy cabbage with chorizo £13.50; Amaretto raspberry trifle £4.75.

Licensees Kathryn and Mark Chambers (freehouse)
Open 11.30 to 2.30, 5.30 to 11, Sun 12 to 2.30, 6.30 to 10.30; bar food and restaurant 12 to 2, 6 to 9; closed 25 Dec
Details Children welcome in family room and restaurant   Car park   Wheelchair access (also WC)   Garden No smoking in eating areas   Background music   Delta, MasterCard, Switch, Visa   Accommodation: 6 rooms, B&B £40 to £85

BEKESBOURNE   Kent   map 3

The Unicorn   NEW ENTRY

Bekesbourne CT4 5ED   TEL: (01227) 830210
off A257 2½m SE of Canterbury

'What a great find!' exclaimed one couple after coming across this 'classic Victorian pub' by a quiet country lane just outside Bekesbourne and close to Howletts Wild Animal Park. There's nothing fussy about the décor, just bare floorboards, wall lamps, simple wooden furniture and – in one corner – an upright piano piled with books of local interest. It seems that most people come here for the genuine atmosphere and the good-value, carefully cooked food. The kitchen happily delivers sandwiches, baguettes and starters like well-flavoured avocado and bacon salad, or smoked cod chowder. Mains take in old stalwarts like splendid lamb's liver and bacon in herby onion gravy as well as slightly more ambitious specials such as confit of duck with ginger sauce, or venison sausages poached in red wine with sweet potato mash. Raspberry Pavlova is a capably handled dessert, otherwise opt for fruit crumble or waffles with maple syrup. Shepherd Neame Master Brew and Adnams Broadside are regularly on draught; also look out for Biddenden Kentish cider and bottles of Whitstable Bay Organic Ale. Three wines are offered by the glass from the modest, affordable list. SAMPLE DISHES: grilled sardines with brown bread £4; marinated spicy chicken salad £7.50; lemon syllabub £3.

Licensees Clive and Cheryl Barker (freehouse)
Open Wed to Sat 11.30 to 2.30, 7 to 11, Sun 12 to 3, 7 to 10.30; bar food Wed to Sun 12 to 2, 7 to 9; closed Sun evenings in winter, 1st week of Jan
Details Children welcome   Car park   Wheelchair access (also WC)   Garden and patio   No music   No dogs No cards

BENTWORTH   Hampshire   map 2

Sun

Sun Hill, Bentworth GU34 5JT   TEL: (01420) 562338
off A339, 3m NW of Alton

The Sun shines brightly from its spot on a narrow country lane just south of the village, not least in summer when colourful hanging baskets and tubs festoon the outside. There are also picnic tables, the better for customers to enjoy the scene. The pub's interior is divided into three interconnecting rooms, a reminder of its origin as a pair of seventeenth century cottages. Low beams, cottagey furniture, patterned curtains, horse brasses and roaring log fires give the place a cosy, homely feel. The stars of the show here are the real ales. A core selection of five regulars, including Hampshire's own Cheriton Pots Ale and Ringwood Best, plus Badger Tanglefoot and Stonehenge Pigswill, are backed up with three or four changing guest beers. A list of 20 wines includes nine by the glass. On the food side, there's a lengthy menu of mostly simple, hearty and traditional dishes ranging from fish pie, and beef in ale stew, to roasted pepper and brie filo tart, and venison in Guinness with pickled walnuts. SAMPLE DISHES: creamy garlic mushrooms £3.50; steak and kidney pie £10; date crumble £3.25.

Licensee Mary Holmes (freehouse)
Open *12 to 3, 6 to 11, Sun 12 to 10.30; bar food 12 to 2, 7 to 9.30*
Details *Children welcome in family room Car park Garden No music Dogs welcome Delta, MasterCard, Switch, Visa*

BERROW GREEN   Worcestershire   map 5

▲ Admiral Rodney Inn NEW ENTRY

Berrow Green, nr Martley WR6 6PL   TEL: (01886) 821375
WEBSITE: www.admiral-rodney.co.uk
on B4197 1m or so N of A44 Worcester to Bromyard road

Set against a hillside on the Worcester Way long-distance footpath, this substantial gabled pub shows all the signs of serious refurbishment. Inside, magnificent old timbers, wall beams and natural floorboards contrast with more up-to-date varnished window frames, stair rails and chunky pine furniture. Real ale is taken seriously in the two linked bars: Wye Valley Bitter is always on draught along with a regularly changing trio of guests from small independent breweries like Woods, Malvern Hills, Weatheroak and Cannon Royal. Bar food is simple, home-made stuff without commercial short cuts, along the lines of chicken and pesto salad, pizzas, omelettes and chilli con carne, backed up by a blackboard of fish from Cornwall: expect anything from bouillabaisse to herb-crusted tuna with red pepper mayonnaise. In the evening there's also a restaurant menu of updated pub dishes like pork loin steaks on celeriac purée with apple compote, and honey-glazed suprême of chicken with poached leeks and chive butter, plus fish from the board. Home-made puddings such as white chocolate cheesecake with blueberry sauce complete the picture. A short, simple wine list kicks off with five by the glass from £2.50, £9.95 a bottle. The pub has its own skittle alley that can be hired for functions. SAMPLE DISHES: coarse pork pâté £4.50; whole roast trout with almond and lime mayonnaise £10; pear tarte Tatin £4.

Licensees Kenneth and Gillian Green (freehouse)
Open *Mon 5 to 11, Tue to Fri 11 to 3, 5 to 11, Sat 11 to 11, Sun 12 to 10.30; bar food Tue to Sun 12 to 2 (2.30 bank hols), all week 6.30 to 9, restaurant all week 7 to 9*
Details *Children welcome Car park Wheelchair access (also WC) Garden and patio No smoking in 1 room Occasional live music Dogs welcome exc in restaurant Delta, MasterCard, Switch, Visa Accommodation: 3 rooms, B&B £40 to £65*

Which? Online subscribers will find The Which? Pub Guide *online, along with other Which? guides and magazines, at* www.which.net. *Check the website for how to become a subscriber.*

BERWICK   East Sussex   map 3

Cricketers Arms

Berwick BN26 6SP   TEL: (01323) 870469
WEBSITE: www.cricketersberwick.co.uk
just off A27 Lewes to Polegate road

Formed from the conversion of two late eighteenth-century brick and flint cottages, the Cricketers is a friendly village local with a charming front garden. It's all agreeably old and worn-looking inside, with gnarled and warped plank tables, old settles, solid wooden doors with old-fashioned latches, low ceilings and a 'cracking log fire'. The cricketing theme is 'not overbearing, just a few photographs and watercolours and a wall-mounted set of wickets being hit by a ball at one end of the bar'. Throughout the three rooms a nice balance has been achieved between eating and drinking, with food (available all day at weekends) firmly from the traditional pub mould: ploughman's, garlic mushrooms, battered cod, steaks, sausages and the like. An inspection meal yielded 'nicely coarse-textured' wild mushroom and bacon pâté – a 'home-made effort' with 'plenty of flavour' – tasty vegetable chilli with garlic bread, and 'rather good' banoffi pie. This is a Harveys of Lewes pub, and the brewery's Best Bitter and seasonal brews are served straight from the cask. Wines of the month are chalked on a blackboard, and around half a dozen are served by the glass. SAMPLE DISHES: rocket salad with red onions and Parmesan £5.25; pan-fried salmon fillets with lime dressing £8; chocolate fudge cake £3.75.

Licensee Peter Brown (Harveys)
Open *winter Mon to Fri 11 to 3, 6 to 11, Sat 11 to 11, Sun 12 to 10; summer Mon to Sat 11 to 11, Sun 12 to 10; bar food Mon to Fri 12 to 2.15, 6.30 to 9, Sat and Sun and all week June, July and Aug 12 to 9; closed 25 Dec*
Details *Children welcome in bar eating areas   Car park   Garden   No music   Dogs welcome   MasterCard, Switch, Visa*

BETCHWORTH   Surrey   map 3

▲ Red Lion

Old Reigate Road, Betchworth RH3 7DS   TEL: (01737) 843336
off A25, 3m E of Dorking

Picnic tables on the patio in front of this old village inn make a great spot to sit in summer and soak up the rural atmosphere – you may even get the opportunity to watch a cricket match on the pitch behind the pub. Inside, the look is quaintly old-fashioned, with banquettes and brown Windsor chairs, red patterned carpet, and a clientele of widely varying ages. The traditional theme continues into the long menus, which list the likes of Cumberland sausages on mash, and steak and kidney pie, but more up-to-date ideas include chilli beef on crispy noodles with hot-and-sour sauce, and deep-fried tempura prawns with chilli dip. Prices on the short wine list start at £12.95 and keep below £20; around half a dozen wines are served by the glass. Real ales include Adnams Broadside, Greene King IPA and Fuller's London Pride. SAMPLE DISHES: deep-fried whitebait £4.50; braised half-shoulder of lamb with red wine jus £13; spotted dick £3.50.

Licensees Alan Podemsky and Tony Wolbrom (Inn House)
Open *11 to 11, Sun 12 to 10.30; bar food Mon to Sat 12 to 2.30, 6 to 9, Sun 12 to 8*
Details *Children welcome   Car park   Wheelchair access (not WC)   Garden and patio   No smoking in eating area   Background music   Amex, Delta, MasterCard, Switch, Visa   Accommodation: 5 rooms, B&B £50 to £75*

BIDDENDEN   Kent   map 3

Three Chimneys ♡ 🍺 🍇

Hareplain Road, Biddenden TN27 8LW   TEL: (01580) 291472
on A262, 2m W of Biddenden

'Very much a community-focused pub', enthused a reporter of this part-timbered,
butter-coloured building (circa 1420), with its ancient, steeply pitched roof supporting not three but two chimneys – the name is a corruption of the French *trois
chemins*, meaning 'three ways'. French officers of the Napoleonic era were impris-
oned locally and were allowed to wander freely, but not beyond the point where the
trois chemins met. The interior reinforces the feeling of great age: interlinked rooms
and windows are small, there are gnarled timbers, and ceilings are low and beamed; it
is all hugely atmospheric. A modern extension – the Garden Room – offers contrast
by way of large windows giving garden views and white cloths on tables. 'Hearty,
unpretentious' dishes are chalked up on blackboards: say, pan-roast loin of venison
with braised red cabbage, roast parsnips and a rich port jus. Starters are a good size and
double up as lunchtime light bites, as well-judged curried parsnip soup garnished
with mature Cheddar and chorizo proved for one visitor. The choice for real beer fans
encompasses Adnams Best Bitter, Shepherd Neame Spitfire Premium Ale and
seasonal ales, all drawn from casks behind the bar. An appetising house selection of
some eight wines available in bottle or by the glass includes Sandhurst Vineyards from
Kent. The main wine list offers lots of flavour for under £15 from the southern hemisphere and plenty from France, but little of that is so readily affordable. Naturally
enough, there's also Biddenden cider. SAMPLE DISHES: Thai-style crab cakes with a
sweet chilli dipping sauce £7; duck leg confit on creamed potatoes and braised Puy
lentils with chorizo and bacon £13; vanilla and strawberry crème brûlée £4.50.

Licensee Craig Smith (freehouse)
Open *11 to 3, 6 (7 Sun) to 11.30; bar food and restaurant 12 to 1.50, 6.30 to 9.45 (7 to 9 Sun)*
Details *Children welcome in eating areas   Car park   Wheelchair access (not WC)   Garden and patio
No music   Dogs welcome   Delta, MasterCard, Switch, Visa*

BIRCH VALE   Derbyshire   map 8

▲ Waltzing Weasel

New Mills Road, Birch Vale SK22 1BT   TEL: (01663) 743402
WEBSITE: www.w-weasel.co.uk
4½m E of Stockport, turn NE off A6 on to A6015, Birch Vale is 2m on

On the edge of the Peak District, the Waltzing Weasel is surrounded by hilly countryside with the impressive Lantern Pike rising in the distance. In fine weather, sit
outside on the stone terrace and appreciate the views; otherwise the main bar area is
cosy and comfortable, with a log fire, upholstered settles, and assorted plain wooden
tables. There's also a small, more formal restaurant with a richly patterned carpet and
an illuminated wall tapestry. The menus avoid pub grub clichés, the bar version
featuring grilled sardines with roasted red peppers and a garlic and anchovy dressing,
followed perhaps by Peak Pie (game and mushrooms in red wine under a puff pastry
lid). There's also a casserole of the day – maybe Italian beef or Moroccan vegetable –
and fish specials are listed on a blackboard. The restaurant menu follows similar lines
but operates on a fixed-price format for two or three courses. Marston's Best Bitter

and Kelham Island Gold are the real ales on offer, while a short wine list includes a few smart bottles, with three by the glass. SAMPLE DISHES: roasted fennel with Parmesan topping £4.75; seafood tart with shrimp sauce £10.50; treacle tart £5.

Licensee Michael Atkinson (freehouse)

Open 12 to 3, 5.30 to 11; bar food and restaurant 12 to 2, 7 to 9

Details Children welcome; no children under 12 in restaurant   Car park   Wheelchair access (not WC)
Garden and patio   No smoking in restaurant   No music   Dogs welcome   Delta, MasterCard, Switch, Visa
Accommodation: 8 rooms, B&B £48 to £108

BISHOP'S CASTLE   Shropshire   map 5

▲ Three Tuns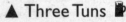

Salop Street, Bishop's Castle SY9 5BW   TEL: (01588) 638797
WEBSITE: www.thethreetunsinn.co.uk
off B4385, just off A488, 8m NW of Craven Arms

Bishop's Castle has a small town centre consisting of narrow, packed streets – on one of which stands the Three Tuns. It consists of a courtyard of buildings that includes a formidably tall brewery producing the fine cask and bottled beers that are served in the pub (and a few other outlets), including XXX Bitter, Steamer, Remergence, Cleric's Cure, and the seasonal Old Scrooge. In the pub is a public bar and a sparsely furnished dining area with a long bar counter, fat black ceiling beams, plain wooden furniture including settles, and candles dripping in bottles. Choose from the blackboard menus, order at the bar and your food will be brought to your table. The style of cooking is as unpretentious and uncluttered as the surroundings, offering dishes such as sweet-cured herrings with dill mayonnaise, pies of either rabbit or game, or, perhaps, salt marsh lamb with garlic potatoes. Produce is local and organic where possible, including rare-breed sirloin steaks. Finish with bread-and-butter pudding or chocolate roulade. Two wines are served by the glass. SAMPLE DISHES: organic smoked salmon pâté £5; beef casseroled in Three Tuns ale £8.50; almond and raspberry cheesecake £3.75.

Licensee Janet Cross (freehouse)

Open Mon to Thur 12 to 3.30, 5 to 11 (11.30 summer), Fri to Sun 12 to 11.30 (10.30 Sun); bar food and
restaurant 12 to 2.30, 7 to 9.30; closed 25 Dec

Details Children welcome   Car park   Wheelchair access (not WC)   Patio   No smoking in restaurant
Occasional live music   Dogs in snug bar only   Delta, Diners, MasterCard, Switch, Visa

BISPHAM GREEN   Lancashire   map 8

Eagle & Child �$ 📭

Malt Kiln Lane, Bispham Green L40 3SG   TEL: (01257) 462297
from M6 junction 27 take A5209 over Parbold Hill, right on B5246, fourth left signposted Bispham
Green; pub ½m on right

Although just a few miles from the M6, the Eagle & Child is a rural pub in an attractive part of Lancashire. Inside, low beamed ceilings, cream-coloured walls hung with country prints, china dogs on the mantelpiece, and plain wooden tables create a rustic look. Food is served in a little no-smoking room, seating about a dozen people mainly at cushioned pews, and in a larger 'anything goes' room, as well as in the bar. The printed menu features such pub staples as steak and ale pie, grilled gammon with pineapple, and battered cod with mushy peas and chips. A blackboard menu of manageable proportions extends the choice, delivering more interesting dishes along the lines of fillet of brill with lobster and pimento linguine, or chump of English lamb with sun-dried tomato and olive mash. An impressive ever-changing choice of guest ales from independent breweries like Hanby, Phoenix and Hart join regulars Thwaites Bitter, Moorhouses Black Cat, Fuller's London Pride and Timothy Taylor Landlord on handpump, and there is a large selection of malt whiskies. House wines are listed on a board above the bar, and the full list has 30 or so bottles, with five by the glass. SAMPLE DISHES: smoked chicken and lentil soup £4.50; confit of duck leg with sage and onion rösti and plum sauce £10; parkin with toffee ice cream £4.

Licensee Monica Evans (freehouse)
Open 12 to 3, 5.30 to 11, Sun 12 to 10.30; bar food and restaurant 12 to 2, 6 to 8.30 (9 Fri and Sat), Sun 12 to 8.30
Details Children welcome in family room Car park Wheelchair access (also WC) Garden No smoking in 1 room Background music Dogs welcome MasterCard, Switch, Visa

BLACKBOYS   **East Sussex**   **map 3**

Blackboys Inn
Lewes Road, Blackboys TN22 5LG   TEL: (01825) 890283
on B2192, 3m E of Uckfield

For centuries this area produced charcoal for the iron foundries at Buxted and Heathfield, and, although the ironworking ceased in the 1800s, the pub that quenched the workers' thirsts is still thriving. The inn is separated from the road by a small green containing some large horse chestnut trees, and ducks can be spotted on the small pond to one side of the pub. Inside there are two bars and a games room, plus a series of interconnecting rooms mainly for dining (food is listed on a carte, a bar snack menu and a blackboard for the specials – perhaps chilli fish, or grilled mushrooms with goats' cheese and roasted tomatoes). This is a Harveys house, so there's Harveys Sussex Best Bitter and Pale Ale, plus seasonal ales, on tap, along with seven wines by the glass. Bar snacks cover the jacket potato/ploughman's/burger/steak spectrum, plus sausage and mash, and perhaps Thai red chicken curry. Restaurant dishes are more elaborate but still substantial. Starters might include confit of duck with hoisin dressing, or tian of crab and avocado with bell pepper and mango dressing, then entrecote steak or whole bass grilled with sea salt, olive oil and lemon juice and served with a salsa verde. Vegetarian dishes might include a butternut squash, spinach and Parmesan tartlet. SAMPLE DISHES: wild mushroom, piquillo pepper and mozzarella bruschetta £6; roast rump of lamb, sweet potato cake, ratatouille £14.50; banoffi pie £3.50.

Licensee Edward Molesworth (Harveys of Lewes)
Open 11 to 3, 5 to 11 (all day Fri and Sun); bar food and restaurant 12 to 2, 6.30 to 9.30; open 25 Dec 12 to 1.30 for drinks only, closed 1 Jan
Details Children welcome in dining room Car park Garden No smoking in dining room Occasional music No dogs in dining room Delta, MasterCard, Switch, Visa

Prices of dishes quoted in an entry are based on information supplied by the pub, rounded up to the nearest 25 pence. These prices may have changed since publication and are meant only as a guide.

BLACKBROOK   Surrey   map 3

Plough   NEW ENTRY

Blackbrook RH5 4DS   TEL: (01306) 886603
off A24, 1¾m SE of Dorking

This unpretentious pub is tucked away on a by-road close to Holmwood Common. It
has a buzzing atmosphere enhanced by terracotta walls, ancient saws fastened to the
ceiling, old treadle machine tables, and local artists' work for sale. There is space for
drinkers, but most people come here to eat. On the huge specials board there could be
pan-fried yellowfin tuna with almonds and sultanas, a rich steak and kidney pudding,
and fillet steak. Local spicy sausages and a ploughman's of Newbury Park blue cheese
with quince jelly are lunchtime options as well as the usual sandwiches, jacket potatoes, pâté, and grilled ham with pineapple, and there are a handful of puddings such as
an 'excellent' terrine of wild fruits with raspberry coulis, and ricotta tart with cinnamon ice cream. Wednesday night is curry night. Beers are Badger Best Bitter, King &
Barnes Sussex and Badger Tanglefoot, while wines are a wide-ranging bunch, with
around 15 by the glass. SAMPLE DISHES: taramasalata with Kalamata olives £3.75; deep-
fried goujons of lemon sole with chips £7; sticky toffee pudding £3.75.

Licensees Christine and Robin Squire (Hall & Woodhouse)
Open 11 to 3, 6 to 11.30, Sun 12 to 3, 7 to 10.30; bar food all week 12 to 2, Tue to Sun 7 to 9; closed 25
and 26 Dec, 1 Jan
Details Children welcome   Car park   Wheelchair access (not WC)   Garden and patio   No smoking in 1 room
Occasional background music   Dogs welcome in 1 room   MasterCard, Switch, Visa

BLAKENEY   Norfolk   map 6

▲ White Horse Hotel ❧

4 High Street, Blakeney NR25 7AL   TEL: (01263) 740574
WEBSITE: www.blakeneywhitehorse.co.uk
off A149, 5m W of Holt

The narrow High Street winds its way down to a small tidal harbour and is lined with
flint-built fishermen's cottages as well as this seventeenth-century former coaching
inn, Blakeney's oldest hotel. Inside, it is all tastefully decorated in creams and dark
wood with lamplight and other soft lighting, and the bar is decorated with works by
local artists. As befits the coastal location, fish features prominently on the bar menu:
cockle chowder, local whitebait, and smoked haddock and prawn pie are typical. Meat
eaters might choose sirloin steak and chips, and lunchers looking for a light bite will
find sandwiches or filled ciabattas. The menu in the restaurant, which is in a
converted stable block overlooking the walled garden and courtyard, offers something
more ambitious, perhaps warm leek and prawn tartlet, followed by grilled fillet of red
snapper on a roasted pepper salad with pesto. Beers from Adnams are on tap, and a
dozen wines from a round-the-world list of around 40 are sold by the glass (with
additional specials chalked up on a blackboard). Prices are reasonable, with the majority of bottles below the £20 mark; there's even a tasty budget alternative to champagne
from Touraine at £16.95 and a good a sprinkling of half-bottles too. SAMPLE DISHES:
grilled goats' cheese with beetroot and walnut dressing £6; pan-fried venison with
onion marmalade and crispy pancetta £15.50; rich chocolate mousse £4.50.

Licensee Dan Goff (freehouse)

Open *11 to 3, 6 (5 summer) to 11, Sun 12 to 3, 6 to 10.30; bar food 12 to 2 (2.15 Sat and Sun), 6 (5 summer) to 9; restaurant Tue to Sun 7 to 9; closed 2 weeks mid-Jan*
Details *Children welcome in family room   Car park   Garden and patio   No smoking in family room and restaurant   Occasional background music   No dogs   Amex, Delta, MasterCard, Switch, Visa   Accommodation: 10 rooms, B&B £40 to £100*

BLANCHLAND   Northumberland   map 10

▲ Lord Crewe Arms   NEW ENTRY

Blanchland DH8 9SP   TEL: (01434) 675251
WEBSITE: www.lordcrewearms.com
off A68, 6½m S of Corbridge

The Abbey of Blanchland dates from the thirteenth century, and on the dissolution of the monasteries the guesthouse and kitchen became first a manor house and then this inn. The imposing building certainly has bags of character, with the gardens created from the old cloisters and an astonishing stone-vaulted Crypt Bar within (once the bishop's chapel); next door is a room 'adapted for eating', with tables and seating arranged around an open fire. Salads, ploughman's and rolls filled with ham and smoked cheese or minute steak are highlights of the printed menu, which also includes such staples as grilled Cumberland sausage with black pudding, apple sauce, onion gravy, mash and peas. The short list of blackboard specials inhabits more ambitious territory: carrot and coriander soup, breast of pheasant stuffed with apple and wrapped in smoked bacon, and grilled cod with a herbed tomato and breadcrumb topping. Wylam Gold Tankard is the one real ale on handpump, and three wines are offered by the glass. A separate entrance leads to the hotel, with its own formal restaurant. SAMPLE DISHES: smoked salmon, prawn and tuna salad £7; rump steak with green peppercorn sauce £9.50; sticky toffee pudding £3.50.

Licensees *Peter Gingell and Alexander Todd (freehouse)*
Open *winter 11 to 3, 6 to 11, Sun 12 to 3, 7 to 10.30, summer 11 to 11, Sun 12 to 3, 7 to 10.30; bar food 12 to 2, 7 to 9, restaurant all week 7 to 9.15, Sun 12.30 to 2*
Details *Children welcome in bar eating area   Wheelchair access (not WC)   Garden   No smoking in restaurant   Background music   Dogs welcome on a lead   Amex, Delta, Diners, MasterCard, Switch, Visa   Accommodation: 21 rooms, B&B £80 to £120*

BLEDINGTON   Gloucestershire   map 5

▲ Kings Head

The Green, Bledington OX7 6XQ   TEL: (01608) 658365
WEBSITE: www.kingsheadinn.net
on B4450 4m SE of Stow-on-the-Wold

The sixteenth-century building, set back from the green in a pretty village in one of the 'wealthiest bits of the wealthy Cotswolds', exudes a general 'classy rural' atmosphere, right down to the rustic furniture, the low, white-painted ceiling beams and large inglenook with an open log fire. The food, too, available in both bar and restaurant, has some bright, modern ideas showing up on the short printed menu or among the handful of blackboard specials. Start perhaps with pressed ham hock terrine with red onion marmalade, or potted salmon, then go on to pan-fried lamb chops with potato and celeriac purée, or fillet of sea bass with braised fennel, new potatoes, cumin and ginger. Lighter dishes are available at lunch, with toasted paninis or baked potatoes featuring alongside smoked chicken Caesar salad or linguine with smoked salmon, but there are hearty classics too: say, Gloucester Old Spot sausages or steak and Hook Norton stew, with British farmhouse cheeses or chocolate fudge brownies to finish. Bass is a permanent fixture on handpump, joined by a couple of guest ales. The six house wines sold by the glass offer a fair range of modern flavours, but the list has its heart in the traditional regions of France. SAMPLE DISHES: chicken liver parfait £5.50; local pheasant and apple cassoulet £9.50; lemon mousse with raspberry coulis £4.

Licensees Archie and Nicola Orr-Ewing (freehouse)
Open 11 to 2.30, 6 to 11, Sun 12 to 3, 6.30 to 10.30; bar food and restaurant 12 to 2, 7 to 9.30 (9 winter); closed 25 and 26 Dec
Details Children welcome in family room and restaurant Car park Garden and patio No smoking in restaurant Occasional live or background music Dogs welcome exc in restaurant Amex, Delta, MasterCard, Switch, Visa Accommodation: 12 rooms, B&B £50 to £90

BODIAM   East Sussex   map 3

Curlew 😊 [NEW ENTRY]

Junction Road, Bodiam TN32 5UY   TEL: (01580) 861394
WEBSITE: www.thecurlewatbodiam.co.uk

Food is certainly the focus at the Curlew: an inspector thought that a steady hand in the kitchen was displaying real flair with 'a freshness in the cooking, wonderful, full flavours'. The building is chunky, white weather-boarded and set at crossroads, with the main door opening outwards straight on to the road – take care! Inside, beams, log-burning stove, hop garlands and plain wood furniture (with white linen in the restaurant) create a classic look. Although very much a restaurant pub – a few food and wine pictures set the tone – drinkers are made welcome with Harveys Best, or Young's on handpump. You can choose from both the bar and restaurant menus in the bar area, mixing things like Mediterranean fish soup (described as 'sheer heaven'), or lobster and salmon sausage on buttered spinach with lobster tandoori sauce, with more traditional pub dishes such as plates of cheese or meat, chicken curry, and fish and chips. Roast pheasant with fondant potatoes, honey-roasted parsnip, cauliflower purée, red cabbage and port sauce is a sophisticated main course, while filled baguettes, say Brie and vine tomato, are a useful proposition at lunchtime. We are unable to comment on the wine list as this was not supplied before the Guide went to press, though we understand that around 200 bottles are featured, with a wide range of prices (from around £12 to close to £2,000). SAMPLE DISHES: smoked garlic and saffron soup £4; pan-fried salmon fillet with braised leek, herb mash and chive cream sauce £14; raspberry crème brûlée with vanilla ice cream £7.

Licensee Andy Blyth (freehouse)
Opening times, other details Not available at time of going to press

BODSHAM   Kent   map 3

Froggies at the Timber Batts 😊 [NEW ENTRY]

School Lane, Bodsham TN25 5JQ   TEL: (01233) 750237
Bodsham signposted off B2068 between Canterbury and Hythe

Next to the village school in deeply rural Kent, this old pub is full of surprises. At first glance the interior seems patriotically English, complete with a huge brick hearth sporting a log fire, dark red carpets, beams and timbers, plus a few decorative touches like a carved stone horse and a piece of sculpted amber on a windowsill – not to mention frog-themed ornaments. There are impeccably kept English real ales, too, including Adnams Bitter, Woodforde's Wherry Best Bitter and Fuller's London Pride, as well as cider from Pawley Farm, Faversham. Up in the 'poacher's corner' of the bar you can get a selection of light meals, including ham, egg and chips, sausages and mash, and baguettes. The real eye-opener, however, is the weekly-changing main menu and list of specials, which promise entirely authentic French country cooking, executed with flair and élan. Dishes are written in immaculate French, with no translations, simply because the chef/proprietor is from France. Those *au fait* with the language should have no trouble with identifying starters like stir-fried freshwater crayfish in a 'brick leave' basket, rock oysters with shallot vinegar, wild rabbit terrine with prunes, or pigeon breasts – which are cooked daringly rare and served with piquant horseradish sauce and a handful of salad leaves. Main courses continue the theme, with fillet of beef and Roquefort sauce, pork fillet in Dijon mustard sauce, roast saddle of lamb, and pavé of sea trout cooked *à point* with cider and sorrel. A separate portable board of desserts is carried from table to table: tarte Tatin, iced nougat with raspberry sauce, and crêpes with apple purée and Cassis sorbet, for example. The wine list is straight out of a French bistro, with bottles identified only by region and appellation and the house wines provided by the owner's cousin. Everything on it is French apart from an Argentinian trio – from a French-owned company. SAMPLE DISHES: warm goats' cheese salad £6; whole sea bass in white butter sauce £13; Cassis sorbet with liqueur £5.

Licensee Joel Yves Gross (freehouse)
Open *winter Tue to Sun 12 to 3.30, 6.30 to 11.30 (10.30 Sun), summer Tue to Fri 12 to 3.30, 6.30 to 11.30, Sat 12 to 11.30, Sun 12 to 10.30; bar food and restaurant Tue to Sun 12 to 2.30 (summer 3.30 Sat and Sun), Tue to Sat 7 to 9.30 (summer 10 Sat)*
Details *Children welcome   Car park   Wheelchair access (not WC)   Garden and patio   Live or background music   Dogs welcome   Delta, MasterCard, Switch, Visa*

BOOTHSDALE   Cheshire   map 7

Boot Inn

Boothsdale, nr Willington CW6 0NH   TEL: (01829) 751375
coming from Chester on A54, turn right to Oscroft Willington, then left at T-junction, then second right up Boothsdale to pub

A narrow, one-track lane curves past this creeper-covered mellow brick and sandstone building before losing itself in a wooded valley. The area, known locally as Little Switzerland, has countless paths that beg to be explored; the leaflet describing six circular walks from the pub is worth picking up in the bar. The interior is on different levels as several cottages were knocked together to create the pub, and low ceilings and beams remain from its origins in the early nineteenth century. A central wood-burning stove stands in the main bar area, with a few benches and tables around its wall, and a snug contains a black-leaded range and old pews. Another room has colour-washed walls and an open log fire, plus there is a light and airy conservatory restaurant with doors to the garden. 'Real' sandwiches and baguettes are served in the bar – honey roast ham with mustards, for instance – where you can also order from the restaurant menu or choose something from the specials board. Main courses take in the traditional: a farmhouse platter of rump steak, pork sausage, liver, bacon, tomato and mushrooms, for example, or Barnsley lamb chops. Grilled goats' cheese and chilli salsa, or salmon fishcakes are typical of the wide choice of starters. Vegetarians are particularly well looked after. Tetley Bitter, Timothy Taylor Landlord and Bass are among the ales on tap, plus perhaps a brew from local Weetwood Ales. The short, fairly priced wine list includes six by the small or large glass, and malt whisky fans will find 30 to choose from. SAMPLE DISHES: fillet of smoked trout with horseradish sauce £6.50; Cumberland sausage with rich onion gravy £8; tipsy cherry trifle £4.50.

Licensee Mike Gollings (Pubmaster)
Open *Mon to Fri 11 to 3, 6 to 11, Sat, Sun and bank hols 11 to 11; bar food and restaurant Mon to Fri 11 to 2.30, 6 to 9.30, Sat, Sun and bank hols 11 to 9.30; closed 25 Dec*
Details *Children welcome in snug and restaurant   Car park   Garden and patio   No smoking in restaurant No music   No dogs   Amex, Delta, Diners, MasterCard, Switch, Visa*

BORASTON   Shropshire   map 5

▲ Peacock Inn

Worcester Road, Boraston WR15 8LL   TEL: (01584) 810506
WEBSITE: www.thepeacockinn.com
on A456, 1¼ m E of Tenbury Wells

The Peacock Inn, which dates from the fourteenth century, is nowadays very much a dining pub, with most of the wooden tables in the warren of little rooms already set. The décor, while traditional, is smart: there's a seating area with leather sofas beside a roaring log fire and some striking floor-to-ceiling panelling, as well as hops draped across oak beams, and sporting prints on the walls. The menu, served throughout, is fairly long, and the style eclectic, but the kitchen keeps things pretty simple, allowing good raw materials to shine. Scallops served in a warm salad with bacon and sherry vinegar have been described by one reporter as 'very good, fresh, nicely timed', while the fillet of English lamb with roasted cherry tomatoes, garlic and a rosemary-scented sauce that followed was 'again nicely timed'. Otherwise there could be crab tart topped with Brie with sauce vierge to start, with main courses of medallions of pork fillet with boudin noir and red wine sauce, or beer-battered cod and chips. Real ales include Hook Norton Old Hooky, Tetley Bitter, and Hobsons Best Bitter, and six wines are sold by the glass or bottle, the rest of the list selected with a keen eye for quality to tempt those willing to spend over £20 or even over £30 a bottle. SAMPLE DISHES: duck liver parfait with Cumberland sauce £4.50; steak and wild mushroom pie £9.25; crème brûlée £4.25.

Licensees James and Alice Vidler (freehouse)
Open *11 to 3, 6 to 11 (10.30 Sun); bar food and restaurant 12 to 2.15, 6.30 to 9.15*
Details *Children welcome in eating areas   Car park   Wheelchair access (not WC)   Garden and patio No-smoking area in bar, no smoking in restaurant   Background music   Dogs welcome in bar only   Delta, MasterCard, Switch, Visa   Accommodation: 6 rooms, B&B £45 to £85*

BOROUGHBRIDGE   North Yorkshire   map 9

▲ Black Bull

6 St James Square, Boroughbridge YO51 9AR   TEL: (01423) 322413
on B6265, ½ m from A1(M) junction 48

Now bypassed by the A1(M), Boroughbridge guarded a crossing over the River Ure and was once the Ninth Legion's camp of Isurium Brigantium, and in 1322 the Battle of Boroughbridge saw the rebel Earl of Lancaster defeated by Edward II's forces. In its main square, on what used to be the Great North Road, is this ancient coaching inn, which shows its age in thick stone walls, beams and a huge fireplace. A printed menu of bar snacks blends traditional and contemporary ideas, ranging from gammon steak with fried egg and chips to wok-fried beef with vegetables and noodles, along with various hot and cold sandwiches – simple bacon with relish perhaps, or roast tomato and basil ciabatta with mozzarella. A blackboard of seasonal specials and fish dishes extends the choice, and the separate restaurant menu is also available in the bar. Regular beers John Smith's and Black Sheep Best are joined by a varying guest ale. The wine list offers 28 bottles priced from £9.50 (a dozen come by the glass too). SAMPLE DISHES: Chinese-style duck salad with hot plum and ginger sauce £5.25; battered haddock with thick-cut chips and mushy peas £9; banana bread-and-butter pudding with toffee sauce £3.

Licensee A.E. Burgess (freehouse)
Open *11 to 11, Sun 12 to 10.30; bar food and restaurant 12 to 2 (2.30 Sun), 6 to 9 (9.30 Fri and Sat)*
Details *Children welcome   Car park   Wheelchair access (also WC)   No-smoking area in bar, no smoking in restaurant   Occasional background music   Dogs welcome   Delta, Diners, MasterCard, Switch, Visa*
Accommodation: 6 rooms, B&B £30 to £56

BOTTLESFORD   **Wiltshire**   map 2

Seven Stars 🍇

Bottlesford SN9 6LU   TEL: (01672) 851325
off A345 at mini-roundabout at North Newnton; follow signs for Woodborough then Bottlesford

Although more or less joined to two other villages, Bottlesford is so tiny that 'blink and you'll miss it'. The Seven Stars stands on its own surrounded by spacious grounds, a lovely old red-brick rambling building: 'even the thatched roof line is not all on one and the same level'. Inside, the 'trad ye olde English' look – roaring log fires, dark wooden panelling – has been given a French touch: not just the chef/land-lord, Philippe Cheminade, but all the staff are decidedly French. The kitchen follows a policy of combining French classic dishes (boeuf à la bourguignonne) with popular English pub food (cottage pie) and the occasional eclectic modern dish (pan-fried pigeon breast with mango and salad). The blackboard may announce 'simple and attractive' vegetarian dishes such as Greek salad or wild mushroom risotto, while the printed menu delivers confit of duck with sautéed potatoes, or timbale of sole, scal-lops, salmon and crayfish tails with white wine sauce. To drink, there's Badger Dorset Best, Fuller's London Pride and Wadworth 6X, alongside local organic cider, a French-led wine list and a range of vintage Armagnacs. Eight house wines at £10.25 a bottle (£2.95 a glass) include unusual grape varieties like Vermentino and Mauzac to offer a better-than-average choice of flavours. Some quite serious French bottles command appropriate prices, but with plenty of good stuff from all around the world at under £20 there's no need to overreach. SAMPLE DISHES: duck foie gras terrine £8; fillet of pork with plums and Armagnac sauce £12.75; French cheeseboard £5.25.

Licensees Philippe and Kate Cheminade (freehouse)
Open *Tue to Sat 12 to 3, 6 to 11, Sun 12 to 3; bar food and restaurant Tue to Sat 12 to 2, 7 to 9.30, Sun 12 to 2*
Details *Children welcome in restaurant   Car park   Wheelchair access (not WC)   Garden and patio   No smoking in 1 dining room   Background music   Dogs by arrangement   Delta, MasterCard, Switch, Visa*

BOUGH BEECH Kent   map 3

Wheatsheaf

Hever Road, Bough Beech TN8 7NU   TEL: (01732) 700254
WEBSITE: www.wheatsheafatboughbeech.co.uk
off B2027 between Edenbridge and Tonbridge

During its lifetime, this typical Wealden building has been a smithy as well as doing duty as an alehouse on and off since the eighteenth century. Inside, its antiquity is evident in such features as a patch of original wattle-and-daub wall dated 1607. The walls are adorned with exotic hunting trophies and unusual musical instruments, while the menus are listed on a huge blackboard. What you can expect is decent, honest food with no frills and value for money. The lengthy repertoire kicks off with starters such as duck and orange pâté or garlic mushrooms on ciabatta with balsamic vinegar and pesto before a big choice of international main courses ranging from pork hock in a fruit compote with mash to Thai green chicken curry. Seafood lovers and vegetarians are well catered for with, say, wok-fried prawns in basil, chilli and olive oil with a mini-paella, or red pepper quiche. Finish perhaps with apple and caramel pancakes or spotted dick. A good choice of real ales includes Harveys Sussex Best Bitter, Old Speckled Hen and Shepherd Neame Master Brew, among others, while the list of 20 wines features four house selections by the glass at £2.95 and £3.95. SAMPLE DISHES: hummus with black olives and pitta bread £6; beef goulash with dumplings, mash and winter vegetables £15; chocolate sponge with hot chocolate sauce £4.50.

Licensee Elizabeth Currie (Enterprise)
Open 11 to 11, Sun 12 to 10.30; bar food 12 to 10
Details Children welcome in bar eating area   Car park   Wheelchair access (not WC)   Garden and patio
Occasional live music   Dogs welcome   MasterCard, Switch, Visa

BOVINGDON GREEN Buckinghamshire   map 3

Royal Oak ✿   NEW ENTRY

Bovingdon Green SL7 2JF   TEL: (01628) 488611
from Marlow town centre take A4155 towards Henley-on-Thames; after 300yds take right turn signposted Bovingdon Green

From the outside, the cream-painted brick building looks like a fairly average roadside pub, with its name scrawled in a modern typeface on the front wall giving no clue that this is a 'first-rate dining pub'. Yet the Royal Oak remains very true to its pubby origins, with no danger of slipping into full restaurant mode. You enter a small, cosy, low-ceilinged bar with a wood-burner; beyond is the open-plan main dining area. The walls are painted deep maroon or cream, the floor is bare boards, tables are simply laid, and plenty of windows give views south over the patio and garden beyond. The menu makes encouraging reading, and some genuinely interesting ideas are at work, with fashionable flavours used inventively. It's divided into 'small plates' (some priced for small or large portions) – say, oak-smoked bacon on bubble and squeak with hollandaise and a poached egg – then 'main meals' of crispy duck leg confit with dauphinois potatoes and cinnamon sauce, with blackboard specials such as a 'superb' starter of pork belly with peach chutney that impressed one visitor, or chorizo, rocket and Parmesan omelette. A separate pudding menu is just as imaginative, with walnut whip fool with lady fingers, and sticky treacle and apple tart typical examples. Beers are a good selection, with Rebellion IPA brewed at nearby Marlow, Brakspear Bitter, and Fuller's London Pride. Wines are taken seriously: a list of some two dozen, which, with a few exceptions, stays well within the affordable bracket, with around 12 offered by the large or small glass. The Royal Oak is a sibling of the Alford Arms, Frithsden (see entry) and the Swan Inn, Denham. SAMPLE DISHES: gnocchi with roast pumpkin, mascarpone and toasted pine nuts £5.75; grilled sea bass fillets with saffron potatoes and rouille £13.25; chocolate brownie with chocolate sauce £4.50.

Licensees David Salisbury and Trasna Rice Giff (freehouse)
Open *11 to 11, Sun 12 to 10.30; bar food 12 to 2.30 (3 Sun), 7 to 10; closed 25 and 26 Dec*
Details *Children welcome   Car park   Wheelchair access (also WC)   Garden and patio   Background music Dogs welcome in bar only   Amex, Delta, MasterCard, Switch, Visa*

BOX   Gloucestershire   map 2

Halfway Inn   NEW ENTRY

Box, nr Stroud GL9 9AE   TEL: (01453) 832631
from A46 follow signs to Amberley, then to Box; pub on the W side of village

From outside the large, cream-painted gabled pub on the edge of Minchinhampton Common looks reassuringly traditional. Step inside and it's quite a surprise. A Spartan interior features a fair quantity of bare modern pine juxtaposed with old-polished floorboards, new roof timbers, and striking orange terracotta walls. It is one large, right-angled space, one part being a long, partitioned bar area, the other set aside for dining. Short menus offer a mix of classic dishes and a few mildly fashionable ideas supplemented by blackboard specials. Ribeye steak with a mushroom flan, dauphinoise potato and green peppercorn sauce is definitely from the traditional camp, as are main-course options such as braised oxtail with mustard dumplings and barley broth, and calf's liver with black pudding mash. But choices may extend to Cornish scallops wrapped in pancetta with steamed buttered parsnip batons and a liquorish cream, to a main course of seared fillet of sea bass with an open clam chowder. Desserts range from good old sticky toffee pudding to îles flottantes. Greene King IPA, Butcombe Bitter and Smiles Best are on handpump, backed up by a guest, and five house wines are available in two sizes of glass. SAMPLE DISHES: pork liver and bacon terrine £4.75; fresh langoustine with lemon mayonnaise and Jersey potatoes with garlic butter £15; apple, prune and butterscotch compote £4.25.

Licensee Matt Walker (freehouse)
Open *winter Tue to Fri 12 to 3, 6 to 11, Sat 12 to 11, Sun 12 to 10.30; summer Tue to Sun 12 to 11; also open bank hol Mons; bar food winter 12 to 2, 7 to 9, summer 12 to 9*
Details *Children welcome   Car park   Wheelchair access (also WC)   Garden and patio   No smoking in restaurant   Background music   Dogs welcome in bar area only   MasterCard, Switch, Visa*

BRAMDEAN   Hampshire   map 2

Fox Inn

Bramdean SO24 0LP   TEL: (01962) 771363
on A272 Winchester to Petersfield road, 3m SE of New Alresford

Legend has it that the one-time Prince of Wales (later George IV) paid a visit to this white-weatherboarded, 400-year-old pub in 1780. Since then, the interior has been comfortably modernised to create a civilised, upmarket feel, with cottagey dark wooden furniture dotted around the open-plan space, lots of swagged burgundy-coloured curtains, and attractive lamps adding to the homely, relaxed atmosphere. The menus offer a safe-and-sound collection of dishes based on ingredients of decent quality, and there's nothing too challenging about the repertoire. Tomato and basil soup is a robust, gutsy version; otherwise you might begin with baked Brie in filo with redcurrant jelly or pan-fried scallops with bacon. Main courses follow the same trend, with anything from roast rack of lamb with rosemary and garlic to fish in the shape of, say, grilled fillet of sea bass, or halibut with lime and chilli butter. The choice of home-made desserts is a selection of classic favourites ranging from summer pudding with clotted cream to chocolate St-Emilion. Ruddles County is on draught, and around 30 modestly priced wines appear on the list, with seven by the glass. SAMPLE DISHES: poached pear, blue cheese and crispy bacon salad £7; pan-fried skate wing with capers £12; treacle tart £4.25.

Licensees Jane and Ian Inder (Greene King)
Open 11 to 3, 6.30 (6 summer) to 11, Sun 12 to 3, 7 to 10.30; bar food 12 to 2, 7 to 9
Details No children   Car park   Wheelchair access (not WC)   Garden and patio   No-smoking area in bar   Background music   Amex, Delta, MasterCard, Switch, Visa

BRAMFIELD   Suffolk   map 6

Queen's Head
The Street, Bramfield IP19 9HT   TEL: (01986) 784214
off A144, 3m S of Halesworth

With it's impressive garden – three-tiered and overlooking an unusual thatched church – and history oozing from an attractive interior, it is no wonder that one visitor described Mark and Amanda Corcoran's centuries-old pub as 'splendidly different all round'. The atmosphere is 'convivial', the main bar has a vaulted ceiling and an immense fireplace, and the food is unpretentious, built around local and often organic supplies, which the kitchen interprets in a generous, enthusiastic manner. Aldeburgh asparagus with melted butter could make a seasonal appearance, or there might be Stonehouse Organic Farm chicken liver and brandy pâté with Cumberland sauce. Exemplary main courses run to Bramfield pork sausages served with an apple and celery sauce and mash, a 'simply wonderful' steak, kidney and Adnams pie, or well-timed plaice fillets with herb butter. Desserts are equally good: 'rich and creamy' home-made vanilla and lemon curd ice cream, say, or apple crumble with custard. On draught are Adnams Bitter and Broadside, plus Crones organic cider. Around 25 wines include a handful of organics and around eight by the glass. SAMPLE DISHES: spinach and coconut soup £3.75; Village Farm lamb steak in a rosemary crust with garlic sauce £11; rich chocolate and brandy pot £4.25.

Licensees Amanda and Mark Corcoran (Adnams)
Open 11.45 to 2.30, 6.30 to 11, Sun 12 to 3, 7 to 10.30; bar food 12 to 2, 6.30 (7 Sun) to 10 (9 Sun); closed 26 Dec
Details Children welcome   Car park   Wheelchair access (not WC)   Garden and patio   No smoking in 2 rooms   No music   Dogs welcome on a lead   Amex, Delta, MasterCard, Switch, Visa

The Guide is totally independent, accepts no free hospitality, carries no advertising and makes no charge for inclusion.

BRAMPFORD SPEKE   Devon   map 1

Agricultural Inn

Brampford Speke EX5 5DP   TEL: (01392) 841591
WEBSITE: www.theagriculturalinn.co.uk
from A377 Exeter to Crediton road, take first right turn after Cowley Bridge roundabout

The appropriately named Agricultural is a large pebbledash building in a deeply rural setting approached down twisting, narrow country lanes. It overlooks a cobbled courtyard at the centre of the village. The interior décor is traditional, and the clientele is mostly made up of the local farming community. The regular menus delve into the modern eclectic repertoire to offer spicy, boldly flavoured dishes – fishcake with chilli and ginger sauce, and a curry of the day – alongside hearty traditional fare such as faggots and mash with onion gravy or steak and kidney pudding, plus a few more unusual ideas like roast rack of lamb with black cherry sauce. Daily specials add a further half-dozen choices. Speke Easy ale is brewed specially for the pub by the local Beer Engine brewery and appears on handpump alongside Fuller's London Pride. The short wine list features around 12 by the glass. SAMPLE DISHES: scallops and bacon on mixed leaves £6; chicken cordon bleu filled with ham and cheese £8.25; apple crumble £3.50.

Licensees Allan and Fern Ferns (freehouse)
Open *Tue to Sat and bank hol Mon 11.45 to 2.30, 6 to 11, Sun 12 to 3, 7 to 10.30; bar food 12 to 2, 6.30 (7 Sun) to 9; closed 25 Dec*
Details *Children welcome   Car park   Wheelchair access (also WC)   Patio   No smoking in eating area Background music   No dogs   Amex, Delta, Diners, MasterCard, Switch, Visa*

BRANCASTER STAITHE   Norfolk   map 6

▲ White Horse

Main Road, Brancaster Staithe PE31 8BW   TEL: (01485) 210262
WEBSITE: www.whitehorsebrancaster.co.uk

From the outside it may seem plain and easy to overlook, but reporters consider this a 'truly special' pub, its beautiful setting equalled by high standards of hospitality, food and drink. The front bar is light and spacious, with scrubbed pine furniture and old photographs and prints on pale yellow walls. To the rear is the conservatory dining area, which opens on to a large terrace – both give splendid views across a wide expanse of marshland towards Scolt Head Island. The daily-changing menu offers a dozen or more options per course with an emphasis on fish and seafood. Alongside cod chowder with spinach, smoked paprika oil and Gruyère croûte, there are locally smoked prawns with lemon and dill mayonnaise for a more straightforward starter, while main courses might include seared tuna loin with Marrakech vegetable tagine, or baked plaice with gnocchi, Spanish black pudding and pesto. Meat eaters might prefer pan-fried guinea fowl with chorizo and spinach risotto. Those who have stayed overnight also praise breakfast. A decent line-up of real ales includes local Woodforde's Nelson's Revenge, and there's also a selection of Belgian wheat beers. Interesting and good bottles keep cropping up on the 50-strong wine list, with a dozen by the glass. A Vermentino from southern France (£12.50) is a tempting oddity while a stretch to just over £20 will bag the highly rated Morton Hawkes Bay Pinot Noir. Dessert offerings run to the rare delights of Mission Hill Icewine (£32.60/half-bottle). SAMPLE DISHES: timbale of crab with potato vinaigrette and herb salad £5.50;

pan-roasted cod with Puy lentils, pancetta, root vegetables and sweet potato chips £13; roast peach frangipane tart £4.

Licensees Cliff Nye and Kevin Nobes (freehouse)
Open 11 to 11, Sun 12 to 10.30; bar food and restaurant 12 to 2.30, 6.45 to 9.15; closed evening 25 Dec (exc for residents)
Details Children welcome   Car park   Wheelchair access (also WC)   Patio   No smoking in dining room
Occasional live or background music   Dogs welcome   Delta, Diners, MasterCard, Switch, Visa
Accommodation: 15 rooms, B&B £48 to £116

BRANSCOMBE   Devon
map 2

▲ Masons Arms 🍺

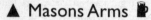

Branscombe EX12 3DJ   TEL: (01297) 680300
WEBSITE: www.masonsarms.co.uk
off A3052, 5m E of Sidmouth

Hidden down tiny lanes that wind around steep hills, the narrow, straggly village of Branscombe is just a mile from the coast. The long stone building that is the Masons Arms is set against quite a steep hillside, and the outside seating area at the side is a whole series of tiny terraces, but fronted by tables under beehive-shaped thatched sunshades. Inside, exposed-stone walls, open fireplaces and beamed ceilings are all present. Beer is serious here (they have a three-day beer festival each summer), and – supplementing Otter Bitter, Otter Ale and draught Bass – guests could include anything from Blackdown, Clearwater, Exe Valley and O'Hanlons, plus Addlestone and Lyme Bay's Jack Rat ciders. The wine list offers nearly 50 wines, with 15 by the glass. Ploughman's and sandwiches are available at lunch only, but the bar menu also offers creamy seafood chowder or basil-marinated goats' cheese tartlet to start, followed by seafood and shellfish stew, lamb, bacon and apricot casserole, steak and kidney pudding, or organically reared Branscombe beef stew with herb dumplings. Desserts range from bread-and-butter pudding to meringue with oranges and cream. The restaurant, now in a separate building, offers a three-course £25 prix fixe, which might run from duck liver parfait, via pan-fried halibut fillet, to chocolate and rum cake. SAMPLE DISHES: tomato and basil soup £3; half a duck glazed with honey, soy sauce and orange £13.50; apple crumble with custard £4.

Licensees Tim Manktelow-Gray, Murray Inglis and Mark Thompson (freehouse)
Open 11 to 11 (11 to 3, 6 to 11 winter), Sun 12 to 10.30; bar food 12 to 2 (2.15 Sat and Sun), 7 to 9; restaurant Tue to Sat 7 to 9
Details Children welcome   Car park   Patio   No-smoking area in bar, no smoking in restaurant   Occasional live music   Dogs welcome   Delta, MasterCard, Switch, Visa   Accommodation: 22 rooms, B&B £30 to £150

BRASSINGTON   Derbyshire
map 5

Ye Olde Gate Inne

Well Street, Brassington DE4 4HJ   TEL: (01629) 540448
just off B3035 Ashbourne to Wirksworth road, 4m W of Wirksworth

The first thing you notice on entering this seventeenth-century creeper-covered inn is the 'spectacular' blackened kitchen range that dominates the main bar. In winter it will be in full blaze, but it is always resplendent with tasteful brasses, copper bedpans and lighted candles, while beams, a flagstone floor, a loudly ticking wall clock and polished wooden tables create a time-stood-still atmosphere. A smaller bar, popular with locals, is darker, reliant on a blazing fire not just for heat but for light, with candles on the scrubbed wooden tables, and high-backed settles. The regularly changing blackboard menu is a catalogue of popular dishes such as lunchtime ploughman's and generously filled baguettes – perhaps rare roast beef with horseradish – as well as steak, mushroom and Guinness pie, Lancashire hotpot, tournedos Rossini, and curries, with New York cheesecake with mixed berry sauce or treacle sponge pudding with custard for dessert. Marston's Pedigree and guest ales are on handpump, and four wines are served by the glass. SAMPLE DISHES: Brie melt with sweet chilli sauce £6; navarin of lamb £11; warm Boston brownie £3.50.

Licensee Paul Scott Burlinson (Wolverhampton & Dudley)
Open Tue to Sat and bank hol Mon 12 to 2.30 (3 Sat), 6 to 11, Sun 12 to 3, 7 to 10.30; bar food Tue to Thur and bank hol Mon 12 to 1.45, 7 to 8.45, Fri to Sat 12 to 2, 7 to 9, Sun 12 to 2
Details No children under 10   Car park   Wheelchair access (also WC)   Garden   No smoking in eating area   No music   Dogs welcome   Delta, MasterCard, Switch, Visa

BREARTON   **North Yorkshire**   map 9

Malt Shovel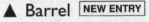

Brearton HG3 3BX   TEL: (01423) 862929
off A61 and B6165, 2m E of Ripley

Tucked away in a tiny hamlet watered by a tributary of the River Nidd, this sixteenth-century inn really manages to pull in the punters despite its remote location. The place oozes character and charming old-world atmosphere, with its bottle-glass windows, log fire, abundant beams and a couple of eponymous malt shovels. The day's menu, chalked on a blackboard, zooms around the world for braised lamb shank with garlic and preserved lemons, chargrilled chicken breast with warm potato and chorizo salad, and potato and tomato curry, ending up back in the North Country with game pie, and haddock in beer batter; sandwiches and ploughman's are also on offer. Puddings are in similar vein, ranging from lemon tart to apple and bramble crumble. Two dozen wines are listed with enthusiastic tasting notes; prices start at £8.95, and all are available by the glass. Beer drinkers can take their pick from a splendid assortment of five regional ales, usually Black Sheep Best Bitter, Daleside Nightjar and Theakston Best plus two guests from eminent local microbreweries such as Durham and Rooster's. SAMPLE DISHES: goats' cheese and leek tart £5.50; pan-fried haddock in Cajun spices £7.25; treacle tart £3.

Licensee Leslie V. Mitchell (freehouse)
Open Tue to Sun 12 to 2.30, 6.45 to 11 (10.30 Sun); bar food Tue to Sun 12 to 2, Tue to Sat 7 to 9; closed 25 and 26 Dec
Details Children welcome   Car park   Wheelchair access (not WC)   Garden and patio   No-smoking area in bar   No music   Dogs welcome on a lead   No cards

BRETTON   **Derbyshire**   map 8

▲ Barrel   NEW ENTRY

Bretton S32 5QD   TEL: (01433) 630856
from A623 follow signs for Foolow, then Bretton

At 1,275 feet above sea level, the Barrel is reputedly the highest pub in Derbyshire and has spectacular views over five counties. 'Shame it was pitch dark,' lamented a reporter who made the winding drive one winter evening and could just about make out 'car headlights way below'. But compensation came from entering a 'real local' run with warmth and enthusiasm, with a roaring fire, lots of highly polished brass and copper, beams hung with old plates and cups, and a kitchen delivering pub staples and hearty country dishes. The printed menu, which offers a range of food from jacket potatoes, sandwiches and omelettes to steak, kidney and Guinness pie, or grilled fillet of plaice with lemon and chive butter, is supplemented by blackboard specials: perhaps hare braised in port with vegetables, or roast pheasant with cranberry and orange sauce. Take a hearty appetite, as portions are robust: pork and nettle sausages on top of a huge mound of mustard mash, with Yorkshire pudding and a pile of plain vegetables, have been described as 'enough to feed three people'. A selection of beers includes Marston's Pedigree, Greene King Abbot Ale, Deuchars IPA and Tetley Bitter, and four house wines come by the glass. SAMPLE DISHES: Brie, spinach and walnut crêpe £5; chicken suprême wrapped in bacon roasted with garlic, thyme and lemon £8.25; spiced orange sponge £4.

Licensee Paul Rowlinson (freehouse)
Open Mon to Fri 11 to 3, 6 to 11, Sat and Sun 11 to 11; bar food 12 to 2.30, 6.30 to 9.30 (9 Sun)
Details Children welcome in eating area   Car park   Wheelchair access (also WC)   Garden and patio   Occasional live music   Dogs welcome   Delta, MasterCard, Switch, Visa   Accommodation: 4 rooms, B&B £45 to £65

BRIDGE   Kent

map 3

White Horse ✿ ✿

53 High Street, Bridge CT4 5LA   TEL: (01227) 830249
take A2050 S from Canterbury and continue into Bridge; pub in centre of village

Bridge is far enough away from Canterbury (and the A2) to feel reassuringly rural, and the White Horse – a white-painted, thatched former coaching inn – sits comfortably at the heart of this sprawling village. It has the look and feel of a pub, with an attractive shaded beer garden behind, and the well-groomed main bar keeps things traditional, with beamed ceilings and a large brick hearth with a log fire. But the White Horse's reputation now hinges on its food, and the kitchen (headed by Ben Walton) works with serious intent: the bar/brasserie blackboard menu is a litany of classy modern dishes peppered with fashionable ingredients and up-to-the-minute techniques. But it is all admirably simple: from home-made fish soup with rouille, or pan-fried scallop and smoked bacon salad with parsley pesto to confit duck leg with red cabbage, mash and apple sauce. Seasonal ingredients are to the fore, most of them from local suppliers. So in winter you may find pheasant and other game featuring plentifully, perhaps in a pork, game and cobnut terrine with red onion chutney and pickles. Finish with vanilla pannacotta with an apple sorbet, or choose a selection from the fine cheese list. Portions are generous, and prices are notably low for this quality of cooking. To the rear of the pub is the separate restaurant, with its own more luxurious, upmarket menu. Despite the focus on food, this remains the kind of pub where locals can call in for a drink. If they do, they will find Shepherd Neame Master Brew Bitter and three guest ales, which might include Fuller's London Pride, Old Speckled Hen, Greene King IPA and Abbot Ale, Adnams Bitter and Hook Norton Old Hooky. There is also a short but decent wine list arranged by country; it opens with eight house wines by the glass from £2.60, or by the bottle from £11.50. SAMPLE DISHES: roasted pear, cobnut and goats' cheese salad £4.75; wild mushroom, Cheddar and herb omelette with rocket salad £6.50; melting chocolate parcel with white chocolate sorbet £5.25.

Licensees Alan and Ben Walton (Enterprise Inns)
Open 11 to 3, 5 to 11, Sun 12 to 5; bar food all week 12 to 2, Mon to Sat 6.30 to 9 (9.30 Fri and Sat), restaurant Wed to Sun 12 to 2, Tue to Sat 6.30 to 9 (9.30 Fri and Sat)
Details Children welcome in bar eating area   Car park   Garden   No-smoking area in bar, no smoking in restaurant   Occasional background music   Dogs welcome   MasterCard, Switch, Visa

BRIGHTON & HOVE   East Sussex   map 3

Basketmakers Arms   NEW ENTRY

12 Gloucester Road, Brighton BN1 4AD   TEL: (01273) 689006

In the North Laines area, this cream-painted pub doesn't stand out visually – a large coaching lamp on one wall signals its presence. You enter into a large single space with part of a partition loosely separating it into two areas, both in the same style: the floor of well-worn dark wood, walls part-panelled, paintwork of oxblood red, and walls plastered with old posters, beer mats, and old cigarette tins. This is a real local, an 'unreconstructed boozer' for 'drinking, chatting and eating if you so wish, no pressure', and it has the laid-back, relaxed air that you might expect in this city. As it is a Gale's pub, a comprehensive range of the brewery's ales are on draught – HSB, Butser, GB, Winter Ale, and Festival Mild – plus guests such as Wells Bombardier Premium Bitter. Daily specials are written up on blackboards – say, steak and mushroom pie, lasagne, or bangers and mash – and there's a printed menu with a long list of sandwiches, ploughman's, jacket potatoes, and simple, straightforward stuff like veggie chilli with garlic bread, hummus with warm pitta bread and feta salad, and home-made 100 per cent beef burger with mild chilli relish. In addition, every Friday 'without fail', locally caught fish in beer batter with chips is served. Coffee has its own section on the menu, and there is a 'proper' machine behind the bar delivering 'properly made' cappuccinos and americanos. From a wine list of some 15 bins, five are by the glass. SAMPLE DISHES: Brie ploughman's £3.75; shepherd's pie £4.50; chicken and smoky bacon pie £4.50.

Licensees Peter and Kate Dowd (Gale's)
Open 11 to 11, Sun 12 to 10.30; bar food all week 12 to 3 (4 Sun), Mon to Fri 5.30 to 8.30
Details Children welcome   Patio   Background music   Dogs welcome on a lead   Amex, Delta, MasterCard, Switch, Visa

Greys   NEW ENTRY

105 Southover Street, Brighton BN2 9UA   TEL: (01273) 680734
WEBSITE: www.greyspub.com

Live gigs and theatrical events are great crowd pullers at this popular pub tucked away on a steep hill away from Brighton's tourist trail. The building, painted petrol blue, consists of one room with lots of dark wood, a cast-iron stove, and walls plastered with posters of musicians and artistes. The food is worth attention: chef 'Spats' Thomson Picken works to a short menu of dishes with a strong French accent – rough-textured duck and pistachio terrine, roast partridge with slices of braised pear and Burgundy sauce, and moules normande with 'ace' chips. There are also a few detours for Liverpudlian pea 'whack' (aka soup), schweinesschnitzel (breaded pork escalope) with mushroom noodles, or roast beetroots with smitaine sauce and cashew nuts (a recipe supplied by composer Sir Harrison Birtwhistle). Bowls of earthy 'potée Lorraine' are served up for 'speedy' meals, and you might finish with rose-petal ice cream or ginger and lime cheesecake. To drink, check out the range of bottled Belgian beers and Breton cider or plump for patriotically English real ales like Harveys Sussex Best Bitter and Timothy Taylor Landlord. A couple of organic wines show up on the short list; four house selections are £1.80 and £2 a glass, £9.50 and £10.50 a bottle. SAMPLE DISHES: Caribbean salad £4.50; coq au vin £10.50; Edwardian trifle £4.25.

Licensees Chris Taylor, Gill Perkins and Ric Blow (Enterprise Inns)
Open Mon 5.30 to 11, Tue to Sat 11 to 11, Sun 12 to 10.30; bar food Tue to Sat 12 to 2, 6 to 9, Sun 12 to 3
Details No children   Patio   Live or background music   Dogs welcome on a lead   Delta, MasterCard, Switch, Visa

BRIGHTWELL BALDWIN   Oxfordshire   map 2

Lord Nelson

Brightwell Baldwin OX9 5NP   TEL: (01491) 612497
WEBSITE: www.lordnelson-inn.co.uk
off B480, 5m SW of M40 junction 6

The quaintly picturesque charms of the small village of Brightwell Baldwin have made it a perfect choice for a location in several episodes of TV detective series *Midsomer Murders*. Not least among those charms are the splendid old stone church and, directly opposite, the Lord Nelson, a white-painted eighteenth-century inn with a red-tiled roof that comes right down to the front verandah. Inside, the low-ceilinged rooms are decorated in pale terracotta; they include a comfortable main bar with a fire, and various eating areas. Several menus and supplementary blackboards offer a wide food choice, not sticking to one particular cooking style but covering a variety of ideas ranging from calf's liver and bacon, or ribeye steak with mushrooms, tomatoes and chips, to red onion, fig and goats' cheese tart with balsamic dressing, or herb-crusted roast cod. Real ales include Good Old Boy from the West Berkshire Brewery, and there's a list of 50-odd wines priced from £11.95, with eight by the glass. SAMPLE DISHES: creamy sautéed mushrooms with garlic and bacon £7; half a duck with classic orange sauce £15.50; lemon posset £5.

Licensees Carole and Roger Shippey (freehouse)
Open 11 to 3, 6 to 11, Sun 12 to 3, 7 to 10.30; bar food and restaurant 12 to 2.30, 6 to 10.30, Sun 12 to 2.30, 7 to 10
Details Car park   Wheelchair access (also WC)   Garden   No-smoking area   Background music   Dogs welcome   Delta, MasterCard, Switch, Visa

BRIMFIELD   Herefordshire   map 5

▲ Roebuck Inn

Brimfield SY8 4NE   TEL: (01584) 711230
WEBSITE: www.theroebuckinn.com
just off A49 Leominster to Ludlow road, 4m W of Tenbury Wells

Set in a village, opposite a pretty church with a half-timbered tower, the cream-coloured Roebuck, with a bow window to the front, dates from the fifteenth century, which is not obvious at first glance. Inside, three linked bar areas have shiny panelled walls from the floor almost to the ceiling and red patterned carpets, while the spacious dining room is a modern space decorated in loud orange, with parquet flooring and some contemporary prints on the walls. The menu, available throughout, is interesting yet straightforward and unpretentious, starters taking in spring rolls of confit duck, or crab ravioli with lemongrass and lobster sauce, while main courses feature humble steak and mushroom pudding alongside grilled sea bass with roast butternut squash and pumpkin oil dressing. A fine cheeseboard makes a good alternative to puddings of glazed lemon tart, or chocolate, amaretti and rum mousse. Real ales stocked are Parish Bitter and Wonderful from the local Wood Brewery, Tetley Bitter, and a changing guest ale. Wines are arranged by style in an enterprising round-the-world list, with plenty of choice under £20. Four house wines from France and Chile are £11, five wines come by the half-bottle, and around a half-dozen are served by the glass. 'Parking can be tight,' commented one visitor. SAMPLE DISHES: pan-seared scallops on apple purée with beetroot and vanilla dressing £6.50; wild venison fillet on celeriac rösti with sloe gin and bay sauce £16; apple and cinnamon suet steamed pudding £4.50.

Licensee Peter Jenkins (freehouse)
Open 11.30 to 3, 6.30 to 11, Sun 12 to 3, 7 to 10.30; bar food and restaurant 12 to 2.15, 7 to 9.30; closed 25 and 26 Dec
Details Children welcome in bar eating area and restaurant   Car park   Patio   No smoking in restaurant No music   Dogs welcome in snug bar   Delta, MasterCard, Switch, Visa   Accommodation: 3 rooms, B&B £45 to £70

BRISTOL   Bristol   map 2

Clifton Sausage

7–9 Portland Road, Clifton, Bristol BS8 4JA   TEL: (0117) 973 1192

Clifton is generally regarded as 'the classy suburb of Bristol', and this self-styled bar and restaurant away from the main drag wears a chic suit of clothes. It's a light, uncluttered space with wooden floors, chunky blond-wood furniture, contemporary artwork, and a bright oatmeal colour scheme. The restaurant, down a few steps, has a tiled sandstone floor and sky-blue and warm yellow walls. Bar snacks (subject to availability) set the tone as regards food: Welsh rarebit, devilled whitebait and so on. As the name suggests, sausages play a starring role: around half a dozen types – including smoky pork with maple syrup, and lamb with mint and apricot – come with onion gravy and a choice of mash or champ. Otherwise, expect British dishes, from crab Scotch eggs and angels-on-horseback to shepherd's pie and smoked haddock fishcakes with parsley and lemon sauce, plus traditional roasts on Sundays. The kitchen occasionally goes walkabout for, say, Stilton, pine-nut and baby spinach salad with Cabernet Sauvignon dressing, and specials throw up a few interesting ideas. Desserts follow suit with the likes of blackberry and apple crumble with bay leaf custard. Local Butcombe Bitter is on handpump, and virtually everything on the curiously arranged wine list is available by the glass. SAMPLE DISHES: warm leek and goats' cheese tartlet £4.50; toad-in-the-hole £9.50; chocolate cheesecake £4.50.

Licensee Peter Austen (freehouse)
Open Mon 6 to 11, Tue to Sat 12 to 11, Sun 12 to 10.30; bar food and restaurant Tue to Sun 12 to 2.30, all week 6.30 to 10
Details Children welcome   Wheelchair access (not WC)   Patio   No smoking in restaurant   Background music   No dogs   Amex, Delta, Diners, MasterCard, Switch, Visa

Spring Gardens

188 Hotwell Road, Hotwells, Bristol BS8 4RP   TEL: (0117) 927 7112
WEBSITE: www.spring-gardens.co.uk

A suntrap balcony overlooks the front of this pub in Bristol's redeveloped docklands, and there's also an attractive paved garden to the rear. Inside, the open-plan bar has dark wood furniture, leather sofas and dark parquet flooring, and lighted candles in the evening give an almost bistro feel, but there is a reassuringly pubby bar counter, and the upstairs room has pool and table football. The short, frequently changing menus are written on a blackboard next to the bar. The choice is varied enough to keep most appetites happy, typically featuring crispy fishcakes with Thai dipping sauce, or tomato and mozzarella salad for starters, with roast sea bass, or pork tenderloin in creamy mushroom sauce to follow. Real ales are Bass and Fuller's London Pride, and there is a short list of wines with three by the glass. Note that booking is essential for Sunday lunch. SAMPLE DISHES: king prawns with garlic, parsley and lemon £5; slow-roast lamb shoulder with rosemary and garlic £8; lime and ginger brûlée £4.50.

Licensees Anna Henderson and Lionel Seigneur (Heritage Pubs Co)
Open Mon to Fri 12 to 11, Sat 5 to 11, Sun 12 to 10.30; bar food Mon to Fri 12 to 2, Mon to Sat 7.30 to 9.30, Sun 12 to 4.30
Details Children welcome   Wheelchair access (not WC)   Garden and patio   Occasional background music; jukebox   Dogs welcome   Delta, MasterCard, Switch, Visa

---

BROADHEMBURY   Devon   map 2

Drewe Arms

Broadhembury EX14 3NF   TEL: (01404) 841267
off A373, 5m NW of Honiton

In an out-of-the-way village of thatched and whitewashed cottages in east Devon's agricultural hinterland, the smart custard-coloured Drewe Arms stands out. Inside, it's the usual warren of small rooms supporting a rather fishy décor – including an eel-trap along with the piscine prints – so you know to expect food that focuses almost entirely on fish as soon as you enter. Ichthyophagy is first apparent in the bar's open sandwiches (half have fishy toppings), then in the blackboard menus, which offer carnivores perhaps only rack of lamb or fillet of beef and a couple of meaty starters along the lines of venison carpaccio and confit of duck. Otherwise the carte and the prix fixe consist of simply treated fish from home waters in nearly every conceivable form, from marinated herrings, and mussels steamed with leeks and garlic, to whole Dover sole with garlic butter, fillet of brill with rémoulade sauce, and turbot with hollandaise. The Otter Brewery's range of ales, from six miles away at Luppitt, is on draught, along with Bollhayes cider, and the somewhat chaotic appearance of the wine list belies a fairly priced selection chosen to suit the cuisine; around ten wines come by the glass. SAMPLE DISHES: spicy crab soup £5; wing of skate with black butter and capers £11; Swedish apple cake £5.50.

Licensees Kerstin and Nigel Burge (freehouse)
Open all week 11 to 3, Mon to Sat 6 to 11; bar food and restaurant 12 to 2, 7 to 9.15; closed 25 and 31 Dec
Details Children welcome in eating areas   Car park   Wheelchair access (also WC)   Garden and patio
No smoking in restaurant   No music   Dogs by arrangement   Delta, MasterCard, Switch, Visa

BROME Suffolk map 6

▲ Cornwallis ♔ ❦

Brome IP23 8AJ TEL: (01379) 870326
WEBSITE: www.thecornwallis.com
at junction of A140 and B1077, midway between Norwich and Ipswich

First impressions of this imposing sixteenth-century dower house, set in grounds 'with room for a horse-racing track', can be rather daunting; this is, after all, a rather grand country hotel. But the 'enticing' bar has the look and feel of a classic old pub, albeit with modern finishing touches. Beams, wood fires, spacious, comfortable seating, and a glassed-over well (said to be 60 feet deep) are principal features, backed up by a good choice of wines and some classy modern food. Snacks or starters might include a salad of Norfolk smoked eel with black pudding, speck and horseradish dressing, or meaty, well-presented ham hock with gherkins, spring onion salsa and parsley jelly – an 'innovative stance on an old idea' for one reporter. Innovation shines through main courses of roast rabbit wrapped in Parma ham with spinach, olive beignets and tarragon cream, or grilled skate wing with artichokes and shallots braised in cider with confit tomatoes and lemon oil. Finish with treacle toffee brûlée with a chocolate finger. A booklet of 25 wines by the glass (£2.75 to £5.80) shows serious intent. Bottle prices on the 100-strong list reflect the smart surroundings, with little under £15, but it's a thoroughly drinkable selection. St Peter's Best Bitter and Adnams Best and Broadside are on handpump. SAMPLE DISHES: linguine of cockles, chorizo and basil £7; Toulouse sausages with a cheese and thyme bhaji, aubergine caviar and beetroot crisps £9.75; apple and walnut trifle with Calvados custard £4.25.

Licensees London and Edinburgh Inns (freehouse)
Open 11 to 11 (10.30 Sun); bar food 11 to 2.30, 6 to 9.45, restaurant 12.30 to 1.45, 6.30 to 9.45
Details Children welcome Car park Wheelchair access (also WC) Garden No-smoking area in bar, no smoking in restaurant Background music No dogs Delta, MasterCard, Switch, Visa Accommodation: 16 rooms, B&B £87.50 to £155

BRYHER Isles of Scilly map 1

▲ Hell Bay Hotel [NEW ENTRY]

Bryher TR23 0PR TEL: (01720) 422947
WEBSITE: www.hellbay.co.uk

The Scilly Isles exist in an environment seemingly untouched by modern life, and the rugged sweep of the Atlantic, wildflowers, soaring sea birds and 'no droning traffic' certainly seems to encapsulate this feeling on Bryher – it takes a helicopter ride or ferry (from Penzance) and a launch from St Mary's to get there. Low-key from the outside and blending well with the environment, Hell Bay is 'a luxury hotel which serves bar meals', noted a reporter, adding that it could 'compete in sophistication with some of the best city-slicker hotels'. Bold modern art by Barbara Hepworth, Ivon Hitchens and Richard Pearce set the tone for the décor and the food, with the bar menu offering modern brasserie fare that's focused on local Scillonian and Cornish producers. The emphasis is on seafood – steamed mussels with garlic and coriander cream, Bryher crab and tomato soup, to start, then a main course of perhaps steamed sea bass with Asian herbs, noodles and ginger. Apart from a few old faithfuls like Hell Bay 'half-pounder' with fries, relish, onion rings and melted Monterey Jack, meat dishes take in crispy duck confit with warm kumquat and pear chutney and steamed sugar-snap peas (in starter or main portions), and chargrilled chicken breast with tomato, basil and olive sauce and roasted vegetables. Scuppered and Natural Beauty from local Ales of Scilly brewery are on handpump, and all of the 11 house wines are available by the glass. SAMPLE DISHES: omelette Arnold Bennett £4.50; honey roasted lamb Henry with minted mash, Puy lentils and lamb jus £9; sticky orange and chilli vodka cake £5.

Licensee A.E. Rodger (freehouse)
Open 12 to 11; bar food and restaurant 12 to 3, 6.30 to 9:30 (7 to 9 restaurant)
Details Children welcome Car park Wheelchair access (also WC) Garden and patio No smoking in dining room No music No dogs Delta, MasterCard, Switch, Visa

BUCKDEN North Yorkshire map 8

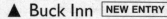

▲ Buck Inn NEW ENTRY

Buckden BD23 5JA TEL: (01756) 760228
WEBSITE: www.thebuckinn.com
on B6160, between Kettleworth and West Burton

On a rise above the village, with views across the western slopes of Wharfedale, this creeper-covered Georgian coaching inn is a useful venue for good-value food and drink. The open-plan interior comprises a flagstone-floored bar plus two spacious carpeted areas, with curved banquettes lining the walls and Old Master copies on the walls. Warm weather brings out the walkers, and the place can get busy, but winter reveals a more relaxed air, with locals popping in for pints of Black Sheep Best Bitter, Timothy Taylor Landlord, Theakston Old Peculier, or Copper Dragon Best Bitter. The menu, chalked on a board, varies with the seasons. Here is a kitchen that can deliver the likes of fishcake with tartare sauce and deep-fried chives, local sausages with creamed mash, caramelised onions and Madeira sauce, and intriguing desserts like orange and Cointreau tart with liqueur ice cream. No comment can be made on the wine as no list was available to us at the time the Guide went to press. SAMPLE DISHES: potato and watercress soup £3.75; steak pie £8; Bakewell tart £4.

Licensee John Fernish (freehouse)
Open 11 to 11, Sun 12 to 10.30; bar food 12 to 2, 6.30 to 9, restaurant 12 to 2 (2.30 Sun), 6.30 to 9.30
Details Children welcome in eating areas Car park Patio No smoking in restaurant Occasional background music Dogs welcome Delta, MasterCard, Switch, Visa Accommodation: 14 rooms, B&B £33 to £72

BUCKLAND Oxfordshire map 2

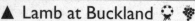

▲ Lamb at Buckland 🏆 🍇

Lamb Lane, Buckland SN7 8QN TEL: (01367) 870484
WEBSITE: www.thelambatbuckland.co.uk
off A420, midway between Faringdon and Kingston Bagpuize

Given the pub's name, it comes as no surprise to find sheep a decorative theme throughout, and one visitor is convinced it is an ever-increasing collection. The beamed bar of this eighteenth-century Cotswold-stone building has a village pub atmosphere, but the restaurant is a different, more refined world of restful blue and yellow, with starched table linen and upholstered chairs. Snacks range from scallop, bacon and endive salad, or scrambled eggs with smoked salmon and prawns, while a full meal might start with three-cheese and red onion tart and proceed to a main course of roast fillet of Kelmscot pork with braised butter beans, Savoy cabbage and Madeira sauce, or sautéed veal sweetbreads in puff pastry, and finish with almond and apricot frangipane tart. Ingredients are first class and are handled by the kitchen with skill. Six interesting and good-quality house wines start at £13.25 and are available by the glass, as are a small number from the more expensive main list, which majors on traditional French wines but dips more than a toe in the warmer waters of the New World; plenty of half-bottles are on offer too. The ales on draught are from Hook Norton. SAMPLE DISHES: pork terrine £5.75; pan-fried escalope of veal with a mushroom, cream and Marsala sauce £15; steamed syrup sponge £4.25.

Licensee Paul Barnard (freehouse)
Open Tue to Sat 11 to 3, 6 to 11, Sun 11 to 4; bar food and restaurant Tue to Sun 12 to 2.30, Tue to Sat 6.30 to 10; closed 24 Dec to 6 Jan
Details Children welcome   Car park   Wheelchair access (not WC)   Garden and patio   No smoking in restaurant   Occasional background music   No dogs   Delta, Diners, MasterCard, Switch, Visa
Accommodation: 1 room, B&B £70 to £145

BUNBURY   Cheshire   map 7

Dysart Arms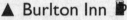

Bowes Gate Road, Bunbury CW6 9PH   TEL: (01829) 260183
WEBSITE: www.brunningandprice.co.uk
off A51, 5m NW of Nantwich

Formerly the village police station, the Dysart Arms is a mellow-brick building opposite the fourteenth-century church of St Boniface. Its large garden enjoys views of the surrounding countryside, while inside are several rooms of varying character: the main bar has quarry-tiled floors, dark ceilings with beams speckled with dried flowers, old maps and *Vanity Fair* cartoons on the walls, and all sorts of other curios, while the stone-floored dining room has rows of bookshelves heaving with old tomes. A long menu lists dishes ranging from seafood casserole to grilled pork loin steak on crushed potatoes, leeks and apple with grain mustard sauce, as well as a selection of upmarket sandwiches. A superior choice of beers features Thwaites Bitter and Timothy Taylor Landlord plus two changing guest ales, perhaps Goldthorn's Gold Bitter and Silver Bullet. From the short wine list, a dozen bottles are also served by the glass. SAMPLE DISHES: chicken liver pâté with piccalilli £4.50; salmon fillet on buttered tagliatelle with coconut pesto £10.25; waffles with honeycomb ice cream, strawberries and raspberry coulis £4.25.

Licensee Darren Snell (Brunning & Price Ltd)
Open 11.30 to 11, Sun 12 to 10.30; bar food Mon to Fri 12 to 2.15, 6 to 9.30, Sat 12 to 9.30, Sun 12 to 9
Details No children under 10 after 6pm   Car park   Wheelchair access (also WC)   Garden and patio
No-smoking area in bar, no smoking in eating areas   Occasional background and live music   Dogs welcome in bar only   Delta, MasterCard, Switch, Visa

BURLTON   Shropshire   map 7

▲ Burlton Inn 🍺

Burlton SY4 5TB   TEL: (01939) 270284
WEBSITE: www.burltoninn.co.uk
on A528, 9m N of Shrewsbury

The tiny village of Burlton is almost non-existent, but its eighteenth-century pub is easily spotted, especially in summer when the building is bright with flowers overflowing from hanging baskets and tubs and filling the pretty garden to the side. The civilised interior is restful and quite understated, with the bar counter and great old hearth of red brick, pale terracotta walls, and untreated ceiling beams, piles of country magazines to read, posies on the tables and no music. Garlic bread topped with red onion and Cheddar, or hot minute steak sandwich are popular snacks; otherwise the menu (served throughout) advertises good-value dishes ranging from home-made soup and duck and orange parfait to steak, kidney and beer pie, grilled bacon chop topped with mustard and parsley butter, and home-made steak burgers. Blackboard specials such as a trio of game sausages with apple mash and onion gravy, or fillets of plaice with lemon and chive cream sauce, extend the choice. Banks's Bitter is the regular beer, supplemented by three frequently changing guests such as Greene King Abbot Ale and Shepherd Neame Spitfire. The list of 20-plus modestly priced wines is unusual in not including a single bottle (except champagne) from France. Around a dozen are sold by the glass. SAMPLE DISHES: caramelised leek and onion tartlet topped with feta £5.75; roast rack of lamb with root mash and rosemary gravy £14; raspberry flummery £4.25.

Licensee Gerald Bean (freehouse)
Open 11 to 3, 6 to 11, Sun 12 to 3.30, 7 to 10.30; bar food 12 to 2, 6.30 to 9.45 (7 to 9.30 Sun); closed bank hol Mon lunchtimes, 25 and 26 Dec, 1 Jan
Details Children welcome in eating area   Car park   Wheelchair access (also WC)   Garden and patio
No music   Small dogs welcome   Delta, MasterCard, Switch, Visa   Accommodation: 6 rooms, B&B £50 to £90

BURNHAM MARKET   Norfolk   map 6

▲ Hoste Arms 🏆 🍇

The Green, Burnham Market PE31 8HD   TEL: (01328) 738777
WEBSITE: www.hostearms.co.uk
on B1155, 5m W of Wells-next-the-Sea

Burnham Market is an affluent village with classy shops and a long, thin, tree-lined green 'where everything happens'. Here you will find the Hoste Arms, a large, prosperous-looking building whose lemon-yellow walls make it hard to miss. The front entrance leads directly into a darkly comfortable and pubby bar (with a huge roaring fire in winter), which has retained much of its original rustic character. Food is not served in here, but only in the several dining rooms – two wood-panelled – and owing to the Hoste's long-standing reputation it is a good idea to book if you wish to eat. From a long menu, you could start simply with Caesar salad, or go for something more ambitious like lasagne of beetroot, caramelised shallots, smoked cherry tomatoes and horseradish hollandaise. Main courses show a similarly broad scope, with at least half a dozen each of fish, meat and pasta choices: baked halibut with Nero pasta and salsa verde, perhaps, or pot-roasted ham hock with apple and Dijon mash. Dessert options might feature Eton mess, or rice pudding brûlée with Asian-spiced plum compote. The wine choice is broad, too, with just enough budget bottles to balance the classier numbers running all the way up to Ch. Pétrus. It's an international selection arranged by style, with an abbreviated list of the cheaper bottles at the front, including ten in three sizes of glass. Real ales are from local brewery Woodforde's – perhaps Wherry Best Bitter – and other breweries like Adnams and Greene King. SAMPLE DISHES: half-dozen Burnham Creek oysters £8; pot-roast ham hock with apple and Dijon mash £9.25; treacle tart with vanilla ice cream £5.25.

Licensee Paul Whittome (freehouse)
Open 11 to 11 (12 to 10.30 winter), Sun 12 to 10.30; restaurant 12 to 2, 7 to 9
Details Children welcome   Car park   Wheelchair access (also WC)   Garden and patio   No smoking in
some restaurant rooms   No music   Dogs welcome   Delta, MasterCard, Switch, Visa   Accommodation:
36 rooms, B&B £78 to £236

BURNHAM THORPE   Norfolk   map 6

Lord Nelson NEW ENTRY

Walsingham Road, Burnham Thorpe PE31 8HL   TEL: (01328) 738241
WEBSITE: www.nelsonslocal.co.uk
off A149/B1155/B1355, 2m SW of Burnham Market

Fans of this unusual 300-year-old pub will be relieved that recent changes have not
altered its distinctive look one jot. New licensee David Thorley has introduced quality
food and a more upmarket feel, but has retained the special atmosphere and, importantly, ale served straight from the barrel. Burnham Thorpe was Lord Nelson's birthplace, and many paintings, bric-à-brac and memorabilia relating to him fill the place –
the pub was formerly known as the Plough but was renamed in 1807 two years after
Nelson's death at Trafalgar. Stone-flagged floors, original wooden settles, and open
fires distinguish the small rooms. Real ales include Greene King IPA and Abbot Ale,
Old Speckled Hen, Woodforde's Wherry and Nelson's Revenge. The daily-changing
menu is an ambitious collection of pub dishes: perhaps local mussels marinière, ribeye
steak with balsamic cherry tomatoes and capers, and local spiced sausages with red
wine onion gravy. Old England has its say with early-evening specials such as steak and
chips, or steak and Guinness pie, but equally there might be Thai-style chicken curry.
Desserts tread the same path with French cherry pudding and tarte au citron lining up
alongside bread-and-butter pudding and Baileys cheesecake. Nine wines are available
by the glass, and the full list includes around three dozen creditable bottles. SAMPLE
DISHES: carrot and ginger soup £3.75; pork fillet stuffed with blue cheese and whole-
grain mustard sauce £11; chocolate marquise £4.75.

Licensee David Thorley (Greene King)
Open 11 to 3 (2.30 Mon to Fri winter), 6 to 11, Sun 12 to 3, 6.30 to 10.30; bar food and restaurant Tue to
Sun 12 to 1.45, Tue to Sat 6 to 8.45; closed Mon winter
Details Children welcome in eating areas   Car park   Wheelchair access (also WC)   Garden and patio   No
smoking in 1 room and restaurant   Live music   Dogs welcome in main bar only   Delta, MasterCard, Switch, Visa

BURNSALL   North Yorkshire   map 8

▲ Red Lion

Burnsall BD23 6BU   TEL: (01756) 720204
WEBSITE: www.redlion.co.uk
on B6160 N of Bolton Bridge

The unspoilt Dales village is surrounded by hills, and at its heart, next to a five-span
bridge over the River Wharfe, is the cosy, rambling Red Lion, fashioned from a
terraced row of old stone cottages; it all presents a 'fine, very English setting'. Inside,
the front snug section has a roaring coal fire, a hunting theme that ranges from the
print on the curtains to the pictures on the walls – the local shoot meets here weekly
in season, with the menus benefiting – and opening up at the rear into a stepped area.

Several menus are in operation, all available throughout, from a light-lunch listing of sandwiches, soups, salads and main courses along the lines of salmon and coriander fishcakes with mango and chilli relish, or eggs Benedict, to ambitious bar blackboards, with a printed version (and slightly higher prices) for the more formal restaurant, ranging from starters of pork, partridge and venison terrine to mains of calf's liver with bubble and squeak and sage and roast garlic sauce. 'The chef here really knows his stuff,' enthused one reporter, pronouncing his daily special of breast of local wood pigeon with rösti and wild mushroom sauce to be 'sensational', and the menu's description of 'absolutely the best lemon tart' was all it promised: 'lovely smooth, tangy filling, thin crisp pastry'. Sunday lunch (restaurant only) honours tradition but could also offer breast of chicken with pak choi and a lime, ginger and chilli dressing. On handpump are well-kept beers from Theakston, along with Old Speckled Hen, Timothy Taylor Best Bitter, and Folly Ale from the local Wharfedale Brewery. The restaurant wine list is available in the bar on request; otherwise, the bar list is a slate of a dozen-plus wines, virtually all also sold by the glass. SAMPLE DISHES: confit of duck with hoisin £6.50; pan-fried medallions of Wharfedale beef fillet with seared foie gras, wild mushrooms and garlic crostini £16.50; sticky toffee pudding with caramel ice cream and butterscotch sauce £6.

Licensee Elizabeth Grayshon (freehouse)
Open 11 to 11.30, Sun 12 to 10.30; bar food 12 to 2.30, 6 to 9.30, restaurant 12 to 2.30, 7 to 9.30
Details Children welcome Car park Wheelchair access (also WC) Garden and patio No-smoking area in bar, no smoking in restaurant No music Dogs welcome Amex, Delta, Diners, MasterCard, Switch, Visa
Accommodation: 15 rooms, B&B £57 to £130

BURPHAM   West Sussex   map 3

George and Dragon
Burpham BN18 9RR TEL: (01903) 883131
2½m up single-track, no-through road signposted Warningcamp off A27, 1m E of Arundel

Well off the beaten track, in the heart of rural Sussex, the George and Dragon shares its car park with the village hall and a playing field and looks out on to pretty Downs scenery. Within are black beams in low ceilings, with a cosy bar area and a posh restaurant. The bar and restaurant menus are quite separate and rather different in style, the former a lot simpler than the latter, although this doesn't mean that dishes are any less interesting or ambitious. Starters range from creamy garlic mushroom tartlet to caramelised goats' cheese with chilli chutney, and main courses from pork goulash to duck confit. Game is served in season, and baguettes, sandwiches and jacket potatoes are also possibilities. The restaurant menu is a set-price affair dealing in roast pigeon breast with red onion marmalade, pan-fried black pudding and a gin and juniper jus, followed by grilled fillet of turbot with king scallops, asparagus and scallop sauce, with pear and ginger crème brûlée to finish. On draught are regional ales from King's Brewery in Horsham, Harveys in Lewes, and Dark Star Brewery near Haywards Heath, and four house wines are served in two sizes of glass. SAMPLE DISHES: smoked salmon parcel filled with salmon mousse £7; roast pheasant with juniper sauce £10; sticky toffee pudding £4.75.

Licensees James Rose and Kate Holle (freehouse)
Open 11 to 2.30, 6 to 11, Sun 12 to 3, 7 to 10.30; bar food all week 12 to 2 (2.30 Sun), Mon to Sat 7 to 9.30, restaurant Tue to Sat 7.15 to 9.30; closed Sun evenings winter
Details No children Car park Wheelchair access (also WC) Patio No smoking in restaurant Background music No dogs Amex, Delta, Diners, MasterCard, Switch, Visa

BUXHALL Suffolk map 6

Buxhall Crown

Mill Road, Buxhall IP14 3DW TEL: (01449) 736521
from Stowmarket take B1115 towards Sudbury and turn right for Buxhall in Great Finborough

The food is the draw at this warm and welcoming country pub that's tucked away near the windmill ('no sails') in Buxhall. Open fires in both bars and a comfortable restaurant decked out with botanical prints and local photographs set the scene for some classy and wide-ranging food that, while displaying imagination, hasn't forgotten typical pub classics. The lengthy blackboard menu could deliver a modish marinated wood pigeon with sautéed strawberries and avocado oil, or more traditional whole grilled plaice with warm tartare sauce. Bar snacks along the lines of hummus with ciabata bread sticks, plus light bites such as ham, egg and chips, and sandwiches, bolster the repertoire. Six ales change on a regular basis, but could see the Earl Soham Brewery's Albert Ale, Woodford Wherry, or Fuller's London Pride on handpump, while the wine list, strong in the New World and listed by style, is all available by the glass. Outside is a patio to the front and a lawn to the side, both set with tables. SAMPLE DISHES: twice-baked goats' cheese soufflé £5; fillet of Aberdeen Angus with a Stilton glaze and port jus £15.25; hot cherry pancakes £4.75.

Licensee Trevor Golton (freehouse)
Open *all week 12 to 3, Mon to Sat 6.30 to 11; bar food 11 to 3, 6 to 11, Sun 11 to 3*
Details *Children welcome   Car park   Wheelchair access   Garden   No smoking in restaurant   Background music   Dogs welcome in 1 bar   Delta, MasterCard, Switch, Visa*

BYLAND ABBEY North Yorkshire map 9

##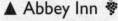

Byland Abbey YO61 4BD TEL: (01347) 868204
WEBSITE: www.bylandabbeyinn.com
off A170, between Thirsk and Helmsley, 2m W of Ampleforth

Standing opposite the haunting ruins of Byland Abbey in a remote spot on the edge of the Vale of York, this square and solid-looking ivy-covered inn was built by monks in the mid-nineteenth century, partly with masonry from the abbey itself. It feels more restaurant than pub, and tables in the two main rooms are all set for eating, complete with flowers and candles, though fireplaces, antique-shop jumble and framed paintings add character. Inventive and varied modern cooking is what to expect: starters take in pan-fried scallops in lemon and butter, alongside chicken liver and foie gras parfait, while mains range from roasted lamb shank with shallots and apricot jus to pasta with griddled aubergine, wild mushrooms and lemon and basil sauce. The wine list puts on a modest air but includes some real goodies from South Africa and a 'Fine French' selection, as well as 20 wines by the glass, from eight house selections at £2.90/£4 to an Old Vine Shiraz at £4.70/£6.50. Beer drinkers will find Black Sheep Best and Tetley Bitter on draught. SAMPLE DISHES: king prawns in filo with garlic and lemon dip £6.75; seared salmon fillet with baby beetroot and crème fraîche £10.50; sticky toffee pudding £5.

Licensees Jane and Martin Nordli (freehouse)
Open *12 to 3, 6.30 to 11; bar food 12 to 2 (3 Sun), 6.30 to 9; closed Sun evening and Mon lunchtime (exc bank hols)*
Details *Children welcome   Car park   Wheelchair access (also WC)   Garden   No smoking in 2 rooms   Background music   No dogs   Delta, MasterCard, Switch, Visa   Accommodation: 3 rooms, B&B £90 to £135*

▲ Manor House Inn

Carterway Heads, Shotley Bridge DH8 9LX   TEL: (01207) 255268
on A68, 3m W of Consett

Don't be put off by the remote location on a windswept hillside – this eighteenth-century pub is well worth the trip. Comfortable accommodation makes staying the night an option worth considering, and nearby Derwent Reservoir is another attraction for summer visitors. The bar has stripped wooden floors and a settle alongside the fireplace, while the lounge has a plusher appearance, with colourful carpets and upholstery, mahogany panelling and rough stone walls. In the dining room, a collection of some 600 milk jugs hangs from the ceiling beams. The printed and blackboard menus offer a wide choice, starting perhaps with sausage, black pudding and mushrooms on bubble and squeak, or a warm bacon and mange-tout salad. Main courses are divided between meat dishes – ranging from steaks to a trio of lamb cutlets with a port and cranberry jus – and fish dishes, such as grilled sardines with herb butter or fillet of sea bass with mushrooms and a creamy herb sauce. Real ales include Theakston Best Bitter and Wells Bombardier Premium, and there's a serious list of wines from around the world, with a good selection by the glass. SAMPLE DISHES: king prawns with sweet-and-sour sauce £5.25; roast duck breast with roasted plums and a piquant sauce £12; fig and almond cake £3.75.

Licensees Chris and Moira Brown (freehouse)
Open *11 to 11, Sun 12 to 10.30; bar food 12 to 9.30, restaurant 12 to 2.30, 7 to 9.30; closed evening 25 Dec*
Details *Children welcome   Car park   Wheelchair access (not WC)   Garden and patio   No smoking in restaurant   Background music in bar   Dogs welcome   Amex, Delta, MasterCard, Switch, Visa Accommodation: 4 rooms, B&B £38 to £70*

Fox and Hounds

Carthorpe DL8 2LG   TEL: (01845) 567433
off A1, 4m SE of Bedale

'Worth the short detour off the A1', thought one reporter of this spick-and-span village-centre pub with loads of parking and a homely character lent by china ornaments, some quite tiny, filling every space. It is best to arrive early in order to grab one of the highly polished tables, as the place rapidly fills and most people are here to eat. There's both a printed menu and a list of blackboard specials, the latter an exciting read that moves quickly from seafood chowder or duck-filled filo parcels with plum sauce to braised lamb shank with root vegetable purée and redcurrant gravy. Grilled black pudding with caramelised apple and onion marmalade could appear on the printed menu, followed by pan-fried sea bass on rösti with red pepper sauce, with champagne and summer fruit jelly with vanilla shortbread to finish. Traditional roasts are the mainstay of the set Sunday lunch, and service is 'attentive and interested'. Black Sheep Best Bitter and Worthington Bitter will keep real ale fans happy. Around three dozen wines feature on the list, and all are available by the glass; house wine starts at £10.95. SAMPLE DISHES: crab tartlet £5.25; steak and kidney pie £9.25; sticky toffee meringue with praline ice cream £4.50.

Licensee Howard Fitzgerald (freehouse)

Open *Tue to Sun 12 to 2.30, 7 to 11; bar food and restaurant 12 to 2, 7 to 10; closed first week Jan*
Details *Children welcome   Car park   Wheelchair access (also WC)   No smoking in restaurant   Background music   No dogs   Delta, MasterCard, Switch, Visa*

CASTERTON   Cumbria   map 8

▲ Pheasant Inn

Casterton, nr Kirkby Lonsdale LA6 2RX   TEL: (015242) 71230
WEBSITE: www.pheasantinn.co.uk
on A683, 1m N of junction with A65

Casterton is on the edge of the Lune Valley beneath the fells, an area favoured by walkers and cavers. At the heart of the hamlet, facing the green, is the Pheasant Inn, a large, sturdy, white-painted building. Inside, it is welcoming and traditional, with a beamed ceiling, carpeted floor and a few country prints on the cream walls. A printed menu advertises the usual sandwiches, ploughman's and home-made soup, but the blackboard of specials moves beyond generous portions of steak and ale pie and gammon steak with pineapple into the likes of a tasty Chinese crab salad with bean sprouts, a satisfying cottage pie with creamy mash, or spiced lamb curry, lemon sole, and rack of lamb, with lemon layer pudding, and plum and apple strudel for dessert. There's a separate restaurant, but the same menu is served throughout. Service is cheerful and attentive. Theakston Best Bitter and Cool Cask, plus Dent Aviator and Black Sheep Best Bitter, are on draught, and six wines by the glass, from £2.40 to £3.25, cover a good range of styles. SAMPLE DISHES: parsnip soup £3; roast crispy duckling with sage and onion stuffing and apple sauce £11.50; lemon meringue roulade £4.

Licensees the Dixon family (freehouse)
Open *12 to 2, 6 to 11 (10.30 Sun); bar food and restaurant 12 to 2, 6 to 9; closed evening 25 Dec*
Details *Children welcome in bar eating area   Car park   Wheelchair access (not WC)   Garden and patio   No smoking in restaurant   Background music   No dogs   MasterCard, Switch, Visa   Accommodation: 10 rooms, B&B £37 to £80*

CASTLE ACRE   Norfolk   map 6

▲ Ostrich Inn

Stocks Green, Castle Acre PE32 2AE   TEL: (01760) 755398
just off A1065 Swaffham to Fakenham road, 4m N of Swaffham

Many years ago there were a dozen Ostrich pubs in the vicinity of Holkam Hall (the estate kept them at one time); now only two are left. With a nod (perhaps) to the spirit of times gone by, this large red-brick building keeps a golden pheasant and parrots in cages in its beer garden. The inn was built in the sixteenth century (nearby are the remains of a twelfth-century priory and a thirteenth-century castle) and is dominated by a large, homely, unpretentious bar warmed by a fire, with beams, wooden tables and photographs of local scenes. The overall value for money has been described as 'excellent' and the pub food 'home cooked and tasty'. Visitors can expect to see salads, sandwiches, and steaks as the mainstay of the bar menu, backed up by pizzas made on the premises, omelettes, burgers, and deep-fried breaded plaice with chips. Specials are chalked up on boards above the bar: say, filo-wrapped king prawns with salad, or steak and kidney pudding, alongside an extensive vegetarian choice that could run to cheese and potato pie or spicy bean burger. An exotic streak runs through desserts, with galatabourica (filo filled with rose-water cream) alongside treacle roly-poly. Greene King ales are on handpump to wash it all down, with three wines by the glass. SAMPLE DISHES: crisp-fried salmon kebabs £5; roast chicken leg stuffed with haggis £5; cassata cheesecake £2.50.

Licensee Raymond Wakelen (Greene King)
Open Mon to Thur 12 to 3, 7 to 11, Fri to Sun 12 to 5, 7 to 11; bar food 12 to 2, 7 to 10; no food 25 and 26 Dec
Details Children welcome in eating area   Car park   Wheelchair access (not WC)   Garden and patio
No smoking in eating area   Live or background music   Dogs welcome on a lead   Amex, Delta, MasterCard, Switch, Visa   Accommodation: 2 rooms, B&B £15 to £30

CASTLE DONINGTON   Leicestershire   map 5

Nags Head Inn

Hill Top, Castle Donington DE74 2PR   TEL: (01332) 850652
4m from M1 junction 24, on B6540, at S end of Castle Donington

Motor racing fans visiting nearby Donington Park may not be immediately drawn to this modest-looking pub on the southern edge of the town when seeking refreshment, but those who are will be rewarded with a friendly atmosphere and superior pub cooking. Décor is traditional – patterned carpet, dark-wood bar and furniture, warming fires – and menus are chalked up on blackboards. They cover a wide range of culinary styles, taking in everything from lemon sole with caper and parsley butter to Cajun-spiced beef fillet with tzatziki dressing. Snack dishes such as Lincolnshire sausage with mash and onion gravy, or beef stir fry with rice, are available at lunchtime and for the earlier part of the evening, along with a selection of sandwiches. Desserts are traditional British favourites such as sticky toffee pudding. Beers are Marston's Pedigree, Banks's Mild and Mansfield Bitter. The wine list is arranged by style and efficiently caters for all tastes, with six house selections available by the glass. SAMPLE DISHES: grilled goats' cheese with cranberry dressing £6; halibut steak with garlic and prawn sauce £14.50; raspberry rice pudding £4.

Licensee Ian Davison (Wolverhampton & Dudley)
Open 12 to 2.30, 5.30 to 11, Sun 12 to 2.30, 7 to 10.30; bar food and restaurant Mon to Sat 12 to 2, 6.30 to 9.15; closed 26 Dec to 2 Jan
Details No children   Car park   Wheelchair access (not WC)   Garden and patio   No smoking in restaurant
No music   Dogs welcome in bar only   Amex, Delta, MasterCard, Switch, Visa

CAUNTON   Nottinghamshire   map 5

Caunton Beck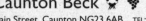

Main Street, Caunton NG23 6AB   TEL: (01636) 636793
in village, just off A616 5m NW of Newark-on-Trent

Breakfast opens proceedings in this revamped sixteenth-century stone pub-cum-eating house next to the village church. Inside, eaters and drinkers will find a beamed bar with floorboards of light-coloured wood, farmhouse-style tables, and walls painted ochre and sand, with comfortable touches like a warming brick fireplace, curtains at the windows and various prints; there's also a more traditional carpeted dining room with cottage-style furniture. The same menu, backed up by blackboard specials, applies in both areas. Sandwiches are always available, but the kitchen really makes its mark with a choice of eclectic dishes running from grilled goats' cheese with poached pear and wilted rocket salad to roast fillet of salmon with red pepper and saffron risotto and coriander oil. In simpler vein, you might also consider pan-fried ribeye steak with lyonnaise potatoes, or grilled lemon sole with beurre noisette, while to finish the choice is between desserts like passion-fruit cheesecake with Cassis sherbet, and farmhouse cheeses with grapes, biscuits and home-made apple and ginger chutney. Ruddles Best Bitter, Springhead Bitter and Marston's Pedigree are on draught. A wine list in descending order of price is a novelty that makes sure everyone casts an eye over reliable smart stuff from Burgundy, the Rhône and some top New World names. These feature among the 25 sold by the glass and there's plenty of action under £15 a bottle too, as well as a host of dessert sweeties. SAMPLE DISHES: seared fillet of tuna niçoise £7.50; breast of Gressingham duck with braised Savoy cabbage and a light plum reduction £14; Morello cherry jelly with Kirsch syrup £4.75.

Licensees Toby Hope and Julie Allwood (freehouse)
Open 8am to midnight, bar food and restaurant 8am to midnight (10pm Sun)
Details Children welcome Car park Wheelchair access (also WC) Garden and patio No smoking in restaurant No music Dogs welcome exc in restaurant Amex, Delta, Diners, MasterCard, Switch, Visa

CAVENDISH   Suffolk   map 6

▲ Bull

High Street, Cavendish CO10 8AX   TEL: (01787) 280245
on A1092 through village

Parts of the Bull, a large inn on the main road through the village, date from the sixteenth century, although much of it is more recent. The open-plan main bar is loosely divided into separate areas for eating and drinking, and a relaxed atmosphere prevails throughout, despite a slightly more formal appearance in the main dining area. Food sticks to a simple and traditional style. Start perhaps with deep-fried Camembert, then choose from a selection of fish dishes such as fillet of sea bass topped with ginger and spring onion, or a steak, a home-made pie, or a curry: chicken balti, say. Vegetarians are given a fair crack of the whip, there are also baguettes with a good choice of fillings, and desserts might run to bread-and-butter pudding, or a cheesecake. This is an Adnams pub, so the brewery's ales are stocked, and six wines are sold by the glass. SAMPLE DISHES: flat mushroom on a croûton topped with goats' cheese and red pesto £5; lamb shank £11; vodka-soaked fruits of the forest meringue £3.50.

Licensee Debbie Hare (Adnams)
Open 11 to 3, 6 to 11, Sun 12 to 10.30; bar food and restaurant Tue to Sat 12 to 2, 6.30 to 9, Sun 12 to 3
Details Children welcome Car park Wheelchair access (also WC) Patio Background music Dogs welcome exc in restaurant Amex, Delta, Diners, MasterCard, Switch, Visa Accommodation: 2 rooms, B&B £35 to £55

CHADLINGTON   Oxfordshire   map 5

Tite Inn

Mill End, Chadlington OX7 3NY   TEL: (01608) 676475
WEBSITE: www.titeinn.com
off A361, 2½m S of Chipping Norton

This seventeenth-century Cotswold pub, built of the distinctive local honey-coloured stone, is in an isolated rural setting on the edge of the village. Inside are three small linked rooms, the middle one the main bar area. Ceilings are low and heavily beamed, walls are painted terracotta and hung with simple pictures of farmyard animals, and there's a tea room look to the cushioned spindle-back chairs, raffia table mats and colourful printed curtains. Real ale is the main draw here: a top-quality selection features Tite Inn Bitter, brewed for the pub by Robinson's, along with Young's Bitter, Hop Back Entire Stout and three guest ales. There is also a draught real cider, usually from Biddenden, and a list of around 20 wines from £11.50, of which six are available by the glass. Menus don't change often but offer a decently varied range of dishes, from boeuf bourguignon through duck sausages with cranberry and brandy sauce to chicken jalfrezi with rice and mango chutney. Lunch options tend to be lighter. SAMPLE DISHES: garlic mushrooms £4.25; salmon fishcakes with hollandaise £9; crème brûlée £4.

Licensee Michael Willis (freehouse)
Open Tue to Sat and bank hol Mon 12 to 2.30, Tue to Sat 6.30 to 11, Sun 12 to 2.30, 7 to 10.30; bar food and restaurant Tue to Sun and bank hol Mon 12 to 2, Tue to Sun 6.45 to 9; closed 25 and 26 Dec
Details Children welcome   Car park   Wheelchair access (not WC)   Garden   No smoking in restaurant
Occasional background music   Dogs welcome   Delta, MasterCard, Switch, Visa

CHADWICK END   West Midlands   map 5

Orange Tree
Warwick Road, Chadwick End B93 0BN   TEL: (01564) 785364
on A4141 on outskirts of village

'This place is about as far removed from a traditional country pub as possible,' commented one inspector of this new breed of modern establishment that's 'very brasserie in its menu, food and décor'. The old pub has been thoroughly and stylishly revamped: earthy colours, coir matting, subdued lighting, low ceilings and beams, and bare-wood tables and chairs all create the mood, while huge niches in the walls are filled with neatly piled logs for the open fires. A large main room is given over to eating, but smaller areas are set aside for just sitting and drinking too. The modern repertoire matches the décor, with a trendy nod to the Mediterranean and beyond; the menu is ambitiously long but laid out in a simple, sectioned style. Crowd-pleasing dishes span the likes of roasted tomato and pepper soup, to scallops with ham, pea and mint risotto, or duck confit with pink peppercorn and smoked bacon mash, or noodles with shrimps, chilli and lemongrass. Beers roll out with Tetley Bitter and Greene King Abbot Ale and IPA, and four wines are served by the glass. Paul Hales is also the licensee at the Crabmill in Preston Bagot (see entry). SAMPLE DISHES: chilli-crusted squid with pineapple and red onion salsa £6.75; whole plaice, lemon pepper and oregano butter £13; baked Alaska £5.

Licensee Paul Hales (freehouse)
Open 11 to 11; bar food and restaurant Mon to Sat 12 to 2.30, 6 to 9.30, Sun 12 to 4.30
Details Children welcome   Car park   Garden   Background music   Dogs welcome   Amex, Delta,
MasterCard, Switch, Visa

CHALGROVE   Oxfordshire   map 2

Red Lion Inn
115 High Street, Chalgrove OX44 7SS   TEL: (01865) 890625
just S of B480, 4m NW of Watlington

At the centre of the village, this handsome white-painted stone pub is owned by the parish church – as it has been since at least 1637. The neat and uncluttered main bar has cream walls hung with Victorian prints, a beamed ceiling, and fireplaces at both ends. Leading off it are two smaller rooms, with a dining room, its décor 'prettily domestic', at the back. Lunch menus offer hearty old-fashioned dishes such as faggots with mushy peas in a Yorkshire pudding with gravy, while evening menus go in for a more upmarket style, starting perhaps with duck and orange pâté and followed by roast rump of lamb on red wine sauce. A variety of sandwiches and warm open baguettes is also available in the bar. Fuller's London Pride, Wadworth 6X and Adnams Bitter are the regular real ales, and there's a wide-ranging list of around 20 wines, of which half a dozen are served by the glass. Parking is available before 7pm in a small public car park; otherwise, park on the road. SAMPLE DISHES: avocado, bacon and Brie salad £4; venison casserole £10; lemon meringue roulade £3.25.

Licensee Annie Shepherd (freehouse)
Open *Mon to Fri 12 to 2.30 (3 summer), 5.30 to 11, Sat 12 to 3, 6 to 11, Sun 12 to 3, 7 to 10.30; bar food and restaurant Mon to Sat 12 to 2, 6 to 9; closed evening 25 Dec*
Details *Children welcome Wheelchair access (also WC) Garden and patio No smoking in restaurant Live or background music Dogs welcome in bar only Delta, Diners, MasterCard, Switch, Visa*

CHAPPEL Essex   map 6

Swan Inn

Chappel CO6 2DD   TEL: (01787) 222353
take Great Tey turning off A1124 at Wakes Colne and cross River Colne to reach pub

---

The River Colne runs right past this 'hearty, honest pub', and from the child-friendly garden at the back there are views of a spectacular high viaduct stretching across the valley. A covered, cobbled courtyard is used for fine weather eating and drinking, while the main bar is heavily beamed, with standing timbers, dark wooden furniture and burgundy-coloured banquettes; the 'old alehouse' feel is enhanced by a large inglenook where a log fire burns on cold days. Fish is the main attraction in the bar and restaurant, thanks to daily deliveries from Billingsgate and Lowestoft. The kitchen keeps things simple and makes admirable use of top-notch ingredients: fried squid and Torbay sole have both been praised, but you might also find anything from grilled scallops with bacon, or poached oak-smoked haddock fillets, to more exotic ideas like butterfish on a bed of spinach with a creamy prawn sauce. Meat comes direct from Smithfield, and the choice runs from various grills and steaks to home-made chicken Kiev. Sandwiches, ploughman's, burgers and the like are also available at lunchtime. Greene King IPA and Abbot Ale plus a guest such as Morland Original are on handpump, and there's an affordably priced list of around 30 wines from £7.50. SAMPLE DISHES: grilled sardines £4.25; poached Scottish salmon with hollandaise £9; fruit crumble £3.50.

Licensee T.L.F. Martin (freehouse)
Open *Mon to Fri 11 to 3, 6 to 11, Sat 11 to 11, Sun 12 to 10.30; bar food 12 to 2.30 (3 Sun), 6.30 to 10; restaurant 12 to 2.30, 7 to 10 (9.30 Sun); no food 25 and 26 Dec*
Details *Children welcome in bar eating area and restaurant Car park Wheelchair access (not WC) Garden and patio No smoking in lounge and restaurant Background music Dogs welcome on a lead Amex, Delta, MasterCard, Switch, Visa*

🍺 *indicates a pub serving exceptional draught beers.*

CHARLTON   West Sussex   map 3

▲ The Fox Goes Free 🍺

Charlton PO18 0HU   TEL: (01243) 811461
off A286 Chichester to Midhurst road, 1m E of Singleton

There's a cottagey charm about this 400-year-old village pub, with its flint walls, peg-tiled roof, and small-paned windows – which is, perhaps, why the Women's Institute chose the place for its first meeting in England in 1915. The two cosy bars – each with settles, chairs, and a fire – offer Ballard's Best Bitter, Fox Goes Free house brew, Old Speckled Hen, and a guest ale along with Addlestone cider. Food is ordered from a long blackboard menu in one of the bars, then brought to one of the two dining rooms. You might begin with duck and port terrine or king prawns in garlic butter before moving on to whole sea bass in lemon and olive oil, chicken breast with bacon, mushrooms and cream, or something simple like chilli con carne. To finish there could be rhubarb tart. Eight wines by the glass feature on the short, international list; house selections are £10.50. SAMPLE DISHES: avocado and Stilton bake £5; duck breast in orange and honey £12.50; sticky toffee pudding £4.50.

Licensee Oliver Ligertwood (freehouse)
Open Mon to Fri 11 to 3, 5.30 to 11, Sat 11 to 11, Sun 12 to 10.30; bar food and restaurant 12 to 2.30, 6.30 to 10.30 (12 to 10.30 Sat and Sun)
Details Children welcome in eating areas   Car park   Wheelchair access (also WC)   Garden and patio
No smoking in 1 room   Live or background music   Dogs welcome exc in restaurant   Delta, MasterCard,
Switch, Visa   Accommodation: 5 rooms, B&B £40 to £60

CHARTHAM HATCH   Kent   map 3

Chapter Arms   NEW ENTRY

New Town Street, Chartham Hatch CT4 7LT   TEL: (01227) 738340
Chartham Hatch signposted on A28 3m SW of Canterbury

The name of this early Victorian pub, a large, rambling building, comes from the fact that it was originally a chapterhouse for Canterbury Cathedral. You enter directly into the main bar – patterned carpet, hop wreaths, and decorative plates – but the most unusual feature is a vast collection of musical instruments hanging from the ceiling: everything from flutes to violins, with old sheet music plastered in between. This reflects the preoccupation with jazz here, with regular live jazz evenings and monthly jazz dinners when diners are encouraged to dress up in 1920s costume. Towards the rear is the popular, cottage-style restaurant. The extensive and 'excessively wordy' printed menu, backed up by blackboard specials, mixes traditional pub staples such as Thai-style fishcakes with sweet chilli and sour cream, or beef suet pudding, with more unusual offerings: monkfish pan-fried with shallots, roasted sweet pepper and baby spinach finished with Chardonnay cream, or lamb shank slowly braised in red wine with shallots and rosemary then roasted in honey. Fruit crumble with custard or dark chocolate and brandy torte may be among desserts. Shepherd Neame Master Brew Bitter, Adnams Broadside and Harveys Sussex Best Bitter are on handpump, and six wines are served by the glass. SAMPLE DISHES: leek, sweet potato and coconut soup £4.25; pork loin and pheasant casserole with dumplings £7.50; sticky toffee sponge pudding with toffee sauce £5.25

Licensees Mr and Mrs A. Richards (freehouse)

Open *11 to 3, 6.30 to 11, Sun 12 to 5; bar food and restaurant all week 12 to 2 (2.30 Sun), Mon to Sat 7
to 9; closed evening 25 Dec*
Details *Children welcome   Car park   Wheelchair access (not WC)   Garden   No smoking in restaurant
Live or background music   Dogs welcome in bar only   MasterCard, Switch, Visa*

CHATBURN   Lancashire   map 8

Black Bull Inn   NEW ENTRY

17 Bridge Road, Chatburn BB7 4AW   TEL: (01200) 440878
follow Chatburn signposts from Clitheroe or from the A59 bypass

The Black Bull stands next to a century-old bridge spanning Heys Brook and close to
one of the small village greens (where it is advisable to park). Inside, the single wood
and tile bar fronts an area 'dedicated to upright drinking', with a line of bar stools
adding support and a 'changing panoply of delights' on handpump, which could
include Harviestoun Brewery's Bitter & Twisted, Black Sheep Best Bitter or Timothy
Taylor Landlord. The lounge, partially separated from the bar by knocked-through
walls, achieves a comfortably lived-in feel with its mongrel mix of chairs and tables,
upholstered benches threading the walls, and paintings displayed for sale. The printed
bar menus offer plenty of choice, from starters of deep-fried Brie in beer batter with
cranberry chutney to wild boar sausage with sautéed black pudding, bacon and a
poached egg. Main courses range from pan-roast halibut with bacon and mushroom
sauce, via a 'mighty fillet' of plaice with cucumber and pink peppercorn sauce, to lamb
steak in an onion and sage sauce. A specials board adds more choice: say, a good-sized
bowl of thick leek and potato soup, red jambalaya consisting of a generous mixture of
pork, chicken, shrimps and tasty spiced sausage on saffron rice, and a game pie 'brim-
ming with meat in a rich gravy'. Lunchtime brings filled rolls and jacket potatoes too.
All 20 or so wines (all under £20) are sold by the glass. SAMPLE DISHES: deep-fried king
prawns with Cajun-spiced tartare sauce £4.50; roast guinea fowl with apple mash and
cider sauce £10.50; jam roly-poly £3.50.

Licensee *Kevin Dale (freehouse)*
Open *Mon 6 to 10.30, Tue to Thur 12 to 2.30, 6 to 11, Fri 12 to 2.30, 4 to 11, Sat 12 to 11, Sun 12 to
10.30; bar food and restaurant Tue to Sat 12 to 2.30, 6 to 9.30, Sun 12 to 9.30*
Details *Children welcome   Wheelchair access (not WC)   Garden   No smoking in restaurant   Occasional
live or background music   Dogs welcome in snug only   Amex, Delta, MasterCard, Switch, Visa*

CHELTENHAM   Gloucestershire   map 5

Beehive   NEW ENTRY

1–3 Montpellier Villas, Cheltenham GL50 2XE   TEL: (01242) 579443
WEBSITE: www.slak.co.uk

Two linked buildings done out in shades of green identify this lively venue on the
corner of two narrow streets near Montpellier Gardens. Expect plenty of action, noise
and music in the 'raucous', trendily retro ground-floor bar, where draught beers
include Goff's Jouster, Marston's Pedigree and Wadworth 6X. At lunchtime you can
also choose from a short menu of baguettes plus a handful of starters and one-plate
dishes ranging from fishcake with spinach cream to Irish stew. In the evening, visitors
wanting to eat would probably do best to head straight upstairs to the high-ceilinged
dining room, which reminded a reporter of a cross between 'a bistro, a nightclub and

a harem', with its bare dark floorboards and sheer navy-blue drapes hanging from the ceiling. The menu is organised restaurant-style, with dishes such as seared Scottish king scallops with crisp black pudding and lemongrass butter based on top-quality ingredients. Main courses are quite straightforward ideas like chargrilled ribeye steak with mustard butter and home-made fries or roast fillet of sea bass on creamed potatoes with mussel cream, while desserts run to pecan tart with honeycomb ice cream or vanilla crème brûlée. The short wine list, opening at £12, draws largely on affordable bottles from France and Australia, although other countries also get a look in. SAMPLE DISHES: Parma ham, rocket and Parmesan salad £5.50; marinated monkfish with Chinese greens and soy dressing £14; chocolate and brandy mousse £5.

Licensee Scott Graff
Open 12 to 11, Sun 12 to 10.30; bar food 12 to 2.30, 6 to 10 (9 Mon and Tue), restaurant Wed to Sat 7 to 10, Sun 12 to 3, 6 to 9
Details No children Wheelchair access (also WC) Garden No smoking in 1 room Background music
Dogs welcome in bar only Delta, MasterCard, Switch, Visa

CHENIES Buckinghamshire   map 3

Red Lion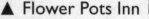

Chenies WD3 6ED TEL: (01923) 282722
off A404, between Chorleywood and Little Chalfont

Landlord Mike Norris has been running this relaxed, cheery pub for 17 years, dispensing an extended range of real ales to locals, commuters and visitors. The jewel in the crown among the range is Lion Pride, brewed especially for the inn by the Rebellion Brewery of Marlow, and it may be joined by Best Bitter from the local Vale Brewery, Wadworth 6X, plus another ale from Rebellion such as Roasted Nuts. Food is ordered at the bar, and the printed menu is augmented by daily specials on the blackboard. Cold snacks and jacket potatoes will satisfy lighter appetites, while those in the market for three courses might choose starters of perhaps three-cheese pâté, or prawns and mushrooms in garlic butter and cream sauce. Then it might be one of the pies – perhaps the never-off-the-menu lamb pie – Cumberland sausage on bubble and squeak with red wine gravy, or a tortilla basket filled with smoked sausage, borlotti beans and peppers in a smoky tomato sauce. A dozen wines are sold by the glass. The beamed dining area is reached through the main bar, and a separate room contains just one table for when only intimacy will do. SAMPLE DISHES: curried sausage and herbed meatballs £5.50; ham and parsley pie £9; rhubarb crumble £3.75.

Licensee Mike Norris (freehouse)
Open 11 to 2.30, 5.30 to 11, Sun 12 to 3, 6.30 to 10.30; bar food 12 to 2, 7 to 10 (9.30 Sun); closed 25 Dec
Details No children Car park Wheelchair access (also WC) Patio No smoking in 1 room No music
Dogs welcome Amex, Delta, Diners, MasterCard, Switch, Visa

CHERITON Hampshire   map 2

▲ Flower Pots Inn

Cheriton SO24 0QQ TEL: (01962) 771318
4m S of New Alresford, off B3046 in Cheriton

Turkey's Delight, Diggers Gold and Village Elder are some of the names you'll encounter at this former farmhouse on the edge of the small village of Cheriton – they are all real ales produced by the Cheriton Brewhouse, which occupies a converted barn across the road from the pub. A fine selection they are too, all poured directly from the cask. To accompany the beers, a short and simple bar menu offers a range of hotpots, jacket potatoes, toasted sandwiches, large filled baps and variations on the ploughman's theme. The pub itself has traditional rustic charm, with a quarry-tiled floor, a log fire and an assortment of wooden tables and chairs. Focal points include a covered well in the bar, while the lounge has a real fire. For non-beer drinkers there are three wines by the glass. SAMPLE DISHES: toasted cheese and prawn sandwich £4.75; jacket potato with coronation chicken £5.25; lamb and apricot hotpot £5.50.

Licensees J.M. and P.M. Bartlett (freehouse)
Open 12 to 2.30, 6 to 11, Sun 12 to 3, 7 to 10.30; bar food (exc Sun and bank hol evenings) 12 to 2, 7 to 9
Details No children   Car park   Wheelchair access (not WC)   Garden   Occasional live music   Dogs welcome on a lead   No cards   Accommodation: 4 rooms, B&B £40 to £60

CHESTER   Cheshire   map 7

Albion

Park Street, Chester CH1 1RN   TEL: (01244) 340345
WEBSITE: www.albioninnchester.co.uk
best reached on foot from city walls between Eastgate and the Groves; a flight of steps off the walls from the Watchtower is virtually opposite the pub

Dating from the 1880s, the Albion is a classic Victorian pub and has been preserved as a 'living museum' since current landlord Mike Mercer took over in 1970. There are three distinct rooms – the vault, the snug and the lounge bar – and décor throughout aims to evoke the period of the First World War with artefacts and pictures, assorted old posters and enamelled advertising signs. The pub has a longstanding reputation as a haven for real ale fans: three regular beers – Timothy Taylor Landlord, Cains Traditional Bitter and Jennings Bitter – are joined by a changing guest, often a local or seasonal brew. The bar menu is a list of simple, hearty dishes that show an admirable dedication to regional produce: haggis pie topped with parsnip mash, Staffordshire oatcakes with various fillings, and boiled gammon with pease pudding and parsley sauce, for example. A specials board extends choice. A handful of wines includes two by the glass at £1.85. Note that the pub is often closed on race days. SAMPLE DISHES: savoury minced beef steak and tatties £7; McConickie's hash (corned beef) with pickled red cabbage £7; lemon cheesecake with caramelised pineapple £3.50.

Licensee Michael Edward Mercer (Inn Partnership)
Open Mon to Fri 11.30 to 3, 5 to 11, Sat 11.30 to 3, 6 to 11, Sun 12 to 2.30, 7 to 10.30; bar food Mon to Fri 12 to 1.45, 5 to 8, Sat and Sun 12 to 2, 7 to 8.30 (8 Sun); restaurant Mon to Fri 5 to 8, Sat 6 to 8.30, Sun 7 to 8 (all opening and food times subject to change and customers are advised to check by phone)
Details No children   No smoking in restaurant   Occasional live music   Dogs welcome   No cards
Accommodation: 2 rooms, B&B £55 per person.

Old Harkers Arms 🍺

1 Russell Street, Boughton, Chester CH3 5AL   TEL: (01244) 344525
WEBSITE: www.brunningandprice.co.uk

A short, pleasant stroll from the city centre along the towpath of the Shropshire Union Canal leads to this former canal-boat chandler's. Though it was a derelict warehouse just fifteen years ago, the brick walls (adorned with assorted framed posters and pictures) and iron pillars and girders give the open-plan interior a timeless look that could fool you into believing it has always been a pub. The long, daily-changing menus represent a veritable pick-and-mix of culinary styles, taking in everything from nachos with melted cheese, sour cream and salsa (in the 'light bites' section) to old-fashioned steak, ale and mushroom pie. To ensure that all sizes of appetite are satisfied, there's also a range of toasted and cold sandwiches. A superb range of well-kept real ales typically includes beers from highly regarded regional brewers such as Thwaites, Phoenix, Caledonian, Moorhouses and Weetwood. There's also Inch's Stonehouse Cider, plus a dozen malt whiskies and a list of 15 wines, all available by the glass. SAMPLE DISHES: steamed mussels in cream and pink peppercorn sauce £4.50; pan-fried chicken on blue cheese and leek potato cake with a mustard and beer sauce £10; banoffi pie £4.

Licensees Catryn Devaney and Barbie Hill (Brunning & Price Ltd)
Open 11.30 to 11, Sun 12 to 10.30; bar food Mon to Fri 12 to 2.30, 5 to 9.30, Sat and Sun 12 to 9.30
Details Children welcome in bar eating area   Wheelchair access (also WC)   No-smoking area   No music
No dogs   Amex, Delta, MasterCard, Switch, Visa

CHICHELEY   Buckinghamshire   map 6

Chester Arms
Bedford Road, Chicheley MK16 9JE   TEL: (01234) 391214
on A422, 3m from M1 junction 14

This stand-alone white-painted pub on the busy road into Bedford is impossible to miss and makes a handy pit stop for those wishing to avoid the M1 services at Newport Pagnell. It is quite unprepossessing within: several interlinked rooms with a basic, traditional pub décor and a bar running the length of the back. Its strength lies in the food on offer: namely fish and seafood delivered daily, and meat and poultry supplied by a local butcher. Treatments are simple, allowing the quality of the produce to stand out: perhaps chargrilled whole gilthead bream, or lamb chops, served with new potatoes and salad, or varying sizes of Aberdeen Angus rump, sirloin or fillet steaks with chips and vegetables. To start, there might be mixed seafood salad, or avocado with crab and crayfish tails, with treacle tart or crème brûlée for dessert. In addition, the lunch menu brings on things like steak and kidney pie and variations on the ploughman's theme. Greene King IPA and Morland Original are on handpump, while wine drinkers can choose from a reasonably priced list, starting at £10.80, with eight available by the glass. SAMPLE DISHES: grilled tiger prawns with garlic butter £6; breast of chicken chasseur £9.25; crème caramel £3.25.

Licensee Phil Hale (Greene King)
Open Tue to Sat 11 to 2.30, 5.30 to 11, Sun 12 to 3; bar food and restaurant Tue to Sun 12 to 2 (1.30 Sat), Tue to Sat 6.30 to 9.30
Details Children welcome in restaurant   Car park   Wheelchair access (not WC)   Garden   No smoking in restaurant   No music   No dogs   Amex, Delta, MasterCard, Switch, Visa

---

Entries are written on the basis of readers' reports, backed up by independent, anonymous inspections. Factual details at the bottom of entries are from questionnaires which the Guide sends to all establishments that feature in the book.

CHICKSGROVE   **Wiltshire**   map 2

▲ Compasses Inn

Chicksgrove SP3 6NB   TEL: (01722) 714318
turn off A30 2m W of Fovant towards Chicksgrove and follow signs for Compasses Inn

Everyone seems to agree that this out-of-the-way sixteenth-century thatched inn is notoriously difficult to track down, but it's well worth the effort. The dimly lit interior gives the impression that nothing much has changed in decades, with low ceilings, thick black beams, and farming implements hung on its part-panelled walls, not to mention an upright piano and a stuffed owl in a glass case. The menu is on blackboards, with additional daily specials written on the canopy of a wood-burning stove in the inglenook. You might begin with mushroom and rosemary soup or baked red pepper stuffed with garlic and anchovies, then move on to say, slow-roast shoulder of lamb, duck breast in Chinese jus, or a warm salad of scallops, crayfish and chorizo. Filled onion loaves, jacket potatoes, and salads are also available at lunchtime, while desserts could range from crème brûlée to chocolate brownie with mixed berries and blackcurrant ice cream. Chicksgrove Churl, brewed for the pub by Wadworth, 6X and Bass are regularly on draught along with a guest ale. Seven wines are sold by the glass from a reasonably priced list of around 30 bottles. SAMPLE DISHES: smoked duck and red onion tartlet £5.50; whole plaice with lemon and pesto dressing £10; chocolate and Kahlùa mousse £4.25.

Licensee Alan Stoneham (freehouse)
Open *Tue to Sun 12 to 3, 6 to 11 (10.30 Sun); bar food Tue to Sun 12 to 2, Tue to Sat 7 to 9*
Details *Children welcome   Car park   Garden and patio   No music   Dogs welcome   Amex, Delta, Diners, MasterCard, Switch, Visa   Accommodation: 4 rooms, B&B £40 to £65*

CHILGROVE   **West Sussex**   map 2

▲ White Horse Inn 🏵 🍇   NEW ENTRY

1 High Street, Chilgrove PO18 9HX   TEL: (01243) 535219
WEBSITE: www.whitehorsechilgrove.co.uk
on B2141 between Chichester and Petersfield

The wisteria-clad eighteenth-century coaching inn on the Chichester to Petersfield road has seen some changes over the last few years. Charles Burton has dispensed with the traditional in favour of a simplified, modern look that goes in for lots of wood in the bar – floorboards, furniture, and plenty burning on the open fire – and smart, uncluttered dining rooms with well-spaced tables covered in white cloths. While locally brewed Ballard's Best and Tetley Bitter are on handpump for real ale lovers, this is the place to leaf through the long 'indulgence list' from the celebrated cellar of classic wines from France and beyond. Much is priced for dreaming rather than drinking but there's also a shorter version for the less intrepid and a good selection by the glass. Bar food dishes range from home-made soups and pâtés to seasonal game, organic meats, and local crab and lobster. An ambitious and more extensive restaurant menu (also served in the bar) brings fideua (Valencian noodle) pasta with sautéed ceps and butternut squash cappuccino, then slow-roast half a Gressingham duck with minted pea purée and a rich Cassis sauce. For racing fans, it is worth noting that the inn is handy for Goodwood. SAMPLE DISHES: Selsey crab and avocado salad £9; seared breast of pheasant £13; lemon tart £6.50.

Licensee Charles Burton (freehouse)
Open Tue to Sat 11 to 3, 6 to 11, Sun 12 to 3; bar food and restaurant Tue to Sun 12 to 2, Tue to Sat 7 to 10
Details Children welcome Car park Wheelchair access (not WC) Garden No smoking in restaurant
Background music Dogs welcome in bar and bedrooms only Delta, MasterCard, Switch, Visa
Accommodation: 8 rooms, B&B £65 to £120

CHILLENDEN   Kent   map 3

Griffins Head

Chillenden CT3 1PS TEL: (01304) 840325
from A2 take Nonnington turn-off; pub 1m past Nonnington on left-hand side

Chillenden is deep in the Kent countryside to the south of Canterbury, and the
ancient Griffins Head is a huge old black and cream half-timbered building with a tall
tiled roof and tiny windows. You enter the main bar, with its large brick inglenook,
plenty of ceiling beams and flagstone floor; to one side is the restaurant, where tables
are formally laid, and on the other side is the bar dining area, with an assortment of
tables of different sizes, shapes and heights. There are hop garlands everywhere,
display cabinets show off various old knick-knacks, and among rows of dusty old
wine bottles is a small gap where the menu blackboards hang. These deliver fairly
upmarket pub food, mostly old-fashioned, along the lines of baked fillet of cod with a
creamy white wine and parsley sauce, as well as a short list of simpler dishes, such as
gammon, egg and chips. Reporters have praised 'simple but effective' mussel and
prawn chowder, tender pan-fried venison with Madeira and mushroom sauce, and
'excellent' raspberry and almond torte. As this is a Shepherd Neame pub, real ale
aficionados will be happy to find that brewery's range on offer. A changing line-up of
four wines by the glass is drawn from a sound, good-value list. SAMPLE DISHES: duck
liver parfait £5; whole roast mallard with port and damson gravy £11; toasted hazelnut
meringue roulade £4.

Licensee Mark Jeremy Copestake (Shepherd Neame)
Open 11 to 11, Sun 11 to 4.30 (later in summer); bar food and restaurant 12 to 2, 7 to 9.30, Sun 12 to 2
Details No children Car park Garden and patio No music Dogs welcome on a lead exc in restaurant
Amex, Delta, MasterCard, Switch, Visa

CHINNOR   Oxfordshire   map 2

Sir Charles Napier 😊 😊 🍇

Sprigg's Alley, Chinnor OX39 4BX TEL: (01494) 483011
*from M40 junction 6 take B4009 to Chinnor; at mini-roundabout in Chinnor turn right and continue up
hill for 2m to Sprigg's Alley*

Set beside the road, high on the Chiltern Hills some two miles from Chinnor, this
remarkable place is a curious cross between pub and restaurant, with a highly eccentric décor that includes giant terracotta pots, unusual sculptures (all for sale) inside
and in the extensive garden, plus quirky objects such as the weighted frying pan used
as a doorstop. Unmatching old tables and chairs contribute to the relaxed atmosphere,
and service is pleasant and unrushed despite crowds of people – especially for Sunday
lunch. Summer specials and winter bar dishes provide plenty of affordable options,
from baked goats' cheese with filo or pheasant boudin blanc to main courses such as
jugged rabbit with mash, and baked salmon with sorrel sauce and crushed new

potatoes. Full restaurant menus also take their cue from the seasons: in winter you might encounter butternut squash risotto before, say, mallard with Jerusalem artichokes, chestnuts and Madeira, while summer ushers in things like asparagus salad with quail's eggs and tarragon or baked Cornish lobster with sauce vierge. Portions are generous, but if you can manage dessert there are concoctions like chocolate tart with marmalade and vanilla ice cream. The exquisite wine list never puts a foot wrong, featuring both classics from Bordeaux, Burgundy and the Rhône – many of them in mature vintages – and New World rising stars. The majority of wines are over £20, but worth the money, and there is a good selection of half-bottles – even wines by the glass aren't your everyday basics. Wadworth 6X and IPA come straight from the barrel. SAMPLE DISHES: onion and basil tart £5.75; navarin of lamb £10.50; hot date cake with toffee sauce £6.50.

Licensee Julie Griffiths (freehouse)

Open Tue to Sat 12 to 3, 6 to 12, Sun 12 to 6; bar food and restaurant Tue to Sat 12 to 2.30, 6.30 to 10, Sun 12 to 3.30; closed 3 days at Christmas

Details Children welcome at L, no children under 7 at D   Car park   Wheelchair access (not WC)   Garden   No-smoking areas   Background music   No dogs   Amex, Delta, Diners, MasterCard, Switch, Visa

---

CHIPPING CAMPDEN   Gloucestershire   map 5

▲ Eight Bells   NEW ENTRY

Church Street, Chipping Campden GL55 6JG   TEL: (01386) 840371
WEBSITE: www.eightbellsinn.co.uk

Built in 1380 of honey-coloured stone, the Eight Bells claims to be the oldest inn in this affluent and picturesque Cotswold village. Exposed stone walls, flagstone floors, numerous fireplaces and tearoom-style furniture set a rustic tone, but the most unusual feature is a glass-covered priest-hole. From the weekly changing menu, expect the likes of smoked haddock and wild mushroom risotto, followed by hearty main courses such as faggots with mushy peas, onion gravy and mash. Daily fish specials might feature pan-fried skate wing with caper and garlic butter and at lunchtime various filled ciabattas are available. Though dishes can sound ambitious, results on the plate generally live up to expectations, showing the professional touch of a chef who has worked in upmarket London hotels. A decent selection of real ales includes Hook Norton Best Bitter and Old Hooky, and Goff's Jouster, and there is also Old Rosie cider. The wine list comes in two parts: the main section covers the world in two dozen bottles, while a short 'fine wines' list includes reputed Italian names. Eight by the glass are £2.80 to £3.50. SAMPLE DISHES: duck liver and walnut parfait with orange marmalade and toasted brioche £5.25; slow-braised oxtail in red wine with baby onions, button mushrooms, carrots and new potatoes £12.50; apple crumble with Chantilly cream £4.25.

Licensees Neil and Julie Hargreaves (freehouse)

Open summer 11 (12 Fri to Sun) to 11, winter 12 to 3, 5.30 to 11; bar food and restaurant 12 to 2.30, 6.30 to 9.30

Details Children welcome in dining room   Garden and patio   No smoking in dining room   Occasional live music   Dogs welcome   Delta, MasterCard, Switch, Visa   Accommodation: 4 rooms, B&B £55 to £85

CHOLMONDELEY Cheshire   map 5

▲ Cholmondeley Arms

Cholmondeley SY14 8BT   TEL: (01829) 720300
WEBSITE: www.cholmondeleyarms.co.uk
on A49, 5½m N of Whitchurch

The school desks, blackboard and easel that occupy the gallery above the bar counter
– along with sporting paraphernalia, bird cages and other oddments – serve as a
reminder that until about 20 years ago this was the village school. Sensitive conversion has retained the building's original character while turning it into a comfortable,
upmarket dining pub. Arches with drapes divide the main space into three distinct
parts, each with bare brick walls washed in pastel shades and adorned with old oil
paintings and photographs; you'll also see a stag's head trophy and the Cholmondeley
coat of arms over a log fire. Regular fixtures on the short bar menu include devilled
kidneys on toast, gammon and pineapple, and fish and chips with mushy peas. These
are supplemented by a long and varied list of blackboard specials, typically featuring
starters like roast asparagus with olive oil and Parmesan, or chargrilled scallop salad
with prawns and baby spinach; mains could include game pie, chicken breast with
mushroom and Dijon mustard sauce, or grilled plaice with butter and herbs. Black
cherry Pavlova, or hot fudged bananas might lurk among desserts. Marston's
Pedigree, Banks's Bitter and Adnams Bitter are on handpump, and seven wines are
sold by the glass from a global list of 30 bottles. SAMPLE DISHES: mushrooms in cream
and Stilton £4.75; rack of lamb with garlic and thyme sauce £10; spotted dick and
custard £4.25.

Licensees Guy and Carolyn Ross-Lowe (freehouse)
Open 11 to 3, 6.30 to 11; bar food 12 to 2.15, 6.30 to 10
Details Children welcome   Car park   Wheelchair access (also WC)   Garden   Occasional background music
Dogs welcome   Delta, MasterCard, Switch, Visa   Accommodation: 6 rooms, B&B £50 to £65

CHRISTMAS COMMON Oxfordshire   map 2

Fox & Hounds 🏵 NEW ENTRY

Christmas Common OX49 5HL   TEL: (01491) 612599
from M40 junction 6 take A40 SE and turn right for village after 2½m

In well-trodden Chilterns walking country, this extended 500-year-old brick and flint
inn confidently juggles the skills required to be both a dining pub and a place for just
having a drink. 'It would be great to take foreigners here, for decent food and old
English ambience,' observed a visitor. The oldest part consists of three small rooms
awash in ochre-brown, with an open fire in one, mismatched dining tables in others,
and a modern restaurant with an open-to-view kitchen to the rear. At lunchtime you
can get ploughman's, 'doorstep sandwiches', and a kipper or roast ham hock with
crusty bread, but the main business is full meals, including pies and steaks.
Ingredients are fresh, and the kitchen flexes culinary muscles for ambitious dishes
such as starters of curried parsnip soup, or boar, pork and apple pâté, and main
courses of slow-cooked lamb shank with roasted Mediterranean vegetables and hassle
back potatoes, and roast suprême of chicken with melted Brie and house chutney.
This is a Brakspear pub, so expect their Ordinary, Special and seasonal brews on
handpump. A handful of organic wines appears on a list that offers 11 by the glass.

SAMPLE DISHES: flaked trout and smoked salmon mousse £6; pan-fried tuna with Asian coleslaw and a chilli, coriander and ginger dressing £13; pear and almond tart £5.50.

Licensee Judith Bishop (Brakspear)
Open *Oct to Easter Mon to Fri 11 to 3, 6 to 11, Sat 11.30 to 11, Sun 12 to 10.30, Easter to Sept Mon to Sat 11.30 to 11, Sun 12 to 10.30; bar food and restaurant 12 to 2.30 (3 Sun), 7 to 9; open 25 Dec 12 to 2 (no food)*
Details *No children Car park Wheelchair access (also WC) Garden No smoking in restaurant Occasional live or background music Dogs welcome MasterCard, Switch, Visa*

CLAVERING Essex   map 3

 ## Cricketers
Clavering CB11 4QT TEL: (01799) 550442
WEBSITE: www.thecricketers.co.uk
on B1038 between Buntingford and Newport, 6m SW of Saffron Walden

Arriving on a frosty winter night, a visitor to this sixteenth-century village pub was heartened by the sight of a roaring log fire in the cosy, beamed bar, where bare brick walls are adorned with traditional pubby artefacts such as horse brasses and copper pans. In finer weather, the patio in front of the pub is a pleasant spot to sit and enjoy a pint of Adnams or Tetley's. The mood throughout is relaxed and unpretentious, and that goes for the food too. Bar menus list a broad choice of homely but interesting dishes with a leaning towards Italian flavours, as in roasted pumpkin risotto with seared king scallops, as well as traditional English dishes (steak and kidney pie, perhaps) and more exotic ideas such as tandoori chicken livers with yoghurt, lime and mint on a poppadum. The separate fixed-price restaurant menu shows a similarly varied style. Most of the 50 wines are under £20 and ten are available by the glass. Landlord Trevor Oliver is Jamie's dad, and has featured in some of his son's TV programmes and commercials. SAMPLE DISHES: chicory salad with avocado and chorizo topped with a deep-fried poached egg £6.50; roasted cod fillet with basil and pine-nut crust on saffron aïoli and ribbon vegetables £12.75; crêpe filled with banana and toffee sauce £5.

Licensee Trevor Oliver (freehouse)
Open *10.30 to 11; bar food and restaurant 12 to 2, 7 to 10; closed 25 and 26 Dec*
Details *Children welcome in eating areas and family room Car park Wheelchair access (not WC) Garden and patio No-smoking area in bar, no smoking in dining room Background music No dogs Amex, MasterCard, Switch, Visa Accommodation: 14 rooms, B&B £70 to £100*

CLAYHIDON Devon   map 2

Merry Harriers
Forches Corner, Clayhidon EX15 3TR TEL: (01823) 421270
off B3170, 6m SW of Taunton at Forches Corner, 2m NE of Clayhidon village

Proximity to junction 26 of the M5, combined with the tranquillity of the Blackdown Hills, makes this welcoming cream-painted and dark-timbered roadside pub a popular spot. The main bar has a cosy, homely feel and a warming log stove, and the friendly and welcoming licensees ensure that the place has a relaxed atmosphere. Locally sourced produce and fresh fish from Brixham feature strongly throughout the menu, though the kitchen takes its ideas from far and wide. Starters of roasted Somerset Brie in nibbed almonds served with pepper confit, or grilled scallops with rosemary and garlic butter, might be followed by confit of Quantock duck on onion marmalade, or Thai chicken curry. To finish, there might be sticky toffee pudding, or treacle tart. A regularly changing selection of good local real ales might include well-kept Otter Ale. There is also Bollhayes cider and apple juice. Ten wines are served by the glass, at £2.50 and £3, from a list of around two dozen bottles. SAMPLE DISHES: green-lipped mussels grilled with pesto £4.50; mixed game and ale casserole with juniper dumplings £12.50; lemon posset £4.

Licensees Barry and Christine Kift (freehouse)
Open *Tue to Sat 12 to 3, 7 to 11, Sun 12 to 3; bar food and restaurant Tue to Sat 12 to 2, 7 to 9, Sun 12 to 2*
Details *No children   Car park   Wheelchair access (not WC)   Garden and patio   No-smoking area in bar, no smoking in restaurant   No music   Dogs welcome on a lead   Delta, MasterCard, Switch, Visa*

CLIFFORD'S MESNE   Gloucestershire   map 5

▲ Yew Tree

May Hill, Clifford's Mesne GL18 1JS   TEL: (01531) 820719
WEBSITE: www.theyewtreeinn.co.uk
off B4222/4216, 4m SE of M50 junction 3

Paul Hackett cooks and his amiable wife Anna is a 'charming and totally unpretentious hostess' at this converted sixteenth-century cider press perched above Clifford's Mesne, on the north slope of May Hill, with a panoramic view over the Leadon Valley towards the Malvern Hills. The sprawling, modern-looking brick façade is softened by colourful hanging baskets and window boxes, while the interior still has some original touches, including a log fire in the bar and beams in the comfortable lounge and restaurant. The kitchen uses local produce extensively, and the style is a blend of traditional and modern ideas. Among starters, you may find frothy asparagus and broccoli soup, or tartare of oak-smoked salmon with prawns, cucumber and crème fraîche. Main courses could include escalope of Brixham inshore cod with champagne, lobster and chive sauce, breast of local pheasant with red cabbage and a claret, game and shallot sauce, and excellent 'strong-tasting' roast loin of Gloucester Old Spot pork with 'deliciously rich' prune stuffing, 'perfect' crackling and a subtly flavoured Pommery mustard gravy. Lemon tart with prune and Armagnac ice cream is a recommended dessert. Shepherd Neame Spitfire Premium Ale, Wye Valley Butty Bach and Fuller's London Pride are on draught, along with oak-conditioned ciders, but the place is best known for its serious list of fine wines. For normal mortals around 20 come by the glass from £3.25 and there are affordable bottles alongside the famous names. SAMPLE DISHES: chicken broth; fillet of Cornish sea bass sautéed in vermouth with dill sauce; sticky toffee pudding with caramel sauce: 2 courses £21.95, 3 courses £27.

Licensee Paul Hackett (freehouse)
Open *Tue to Sat 12 to 3, 6.30 to 11, Sun 12 to 3; bar food and restaurant 12 to 2, 7 to 9, Sun 12 to 2; closed 2 to 22 Jan*
Details *Children welcome   Car park   Wheelchair access (also WC)   Garden and patio   No smoking in bar and restaurant   Background music   Dogs welcome   Delta, MasterCard, Switch, Visa   Accommodation: 2 rooms, B&B £55 to £70*

CLIPSHAM   Rutland   map 6

Olive Branch 🏵 🍺 🍇

Main Street, Clipsham LE15 7SH   TEL: (01780) 410355
1½m off A1 at Ram Jam Inn junction, 8m N of Stamford

Clipsham doesn't appear to consist of anything more than this popular pub and a couple of houses, and even the pub looks more like a farmhouse, being quite low and set at right angles to what looks like an unused barn. There's a lawn and a gravel patio with trestle tables, while the interior is a quirky but relaxed mix of sisal matting, tiled floors, wooden tables and chairs, pews, pale pastel walls, log fires and lamplight. The house beer comes from the local Grainstore Brewery, and others might include one from the Fenland microbrewery in Cambridgeshire, and guests such as Greene King Abbot Ale and Timothy Taylor Landlord. Blackboards draw attention to food, cigars and bin-ends and special purchases of wines. The wine selection here and on the printed list is outstanding both for quality and value, and manageably brief. It is enthusiastic without being snobbish, taking in clarets from some of the best vintages of the last 30 years on the one hand and offering a simple guide to wine styles on the other. Ten wines can be had by the glass. More boards offer soups, hot sandwiches and a good-value two- or three-course set lunch: say, potted shrimps, venison casserole, and Eton mess. The printed carte encompasses the homely (pork and Stilton pie with home-made piccalilli, or fish and chips with tomato sauce and minted peas), the exotic (poached sea bass with a sweetcorn and coconut rice cake and Thai curry sauce), and the somewhat indulgent (chocolate brownie with white chocolate sauce and crème fraîche). SAMPLE DISHES: crab and avocado salad with prawn toast and lime and ginger dressing £6.75; roast chicken breast with Savoy cabbage and fricassee of wild mushrooms £10.50; vanilla pannacotta with spiced plum compote £5.

Licensees Marcus Welford, Sean Hope and Ben Jones (freehouse)
Open 12 to 3 (5 Sat), 6 to 11, Sun 12 to 6; bar food and restaurant Mon to Sat 12 to 2, 7 to 9, Sun 12 to 3
Details Children welcome   Car park   Garden and patio   No-smoking areas   Occasional background music
Dogs welcome in bar only   MasterCard, Switch, Visa

COCKWOOD   Devon   map 1

Anchor Inn 🍺 🍇

Cockwood EX6 8RA   TEL: (01626) 890203
WEBSITE: www.anchorinncockwood.com
off A379, on W side of River Exe estuary opposite Exmouth

A lovely harbour's-edge setting with estuary views is, one of this sixteenth-century pub's prize assets, but just as appealing are the atmospheric low-ceilinged bar, with old lamps hanging from the beams, and the particularly friendly welcome. Real ale fans will also appreciate the line-up of Bass, Fuller's London Pride, Wadworth 6X, Otter Ale and Greene King Abbot Ale and Old Speckled Hen. And for wine lovers there's a list of 30-odd good-value bottles – nine of them are also available by the glass – plus blackboard specials and a 'reserve list' of 300 more that includes some real gems. The lengthy menus offer plenty of variety, with an emphasis on seafood: mussels are served in 30 different ways, oysters in 8 ways and scallops in 14 ways. The rest of the menu goes in for simple, mostly traditional snacks and main dishes, including hot roast beef sandwich, faggots and peas, potted seafood pie, and salmon steak with lemon butter. To finish, choose from 12 versions of treacle tart. There's also a separate but similarly eclectic restaurant menu. SAMPLE DISHES: avocado with crab-meat and prawns £5; tuna steak in tomato, garlic and herbs £7.50; treacle tart with banana chips £3.75.

Licensees Terry Morgan and Alison Sanders (Heavitree Brewery)
Open 11 to 11, Sun 12 to 10.30; bar food and restaurant 12 to 3, 6.30 to 10, Sun 12 to 2.30, 6.30 to 9.30; closed 25 Dec evening, no food all day
Details Children welcome in bar eating area   Car park   Wheelchair access (also WC)   Patio   No smoking in restaurant   Background music   Dogs welcome exc in restaurant   Amex, Delta, Diners, MasterCard, Switch, Visa

CODFORD   Wiltshire   map 2

▲ George Hotel 😋 NEW ENTRY
High Street, Codford BA12 0NG   TEL: (01985) 850270

This old roadside inn has been given a new lease of life by Boyd McIntosh and Joanne Fryer (both ex Howard's House Hotel in nearby Teffont Evias). The unpretentious, contemporary refurbishment with a Mediterranean vibe (lots of terracotta) has been tastefully done, incorporating a bold lounge with large, burgundy sofas and big mirrors; and a bar area where one end is set out for dining with an assortment of scrubbed wood and polished tables. The end result combines pubby roots with high-end gastro-pub dining and excellent service. The cooking has a light touch, using first-rate ingredients to create clear flavours and balanced combinations. Expect fresh ideas: for example, starters of warm tartlet of wood pigeon breast, creamy wild mush-rooms and coriander; and salad of Black Forest ham, sun-blushed tomatoes and garlic croûtons with balsamic dressing. Main courses might run to roast loin of Wiltshire lamb, Savoy cabbage and bacon and a light mint jus; or crisp battered fillets of gurnard with basil potato, caper and tomato cream. Finish with something like soft poached pear with vanilla ice cream and raspberry coulis. Three real ales are on handpump, rotating among Ringwood Best, Hop Back GFB, Timothy Taylor Landlord, Shepherd Neame Spitfire and Greene King Abbot Ale. On the 40-plus wine list four are available by the glass. SAMPLE DISHES: chargrilled chicken, black pudding and fried egg stack £7; caramelised breast of duck, sautéed wild mushrooms, smoked tea and port sauce £12; vanilla and rosemary pannacotta, mango coulis and shortbread fingers £4.25.

Licensees Boyd McIntosh and Joanne Fryer (freehouse)
Open Mon and Wed to Sat 12 to 2.30, 6.30 to 11, Sun 12 to 3, 7 to 10.30; bar food 12 to 2.30, 6.30 to 11
Details Children welcome in dining room   Car park   Patio   No-smoking area in bar   Background music No dogs   Delta, Diners, MasterCard, Switch, Visa   Accommodation: 3 rooms, B&B £45 to £65

COLDHARBOUR   Surrey   map 3

▲ Plough Inn 🍺

Coldharbour RH5 6HD   TEL: (01306) 711793
4m S of Dorking, signposted Leith Hill and Coldharbour

Even though it is near the National Trust's Leith Hill (one of the best viewpoints in the south-east), this is not the most beautiful pub to look at – though 'handsome enough' in a four-square Georgian manner that belies its seventeenth-century origins. But it does come with a built-in brewery. The Leith Hill Brewery supplies the Plough with Crooked Furrow Bitter ('good stuff,' mumbled one enthusiast) and Tallywhacker Porter, and these sit alongside guest ales, Timothy Taylor Landlord and Shepherd Neame Spitfire. Inside, there are beams and white plaster, but not the folksy over-busyness that many pubs succumb to – and in an old barn outside the main building there's a large family room. Food, listed on blackboards, can be eaten in the two bar areas or the restaurant and focuses on simple dishes done well. There are starters like pan-fried baby squid with garlic butter, while main dishes may include confit of duck on mashed potato with citrus jus, or chargrilled escolar (a kind of Spanish mackerel) with lemon and herb butter. There's a short children's menu too. Sweets take in bread-and-butter pudding and custard. House wine starts at £9.90, and six are available by the glass from £2.60. SAMPLE DISHES: king prawns pan-fried in garlic and herb butter £8; roast poussin with sage, lemon and onion stuffing £10; chilled lemon tart £4.50.

Licensees Richard and Anna Abrehart (freehouse)
Open 11.30 to 11, Sun 12 to 10.30; bar food and restaurant 12 to 3, 7 to 9.30, Sun 12 to 3
Details Children welcome in family room Car park Wheelchair access (also WC) Garden No smoking in dining room Occasional background and live music Dogs in bar only MasterCard, Switch, Visa
Accommodation: 6 rooms, B&B £55 to £85

COLEBY Lincolnshire   map 6

▲ Bell Inn

3 Far Lane, Coleby LN5 0AH TEL: (01522) 810240
on A607 from Grantham to Lincoln, take second left after Boothby Graffoe

The Bell is in a pretty village close to the church, and despite some recent 'sprucing up' it retains a decidedly traditional, cosy feel. Eating is taken seriously here, as one glance at the restaurant menu (also served in the bar) will reveal – an extensive and varied list with something for everyone. Typical are roast tenderloin of pork with sage and onion boulangère and slow-roast tomatoes, and salmon poached with mushrooms and leeks in a white wine and cream sauce. Those with a lighter appetite could opt for grilled haddock on spinach with mashed potato and cheese sauce, or chicken tikka with raita, and both starter and main-course portions are offered of such things as fishcakes on a tomato and goats' cheese salsa, and tagliatelle with chicken, mushrooms and peas in a cream sauce. Sandwiches and tapas are available in the bar, and among desserts might be lemon meringue pie or, for the more adventurous, candy shop terrine – layers of chocolate and sweets. Draught Bass, Black Sheep Best Bitter and Adnams Best are on tap for beer drinkers; for wine lovers there's a choice of six by the glass or a list of around 30 bottles, mostly from France. Prices are good and half a dozen also come in half-bottles. SAMPLE DISHES: slow-cooked pig's cheek with creamed cassoulet sauce £4.75; chicken breast stuffed with dolcelatte, mushrooms and bacon £9.50; sticky toffee pudding £4.

Licensees Troy Jeffrey and Robert Chamberlain (Pubmaster)
Open 11.30 to 2.30, 5.30 to 11, Sun 12 to 10.30; bar food and restaurant Mon to Sat 11.30 to 2.30, 5.30 to 9 (9.30 Fri and Sat), Sun 12 to 8
Details Children welcome in eating areas Car park Wheelchair access (not WC) Patio No smoking in 1 eating area Background music Dogs welcome in bar only Delta, MasterCard, Switch, Visa
Accommodation: 3 rooms, room only £34.50

COLEFORD   Devon   map 1

New Inn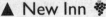

Coleford EX17 5BZ   TEL: (01363) 84242
WEBSITE: www.reallyreal-group.com
off A377 Exeter to Barnstaple road, 4m W of Crediton

Among the characters you might encounter at this thirteenth-century thatched inn in
a charming Devon village are Captain the blue-fronted Amazon parrot, and the resident ghost of a former monk who drowned in the nearby stream. The main bar has a
timeworn feel, while the lower bar has more atmosphere, with its heavy beams and
sturdy old furnishings. Flagstone floors, simple furniture and assorted bric-à-brac
characterise the main dining area to the rear. The long, eclectic menus offer starters
ranging from wild mushroom tart with salsa verde to fish goujons with sweet chilli
salsa, followed by faggots with herbed mash and sweet onion gravy or perhaps pan-
fried lamb noisettes with Puy lentils and rosemary jus. A couple of daily blackboard
specials add further options. Badger Best is on draught, and six wines are available by
the glass. The list of around 50 reds and whites organised by grape variety efficiently
covers a wide range of flavours, with plenty of options under £15 and a good showing
of half-bottles. SAMPLE DISHES: pigeon breast and smoked bacon salad with redcurrant
dressing £5; beef fillet with wild mushroom stroganoff £14; crème brûlée £4.

Licensee Paul Butt (freehouse)
Open 12 to 2.30, 6 to 11, Sun 12 to 2.30, 7 to 10.30; bar food and restaurant 12 to 2, 7 to 10
Details Children welcome   Car park   Wheelchair access (not WC)   Garden   No smoking in restaurant
Background music   No dogs in restaurant   Amex, Delta, Diners, MasterCard, Switch, Visa   Accommodation:
6 rooms, B&B £55 to £80

COLESHILL   Buckinghamshire   map 3

Red Lion

Village Road, Coleshill HP7 0LN   TEL: (01494) 727020
village signposted off A355 S of Amersham; once in village, go past sign for school; pub opposite church

Coleshill is a big, sprawly village, and the Red Lion, looking much like a private residence, is opposite the church – look for picnic tables on the grassy area in front.
Inside, the walls are painted a cheery yellow; above the bar are lots of photographs and
plaques to do with local matters, and village events are announced on notices in the
entrance porch. There is no restaurant, just a few tables in the bar, which can be
reserved. The printed menu lists jacket potatoes, ploughman's, sandwiches and
snacks like smoked salmon and scrambled egg, but the real business is chalked up on
blackboards: perhaps steak and mushroom pie, hot poached salmon, or vegetable
quiche, with apple strudel or toffee sponge pudding to finish. Greene King IPA and
Banks's Bitter are the regular beers, with Rebellion IPA and Smuggler, Archers
Village Bitter or Vale Brewery's Wychert Ale among the guests. Four wines are sold
by the large or small glass. SAMPLE DISHES: buck rarebit £5.25; grilled liver with onion
gravy £7; rhubarb crumble £3.50.

Licensees Christine and John Ullman (Innspired Pubs & Taverns)
Open Mon to Fri 11 to 3.30, 5.30 to 11, Sat 11 to 11, Sun 12 to 5, 7 to 10.30; bar food (exc Sun evening)
12 to 2.15, 7 to 9
Details Children welcome   Car park   Garden and patio   No music   Dogs welcome on a lead   No cards

COLKIRK **Norfolk** map 6

Crown NEW ENTRY

Colkirk NR21 7AA   TEL: (01328) 862172
off B1146, 1m S of Fakenham

This Greene King tenancy is a popular dining pub, with a friendly, cheerful atmosphere, where customers can tuck into a wide selection of well-cooked food chalked on blackboards. For one group of visitors 'the tidy, unassuming, homely' Crown proved to be an 'excellent local village pub', just the place for a traditional-style Sunday lunch. Try, for a first course, cream of mushroom soup, or duck liver and port pâté. Roast beef is mandatory, 'tasty, lean and well cooked', with good Yorkshire pudding, as is loin of pork with tangy apple sauce and crisp crackling, or rebel and go for smoked salmon and prawn omelette, or lamb and apricot casserole. Lemon cheesecake with a scoop of vanilla ice cream is likewise a must. The well-kept beers are Greene King IPA, Abbot Ale and a guest, and all of the two dozen or so bottles on the wine list are available by the glass. SAMPLE DISHES: mushroom and Stilton vol-au-vent £4.50; chicken fillet with oriental ginger sauce £8.50; bread-and-butter pudding £3.50.

Licensee Roger Savell (Greene King)
Open *11 to 3, 6 to 11, Sun 12 to 3, 7 to 10.30; bar food 12 to 1.30, 6.30 to 9*
Details *Children welcome   Car park   Wheelchair access (also WC)   Garden and patio   No smoking in dining room   Live music   Dogs welcome in bar   Delta, Diners, MasterCard, Switch, Visa*

COLLINGHAM **Nottinghamshire** map 5

King's Head

6 High Street, Collingham NG23 7LA   TEL: (01636) 892341
on A1133 N of Newark-on-Trent

The red-brick building beside a busy road may look unassuming, but the interior is something else. The style is modern and simplistic; the lengthy bar counter is topped with brushed aluminium, and the quarry-tiled floor complements the cream-painted walls and pine furniture. A small arch separates the bar from the L-shaped restaurant, where a maple floor, tiger-skin-patterned banquette covers, and paintings that juxtapose traditional portraits of Henry VIII and other kings' heads with abstract works create a striking contemporary look. Food is available throughout, with chef/owner Jamie Matts responsible for the bright, modern ideas and sound cooking skills seen in a starter salad of king prawns, chicken, bacon and goats' cheese with a Thai dressing, and main courses of roast confit of duck with sage and onion mash and balsamic vinegar sauce. Classic pub favourites are not neglected, and the specials board might list sautéed garlic mushrooms served with warm naan bread as well as lasagne, braised beef with mash, fish, chips and mushy peas, and apple and sultana crumble with 'a nice, smooth custard'. Themed evenings – Chinese or French, say – and a monthly food and drink quiz with its own menu are added attractions. Baguettes are possibilities at lunchtimes, and breakfast, morning coffee and cakes are served between 9.30 and noon. For beer drinkers, regular Timothy Taylor Landlord is supplemented by weekly-changing guest ales. Five wines are sold by the glass, and the annotated list runs to 20 bottles. SAMPLE DISHES: spinach and nutmeg soup £4.25;

pork steak topped with spinach and mozzarella served with sherry sauce £11; honey and whisky cheesecake £4.

Licensee Jamie Matts (freehouse)
Open 11 to 11, Sun 12 to 6; bar food and restaurant 12 to 2, 6 to 9, Sun 12 to 4
Details Children welcome Car park Wheelchair access (not WC) Patio No smoking in restaurant
Occasional live music Dogs welcome in bar only Delta, MasterCard, Switch, Visa

COLN ST ALDWYNS   Gloucestershire   map 2

 New Inn   NEW ENTRY

Coln St Aldwyns GL7 5AN   TEL: (01285) 750651
WEBSITE: www.new-inn.co.uk
off B4425, Cirencester to Burford road, 2m SW of Bibury

The New Inn, new some 400 or so years ago, is an imposing ivy-covered building whose large, arched passageway at the back (surmounted by a row of ancient pigeon-holes) hints at its former life as a coaching inn. Exposed-stone walls, plus the odd bit that's plastered and painted deep pink, open hearths, and simple wooden furniture distinguish the bar areas, where handpumped ales include Hook Norton Best Bitter and Butcombe Bitter. The Courtyard Bar menu offers fairly simple yet contemporary pub dishes: say, savoury Welsh rarebit on brioche, or deep-fried tiger prawns in filo with chilli jam. Braised shank of lamb, faggots and peas, and steak and mushroom pie are the kind of things to expect for main courses, and there could be warm apricot panettone bread-and-butter pudding, or apple and mixed fruit crumble with crème anglaise to finish. Lunchtime sandwiches and baguettes are listed on a blackboard. A fixed-price menu operates in the separate restaurant, with such dishes as 'nicely timed' Scottish mussels with tarragon mustard cream to start, then saddle of rabbit stuffed with chicken and sage mousse served with potato purée, wilted spinach and peppercorn sauce. Eight wines on the short bar version of the wine list are served by the glass from £3.10. SAMPLE DISHES: salmon and potato fishcake with citrus herb mayonnaise £5.25; spicy apricot and cumin lamb with coconut rice £9.50; chocolate and Baileys cheesecake £4.75.

Licensees Mr and Mrs Roger Kimmett (freehouse)
Open 11 to 11, Sun 12 to 10.30; bar food 12 to 2 (2.30 Sun), 7 to 9, restaurant Mon to Sat 7 to 9, Sun 12 to 2.30, 7 to 9
Details Children welcome in bar eating area; no children under 10 in restaurant Car park Garden
No smoking in restaurant No music Dogs welcome exc in restaurant and residents' lounge Delta, Diners, MasterCard, Switch, Visa Accommodation: 14 rooms, B&B £90 to £155

COLSTON BASSETT   Nottinghamshire   map 5

 Martins Arms 🏵 📖

School Lane, Colston Bassett NG12 3FD   TEL: (01949) 81361
off A46 Leicester to Newark road, 4m S of Bingham

'Quirky country charm' sums up part of the appeal of this attractive old inn. It began life as a farmhouse on the Colston Bassett Estate and stands in the heart of the village, close to the Market Cross (now a National Trust monument). These days it plies its trade as a classic upmarket Shires hostelry with a strong reputation for imaginative pub food. The bar menu always kicks off with a soup (artichoke and mushroom has been deemed 'earthy and wholesome') and it could also feature, say, rabbit and truffle terrine with elderberry and quince compote, baked mackerel with Sicilian crumbs and lemon potatoes, or balsamic-braised belly of pork with pak choi; at lunchtime you can also get sandwiches and ploughman's with Colston Bassett Stilton or Melton Mowbray pork pie. There's also no shortage of choice on the ambitious à la carte menu that serves both the print-festooned bar and the antique-furnished restaurant, the kitchen flexing its muscles for the likes of pigeon and pig's trotter risotto with peas, duck breast with figs, roasted red onions and mustard leaves, or monkfish, haricot bean and fennel stew with crème fraîche and anchovies. Puddings maintain interest with the likes of white peach, thyme and rose-water tarte Tatin, or chocolate and banana bread-and-butter pudding. Drinks are also up to standard, with spot-on real ales like Black Sheep Best Bitter, Bateman XB, Adnams Bitter and others supplemented by guests such as Elgood's Black Dog Mild. Apart from the house bottles, £15.25 is the entry point for a wine list with impeccable pedigree. SAMPLE DISHES: steamed mussels with Stilton, chives and spring onions £8; cassoulet £17.50; chocolate and orange soufflé cake £5.50.

Licensees Lynne Strafford Bryan and Salvatore Inguanta (freehouse)
Open *12 to 3, 6 to 11, Sun 12 to 3, 6.30 to 10.30; bar food all week 12 to 2, Mon to Sat 6 to 10; restaurant all week 12 to 1.30, Mon to Sat 6 to 10; closed evening 25 Dec*
Details *Children welcome in family room and restaurant   Car park   Wheelchair access (also WC)   Garden No smoking in snug and restaurant   No music   No dogs   Amex, MasterCard, Switch, Visa   Accommodation: 2 rooms, B&B £35 to £65*

COLTISHALL   Norfolk   **map 6**

▲ King's Head

26 Wroxham Road, Coltishall NR12 7EA   TEL: (01603) 737426

From the road the King's Head appears to be an unpretentious roadside pub, and it is only when you pull into the spacious car park that you spot moorings and a small jetty – the River Bure meanders along a short distance away. Within it is 'cosily homely' with a winter coal-burning fire in the main bar, large, polished wood dining tables, and blackboard menus offering quite an ambitious selection for such a rural place. Although the bar menu deals in dishes like open steak sandwich, sausages, and burgers, an à la carte menu available both in the bar evenings and in the non-smoking restaurant offers, say, hot-smoked salmon in a risotto of fennel and shallots, or smoked Norfolk eels with a warm potato and beetroot salad. Main courses include breast of pigeon with chicory and orange salad, sautéed potatoes and pancetta, or Gunton Park fillet of venison with half a roast mallard served with fondant potatoes, braised red cabbage and two sauces (plus, of course, Sunday roasts). Finish with hot apple and berry crumble with vanilla ice cream and crème anglaise. A diverse (illustrated) wine list provides ten by the glass and a sprinkling of half-bottles. SAMPLE DISHES: chicken liver and foie gras pâté £6; sea bass with king prawns and scallops with fresh tagliatelle £15; soufflé beignets filled with Grand Marnier cream with raspberry coulis £4.50.

Licensee Kevin Gardner (freehouse)
Open *11 to 3, 6 to 11, Sun 12 to 10.30; bar food Mon to Sat 12 to 2, Sun to Thurs 6 to 7; restaurant all week 7 to 9*
Details *Children welcome in bar eating area   Car park   Patio   No smoking in dining room   Background music   No dogs   Amex, Delta, MasterCard, Switch, Visa   Accommodation: 4 rooms, B&B £25 to £55*

COMPTON   Surrey   map 3

Withies Inn   NEW ENTRY
Withies Lane, Compton GU3 IJA   TEL: (01483) 421158
village on B3000, just off A3 SW of Guildford

Hugh and Brian Thomas have been in residence at this whitewashed village pub since 1979. Outside is a lawn with a weeping willow and lots of picnic tables, while the dimly lit, beamed bar has tiny curtained windows, horse brasses and a log fire to provide warmth in inclement weather. Bar snacks consist mostly of light dishes: a couple of soups, a pair of pâtés, ploughman's, and quiche plus a selection of sandwiches and jacket potatoes. The restaurant at the front, run by uniformed staff, has its own menu. Fish shows up well in the shape of pan-fried sardines, Arbroath smokies with lemon mayonnaise, and poached halibut with prawns and brandy sauce, while meat eaters could opt for, say, beef Wellington, chicken Kiev, or something from the chargrill; also look for seasonal specials ranging from asparagus to wild duck. The choice of real ales includes Hogs Back TEA, Greene King IPA and King & Barnes Sussex, and the wine list features around nine by the glass from £3. SAMPLE DISHES: melon and Parma ham £6.25; beef stroganoff £14; treacle tart £4.50.

Licensees Hugh and Brian Thomas (freehouse)
Open 11 to 3, 6 to 11, Sun 11 to 3; bar food and restaurant all week 12 to 2.30, Mon to Sat 7 to 10
Details Children welcome   Car park   Wheelchair access (not WC)   Garden and patio   No music   No dogs
Amex, Delta, Diners, MasterCard, Switch, Visa

CONSTABLE BURTON   North Yorkshire   map 8

▲ Wyvill Arms
Constable Burton DL8 5LH   TEL: (01677) 450581
on A684, 3½m E of Leyburn

This large creeper-clad roadside inn is easily spotted as you travel along the main road from Leyburn. Its attractive gardens were lovingly restored from their sorry state when the current owners took over in 1999. They have also done a good job on the seventeenth-century building, restoring the large main bar to a smart if somewhat old-fashioned style, with old photographs and watercolours covering the walls, and an attractively rustic-looking stone fireplace. Landlord Nigel Stevens is a friendly presence in the bar and seriously enthusiastic about his food. The menus offer a huge choice, with 'old favourites' like steak and mushroom pie and gammon steak with egg as well as more sophisticated main courses, such as roast suckling pig with mustard mash, poached apple and cider sauce, or lamb shank with mushy peas, mash and a rich rosemary and thyme jus. Fishy options run to pan-fried sea bream with vanilla and coral sauce and proper fish and chips, and there's a shorter bar lunch menu of sandwiches, pasta and risotto. To drink, there are Theakston Best, John Smith's Bitter and Black Sheep Best Bitter, and some eight wines by the glass from the diverse list of 40-odd bins. SAMPLE DISHES: trout and saffron pâté £5; fillet of pork with cream, brandy and prune sauce £11; Baileys-soaked bread-and-butter pudding £4.

Licensee Nigel Stevens (freehouse)
Open 11.30 to 3, 6 to 11, Sun 12 to 3, 7 to 10.30; bar food and restaurant 12 to 2 (2.30 summer), 6.30 to 9
Details Children welcome   Car park   Wheelchair access (also WC)   Garden and patio   No smoking in restaurant   Occasional live or background music; jukebox   Dogs welcome on a lead in bar only   Amex, Delta, MasterCard, Switch, Visa   Accommodation: 4 rooms, B&B £34 to £56

CONSTANTINE Cornwall map 1

▲ Trengilly Wartha Inn 🍴 🍺 🌿

Nancenoy, Constantine TR11 5RP TEL: (01326) 340332
WEBSITE: www.trengilly.co.uk
off A394 Falmouth to Helston road, between Constantine and Gweek

The pub name means 'settlement above the trees', and from its terrace and peaceful garden you can gaze across acres of meadows to the valley and river below. This is an Area of Outstanding Natural Beauty hidden away down steep and muddy lanes, but despite the tortuously out-of-the-way location the car park may well be full to overflowing. The farmhouse décor might seem rather well worn these days, with its eclectic mix of furnishings, beer mats on the beams and paintings by local artists brightening up the walls, but the whole place feels rather like a homely 'French-style auberge'. The kitchen makes admirable use of local and organic produce for a bar menu that ranges from chicken liver and port pâté with home-made chutney, or ploughman's, to 'Trengilly Classics' like crab cakes with white wine sauce, beef stroganoff, and – of course – Cornish pasty. The specials board (which is also the restaurant menu) casts its net further afield for impressive ideas like beetroot and herbed goats' cheese salad with walnut dressing, or confit of Cornish lamb on haricot bean and gammon ragoût with mint oil. In addition there are fish dishes like wild sea bass fillets with chicory, fennel and potato in pink grapefruit dressing, plus desserts such as chocolate terrine with brandied cherries and clotted cream. The inn also manages to maintain a happy balance between eating and drinking. Well-kept ales from the cask always include Sharp's Cornish Coaster, plus others from Skinner's and the Doghouse Brewery. The owners' wine business has moved out to Penryn but keeps bar, restaurant and take-away customers well supplied with a mix of trusted names and offbeat discoveries at good prices. Ten come by the glass for £2.70 to £3.90 and there's a shortlist of recommendations by style to save wading through the 250-strong full bottle selection. SAMPLE DISHES: pork and prawn spring roll with bean shoots and a sweet chilli and lemongrass dipping sauce £5.50; Cornish venison loin fillet on a crisp red onion galette with a red wine glaze £14.25; trio of brûlées £4.25.

Licensees Michael Maguire and Nigel Logan (freehouse)
Open 11 to 3, 6.30 to 11, Sun 12 to 3, 7 to 10.30; bar food 12 to 2.15 (2 Sun), 6.30 (7 Sun) to 9.30; restaurant 7.30 to 9.30; no food served 25 Dec
Details Children welcome Car park Wheelchair access (not WC) Garden No smoking in family room, conservatory or restaurant Occasional background music Dogs welcome Amex, Delta, Diners, MasterCard, Switch, Visa Accommodation: 8 rooms, B&B £49 to £96

CORSCOMBE Dorset map 2

▲ Fox Inn 🍴

Corscombe DT2 0NS TEL: (01935) 891330
off A356, 6m SE of Crewkerne

The thatched, custard-coloured Fox is not in Corscombe but outside the village opposite a brook in a web of narrow, twisting country lanes. The traditional interior has stone floors, pine furniture, beams aplenty and blue-check tablecloths, plus assorted country prints, some stuffed owls, and, unsurprisingly, a fox's head. The 'little bar', the stables, the conservatory and country kitchen dining room offer a choice of settings for diners, who can also eat in the bar. Here the restaurant's long menu is supplemented by blackboards listing daily specials, with fish a mainstay: say, whole roast sea bass with garlic and mushrooms. But meat eaters are not neglected: witness a warm salad of pigeon breast with bacon to start, and a main course of fillet of local venison with a rich game sauce. Exmoor Ale, Fuller's London Pride and Stowford Press cider are regularly served. A wine list was not available for the Guide to see this year, and therefore we cannot venture an assessment. SAMPLE DISHES: local goats' cheese salad £5; West Bay lemon sole £18; rhubarb crumble £4.

Licensees Clive Webb and Margaret Hannell (freehouse)
Open 12 to 3, 7 to 11, Sun 12 to 4, 7 to 10.30; bar food and restaurant 12 to 2, 7 to 9 (9.15 Fri and Sat)
Details Children welcome Car park Wheelchair access (not WC) Garden No smoking in restaurant
Occasional live music No dogs Amex, Delta, MasterCard, Switch, Visa Accommodation: 4 rooms, B&B £55
to £100

CORSLEY   Wiltshire   map 2

Cross Keys

Lyes Green, Corsley BA12 7PB   TEL: (01373) 832406
take right turn at Chapmanslade off A3098 from Frome

Among the attractions of this dining pub in a small village on the edge of Salisbury Plain are traditional pub games such as cribbage and skittles, which can be played in the quarry-tiled bar by the warmth of a log fire, along with a pint of Wadworth 6X, Henry's Original IPA or JCB. Another crowd puller is the food, served in the separate dining area, with its black beams, cream walls and big pine tables dressed with flowers and candles. The menus offer plenty of tempting options in a modern, eclectic vein. Blackboards of fish specials might include fried skate with pizzaiola sauce, or Brixham crab cakes with sweet chilli dressing, while another blackboard offers 'comfort zone' dishes such as braised beef and 6X pie. The printed menu aims to be more upmarket, with the likes of roast rack of lamb with a minted pear and red wine sauce. A list of around two dozen wines features six by the glass. SAMPLE DISHES: grilled goats' cheese on red onion marmalade £5.25; pan-fried duck breast on apple compote with red wine sauce £12.25; apple and cinnamon crumble with custard £4.

Licensees Fraser Carruth and Wayne Carnegie (Wadworth)
Open 12 to 3, 6.30 to 11, Sun 12 to 4, 7 to 10.30; bar food and restaurant all week 12 to 2.30, Mon to Sat
7 to 9.30; closed evenings 25 Dec and 26 Dec, 1 Jan
Details Children welcome in restaurant Car park Garden Background music Dogs welcome
MasterCard, Switch, Visa

CORTON   Wiltshire   map 2

▲ Dove Inn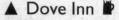

Corton BA12 0SZ   TEL: (01985) 850109
WEBSITE: www.thedove.co.uk
off A36, 5m from Warminster

This pretty mid-nineteenth-century inn in an off-the-beaten-track village close to the River Wylye saw a change of ownership in October 2003. The new licensees have wisely retained the welcoming, unpretentious pubby feel in the bar, emphasised by exposed-brick walls, flagstone floors, pine tables and a central open fireplace – backed up by a decent selection of real ales that might include Butcombe Bitter, Timothy

Taylor Landlord, and Crop Circle from the local Hop Back Brewery. The emphasis remains firmly on dining, and blackboards advertise snacks such as sandwiches, plough-man's and sausages as well as more substantial dishes like cod in a pesto crust with balsamic dressing, beef and stout pie, baked whole sea bass, and chicken curry. On the printed menu you can expect duck foie gras terrine, classic beef stroganoff, rack of lamb, and a range of steaks with a choice of sauces. From a list of some 33 bottles, nine wines are offered by the glass. SAMPLE DISHES: duck foie gras terrine £6.75; medallions of pork with Calvados sauce £14.25; mango cheesecake £4.50.

Licensees Michael and Beverley Wilson (freehouse)
Open 12 to 2.30 (3 Fri and Sat), 6 to 11, Sun 12 to 3, 7 to 10.30; bar food and restaurant 12 to 2 (2.30 Fri to Sun), 7 to 9 (9.30 Fri and Sat)
Details Children welcome in eating areas   Car park   Wheelchair access (also WC)   Garden and patio
No smoking in restaurant   Background music   Dogs welcome   Delta, MasterCard, Switch, Visa
Accommodation: 5 rooms, B&B £49.50 to £70

COTHERSTONE   Co Durham   map 10

▲ Fox & Hounds

Cotherstone DL12 9PF   TEL: (01833) 650241
on B6277, 3m NW of Barnard Castle

Overlooking a steeply sloping green in a small village above a valley, this white-painted slate-roofed building is a comfortable old local with a friendly atmosphere. Sketches of wild animals on the walls, old kettles in recesses in the thick stone walls, and stone bottles on the floor provide a decorative theme in the laid-back main bar, where beers from the Hambleton brewery are offered alongside Black Sheep Best Bitter. There is also a list of around 30 wines, mostly under £15, with seven by the glass. The bar lunch menus offer a choice of straightforward dishes made with local produce: sausages on mustard mash with onion gravy, for example, or a warm salad of bacon and apple with Cotherstone cheese. A full à la carte menu takes over in the evening, incorporating a few more sophisticated dishes into the repertoire, such as rack of Teesdale lamb with cranberry, orange and rosemary sauce, or roast salmon on watercress mash with lemon and lime dressing. SAMPLE DISHES: pan-fried Dublin Bay prawns in lemon and herb butter £4.50; pork tenderloin in mushroom and Marsala cream £10; hazelnut meringue in butterscotch sauce £3.75.

Licensees Ian and Nichola Swinburn (freehouse)
Open 12 to 2 (2.30 summer), 7 to 11 (10.30 Sun); bar food 12 to 2, restaurant 12 to 2, 7 to 9 (9.30 Fri and Sat summer); closed 25 and 26 Dec
Details Children welcome in family room and restaurant   Car park   Wheelchair access (not WC)   Patio
No smoking in restaurant   No music   Guide dogs only   Delta, MasterCard, Switch, Visa   Accommodation: 3 rooms, B&B £42.50 to £65

COTTESMORE   Rutland   map 6

Sun Inn

25 Main Street, Cottesmore LE15 7DH   TEL: (01572) 812321
on B668, 4m NE of Oakham

This small pretty village is close to RAF Cottesmore, although 'happily, this does not really impinge'. The attractive white-painted and thatched seventeenth-century pub is set well back from the road, bright with hanging baskets, shaded by an old yew, and offering a 'congenial atmosphere'. Within are beamed low ceilings, country-style furniture, open fires and an abundance of china suns. The kitchen looks to sunnier climes for inspiration, turning out feta cheese Greek salad, and pasta with aromatic chicken and baby octopus. From closer to home comes gammon and eggs, or braised fillet of beef with horseradish dumplings in a port, Seville orange and winter root casserole, with that very British dessert – sticky toffee pudding with vanilla ice cream – to finish. On draught are Adnams Bitter, Everards Tiger Best and Marston's Pedigree. A couple of wines are sold by the glass, the full list running to 14 bottles starting at £9.50. SAMPLE DISHES: mussels Parmesan £3.75; beef lasagne £6.25; roast vanilla strawberries with Grand Marnier syrup on hazelnut shortbread with Marsala cream £4.

Licensee David Johnson (Everards)
Open *Tue to Sat 11.30 to 2.30, 6.30 to 11, Sun 12 to 3, 7 to 10.30; bar food and restaurant Tue to Sun 12 (12.30 Sun) to 2, Tue to Sat 7 to 9*
Details *Children welcome   Car park   Garden and patio   No smoking in restaurant   Background music Dogs welcome   Delta, MasterCard, Switch, Visa*

COWDEN   Kent   map 3

Fountain Inn
Cowden TN8 7JG   TEL: (01342) 850528
from A264 take B2026 towards Edenbridge; Cowden first left

At its heart a true country local, the Fountain still retains its separate entrance doors to public and lounge bars. The former is heavy with dark beams and the flicker of a fruit machine, while the lounge has just four veneered tables accompanied by wooden chairs and a busy red carpet. What it may lack in modern-day refinement it certainly makes up for in genuine, workaday friendliness. Food reflects the atmosphere, with uncomplicated, honest dishes and ambition that's sensibly limited. The compact handwritten menu features parsnip, sage and potato soup, or smoked mackerel pâté to start, with such main courses as calf's liver with smoked bacon, mash and a red wine and balsamic jus, or ribeye steak with bubble and squeak and home-made chutney, alongside pub classics of home-cured ham, eggs and chunky chips and steak sandwich. Drinkers are catered for with Harveys Sussex Pale Ale and Best Bitter, plus a guest beer, while the short wine list features a handful by the glass. SAMPLE DISHES: smoked trout salad with a poached egg and basil dressing £5.25; black pudding and smoked bacon hash £9; sticky toffee pudding £4.50.

Licensees John and Maria E'Vanson (Harveys)
Open *11.30 to 3, 6 to 11.30, Sun 12 to 10.30; bar food Tue to Sun 11.30 to 3, Tue to Sat 6 to 11.30*
Details *Children welcome   Car park   Garden   Background and occasional live music   Dogs welcome Delta, MasterCard, Switch, Visa*

COXWOLD   North Yorkshire   map 9

▲ Fauconberg Arms
Coxwold YO61 4AD   TEL: (01347) 868214
WEBSITE: www.fauconbergarms.co.uk
off A19 7m S of Thirsk; pub on main street in middle of village

From the front, this building of golden sandstone and pantiles could be mistaken for a private house: it's a comfortably unflashy kind of place. Through the front door is a domestic-looking carpeted hallway leading to the lounge bar which – in season – is dominated by an enormous wood-burning fire; oak furniture, of various ages, stands on part-flagstoned floors under the beamed ceiling. Sandwiches and snacks are served in the bar at lunchtime, along with straight-and-true ideas like potted Wensleydale cheese with home-made chutney and oatcakes, or smoked chicken with curried mayonnaise, followed by, say, a trio of game sausages with mash and red onion marmalade, or baked cod with roast vegetables and tomato sauce. The specials board has a good choice of desserts. The restaurant boasts a more elaborate up-market menu along the lines of seared scallops with sweet chilli and lobster oil dressing, and chargrilled fillet steak with foie gras and Madeira jus, before desserts such as rhubarb crumble tartlet or hazelnut parfait with passion fruit and raspberry sauce. Sunday lunch brings on traditional roasts with all the trimmings. Guest ales from Black Sheep, Cropton and Daleside often make an appearance alongside regular John Smith's Bitter and Theakston Best Bitter. Four wines are sold by the glass from a serviceable and well-priced list of two dozen bins. SAMPLE DISHES: smoked salmon and prawn mousse £5; roast minted shoulder of lamb with rosemary, garlic and port gravy £9.50; pistachio brûlée £4.50.

Licensee Julie Gough (freehouse)
Open 11 to 3 (2.30 winter), 6.30 to 11, Sun 12 to 3, 6.30 to 10.30; bar food 12 to 2.30, 6.30 to 8.30, restaurant Wed to Sat 7 to 9.30, Sun 12 to 2.30
Details Children welcome   Car park   Patio   No smoking in restaurant   Background music   Dogs welcome exc in restaurant   MasterCard, Switch, Visa   Accommodation: 4 rooms, B&B £35 to £60

CRANK   Merseyside   map 7

Red Cat 🍇
8 Red Cat Lane, Crank WA11 8RU   TEL: (01744) 882422
follows signs for Crank from junction of A580 and A570

This 1900-ish stone terraced building sits on a junction at the north end of the village, its leaded windows and hanging baskets looking across fields to Billinge Hill, Merseyside's high point (587ft). Inside, it feels pretty much the village pub, but the kitchen's ambitions reach higher. There's a fairly standard bar menu (lasagne, ribeye steak, etc.), but go instead for the set meals (2 courses for £9) or check the lengthy specials board for starters like Bury black pudding with bacon and pepper sauce, or such mains as wild Lune salmon with poached samphire and sorrel sauce, or loin of free-range Bowland pork with asparagus and girolle sauce. Seasonal game has pleased reporters, too, and, if there is room for dessert, chocolate and raspberry torte with white chocolate ice cream could be just the thing. Theakston Best Bitter and Old Speckled Hen are on draught, but for wine-bibbers the real attractions come with corks in. Wine lists follow a similar pattern to the menus: a laminated bar list offers a good spread that mostly stays under £15, but it's more rewarding to browse the blackboard for excellent-value bin-end specials, or you can go for full immersion in the 500-plus fine wine list majoring on premium French, Italian and Californian offerings. Only three come by the glass but half-bottles add to the possibilities. SAMPLE DISHES: chicken liver pâté with Theakstons, apple chutney and toast £4; grilled duck breast with fresh raspberries and brandy and parsley jus £11; glazed figs with mascarpone and maple syrup £4.

Licensee Ian Martin (Pubmaster)
Open 12 to 11, Sun 12 to 10.30; bar food and restaurant Wed to Sat 12 to 2, 6 to 9.30, Sun 12 to 8
Details Children welcome   Car park   Wheelchair access (also WC)   Patio   No smoking in restaurant No music   Guide dogs only   Delta, MasterCard, Switch, Visa

CRAYKE   **North Yorkshire**   map 9

▲ Durham Ox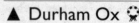

Westway, Crayke YO61 4TE   TEL: (01347) 821506
WEBSITE: www.thedurhamox.com
off A19, 2m from Easingwold

The Ox may look quite ordinary from the outside, but inside, it is civilised and smart and, with its low ceilings, panelled walls, a blazing fire and a genuinely warm welcome, retains the atmosphere of an old village pub. The bar area has sofas and low tables set informally for eating, but there is a separate restaurant and crisp white linen aplenty for those who prefer more formal surroundings. The menu, served throughout, is a neat combination of the classical and the traditional, with an evident high level of ambition. The scope of the cooking is wide enough to take in simple starters of ham and free-range egg terrine with bean salad and tomato chutney, and straightforward main courses like grilled fillet of salmon with creamed leeks and new potatoes alongside more ambitious dishes such as goose liver parfait with red onion chutney, and braised lamb shank with spicy chickpea ragoût. Local game, as in a casserole with herb dumplings and root vegetables, and grilled free-range chicken (from Loose Birds of Harome) also figure, and so does a selection of Yorkshire farmhouse cheeses. A decent selection of real ales includes Wells Bombardier Premium Bitter and Theakston Black Bull, and wines, organised by price, have a good selection under £20, along with pricier bottles. There is a bias towards France, but producers from elsewhere are by no means neglected; around ten wines are offered by the glass. SAMPLE DISHES: Cajun salmon and crab salad with chilli dressing £5.75; baked cod fillet with chorizo and provençale vegetables £13.50; Ampleforth apple crumble with clotted cream £5.

Licensee Michael Ibbotson (freehouse)
Open *Mon to Fri 12 to 3, 6 to 11, Sat 12 to 11, Sun 12 to 10.30; bar food and restaurant 12 to 2.30 (3 Sun), 6 to 9.30 (10 Sat, 8.30 Sun); open 11 to 2.30 25 Dec (no food)*
Details *Children welcome in bar eating area   Car park   Wheelchair access (not WC)   Garden and patio No smoking in restaurant   Occasional live or background music   No dogs   Amex, Delta, MasterCard, Switch, Visa   Accommodation: 8 rooms, B&B £50 to £120*

CRAZIES HILL   **Berkshire**   map 3

Horns

Crazies Hill RG10 8LY   TEL: (0118) 940 1416
off A4 at Kiln Green, 3m N of Twyford

The eponymous horns above the front door, and around the restaurant, give a clue to the building's past life as a Tudor hunting lodge. The interior has been remodelled but still retains the character and fabric of the old building through exposed beams and timbers, winter fires, and solid stripped-wood furniture, all offset by 'pastel Mediterranean-coloured walls'. Behind the bar is a cosy snug, while an eighteenth-century 'character-packed' barn (now the no-smoking restaurant) delivers a quarry-tiled floor, more exposed beams, timbers, brickwork, and hunting pictures and mementoes as well as stags' horns. The menu hits a traditional note with the odd journey to far-reaching shores, taking in Brie and cherry tomato tartlet with baby spinach salad, and tortilla chips with spicy salsa, melted cheese and sour cream among starters, with pork and leek sausages with spring onion mash, or sea bass fillet on a bed of roasted Mediterranean vegetables typical of main courses. Quality ingredients and good timing are uppermost, seen especially in a generous dish of pan-fried beef medallions on rösti with wild mushroom and red wine jus that made up one inspection meal. No surprises with puddings: they stay close to home with familiar, comfort-style offerings of bread-and-butter pudding and rhubarb crumble. Beers are from Brakspear, and nine wines are sold by the glass from a short but varied list. SAMPLE DISHES: tomato and basil soup £4.25; Barbary duck breast with stir-fried chilli noodles and mango salsa £14; treacle tart £4.25.

Licensee Andy Hearn (Brakspear)

Open 11.30 to 2.30 (3 Sat), 6 to 11, Sun 12 to 5; bar food and restaurant Mon to Sat 12 to 2 (2.15 Sat), 7 to 9.30, Sun 12 to 4; closed 25 Dec

Details Children welcome in family room and eating areas lunchtime only   Car park   Wheelchair access (also WC)   Garden   No smoking in restaurant   No music   Dogs welcome on a lead in bar area only   Delta, MasterCard, Switch, Visa

CRONDALL   Hampshire   map 3

Hampshire Arms ✿

Pankridge Street, Crondall GU10 5QU   TEL: (01252) 850418
WEBSITE: www.thehampshirearms.co.uk
from M3 junction 5 take A287 towards Farnham; turn left opposite petrol station and continue approx 3m

It's all change at this 250-year-old pub. Refurbishment has introduced a more modern note, updating the restaurant and giving it a separate entrance, and shoehorning in a lounge and brasserie-cum-deli. The pubby roots are apparent in a small locals' bar that has retained its regular dark wood furniture and open winter fire, and as this is a Greene King pub, Abbot Ale and IPA, plus a guest beer, are on handpump. Paul Morgan's cooking buzzes with enthusiasm, and his modern dishes are well presented, robust and generous, with dinner even including freebies (canapies, amuse bouche and pre-dessert), and there can be a lot going on the plate – sea bass on fennel, celery and leeks braised in orange and served with an open ravioli of scallop and crayfish mousse, accompanied by lobster oil and garnished with clams, for example. Lunch is a more straightforward affair, with things like liver and bacon with black pudding, bubble and squeak and French fried onions, or pesto chicken with sun-dried tomato risotto and rocket salad. The deli and brasserie had not yet opened when we inspected, but the deli will sell pickles, hams and salami as well as pre-prepared dishes to take way; the brasserie is expected to offer simple steaks and meats to order. An enterprising and reasonably priced wine list globe-trots, though has a soft spot for France. Around ten wines are served by the glass from £3.25. SAMPLE DISHES: game terrine with piccalilli chutney £6.25; seared tuna, baby roasted tomatoes, marinated green beans with a Mediterranean poached egg £17; passion-fruit parfait with mango, pineapple and chilli salsa and a mango cream £6.

Licensee Paul Morgan (Greene King)

Open 11 to 3.30, 5.30 to 11.30, Sun 12 to 10.30; bar food and restaurant 12 to 2, 7 to 9.30

Details Children welcome in eating areas   Car park   Wheelchair access (also WC)   Garden   No smoking in dining room   Background music   Dogs welcome in public bar   Amex, Delta, MasterCard, Switch, Visa

CROSLAND HILL　　West Yorkshire　　　　map 8

Sands House

Blackmoorfoot Road, Crosland Hill HD4 7AE　TEL: (01484) 654478
off A62, 2m SW of Huddersfield town centre

Veteran traffic lights, telephone boxes and the like in the children's play area should prepare you for the interior of this old stone pub on the outskirts of Huddersfield, where town and moorland meet. The place is owned by the Unique Pub Company, a name to some extent justified by the miscellaneous collection of clocks inside hanging from the ceilings and propped on shelves. It's a busy place, popular with local drinkers as much as those out for a celebratory meal; the keynote is robust, hearty food, but that doesn't exclude some imaginative touches on the menu. Start perhaps with duck spring roll in ginger dressing, or curried parsnip soup, and continue with pork fillet in creamy pepper sauce, or beef Wellington in red wine sauce, both served with plenty of fresh vegetables. Those with old-fashioned Yorkshire appetites may be able to cope with hot chocolate fudge cake, or bread-and-butter pudding. Old Speckled Hen, Boddingtons Bitter, John Smith's, Tetley Bitter, Courage Directors and a guest ale are all available. Five wines come by the glass. SAMPLE DISHES: salmon, tuna and prawn fishcakes £4.75; chicken breast stuffed with Camembert £8; treacle sponge £3.25.

Licensee Bob Buckley (Unique Pub Company)
Open *Mon to Sat 11.30 to 11, Sun 12 to 10.30; bar food and restaurant 11.30 to 9.30*
Details *Children welcome in bar eating area　Car park　Garden　No smoking in dining room　Background music　No dogs　Amex, Delta, Diners, MasterCard, Switch, Visa*

CROSTHWAITE　　Cumbria　　　　map 8

▲ Punch Bowl Inn 😕 😕

Crosthwaite LA8 8HR　TEL: (015395) 68237
WEBSITE: www.punchbowl.fsnet.co.uk
off A5074, 3m S of Windermere

This well-established seventeenth-century southern Lakeland inn is very much an upmarket dining pub; 'more of a restaurant with a bar' mused one reporter, who found the dining room full (bookings preferred), while the spacious, multi-level bar area was empty. But at heart the Punch Bowl remains a pub, with low ceilings, beams, log fires, and ales from Black Sheep (Best Bitter, Special Ale and Riggwelter), as well as Coniston Bluebird Bitter. In the kitchen, Steven Doherty heads straight for the cosmopolitan world of baked goats' cheese on filo with roast beetroot, crumbled Roquefort and walnut oil dressing, and roast breast of duck on spring onion mash with Chinese-style hoisin and oyster mushroom sauce. Elsewhere on the à la carte menu there are more traditional encounters along the lines of a 'perfect' fell-bred ribeye steak served with a 'good classic' pepper sauce, while on the good-value set two- or three-course lunch might be cream of wild mushroom soup, roast chicken with apple, sage and onion stuffing and pork and chive sausage, and lemon tart. Puddings range from Tunisian-style orange cake to soft chocolate and ginger tart. With 20 wines by the glass to choose from on the succinct and imaginative wine list, with the same number by the litre and half-litre, diners will find ample choice for matching wine with food. Eating on the patio, with views over the Lyth Valley, is pleasant in warm weather. SAMPLE DISHES: Cullen skink £5.50; boned and rolled stuffed saddle of rabbit with tomato and tarragon jus £14; steamed white chocolate pudding with anglaise and poached damsons £4.50.

Licensee Marjorie Doherty (freehouse)
Open 11 to 11, Sun 12 to 10.30; bar food and restaurant Tue to Sun 12 to 2, Tue to Sat 6 to 9; closed 4 weeks Nov to Dec, 25 Dec
Details Children welcome   Car park   Wheelchair access (not WC)   Patio   No smoking in restaurant
No music   Guide dogs only   MasterCard, Switch, Visa   Accommodation: 3 rooms, B&B £37.50 to £70

CROWCOMBE   Somerset   map 2

▲ Carew Arms   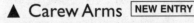 NEW ENTRY

Crowcombe TA4 4AD   TEL: (01984) 618631
WEBSITE: www.thecarewarms.co.uk
Crowcombe signposted off A358 between Taunton and Minehead

Crowcombe is a sleepy village tucked below the Quantock Hills and offers great walks and views in equal proportions. Until quite recently the Carew Arms was a run-down village local, but it is an example of what an injection of cash, big plans and plenty of enthusiasm can do. The classic front bar has changed little, its laid-back, relaxed atmosphere enhanced by flagstones, scrubbed tables, rustic benches and a wood-burning fire, and complemented by a hatchway-style bar dispensing tiptop Exmoor Ale alongside guests like Butcombe Gold or Otter Ale. At the back, the old skittle alley has been transformed into a long restaurant with French doors leading on to a terrace. Here, good use is made of local produce in dishes that acknowledge pub favourites (such as gammon, egg and chips), especially at lunchtimes when the menu is available in the bar. But there are far more promising things to be had: starters of butterflied sardines coated in Parmesan breadcrumbs, for example, or seared king scallops with orange, vanilla and cardamom sauce, and main courses of chicken and pea risotto, and sautéed kidneys en croûte with a creamy mustard sauce. Bread-and-butter or treacle pudding couldn't be a more traditional way to finish. Eight wines by the glass are £2.75 and £2.95. SAMPLE DISHES: chicken ravioli with truffle cream dressing £5.50; homemade faggots with mash and Madeira gravy £8.50; passion-fruit tart £4.25.

Licensee R.A. Ambrose (freehouse)
Open 11 to 4, 6 to 11 (summer Sat and Sun 11 to 11); bar food and restaurant all week 12 to 2.15, Mon to Sat 6.45 to 10
Details Children welcome in restaurant   Car park   Wheelchair access (not WC)   Garden and patio
No smoking in restaurant   Occasional live or background music   Dogs welcome exc in restaurant
MasterCard, Switch, Visa   Accommodation: 5 rooms, B&B £47 to £110

CUDDINGTON   Buckinghamshire   map 2

Crown

Aylesbury Road, Cuddington HP18 0BB   TEL: (01844) 292222
WEBSITE: www.thecrowncuddington.co.uk
off A418, 4½m W of Aylesbury

'Cuddington looks unspoilt and very tidy: lots of thatched roofs, an impressive church, and a sign opposite the white-painted pub – also thatched – that says "Buckinghamshire's best-kept village",' notes a reporter. The Crown is a popular venue for food and drink. The three interconnecting dining areas are filled with fairly close-set wooden tables, with mirrors and prints on the walls, creating a comfortable, cosy, cheerful atmosphere. The printed menu lists the usual sandwiches and salads as well as beer-battered fish, chips and mushy peas, and more interesting dishes like hot-smoked salmon with creamed horseradish sauce, and calf's liver with crispy pancetta and red wine jus, while a blackboard gives the daily specials. There's been praise for seared scallops with chilli jam and crème fraîche as well as a Sunday lunch special of roast beef with 'first-class' gravy and Yorkshire pudding. Dessert could be hot pecan pie with vanilla ice cream or ginger sponge with golden syrup and custard. As this is a Fuller's house, expect London Pride on draught alongside the brewery's seasonal Summer Ale or Jack Frost, plus guests such as Adnams Bitter. The wine list of 20-odd bottles from £10.95 to £35 includes six by the glass. SAMPLE DISHES: tomato, basil and mozzarella tartlet £6; fillet of cod in a herb crust £10.50; apple and cinnamon flan £4.50.

Licensee David Berry (Fuller's)

Open *12 to 3, 6 to 11, Sun 12 to 10.30; bar food and restaurant 12 to 2, 6.30 to 9.30, Sun 12 to 8*

Details *Children welcome   Car park   Wheelchair access (also WC)   Garden and patio   No-smoking area in restaurant   Background music   Guide dogs only   Delta, MasterCard, Switch, Visa*

CULMSTOCK   Devon   map 2

▲ Culm Valley Inn 🍺 🍇

Culmstock EX15 3JJ   TEL: (01884) 840354
about 2m off A38 W of Wellington

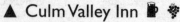

Once a railway hotel (the track ran through what is now the car park), this highly individual inn stands on the edge of the village by the stone bridge over the River Culm, deep in the Blackdown Hills. If you like walking and enjoy real ale, it's a must. Up to eight regularly changing beers from independent West Country breweries are generally in stock, such as Cotleigh Tawny, O'Hanlon's Wheat and Glastonbury Hedgemonkey – but that's only part of the story. You can also sample Burrow Hill cider and Somerset cider brandy from Julian Temperley, as well as home-made sloe vodka. Owners Richard and Lucy Hartley have left well alone as regards the interior, which has a truly relaxed feel, with its dim lighting, stripped bar, books, piano and unmatching tables. By contrast, the modern dining area to the rear is done out in 'Ikea style', with an open kitchen. The food suits the pub perfectly. What you get is an eclectic choice of regularly changing dishes at different prices to suit virtually all appetites and pockets; ingredients (including organic produce where possible) are true to the region, but the inspiration is global. Brill with quince aïoli, squid braised in olive oil with spinach, tomato and 'a bit of chilli', Lebanese 'fatayer' (yeast dough stuffed with roasted squash, feta and pine nuts) or 'chitarnee' (free-range chicken breast 'as cooked by Indian Jews in Baghdad') are typical of the kitchen's style. A plate of Spanish tapas makes a palate-tingling starter, and you might finish with, say, chocolate marquise or Italian lemon tart. Wines are an enjoyable jumble of good New World names and little-known French producers imported by Richard Hartley and his brother. Prices are good, there are mature vintages to be had and everything comes by the glass. SAMPLE DISHES: provençale fish soup £6; pheasant breast with chestnuts, pancetta, mace and tomato £9; treacle and lemon tart £4.

Licensees Richard and Lucy Hartley (freehouse)

Open *12 to 3, 6 to 11, Sun 12 to 10.30; bar food and restaurant all week 12 to 2, Mon to Sat 7 to 9; closed 25 Dec; may open all day in good weather in summer*

Details *Children welcome   Car park   Wheelchair access (not WC)   Garden   Occasional live music   Dogs welcome   No cards   Accommodation: 3 rooms, B&B £40 to £60*

DACRE BANKS   North Yorkshire   map 8

▲ Royal Oak

Oak Lane, Dacre Banks HG3 4EN   TEL: (01423) 780200
WEBSITE: www.theroyaloak.uk.com
from B6165 Ripley to Pateley Bridge road, turn S onto B6165 at Summerbridge; pub is ½m on left

This good, solid Yorkshire inn dates from 1752, its intricately interlinked interior
oozing character and warmth. There are several beamed rooms, some wood-panelled,
some cream-washed, some stone-flagged (one has a pool table, another a wood fire).
One bar serves them all with well-kept beers from local brewers, such as Rudgate,
Viking and Yorkshire Dales bitter, and Old Dacre Ale (specially brewed for the Royal
Oak). Accompany these with salads, sandwiches, or giant Yorkshire puddings filled
with the likes of beef chilli or sausage and onion gravy; alternatively you can tackle a
full meal – starting perhaps with devilled kidneys or baked sardines, then on to rabbit,
ham and mushroom pie, or honey-roast Nidderdale pheasant in a balsamic and
caramelised onion sauce. It's sheep country round here, so local lamb should be a
good choice too, but there's also plenty for fish-fans (gratin of whole lemon sole,
perhaps), and vegetarians are not forgotten. Sweets, on a blackboard, might include
lemon tart or summer pudding. Wines, mostly non-French and under £20, start with
six house wines (also available by the glass) at £10. There's a terrace and a pétanque
piste in front, and a terrace and a small garden behind surveys the gentle, comfortable
contours of Nidderdale. SAMPLE DISHES: chicken and Stilton pancake £5.50; traditional lamb hotpot £8; chocolate cookie cake £3.50.

Licensee Stephen Cock (freehouse)
Open *11.30 to 3, 5 to 11, Sun 12 to 3, 7 to 10.30; bar food 12 to 2, 6.30 to 9, Sun 12 to 2.30, 7 to 9;
closed 25 Dec*
Details *Children welcome in bar eating area   Car park   Wheelchair access (also WC)   Garden and patio
No-smoking area in bar, no smoking in dining room   Background music   Guide dogs only   Delta, MasterCard,
Switch, Visa   Accommodation: 3 rooms, B&B £30 to £60*

DARGATE   Kent   map 3

Dove

Plum Pudding Lane, Dargate ME13 9HB   TEL: (01227) 751360
signposted off A299, 4m SW of Whitstable

The Dove is a sturdy brick building at a three-way road junction at the centre of a
picture-postcard village. Inside, the look is fresh, simple and well kept: a series of
small opened-up rooms lead off one another, with walls painted a pale lemony yellow
or covered with honey-coloured pine panelling, floors are bare boards, tables
scrubbed deal, and chairs plain kitchen, with candles, flowers, and an open fire. Over
the years, Nigel Morris has built up a solid local reputation for producing high-class
pub food. At lunchtime you can get baguettes not only filled with ham and salad but
also with minute steak and glazed onions, an outstanding warm salad of marinated
chicken scented with mint, and excellent-value specials such as cassoulet. The printed
carte extends the focus on dishes with a cosmopolitan modern flavour: baked wild
mushroom and Bayonne ham tart, and whole pan-fried crevettes flavoured with pickled ginger and herbs to start, followed by grilled wild sea bass with confit of fennel
and sweet pepper, or roast breast of duck on a bed of tapenade-flavoured crushed

potatoes. A first-class hot chocolate pudding gets the thumbs up, or there could be British and Irish cheeses as an alternative to dessert. This being a Shepherd Neame house, Master Brew Bitter is on tap, and six wines are served by the glass. SAMPLE DISHES: sardines grilled with garlic and olive oil £5.25; roast crown of local pheasant on braised red cabbage £14.25; orange and passion-fruit crème brûlée £5.

Licensees Nigel and Bridget Morris (Shepherd Neame)
Open *Tue to Sat 12 to 3, 6 to 11, Sun 12 to 3, 7 to 10.30; bar food Tue to Sun 12 to 2, Wed to Sat 7 to 9*
Details *Children welcome in family room Car park Garden and patio No music Dogs welcome Delta, MasterCard, Switch, Visa*

DARTINGTON Devon map 1

▲ White Hart ☺ NEW ENTRY

Dartington Hall, Dartington TQ9 6EL TEL: (01803) 847111
from A384 follow signs for Dartington and then to Dartington Hall

'The setting must be unique,' mused a reporter. 'Where else would you find a pub set bang in the centre of a 1,000-acre estate that incorporates 28 acres of magnificent gardens, a college of art, an international summer school, and a centre for concerts, films, lectures and theatre?' On top of all this, the White Hart is housed in the former kitchens of the fourteenth-century Dartington Hall, described by Nikolaus Pevsner as 'the most spectacular domestic survival of late-medieval England'. The interior blends historical features with contemporary light oak furnishings, modern art and subtle lighting and has a tremendous buzz, especially in the evenings when lecturers, students, musicians, artists and audiences are cheerfully mixed. Above-average food is built around local, free-range and organic ingredients with the menu acknowledging producers: Cheddar cheese and air-dried ham from Denhay Farms, local cheeses from Ticklemore Cheese Shop in Totnes, Brixham fish, Dart sea trout, and beef and lamb from Chris McCabe of Totnes. Local game, smoked bacon and pistachio terrine with fruit chutney, or mussels steamed with white wine, shallot and parsley, could open a meal that goes on to Devon lamb casseroled Moroccan-style, or pan-fried pigeon breast with root vegetable purée and bacon and red wine sauce, with bitter chocolate tart to finish. Local ales on handpump include Princetown Dartmoor IPA and White Hart Ale, and there's also local Luscombe cider. The short wine list features a couple of English wines and around ten by the glass. SAMPLE DISHES: grilled goats' cheese with beetroot and walnut salad £5.25; Dartington beef burger with melted Cheddar and caramelised onions £6; crème brûlée £4.

Licensees Adam Powell, Nick Edwards and Rob Gould (freehouse)
Open *11 to 11, Sun 12 to 10.30; bar food and restaurant 12 to 2, 6 to 9*
Details *Children welcome in restaurant Car park Wheelchair access (also WC) Garden and patio No smoking in restaurant Occasional live or background music No dogs Delta, MasterCard, Switch, Visa Accommodation: 51 rooms, B&B £75 to £150*

▲ *indicates where a pub offers accommodation. At the end of the entry information is given on the number of rooms available and a price range, indicating the cost of a single room or single occupancy to that for a room with two people sharing.*

DEDHAM   Essex   map 3

▲ Sun Inn    NEW ENTRY

High Street, Dedham CO7 6DF   TEL: (01206) 323351
WEBSITE: www.thesuninndedham.com
follow Dedham signposts from A12 at Stratford St Mary N of Colchester

London gastro-pub owner Piers Baker moved out of town to take over and refurbish this fifteenth-century coaching inn deep in the heart of Constable country. The building still has its quota of old black timbers, although the interior is now done out in primrose-yellow, with ceiling spotlights and walls covered with paintings and photographs (many for sale). There are newspapers to read, board games to play and plenty of space outside when the weather permits. The mood is congenial, relaxed and family-friendly, with jazz and Latin American background music adding to the atmosphere. As regards food, the kitchen draws heavily on Italian, Spanish and Moroccan cuisine for a daily-changing menu that shows a keen eye for local ingredients, including rare breeds. Meals begin with a basket of warm bread and olive oil before starters such as linguine al' amatriciana or calf's liver risotto with sage, lemon, garlic and Parmesan. Elaborately conceived main courses might include pheasant confit with star anise and cinnamon, Puy lentils, peppers and fig compote, or baked cod fillet with salsa fresca, braised fennel and baby carrots with green beans, white wine, cumin and ginger. At lunchtime you can also get sandwiches on baked ciabatta. Cheeses are generally French, and the choice of desserts might include Mrs Smith's crème caramel with orange and almond biscotti. East Anglian breweries are admirably represented on the handpumps, with Adnams Broadside, Earl Soham Victoria Bitter and perhaps Crouch Vale Essex Blond lining up alongside Timothy Taylor Landlord. The small but perfectly formed wine list is sourced from ambitious modern producers and includes a dozen by the glass from £2.50. SAMPLE DISHES: field mushroom soup with rosemary and truffle oil £4; baked fillet of salmon with parsley rice and yoghurt salsa £9.50; mixed melon salad with ice cream £4.

Licensee Piers Baker (freehouse)
Open 12 (11 summer) to 11, Sun 12 to 10.30; bar food 12 to 2.30 (3 Sat and Sun), 7 to 9.30 (10 Fri and Sat); closed Sun evenings winter, 25 and 26 Dec
Details Children welcome   Car park   Garden and patio   No-smoking area in bar, no smoking in eating area
Background music   Dogs welcome   MasterCard, Switch, Visa   Accommodation: 4 rooms, B&B £55 to £120

DIDMARTON   Gloucestershire   map 2

▲ Kings Arms Inn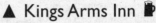

The Street, Didmarton GL9 1DT   TEL: (01454) 238245
on A433 SW of Tetbury

This seventeenth-century Cotswolds coaching inn is on a busy thoroughfare, but there's a lovingly tended garden, with lawns, dry-stone walls, apple trees, and a boules pitch at the back. It's an attractive pub: the bars are surprisingly unpretentious, with a real fire and a friendly atmosphere, and there's a separate no-smoking restaurant. The menu here, also available in the bar, is an ambitious choice that could open with home-cured gravad lax with warm blinis, herb salad, and sweet Dijon mustard dressing, or warm goats' cheese and home-smoked chicken tart with basil oil dressing. Main courses could range from chump of Cornish lamb with mint and pea risotto and a 'very good' tomato and balsamic dressing to a special of fillet of red mullet with buttered green vegetables, creamed potato and sauce vierge, followed by a pavlova of 'fudgy brown sugar meringues' with spicy poached pineapple or sticky toffee pudding for which they are evidently renowned. A blackboard of specials extends the range even further, and home-made, very fresh bread is worth a separate mention. Though this is principally a dining pub, beers are a strong suit, regular Uley Bitter, Butcombe Bitter and Gold being supplemented by changing guests. Nine wines come by the glass from a list of 30-odd bottles, starting at £10.95. SAMPLE DISHES: salad of tea-smoked chicken suprême with Moroccan potato salad and smoked paprika aïoli £5.75; roast fillet of sea bass with tarragon beurre blanc £14; glazed pistachio brûlée topped with roast strawberries £5.

Licensees Nigel Pushman and Zoe Coombs (freehouse)
Open Mon to Thur 11 to 3, 6 to 11, Fri and Sat 11 to 11, Sun 12 to 10.30; bar food and restaurant 12 to 2 (2.30 Sat and Sun), 7 to 9.30 (9 Sun)
Details Children welcome   Car park   Garden   No smoking in restaurant   No music   Dogs welcome exc in restaurant and front bar   Delta, MasterCard, Switch, Visa   Accommodation: 4 rooms, B&B £45 to £80

DODDISCOMBSLEIGH   Devon

map 1

▲ Nobody Inn 🕸 🍺 🌿

Doddiscombsleigh EX6 7PS   TEL: (01647) 252394
WEBSITE: www.thenobodyinn.co.uk
3m W of A38, Haldon Racecourse exit

'Well worth the . . . drive through narrow lanes,' exclaimed one reporter, who found Nick Borst-Smith's 'wonderful' sixteenth-century thatched inn 'consistently good in every department': good food, magnificent West Country cheeses, excellent wines and whiskies, plus 'a peaceful night's sleep in a homely bedroom'. Indeed, wines are a serious business here, with 20-plus by the glass drawn from an 800-strong list that is probably unrivalled by any other in the Guide, not just for range but for value too. Mark-ups to drink 'inn' are minimal and quality is high across the board. Some 250 whiskies of various descriptions are kept, too. Beer lovers will find fine cask-conditioned ales such as the proprietary Nobody's Bitter from Branscombe Vale, and Teign Valley Tipple; there's also cider from Branscombe Farm and Heron Valley. The dark, beamed interior is filled with ancient settles, antique tables, hunting prints, and horse brasses and copper pots decorating the glowing inglenook fireplace. Behind a partition is a more formal restaurant area with a separate menu. Seasonal bar food focuses on simple country cooking, whether a classic lunchtime countryman's lunch of local Cheddar and blue cheese (from a selection of around 40 local cheeses), or heartier pot-roast pheasant with game and juniper sauce, followed perhaps by stem ginger pudding with ginger sauce. There's a more contemporary approach in the restaurant, where roasted squash and nutmeg soup, silverside of veal with a ratatouille of caramelised onion, mushrooms, pepper and chicory, and bitter chocolate, coffee and cardamom cake are typical. SAMPLE DISHES: mushroom risotto £4.50; chunky lamb casserole £9; baked apple with mixed fruit and brandy £4.50.

Licensee Nick Borst-Smith (freehouse)
Open 12 to 2.30, 6 to 11, Sun 12 to 3, 6 to 10.30; bar food 12 to 2, 7 to 10; restaurant Tue to Sat 7.30 to 9; closed 25, 26 and 31 Dec, 1 Jan
Details No children   Car park   Patio   No smoking in restaurant   No music   Guide dogs only   Amex, Delta, MasterCard, Switch, Visa   Accommodation: 7 rooms, B&B £23 to £70

DONHEAD ST ANDREW Wiltshire map 2

Forester ✿ NEW ENTRY

Lower Street, Donhead St Andrew SP7 9EE TEL: (01747) 828038
pub signposted off A30 4m E of Shaftesbury

Down a narrow village lane lined with smart stone houses and quaint thatched cottages stands the smartly thatched, fourteenth-century Forester, gable end on to the lane. 'You can see it has been lovingly attended to,' noted a visitor, taken by the smart new signs, neat side terrace with chunky benches, and landscaped garden. The interior lives up to expectations, with a big wood-floored and beamed bar on two levels, warm and welcoming, with a blazing log fire in the inglenook, and a stylish restaurant that has plenty of exposed stone and terracotta-coloured half-panelled walls with work by local artists. Food is taken seriously here, and the constantly changing blackboard menu shows a kitchen that revels in its modern approach. Tagliatelle with artichokes, oyster mushrooms, tomatoes and cream sauce, for example, has been described as 'one of the best vegetarian pasta dishes tasted'. Other good things include starters like a pan-fried crab cake with piri-piri or butternut squash and radicchio risotto with chilli, herbs and crème fraîche, and main courses of chargrilled beef fillet with rösti, rocket, spinach and Madeira, or pan-fried medallions of monkfish with crab risotto and bouillabaisse sauce. Real ales include Wadworth 6X, Bass and Ringwood Best Bitter, and around ten wines are served by the glass. SAMPLE DISHES: cream of asparagus soup £3.50; smoked haddock and leek fishcakes with coriander cream £10.50; apricot and honey crème brûlée £4.25.

Licensee Darren Morris (freehouse)
Open *12 to 3, 6.30 to 11, Sun 12 to 3, 7 to 10.30; bar food and restaurant 12 to 2, 7 to 9.30*
Details *Children welcome Car park Wheelchair access (not WC) Garden and patio No smoking in restaurant No music Dogs welcome in main bar only MasterCard, Switch, Visa*

DOWNHAM Lancashire map 8

Assheton Arms

Downham BB7 4BJ TEL: (01200) 441227
WEBSITE: www.assheton-arms.co.uk
3m NE of Clitheroe; turn off A59 for Chatburn, thence follow sign to Downham

More hamlet than village, Downham comprises a few houses, post office and phone box, plus this popular local pub on a rise just opposite the church. Outside are tables for summer drinking; inside is a rambling, low-ceilinged bar with horse brasses and copper pots on the walls, solid oak tables and wing-back settles. Boddingtons Bitter and Marston's Pedigree are on handpump and they also dispense Hoegaarden beer, while everything on the highly affordable list of 18 wines is available by the glass (from £2.50). An extensive printed menu (including sandwiches and children's dishes) is supplemented by an impressive choice of blackboard specials. Fish is well represented, from starters of devilled whitebait, or shell-on prawns and garlic mayonnaise, to main dishes ranging from grilled fillet of plaice with parsley butter to poached salmon fillet in prawn and cucumber sauce. Vegetarians are offered things like Italian-style courgettes with pesto and mozzarella, while resolute carnivores could opt for a trio of lamb · cutlets, a peppered sirloin steak, or venison, bacon and cranberry casserole. Home-made puddings complete the picture. SAMPLE DISHES: potted Morecambe Bay shrimps £5.25; chicken and mushroom pie £7.50; jam roly-poly £4.

Licensees David and Wendy Busby (Enterprise Inns)
Open *12 to 3, 7 to 11, Sun summer 12 to 11; bar food 12 to 2, 7 to 10, Sun winter 12 to 2.30, 7 to 10, summer 12 to 10; closed 1st week Jan*
Details *Children welcome   Car park   Wheelchair access (also WC)   Patio   No-smoking area in bar Background music   Well-behaved dogs welcome   Amex, Delta, MasterCard, Switch, Visa*

DREWSTEIGNTON   Devon   map 1

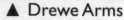 Drewe Arms

Drewsteignton EX6 6QN   TEL: (01647) 281224
2m S of A30, 8m W of Exeter

The long, low, thatched pub stands next to the church in a pretty village high above the wooded slopes of the Teign Valley. It's 'a gem of a rural pub', once totally in a time warp, where Britain's longest-serving landlady, Mabel Mudge, clocked up 75 years before retiring in 1996, aged 99. Thanks to the enthusiasm of Colin and Janice Sparks, everything remains simple and unspoilt, from the classic front bar to a room opposite, rarely used in Mabel's days, furnished with sturdy pine tables, settles and chairs, with photographs of Mabel and old characters who used to frequent the place, and a good log fire. Mabel's Kitchen is a small restaurant named in her memory, with her old cooking range, dresser and cupboards intact. A blackboard in the flagged passageway is a regularly changing slate of country-style dishes that might include corned beef hash, steak and kidney pie in a herb pastry crust, pistachio- and almond-stuffed pheasant with juniper sauce, and sea bass on leek gratin. At lunchtime there are hearty soups, sandwiches and ploughman's, desserts are old favourites such as chocolate sponge pudding or treacle sponge, and Tuesday evening is steak night. Real ales include Bass and Gale's HSB, and also on draught is local farm cider. The National Trust's Castle Drogo, which looks medieval but was built in the early twentieth century, is nearby. SAMPLE DISHES: sausages on bubble and squeak with chutney £8; baked smoked haddock with Stilton and a poached egg £10; apricot and vanilla rice pudding £4.

Licensees Colin and Janice Sparks (Whitbread)
Open *11 to 3 (2.30 winter), 6 to 11, Sun 12 to 3, 7 to 10.30; bar food and restaurant 12 to 2.30, 6.30 to 9.30*
Details *Children welcome in eating areas   Wheelchair access (also WC)   Garden and patio   No smoking in restaurant   No music   Dogs welcome in bar only   Delta, MasterCard, Switch, Visa   Accommodation: 3 rooms, B&B £60 (double room)*

DUNSTAN   Northumberland   map 10

Cottage Inn

Dunstan NE66 3SZ   TEL: (01665) 576658
WEBSITE: www.cottageinnhotel.co.uk

Dunstan is a short distance from the sea and from the fishing village of Craster, so it's no surprise that Craster crab makes an appearance on menus at this old stone inn set in large gardens. But there are also meaty main courses such as braised steak cooked with a sauce of tomatoes, paprika, caraway garlic and peppers, sitting alongside fishy ones like poached salmon served with lime sauce and pickled sea grass, while for vegetarians there's spinach and ricotta cannelloni. Snacks and sandwiches are also available. Real ales might include local Wylam Bitter or Belhaven Best, and the short wine list features four house wines at £8.95 plus ten or so 'specials' at £10.75 a bottle, £2.75 a glass. Dining is spread over several areas, all with a traditional feel, with lots of beams, wood panelling, leaded glass and brick fireplaces – as well as the bar, covered patio, and no-smoking conservatory, there is the Harry Hotspur restaurant, which is decorated with murals depicting the local hero. SAMPLE DISHES: Craster crab soup £4.25; breast of pheasant £10.75; summer pudding with cream £4.

Licensee Zoe Finlay (freehouse)
Open 11 to 11; bar food and restaurant 12 to 2.30, 6 (7 Sun) to 9.30
Details Children welcome   Car park   Wheelchair access (also WC)   Garden and patio   No smoking in conservatory and restaurant before 9pm   Live or background music; jukebox   Guide dogs only   Delta, MasterCard, Switch, Visa   Accommodation: 10 rooms, B&B £25 to £69

EARLS COLNE   Essex   map 3

Carved Angel

Upper Holt Street, Earls Colne CO6 2PG   TEL: (01787) 222330
WEBSITE: www.carvedangel.com
on A1124 between Halstead and Colchester

The cream-painted fifteenth-century pub on a bend in the main road running through the pleasantly unspoilt village of Earls Colne looks unassuming, but that all changes once inside. A stylish look introduces bright contemporary colours, modern prints and plenty of light and space, only the ceiling timbers giving a sign as to the real age of the building. A few sofas are among the wooden tables, but this is primarily a dining pub. That said, real ale fans will be pleased to note that Greene King IPA, Adnams Bitter and a guest beer – say, one from local Mighty Oak Brewery – are dispensed at the bar. Food is listed on blackboards, and the choice is plentiful and imaginative: perhaps onion fondue topped with a poached egg and glazed cheese sauce to start, followed by fillet of sea trout on a crisp risotto cake with saffron sauce, or a traditional Cumberland sausage curl with herb mash and red wine jus; a separate sandwich menu is available for lunch. Desserts are equally appealing: say, pear and almond tart with crème fraîche, or chocolate marquise with sauce anglaise. The short wine list is not the cheapest around, offering limited choice under £15, although blackboards list better-value options, and there are around 14 by the glass. SAMPLE DISHES: red onion tarte Tatin with chive sour cream £4.75; lamb rump with provençale sauce £14; passion-fruit bavarois with raspberry coulis £4.50.

Licensees Melissa and Michael Deckers (freehouse)
Open 11.30 to 3, 6.30 to 11, Sun 12 to 3.30, 6.30 to 10.30; bar food 12 to 2 (2.30 Fri to Sun), 7 to 9 (10 Fri and Sat); closed 26 Dec, 1 Jan
Details Children welcome in games room and eating area   Car park   Wheelchair access (not WC)   Garden and patio   No-smoking area in bar   Background music   Guide dogs only   Delta, MasterCard, Switch, Visa

Licensing hours and bar food times are based on information supplied by each establishment and are correct at the time of going to press. It is advisable to check these, however, before making a lengthy journey as they are often subject to change, especially in winter months.

▲ Mole and Chicken

Easington HP18 9EY   TEL: (01844) 208387
WEBSITE: www.moleandchicken.co.uk
from M40 junction 7 take A329 towards Aylesbury; at Thame take B4011 to Long Crendon; turn right into Carters Lane opposite Chandos Arms and follow signs to Easington

Splendid views of surrounding countryside are among the attractions of this nineteenth century inn, and the terraced garden makes the most of the setting. Originally the village store and later a pub known as the Rising Sun, it takes its unusual current name from the nicknames of a pair of previous owners and these days is styled as a 'country restaurant', with service by well-drilled, uniformed young staff. Flagstone floors, log fires, beamed ceilings and a bar counter where you can sit and sup hand-pulled ales (Hook Norton Bitter, Vale Best Bitter and Fuller's London Pride) give it the look of a traditional pub, but eating is the main business, and booking is advised. Blackboard menus offer a good mix of modern and traditional flavours in dishes such as roast pig cheeks on leek and potato mash with red wine, plum and shallot sauce; fried sea bass with roast vegetables and sun-dried tomato; and butternut squash and spinach risotto with nutmeg and basil oil. Desserts range from banoffi pie to tiramisù. Over 40 malt whiskies are available, and a global list of 30 wines includes five by the glass. SAMPLE DISHES: chicken breast satay £6; baked cod fillet with mussels, saffron and white wine £14; triple chocolate marbled parfait £5.

Licensee Shane Ellis (freehouse)
Open 12 to 2.30, 6 to 11, Sun 12 to 10.30; bar food 12 to 2, 7 to 9.30
Details Children welcome   Car park   Wheelchair access (not WC)   Garden   Background music   No dogs
Amex, Delta, MasterCard, Switch, Visa   Accommodation: 5 rooms, B&B £50 to £65

▲ Horse & Groom NEW ENTRY

East Ashling PO18 9AX   TEL: (01243) 575339
WEBSITE: www.horseandgroom.co.uk
on B2178 a few miles NW of Chichester

The Horse & Groom, which dates from the seventeenth century, is, according to a reporter, 'one of those rare, unpretentious pubs, a winter-warming one with two of the cosiest, simple bars to be found anywhere in the area'. One of the bars comes complete with a 'black iron monster' of a stove, while the other has a fireplace. In both, you can open the drawers of any scrubbed pine table and unearth a cribbage board or a pack of cards – 'it's that kind of pub'. Ploughman's, jacket potatoes, sandwiches and things with chips, such as scampi, are offered on the printed menu, but the best stuff is listed on the huge blackboard. Braised pheasant with juniper and red wine has been heartily endorsed, as has calf's liver with bacon and forestière sauce; chicken, steaks, and omelettes also feature, and home-made desserts run to treacle tart and bread-and-butter pudding. Hop Back Summer Lightning and Young's Bitter are on draught, together with a guest, and six wines come by the glass, with the full list running to around 20 bottles. To the back is a sheltered beer garden. The pub can get busy when there are race meetings at nearby Goodwood. SAMPLE DISHES: whitebait with tartare sauce £5; steak and mushroom pie £10; apple and blackberry crumble £4.75.

Licensee Michael Martell (freehouse)
Open 12 to 3, 6 to 11, Sun 12 to 6; bar food and restaurant 12 to 2.15, 6 to 9.15, Sun and bank hols 12 to 2.30
Details Children welcome Car park Wheelchair access (also WC) Garden and patio No smoking in restaurant No music Dogs welcome exc in restaurant Amex, Delta, MasterCard, Switch, Visa
Accommodation: 11 rooms, B&B £40 to £70

EAST CHILTINGTON East Sussex map 3

Jolly Sportsman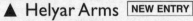
Chapel Lane, East Chiltington BN7 3BA TEL: (01273) 890400
WEBSITE: www.thejollysportsman.com
on B2116 E of Plumpton turn N signposted East Chiltington, continue approx 1½m then first left (pub signposted)

This pub and restaurant, hung with tiles and custard-coloured weatherboarding, is one of the most sought-after and popular eating places in the area, although having just a pint – one of a constantly changing range of ales generally from microbreweries and served from the barrel – is a possibility in the small bar or large, attractive garden. Elsewhere, bare floorboards, walls painted pink and green, and a cacophony of contented customers create an atmosphere that is more modern bistro than pub, and judging by the menu it is easy to see why. Dishes like duck breast with ham, grilled artichoke and pickled figs, and roast halibut steak with capers, tomato and saffron reveal a kitchen with a sensible approach to raw ingredients, producing clear, strong flavours. Alternatives might be fennel and roast tomato soup, or Thai crab beignets with chilli jam, and then marinated rump of lamb with aubergine and piquillo pepper stew. Up-to-the-minute components appear at dessert stage too: say, chestnut and orange charlotte, or apricot, walnut, ginger and toffee pudding. A set-price two- or three-course lunch is served from Tuesday to Saturday. The wine list confidently achieves excellence at all levels, without laying on any pretensions. Nine wines by the glass (in three sizes) give a sample of the range on offer rather than sticking with the budget basics; the selection of half-bottles is extensive, and the full list of around 150 wines will leave you spoilt for choice whatever your budget or preferences. SAMPLE DISHES: pigeon breast and wild mushroom risotto £6.50; cod fillet in a Dijon mustard and herb crust £13.50; hot apple tart with Calvados sauce £6.

Licensees Bruce and Gwyneth Wass (freehouse)
Open Tue to Sat and bank hol Mon 12 to 2.30, 6 to 11, Sun 12 to 4; bar food and restaurant Tue to Sat and bank hol Mon 12.30 to 2, 7 to 9 (10 Fri and Sat), Sun 12.30 to 3; closed 4 days Christmas
Details Children welcome Car park Wheelchair access (also WC) Garden and patio No smoking in restaurant No music Dogs welcome Delta, MasterCard, Switch, Visa

EAST COKER Somerset map 2

▲ Helyar Arms NEW ENTRY
Moor Lane, East Coker BA22 9JR TEL: (01935) 862332
WEBSITE: www.helyar-arms.co.uk
East Coker signposted off A37 3m S of Yeovil

When he retired as chairman of the Restaurant Association, Ian McKerracher bought an old farmhouse a few doors down from the Helyar Arms – a superb Grade II listed fifteenth-century inn with a pillared stone porch and mullioned windows. Within months, fed up with the pub serving freezer food and with the lease up for grabs, he became a pub landlord. He's thrown out the freezers and focuses on producing fresh food from local produce; given the fact that this is still the village pub complete with a local drinking crowd and pub games, he manages a good balance between dining and drinking. The seasonally changing menu (enhanced by daily blackboard specials) delivers modern touches to traditional dishes. Typical of starters is twice-baked cheese soufflé, or duck and apricot terrine with tomato compote, with main courses ranging from sautéed Somerset pork loin with grain mustard cream sauce to a perfectly cooked Somerset farm sirloin steak with pepper sauce, while locally made Lovington's ice creams and sorbets compete with hot chocolate fondant pudding for dessert. On handpump are Bass, Fuller's London Pride, Flowers Original and often a guest, and the wine list is a global selection with around a dozen by the glass. SAMPLE DISHES: smoked duck breast salad £5.75; roast baby spring chicken with truffle sauce £12.50; coffee and chocolate trifle £5.

Licensee Ian McKerracher (Punch Taverns)
Open *11 to 11, Sun 12 to 10.30; bar food and restaurant 12 to 2.30, 6.30 to 9.30, Sun 12 to 4.30 Jan to Easter, 12 to 9 rest of year; closed Sun evenings Jan to Easter*
Details *Children welcome   Car park   Wheelchair access (not WC)   Garden   No-smoking area in bar, no smoking in restaurant   Occasional live or background music   Dogs welcome   Amex, Delta, MasterCard, Switch, Visa   Accommodation: 6 rooms, B&B £59 to £80*

EAST DEAN   **East Sussex**   **map 3**

Tiger Inn

The Green, East Dean BN20 0DA   TEL: (01323) 423209
off A269 Seaford to Eastbourne road, 4m W of Eastbourne

A long terrace of houses forms one side of the village green, and it is here, at the end, that you will find the Tiger Inn. Close proximity to the coast and Birling Gap makes it a popular tourist spot, and parking spaces and outside tables fill up fast on fine days. The low and dark bar has photographs and prints of local interest alongside 'two stuffed tiger heads and other taxidermy such as pheasants, a fox and a trout'. The menus, written on a blackboard, take in everything from light dishes or starters of Breton fish soup, country pâté, or locally smoked salmon to a generous portion of fish pie made with cod, salmon and smoked haddock, or grilled fillet of halibut on creamed leeks with lemon and rosemary butter, while slow-roast shank of local lamb, and a casserole of Sussex pork, cider and root vegetables fly the flag for carnivores. Chocolate roulade or pecan pie may show up at dessert stage. Regular ales on handpump are Harveys Sussex Best Bitter and Adnams Bitter alongside a guest such as Brakspear Bitter. The blackboard of wines lists some 40 bottles, and a dozen are served by the glass; the bin-ends are worth considering too. SAMPLE DISHES: gravad lax with mustard and dill sauce £7; beef casseroled in Burgundy with smoked bacon £8; French lemon tart £3.50.

Licensee Nick Denyer (freehouse)
Open *Mon to Fri 11 to 3, 6 to 11, Sat 11 to 11, Sun 12 to 10.30; bar food Mon to Sat 12 to 2, 6.30 to 9 (9.30 Fri and Sat), Sun 12 to 2, 6 to 8*
Details *No children   Car park   Patio   No music   No cards*

EAST END   Hampshire   map 2

East End Arms ✿

Main Road, East End SO41 5SY   TEL: (01590) 626223
off B3054, 2m E of Lymington; follow signs for Isle of Wight ferry and continue past terminal for 3m

Tucked away on the southern edge of the New Forest close to the Solent, this white-washed pub looks quite unassuming from the outside. Behind the green door is a convivial, unselfconscious and unspoilt interior complete with two bars, a stone floor and 'lived-in' furniture; photographs of rock stars and other celebrities line the walls – not surprising, since the place is owned by John Illsley from the band Dire Straits. Lunch is a blackboard of robust main dishes including fish pie, 'obviously home-made' chicken dhansak, rabbit casserole, and pan-fried pork loin, backed up by assorted baguettes. Fish from the South Coast gets a good airing on the more ambitious evening menu, which kicks off with starters like monkfish cannelloni, or baked Parma ham with a free-range egg, before grilled halibut with Cape Malay butter, roast spiced cod with shrimps and peas, or slow-roast lamb with Parmesan mash and basil stock. Puddings tread a familiar, comforting path, taking in the likes of apple crumble, treacle tart, and rhubarb fool along the way. Fortyniner and Best Bitter from the nearby Ringwood Brewery are on draught, and the concise wine list includes a pair of organics and four commendable offerings by the glass. The pub has a small lawn and garden for fair-weather eating and drinking. SAMPLE DISHES: salmon cake with tartare sauce £5; braised guinea fowl with onions and Brussels sprouts £12; honeycomb ice cream £4.50.

Licensees P. and J. Sykes, and J. Willcock (freehouse)
Open *11.30 to 3, 6 to 11 (9 Mon), Sun 12 to 9; bar food and restaurant Tue to Sun 12 to 2, Tue to Sat 7 to 9;*
no food first 2 weeks Mar and first 2 weeks Oct
Details *Children welcome   Car park   Wheelchair access (also WC)   Garden   Background music*
Dogs welcome in bar only   Amex, MasterCard, Switch, Visa

EASTGATE   Norfolk   map 6

Ratcatchers Inn

Easton Way, Eastgate NR10 4HA   TEL: (01603) 871430
10m NW of Norwich off B1149 Holt road, 1m SE of Cawston

It may not be the easiest pub to find (especially in the dark), as the village of Eastgate spreads out in all directions, yet the Ratcatchers still manages to pack in the crowds. Food is clearly the main attraction, judging from the layout of the place: off the bar, there's a conservatory in one direction and a dining room in the other, with the same menu served throughout. The regular repertoire has its full share of pub stalwarts, vegetarians are well catered for, and the kitchen takes account of East Anglian produce in the shape of smoked mackerel from the Cley smokehouse, locally produced sausages (including a smoked version served with Norfolk mustard), and some fish from Lowestoft. Home-made pies with a choice of puff or shortcrust pastry are also something of a speciality: expect anything from beef and ale to 'fowl and fungi' (chicken and mushroom to you and me). Blackboard specials add a touch more adventure with, perhaps, sizzling char-roast lamb cutlets, skate wing with melted butter, balsamic vinegar and white wine, or pork fillet with brandy-soaked apricots wrapped in bacon. Adnams Bitter, Hancock's Ratcatchers, Greene King IPA and others are generally on draught. The good-value wine list makes extravagant claims for its well-chosen bottles but gives an accurate guide to flavours. Eight come by the glass from £2.50. SAMPLE DISHES: cheese fritters with sweet-and-sour sauce £5; peppered chicken breast flamed in brandy £10.75; fresh fruit meringue with cream £4.

Licensee Peter McCarter (freehouse)

Open Mon to Fri 11.45 to 3, 6 to 11, Sat 11.45 to 10, Sun 11.45 to 9; bar food and restaurant Mon to Fri 12 to 2, 6 to 10, Sat 12 to 10, Sun 12 to 9

Details Children welcome Car park Wheelchair access (not WC) Garden No smoking in restaurant and conservatory Background music No dogs Delta, MasterCard, Switch, Visa

EAST HADDON Northamptonshire map 5

▲ Red Lion Hotel

Main Street, East Haddon NN6 8BU TEL: (01604) 770223
WEBSITE: www.redlionhoteleasthaddon.co.uk
off A428, 8m NW of Northampton

Sedate and gentrified, this attractive thatched inn built of local stone is one of the focal points of East Haddon village life. Inside, all is cosy, homely and cottagey, with dark beams and red-upholstered furniture set off by floral cushions and curtains, and décor in the line of country-themed pictures, crockery and horse brasses. The bar menus offer a traditional assortment of mostly classic pub dishes including home-made pâté, fishcakes, pot-roast lamb shank and so on, bolstered by a cold buffet and sandwiches (not available Saturday evening and Sunday lunchtime), followed by desserts along the lines of Bakewell tart or bread-and-butter pudding. The restaurant menu goes in for more complex dishes like mushroom and Parmesan ravioli, followed by escalope of salmon on a bed of buttered spinach with a light shellfish bisque. Wells Eagle IPA and Bombardier Premium Bitter, Old Speckled Hen and Adnams Broadside are on handpump, and there is a respectable, fairly priced list of around 50 wines, with house selections at £13 and seven by the glass. SAMPLE DISHES: smoked salmon with lemon and caper dressing £9; honey-roast duckling with apple and Calvados sauce £13; blueberry cheesecake £4.50.

Licensee Ian Kennedy (Charles Wells)

Open 11 to 2.30, 6 to 11, Sun 12 to 2.30, 7 to 10.30; bar food and restaurant all week 12 to 2, Mon to Sat 7 to 9.30; closed 25 Dec

Details Children welcome in eating areas Car park Wheelchair access (also WC) Garden and patio No smoking in restaurant Background music No dogs Amex, Delta, Diners, MasterCard, Switch, Visa Accommodation: 5 rooms, B&B £60 to £75

EAST LANGTON Leicestershire map 5

▲ Bell Inn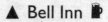

Main Street, East Langton LE16 7TW TEL: (01858) 545278
WEBSITE: www.thebellinn.co.uk

Renowned as the home of the Langton Brewery, which is housed in outbuildings, this sixteenth-century pub stands just across the road from the cricket ground. No doubt thirsty sportsmen make a beeline for the bar after a match to sample pints of Caudle Bitter, Bowler Strong Ale and Boxer Heavyweight, along with Greene King Abbot Ale. Inside, all is thoroughly traditional, with beamed ceilings, exposed-stone walls, a log fire and a sit-up-and-beg piano 'awaiting a player'; there's also a bright, spick-and-span quarry-tiled restaurant. Reporters have been pleased with samples from the lunch menu, including plump mussels in white wine and garlic crème, char-grilled chicken breast with asparagus and tagliatelle, and meaty Lincolnshire sausages with mash and onion gravy. You can also get assorted ciabattas and wraps, plus a selection of savoury tarts. The evening calls into play a more international repertoire spanning everything from Irish lamb stew to Thai duck red curry with jasmine rice and flat bread. Sunday lunch is a carvery. The adequate list of around 20 quaffable wines includes six by the glass, and there's a board of bin-ends. SAMPLE DISHES: papaya, melon and strawberry salad £5.50; seared tuna steak on sautéed French beans and roasted peppers in a light garlic and lemon oil £14; red berry meringue with cream £4.50.

Licensee Peter John Faye (freehouse)
Open 11.30 to 2.30, 6.30 to 11 (summer 11 to 11 Sat and Sun); bar food and restaurant 12 to 2, 7 to 9.30 (summer 12 to 9.30 Sat and Sun)
Details Children welcome in eating areas   Car park   Wheelchair access (also WC)   Garden   No smoking in restaurant   Live or background music   Dogs welcome   Delta, MasterCard, Switch, Visa   Accommodation: 2 rooms, B&B £39.50 to £80

EAST LAVANT   West Sussex   map 3

▲ Royal Oak ✿

Pook Lane, East Lavant PO18 0AX   TEL: (01243) 527434
WEBSITE: www.sussexlive.co.uk/royaloakinn

There may be low ceilings, beams and an old fireplace, as well as the odd farming implement, but this one-room local has morphed into a stylish dining pub. A new extension has been tacked on, and customers can sip aperitifs on sofas by the bar, although real ales include Ballard's, Hall & Woodhouse Badger and Sussex Bitter. On the food front, there are obvious restaurant overtones, particularly among starters (seared king scallops with lemon risotto and truffle oil, or tian of roasted vegetables with salsa verde, for instance), while main courses strike a more robust, traditional note: honey- and clove-roast ham with hand-cut chips and a free-range egg, salmon and cod fishcakes with spinach and parsley sauce, and calf's liver and bacon with mash and a red wine and shallot sauce. Puddings, too, are straight out of the comfort zone: warm sticky apple sponge with Calvados crème fraîche, and banana bread-and-butter pudding with Baileys custard. Wine prices start at £11 (from around £3 per glass), but the list doesn't really get into gear until it passes the £15 mark – whereupon it accelerates rapidly towards a selection of top-class French classics, albeit in fairly young vintages. SAMPLE DISHES: carpaccio with rocket and Parmesan salad and honey-roasted figs £7; tenderloin of pork with port jus £14.50; orange and passion-fruit tart with caramelised kiwi fruit £5.50.

Licensee Nick Sutherland (freehouse)
Open 12 to 11; bar food and restaurant 12 to 3, 6 to 9.30
Details Children welcome   Car park   Wheelchair access (also WC)   Garden and patio   No music   Guide dogs only   Amex, Delta, Diners, MasterCard, Switch, Visa   Accommodation: 6 rooms, B&B £50 to £150

Food mentioned in the entries is available in the bar, although it may also be possible to eat in a dining room.

EASTON   Hampshire   map 2

Chestnut Horse

Avington Park Lane, Easton SO21 1EG   TEL: (01962) 779257

'Bags of character' at this small village hostelry, whose series of five, cosy, interconnecting rooms are set around a bar. In the two bar rooms are roaring fires, log baskets, tankards, teapots and even chamber pots hanging from the dark-boarded ceiling, and walls throughout are hung with a cornucopia of pictures, mirrors and crockery, and every shelf, nook and cranny is filled with bric-à-brac. Locally brewed Chestnut Horse Bitter is on draught along with Courage Best and Fuller's London Pride, and from a list of 40-odd wines around ten come by the glass. But food is also at the heart of the operation, and the place can get busy, thanks to the popularity of a set-price (£12.95 for two courses) lunchtime and early-evening menu that may include Caesar salad, followed by confit of duck with green beans and string chips. Sandwiches and ploughman's are also available at lunchtime, while the full menu has old favourites like bangers and mash, fish 'n' chips (medium or massive portions offered), and steak and salad. Look to the specials lists for the likes of local pheasant braised in wine, or seared scallops on asparagus. SAMPLE DISHES: Thai fishcake with rocket and sweet chilli sauce £5; steak and kidney pudding £14.50; treacle and lemon tart £4.50.

Licensees John and Jocelyn Holland (freehouse)
Open 11 to 3.30, 5.30 to 11, Sun 12 to 6 (10.30 summer); bar food and restaurant 12 to 2.30, 6.30 to 9.30, Sun 12 to 4.30 (8.30 summer)
Details Children welcome   Car park   Wheelchair access (not WC)   Garden and patio   No smoking in restaurant   Occasional background music   Dogs welcome   Delta, MasterCard, Switch, Visa

EAST TYTHERLEY   Hampshire   map 2

Star Inn

East Tytherley SO51 0LW   TEL: (01794) 340225
WEBSITE: www.starinn-uk.com
off B3084 Romsey road, N of Lockerley

The sixteenth-century brick-built inn stands opposite the cricket pitch in a lovely rural position on a lane linking Lockerley and the Tytherleys. In summer the terrace is ablaze with colourful pots, hanging baskets and a rose-covered loggia, while the much-modernised interior is comfortable and welcoming, with a roaring winter fire, a pubby bar area, and a traditional restaurant with dark wooden furnishings and plush banquettes. This is a place that caters for all-comers, be they skittle players (the skittle alley is off the bar), walkers, real ale fans (Ringwood Best, plus a guest), cricket teams, or local foodies. This is reflected in the wide range of food on offer: sandwiches or jacket potatoes for the walkers, perhaps, cod and chips for the traditionalists, sausage and mash for the skittle players, maybe, and woodland mushroom timbale with pan-fried foie gras and cep jus, and grilled fillets of sea bass with braised fennel and asparagus with langoustine jus for the more adventurous. Of the 30-odd wines listed, ten are available by the glass; prices start at £9.50 a bottle (£2.50 a glass). SAMPLE DISHES: duck liver pâté £5.25; steak, kidney and Guinness pie £7.50; orange marmalade pudding with custard £4.50.

Licensees Paul and Sarah Bingham (freehouse)
Open Tue to Sat 11 to 2.30, 6 to 11, Sun 12 to 2, 7 to 10.30; bar food and restaurant 12 to 2, 7 to 9 (9.30 Fri and Sat); closed evening 25 Dec, 26 Dec

Details *Children welcome   Car park   Wheelchair access (also WC)   Garden and patio   No smoking in restaurant   Occasional live music   Dogs welcome exc in bedrooms   Delta, MasterCard, Switch, Visa Accommodation: 3 rooms, B&B £45 to £70*

EAST WITTON   North Yorkshire map 8

▲ Blue Lion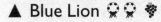

East Witton DL8 4SN   TEL: (01969) 624273
WEBSITE: www.thebluelion.co.uk
on A6108 Masham to Leyburn road, 2m SE of Middleham

Set amid the Dales, some way off the beaten track, is the small rural village of East Witton, and at its centre is this handsome eighteenth-century coaching inn. The front door leads directly into a warm, snug, flagstone-floored bar with a convivial and welcoming atmosphere. Much of the clientele are locals, but friendly young staff, clad smartly in black and white, make everyone equally welcome. On one wall, above a huge fireplace, is a vast blackboard listing as many as 20 main-course choices (starters are on further boards over the bar counter), which are scrubbed out and replaced according to availability. The cooking brings fine Yorkshire produce to the fore. Among starters might be roast scallops with lemon risotto, or bubble and squeak with crisp black pudding and red wine sauce, as well as a few more upmarket dishes such as a warm salad of sautéed wood pigeon and smoked foie gras with a grain mustard and beetroot dressing. To follow there may be roast partridge with game sauce, cabbage and chorizo, or beef and onion suet pudding with onion sauce. Well-kept real ales come from the local Black Sheep and Theakston breweries, while wine drinkers have 12 flavoursome, good-value choices by the bottle, glass or half-litre. The full wine list serves up classic vintages alongside fresh modern flavours from around the world, with serious bottles in both categories. SAMPLE DISHES: duck and orange terrine with grain mustard salad and toasted brioche £5.50; sautéed pheasant breast wrapped in bacon with wild mushroom, prune and winter vegetable risotto £14; raspberry and white chocolate trifle £5.75.

Licensee *Paul Klein (freehouse)*
Open *11 to 11, Sun 12 to 10.30; bar food 12 to 2.15, 7 to 9.30 (9.45 weekends); restaurant all week 7 to 9.30 (9.45 weekends), Sun 12 to 2.15*
Details *Children welcome   Car park   Wheelchair access (also WC)   Garden and patio   No music Dogs welcome   Delta, MasterCard, Switch, Visa   Accommodation: 12 rooms, B&B £53.50 to £89*

EAST WOODLANDS   Somerset map 2

Horse & Groom

East Woodlands BA11 5LY   TEL: (01373) 462802
off A361, 2m S of Frome; village signposted off Frome bypass

The Horse & Groom, a remarkably out-of-the-way pub on the edge of the Longleat Estate, is also known as the Jockey locally, should you get lost and require directions. Tables cover the lawn to the front, and there are more in the secluded garden at the side, while hanging baskets provide extra colour. Within the seventeenth-century building both furniture and décor are comfortable and well worn, with the lounge bar sporting a couple of deep armchairs and sofas; there are inglenooks and stone-flagged floors. Butcombe Bitter, Branscombe Vale Branoc, Wadworth 6X and Timothy

Taylor Landlord are on handpump, and Stowford Press cider is also stocked. The restaurant is in a conservatory-style extension, and the printed menu here might offer a warm salad of Barbary duck breast with scallops and an orange, honey and grain mustard dressing as a starter, with the specials board perhaps producing a main course of whole sea bass stuffed with sun-dried tomatoes, olives and crushed chillies. The bar menu is more traditional, in the shape of gammon steak and pineapple, lamb's liver with onion gravy, or sausages and mash. Six wines on the 32-strong reasonably priced list come in two sizes of glass. SAMPLE DISHES: cheesy garlic mushrooms on granary toast £4.25; bacon chop grill with mustard mash £8; lemon and lime meringue pie £4.

Licensee Kathy Barrett (freehouse)
Open *Tue to Sat 11.30 to 2.30, Mon to Sat 6.30 to 11, Sun 12 to 3, 7 to 11; bar food and restaurant Tue to Sun 12 to 2, Tue to Sat 6.30 to 9; also open bank hol Mon (limited menu)*
Details *Children welcome in eating areas   Car park   Wheelchair access (also women's WC)   Garden No smoking in restaurant   No music   Dogs welcome on a lead exc in restaurant   MasterCard, Switch, Visa*

EBBESBOURNE WAKE   **Wiltshire**   map 2

▲ Horseshoe Inn 🍺 [NEW ENTRY]

Ebbesbourne Wake SP5 5JF   TEL: (01722) 780474
village signposted off A30 W of Fovant between Salisbury and Shaftesbury

---

The Bath family work hard to preserve the timeless, unchanging atmosphere of their mellow-brick eighteenth-century inn in an Ebble Valley village, accessed by narrow lanes, which 'seems to have escaped the hustle and bustle of modern-day life'. Beer (usually Ringwood Best, Adnams Broadside and Wadworth 6X, with guests such as Stonehenge Pigswill and Butcombe Bitter) is drawn straight from the barrel in the bar, which has a huge inglenook with a winter log fire, an assortment of rustic furniture and an extensive collection of old tools and rural artefacts; a second bar is tiny, with a few simple tables and chairs, and the restaurant has a small conservatory extension. Honest home cooking is the trademark here, whether traditional favourites like thick home-made soup, lamb's liver and bacon, locally made faggots, and popular Sunday roasts, or seasonal game and roast duck and fish specials. Six wines are available by the glass. Climbing roses and honeysuckle around the door plus a flower-filled garden make this a lovely spot for a summer evening's drink. SAMPLE DISHES: salmon and trout pâté £6.25; steak and kidney pie £9.50; plum crumble £4.

Licensees Anthony and Patricia Bath (freehouse)
Open *Mon 6.30 to 11, Tue to Sat 12 to 3.30, 6.30 to 11, Sun 12 to 3.30, 7 to 10.30; bar food and restaurant Tue to Sun 12 to 2, Tue to Sat 7 to 9.30; open 12 to 1, 25 Dec (no food), closed 26 Dec*
Details *Children welcome in eating areas   Car park   Garden   No smoking in restaurant   Occasional background music   No dogs   MasterCard, Switch, Visa   Accommodation: 2 rooms, B&B £40 to £60*

ELKESLEY   **Nottinghamshire**   map 9

Robin Hood Inn

High Street, Elkesley DN22 8AJ   TEL: (01777) 838259

This attractive pub stands in the centre of a small village just off the A1, making it a useful stopping place for travellers as well as a popular local watering hole. Outside, stuccoed walls are painted in a delicate primrose and decked with troughs of plants;

there's a large garden with a children's play area. Inside, the bar is comfortably appointed, and the restaurant is colourfully decorated, with dark wood furniture, a multi-hued carpet, and framed retro posters on walls painted in shades of cream, plum and eau-de-nil. The long menus offer plenty of variety, main dishes ranging from beef with mushrooms and bacon braised in red wine to chicken curry. Daily specials are listed on a blackboard, including the soup of the day – perhaps mushroom with greens – and fish dishes such as fillet of salmon roasted with peppers served with vermouth butter sauce. Beers are Marston's Pedigree, Flowers IPA, and Boddingtons Bitter, and the wine list runs to a dozen or so reasonably priced bottles, of which six come by the glass. SAMPLE DISHES: salmon fishcake with spinach and lemon butter sauce £6; pan-fried chicken suprême with mushrooms in cream, white wine and Dijon mustard sauce £10; crème brûlée with raspberries £4.50.

Licensee Alan Draper (Enterprise Inns)
Open 11.30 to 3, 6.30 to 11, Sun 12 to 3, 7 to 10.30; bar food and restaurant all week 12 to 2, Mon to Sat 6.30 to 9; closed evening 25 Dec
Details Children welcome Car park Wheelchair access (also WC Garden No-smoking area in bar, no smoking in restaurant Occasional live or background music Dogs welcome Delta, MasterCard, Switch, Visa

ELSTED **West Sussex** map 2

Three Horseshoes 🍺
Elsted GU29 0JY TEL: (01730) 825746
3m S of A272, 3m W of Midhurst

This hugely atmospheric old pub is set high above a bank overlooking the road, backing on to the north slope of the South Downs. The four linked rooms may be quite small but are redolent of the building's sixteenth-century origins: walls of bare red brick with wooden studwork and dadoes, wooden floors, worn tiles, ancient pews and settles, even doors, and an ancient brick and stone fireplace. True to its Old England atmosphere, excellent real ales include Cheriton Pots Ale, Ballard's Best Bitter, Timothy Taylor Landlord, and Hop Back Summer Lightning; wines run to only around a dozen bottles, with just one red and two whites served by the glass. On blackboards might be mozzarella and bacon salad, or a hearty soup, with substantial main courses of pheasant breast with shallots, cider and prunes, or local pork sausages with mash and onion gravy. In season, expect lots of venison, crab and lobster. In summer, the part-brick, part-stone façade is heavily covered in climbing roses and the large lawned garden, with well-spaced trestle tables, comes into its own. SAMPLE DISHES: prawn mayonnaise wrapped in smoked salmon £7; chicken with Dijon mustard sauce £9; treacle tart £5.

Licensee Sue Beavis (freehouse)
Open 11 to 2.30, 6 to 11, Sun 12 to 3, 7 to 10.30; bar food and restaurant 12 to 2, 7 to 9
Details Children welcome Car park Garden No smoking in restaurant No music Dogs welcome in bar Delta, MasterCard, Switch, Visa

Which? Online subscribers will find The Which? Pub Guide *online, along with other Which? guides and magazines, at* www.which.net. *Check the website for how to become a subscriber.*

ELTERWATER   **Cumbria**   map 8

▲ Britannia Inn 🍺

Elterwater LA22 9HP   TEL: (015394) 37210
WEBSITE: www.britinn.co.uk
off A593, 3m W of Ambleside

A lovely setting in the Langdale Valley makes this whitewashed Lakeland gem of a pub a prime target and perennial favourite with walkers, sightseers and outdoor types. There are window boxes and plenty of picnic tables outside by the village green; otherwise it can be quite a scrum in the tiny, three-table bar and separate 'back bar', both of which have open fires, beams and flagstone floors. The food on offer is just what you might expect: hefty helpings of simple, unpretentious pub grub with a few more adventurous dishes and a fondness for local produce, including Lakeland lamb (perhaps roasted and served with minted redcurrant jus), steaks from organically reared Dexter beef, and Cumberland sausages from Waberthwaite. There are also a few dishes from further afield such as lamb rogan josh, or red pesto and sweet pepper filo tart, plus desserts ranging from jam roly-poly to poached pear in mulled wine. Fans of real ale should have a field day here, with top-notch names such as Jennings Bitter, Coniston Bluebird, Timothy Taylor Landlord and guest brews on the hand-pumps. If wine is required, there's also a useful list of around 20, with three by the glass as well as country wines from Lindisfarne. SAMPLE DISHES: smoked salmon and prawn platter with lemon mayonnaise £4.50; braised shoulder of lamb with red-currant and rosemary sauce £10.25; blackberry and apple pie £4.

Licensees Clare Woodhead and Chris Jones (freehouse)
Open 10.30 to 11, Sun 12 to 10.30; bar food and restaurant 12 to 3.30, 6.30 to 9.30
Details Children welcome   Car park   Wheelchair access (not WC)   Patio   No smoking in hallway, restaurant or residents' lounge   No music   Dogs welcome exc in restaurant   Amex, Delta, MasterCard, Switch, Visa   Accommodation: 9 rooms, B&B £58 to £92

ELTON   **Cambridgeshire**   map 6

Black Horse

14 Overend, Elton PE8 6RU   TEL: (01832) 280240

This seventeenth-century pub, by the village church, is a light-coloured stone build-ing, typical of the local style, with a covered patio and an extensive garden overlooking open countryside. Inside, the décor in the main bar is 'tasteful and homely', with a 'real pub' look and a rustic feel. One of the two dining rooms has bright murals, while the other is more formal. Food-wise, plenty of choice is offered by a long blackboard menu, backed up by a bar sandwich menu and a separate blackboard for puddings. Start perhaps with dressed crab or chicken Caesar salad (also available as a main-course portion). Among main courses are simple, traditional ideas such as game pie, but if you fancy something more exotic you could go for ostrich fillet with onion marmalade. Several appealing fish options are usually available too, among them perhaps fillet of sea bass with king prawns and hollandaise. Regular draught Bass is joined by a guest ale, perhaps Nethergate Augustinian Ale, while all dozen house selections on the wine list are sold in two sizes of glass as well as by the bottle; there's also a short list of fine wines. SAMPLE DISHES: rollmop herrings with salad and mayon-naise £5; pan-fried goose breast with pear and ginger chutney £15; apple pie £5.

Licensee John Clennell (freehouse)
Open *12 to 3 (5 Sun), 6 to 11; bar food all week 12 to 2.30 (3 Sun), Mon to Sat 6 to 9.30*
Details *Children welcome   Car park   Garden and patio   No smoking in 1 room   No music   Dogs welcome*
Amex, Delta, MasterCard, Switch, Visa

EMPINGHAM   Rutland   map 6

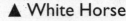 White Horse

Main Street, Empingham LE15 8PS   TEL: (01780) 460221
WEBSITE: www.whitehorserutland.co.uk
on A606 midway between Oakham and Stamford

Rutland Water is a major attraction in the area for those interested in watersports and
angling, but for those who seek good-value pub food the White Horse is a natural
focal point. Originally the courthouse of this pretty, rural village, the long, stone-built
inn shows much character, with low, beamed ceilings, exposed-stone pillars,
patterned carpets and dark wooden furniture giving the bar a traditional look. There's
also a large open log fire to provide warmth on cold winter days, and the separate
dining room is similar in style, with a wood-burning stove and a Welsh dresser
garlanded with hops. The printed menus and daily blackboard specials provide plenty
of choice in a predominantly simple, hearty style: thick and satisfying asparagus soup,
lightly battered scampi with freshly cooked fries, and rosemary-coated Barnsley chop
with a flavour-packed red wine sauce. Ruddles Best Bitter, though no longer brewed
in Rutland, adds a local flavour to the beer line-up, while two dozen wines cover a
wide range of styles and nationalities, with prices starting at £10.50. SAMPLE DISHES:
garlic- and rosemary-crusted Brie with cranberry and orange sauce £5.25; pork
medallions with Stilton and smoked bacon cream sauce £10; mandarin cheesecake £4.

Licensees Ian and Sarah Sharp (Unique Pub Company)
Open *8am to 11 (10.30 Sun); bar food 12 to 2.15, 7 to 9.30 (9 Sun)*
Details *Children welcome   Car park   Wheelchair access (also WC)   Garden and patio   No smoking in
eating area   Background music   No dogs   Amex, Delta, MasterCard, Switch, Visa   Accommodation: 13 rooms,
B&B £45 to £65*

EVERSHOT   Dorset   map 2

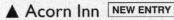 Acorn Inn   NEW ENTRY

28 Fore Street, Evershot DT2 0JW   TEL: (01935) 83228
WEBSITE: www.acorn-inn.co.uk

This sixteenth-century village inn, close to the church, was Thomas Hardy's inspiration for the Sow and Acorn in *Tess of the D'Urbervilles*. Of its two rooms, the back bar is
the livelier; the front bar and dining area is uncluttered and stylish, with white table
linen, wood panelled walls, tiled floors and a stone fireplace. Simple bar food options
include provençale pork with rice, rump steak with chips, and various open sandwiches, but the separate restaurant menu is the main focus of culinary attention.
Ingredients are mostly locally sourced, though the cooking style shows wider influences, with dishes ranging from kedgeree with a poached quail egg as a starter, via
pan-fried beef fillet with marinated chicken livers and Madeira jus to caramelised
Gressingham duck breast on honey and soy noodles with Thai dressing. There's also
a board of daily-changing fish specials such as pan-fried turbot with mussels and chive

sauce, and among desserts may be chocolate mousse or fig tart. Beers include Fuller's London Pride, Butcombe Bitter and Shepherd Neame Spitfire, plus Stowford Press cider, and there are three wines by the glass from a list of 20 varied international bottles. SAMPLE DISHES: seared red mullet fillets on warm fennel, carrot and coriander salad £6; baked lemon sole with tarragon sauce £14; clafoutis £5.

Licensees Todd and Louise Moffat (freehouse)
Open 11 to 11, Sun 12 to 10.30; bar food and restaurant 12 to 2, 7 to 9.30
Details Children welcome   Car park   Wheelchair access   Patio   No smoking in dining room   Occasional live music; jukebox   Dogs welcome exc in dining room   Amex, Delta, MasterCard, Switch, Visa
Accommodation: 9 rooms, B&B £75 to £130

EWEN   Gloucestershire   map 2

 ## Wild Duck Inn

Drakes Island, Ewen GL7 6BY   TEL: (01285) 770310
off A429 Cirencester to Malmesbury road, 3m SW of Cirencester

---

Dating from the fifteenth century, this well-tended and seriously busy Cotswold-stone pub consists of a linked group of buildings around a courtyard fronted by a central clock tower. Inside is a 'rabbit warren' of irregularly shaped rooms with dark red walls, honey-coloured plaster and blackened beams garlanded with bunches of hops. Mirrors and eclectic oil paintings break up the space. The printed menus change daily, and the kitchen seems to be geared towards substantial one-dish meals. Plenty of pub favourites show up at lunchtime: perhaps burgers, ploughman's, fish pie and the like alongside a few more upmarket starters such as prawn 'panko' with a light Thai salad and honey and ginger dressing. Main courses in the evening also run to roast Gressingham duck with port and redcurrant sauce, or griddled chicken breast with roast aubergine, chorizo and chickpea couscous and a warm orange and thyme dressing, alongside steaks and beer-battered fish. To finish, there are carefully chosen cheeses and desserts such as warm hazelnut tart with pistachio ice cream. Real ales are mostly familiar names like Theakston XB, Smiles Best, and Courage Directors, plus the house brew, Duck Pond Bitter. With 27 wines by the glass and a host of bottles under £15 there's no shortage of good value drinking here, while pricy French classics give the list a more serious complexion. SAMPLE DISHES: tuna carpaccio on tomato and red onion salad £7.50; slow-roast belly pork with cider gravy £12; orange and stem ginger pudding with sauce anglaise and an apple and apricot compote £4.75.

Licensee Dino Mussell (freehouse)
Open 11 to 11, Sun 11 to 10.30; bar food and restaurant 12 to 2 (2.30 Sun), 6.30 to 10
Details Children welcome   Car park   Wheelchair access (also WC)   Garden and patio   Live or background music   Dogs welcome   Amex, Delta, MasterCard, Switch, Visa   Accommodation: 11 rooms, B&B £60 to £100

EXFORD   Somerset   map 1

▲ Crown Hotel

Park Street, Exford TA24 7PP   TEL: (01643) 831554
WEBSITE: www.crownhotelexmoor.co.uk
on B3224, 12m SW of Minehead

Set in three acres of gardens in a pretty Exmoor village and surrounded by beautiful moorland, the Crown is a seventeenth-century coaching inn and sporting hotel.

Those interested in country pursuits will be keen to take advantage of the stables and livery services, while everybody else will appreciate the comfortable, old-fashioned bar, which has a hunting theme to the décor in the shape of fox masks and deer hooves on the walls. Bar menus offer a varied and imaginative choice of fashionable and traditional dishes – confit duck leg with beetroot and pickled walnuts contrasts with chicken liver parfait with apple chutney among starters, while main courses range from mushroom and Parmesan risotto to braised lamb shank with rosemary sauce. Pudding choices include chocolate parfait and crème brûlée. A fine selection of beers from southwest England includes Exmoor Ale, Fox and Gold, Clearwater Crown and St Austell Tribute. Prices start at around £13 on the list of 42 mostly French wines. Three are available by the glass. The separate restaurant serves a fixed price three-course menu. SAMPLE DISHES: grilled goats' cheese with orange and pine nut salad £4.50; roast chicken breast with mushroom sauce £9.50; orange bread-and-butter pudding £4.

Licensee Hugo Jeune (freehouse)
Open winter Mon to Fri 11 to 2.30, 6 to 11, Sat and Sun 11 to 11, summer all week 11 to 11; bar food and restaurant 12 to 2, 7 to 9.30
Details Children welcome in bar eating area   Car park   Wheelchair access (also WC)   Garden
No smoking in dining room   Background music   Dogs welcome   Amex, Delta, MasterCard, Switch, Visa
Accommodation: 17 rooms, B&B £47.50 to £57.50

EXTON   Rutland   map 6

▲ Fox and Hounds   NEW ENTRY

19 The Green, Exton LE15 8AP   TEL: (01572) 812403
WEBSITE: www.foxandhoundsrutland.com

'Much improved under the stewardship of Valter (the Italian landlord) and his English wife Sandra,' commented a reporter after a visit to this good-looking three-storey stone-built coaching inn not far from Rutland Water. The creeper-covered building faces a small green edged with mature trees, and inside it has a genuinely 'homely feel', with rust-coloured sofas, dark wooden tables, standard lamps and a log fire in the lounge bar. Given the landlord's nationality, it's no surprise to find bruschetta, antipasti, and plenty of pasta on the restaurant menu; there's also a separate menu devoted to pizzas of every description. Away from the Mediterranean, you might encounter a warm salad of seared scallops and smoked salmon with dill dressing, not to mention gammon steak with fries, or even steak and kidney pie. The 'casual lunch' menu revolves around jacket potatoes, ploughman's, and sandwiches (made with ciabatta if you wish), while desserts could include lemon meringue pie. Beers from the Grainstore Brewery in nearby Oakham are on handpump alongside Marston's Pedigree and Timothy Taylor Landlord, and there's a decent wine list with the emphasis on Italy and Australia. SAMPLE DISHES: baked Camembert with cranberry sauce £4.25; breast of chicken with roasted peppers on a bed of linguine £9; chocolate bread-and-butter pudding £4.

Licensees Valter and Sandra Floris (freehouse)
Open 11 to 3, 6 to 11, Sun 12 to 3, 7 to 10.30; bar food and restaurant all week 12 to 2, restaurant Mon to Sat 6.30 to 9
Details Children welcome   Car park   Wheelchair access (not WC)   Garden   No smoking in restaurant
Background music   Dogs welcome in bar only   Delta, MasterCard, Switch, Visa   Accommodation: 4 rooms,
B&B £28 to £42

Plough

Main Street, Fadmoor YO62 7HY · TEL: (01751) 431515

Low ceiling beams, old paraffin lamps (now electric) and a wood-burning range are reminders that this is an untarnished village pub with a genuinely rustic atmosphere. The carpeted lounge is comfortable and homely, while the restaurant is a tad more formal. The menus offer a generous choice at both lunchtime and in the evening: perhaps pan-fried black pudding with caramelised onions and apple sauce, or duck and mango spring rolls with sweet chilli and ginger dip to start, and main courses of slow-roast shank of lamb, braised beef brisket, and a chunk of halibut wrapped in puff pasty and served with a rustic tomato, garlic and parsley sauce. Firm lunchtime favourites include lasagne, battered fillet of haddock, and grilled gammon steak with mushrooms, tomato, a fried egg, pineapple and chips. On draught is Black Sheep Best Bitter, plus a guest in summer. All six house wines are sold by the glass at £3 (£11.95 a bottle), and there are a further 20 or so bottles to choose from. SAMPLE DISHES: wild mushroom and noodle soup £3.50; medallions of monkfish wrapped in Loch Fyne smoked salmon with a Thai lemongrass and coriander sauce £13.50; caramelised lemon tart £4.50.

Licensee Neil Nicholson (Holf Leisure)

Open 12 to 2.30, 6.30 (7 Sun) to 11.30; bar food and restaurant 12 to 1.45 (2 Sun), 6.30 to 8.45 (8.30 Sun); closed 25 and 26 Dec, 1 Jan

Details Children welcome   Car park   Garden and patio   No smoking in restaurant   Occasional background music   No dogs   Delta, MasterCard, Switch, Visa

Inn at Farnborough ✿ ❀   NEW ENTRY

Farnborough OX17 1DZ   TEL: (01295) 690615
WEBSITE: www.theinnatfarnborough.co.uk

In a tiny village, this big, well-cared-for pub consists of a cluster of honey-coloured stone buildings that might once have been a farm. A classy front porch leads to the spacious interior, which also has an 'artistic farmhouse' feel, with its heavily beamed ceilings, boarded floors and modern prints. This is a pub that genuinely welcomes children, and everyone is helpfully served by bright, committed staff. One menu runs throughout the place, and it's resolutely based on high-quality produce: check out the printed list of suppliers. The style is modern and generous without being over-pretentious, and the kitchen also knows how to bake bread. Roast rump of Lighthorne lamb marinated in rose harissa with roast vegetables and sweet pepper jus impressed an inspector, as did a starter of sautéed scallops, calamari and king prawns provençale. Elsewhere you might find wild mushroom and celeriac risotto, confit of Gressingham duck in a plum glaze with black pudding and spring onion mash or – in simpler vein – ciabatta rolls filled with pork and leek sausages. A separate dessert menu (with matching 'sticky' wines) spans everything from sticky toffee pudding to baked dark chocolate tart with bourbon ice cream. Well-known names like Greene King Abbot Ale and Ruddles County are on handpump. A crisply presented wine list showcases all the key New World varieties including emerging specialities such as Australian Verdelho and New Zealand Pinot Gris. France adds some southern upstarts to the classic regions and runs to a few bottles for deeper pockets. House wines start at £9.95 and ten by the glass cover all levels of the sub-£20 range. Farnborough Hall (National Trust) is close by. SAMPLE DISHES: Warwickshire game terrine with spiced beetroot and peppercorn chutney £6; chargrilled fillets of sea bass with borlotti bean stew and chorizo £14; orange and Grand Marnier crème brûlée £5.

Licensees Anthony and Jo Robinson (freehouse)
Open Mon to Fri 12 to 3, 6 (5 Fri) to 11, Sat and Sun 11 to 11; bar food and restaurant 12 to 2.30 (4 Sun and bank hols), 6 to 10
Details Children welcome   Car park   Wheelchair access (also WC)   Garden   No smoking in restaurant Occasional background music   Dogs welcome   Amex, Delta, Diners, MasterCard, Switch, Visa

FARNHAM   Dorset   map 2

▲ Museum Inn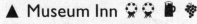
Farnham DT11 8DE   TEL: (01725) 516261
off A354, 9m NE of Blandford Forum

Built in the seventeenth century, this part-thatched country inn was extended in the nineteenth century by General Augustus Lane Fox Pitt-Rivers, who is known as the father of modern archaeology, to provide accommodation for visitors to his museum (now closed) – hence the pub's name. It's a strikingly handsome building, and sympathetic refurbishment has brought it up to date while retaining its original character: beige-coloured flagstones, bare wooden tables, and quirky touches such as a stuffed fox curled up in a disused bread oven. It's a popular place, but well-drilled, friendly staff cope well with the crowds. At lunchtime, upmarket sandwiches are available, while the menu offers a modern version of hearty country cooking with lots of bold, fashionable flavours. Start perhaps with chicken liver parfait with date and apple chutney, or crispy Parma ham, peppers and rocket bruschetta with basil, olives and sardines. Main courses continue in similar vein: fishcake with a poached egg and a white wine, chervil and lemon velouté rubs shoulders with braised lamb shank with rosemary and garlic, crushed sun-blush tomatoes, olives and new potatoes. And to finish there might be Granny Smith apple mousse with Calvados sorbet. The same menu is offered in the separate Shed Restaurant (limited opening). Three real ales are always on offer, usually from small, independent local breweries, typically including Ringwood Best, Hop Back Summer Lightning, and Palmers Dorset Gold. Thatcher's cider is also on draught. Nine house wines are available by the glass from £3, or by the bottle at £11, and the full restaurant list has plenty of good drinking at fair prices, with France the mainstay. A selection of superior vintage ports might tempt anyone wanting to splash out. SAMPLE DISHES: wood pigeon terrine with pickled apples and dates £6; roast sea bass with capers, aïoli and lemon £15; rhubarb and ginger crumble with vanilla ice cream £5.50.

Licensees Vicky Elliot and Mark Stephenson (freehouse)
Open 12 to 3, 6 to 11, Sun 12 to 3, 7 to 10.30; bar food 12 to 2 , 7 to 9.30, Sun 12 to 3, 7 to 9; restaurant Sun 12 to 3, Fri and Sat 7 to 9.30
Details Children welcome   Car park   Wheelchair access (also WC)   Garden and patio   No smoking in restaurant   Occasional live music   Dogs welcome   Delta, MasterCard, Switch, Visa   Accommodation: 8 rooms, B&B £65 to £95

FARTHINGSTONE   **Northamptonshire**   map 5

Kings Arms   NEW ENTRY

Main Street, Farthingstone NN12 8EZ   TEL: (01327) 361604

Reporters confirm that this slightly Gothic-looking pub is an 'extraordinary' rural gem. On the edge of the village in peaceful countryside close to the National Trust-owned Canons Ashby House, it looks every inch the classic country pub: untarnished and unadulterated in the best sense of the words. There's one main bar room with a stone-flagged floor, but a huge old high-backed settle acts as a room divider, so you appear to enter an entrance room that is kitted out like an old-fashioned front parlour, with an ancient three-piece suite, upright piano and a couple of bar tables and chairs in the window; books, prints, knick-knacks, and china ornaments cover every surface. You then step into the bar proper, with its wood-burning fire at one end, wooden tables, benches, rough-stone walls, horse brasses and board games piled on the bar counter. There's a further public bar (beyond the fire) that is more sparsely furnished. Food-wise, the emphasis is on plates of British farmhouse cheeses – a weekly-changing blackboard menu lists the likes of Appleby's Cheshire, Cotherstone, Colston Bassett, Waterloo (a kind of British Brie), Westcombe Cheddar – backed up by home-made soups, Cumberland sausage and mash, a smoked fish platter, and that's pretty much it. A further blackboard advertises vacuum-packed retail purchases to take away, such as wild Argyll venison steaks and Loch Fyne smoked salmon. Hook Norton Best Bitter is on offer along with Bateman XB, Timothy Taylor Landlord and Jennings, and there are a few wines by the glass. The pub is open only on certain evenings during the week, and food is served only at weekend lunchtimes: see details below. SAMPLE DISHES: home-made soup £4; Kings Arms cheese platter £6; Yorkshire pudding with steak and kidney £6.25.

Licensees Paul and Denise Egerton (freehouse)
Open Tue, Thur and Fri 7 to 11, Sat and Sun 12 to 3, 7 to 11; bar food Sat and Sun 12 to 2; closed 25 and 26 Dec, 1 Jan
Details Children welcome in bar eating area   Car park   Garden   Occasional live music   No dogs   No cards

FENSTANTON   **Cambridgeshire**   map 6

King William IV

High Street, Fenstanton PE28 9JF   TEL: (01480) 462467

The major claim to fame of this secluded fenland village is that Capability Brown was lord of the manor. Interesting local features include the seventeenth-century lock-up, with a clock on its east well, and this mainly eighteenth-century brick-built pub. Its bar has a brick and studwork counter, a low, beamed ceiling, and a brick fireplace, while the other end of the building has two dining rooms, one low-ceilinged and cosy, the other a lighter room with large windows. Lunch menus take in sandwiches, jacket potatoes and ploughman's as well as simple main courses like baked fishcake or chicken burrito. The main menu goes in for more elaborate fare, with starters such as mulled pear with Stilton and walnut dressing, followed perhaps by roast pheasant in an onion, brandy and parsley cream sauce, or something from the handful of daily fish specials. This is a Greene King pub, with Abbot Ale and IPA on draught, plus a guest beer. Nine house wines come by the bottle from £9, or by the large or small glass. SAMPLE DISHES: melon cocktail with lychees, lime syrup and mint £5; chicken breast on creamed leeks with saffron and toasted focaccia £11.25; cinnamon meringue with caramel ice cream £4.50.

Licensee Mrs D.T. Amps (Greene King)
Open _11 to 3.30, 6 to 11, Sun 12 to 10.30; bar food and restaurant Mon to Sat 12 to 2.15, 7 to 9.45, Sun 12 to 3.30_
Details _Children welcome in eating areas   Car park   Wheelchair access (not WC)   Patio   No smoking in restaurant   Background and live music   Dogs welcome in bar only   MasterCard, Switch, Visa_

FERNHURST   West Sussex   map 3

King's Arms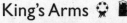

Midhurst Road, Fernhurst GU27 3HA   TEL: (01428) 652005
on A286, 1m S of Fernhurst on sharp bend

An unusual tiled porch runs the length of this compact 300-year-old inn (bright with hanging flower baskets in the summer), while a large barn is used for functions. It may look unassuming, but this is a place with aspirations – most of which relate to the output of the kitchen. Specials cover familiar bar snack ground with shepherd's pie, corned beef hash and pork sausages with bubble and squeak, but most of Michael Hirst's gastro-energies are channelled into the main menu, which moves rapidly into the world of cosmopolitan modern cooking. Carpaccio of beef fillet is served as a starter with baby courgette fritters and lemon and Parmesan dressing, for example, and a main course of roast loin of pork is accompanied by caramelised apples, a shallot and Stilton Tatin and buttered Savoy cabbage. Desserts are pretty arty: dark chocolate and Cointreau mousse, or lemon and lime crème brûlée. Any doubts that this is still a pub should be quelled by the five real ales on handpump: King's Arms Bitter, brewed by Ventnor Brewery, Ringwood Best, and Yankee from Rooster's in North Yorkshire are just three examples from a regularly changing list; there's also genuine Dublin-brewed Guinness on tap. The no-smoking room at the back has a strong oenological theme, with labels, cartoons, corkscrews and much more on display. The wine list is a globetrotting selection, with a collection of fine wines and ten by the glass from £2.75. SAMPLE DISHES: brown potted shrimps £6; seared king scallops with sun-blush tomatoes, asparagus and saffron risotto £15; banana and toffee pie £5.25.

Licensees Michael and Annabel Hirst (freehouse)
Open _11.30 to 3, 5.30 (6.30 Sat) to 11, Sun 12 to 3; bar food and restaurant all week 12 to 2.30, Mon to Sat 7 to 9.30_
Details _Children welcome in eating areas exc under-14s after 7pm   Car park   Garden   No smoking in 1 room   No music   Dogs welcome in bar only   Delta, MasterCard, Switch, Visa_

FERRENSBY   North Yorkshire   map 9

▲ General Tarleton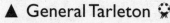

Boroughbridge Road, Ferrensby HG5 0PZ   TEL: (01423) 340284
WEBSITE: www.generaltarleton.co.uk

Easily found along country roads not far from the A1, the General Tarleton, a former coaching inn, is more restaurant-with-rooms than traditional pub. It even looks as if it's in two halves: a white-painted brick and pebbledash part for the pub, and a stone-built wing converted to provide accommodation and a restaurant. The last, spread over two floors, has its own menu, but eating and drinking options are flexible, and the beamed bar/brasserie has an informal, pubby feel. With the relaxed atmosphere helped along by a log-burning fire and cosy alcoves, it is still possible to drop in just for a sandwich (lunchtimes only) and a pint – beers come from Yorkshire brewers Timothy Taylor and Black Sheep – but it will be hard to resist the menu of ambitious modern brasserie food. Typical options have included starters of queenie scallops grilled with garlic, Gruyère and Cheddar, or a pressing of Yorkshire ham and foie gras, and main courses of slow-braised shoulder of lamb, and Birstwith Angus steak and ale pudding. Finish with glazed lemon tart, or a selection of English farmhouse cheeses. The impressive wine list is arranged by grape variety and style, with a healthy mix of quality names from Old World and New and over a dozen by the glass from £2.40. The own-label house wines at £13.95 are the only 'budget' bottles on the list. The pub is connected by common ownership and passion to the Angel in Hetton. SAMPLE DISHES: provençale fish soup £5.75; roast grey partridge with thyme and port jus £12.25; gingerbread rice pudding £5.

Licensee John Topham (freehouse)

Open 12 to 3, 6 to 11 (10.30 Sun); bar food 12 to 2.15, 6 to 9.15 (8.30 Sun); restaurant Sun 12 to 1.45, Mon to Fri 6 to 9.15, Sat 6.45 to 9.30

Details Children welcome   Car park   Wheelchair access (not WC)   Garden   No-smoking area in bar, no smoking in restaurant · Occasional live music   Dogs welcome   Amex, MasterCard, Switch, Visa Accommodation: 14 rooms, B&B £75 to £110

FLETCHING   East Sussex   map 3

▲ Griffin Inn

Fletching TN22 3SS   TEL: (01825) 722890
WEBSITE: www.thegriffininn.co.uk
off A272, between Maresfield and Newick, 3m NW of Uckfield

At the heart of the village, this sixteenth-century pub enjoys a beautiful setting, with panoramic countryside views from its splendid garden. On entering the saloon bar, expect roaring log fires, horse brasses, pictures and decorative plates on wood-panelled walls, and typically varied dark wooden pub furniture, the tables adorned with church candles and flowers. The atmosphere is that of a traditional village inn, so you may well encounter locals reading newspapers and eating their supper at the bar (there is also an adjoining public bar). The restaurant to the rear has its own ambitious upmarket menu, but those who eat in the bar are not sold short, with a wide-ranging list of appealing modern ideas ranging from tiger prawn bisque or roasted garlic and herb risotto for starters to main courses of Thai curry with butternut squash, spinach and coconut, slow-roast lamb shank in red wine with herb mash, or a salad of baby beetroot, broad beans, quail's eggs and Jersey potatoes. Real ales include Harveys Sussex Best Bitter, King's Horsham Best and Badger Tanglefoot. A dozen wines under £15 a bottle are listed by the glass on a blackboard but for those with more to spend it's worth perusing the excellent list which features over 50 more bottles, mostly from Europe, a seasonally themed page of specials and some high-priced classics. SAMPLE DISHES: chargrilled asparagus with Parmesan shavings £6; confit of Barbary duck leg with braised Puy lentils £10.50; raspberry cheesecake £5.

Licensees James Pullan and John Gatti (freehouse)

Open 12 to 3, 6 to 11 (10.30 Sun); bar food and restaurant 12 to 2.30, 7 to 9.30 (9 Sun); closed 25 Dec; restaurant closed Sun evening winter

Details *Children welcome   Car park   Wheelchair access (also WC)   Garden and patio   No smoking in restaurant   Occasional background music   Dogs welcome   Amex, Diners, MasterCard, Switch, Visa Accommodation: 8 rooms, B&B £50 to £120*

FONTHILL GIFFORD   Wiltshire   map 2

▲ Beckford Arms

Fonthill Gifford SP3 6PX   TEL: (01747) 870385
take minor road off B3089 at Fonthill Bishop and follow signs to Fonthill Gifford

Built in the eighteenth century, this substantial stone inn was named after the eccentric millionaire and author William Beckford, who attempted to erect an extravagant 'Gothic dream palace' (Fonthill Abbey) on the Fonthill Estate. Behind the pub is a peaceful terrace and raised garden for summer days, and the place still supports a lively locals' bar. In the tastefully rustic main bar there's a highly sought-after window seat, plus a stone fireplace, huge scrubbed pine tables and ornate mirrors. Beyond is a dining area with terracotta walls and plants, and also an airy Garden Room with picture windows. At lunchtime you can get upmarket ciabatta sandwiches and a mixed bag of traditional stalwarts and modern ideas ranging from prawn cocktail and ham and eggs to grilled goats' cheese with walnuts and parsley pesto or breast of Barbary duck with spiced rhubarb and ginger compote. The evening menu shows a touch more elaboration, with dishes like medallions of Wiltshire pork with caramelised apple, Calvados and cider, while desserts take a familiar route for treacle sponge and pecan pie. Draught beers are well-known names like Fuller's London Pride, Greene King Abbot Ale and Timothy Taylor Landlord, and the varied list of around 25 wines includes seven by the glass. SAMPLE DISHES: Thai crab and sweetcorn fishcake with chilli mayonnaise £6; fillet of Scottish beef with a red wine and crushed black peppercorn sauce £17; apple pie £4.50.

Licensees Karen and Eddie Costello (freehouse)
Open *12 to 11 (10.30 Sun); bar food 12 to 2, 7 to 9*
Details *Children welcome   Car park   Garden and patio   Background music   Dogs welcome on a lead Delta, MasterCard, Switch, Visa   Accommodation: 4 rooms, B&B £40 to £85*

FORD   Buckinghamshire   map 3

▲ Dinton Hermit

Water Lane, Ford HP17 8XH   TEL: (01296) 747473
off A418, 4m SW of Aylesbury

In a hamlet next to Dinton, this pub takes its name from one John Bigg, the Dinton-born clerk to Simon Mayne, one of the signatories to Charles I's death warrant. Mayne ended his days in the Tower of London, while Biggs ended his as a cave-dwelling hermit, dying in 1696. The stone cottage has been much extended, with a recent barn conversion adding smart up-to-date bedrooms, but the bar retains a characterful pubby appeal through black beams, exposed-stone walls and a warming winter fire. Real ales on tap include Adnams Bitter, Fuller's London Pride and Wychert Ale. A winter menu might begin with Devon crab cakes with coriander salsa, or chicken liver and cognac pâté with onion marmalade, and go on to a trio of lamb loin cutlets with potato and red onion rösti and a mint and honey jus, or pot-roast guinea fowl with raisins, pine nuts, orange zest and sherry, and there's roast beef, lamb or chicken on Sundays. A 40-strong wine list has four by the glass. SAMPLE DISHES: crispy duck salad with warm plum and star anise dressing £6.50; braised ham hock with butter beans, tarragon and mature Cheddar £12.50; strawberry crème brûlée £5.50.

Licensees John and Debbie Collinswood (freehouse)
Open 11 to 11, Sun 12 to 10.30; bar food 12 to 2, 7 to 9; closed 25 Dec
Details Children welcome   Car park   Garden and patio   Background music   Dogs welcome exc in restaurant   Amex, Delta, MasterCard, Switch, Visa   Accommodation: 13 rooms, £80 to £125.

FORDHAM   Cambridgeshire   map 6

White Pheasant

21 Market Street, Fordham CB7 5LQ   TEL: (01638) 720414

Set right on the corner of the A142 beside the turning to Burwell, this large, white painted seventeenth-century inn is easy to spot. Inside, the light, airy main bar's atmosphere mixes traditional pub and relaxed restaurant – walls hung with prints and bric-à-brac, background music, tables laid for food, a good log fire. Frequently changing ales may include Hobson's Choice from City of Cambridge Brewery, or Woodforde's Wherry and Nelson's Revenge, and the 40-bin wine list offers 14 by the glass and (barring a dozen 'fine' wines) keeps bottle prices under £20. Attentive service complements generous portions and fresh ingredients. Choose from bar snacks (bacon and black pudding sandwich, say, or gammon steak with fried egg and sautéed potatoes) or an evening menu (supplemented by a specials board with many fish and game dishes) that doesn't overlook vegetarians and gluten-allergics. The latter may offer starters like sun-dried tomato and spring onion crab cakes with coriander relish and balsamic reduction, or wild mushroom tortellini with basil butter sauce and Parmesan. Then peppered fillet of English beef with horseradish mash, roast baby shallots, crispy pancetta and brandy jus, or Swiss chard and ricotta cannelloni baked with white wine, cream and Gruyère. SAMPLE DISHES: smoked haddock and grain mustard chowder £5; salami-wrapped poached pheasant suprême stuffed with watercress and shiitake mushrooms £16; vanilla poached pears £4.50.

Licensee Elizabeth Meads (freehouse)
Open 12 to 3, 6 to 11, Sun 12 to 3, 7 to 10.30; bar food and restaurant Mon to Sat 12 to 2.30, 6 to 9.30, Sun 12 to 2.30, 7 to 9
Details Children welcome   Car park   Garden   No-smoking areas   Background music   Guide dogs only   Amex, Delta, MasterCard, Switch, Visa

---

FORDWICH   Kent   map 3

Fordwich Arms

King Street, Fordwich CT2 0DB   TEL: (01227) 710444

Fordwich claims to be the smallest town in Britain, by virtue of its ancient town hall, a tiny half-timbered building. In truth, Fordwich is more of a village but is really a residential suburb of Canterbury, albeit a posh one, with the River Stour running through the middle and the Fordwich Arms on its bank. It's an unusual-looking building of traditional red brick with elaborate Victorian Gothic styling. Inside, the main bar is 'awash with chintz – heavily patterned pink floral wallpaper and matching curtains', and all around the room on shelves, mantelpieces and windowsills are assorted knick-knacks, dried flower displays and leather-bound editions of classic novels; the dining room is a little more sedate. The printed menu delivers standard bar snacks, with blackboard specials (which are the same as in the restaurant) adding more interest. Thick and flavoursome pea and bacon soup, and rabbit in ale with dumplings have made recent appearances. Otherwise, there could be breast of chicken stuffed with bacon and chestnuts, roast pheasant with root vegetables and port sauce, and beef curry with rice and naan. Puddings might run to rich chocolate torte and iced banoffi brûlée. Beers include Shepherd Neame Master Brew Bitter, Flowers Original and Wadworth 6X, and 13 wines are sold by the glass. SAMPLE DISHES: garlic-fried king prawns £5.25; lamb's liver and bacon £9; chocolate and orange sponge pudding £4.

Licensees Mr and Mrs Sean O'Donnell (Enterprise Inns)

Open 11 to 11, Sun 12 to 3, 7 to 10.30; bar food and restaurant (exc Sun evening) 12 to 2.30 (2 Sun), 6.30 to 9.30

Details Children welcome in restaurant   Car park   Wheelchair access (also WC)   Garden and patio No smoking in restaurant   Occasional background music   Dogs welcome exc in restaurant   Delta, MasterCard, Switch, Visa

---

FORTON   Lancashire   map 8

Bay Horse Inn ✿ 🍺

Bay Horse, Forton LA2 0HR   TEL: (01524) 791204
WEBSITE: www.bayhorseinn.com
from M6 junction 33 take A6 towards Preston; take second left-hand turn; pub on right

Look for the Trough of Bowland signs if you are making your way to this immaculately kept black and white pub in a tiny village just minutes from the M6. From the outside it looks inviting, with window boxes and tables on the patio. The interior still feels like a genuine rural pub, with a bar in one corner dispensing excellent Lancastrian beers like Moorhouses Pendle Witches Brew and Thwaites Lancaster Bomber alongside guests such as Ridleys Rumpus or Adnams Fisherman. But the main emphasis is on food, and most visitors head for the spotless dining room where tables are laid with linen cloths and there's artwork on the walls. It is all very sedate, civilised and comfortable. The regular printed menu is bolstered by a specials board hung over the fire, and there's no doubting the kitchen's commitment to Lancastrian and North Country produce. Goosnargh chicken might be the starting point for a classy pressed terrine with Italian ham and Garstang blue cheese, while Goosnargh duckling could be slowly cooked and served with potato purée, roast figs and elderberry wine and honey sauce. Bowland lamb also puts in an appearance (roast rack has been served with a feather-light, 'almost soufflé-like' polenta cake scented with thyme), and from further afield you can expect Morecambe Bay potted shrimps and Cumbrian fell-bred beef with goats' cheese mash and a wild mushroom and Madeira sauce. Fruit tarts and cheesecakes share top billing when it comes to desserts. A serviceable list of around 30 affordably priced, mostly familiar wines includes around ten by the glass. As we go to press the team here is opening a second pub, The Borough at Dalton Square, Lancaster. SAMPLE DISHES: smoked chicken Caesar salad £5.50; seared salmon fillet with sweet chilli dip £13; warm treacle, walnut and fig tart with toffee ice cream £4.75.

Licensee Craig Wilkinson (Creation Foods)
Open Tue to Sat 12 to 2, 6.30 to 11, Sun 12 to 4, 8 to 10.30; bar food Tue to Sat 12 to 1.30, 7 to 9.15,
Sun 12 to 3
Details Children welcome in eating areas   Car park   Wheelchair access (not WC)   Garden and patio
No smoking in eating areas   Background music   No dogs   Delta, MasterCard, Switch, Visa

FOSS CROSS   Gloucestershire   map 2

▲ Hare & Hounds   NEW ENTRY

Foss Cross GL54 4NW   TEL: (01285) 720288
on A429, 6m N of Cirencester

A few miles from tourist-trap Bibury, with its National Trust Arlington Row of
ancient cottages (not open to the public), Foss Cross is nothing more than a crossroads on the 'dead straight' Roman Fosse Way, with the Hare & Hounds the one
'isolated' pub. It's an ancient Cotswolds building of pale honey-coloured stone, with a
big patio area and lawned garden. Inside, the interior has been left uncluttered and
treated with respect: colours are natural or white, with floors of old oak boards or
honey-coloured limestone flags, and tables of stripped wood; no background music is
a bonus. Chef/landlord Geraldo Ragosa is Italian-born, and there's a Mediterranean
echo to the menu. On the whole, dishes play it safe with tried and tested combinations, such as starters of duck and chicken liver pâté with orange and white onion
marmalade, and main courses of roast rack of lamb cooked in honey and ginger with a
mint and white wine sauce, or Italian-style breast of chicken with tomatoes, basil,
oregano and olives on a bed of linguine. Puddings are mainly traditional English pies,
trifles and sponges. Arkell's 2B and 3B are on handpump, and five red and five white
wines are available by the glass. SAMPLE DISHES: cream of butternut squash and chive
soup £4.50; spatchcock poussin roasted with garlic and kumquats with caper sauce
£13; stem ginger and ricotta cheesecake with almond and whisky sauce £5.

Licensees Angela Howe and Geraldo Ragosa (Arkell's)
Open 10 to 11, Sun 12 to 11; bar food and restaurant 12 to 2.30, 6 to 9.30, Sun 12 to 3, 7 to 9
Details Children welcome   Car park   Wheelchair access (also WC)   Garden and patio   No-smoking area in
bar, no smoking in restaurant   Occasional live or background music   Dogs welcome   Delta, MasterCard,
Switch, Visa   Accommodation: 10 rooms, B&B £50 to £70

FOTHERINGHAY   Northamptonshire   map 6

Falcon Inn 🏵 🌳

Fotheringhay PE8 5HZ   TEL: (01832) 226254
WEBSITE: www.huntsbridge.com

Fotheringhay's mighty church dominates the scene in this quiet village and casts its
shadow over the pretty-looking Falcon. Windsor chairs, flowers, discreet soft colours
and properly laid tables lend an air of modern comfort, and the main dining area is in
a handsome conservatory extension; there's also a separate tap bar (with its own
entrance and dartboard), which is popular with locals. Ray Smikle cooks with an eye
on current trends, turning his hand to sweet potato, plantain and roast pepper soup,
escalope of pork with couscous salad and harissa, and breast of chicken with roast
butternut squash, radicchio, pancetta, red onions and tarragon pesto. Fish tends to
play second fiddle, but you might notice, for example, roast fillet of salmon with

minted courgettes, salsa verde and lemon butter sauce. Hand-cut chips are a must, and desserts could include winter fruit and Armagnac tart. Eat as much or as little as you want: there's even a blackboard listing snacks like open sandwiches and Greek burgers. The Falcon is part of the Huntsbridge Group (see the entries for the Old Bridge at Huntington, the Pheasant at Keyston and the Three Horseshoes at Madingley), which is famed for its pedigree wine lists. A dozen or more are offered by the glass from £3 to £7.50, and there's an impressive back-up of sherries and dessert wines. The main slate of around 100 bins is arranged by style and divided into 'under £20' and 'top-class' sections with useful, knowledgeable notes. If it's beer you've come for, there are East Anglian brews from Adnams, Greene King and guests. SAMPLE DISHES: pork rillettes with cranberry pickle £5.50; Thai-style fishcake with marinated Thai vegetables and chilli sauce £9.75; queen of puddings £5.50.

Licensees John Hoskins and Ray Smikle (freehouse)
Open 12 to 3, 6 to 11 (10.30 Sun); bar food and restaurant 12 to 2.15, 6.30 to 9.30
Details Children welcome Car park Wheelchair access (also WC) Garden No smoking in conservatory
No music Dogs welcome Amex, Delta, Diners, MasterCard, Switch, Visa

FOWLMERE   **Cambridgeshire**   map 6

Chequers
High Street, Fowlmere SG8 7SR   TEL: (01763) 208369
off B1368, between A10 and A505, 5m NE of Royston

This place has seen some comings and goings in 500 years. In the sixteenth century it doubled as a chapel of rest for coffins journeying between London and Cambridge; in the seventeenth Samuel Pepys spent a night here; and in the twentieth pilots from Fowlmere aerodrome sought distraction from two world wars (the pub sign's two sides bear the chequered colours of 19 Squadron RAF and 339 Fighter Group USAF). It is still a popular, upmarket haunt, warmed by a huge log-burning inglenook, and its laminated menu and the blackboard offer plenty of food for thought. Elaborate offerings might include poached black pudding on a potato, chilli, mango and ginger stew, then maybe roast loin of wild venison with pepperdews, port and veal jus, Parisienne potatoes and rocket and raw mushroom salad. Irish farmhouse cheeses might offer a simpler finish than desserts like pan-fried Russet apples with Muscovado sugar laced with Calvados and served with Belgian bourbon vanilla ice cream. Adnams Bitter and a guest ale are on draught, but there are also 30 malt whiskies, and house table wines (also available by the glass) are all under £12. The wine list is half French, but alongside pricey bottles, there are some canny choices under £20. SAMPLE DISHES: creamed mushrooms with white wine and tarragon in a filo case £5; roast salmon fillet and freshwater prawns with creamed basil sauce, herb tagliatelle and mange-tout £11.25; dark chocolate mousse with whipped cream, 'glaced' mango and Amaretti biscuits £4.75.

Licensees Norman and Pauline Rushton (freehouse)
Open 12 to 2.30, 6 to 11, Sun 12 to 3, 7 to 10.30; bar food and restaurant 12 to 2, 7 to 10, Sun 12 to 3, 7 to 9.30; closed 25 Dec
Details Children welcome Car park Wheelchair access (not WC) Garden and patio No smoking in restaurant No music No dogs Amex, Delta, Diners, MasterCard, Switch, Visa

FRAMPTON MANSELL   Gloucestershire   map 2

White Horse 🏵 🍇

Cirencester Road, Frampton Mansell GL6 8HZ   TEL: (01285) 760960
on A419, about 7m W of Cirencester, at junction with road to Frampton Mansell

The A419 may be always busy outside the door of this unpretentious-looking old stone pub, but, within, the simplicity of the tables and décor suggest a rural retreat. In just a few years, Emma and Shaun Davis have created a stylish pub-restaurant, with the emphasis more on 'restaurant' than 'pub'. A fittingly ambitious modern British menu offers starters of lambs' sweetbreads with lardons, roasted baby onions and a port and thyme jus, or quail's eggs en croûte with buttered spinach and basil pesto. Main courses range from slow-braised belly pork with noodles, caramelised baby apples and soy and balsamic to grilled monkfish tail with roasted cherry tomatoes and a parsley and saffron cream. There is no real distinction between bar and restaurant, but a separate lunchtime bar menu, listed on a blackboard and available throughout, lists simpler dishes along the lines of battered cod with tartare sauce, and home-glazed ham with egg and home-made chips as well as filled baguettes. Although food is the main business, drinkers are encouraged – to that end, the bar area is furnished with a large sofa and comfortable chairs where you can relax while enjoying a pint of Uley Bitter, Hook Norton Best or perhaps Arkells Summer Ale in season. If you prefer wine, there is a choice of six by the glass, representing each of the styles used to arrange the list of around 40 bottles. It's an interesting mix, and quality is good, with prices starting at £11.50 and almost all under £20. SAMPLE DISHES: tomato and thyme soup £3.50; red mullet with pineapple and chilli relish, coriander and lemon dressing £12; lemon posset with poached berries and spun sugar £4.25.

Licensees Emma and Shaun Davis (freehouse)
Open *11 to 3, 6 to 11; bar food 12 to 2.30 (3 Sun); restaurant 12 to 2.30 (3 Sun), 7 to 9.45; closed Sun evening, 24 to 26 Dec, 1 Jan*
Details *Children welcome in eating areas   Car park   Wheelchair access (not WC)   Garden   No cigars/pipes in restaurant   No music   Dogs welcome   MasterCard, Switch, Visa*

FRITHSDEN   Hertfordshire   map 3

Alford Arms

Frithsden HP1 3DD   TEL: (01442) 864480
turn left at Water End off A4146, head towards Frithsden and Nettleden. Turn left at junction, next right, pub is 100yds on right

An old cream-painted inn on the edge of the village, the Alford is a gastro-pub with the emphasis on gastro rather than pub, though one corner is reserved for drinkers, who also enjoy the benefit of a log fire. The dining area has a cosy, intimate feel thanks to soft lighting, chintz curtains and warm coral-coloured walls adorned with prints and pewter pans. Imaginative menus provide plenty of choice, starters taking in everything from duck livers with damson and smoked paprika to smoked haddock, potato and parsley broth, while main courses might feature salmon and herb fishcake with tartare sauce and buttered greens, alongside lamb rump with Puy lentils and roasted root vegetables. Careful cooking and stylish presentation means it all eats as well as it reads, and a young, energetic and able serving team ensure that everything runs smoothly. There's a short global wine list, with a good choice by the glass or half bottle, and beers include Morrell's Oxford Blue, Marston's Pedigree and Brakspear Bitter. SAMPLE DISHES: oak-smoked bacon on bubble and squeak with hollandaise and poached egg £5.75/£11; calf's liver and bacon on Parmesan mash with onion gravy £11.75; vanilla pannacotta with blackberry compote £4.25.

Licensees David and Becky Salisbury (freehouse)
Open 11 to 11, Sun 12 to 10.30; bar food 12 to 2.30, 7 to 10, Sun 12 to 3, 7 to 9.30
Details Children welcome Car park Patio Background music Dogs welcome in bar only Amex, Delta, MasterCard, Switch, Visa

FRODSHAM Cheshire   map 7

Netherton Hall 🍺

Chester Road, Frodsham WA6 6UL   TEL: (01928) 732342
WEBSITE: www.nethertonhall.com
on A56 Warrington to Chester road, on the SW edge of Frodsham

Handsome, ivy-clad Netherton Hall was built in the Georgian period as a farmhouse and converted into a pub relatively recently. Surrounded by landscaped gardens, it enjoys views of nearby Frodsham Hill and feels secluded despite being close to the motorway. The open-plan interior is divided into several distinct areas around a central brick and tile bar, and although it tends more towards the restaurant end of the scale the atmosphere is suitably informal, and a simple bar snacks menu lists sandwiches, omelettes and pasties. More interesting are the long and eclectic blackboard menus: here, duck spring rolls with plum sauce appear next to grilled sardines with lemon and parsley butter for starters, while main courses might include teriyaki-style tuna, pan-fried venison steak with a chestnut, thyme and port reduction, and vegetarian haggis on roast aubergine. Drinkers are well served too, with well-kept real ales including Greene King IPA and Abbot Ale, Timothy Taylor Landlord and Ram Tam, and Jennings Cumberland Bitter, as well as a good selection of whiskies and 30 wines from £9.95, 17 of which come by the glass. SAMPLE DISHES: pan-fried crab cakes with dill mayonnaise £5.25; roast pork fillet wrapped in Parma ham with cider apple sauce £13.50; tiramisù £4.75.

Licensee H. Sharter (Punch Group)
Open 12 to 11, Sun 12 to 10.30; bar food and restaurant 12 to 2.30, 6 to 9
Details No children Car park Wheelchair access (not WC) Garden and patio No-smoking area in bar, no smoking in restaurant Background music No dogs Amex, Delta, MasterCard, Switch, Visa

FROGGATT Derbyshire   map 8

▲ Chequers Inn

Froggatt Edge, Froggatt S32 3ZJ TEL: (01433) 630231
WEBSITE: www.chequers-froggatt.com
off A623 just N of Calver

Froggatt Edge, in the heart of the Peak District, is a popular spot with walkers, but those who prefer more leisurely pursuits can enjoy splendid views from the woodland garden of this sixteenth century inn. Inside, décor has the homely feel of a country cottage, with simple wooden furniture, polished dark wood floorboards, pine dressers full of crockery, and country-themed prints on pale yellow walls. A regular menu plus daily specials provide an appealing choice of dishes ranging from traditional favourites like sausages and mash with shallot gravy to more modern and ambitious ideas such as grilled salmon with Mediterranean vegetables and Vermouth sauce. Superior sandwiches are also available – one reporter praised the poached salmon and lime mayonnaise version, as well as the 'moist, almondy' Bakewell tart for dessert. Real ales on draught are Charles Wells Bombardier and Greene King Abbott Ale, and there's a list of 30 wines, eight of which are available by the glass from £2.50/£3.65. SAMPLE DISHES: glazed goats' cheese with roasted vegetables and mustard dressing £5.25; pork fillet with apple and plum marmalade and apple jus £15; Bakewell pudding £4.25.

Licensees Jonathan and Joanne Tindall (freehouse)
Open Mon to Fri 12 to 3, 6 to 11, Sat 12 to 11, Sun 12 to 10.30; bar food Mon to Fri 12 to 2, 6 to 9.30, Sat 12 to 9.30, Sun 12 to 9
Details Children welcome   Car park   Garden and patio   No-smoking area   Background music   No dogs
Amex, Delta, MasterCard, Switch, Visa   Accommodation: 5 rooms, B&B £50 to £80

FULBECK   **Lincolnshire**   map 6

▲ Hare & Hounds
The Green, Fulbeck NG32 3JJ   TEL: (01400) 272090

At the centre of the village overlooking the green, the Hare & Hounds is a charming and well-preserved seventeenth-century coaching inn. Two interconnecting bar areas have beamed ceilings, fireplaces, dark wood cottage-style furniture and a relaxed, welcoming atmosphere. There is also a separate restaurant to the rear with a menu of hearty but stylish country cooking, such as roast salmon on buttered leeks with dill cream, or chicken breast stuffed with garlic cream cheese, basil and sun-dried tomato. This menu is available throughout, but there's also a simpler bar menu of dishes such as steaks, salads, and Lincolnshire sausages and mash, plus specials including pies of steak and Stilton, or salmon and broccoli. A good range of real ales features Bateman XB, Fuller's London Pride, Hook Norton Best Bitter and Greene King IPA, plus regularly changing guests. The wine list opens with a page of ten varied, good-value house selections available by the bottle (from £10) and large or small glass; the full list runs to 40-plus well-chosen bottles. SAMPLE DISHES: pâté with red onion marmalade £6; crisp-roast half-duck with orange and Cointreau sauce £14.25; tipsy bread-and-butter pudding £4.50.

Licensees David and Alison Nicholas (freehouse)
Open 12 to 2.30 (2 winter), 6 (7 Sun) to 11 (12 to 11 Sat and Sun Apr to Oct); bar food and restaurant 12 to 2, 6 to 10
Details Children welcome   Car park   Wheelchair access (not WC)   Garden and patio   No-smoking area in bar, no smoking in restaurant   Background music   Dogs welcome exc in restaurant   MasterCard, Switch, Visa
Accommodation: 8 rooms, B&B £39.50 to £50

GALPHAY   **North Yorkshire**   map 8

Galphay Arms ✿
Galphay HG4 3NJ   TEL: (01765) 650133
of B6265, 4½m W of Ripon

Visitors to Fountains Abbey should take note of the Galphay Arms a few miles away. The pub, parts of which date from around 1800, is a neat, compact stone building rescued from a run-down state. The current owners put a great deal of effort into the renovation, and according to a seasoned inspector the results are impressive. Enter into a reception area with leather armchairs and a blazing log fire, then move to the main bar area, comfortably furnished and panelled with dark wood. Beyond is the dining area, done out in pale green and with well-spaced pine tables. Simple sandwiches and snacks are served in the bar, but the main menu offers plenty of options for those seeking a full and leisurely meal, and the cooking is refreshingly simple and unpretentious. Among starters might be ham hock terrine with spiced apple and plum chutney, or crab fritters with a sweet dipping sauce, while main course choices typically take in wild mushroom and brie risotto, or duck breast with red cabbage and oranges. First-class raw materials give simple dishes such as fish pie a strong impact. Beers are Black Sheep Bitter and John Smith's Cask Ale, and there are six wines by the glass from a list of around 45 bottles, mostly under £20. SAMPLE DISHES: goats' cheese tartlet £5; chicken breast wrapped in locally cured bacon with creamed wild mushrooms £10; sticky toffee pudding £4.25.

Licensees Robert and Samantha MacArthur (freehouse)
Open Wed to Mon 12 to 3, 6.30 to 11; bar food Wed to Mon 12 to 2, 6.30 to 10; closed lunchtime Nov, Feb and Mar
Details Children welcome Car park Occasional live music No dogs Amex, Delta, Diners, MasterCard, Switch, Visa

GEDNEY DYKE   Lincolnshire   map 6

Chequers

Main Street, Gedney Dyke PE12 0AJ   TEL: (01406) 362666
WEBSITE: www.chequerspub.co.uk
just off B1359, from Gedney roundabout on A17, 3m E of Holbeach

The Chequers remains 'very much a food-orientated pub', surrounded by marshes, wildfowl and a vast expanse of sky. Homely, welcoming and well worn, the beamed bars have real fires, and there's a separate, modern conservatory restaurant; bar snacks and blackboard specials are available throughout. Breast of chicken stuffed with bacon and topped with mozzarella and sun-dried tomato sauce, or haunch of venison with potato and celeriac galette and wild mushroom sauce might feature on the board, while the printed menu sticks with tradition, offering sandwiches, ploughman's and the like but ringing the changes with a burger made with wild boar and apple and served with home-made tomato chutney. A 'well-flavoured' crab and Parmesan tartlet with cucumber balsamic dressing, or confit of bacon with a grain mustard dressing with chutney and salad make good starters, bread is home made, and service is 'attentive and helpful'. Real ales are Elgood's Black Dog Mild, from Wisbech, and Adnams Best Bitter and Greene King Abbot Ale. Ten wines by the glass head up a list that offers a sound international choice at good prices. SAMPLE DISHES: cheese-filled pasta with tomato and basil sauce £5.50; roast leg of Gloucester Old Spot pork with black cherry sauce £10.50; orange and apple crumble with crème anglaise £5.

Licensees Sarah Tindale and Adrian Isted (freehouse)
Open Tue to Sun 12 to 2, 7 to 11 (10.30 Sun); bar food and restaurant 12 to 2, 7 to 9
Details Children welcome Car park Wheelchair access (also WC) Garden and patio No smoking in 1 room Background music No dogs Amex, Diners, MasterCard, Switch, Visa

GODMANCHESTER Cambridgeshire map 6

Exhibition

London Road, Godmanchester PE29 2HZ   TEL: (01480) 459134
along A1198 towards Wood Green, take first right to Godmanchester; pub is 300yds on right

This is an attractive old building in a village of water meadows and timber-framed houses. It has been extensively modernised, but the beams and shape of the old house can still be seen. The stone-flagged main bar is a surprise, with re-created shop fronts along the outside wall (post office, gallery, stores) creating the distinct impression that you're sitting in a Victorian street; the dining room is particularly 'olde worlde' too. The food is cooked to order and, even if the place is busy, 'worth waiting for'. Several blackboard menus provide a range of choice and interest for all appetites and tastes: perhaps mackerel and salmon brochettes with roast beetroot oil and roquette salad to start, followed by chargrilled Tuscan-style pigeon marinated in red wine, olive oil, sage and garlic and served with celeriac purée, wilted greens and a red wine dressing. Greene King IPA and Fuller's London Pride, plus a changing guest beer, and six wines by the glass offer various combinations of liquid accompaniments. SAMPLE DISHES: risotto of spiced chicken livers with Parmesan and a Madeira vinaigrette £5; honey-glazed lamb shank with pumpkin purée and wilted spinach £11; Baileys crème brûlée with chocolate ice cream and brandy-snap basket £4.25.

Licensee J.W. Middlemiss (Unique)
Open *Mon to Thur 11.30 to 3.30, 5.30 to 11.30, Fri and Sat 11.30 to 11.30, Sun 12 to 10.30; bar food and restaurant 12 to 2.15, 6.30 to 9.45, Sun 12.30 to 3, 6.30 to 9.30*
Details *Children welcome in restaurant   Car park   Wheelchair access   Garden   No smoking in restaurant Background and occasional live music   No dogs   Amex, Delta, MasterCard, Switch, Visa*

GOUDHURST Kent map 3

Green Cross Inn ☺

Station Road, Goudhurst TN17 1HA   TEL: (01580) 211200
WEBSITE: www.greencrossinn.co.uk
on A262, 3m E of A21 and 1m W of village

This tall and solid-looking roadside pub is in a rural setting just outside Goudhurst. Step through the front porch directly into the light, airy and very clean and neat-looking main bar, with its large stuffed trout in a display case over the brick fireplace. There's quite a buzz in the atmosphere, and, though the emphasis is on eating, you can expect to find a gaggle of locals just chatting and drinking around the small central bar counter. Bar menus keep things simple, unpretentious and mostly traditional, with the likes of salmon fishcakes with tartare sauce, sausages in Yorkshire pudding with onion gravy, or 'cataplana', a hearty Spanish dish of mussels with chorizo and bacon in a thin, spicy, tomato- and garlic-flavoured broth. Classic fish and seafood dishes are the speciality of the separate restaurant menu that runs through, say, smoked eel and whole Dover sole (or wild duck cassoulet) to zabaglione. An above-average range of real ales includes Harveys Sussex Best and local Larkins Best, and the list of 50 assorted wines includes five house selections from £10, also available by the glass. SAMPLE DISHES: avocado and prawns £4.25; moules et frites £8; pannacotta with strawberry coulis £4.25.

Licensees Eleuterio and Caroline Lizzi (freehouse)
Open 11 to 3, 6 to 11; bar food and restaurant 12 to 2.30, 7 to 10; closed Sun evenings winter
Details Children welcome Car park Garden No smoking in restaurant Occasional background music
Dogs welcome in bar only MasterCard, Switch, Visa

GRASMERE Cumbria map 10

Travellers Rest

Grasmere LA22 9RR TEL: (015394) 35604
WEBSITE: www.lakedistrictinns.co.uk
on A591 Keswick road, ½m N of Grasmere

Its location, close to the tourist hot spots of Grasmere and Ambleside, means that this sixteenth-century coaching inn gets more than its fair share of tourists and walkers (it stands on the coast-to-coast long-distance walk). So successful is the place that food can be slow in coming at busy times, despite the touch-screen ordering system. Jennings Bitter, Cumberland Ale, Cocker Hoop and Sneck Lifter are on handpump, along with guest ales, and the wine list, starting at £10.25 and staying under £18, offers ten by the glass. The menu and specials are mainly sure-fire favourites like starters of prawns in garlic butter and main courses of chargrilled steak, steak and kidney in Jennings ale pie, or gammon and eggs. Puddings include pear and chocolate tart or coffee and cardamom ice cream. There are also lunchtime sandwiches and a children's menu (lots of chips). SAMPLE DISHES: wild mushrooms in garlic sauce £4; chicken with pumpkin and chickpeas £9; apricot and raspberry roulade £4.

Licensee Lynne Sweeney (freehouse)
Open 11 to 11, Sun 11 to 10.30; bar food and restaurant winter 12 to 3, 6 to 9.30, summer 12 to 9.30
Details Children welcome Car park Patio No smoking in restaurant Background music Dogs welcome
exc in restaurant Delta, MasterCard, Switch, Visa Accommodation: 8 rooms, B&B £50 to £88

GREAT HINTON Wiltshire map 2

Linnet

Great Hinton BA14 6BU TEL: (01380) 870354
just S of A361, about 2m E of Trowbridge

Visitors planning a day taking in the National Trust's Great Chalfield Manor and the Courts Garden at Holt would do well to include the lovely, old red-brick Linnet as a pit stop. It's very much a dining pub (offering good value for money), with 'extremely pleasant' service and a neat, spick-and-span interior including a beamed bar and dining area painted in pale terracotta and filled with flowers and evening candles. First-class raw materials and good timing distinguish dishes as diverse as steamed Thai-style mussels, and a 'perfect' chicken liver and roasted black pudding parfait with spicy pear chutney. Mains such as chargrilled ribeye steak teamed with a grouse and smoked bacon sausage and port and thyme sauce, or 'impeccably prepared' roast rump of lamb with red wine, smoked bacon and orange risotto, show equal care. Finish with white chocolate and raspberry ripple cheesecake, or ice cream, which, like the bread, is home made, with good flavour combinations. This is a Wadworth house, offering 6X and IPA for real ale drinkers, while for wine fans there are eight by the glass. SAMPLE DISHES: crispy duck pancake on mango salsa with plum sauce £5.25; roast loin of monkfish on avocado and shallot relish with roasted tomato sauce £13.75; warm cherry and almond tart with double vanilla ice cream £4.75.

Licensee Jonathan Furby (Wadworth)

Open *Tue to Sat 11 to 2.30, 6 to 11, Sun 11 to 2.30, 7 to 10.30; bar food and restaurant Tue to Sun 12 to 2, 6.30 to 9 (9.30 Fri and Sat); closed 25 and 26 Dec, 1 Jan*

Details *Children welcome   Car park   Wheelchair access (also WC)   Patio   No smoking in restaurant Occasional background music   Dogs welcome in bar only   Amex, Delta, Diners, MasterCard, Switch, Visa*

GREAT TEW   Oxfordshire   map 5

▲ Falkland Arms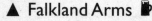

Great Tew OX7 4DB   TEL: (01608) 683653
WEBSITE: www.falklandarms.org.uk

An archetypal pub in an archetypal Oxfordshire village, this part-thatched Cotswold-stone inn consists of a row of tiny terraced cottages that are now thoroughly festooned with creeper. The inn actually dates from the sixteenth century, although its current name refers to the Falkland family who inherited the manor of Great Tew some years later. Visitors marvel at its gloriously preserved interior, which is a fascinating mix of oak beams and settles, flagstone floors, and an inglenook, with wooden shutters at the windows and a vast collection of jugs and vessels hanging from the ceiling. Above the bar counter is a prodigious array of beer mats – a reminder that the place is famed for its spectacular selection of draught beers: half a dozen are normally on handpump, including Wadworth 6X and IPA plus guest ales, alongside Inch's Harvest dry cider. In addition, there are some 15 conventional wines (mostly from the New World), plus about the same number of traditional English country wines, with 22 served by the glass. The kitchen takes a traditional view of things, with dishes honestly prepared and totally in harmony with the surroundings. The evening blackboard advertises robust soup (perhaps cream of courgette with rosemary) with crusty bread, or spicy chicken liver and bacon salad, before the likes of slow-cooked lamb shank 'on a great mound of luscious mash', poached fillet of smoked haddock with a poached egg, or something a little more modern like roast Barbary duck breast on rösti with port and sage jus. At lunchtime there are baguettes, jacket potatoes, and heart-warming dishes such as beef and beer stew with dumplings. Desserts range from sticky toffee pudding to pear tarte Tatin. SAMPLE DISHES: deep-fried crispy whitebait with garlic mayonnaise £6; breast of chicken with bacon, mushrooms and Stilton sauce £9.50; bread-and-butter pudding with vanilla ice cream £4.25.

Licensee Paul Barlow-Heal (Wadworth)

Open *Mon to Fri 11.30 to 2.30, 6 to 11, Sat 11.30 to 3, 6 to 11 (11.30 to 11 summer), Sun 12 to 3, 7 to 10.30 (12 to 10.30 summer); bar food 12 to 2, restaurant Mon to Sat 7 to 8; closed evenings 25 and 26 Dec, 1 Jan*

Details *Children welcome in eating area at lunchtime   Wheelchair access (not WC)   Garden and patio No smoking in restaurant   Live music Sun evening   Dogs welcome on a lead   Amex, Delta, MasterCard, Switch, Visa   Accommodation: 5 rooms, B&B £65 to £80*

Many pubs have separate restaurants with very different menus. These restaurants have not been inspected. A recommendation for the pub/bar food does not necessarily imply that the restaurant is also recommended.

GREAT WHITTINGTON Northumberland map 10

Queens Head Inn ✣

Great Whittington NE19 2HP TEL: (01434) 672267
from A68 4m N of Corbridge turn E on B6318 at Stagshaw roundabout, then left to village

A large dining extension testifies to the main business at this updated early seventeenth-century stone pub in a charming, out-of-the-way village overlooking lovely countryside. The restaurant menu – also available in the bar – is a mixed bag of modern ideas, from pan-fried scallops with bacon and green bean salad, or warm ciabatta bread topped with roasted peppers, black olives, feta and basil oil, to fillet of halibut on 'ribbons' of fresh pasta with a leek and king prawn ragoût, or medallions of venison with a confit of honey-roasted parsnips and caramelised chestnuts and a herb and Burgundy glaze. There's also a fixed-price menu at lunchtime, which always includes a choice of roasts on Sundays. Queens Head and Hambleton Bitter (brewed near Thirsk) are on draught, and three wines come by the glass from a list of about 30 that is spread fairly between the Old and New Worlds with a useful clutch of halves. SAMPLE DISHES: deep-fried black pudding with apple and raisin chutney £6; honey-roast gammon with caramelised onions and mustard sauce £12; sticky toffee pudding with butterscotch sauce £4.50.

Licensee Ian Scott (freehouse)
Open *Tue to Sat and bank hol Mon 12 to 2.30, 6 to 11, Sun 12 to 2.30; bar food and restaurant Tue to Sat and bank hol Mon 12 to 2, 6.30 to 9, Sun 12 to 2*
Details *Children welcome in eating areas Car park Wheelchair access (also WC) No smoking in restaurant Background music Guide dogs only Delta, MasterCard, Switch, Visa*

GREAT WOLFORD Warwickshire map 5

▲ Fox & Hounds Inn

Great Wolford CV36 5NQ TEL: (01608) 674220
off A44, 3m NE of Moreton-in-Marsh

Chatty new licensees and a new chef are now in residence at this gentrified Cotswold country pub built around a courtyard. The inn has been trading since 1540, and it looks the part, with ancient shiny flagstones, beams garlanded with dried hops, and a great hearth helping to give the place an unashamedly cosy, rustic feel. If food is what you're after, peruse the day's blackboard menu. The kitchen makes capable use of high-quality fresh supplies: witness a chargrilled venison steak on roasted root vegetables with grain mustard cream and red wine jus. Elsewhere, expect anything from wild boar sausages, or ostrich medallions with mulled pears, to grilled gammon with all the trimmings. Grilled swordfish topped with tapenade and anchovy fritters is a typical fish alternative, while vegetarians might be offered wild mushroom and leek strudel. Desserts inhabit the traditional world of chocolate brownies and sticky toffee pudding. At lunchtime (Tuesday to Saturday) you can also get sandwiches, baguettes and a handful of 'light bites' such as home-made terrine or garlic mushrooms. Well-kept Hook Norton Best Bitter, Bass and a guest beer – perhaps from Dow Bridge Brewery in Leicestershire – are on draught; the pub also boasts 160 different malt whiskies, and eight wines are served by the glass from a list of about two dozen. SAMPLE DISHES: roast figs and Parma ham £5.50; grilled fillets of plaice with capers, smoked cherry tomatoes and lemon butter £13.75; warm Bakewell tart with crème anglaise £4.25.

Licensees Paul and Veronica Tomlinson (freehouse)
Open Tue to Sat 12 to 2.30, 6 to 11, Sun 12 to 3, 6 to 10.30; bar food Tue to Sun 12 to 2, Tue to Sat 6.45 to 9; closed 10 days early Jan
Details Children over 10 welcome in eating area　Car park　Wheelchair access (also WC)　Patio
No smoking in eating area　Occasional background music　Dogs welcome　MasterCard, Switch, Visa
Accommodation: 3 rooms, B&B £45 to £70

GREAT YELDHAM　Essex　map 6

White Hart 🏵 🌺

Poole Street, Great Yeldham CO9 4HJ　TEL: (01787) 237250
on A604 between Haverhill and Halstead, 6m NW of Halstead

'Standards remain consistently high' at this premier-league pub/restaurant that's set back from the main road just south of the village. Through the door of this striking, rambling half-timbered Tudor building is a roomy and elegant bar with well-spaced armchairs and an atmosphere of wellbeing and traditional creature comforts (including a log fire in winter). To one side is a slightly more formal restaurant complete with polished floorboards, antique tables and two enormous inglenooks at either end. You can choose to eat where you like. The 'light menu' (available for lunch and dinner) promises a selection of sandwiches, farmhouse cheeses from Jeraboam, and grilled Lincolnshire sausages with mash and gravy, while the full works is a wide-ranging assortment of seasonally aware dishes spanning everything from pan-fried saddle of rabbit on colcannon, roasted beetroot and salsify, to rack of lamb with fondant potato, swede and carrot mash and mint jus. Fish is particularly well handled, with imagination on show in dishes such as whole grilled sea bass with roasted plum tomatoes and olives with flat parsley pesto. Adnams is the house bitter, although there are always guest ales, plus six Belgian bottled beers and oak-matured scrumpy. The outstanding list of 80 wines arranged by style is a joy to choose from, whatever your budget. Thirteen come by the glass from £3 to £5.25 and the full selection will get wine-lovers' pulses racing with exciting European names like Planeta and Olivier Leflaive mixing with New World classicists Henschke and Fromm – but there's good stuff under £15 too. An impressive range of champagne opens proceedings and sweet wine fans are well catered for come dessert time. SAMPLE DISHES: aromatic duck pancake with hoisin sauce £6.50; local roast partridge with a prune and apricot farce with roasted cabbage £15.25; fig tart with rum and raisin cream £5.50.

Licensee John Dicken (freehouse)
Open 11 to 11, Sun 12 to 10.30; bar food 12 to 9.30; restaurant 12 to 2, 6.30 to 9.30
Details Children welcome　Car park　Wheelchair access (also WC)　Garden and patio　No smoking in restaurant　No music　Guide dogs only　Amex, Delta, Diners, MasterCard, Switch, Visa

GRETA BRIDGE　Co Durham　map 10

▲ Morritt Arms 🌺

Greta Bridge DL12 9SE　TEL: (01833) 627232
WEBSITE: www.themorritt.co.uk
off A66, 6m E of Bowes

This splendidly rural Georgian coaching inn is beside a narrow, high-arched bridge spanning the river Greta. Inside, the walls of the Dickens Bar, so called because the author reputedly stayed here in 1839 while researching *Nicholas Nickleby*, are covered with murals depicting characters from his novels. A large curving wooden bar takes up one end of the room, while a stuffed black bear guards the other end; in between are an open fire, a mongrel selection of chairs, settles and Britannia tables and a shelf of pewter mugs and teapots. The hotel also has comfortable beamed lounges, a brightly decorated bistro and a separate panelled restaurant. Lunch offers an interesting mix of sandwiches and baguettes and a set menu that might feature a salad of Swaledale cheese with lyonnaise potatoes, rocket, chilli beetroot and parsnip crisps among starters, and main courses like rump of Teesdale lamb with garlic mash and cassoulet. The blackboard expands choice with fish mixed grill with pesto mash and tomato essence, Mainsgill Farmhouse sausages with Wensleydale cheese and chive mash, and steak and kidney pie, while treacle and orange tart with vanilla ice cream could put in an appearance at dessert. Real ales come in the form of Timothy Taylor Landlord, Jennings Cumberland Ale and Black Sheep Best Bitter. A dozen wines are offered by the glass from a 160-strong list arranged by grape variety and then by region – and there's plenty of choice whichever way you choose to look at it. At the time of going to press, the wine list was in the process of being updated. SAMPLE DISHES: grilled seafood in garlic and chilli butter £6.50; chicken casseroled with tomatoes and woodland mushrooms £12; bread-and-butter pudding £5.

Licensee Barbara-Anne Johnson (freehouse)
Open 11 to 11, Sun 12 to 10.30; bar food 12 to 5 (3 Sun), 6 to 9.30 (9 Sun), restaurant 12 to 2, 7 to 9 (8.30 Sun)
Details Children welcome   Car park   Wheelchair access (also WC)   Garden and patio   No-smoking area in bar, no smoking in restaurant   Occasional live music   Dogs welcome exc in eating areas   Amex, Delta, MasterCard, Switch, Visa   Accommodation: 23 rooms, B&B £59.50 to £106.50

GRIMSTHORPE   Lincolnshire   map 6

▲ Black Horse Inn
Grimsthorpe PE10 0LY   TEL: (01778) 591247

New ownership towards the end of 2003 at this early eighteenth-century coaching inn, its creeper-covered front looking out over Grimsthorpe Castle, has rung a few changes. Enter through a small dining area to reach the beamed bar, where Wells Bombardier Premium Bitter and White Squall and Bear Island from Newby Wyke are dispatched. Bar food runs from a range of fillings for sandwiches, baguettes, ciabatta and baked potatoes, to traditional pub dishes including Lincolnshire sausage and mash, lasagna verdi, and beef and ale stew. The main dining room, with wood-block flooring, exposed stone walls and a stone fireplace, offers plenty of choice. Starters range from smoked chicken with tapenade and quail's eggs to a plum tomato and mozzarella stack with pesto, and main courses typically include grilled tuna steak with Mediterranean vegetables, and duck kebabs marinated in honey, ginger and orange served with egg noodles and chilli and coriander sauce. Eight wines are sold by the glass, and the full slate of 40 bins is arranged by style, with good choice under £20. SAMPLE DISHES: moules marinière £6; escalope of veal cordon bleu £14.75; apple and mixed-fruit crumble £4.25.

Licensee Shaun Gilder (freehouse)
Open 12 to 2, 6 to 11, Sun 12 to 4, 7 to 10.30; bar food and restaurant Mon to Sat 12 to 2, 6 to 9, Sun 12 to 4 (restaurant occasionally closes later evenings)
Details Children welcome   Car park   Garden and patio   No smoking in restaurant   Background music   No dogs   Amex, Delta, Diners, MasterCard, Switch, Visa   Accommodation: 6 rooms, B&B £45 to £80

GUNWALLOE   Cornwall   map 1

▲ Halzephron Inn

Gunwalloe TR12 7QB   TEL: (01326) 240406
from A3083 4m S of Helston take small lane towards Church Cove

Atmosphere and drama are provided in abundance here. The 500-year-old pub stands on an exposed headland of the Lizard peninsula – whose name means 'hell's cliff' – with views of Mount Spey in the background. Inside, it's all low-beamed ceilings and cosy corners, and lively crowds of drinkers and diners provide a warm and welcoming atmosphere. And you'll be equally welcome whether you're here to sample the real ales from Sharp's or the superior pub grub. Children will find much to entertain (or distract) them in the family room. The printed menu features mostly simple and traditional dishes such as prawn cocktail, tagliatelle bolognese, or chargrilled steak. More interesting is the daily-changing specials board, which might feature smoked fish pâté with toasted brioche to start, followed by peppered venison loin with bramble jus, or pan-fried cod steak with pancetta and wild mushrooms. Five house wines at £11.50 a bottle or £2 a glass open a list of 60 reasonably priced bottles. SAMPLE DISHES: pan-fried pigeon breasts with poached baby pears and a redcurrant and juniper sauce £6.50; seared salmon on pasta, fennel and asparagus with asparagus velouté £13.50; chocolate and Amaretto praline torte £5.

Licensee Angela Thomas (freehouse)
Open 11 to 2.30, 6 (6.30 winter) to 11, Sun 12 to 2.30, 6 (6.30 winter) to 11; bar food and restaurant 12 to 2, 7 to 9 (6.30 to 9.30 July and Aug); closed 25 Dec
Details Children welcome in family room   Car park   Garden and patio   No smoking in restaurant
Occasional live music   No dogs   Amex, Delta, MasterCard, Switch, Visa   Accommodation: 2 rooms, B&B £44 to £78

HALAM   Nottinghamshire   map 5

Waggon & Horses   NEW ENTRY

Mansfield Road, Halam NG22 8AE   TEL: (01636) 813109

William and Rebecca White run a busy, happy set-up in this simple-looking red-brick and stucco village pub. Drinkers and eaters are cheerfully accommodated in the beamed bar and dining room, with its brick fireplace and cricketing prints hanging on the walls, and the kitchen also finds time to produce a range of ready-made meals for home consumption. Those wanting to eat in the pub will find a wide-ranging menu spanning everything from loaded potato skins filled with bacon and sun-dried tomatoes to specials such as pan-fried John Dory with spring onion mash and soy dressing. Reporters have found plenty to enjoy, including neatly presented smoked mackerel pâté garnished with strips of courgette and spring onion, mushroom risotto with Parmesan and pesto, and hearty roast loin of pork with apricot stuffing, apple sauce and onion gravy. To finish, British cheeses are the order of the day; otherwise choose a dessert like bitter chocolate tart with raspberry and vanilla cream. This is a Thwaites pub with a decent range of its cask ales, such as Premium Smooth, Good Elf and Lancaster Bomber. Seven wines are served by the glass from a decent list of around two dozen bottles. SAMPLE DISHES: shallow-fried Cropwell Bishop Stilton with tomato and chilli jam £6; slow-roast shoulder of lamb with redcurrant, garlic and rosemary £11; lemon and ginger cheesecake with orange coulis £4.

Licensees William and Rebecca White (Daniel Thwaites)
Open Mon to Fri 11 to 3, 5 to 11, Sat 12 to 11, Sun 12 to 10.30; bar food and restaurant Mon to Sat 12 to 2.30, 6 to 9.30, Sun 12 to 4; closed 25 and 26 Dec
Details Children welcome Car park Garden No smoking in restaurant Background music Dogs welcome Delta, MasterCard, Switch, Visa

HALFWAY BRIDGE   West Sussex   map 3

▲ Halfway Bridge Inn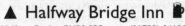
Halfway Bridge GU28 9BP   TEL: (01798) 861281
WEBSITE: www.thesussexpub.co.uk
on A272, midway between Midhurst and Petworth, just S of Lodsworth

The unassuming brick and tile-hung pub is shielded from the busy A272 by a pretty front garden with a worn herringbone brick path and rustic wood seating. But push through the small white door and the interior proves to be cosy and full of character. The two dining areas and long bar have no fewer than five fireplaces, one an old iron range, and wooden tables of all shapes and sizes blend skilfully with the wooden floors. The blackboard menu is supplemented by daily specials, and at lunchtime sandwiches are available, along with lighter meals that can also be taken as starters: warm salad of scallops and bacon, or tiger prawns sautéed in garlic, for instance. Main courses are things like local organic sausages with grain mustard mash and onion gravy, or wild boar steak with caramelised apples and Calvados jus. Lemon and lime tart with passion-fruit sorbet might be among the desserts. Well-kept Gale's HSB, Harveys Sussex Best and Cheriton Pots Ale are the regular real ales, and there's a regularly changing guest. Six wines are sold by the glass. The bedrooms are in a converted barn. SAMPLE DISHES: ricotta and bean pâté with herb foccacia £7; roast half-shoulder of lamb with garlic and rosemary sauce £15.50; Eton mess £4.25.

Licensees Simon and James Hawkins (freehouse)
Open 11 to 3, 6 to 11, Sun 12 to 3, 7 to 10.30; bar food and restaurant 12 to 2 (2.30 Sat and Sun), 7 to 10; closed 25 Dec
Details No children Car park Garden and patio No smoking in 1 eating area No music Dogs welcome on a lead in bar Delta, MasterCard, Switch, Visa Accommodation: 8 rooms, B&B £45 to £100

HALIFAX   West Yorkshire   map 8

▲ Shibden Mill Inn
Shibden Mill Fold, Shibden, Halifax HX3 7UL   TEL: (01422) 365840
WEBSITE: www.shibdenmillinn.com
off A58 Halifax to Leeds road

Any difficulties in finding this out-of-the-way inn are more than outweighed by the prospect of sampling its adventurous food and drink. Though it has a real inn feel – low beams, rich colours, antique furniture, and open fires – most of the space is given over to dining. Expect good, sound cooking and some fresh ideas, even among bar snacks – look out for macaroni cheese with smoked cod fritters, and a selection of British tapas in starter or main-course sizes. On the restaurant menu, warm red mullet and crayfish tails, or corned beef hash with grilled foie gras and apple butter might be among the starters, while main courses have included slow-roast pork shank with chorizo, cabbage and potato, and grilled fillet of sea bass with a crab tart and roasted artichokes. Finish with something like hot cinder toffee soufflé with treacle sauce, or iced white chocolate parfait with mulled wine berry compote; cheese on toast with tomato relish and a glass of port is a savoury alternative. A good choice of real ales includes John Smith's Bitter and their own Shibden Mill Inn ale plus a couple of guests – among them perhaps Timothy Taylor Landlord – while the wine list focuses on good-value everyday drinking (much from the Antipodes and South America), opening with half a dozen bottles at £9.90. Twelve wines come by the glass. SAMPLE DISHES: shepherd's pie tart £5; cold flaked ham hock with egg and chips and pineapple chutney £8; warm rhubarb charlotte with ginger and rhubarb ice cream £4.25.

Licensee S.D. Heaton (freehouse)
Open *Mon to Fri 12 to 2.30, 5.30 to 11, Sat 12 to 11, Sun 12 to 10.30; bar food and restaurant 12 to 2, 6 to 9.30, Sun 12 to 7.30; closed evenings 25 and 26 Dec, 1 Jan*
Details *Children welcome   Car park   Wheelchair access (also WC)   Garden and patio   Background music No dogs   Amex, MasterCard, Switch, Visa   Accommodation: 12 rooms, B&B £65 to £115*

HAMBLEDEN   Buckinghamshire   map 3

▲ Stag & Huntsman Inn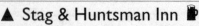

Hambleden RG9 6RP   TEL: (01491) 571227
off A4155 Henley to Marlow road, 1m from Mill End

In a picture-postcard village of brick and flint cottages, this cheery country pub certainly looks the part. Inside, it is all nooks and crannies, although the place is divided up into three distinct areas: a bar at the front used mainly for drinking, to one side a dining room prettily set with green tablecloths, and a lounge warmed by a log fire in winter. One menu runs throughout. Regular items like salade niçoise, ploughman's and main dishes such as chilli, mixed grill, and salmon fishcakes are bolstered by a board of specials that generally include game in season (look for the Hambleden venison sausages). To finish, there are fruit crumbles, cheesecake and ice creams. Real ales are taken seriously here, with regulars like Rebellion IPA and Wadworth 6X backed up by guest ales from the West Country. Thatcher's cider is also on tap, and four house wines (from £2.60 a glass, £10.25 a bottle) kick off the short but serviceable list. Barbecues are held in the beer garden in summer. SAMPLE DISHES: game terrine £5.50; marinated loin of pork with apple and cider sauce £9.50; chocolate brownie with chocolate sauce £4.25.

Licensee Andy Stokes (freehouse)
Open *11 to 2.30 (3 Sat), 6 to 11, Sun 12 to 3, 7 to 10.30; bar food and restaurant all week 12 to 2, Mon to Sat 7 to 9.30; closed 25 Dec, evenings 26 Dec and 1 Jan*
Details *Children welcome in eating areas   Garden   Background music   Dogs welcome in bar only   Delta, MasterCard, Switch, Visa   Accommodation: 3 rooms, B&B £58 to £68*

HANDLEY   Cheshire   map 7

Calveley Arms

Whitchurch Road, Handley CH3 9DT   TEL: (01829) 770619
WEBSITE: www.calveleyarms.co.uk
off A41, 6m S of Chester

Dating in part from the early seventeenth century, the Calveley is an archetypal old village inn opposite the venerable church. In summer, barbecues are held in the garden, often to musical accompaniment, and boules is played, or you can just enjoy the views of the distant Clwydian mountains. The eclectic interior décor features water jugs, hop bines, country prints, old photographs, assorted brass artefacts and even a pair of old wooden skis. In keeping with the characterful look, menus are bound in covers from old children's annuals and agricultural supplies catalogues, while daily specials – predominantly fish – are chalked on a board. Battered squid rings and garlic mushrooms are typical starters, while main courses take in everything from gammon steak with pineapple to pasta carbonara or curry with poppadoms and chutney. Regular Greene King IPA is joined by two frequently changing guest ales, and there are around two dozen wines from £9.50, with half a dozen by the glass. SAMPLE DISHES: sliced roast duck breast with wild berry dressing £4.50; sea bass with a lemon and herb crust and tomato butter sauce £11; bread-and-butter pudding £3.50.

Licensee Simon Grant Wilson (Enterprise Inns)
Open 12 to 3, 6 to 11, Sun 12 to 3, 7 to 10.30; bar food 12 to 2.15, 6 to 9.30, Sun 12 to 2.30, 7 to 9; closed evening 25 Dec
Details Car park   Wheelchair access (also WC)   Garden   Background music   Dogs by arrangement   Delta, MasterCard, Switch, Visa

HAROME   North Yorkshire   map 9

▲ Star Inn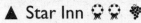

Harome YO62 5JE   TEL: (01439) 770397
WEBSITE: www.thestaratharome.co.uk

Harome is a picture-postcard Yorkshire village just off the main road to Scarborough, with the Star shining at its heart. The fourteenth-century, part-thatched cruck-framed longhouse works as a pub, as a restaurant – what was the byre is now the dining room, and the original parlour and dairy are now the bar – and offers the sort of bedrooms that put many hotels to shame. Good cheer prevails within, helped by surroundings of low beams, open fires and pews, as does some seriously accomplished, straightforward cooking, which can be enjoyed in the restaurant, with its bare wooden tables and spindle-backed chairs, or in the main bar. (Note that bookings are not taken in the bar but are advisable for the restaurant.) Local supplies influence the menus, with the kitchen's imaginative and skilfully cooked output represented by a starter of risotto of Rievaulx partridge with Fadmoor curly kale, braised chestnuts and white truffle oil, and a main course of roast leg of Ryedale lamb with celeriac purée, followed by baked ginger parkin with rhubarb ripple ice cream, hot spiced syrup and rhubarb schnapps. No less appealing are lunchtime sandwiches and buns – perhaps crayfish and prawn cocktail – a 'posh ploughman's' of cold meats and British cheeses, and grilled black pudding with pan-fried foie gras, apple and vanilla chutney and scrumpy reduction. Real ales include Cropton Two Pints, Endeavour, John Smith's Bitter, Black Sheep Best, and Riggwelter. An interesting selection of ten house wines is available by the glass from £3 to £4.95; the main wine list of some 100 bins has no truck with budget bottles but concentrates on high quality with equal success in both France and the New World. SAMPLE DISHES: cassoulet of smoked Hartlepool haddock with home-baked beans, grain mustard and herbed Wensleydale crust £6.25; pan-fried calf's liver with smoked bacon dressing £14; lemon tart with raspberry coulis £6.50.

Licensees Andrew and Jacquie Pern (freehouse)
Open *Mon 7.45 to 11, Tue to Sat 11.30 to 3, 6.15 to 11, Sun 12 to 10.30; bar food and restaurant Tue to Sat 11.30 to 2, 6.30 to 9.30, Sun 12 to 6; closed 25 Dec, 2½ weeks Jan, bank hols*
Details *Children welcome   Car park   Wheelchair access (not WC)   Garden   No smoking in restaurant Occasional background music   No dogs   Delta, MasterCard, Switch, Visa   Accommodation: 11 rooms, B&B £90 to £195*

HARROGATE   North Yorkshire   map 9

Old Bell Tavern   NEW ENTRY

6–7 Royal Parade, Harrogate HG1 2SZ   TEL: (01423) 507930
WEBSITE: www.markettowntaverns.co.uk

The Bell has a long history as an inn, as it was in business before the construction of the Georgian terrace of which it now forms a part. In more recent times it was the sales showroom of Farrah's toffee before reverting in the late 1990s to its original role. Nowadays it is part of a small Yorkshire chain whose aim is to recall a pure pub ambience: no children, fruit machines or music, with the emphasis on quality beers and above-average food. Indeed, an extensive choice of real ales ranges from regulars such as Timothy Taylor Landlord, Black Sheep Best Bitter, and Caledonian Deuchars IPA to five guests, and the vision has been updated to embrace a good selection of globally sourced wines, with eight by the standard or large glass. The former shop windows illuminate a pair of rooms with wooden floors, a mix of wooden tables and Sunday school chairs. Good, substantial, bistro-style food is offered on a printed menu that takes in four or five starters (among them a soup of the day, chicken liver pâté with tomato chutney, and smoked salmon), and half a dozen mains: say, lasagne, salmon steak in a herbed crumb topping with a crème fraîche and dill sauce, and Cumberland sausage with leek mash and onion gravy. Daily dishes, both starters and main courses, are chalked up on boards, and in the evening an upstairs brasserie offers much from the downstairs menu and more. SAMPLE DISHES: black pudding on apple mash with red onion confit £4; fish pie £7; bread-and-butter pudding £4.

Licensees Simon Midgley and Andrew Bates (Market Town Taverns plc)
Open *12 to 11 (10.30 Sun); bar food 12 to 2.30, 6 to 9.30; restaurant Mon to Thur 7 to 9.30, Fri and Sat 6 to 10; closed 25 Dec*
Details *No children   No-smoking area in bar, no smoking in restaurant   No music in bar, background music in restaurant   Dogs welcome   Delta, MasterCard, Switch, Visa*

HASSOP   Derbyshire   map 9

Eyre Arms

Hassop DE45 1NS   TEL: (01629) 640390
on B6001, 2m N of Bakewell

This creeper-covered roadside pub dates from the seventeenth century and takes its name from the one-time owners of Hassop Hall, which dominates the hamlet. The Eyres' coat of arms can be seen on the pub's sign and above the impressive fireplace in the main bar. There is no restaurant, but the long bar menu takes in main courses such as steak and kidney pie and Grand Marnier duckling, while an Indian influence appears in Eastern-style lamb cooked with coconut, black pepper and spices. Fish, steaks, and pasta are other headings on the menu, and there are six interesting options for vegetarians, including bulgur wheat and walnut casserole. Blackboard specials point up more interest, from broccoli and Cheddar soup to braised pheasant in Madeira, or sea bass with a sweet pepper sauce. Sandwiches, ploughman's and jacket potatoes are also available at lunchtime, and puddings include, appropriately, Derbyshire pie as well as things like carrot cake and bread-and-butter pudding. On handpump are Black Sheep Special Ale, Marston's Pedigree, and John Smith's Bitter, and three wines are sold by the glass. SAMPLE DISHES: Derbyshire oatcake filled with Cheddar cheese and asparagus £4; local trout baked with butter and almonds £8.25; sticky toffee pudding £3.50.

Licensee Lynne Smith (freehouse)
Open 11 to 3, 7 (6.30 summer) to 11; bar food 12 to 2, 6.30 to 9
Details Children welcome in eating area   Car park   Wheelchair access (not WC)   Garden   No-smoking area in bar, no smoking in eating area   Occasional background music   No dogs   Delta, Diners, MasterCard, Switch, Visa

HATHERSAGE   Derbyshire   map 9

▲ Plough Inn

Leadmill Bridge, Hathersage S32 1BA   TEL: (01433) 650319
WEBSITE: www.theploughinn-hathersage.com
on B6001, 1m S of Hathersage

Standing in its own grounds by the River Derwent in the heart of the Peak District National Park, this handsome converted sixteenth-century corn mill is the sort of place that might inspire customers to wax lyrical. It is a warm, welcoming pub with comforts aplenty in its convivial open-plan, split-level bar and cottagey dining room. Bar meals (not served in the restaurant in the evening) are hearty, down-to-earth classics like Cumberland sausage and mash backed up by a home-made curry, roast and pie 'of the day'. By contrast, the restaurant menu zooms rapidly into the realms of smoked beef teriyaki with a salad of white radish and tomato jam, and confit of belly pork with braised pig's cheeks, caper mash and braised cabbage, while desserts could include anything from fruit crumble to cappuccino crème brûlée. Theakston Best and Old Peculier are top of the real ale billing, with a supporting cast of two regularly changing guests; the 50-strong wine list – organised by style – has 18 by the glass (from £2.75) plus a 'connoisseurs collection' with plenty of decent drinking for around £20 a bottle. Stylish, well-equipped accommodation is in separate buildings across the cobbled courtyard. SAMPLE DISHES: warm chicken livers with bacon, pine nuts and new potato salad £7; roast salmon on champ with thyme butter sauce and mustard lentils £13.25; dark chocolate tart with white chocolate ice cream £4.

Licensee Bob Emery (freehouse)
Open 11 to 11, Sun 12 to 10.30; bar food and restaurant Mon to Fri 11.30 to 2.30, 6.30 to 9.30, Sat 11.30 to 9.30, Sun 12 to 9; closed 25 Dec
Details Children welcome exc in restaurant evenings   Car park   Wheelchair access (not WC)   Garden No smoking in restaurant   Background music   No dogs   MasterCard, Switch, Visa   Accommodation: 5 rooms, B&B £49.50 to £99.50

NEW ENTRY   *indicates that the pub was not a main entry in the previous edition.*

HAWKLEY   **Hampshire**   map 2

Hawkley Inn 🍺

Pococks Lane, Hawkley GU33 6NE   TEL: (01730) 827205
off A325, 2½m N of Petersfield

Hidden away, or, depending on your map-reading/road-sign skills, lost down country lanes, this unpretentious pub hits just the right note as an honest country pub. Two rooms on either side of the bar are furnished with cottagey tables and chairs and have open fires in winter, and a well-trodden carpet emphasises that this is a down-to-earth meeting place with no airs and graces. We hope readers of last year's entry weren't too disappointed to discover that the 'huge mouse's head' above the fireplace is in fact a moose's head. Wines are not a main feature (only two are offered), but beers are a good collection that changes frequently: among them might be Ballard's Trotton Bitter and Nyewood Gold, brewed in nearby Petersfield, Cottage Golden Arrow and Alton's Pride, from the Triple fff Brewing Company – and for cider drinkers there's the pub's own Swamp Donkey. Generous, robust dishes are listed on two black-boards, including perhaps faggots in onion gravy, spicy meatballs with noodles in tomato and coriander sauce, and cider sausages served with mash and vegetables. Rolls and ploughman's are also listed, together with familiar desserts like treacle tart, and the evenings see the addition of perhaps rump steak, or grilled duck breast in green peppercorn sauce. Despite its rural location, the pub can get packed. SAMPLE DISHES: beef and noodle soup £5; ham and leek pancakes £9; chocolate pudding £3.75.

Licensee A. Stringer (freehouse)
Open *12 to 2.30 (3 Sat), 6 to 11, Sun 12 to 3, 7 to 10.30; bar food 12 to 2, 7 to 9.30, Sun 12 to 2*
Details *Children welcome before 8pm   Wheelchair access (not WC)   Patio   No-smoking area in bar
Background and occasional live music   Dogs welcome   MasterCard, Visa*

HAWKSHEAD   **Cumbria**   map 8

▲ Queen's Head Hotel

Main Street, Hawkshead LA22 0NS   TEL: (015394) 36271
WEBSITE: www.queensheadhotel.co.uk
on B5285, 4m S of Ambleside

Rough black ceiling beams, handsomely panelled walls and bar counters, plus pictures, decorative brass and china define the décor in this solid black and white village pub. Drinkers can take their pick from a selection of Robinson's draught beers, including Frederics, Hartleys XB, and Cumbria Way; alternatively, a dozen wines are served by the glass on the extensive, keenly priced list. Those looking for food can eat in the bar or restaurant from a wide-ranging menu that takes in everything from tradi-tional Cumberland sausage and mash with white onion sauce to marinated pork fillet roasted on rhubarb with potato and sage rösti. There's also a daily fish menu that might feature, say, Esthwaite Lake organic trout baked with olives, tomato and basil or roast orange tilapia with ginger and orange and lemon butter. Start with chicken liver pâté laced with tequila or pear and Roquefort salad and finish with a dessert such as sticky date pudding. SAMPLE DISHES: squashed cherry tomato and olive salad with coriander and crème fraîche £4.75; slow-roast lamb with rosemary-scented sauce £10.50; cherry and chocolate cheesecake £4.50.

Licensee Anthony Merrick (Robinson's)
Open 11 to 11, Sun 12 to 10.30; bar food and restaurant 12 to 2.30, 6.15 to 9.30
Details Children welcome   Wheelchair access (not WC)   No-smoking area in bar, no smoking in restaurant
Background music   No dogs   Delta, MasterCard, Switch, Visa   Accommodation: 14 rooms, B&B £30 to £110

HAYDON BRIDGE   Northumberland   map 10

General Havelock Inn

9 Ratcliffe Road, Haydon Bridge NE47 6ER   TEL: (01434) 684376
on S side of A69, 6m W of Hexham, 100yds from junction with B6319

Proximity to the South Tyne river is part of the lure at this welcoming, 200-year-old
inn right in the heart of the village. It may front the road, where the main bar is
located, but further back – in a converted barn – is an attractive room with the bonus
of views over the river. The main restaurant menu is a regularly changing, fixed-price
affair that might kick off with soup – say, pea, mint and potato – or deep-fried crab
cakes with ginger dressing, before roast rack of lamb with green peppercorn sauce.
Cheeses (many from the North Country) make a pleasing alternative to desserts such
as Italian-style rice pudding. Otherwise, stay with the bar menu, which offers heartier
stuff in the shape of deep-fried cheese croquettes with tomato mayonnaise dip, or
Cumberland sausage with onion gravy, followed by glazed lemon tart. Beer drinkers
will find a forthright contingent of locally brewed ales from within a 40-mile radius,
including, perhaps, Wylam Whistlestop, Hesket Newmarket, Yates Fever Pitch, Big
Lamp Prince Bishop Ale, and Geordie Pride from the Mordue Brewery in
Shiremoor. Those with a taste for the grape will find a satisfyingly fruity, if less adventurous, selection. The list of around 20 sound bottles stays mostly below £15, with
two wines by the glass at £1.95 and four half-bottles. SAMPLE DISHES: potato wedges
with garlic mayonnaise £1.50; chicken, leek and Cheddar pie £6.75; Italian-style
chocolate cake £4.50.

Licensee Gary Thompson (freehouse)
Open Tue to Sat 12 to 2.30, 7 to 11, Sun 12 to 2.30, 8 to 10.30; bar food and restaurant Tue to Sun 12 to
2, Tue to Sat 7 to 9
Details Children welcome   Wheelchair access (also WC)   Garden   No-smoking area in bar, no smoking in
restaurant   Occasional live music   Dogs welcome   Delta, MasterCard, Switch, Visa

HAYFIELD   Derbyshire   map 9

Sportsman

Kinder Road, Hayfield SK22 2LE   TEL: (01663) 741565
from centre of Hayfield (off A624 Glossop to Chapel-en-le-Frith road) follow campsite signs; pub is ½m
on left

The Sportsman may be a bit off the beaten track on a narrow, unclassified road that
climbs out of Hayfield and continues on to Kinder Scout, but it has bags of character.
It's a place where, in wintertime, locals quietly enjoy its log fire and small warren of
cosy seating areas with prints, lanterns and guns on the walls. Then spring brings the
walkers onto the moors once more, and incomers arrive to share the Thwaites beer –
Bitter and Lancaster Bomber, plus a third that changes sporadically – and the 20 or
more single malts behind the bar (there's also a brief wine list that includes two served
by the glass). Thirst slaked, they can refuel from a menu that starts with black

pudding and mustard sauce, or warm asparagus tart, then moves on to a traditional hotpot of lamb and vegetables, a selection of steaks, or fresh plaice grilled in butter. Puddings should not be ordered lightly – portions are not mean here and may take some walking off. SAMPLE DISHES: peppered mackerel with horseradish £4.75; farmhouse grill £9; rhubarb and ginger cobbler £4.75.

Licensee John Dunbar (Thwaites)

Open *all week (exc Mon lunchtime) 12 to 3, 7 to 11; bar food 12 to 2, 7 to 9; closed 25 Dec*

Details *Children welcome   Garden and patio   Background music   Dogs welcome exc in bedrooms   Amex, Delta, MasterCard, Switch, Visa   Accommodation: 6 rooms, B&B £30 to £50*

HAYTOR VALE   Devon   map 1

▲ Rock Inn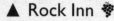

Haytor Vale TQ13 9XP   TEL: (01364) 661305

WEBSITE: www.rock-inn.co.uk

turn off A38 at Bovey Tracey on to A382; after 2m join B3387 to Haytor, then left at phone box

Formerly a coaching inn, the Rock Inn is nowadays more of an upmarket gastro-pub, though old-fashioned values prevail, exhibited both in the warm welcome and in the décor – the series of small rooms have smart patterned carpets, dark wood furniture and welcoming fires. Tables are set with proper napkins and tall wine glasses, emphasising the fact that dining is the main business (booking is advised). At lunchtime, expect simple bar snacks, sandwiches and salads, plus main courses such as salmon fillet on spinach with sauce vierge. Dinner options are more ambitious, ranging from duck breast on braised cider cabbage with apple jus, to pan-fried sea bass on roasted fennel with vanilla sauce. Dartmoor Best, Old Speckled Hen and Bass are the regular real ales. The wine list puts serious French offerings up front, but beyond these are more affordable bottles and a good global range that includes the excellent Nativa organic Cabernet Sauvignon from Carmen in Chile. Six are available by the glass. SAMPLE DISHES: chicken liver parfait with red onion marmalade and Melba toast £7; roast monkfish on crushed potato with chorizo and paprika oil £15; sticky toffee pudding with pecan sauce £4.50.

Licensee Christopher Graves (freehouse)

Open *11 to 11 (10.30 winter); bar food and restaurant 12 to 2.30 (4 Sun), 6.30 to 9; closed 25 Dec, evening 26 Dec*

Details *Children welcome   Car park   Wheelchair access (not WC)   Garden and patio   No-smoking area in bar, no smoking in restaurant   No music   No dogs   Amex, Delta, Diners, MasterCard, Switch, Visa   Accommodation: 9 rooms, B&B £60 to £95.50*

HEDLEY ON THE HILL   Northumberland   map 10

Feathers Inn ✿ 🍺

Hedley on the Hill NE43 7SW   TEL: (01661) 843607

from New Ridley, signposted from B6309 N of Consett, follow sign for Hedley on the Hill

Hedley on the Hill 'is not the easiest of places to find', commented a visitor, but, once found, the centrally located, stone-built pub compensates with magnificent views and high standards. Two homely bars share the central bar counter and are warmed by winter fires; one is popular with locals, while the other is smaller and quieter; a further room leads off this. The blackboard menu changes weekly, but popular items like ham (honey-roast, served perhaps with mango chutney) and Cumberland sausage (with braised onions and cider, or grain mustard sauce) are on all the time. The food has received plaudits, ranging from 'utterly delicious' spiced parsnip soup, or Bywell (local) smoked duck with redcurrant jelly, to a leek and mature Cheddar tart served with a good salad and plain boiled new potatoes, or chicken breast in a creamy sauce with herbs, garlic and mushrooms. Ales, from local breweries, include Workie Ticket from Mordue, Hadrian Gladiator and Yates Bitter. Wines by the glass are limited, but there's an interesting choice by the bottle. SAMPLE DISHES: mushroom and celery soup £3.50; beef casseroled with tomatoes, white wine, olives and oregano £9; citrus tart £4.50.

Licensee Marina Atkinson (freehouse)
Open Mon to Fri 6 to 11, Sat and bank hols 12 to 3, 6 to 11, Sun 12 to 3, 7 to 10.30; bar food Tue to Fri 7 to 9, Sat, Sun and bank hols 12 to 2.30, 7 to 9; closed 25 Dec
Details Children welcome in 2 rooms   Car park   Garden   Occasional live music   Guide dogs only   Switch

HEMINGFORD GREY   Cambridgeshire   map 6

Cock

47 High Street, Hemingford Grey PE28 9BJ   TEL: (01480) 463609
WEBSITE: www.cambscuisine.com
follow signs for Hemingford Grey from A14 just W of Huntingdon

This seventeenth-century pub in a street of thatched and timbered cottages looks every inch the village local. But the place consists of two contrasting rooms: one is a simple, plain locals' bar dispensing real ale from East Anglian breweries, including Elgood's Black Dog, Woodforde's Wherry Best Bitter and Adnams Bitter, plus a guest from Oakham Ales; the other is a spacious, light, modern restaurant offering simple, gutsy food in modern brasserie mode. Blackboards list fresh fish specials and home-made sausages, such as Moroccan lamb, Toulouse, or chicken, lemongrass and ginger, which come with mix-and-match kinds of mash and sauces. There's also a short à la carte of, say, venison carpaccio with herb oil and tomato jam to start, then pheasant breast with crépinette and orange and redcurrant sauce, and sticky toffee pudding to finish. A good-value bar lunch selection includes sandwiches, a soup, and perhaps fishcake with salsa verde, or game, cider and mushroom pie; there's always a choice of roasts for Sunday lunch, and the cheeses are British and Irish. Wine drinkers are well served by a selection of eleven or by two sizes of glass and a colourful list that covers most bases, with good choice under £15. A sister establishment (though more restaurant than pub), the Crown and Punchbowl, is located in nearby Horningsea. SAMPLE DISHES: leek terrine with Cashel Blue and green peppercorns £5; rolled pork belly with chestnuts and potato and apple rösti with rosemary sauce £12; chocolate and pecan torte £4.50.

Licensees Oliver Thain and Richard Bradley (freehouse)
Open 11.30 to 3, 6 to 11, Sun 12 to 4, 6.30 to 10.30; bar food and restaurant all week 12 to 2.30, Mon to Sat 6.45 to 9.30
Details No children under 8 evenings   Car park   Wheelchair access (not WC)   Garden   No smoking in restaurant   Occasional live music   Dogs welcome exc in restaurant   MasterCard, Switch, Visa

---

Feedback on pubs in the Guide, and recommendations for new ones, are very welcome.

▲ Angel Inn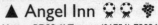

Hetton BD23 6LT   TEL: (01756) 730263
WEBSITE: www.angelhetton.co.uk
off B6265, 5m N of Skipton

At its core the Angel is a long village inn of local stone which has expanded into adjoining cottages so that the interior rambles through several rooms with open fires. Beams, nooks and crannies, and lots of polished wood keep the look tastefully traditional, while pink walls are hung with chef cartoons and an assortment of photographs and awards, highlighting the ambitions and standing of the kitchen. It is advisable to book in the bar (and always in the restaurant). Blackboards supplement the bar/brasserie menu too, expanding the clever mix of classic pub dishes and interesting specialities based on top-notch ingredients. Starters range from the never-off-the-menu little pastry moneybags of seafood with lobster sauce to home-made black pudding on buttered spinach with Puy lentils. Main courses can be as traditional as Lishman's prize-winning pork sausages with mash and rich onion gravy, or as European as steamed fillet of cod on a bed of clams and chorizo served with soft peppers and saffron potatoes. The restaurant amplifies such dishes with, say, carpaccio, followed by wood pigeon breast with a game sausage and thyme jus, then chocolate tart. Timothy Taylor Landlord, Black Sheep Best Bitter and Worthington Bitter are on handpump, but the Angel is best known for its list of over 150 wines, which has strength in depth when it comes to classic regions like Bordeaux and Burgundy, and the Italian selection is good too. Bargain hunters will have a tough time of it, however – the house white and red are the only bottles under £15 – but can still drink well from the 14-strong by-the-glass selection or the impressive collection of half-bottles. Head east to Ferrensby and you'll find the Angel's sibling, the General Tarleton. SAMPLE DISHES: roasted butternut squash and sage risotto £5.75; confit shoulder of lamb with a tomato and black olive sauce £11; poached pear in spiced red wine £4.25.

Licensees Denis Watkins and Bruce Elsworth (freehouse)
Open *Sun to Fri 12 to 3, 6 to 10 (10.30 summer), Sat 12 to 3, 6 to 11.30; bar food Mon to Sat 12 to 2.15, 6 to 8.30 (9 Sat), Sun 12 to 2.30, 6 to 8.30, restaurant Mon to Sat 6 to 9, Sun 12 to 2; closed 25 Dec*
Details *Children welcome in bar eating area   Car park   Wheelchair access (not WC)   Patio   No smoking in snug, lounge bar and part of restaurant   No music   No dogs   Amex, MasterCard, Switch, Visa*
Accommodation: 5 studio suites, B&B £120 to £170

Dipton Mill 🍺

Dipton Mill Road, Hexham NE46 1YA   TEL: (01434) 606577
2m S of Hexham, beyond Hexham racecourse

Here is a creeper-clad pub in a jewel of a location, a dell with a river and mill stream 'all gurgling past', with a pretty rear garden approached over a narrow wooden bridge. Within, the L-shaped bar has two open fires, one in an inglenook, the other in a more homely red-brick fireplace, and there are small, low tables and deep-red upholstery. The blackboard menus offer a nice, simple choice of soups – say, leek and potato, or spiced parsnip – then haddock baked with tomato and basil, mince with dumplings, or lamb leg steak in wine and mustard sauce. Pick a ploughman's and you have a dozen cheeses to choose from (only Stilton and Cheddar come from further away than Barnard Castle). In addition, there are sandwiches, such as home-roast chicken or beef, and salads, and desserts might run to chocolate rum truffle torte or plum crumble. Hexhamshire beers are from a brewery two miles away run by licensee Geoff Brooker; these are Shire Bitter, Devil's Elbow, Devil's Water (named after a local stream), Whapweasel, and a Christmas special called Old Humbug. There's also Old Rosie cider, and all 16 of the good-value wines are served by the glass. SAMPLE DISHES: carrot and celery soup £1.75; pork fillet with apple, orange and ginger £6.50; raspberry roulade £2.

Licensee Geoff Brooker (freehouse)
Open _12 to 2.30, 6 to 11, Sun 12 to 3, 7 to 10.30; bar food 12 to 2.30, 6.30 to 8.30; closed 25 Dec_
Details _Children welcome   Wheelchair access (also WC)   Garden and patio   No music   No cards_

HEYDON   Cambridgeshire   map 6

King William IV
Heydon SG8 8PN   TEL: (01763) 838773
take B1039 towards Royston, turn right at Great Chishall and follow road to Heydon; pub on right-hand side past animal sanctuary

The interior of this country inn is so spacious and rambling that one reader felt a 'feeling of freedom'. Masses of candlelight and low lamplight create warmth in the evening, and the 'gazillions' of horse brasses and pieces of antique agricultural implements is endearingly over the top; every available space is crammed with horse collars, chains, churns and so on. This is a popular dining pub, and two of the rooms are given over to eating, but the same menu is available wherever you sit. The food is presented restaurant-style on big white plates, and the lengthy printed menu ranges from soup and Cajun chicken Caesar salad to main courses of steak and kidney pudding and whole sea bass baked in rice paper with Thai spices, with an admirable list of vegetarian options, and things like treacle pudding with custard for dessert. Light snacks or lunch take in jacket potatoes, ploughman's and baguettes. For beer drinkers, City of Cambridge Hobson's Choice, Adnams Bitter, Fuller's London Pride and Greene King IPA are all regulars, while a 24-strong list of wines offers ten by the glass. SAMPLE DISHES: tomato and crispy Parma ham tartlet £6.25; local venison Wellington with foie gras and Madeira sauce £17; toffee pecan cheesecake £3.75.

Licensee Elizabeth Nicholls (freehouse)
Open _12 to 2.30, 6 to 11, Sun 12 to 3, 7 to 10.30; bar food and restaurant 12 to 2, 6.30 to 10, Sun 12 to 2.30, 7 to 9.30_
Details _Children welcome   Car park   Wheelchair access (also WC)   Garden   No-smoking area in bar, no smoking in restaurant   Background music   No dogs   Delta, MasterCard, Switch, Visa_

HEYTESBURY   Wiltshire   map 2

▲ Angel Coaching Inn
High Street, Heytesbury BA12 0ED   TEL: (01985) 840330
just off A36, 2m E of Warminster

In a village strung along the River Wylye, with Salisbury Plain to the north, this old coaching inn has seen plenty of improvements since the eighteenth century, the very latest being a total remodelling in early 2004. A reporter was impressed by the upmarket, rustic-chic tone that mixes scrubbed wood beams and timbers, log fire, bare boards, exposed brick, comfy sofas and contemporary lighting, while high-backed leather chairs make 'a sophisticated statement' in the dining room. Antony Worrall Thompson is responsible – he is a partner in the business and the Angel is inspired by his Notting Grill restaurant. Menus are built around the chargrill and that means steaks – rump sirloin or fillet – properly hung and served with a choice of sauces (béarnaise, say, or au poivre), 'decent fat' chips and 'nice, crisp' salad. Separate menus describe lunchtime favourites, say roast beef and horseradish roll, free-range pork sausage, mash and onion gravy, or smoked haddock and salmon fishcake, while the evening carte offers fried chilli squid with spring onion to start, and the likes of baked fillet of sea bass with fennel and leek fondue as an 'Alternative Choice' to the signature steaks. Our visit was not long after the refurbishment, so more reports please. Greene King Abbot Ale, Wadworth 6X and Ruddles County are on draught. SAMPLE DISHES: baked field mushroom with Stilton rarebit and tomato-basil salad £7; pan-fried calf's liver with dry-cured bacon and mash £14; classic crème brûlée £4.

Licensees Tim Etchellis and Mark Wilderspin (Greene King)
Open 11 to 11, Sun 12 to 10.30; bar food and restaurant 12 to 2.30 (2 Sun), 7 to 9.30 (9 Sun); open 25 Dec 12 to 2 (restaurant closed)
Details Children welcome   Car park   Patio   No smoking in restaurant   Background music   Dogs welcome Amex, Delta, MasterCard, Switch, Visa   Accommodation: 6 rooms, B&B £60 to £75

HIGHCLERE   Hampshire   map 2

▲ Yew Tree   NEW ENTRY

Hollington Cross, Andover Road, Highclere RG20 9SE   TEL: (01635) 253360
on A343, 5m S of Newbury

The Yew Tree has taken the contemporary dining pub route, although the sympathetic remodelling retains the old fabric and character of the seventeenth-century building and offers tables for drinkers but includes that seemingly modern-day dining pub requirement – an elegant restaurant. Though the bar area continues the restaurant's theme, it's more robust and pays homage to its pub roots with a huge inglenook, church pews, old timbers and beams, and Fuller's London Pride and a guest ale that changes with every barrel. Available throughout the bar and restaurant is a generous, modern British repertoire that ranges from a good, thick bowl of watercress and apple soup, or 'perfectly timed' crayfish and herb risotto, to 'first-rate' pan-fried calf's liver with bacon, horseradish mashed potato and onion gravy, or duck confit with bubble and squeak. Equally appealing could be steamed Scottish sea bass with stir-fried pak choi, spring onions and ginger and a chilli and red pepper salsa, or the traditional Sunday roast of tender pork loin with all the trimmings that impressed one visitor. The kitchen makes a big show of presentation, which runs through to desserts of warm apple and cinnamon tart with vanilla ice cream, for example. Eight wines are available by the glass. SAMPLE DISHES: pheasant terrine with Calvados-dressed salad £4.25; breast of free-range chicken stuffed with white crabmeat and dill on cognac sauce £12.25; chocolate and hazelnut semifreddo £5.

Licensee Eric Norberg (freehouse)
Open 12 to 11, Sun 12 to 10.30; bar food and restaurant 12 to 3, 6 to 10, Sun 12 to 4, 7 to 9
Details Children welcome   Car park   Patio   No smoking in restaurant   Live or background music   Dogs welcome   Amex, Delta, MasterCard, Switch, Visa   Accommodation: 6 rooms, B&B £60

HIGHER BURWARDSLEY   Cheshire   map 7

▲ Pheasant Inn

Higher Burwardsley CH3 9PF   TEL: (01829) 770434
off A41 6m SE of Chester, signposted Tattenhall and Burwardsley

Down a twisting lane on the western side of Cheshire's stunning Sandstone Edge, this 'convivial country dining pub' was once several sandstone and half-timbered cottages. Straggling alongside a no-through road, it has sublime views westwards over the Cheshire Plain to mountainous North Wales and northwards to Liverpool Cathedral. A rather stark, open-plan interior is split into distinct areas by the generous use of sandstone-block pillars and timber-framed dividers, all beneath a heavily timbered ceiling. The furniture is mostly of wood, and an island log fire is a feature at one end, with an old range in an inglenook in a rear room. The printed menu, available throughout, is long and varied enough to accommodate all tastes. Among starters might be black pudding tarte Tatin, or game terrine, and main courses could run to braised pig's cheek with stewed apple, white pudding, Puy lentils and a rich jus, or fillet steak Rossini. The full range of Weetwood ales is on draught, and nine wines are served by the glass. Those wonderful views can be enjoyed from the patio and garden, where a seaside-style pay telescope has been installed. SAMPLE DISHES: French onion soup with wholegrain mustard crisps £3.75; poached cod on fennel and radicchio risotto with cockle and calamari beurre blanc £14.50; crème brûlée, £5.25.

Licensee Simon McLoughlin (freehouse)
Open *12 to 11, Sun 12 to 10.30; bar food Mon to Sat 12 to 2.30, 6.30 to 9.30, Sun 12 to 5, 6.30 to 8.30*
Details *Children welcome   Car park   Wheelchair access (also WC)   Garden and patio   No-smoking area*
Background music   No dogs   Amex, Delta, Diners, MasterCard, Switch, Visa   Accommodation: 10 rooms, B&B
£55 to £80

HIGHER SUTTON   Cheshire   map 8

Hanging Gate Inn   NEW ENTRY

Higher Sutton SK11 0NG   TEL: (01260) 252238
from A523 S of central Macclesfield, take signposted turn-off for Sutton and Langley; 250yds past Kings Head aqueduct, turn left for Langley; turn right immediately past Church Inn; pub is 2m on, on right after a steep hairpin bend

Dating from 1621, this small old rural pub clings to a steep slope on the edge of open moorland, high above Rossen Dale, with endless panoramas sweeping west across Croker Hill and Sutton Common to the Cheshire plains and beyond. The building sags beneath large gritstone tiles and steps down the hillside in a challenging tumble of levels. At the lowest end is a stone patio with a few bench tables; one of the middle levels has an adjoining lawned area, again set with tables. You enter via a tiny, flag-floored, black-beamed bar with an open fire, a few stools and room for a couple of modest tables, nothing more; the whole pub is maybe only 20 feet wide. What it lacks for in width it makes up for in depth: the next room is a cosy lounge, then a few steps lead down to a tiny, intimate snug, and down another flight of steps is the lowest room – the View Room – with magnificent vistas, a winter fire, and maybe ten tables. There are no printed menus; each room (apart from the snug) has blackboards offering well-prepared, generously portioned, good-value food using local produce. Starters could include grilled sardines, with main courses of garlic and ginger chicken, grilled fillet steak, or roast duckling, with chocolate fudge cake and locally made ice creams among desserts. The Hanging Gate is tied to Manchester's Hydes Brewery and offers real ales in the form of Best Bitter, Jekyll's Gold Premium Ale, and changing seasonal brews. A small blackboard lists around half a dozen wines by the glass or bottle. SAMPLE DISHES: marinated herrings in dill £4; grilled lamb cutlets £11; sticky toffee pudding £3.

Licensees Peter and Paul McGrath
Open *Mon to Fri 12 to 3, 7 to 11, Sat and Sun 12 to 11; bar food all week 12 to 2, Mon to Sat 7 to 9*
Details *Children welcome in eating area   Car park   Wheelchair access (not WC)   Garden   No-smoking area in bar, no smoking in eating area   Background music   No dogs   Amex, Delta, Diners, MasterCard, Switch, Visa*

HINDON   Wiltshire   map 2

▲ Angel Inn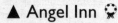

High Street, Hindon SP3 6DJ   TEL: (01747) 820696
WEBSITE: www.theangelhindon.fslife.co.uk
1m from A350 between Warminster and Shaftesbury

Hindon is a tiny and 'totally rural' village just off the busy A303, and this long, grey-stone Georgian coaching inn sits solidly at a staggered crossroads. It is smart within, with an open-plan bar area in rich dark brown, a small lounge with deep, comfortable sofas, and a restaurant that's all cream and glass with ceiling spotlights and huge, square evening candles. This is a pub where food takes centre stage, the menu (served throughout) an ambitious collection of upmarket pub dishes with brasserie leanings: crispy fishcakes with lemon and dill mayonnaise, pan-fried calf's liver with herbed mash, bacon and whole-grain mustard sauce, and braised belly pork with parsnip mash, black pudding and sage and cider sauce. The food is pitched exactly right for the surroundings: what the kitchen delivers is a range of fresh, honestly prepared dishes with bags of flavour. Home-cured gravad lax comes with an excellent mustard and dill dressing, and roast English partridge is a perfect combination of gamey breast, confit leg, a local butcher's chipolata ('totally unlike the usual product'), braised red cabbage, chestnuts and a rich game jus. Desserts range from treacle tart with black treacle ice cream to poached Williams pear with mulled wine jelly and clotted cream. Wadworth 6X, Ringwood Best Bitter and Fuller's London Pride are on draught, and the wine list, strongest in France and Australia, is backed up by a slate of cheaper bottles on a blackboard over the bar; some six are served by the glass. This is great walking country, with two long-distance footpaths, the Wessex Ridgeway and the Monarch's Way, running through Hindon. The Angel changed hands in summer 2004, after our inspection, and we were told that chef Matthew Laughton was set to continue. SAMPLE DISHES: herring roe pan-fried with capers, bacon, lemon and parsley £5.25; rabbit poached in olive oil served with tagliatelle and a wild mushroom, bacon and watercress creamed sauce £12; dark chocolate pot with vanilla and mascarpone cheesecake and kumquat marmalade £5.

Licensee Catherine Trant
Open *winter 11 to 3, 6 to 11, summer 11 to 11; bar food and restaurant all week 12 to 2.30, Mon to Sat 6.30 to 9.30; closed 26 Dec*
Details *Children welcome in bar eating area   Car park   Wheelchair access (not WC)   Garden   No smoking in restaurant   No music   Dogs welcome exc in restaurant   Delta, MasterCard, Switch, Visa   Accommodation: 8 rooms, B&B £30 to £75*

HINTON CHARTERHOUSE   Bath & N.E. Somerset   map 2

▲ Rose & Crown

High Street, Hinton Charterhouse BA2 7SN   TEL: (01225) 722153
on B3110 6m S of Bath

This solid stone building in the heart of the village has a pantiled roof and (from the front, at least) the sort of strictly symmetrical façade that makes one think of doll's houses. All is neat and tidy in the bar with its attractive wood panelling, red carpets and splendid fireplace, not to mention a full quota of sporting prints and old photos of the pub in days gone by. A few specials, such as goats' cheese and red onion marmalade tartlets, or pheasant breast with red wine and cherry sauce, jazz up a menu that celebrates the virtues of decent, simple food when it is cooked simply and decently: expect the likes of grilled sea bass with lemon and cracked black pepper butter, steak and ale pie, and grilled Barnsley chop with redcurrant and mint gravy. Fuller's London Pride and Butcombe Bitter are on draught, and the pub has a minimal wine list with several available by the glass. SAMPLE DISHES: chicken liver pâté £3.75; fried skate wing with green peppercorns £9; apricot, almond and brandy trifle £3.75.

Licensees Paul and Rosemary Harris (freehouse)
Open 11 to 2.30, 5.30 to 11, Sun 12 to 3, 7 to 10.30; bar food and restaurant 11 to 2, 6 (7 Sun) to 9.30
Details *Children welcome in eating areas   Car park   Wheelchair access (also WC)   Patio   No smoking in dining room   No music   No dogs   Delta, MasterCard, Switch, Visa   Accommodation: 4 rooms, B&B £45 to £65*

HOGNASTON   Derbyshire   map 5

▲ Red Lion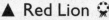

Main Street, Hognaston DE6 1PR   TEL: (01335) 370396
WEBSITE: www.lionrouge.com

In the well-watered countryside between Ashbourne and Matlock, this unpretentious whitewashed pub in a quiet village is quite a find. Log fires warm the large L-shaped stepped-level area around the panelled bar, with its mixture of farmhouse tables, chairs and settles under a beamed ceiling. White walls, some brick, are hung with old prints, oils, watercolours and photographs, and there's even a grandfather clock, The menu, chalked on blackboards, is served throughout the pub and offers fresh, good-quality, good-value food of some ambition. Start with goats' cheese tartlet blended with herbs, sun-dried tomatoes and red onions, or marinated cod kebabs in a strawberry and pink peppercorn sauce. Main courses run from shank of slow-cooked lamb with mashed potato and rich mint gravy, through boeuf bourguignon, to chicken fajita with guacamole, sour cream and mixed salad. Desserts, also drawn from near and far, run a gamut from sticky toffee pudding to American-style blueberry cheesecake. Service is welcoming, and the atmosphere warm, welcoming and buzzy. Marston's Pedigree, Old Speckled Hen and Bass are on draught, and the wine list is short and to the point, encompassing a trio of South African house wines available by the glass, plus another five white, six red and three champagnes. SAMPLE DISHES: potted brown shrimps with mildly spiced butter £5.50; whole sea bass with prawns, Pernod and chive sauce £12; jam roly-poly and custard £5.

Licensee Philip Price (freehouse)
Open 12 to 3, 6 (7 Sun) to 11; bar food and restaurant Tue to Sun 12 to 2, Mon to Sat 6.30 to 9; closed 25 Dec
Details *Children welcome in restaurant   Car park   Wheelchair access (also WC)   Patio   No smoking in*

restaurant   Occasional live or background music   Dogs welcome exc weekend evenings   Amex, Delta,
MasterCard, Switch, Visa   Accommodation: 3 rooms, B&B £50 to £80

HOLCOMBE   Somerset   map 2

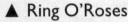

▲ Ring O'Roses

Stratton Road, Holcombe BA3 1EB   TEL: (01761) 232478
WEBSITE: www.ringoroses.co.uk
from Stratton-on-the-Fosse, on A367, follow signpost for Holcombe; pub is to the left after crossroads,
before the village

This very rural and much extended inn was originally a farm cottage. It dates from the
sixteenth century, and the unusual name, taken from the nursery rhyme, refers to a
time when the plague devastated the old village of Holcombe. Spacious, with well-
spaced tables in the dining area, this is a serious-minded country hotel that takes a
grown-up view of relaxation and comfort, with newspapers to read by the log fire in
the oak-panelled bar and a peaceful garden overlooking Downside Abbey. Bar and
restaurant menus are available throughout, and the style of the latter is ambitious,
with starters such as smoked duck breast with marinated vegetables and rice noodles
with teriyaki sauce, and main courses of chargrilled monkfish with plum tomato
sauce, oregano oil and roasted garlic. Bar food is simple fare such as toad in the hole,
chilli beef, or chicken tagliatelle, as well as a range of salads, sandwiches, jacket potatoes, and pies. Otter and Blind Man's Breweries supply the real ales, and there is also
an excellent range of bottled ciders. The wine list is a compilation of around 35
bottles, starting with seven house wines at £9.75, or £3.35 a large glass. SAMPLE
DISHES: chargrilled black pudding on a hot buttered croûte with poached egg and
fresh truffle £5.25; rack of English lamb with celeriac purée, red wine sauce and
redcurrant jelly tartlet £13.25; white chocolate bread-and-butter pudding £4.25.

Licensee Richard Rushton (freehouse)
Open *Mon to Fri 11.30 to 11, Sat 11.30 to 1.45, 7 to 11, Sun 12 to 2.30, 7 to 10.30; bar food Mon to Sat
12 to 1.45, restaurant Mon to Sat 12 to 2 , 7 to 9, Sun 12 to 1.30, 7 to 8.30*
Details *Children welcome in restaurant   Car park   Wheelchair access (also WC)   Garden   No smoking in
restaurant   Background music   Dogs welcome in bar only   Delta, MasterCard, Switch, Visa   Accommodation:
8 rooms, B&B £65 to £95*

HOLLINGTON   Derbyshire   map 5

Red Lion Inn ✿

Main Street, Hollington DE6 3AG   TEL: (01335) 360241

This white-painted country pub is on the edge of the village surrounded by fields. It's
been smartly modernised within (a list of publicans from 1786 to the present day gives
the age away), the mix of period features and modern touches working well together,
especially the contrast of bare brick walls with cream- or red-washed plaster. People
come primarily to eat, although there is ample space for drinkers, with Marston's
Pedigree and a weekly-changing guest on handpump. The bar is split in two, with
traditional pub tables and chairs to the right and a smaller area filled with dark red
leather chesterfields to the left, plus two dining rooms, the larger a pleasant light room,
very cottagey in looks and traditionally furnished, to the side. For those wanting just a
simple snack, bar food is a small slate of creamy garlic mushrooms, toad-in-the-hole,

steak and ale pie, and ribeye steak, but the main action is on the huge, regularly changing blackboards. Starters might run to thick, richly flavoured cream of brown onion soup with a mature Cheddar flute (basically a split baguette toasted with Cheddar), and goats' cheese soufflé with red onion marmalade and fresh home-made rosemary bread, while main courses could include grilled halibut steak on warm lemon butter sauce, or pan-fried fillet steak topped with melting Stilton on red wine syrup, with lemon crème brûlée for dessert. A short wine list features around 15 bottles plus half a dozen or so by the glass. SAMPLE DISHES: goats' cheese wrapped in smoked pancetta with roasted peach chutney £5; honey-glazed ham hock with Madeira jus £13; chocolate fudge brownie with home-made honeycomb crunch ice cream £4.25.

Licensee Robin Hunter (Pyramid)

Open 12 to 3, 6 to 11, Sun 12 to 3, 6 to 10.30; bar food and restaurant all week 12 to 2, Tue to Sun 6.30 to 9

Details Children welcome   Car park   Wheelchair access (also WC)   Garden and patio   No smoking in restaurant   Live or background music   Dogs welcome   MasterCard, Switch, Visa

HOLY CROSS   Worcestershire   map 5

Bell and Cross ✿

Holy Cross DY9 9QL   TEL: (01562) 730319
off A491, SE of West Hagley

Right on the crossroads at the centre of a tiny village, this tall custard-coloured pub is exceptionally busy for its rural location. This may be due to the fact that Roger Narbett has been a well-known figure on the Midlands restaurant scene for many years. Inside, the walls of the series of small rooms are crammed with prints, photographs and framed portraits, and the no-smoking restaurant, with its red walls and ceiling, has jars of preserves on the windowsill and little terracotta pots with miniature trees on the tables. There's plenty of ambition at work here – witness ham hock pâté with brandy, plum and fig compote, and main courses of slow-cooked daube of Cornish lamb with spicy sausages and baby onion garlic mash, or roasted pavé of Highland cod with smoked haddock brandade and balsamic tomato. Desserts might include anything from a warm Belgian waffle with banana and toffee ripple ice cream to tiramisù with biscotti. At lunchtime you can also get 'sarnies' and 'light bites': say, Indian-spiced chicken Caesar salad, or Parma ham, cannellini bean and mozzarella salad. Timothy Taylor Landlord, Banks's Mild and Bitter, and Marston's Pedigree are among the beers on draught, and the short list of around 30 wines includes some decent stuff, with about ten by the glass. SAMPLE DISHES: Cheddar cheese and confit tomato soup £3.75; honey-seared suprême of chicken with smoked ham and leek risotto and tarragon jus £11; treacle tart with vanilla ice cream £5.

Licensee Jo Narbett (Enterprise Inns)

Open 12 to 3, 6 to 11, Sun 12 to 3, 7 to 10.30; bar food and restaurant Mon to Sat 12 to 2, 6.30 to 9.15 (9.30 Sat), Sun 12 to 2.30; closed 25 Dec, evening 26 Dec, 31 Dec, evening 1 Jan

Details Children welcome in restaurant   Car park   Wheelchair access (not WC)   Garden and patio   No smoking in restaurant   Background music   No dogs   MasterCard, Switch, Visa

Report forms are at the back of the book; write a letter if you prefer; or email your pub report to whichpubguide@which.net.

▲ Crown and Anchor Hotel

Market Square, Holy Island TD15 2RX   TEL: (01289) 389215
WEBSITE: www.crownandanchorinn.fsnet.co.uk

On the edge of the village, facing south with views over the ruined priory, the Farne Islands, Bamburgh Castle and the famous Lindisfarne Castle (National Trust), the Crown and Anchor provides sustenance for modern-day pilgrims, tourists and locals. Blackboards in the small bar and in the restaurant list wines and specials of the day, and David Foxton's menus are always interesting (and quite enterprising in the evenings), stepping out with modish dishes such as oxtail soup with manzanilla and horseradish cream, grilled gilthead bream with caper berries, roast shank of salt-marsh lamb, and a salad of Serrano ham with rocket and Parmesan. Blueberry mille-feuille could head up desserts. For beer drinkers there's Caledonian Deuchars IPA and a weekly-changing guest, and wine lovers can choose from nine wines by the glass. Often referred to as Lindisfarne, Holy Island is a tidal island reached by a cause-way which is impassable some two hours before high tide and three hours after (tide tables are displayed at the causeway or phone ahead). SAMPLE DISHES: cream of broc-coli and blue cheese soup £2.50; roast Piperfield pork with seasonal vegetable broth £9.75; dark chocolate pots with polenta biscuits £4.50.

Licensee David Foxton (freehouse)
Open 11 to 11, Sun 12 to 10.30; bar food 12.15 to 2.30, restaurant Tue to Sat 6.30 to 8.30; closed 3 to 6 winter, all weekdays Dec to Mar
Details Children welcome in restaurant   Wheelchair access (also WC)   Garden   No smoking in restaurant   Background music   No dogs   Delta, Diners, MasterCard, Switch, Visa   Accommodation: 5 rooms, B&B £45 to £80

▲ Cheshire Cheese Inn

Edale Road, Hope S33 6ZF   TEL: (01433) 620381
WEBSITE: www.cheshire-cheese.net
on A625 between Chapel-en-le-Frith and Hathersage; leave Hope by unclassified road to Edale; pub is on left after ½m

This snug, traditional and utterly unpretentious inn dates from the sixteenth century and is popular with walkers, tourists and locals. It is at the heart of the Peak District National Park, with Castleton and its caverns, the Ladybower and Derwent Reservoirs, and wild open moorland all within easy reach. The three rooms are on different levels, including a small bar with a log fire, beams and heavy cottage-style furniture and lots of old prints and maps on the walls. Visitors can quench their thirst with a pint of one of the good line-up of hand-pulled real ales, among them Black Sheep Best Bitter, Wentworth Pale Ale, Timothy Taylor Landlord, Barnsley Bitter, and Acorn Brewery Gold, and satisfy their hunger with something from the printed menu or the blackboard of specials. You could start with a bowl of moules, or savoury Brie wedges, and go on to a hearty pie – perhaps chicken and mushroom – or a medley of local butcher's sausages, and end with sticky toffee pudding or syrup sponge. Vegetarians get a good deal, and Sunday lunch delivers traditional beef and pork dinners. Around a dozen wines are served by the glass, with bottle prices starting at £7.50. SAMPLE DISHES: garlic mushrooms £4.50; grilled cod with lemon and cracked black pepper £9; chocolate pudding with chocolate sauce £3.75.

Licensee David Helliwell (freehouse)
Open *Mon to Fri 12 to 3, 6.30 to 11, Sat 12 to 11, Sun 12 to 4, 6.30 to 10.30; bar food 12 to 2 (2.30 Sat and Sun), 6.30 to 8.30 (9 Sat, 8 Sun)*
Details *Children welcome in eating areas   Car park   Wheelchair access (not WC)   Garden and patio No smoking in eating areas   Background music   Dogs welcome   Amex, Delta, MasterCard, Switch, Visa Accommodation: 3 rooms, B&B £65 to £75 (double room)*

HOPTON WAFERS   Shropshire   map 5

▲ Crown Inn

Hopton Wafers DY14 0NB   TEL: (01299) 270372
WEBSITE: www.crownathopton.co.uk
on A4117, 2m W of Cleobury Mortimer

This prosperous, long-established country inn offers a number of places in which to eat and drink, both inside and out. A paved terrace at the front contains picnic tables and parasols, then there's a steep drop to the lawned gardens that run down to a stream. Inside, its decorative style is traditional, with exposed timbers in bar, restaurant and bedrooms. The Rent Room bar is so called because this was where stewards once collected rents from tenant farmers, while the restaurant takes the name of Poacher's and has a separate menu. Blackboards list the bar choices: perhaps chicken liver parfait, or salade niçoise, followed by generous main courses of half a shoulder of local lamb roasted with mint and mango and served with a Burgundy and redcurrant gravy, or steak and kidney pie. In the restaurant there might be seared pigeon breasts with spring onions, peppers and bean sprouts in a spicy Thai dressing to start, followed by chargrilled Hereford beef fillet with beetroot risotto and a port reduction. Four real ales are usually stocked, among them Timothy Taylor Landlord and Hobson's Best, plus always a guest. The global wine list rarely breaches the £20 mark; ten wines are available by the glass. SAMPLE DISHES: Stilton pâté £4.75; venison casserole with parsnip mash £8.75; Bakewell tart with custard £4.

Licensee Howard Hill-Lines (freehouse)
Open *12 to 3, 6 to 11 (10.30 Sun); bar food and restaurant 12 to 2.30, 6.30 to 9.30 (9 Sun)*
Details *Children welcome in bar eating area; no children under 7 in restaurant   Car park   Garden and patio No smoking in eating areas   Background music   No dogs in eating areas   Amex, Delta, MasterCard, Switch, Visa   Accommodation: 7 rooms, B&B £47.50 to £75*

HORNDON ON THE HILL   Essex   map 3

▲ Bell Inn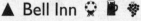

High Road, Horndon on the Hill SS17 8LD   TEL: (01375) 642463
WEBSITE: www.bell-inn.co.uk
off M25 junctions 30 and 31, signposted Thurrock, Lakeside; take A13, then B1007 to Horndon

In the Middle Ages this ancient hostelry was used as a stopover by pilgrims and merchants waiting for low tide, when they could cross the Thames at Higham's Causeway. Five centuries on, it still looks the part, with flagstone floors, standing timbers, a collection of foundry memorabilia, a longcase clock, and normally a bustle of people. Those who come in for just a drink use the front bar, while the back bar next to the restaurant is where those wishing to eat may settle (note that bar tables are not bookable). The modern and imaginative restaurant menu (which is also served in the bar) shows a good deal of ambition and invention: to start, there might be squid stuffed with braised oxtail, carpaccio and squash purée, while main courses could include pan-fried zander with crab mayo and an egg poached in red wine, or parsnip risotto with Parmesan and parsnip froth, as well as beer-battered cod, and smoked bacon macaroni cheese. Completing the picture are complex desserts like blood orange pannacotta with marzipan and almonds dipped in white chocolate. Additional touches, such as stylish presentation, add to the feeling that this is a well-run operation that knows what it's doing. Sandwiches are available in the bar at lunchtime along with simple dishes like roast sausages with parsley and truffle sauce or pan-fried lambs' kidneys with mustard and sage. Around 16 wines are offered by the glass from an irreverent house list. The main wine list runs to some serious aged Bordeaux and Burgundy but is sprinkled with good choices from around the world at fair prices. All wines are also available to buy at take-away prices. Real ale buffs can choose from a selection that includes Greene King IPA, Bass, Crouch Vale Brewers Gold and Morland Original. SAMPLE DISHES: chicken Caesar salad £7; grilled cod fillet with white beans and watercress £8.50; pears poached in mulled wine with cinnamon rice pudding £5.50.

Licensee J.S.B. Vereker (freehouse)
Open Mon to Fri 11 to 2.30, 5.30 to 11, Sat 11 to 3, 6 to 11, Sun 12 to 4, 7 to 10.30; bar food and restaurant 12 to 1.45, 6.45 to 9.45; no food bank hol Mons, closed 25 and 26 Dec
Details Children welcome   Car park   Wheelchair access (also WC)   Garden   No smoking in restaurant   No music   Dogs welcome on a lead in bar only   Amex, Delta, MasterCard, Switch, Visa   Accommodation: 5 rooms, room only £50 to £85

HORRINGER   Suffolk   map 6

Beehive
The Street, Horringer IP29 5SN   TEL: (01284) 735260
on A143, 3m SW of Bury St Edmunds

Horringer is within striking distance of Ickworth House and Gardens (NT), and on the main road through it a beehive on the front lawn marks out this well-kept, welcoming brick-and-flint pub. Enter through the rear, past the small leafy beer garden, into a network of small rooms decorated in a simple, cottagey style, with hessian flooring and a mix of traditional pictures and old photographs. The place has retained its unspoilt, informal atmosphere, although most customers are now attracted by the food. Strips of blackboard hung opposite the bar advertise the day's specials which always feature plenty for fish-fanciers and meat-eaters alike. Typically you might find anything from salmon and crayfish-tail terrine with lemon dressing, or twice-baked cheese soufflé with marinaded artichokes, to slow-braised oxtails or home-made pork, apple and leek sausages on creamy mash. There's also a selection of lighter dishes, such as warm 'three cheese' and broccoli tart, or Suffolk ham with French bread, and you might conclude with chocolate and Grand Marnier mousse or lemon posset. This is a Greene King pub with IPA and Abbot Ale on draught, alongside Old Speckled Hen; alternatively dip into the affordably priced list of around 30 wines (from £10.95), eight of which are offered by the glass. SAMPLE DISHES: chicken liver parfait with home-made chutney £5; sea bass on sun-ripened tomato and pesto potatoes £14; raspberry crème brûlée £4.

Licensee Gary Kingshott (Greene King)
Open 11.30 to 3, 7 to 11 (Sun 10.30); bar food (exc Sun evening) 12 to 2, 7 to 9.30 (closing times may vary)
Details Children welcome   Car park   Wheelchair access (not WC)   Garden and patio   No music   No dogs
Delta, MasterCard, Switch, Visa

HORSTEAD   Norfolk   map 6

Recruiting Sergeant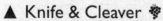

Norwich Road, Horstead NR12 7EP   TEL: (01603) 737077
on B1150 Norwich to North Walsham road, 7m N of Norwich

Military prints decorate this long, white pub set back a little from the road through
the village. The main bar extends the length of the place, with an L-shaped counter
separating the front from the quieter back section that opens on to the garden behind.
A chatty atmosphere prevails, thanks largely to a 'cheerful group' of young staff who
keep things moving along. The regular carte is supplemented by daily printed menus
with the spotlight on fish delivered fresh from the Norfolk coast. Cod in beer batter,
Brancaster mussels, and conger eel have all been endorsed, but the repertoire extends
to pan-fried sardines with Greek salad and mint dressing, monkfish tails with a crab
and spring onion cake and thermidor sauce, and John Dory with bouillabaisse. Meat
eaters are also well served by, say, roast beef and Yorkshire pudding, or Barbary duck
breast with apple and potato rösti and a cider and honey jus. A fine brigade of mostly
East Anglian beers includes Adnams Bitter and Broadside, Greene King Abbot Ale,
Woodforde's Wherry or Nelson's Revenge plus Queen's Shilling (brewed for the pub
by Courage). There's also a well-spread, affordable list of around 25 wines, with ten
available by the glass (from £2.30). SAMPLE DISHES: butternut squash and chorizo soup
£4; mixed seafood paella £12; orange and Cointreau pannacotta £4.

Licensee Matthew John Colchester (freehouse)
Open 11 to 11, Sun 12 to 10.30; bar food and restaurant 12 to 2, 6.30 to 9 (9.30 Thur to Sat); no food
25 Dec, closed 26 Dec
Details Children welcome   Car park   Wheelchair access (also WC)   Garden and patio   No-smoking area in
bar, no smoking in restaurant   Background music   Dogs welcome on a lead   Delta, MasterCard, Switch, Visa

HOUGHTON CONQUEST   Bedfordshire   map 6

▲ Knife & Cleaver 🌺

The Grove, Houghton Conquest MK45 3LA   TEL: (01234) 740387
WEBSITE: www.knifeandcleaver.com

The Knife & Cleaver has grown over the years, extending into a large conservatory
dining room to the rear and, across a courtyard, to some ground-floor bedrooms.
With the bar area now a pleasant lounge devoted to pre-meal drinks and food ordering, the swinging sign outside proclaiming 'restaurant-with-rooms' is no surprise.
But Bateman XB and Fuller's London Pride are on draught, with Stowford Press for
cider drinkers, and the bar menu is an appealing mix of pub favourites and more
unusual ideas, showing that the place hasn't lost sight of its origins. Interesting filled
baguettes and ciabattas, as well as ploughman's, are there for those after just a snack,
and among starters might be pheasant and wild mushroom terrine, and marinated
herring fillets with a lobster and dill dressing. Confit of duck leg with an apple, potato
and celeriac cake, or pork and Stilton sausages with parsnip and honey mash show the

range of main courses, and desserts could well include pear and frangipane tart with an unusual English Brie ice cream. Fish is the main thrust of the restaurant menu, although something like rack of Welsh lamb with layered Mediterranean vegetables and an olive and garlic jus might make an appearance among meat dishes. Wines come on two lists, the first offering around 20 by the glass or 50cl carafe, the second a full restaurant list, grouped by style, that sweeps happily from £11 basics to expensive French classics. SAMPLE DISHES: smoked haddock chowder £5; salmon and shrimp fishcake £6.50; sticky toffee pudding with Calvados toffee sauce £3.75.

Licensees David and Pauline Loom (freehouse)
Open *all week (exc Sun evening) 12 to 2.30, 7 to 11; bar food 12 to 2.30 (2 Sat), 7 to 9.30 (no bar food served when restaurant is busy, usually Sat evening and Sun lunchtime: best to phone at weekends); restaurant (exc Sat lunchtime) 12 to 2.30, 7 to 9.30; closed bank hol Mon evenings, 27 to 30 Dec*
Details *Children welcome in eating areas   Car park   Wheelchair access (not WC)   Garden and patio No smoking in restaurant   Background music   Dogs in bedrooms only   Amex, Delta, Diners, MasterCard, Switch, Visa   Accommodation: 9 rooms, B&B £53 to £78*

HUNTINGDON   Cambridgeshire   map 6

▲ Old Bridge Hotel 🍷🍷 🍇

1 High Street, Huntingdon PE29 3TQ   TEL: (01480) 424300
WEBSITE: www.huntsbridge.co.uk
off Huntingdon ring road, by river

There's a simple rule to finding the Old Bridge: just stay with Huntingdon's one-way system as it swings around town and you will eventually come to this handsome eighteenth-century building – right on the road by the bridge spanning the Great Ouse. As a member of the Huntsbridge Group, it follows the same formula successfully applied at its sister establishments (see the Three Horseshoes, Madingley, the Pheasant Inn, Keyston, and the Falcon, Fotheringhay), combining the virtues of the informality of a pub with some seriously good cooking. Chef Martin Lee offers two well-balanced menus: an à la carte for the bar areas, including the spacious and relaxing lounge, the smaller bar with a winter log fire, and in the informal Terrace Restaurant; in the separate Dining Room there is a three-course set menu for £36. The cooking style is distinctly modern, displaying lots of bright Mediterranean influences, as well as some from further afield, alongside more traditional ideas. This can result in such dishes as seared fillet of salmon with wok-fried greens and a saffron and coriander dressing appearing on the menu next to bangers and mash with onion and Dijon mustard sauce. Game is handled confidently – perhaps roast Suffolk partridge with garlic polenta and thyme sauce – as is seafood – perhaps a starter of peppered tuna and salmon sushi with wasabi, pickled ginger, soy, coriander and cress. Sandwiches are an alternative, and among puddings may be pineapple and coconut Bakewell tart. Adnams Bitter is the regular real ale; this is accompanied by three guests, one of which may be from a local brewery, such as City of Cambridge, Potton or Elgood's. Wine is a passion here, with 14 by the glass priced from £3 to £7.50 and covering an exciting range of flavours; good sherry is on offer too. The full list of around 300 bottles starts off with an appetising 'under-£20' selection arranged by style, but makes no bones about encouraging customers to spend more on the outstanding range of 'top-class' bottles. SAMPLE DISHES: roast butternut squash and lentil soup £4.75; roast pheasant with parsnip purée, roast shallots, cavolo nero and roast potatoes £14.75; Valrhona chocolate and hazelnut mousse with hazelnut ice cream £7.

Licensees John Hoskins and Martin Lee (freehouse)
Open 12 to 11, Sun 12 to 10.30; bar food and restaurant 12 to 2.30, 6.30 (7 Sun) to 10
Details Children welcome   Car park   Wheelchair access (also WC)   Garden   No smoking in restaurant
Occasional live music   Dogs welcome   Amex, Delta, Diners, MasterCard, Switch, Visa   Accommodation:
23 rooms, B&B £85 to £180

HUTTON MAGNA 😟   Co Durham   map 10

Oak Tree Inn 😟   NEW ENTRY
Hutton Magna DL11 7HH   TEL: (01833) 627371
WEBSITE: www.elevation-it.co.uk/oaktree
village just N of A66 about 7m NW of Scotch Corner

Booking is essential at this village pub/restaurant, which from the outside doesn't
look much like a hostelry at all. Inside, it is deceptively large, with an unpretentious
homely bar area at the front, where there's a stand with newspapers to browse
through and real ales including Black Sheep Best Bitter, Timothy Taylor Landlord
and a guest such as Wells Bombardier Premium Bitter on handpump. Towards the
rear is the dining area, with its bottle-green walls and square polished wooden tables.
The blackboard menu changes daily and is based resolutely on what is freshly available from the market. The kitchen comes up with some intriguing twists on classic
ideas. To start, there might be a spring roll packed with sautéed vegetables around a
core of feta with sweet chilli jam, curry-spiced spaghetti with mussels, or home-cured
gravlax accompanied by a warm poached egg, avruga caviar and crème fraîche. Main
courses are in similar vein: roast fillet of organic salmon might be served with white
beans, broccoli and Toulouse sausages, and vegetarians could home in on a warm
salad of roasted peppers and goats' cheese with cured tomato. The choice of desserts
runs to banana tart with superb rum and raisin ice cream ('a perfect combination, very
well executed,' thought one recipient). The whole place is charmingly run by an
enthusiastic husband and wife team: he cooks, she serves behind the bar. The main
list of around two dozen wines has some interesting offerings (although vintages are
absent), and four house selections come by the glass; a separate list of 'specials' moves
into more serious territory. SAMPLE DISHES: game tart with cauliflower cream £4.75;
pan-fried fillets of sea bass with green beans, roast scallops and ginger £14.50; poached
plums with honey and yoghurt ice cream £4.75.

Licensees Alastair and Claire Ross (freehouse)
Open Tue 6 to 11, Wed to Fri 12 to 3, 6 to 11, Sat 12 to 11, Sun 12 to 10.30; bar food Wed to Sun 12 to 2,
Tue to Sat 6.30 to 9 (booking is advised); closed 1 week Jan
Details Children welcome in eating area   Car park   No smoking in eating area   Background music
Dogs welcome   Delta, MasterCard, Switch, Visa

ICKLESHAM   East Sussex   map 3

Queens Head 🍺
Parsonage Lane, Icklesham TN36 4BL   TEL: (01424) 814552
just off A259 2m W of Winchelsea

It's easy to miss the sharp, narrow turn into the lane leading to the Queens Head, but
once there you will find plenty of parking spaces, as well as a boules pitch and a large
grassed garden with picnic tables. Inside, the compact interlinked rooms around a

central bar have an old-world feel (the building dates from 1631), with ceilings at different heights and, hanging from them, artefacts ranging from old-fashioned agricultural tools to an ancient delivery bike. The good-value cooking is of the no-frills traditional English variety. The standard menu lists things like deep-fried Brie with cranberry sauce, steak in French bread, chicken, ham and mushroom pie, a daily curry, and ham and eggs. More interesting are the blackboard specials, which might include seasonal game. Desserts are from the chocolate fudge cake and raspberry cheesecake school. Real ales are a strong point: up to six are offered at a time, including something from Harveys, Greene King and Woodforde's and Courage Directors. Wines are not bad either – the short list offers plenty of choice by the glass. Visit on Tuesday evenings for live music. SAMPLE DISHES: smoked mackerel horseradish £4.25; Stilton and apricot macaroni cheese £6.75; banoffi pie £3.25.

Licensees Ian Mitchell and Lee Norcott (freehouse)
Open 11 to 11, Sun 12 to 10.30; bar food Mon to Fri 12 to 2.45, 6.15 to 9.45, Sat and Sun 12 to 9.45; closed evenings 25 and 26 Dec
Details No under-12s after 8.30pm Car park No-smoking areas Live or background music Amex, Delta, Diners, MasterCard, Switch, Visa

ICKLINGHAM Suffolk

map 6

Red Lion
The Street, Icklingham IP28 6PS TEL: (01638) 717802

Neat lawns separate this smartly white-painted and thatched old pub from the main road that runs through the small village of Icklingham, and a warm and welcoming atmosphere is created inside by an oriental rug, large winged armchairs and a huge inglenook. Bar meals tend to be simple dishes like pork chops with apple and cider sauce, or sausages with mash and onion gravy. The main menu shows a slightly more elaborate style, as in guinea fowl suprêmes on baby spinach with white wine and mushroom sauce, or chicken breast stuffed with herb and garlic cream cheese and served with a whole-grain mustard sauce. Choice is extended further with a seasonal game menu and a blackboard of fish specials. This is a Greene King pub serving IPA and Abbot Ale. Of the list of 16 wines, a couple are served by the glass; country wines such as elderberry and silver birch are also available. SAMPLE DISHES: breadcrumbed Brie on red fruit coulis £6; rack of lamb with sauce chasseur £16; sticky toffee pudding £4.75.

Licensees Elizabeth Mason and David Grinling (Greene King)
Open 12 to 3, 6 to 11, Sun 12 to 2.30, 7.15 to 10.30; bar food and restaurant 12 to 2.30, 6 to 10
Details Children welcome Car park Wheelchair access (also WC) Garden Background music No dogs Delta, MasterCard, Switch, Visa

IDDESLEIGH Devon

map 1

▲ Duke of York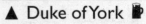
Iddesleigh EX19 8BG TEL: (01837) 810253

This thatched old Devon longhouse standing by the church and surrounded by old cottages sits in a classic English scene. Inside, it is cosy and welcoming: low ceilings, small rooms, cavernous fireplace, dartboard, and old prints and banknotes decorating the walls. The effect is reinforced by real ales, which are a particular strength;

Cotleigh Tawny Bitter and Adnams Broadside are joined by guests from West Country brewers like Sharp's and Exe Valley. A dozen wines are available by the glass too. Result: a comfortable hubbub of voices, 'lots of dogs, chatting drinkers and contented eaters', all testifying to the pub's popularity. One of the walls is covered with a large board detailing the extensive menu, and bar food encompasses standards such as ham, egg and chips, jumbo sausages, steak and kidney pudding, and cottage pie. In the evenings a more ambitious fixed-price menu is also offered in the separate restaurant area. This might offer you duck breast hot-smoked with orange peel and Grand Marnier and served with Cumberland sauce, followed by monkfish sautéed with shallots and mushrooms in a Pernod and cream sauce, plus date, almond and marzipan bread-and-butter pudding to follow. SAMPLE DISHES: crab mayonnaise £5.50; sea bass filled with pine nuts and smoky bacon £11; blackcurrant crumble £3.50.

Licensees Jamie Stuart and Pippa Hutchinson (freehouse)
Open 11 to 11, Sun 12 to 10.30; bar food 11 to 10; restaurant 6.30 to 9.30
Details Children welcome   Garden   Occasional live music   Dogs welcome   Delta, Diners, MasterCard, Switch, Visa   Accommodation: 7 rooms, B&B £25 to £50

IGHTHAM COMMON   Kent   map 3

Harrow Inn

Common Road, Ightham Common TN15 9EB   TEL: (01732) 885912
from A25 Sevenoaks to Borough Green road, take turning signposted Ightham Common; pub about ½m on left

While this charming old Kentish ragstone pub still functions as a cheery village local, it clearly sets out its stall on the food front. Blackboards are dotted around the panelled walls in the little bar, and beyond is a softly lit, cosy room with a black-and-white-tiled floor and turquoise paintwork. There's also a smartly laid-out dining room-cum-conservatory with its own menu. The bar menu is a lengthy affair, and it steers clear of anything too modish: deep-fried Camembert might come with gooseberry preserve or perhaps rhubarb compote, and other typical options could include tomato and anchovy salad, pan-fried calf's liver with crispy bacon, and Goan chicken – not to mention scampi and chips. Specials add more variety in the shape of, say, pan-fried sea bass fillet with spinach and lobster sauce, or mushroom florentine. Finish with something fruity like summer pudding or oranges in caramel. Greene King IPA and Abbot Ale are on handpump along with guests. Ten wines of the month, by glass or bottle, feature on a blackboard over the bar and there's a straightforward printed list. Ightham Mote (National Trust) is not far away. SAMPLE DISHES: goats' cheese and caramelised red onion tart £6.50; lamb shank with mash, shallots and red wine jus £11; Belgian apple pie £4.50.

Licensee John Elton (freehouse)
Open Tue to Sun 12 to 3, Tue to Sat 6 to 11; bar food and restaurant 12 to 2, 6 to 9; closed 1 Jan
Details Children welcome in family room   Car park   Wheelchair access (not WC)   Patio   No smoking in restaurant   Background music   No dogs   MasterCard, Switch, Visa

🏵 *indicates a pub serving outstanding bar food, backed up by all-round excellence in other departments, such as service, atmosphere and cleanliness.*

ILKLEY   West Yorkshire   map 8

Bar t'at 🍺

7 Cunliffe Road, Ilkley LS29 9DZ   TEL: (01943) 608888

This stylish ale and wine bar in the centre of town doffs its flat cap to that most famous of all Yorkshire dialect songs ('On Ilkley Moor...' etc., etc.). Beer advertisements and memorabilia decorate the ground-floor bar, which stocks a vast array of bottled beers from all corners of the globe, as well as a goodly line-up of real ales, including Deuchars IPA, Timothy Taylor Landlord, Black Sheep Best Bitter and four regularly changing guests. There's also a fair selection of reasonably priced wines, including eight by the glass (from £2.50). In the cellar, reached via a spiral staircase, is a no-smoking dining room with pews, bare wooden tables and chairs, and an open-plan kitchen hatch. At lunchtime you can get sandwiches, ciabatta melts, a home-made stew, and a mixed bag of main dishes ranging from haddock goujons in beer batter to home-made Toulouse sausage with creamy leek mash, or mussels in Thai red curry sauce. The evening menu (and specials board) adds a few more main dishes in the shape of, say, Portuguese-style pork loin steaks, vegetable and mixed-bean casserole with olives and basil, and grilled sirloin steak. SAMPLE DISHES: king prawns in filo with chilli dip £4.50; minted shoulder of lamb with cranberry and mint gravy £9.50; treacle tart £3.50.

Licensees Stella Jane Mallinson and Michael Frazer Barnes (freehouse)
Open 12 to 11 (10.30 Sun); bar food and restaurant 12 to 2.30, 6 to 9; closed 25 Dec
Details Children welcome in restaurant   Wheelchair access (not WC)   Garden   No-smoking area in bar, no smoking in restaurant   No music   Dogs welcome in bar only   Delta, MasterCard, Switch, Visa

ILMINGTON   Warwickshire   map 5

▲ Howard Arms 🍺 🌼

Lower Green, Ilmington CV36 4LT   TEL: (01608) 682226
WEBSITE: www.howardarms.com

Overlooking the small village green, this large inn built of ochre-coloured stone was originally two separate houses. There is a significant difference in character (and floor level) between the two halves: the main bar has flagstone floors, an enormous stone inglenook and a long bar counter, while the dining area has bare old floorboards, mustard-coloured walls, and giant worm-eaten ceiling beams. Food is listed on numerous blackboards throughout, with around a dozen varied options per course. Chargrilled pork cutlet on braised red cabbage with Calvados sauce, or pan-fried calf's liver on buttered onions with crisp bacon represent the more conservative side of the repertoire, but there might also be devilled mackerel fillets with beetroot and horse-radish purée, or pumpkin, leek and butter-bean stew with Gruyère profiteroles. A superlative line-up of real ales features Genesis from the North Cotswold Brewery alongside Everards Tiger Best and guests, which might include Timothy Taylor Landlord or Adnams Broadside. The house wine list offers varied drinking by the glass or bottle, but anyone with more than £15 in their pocket should turn to the 'small yet interesting selection of some rather nice wines' for some very well chosen bottles. SAMPLE DISHES: smoked haddock kedgeree with a poached egg and hollandaise £5.50; lamb shank braised with orange, port and juniper £13.50; apricot and almond tart with mascarpone £5.

Licensees Rob Greenstock and Martin Devereux (freehouse)
Open 11 to 2, 6 to 11; bar food Mon to Sat 12 to 2, 7 to 9 (9.30 Fri and Sat), Sun 12 to 2.30, 6.30 to 8.30; closed 25 Dec and evening 31 Dec
Details Children welcome in eating areas before 8pm   Car park   Wheelchair access (not WC)   Garden and patio   No smoking in 3 rooms   No music   No dogs   Delta, MasterCard, Switch, Visa   Accommodation: 3 rooms, B&B £52 to £94

IRONBRIDGE   Shropshire

map 5

▲ Malthouse

The Wharfage, Ironbridge TF8 7NH   TEL: (01952) 433712
WEBSITE: www.malthousepubs.co.uk
in centre of Ironbridge, 200yds from bridge

On a road that winds its way along the river, this country pub/bar/restaurant-with-rooms comprises a number of attached but dissimilar buildings around a cobbled courtyard. The bright, spacious Jazz Bar is the part that most resembles a traditional pub, and, as the name suggests, it is also frequently a live music venue. To wet your whistle, you can sample Flowers IPA, Boddingtons Bitter or a guest ale such as Old Speckled Hen; alternatively, try something from the global list of over 40 wines. There is also a simple but cosmopolitan bar menu with starters including prawn and sweetcorn cakes with sweet chilli sauce, and warm spiced beef salad with a balsamic, pine-nut and basil dressing, before main courses ranging from chicken and red wine casserole with braised rice to blackened Cajun salmon with spinach and mussel stew. In between are various 'snacks and nibbles' like goats' cheese and Parma ham crostini, garlic mushrooms with smoked bacon and parsley sauce, and vegetable crudités with dips. The main part of the Malthouse is given over entirely to dining, with an ambitious modern menu taking in busy-sounding dishes such as crab and lobster ravioli with yellow pepper sauce and green pepper oil, and escalope of pork with Brussels champ mash, warm cranberry and chestnut compote and a thyme and port sauce. SAMPLE DISHES: three-cheese macaroni with green chilli relish £5; grilled ribeye steak with peppercorn butter £11; pear and vanilla cheesecake £3.50.

Licensee Alexander Nicoll (Pubmaster)
Open 12 to 11 (10.30 Sun); bar food 12 to 2.30, 5.30 to 9, restaurant 12 to 2, 6.30 to 9.45; closed 25 Dec
Details Children welcome   Car park   Wheelchair access (not WC)   Patio   No smoking in restaurant   Live or background music   Dogs welcome   Delta, MasterCard, Switch, Visa   Accommodation: 9 rooms, B&B £55 to £70

ITTERINGHAM   Norfolk

map 6

Walpole Arms 🍺

The Common, Itteringham NR11 7AR   TEL: (01263) 587258
WEBSITE: www.thewalpolearms.co.uk

This brick-built former farmhouse, fronted by a wide lawn and festooned at night with fairy lights, stands right in the village centre. In the large, comfortable green-carpeted bar, with its low ceiling, light-coloured oak beams and studs, the brick-fronted counter serves East Anglian beers: Adnams Bitter and Broadside, and Woodforde's Walpole specially brewed for the pub, plus guests (maybe from Buffy's and Wolf) and strong French and Belgian beers. Over the fireplace a blackboard lists snacks such as pork, prune and vegetable pie with handcut chips, and pickled herrings with Baltic potato salad and beetroot. There's more formality across the farmyard in the restaurant in the old cart shed. Here you'll find smoked eel fritters with pickled red cabbage, or Asian-style carpaccio of venison with kimchie cabbage and mango, preceding lamb shank with little gem, mint, roast baby onions and garlic mash, or fillet of brill with cauliflower cheese, pommes allumette and red wine jus. Sweets may include pumpkin pie with Seville orange custard. Blackboards advertise weekly wine specials and 15 good-value house wines spanning a range of styles and available by the glass, as are a host of sherries, ports and dessert wines. The printed wine list sticks to a manageable 50-odd bottles, with a fair range under £20. Eight wines are available in half-bottles. SAMPLE DISHES: boudin blanc sausage of mushroom and foie gras with roast squash £5.25; Morston mussels with leeks, white wine, cream and crusty bread £9; caramelised banana with gingerbread and butterscotch ice cream £5.25.

Licensees Richard Bryan and Christian Hodgkinson (freehouse)
Open Mon to Sat 12 to 3, 6 to 11, Sun 12 to 10.30; bar food and restaurant 12 to 2 (3 Sun), 7 to 9 (9.30 summer); no bar food Sun evening; closed evening 25 Dec
Details Children welcome in bar eating area and restaurant   Car park   Wheelchair access (also WC)   Garden and patio   No smoking in dining room   Background music   Dogs welcome on a lead in bar only   Delta, MasterCard, Switch, Visa

KEIGHLEY   West Yorkshire   map 8

Quarry House Inn
Bingley Road, Lees Moor, Keighley BD21 5QE   TEL: (01535) 642239
off A629, 2m E of Haworth

Visitors wishing to escape the Brontë tourists overrunning Haworth would do well to remember that the Quarry House Inn is just a couple of miles away. The drive up to Lees Moor gives superb views over the Worth Valley, and the pub's own merits (which make booking advisable at weekends) justify the journey too. The pub has two strings to its bow: decent traditional beer (well-kept Yorkshire brews: Timothy Taylor Best Bitter, Golden Best and Landlord, together with Tetley Bitter) and decent traditional food. The dining areas have pink-clothed tables and spindle-back chairs, and food is listed on a carte plus blackboards of daily specials. Creamy garlic mushrooms or home-made soup are typical starters, with mains taking in the usual lasagne, steaks, grills, Cumberland sausage, or breast of chicken with a white wine, tarragon, mushroom and cream sauce. Fish eaters can choose among breaded haddock fillets, fillet of Scottish salmon, and whole-tail scampi with tartare sauce from the printed menu or from the regularly changing fish specials board. Tasty, tender roasts (beef, lamb, pork, chicken) feature at Sunday lunch. About 35 wines, from both Old and New Worlds, are listed on a blackboard; all are served by the glass. SAMPLE DISHES: chicken liver pâté £4; fillet steak with pepper, brandy and cream sauce £13.75; apple pancake stack £3.

Licensee C.M. Smith (freehouse)
Open 12 to 3, 7 to 12; bar food and restaurant 12 to 2, 7 to 10; closed 25 and 26 Dec, 1 Jan
Details Children welcome   Car park   Garden   No smoking in restaurant   Background music   Dogs welcome in bar only   Delta, MasterCard, Switch, Visa

See 'How to use the Guide' at the front of the book for an explanation of the symbols used at the tops of entries.

▲ Walter de Cantelupe Inn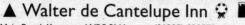

Main Road, Kempsey WR5 3NA   TEL: (01905) 820572
WEBSITE: www.walterdecantelupeinn.com

First of all, a history lesson. In the thirteenth century the village of Kempsey played a key role in Simon de Montfort's campaign against Henry III, and the inn is named after one of de Montfort's supporters who was Bishop of Worcester. These days its claim to fame is a winning combination of top-notch pub food and splendid beer. The décor is artistic – in an unpretentious way – with an almost baroque colour scheme (as in red curtains with a gold fleur-de-lis print) and quirky touches such as a giant antique gramophone. Alongside the honours board for the de Cantelupe Golf Society is another board that makes much more interesting reading: it lists the kitchen's output for the day. Though the cooking style is essentially simple, the repertoire covers a lot of territory, from Barnsley chop with minted gravy to baked sea bass on a bed of mozzarella, basil and tomato, and the focus is firmly on local ingredients: pork and leek sausages are hand-made nearby, roast Gressingham duck might be served with a sauce made from local honey and thyme, and the kitchen also produces its own chutneys. To back up the food, there's a fine selection of superior real ales including Everards Beacon Bitter, Timothy Taylor Landlord, and King's Shilling from the local Cannon Royall Brewery, plus some decent guest beers. At least six wines from the global list are generally available by the glass; house wine is £9.95. SAMPLE DISHES: cream of mushroom soup £3.50; steak and kidney pie £8; summer pudding £3.50.

Licensee Martin Lloyd-Morris (freehouse)
Open Tue to Sat 12 to 2.30, 6 to 11, Sun 12 to 3, 7 to 10.30; bar food Tue to Sat 12 to 2 (2.30 Sat summer), 6.30 to 9 (10 Fri and Sat), Sun 12 to 3; closed 25 and 26 Dec, 2 weeks late Jan to early Feb
Details Children welcome in eating areas before 8.15pm   Car park   Patio   No smoking in eating areas
Occasional live or background music   Dogs welcome on a lead   Amex, Delta, MasterCard, Switch, Visa
Accommodation: 3 rooms, B&B £29 to £70

Chequers Inn

Pertenhall Road, Brook End, Keysoe MK44 2HR   TEL: (01234) 708678
WEBSITE: www.bigfoot.com/~chequers
on B660, 8m N of Bedford and at N end of Keysoe

The neat, well-maintained cream building with its dormer windows, tidy front garden and small car park entrance can easily be mistaken for a private house. Once identified, the pub's rural location brings the bonus of a pleasant terrace and garden with a children's play area and, within, a welcome that is genuine and warm. Mid-twentieth-century modernisation may have robbed the place of any real sense of age (although there are some fiercely low beams), but the main emphasis here is the food. Traditional it may be, but raw materials are good and everything is cooked with care. A printed menu strays no further than popular steaks, chilli, chicken curry, or a range of sandwiches (plus a short, familiar children's menu), and you need to look to the specials board for more interesting choices: generous country dishes such as a thick, warming, 'properly made' vegetable soup, or collar of bacon with parsley sauce, alongside the more usual lamb shank with minted gravy. Fuller's London Pride and Hook Norton Best Bitter are on handpump, and four wines are served by the glass from a short list. SAMPLE DISHES: garlic mushrooms on toast £3.75; steak and ale pie £6.50; caramel walnut meringue £2.75.

Licensee Jeffrey Kearns (freehouse)

Open *Mon and Wed to Sat 11.30 to 2.30, 6.30 to 11, Sun 12 to 2.30, 7 to 10.30; bar food and restaurant 12 to 2, 7 to 9.30*

Details *Children welcome in family room and restaurant　Car park　Wheelchair access (also WC)　Garden and patio　No-smoking area in bar　Occasional background music　No dogs　MasterCard, Visa*

KEYSTON　　Cambridgeshire　　　　　　　　　　　　　　　　　　map 6

Pheasant Inn 🏆 🏆 🍇

Loop Road, Keyston PE28 0RE　TEL: (01832) 710241
on B663, just S of junction with A14

Keyston may be a rural village but it is affluent, and the long, thatched Pheasant at its heart looks prosperous and traditional. The inn has all the trappings of an old English village pub, with lots of beams, a fire, stuffed pheasants, and hunting prints. It shares the same informal approach to eating and drinking as its sister establishments in the Huntsbridge Group, the Three Horseshoes, Madingley, the Old Bridge, Huntingdon, and the Falcon, Fotheringhay (see entries), which means that one menu is served throughout, both in the more formal restaurant and the relaxed lounge, and you can eat as much or as little as you like, from a full three-course meal to a light dish of risotto with roast pumpkin, oregano and Parmesan. As that dish might suggest, modern themes prevail in the cooking, and no small degree of invention is at work. Braised pork belly might come with noodles, cavolo nero and Thai broth, and haunch of venison with parsnip mash, red cabbage, cranberry relish and red wine sauce. Those wanting something more traditional might start with coarse-cut country pâté with piccalilli, and move on to bangers and mash with white onion sauce. The place confirms its pub credentials with its selection of fine real ales, which includes Adnams Best Bitter alongside two guests, of which regulars come from the local Potton Brewery. As with its sister establishments, the wine list here will gladden the heart of any wine lover. The 14 wines by the glass (from £3 to £7.50) or the selection of aperitif sherries offer plenty to relish while browsing the list of over 100 wines arranged into 'under £20' and 'top-class' sections. SAMPLE DISHES: carpaccio of tuna with ginger, lime and coriander £7.50; loin of Cornish lamb with boulangère potatoes, cavolo nero and redcurrant jelly £14.75; apple and date pie with Calvados sauce £5.75.

Licensee John Hoskins (freehouse)

Open *12 to 3, 6 to 11, Sun 12 to 2.30, 6 to 10.30; bar food and restaurant 12 to 2.15, 6.30 to 9.30 (7 to 9 Sun)*

Details *Children welcome　Car park　Wheelchair access (not WC)　Patio　No smoking in restaurant Occasional live music　Dogs welcome in main bar only　Delta, MasterCard, Switch, Visa*

Prices of dishes quoted in an entry are based on information supplied by the pub, rounded up to the nearest 25 pence. These prices may have changed since publication and are meant only as a guide.

KINGSDON Somerset map 2

Kingsdon Inn

Kingsdon TA11 7LG TEL: (01935) 840543
village signposted off B3151 Ilchester to Street road, just N of A372

This charming thatched and stone building is in an 'appealing little village', yet close enough to the area's major trunk road – the A303 – to attract travellers prepared to detour for something in the way of food and drink. Four rambling, interlinked dining areas, 'all very cottagey in décor and furnishings', are accessible from the spacious bar area, the lower part of which, with its stone floor, raised hearth with roaring log fire and stripped deal tables, is the best part in which to sit. Blackboards list pub classics such as ploughman's and steak and kidney pie for lunch, giving way to more inventive dinner menus, with starters often also available at lunch as a snack or starter. Reporters have been impressed by the quality of simple lunch dishes such as walnut, leek and Stilton pie, and well-presented liver and bacon with separate dishes of sautéed potatoes and vegetables. Evening choices range from starters of king prawns in lime and ginger to grilled whole lemon sole, or wild rabbit in Dijon mustard and white wine sauce. On draught are Butcombe, Cotleigh Barn Owl and Otter bitters as well as Burrow Hill farmhouse cider. A fair selection of malt whiskies is available, plus around ten wines by the glass from £3. The wine list of some 50 bins (seven of them in halves) is arranged by style and stays mainly under £20. SAMPLE DISHES: crab and prawn Mornay £5.50; rack of lamb with port and redcurrant sauce £14; lemon crunch £4.

Licensees Leslie and Anne-Marie Hood (freehouse)
Open 12 to 3, 6.30 to 11, Sun 12 to 3, 7 to 10.30; bar food 12 to 2, 6.30 to 9.30 (9 Sun); closed 25 and 26 Dec, 1 Jan
Details Children welcome in bar eating area; no children under 12 after 8pm Car park Wheelchair access (not WC) Garden No-smoking area Background music No dogs Delta, MasterCard, Switch, Visa

KINTBURY Berkshire map 2

▲ Dundas Arms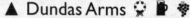

Station Road, Kintbury RG17 9UT TEL: (01488) 658263
WEBSITE: www.dundasarms.co.uk
1m S of A4, between Newbury and Hungerford

Wedged between the Kennet and Avon Canal on one side and the River Kennet on the other, with a line of picnic-style tables strung out along the canal, plus a few over-looking the river, this white, eighteenth-century pub really comes into its own in summer. Inside, the décor is predominantly modern, with some bright splashes of colour, and the public bar has a green ceiling, wood-panelled dado and cream walls hung with prints. Well-kept handpumped ales include Barbus Barbus from Butts in Hungerford, Adnams Bitter, Good Old Boy from West Berkshire at Yattendon, and Morland Original Bitter. The food (there isn't any on Sundays) mixes old faithfuls with exotics: starters could include chicken liver, tequila and cranberry pâté, salad of warm smoked breast of duck, and leek and potato soup. Main dishes may take in grilled ribeye steak, grilled tuna steak with a mango, orange and chilli salsa, pan-fried sea bass fillet with crab risotto, and roast pheasant with bacon gravy and bread sauce. Among puddings, you might find brown sugar meringues with cream, or iced orange soufflé. An enterprising wine list starts at £14 and has much under £20; there are a good number of half-bottles too. Wine lovers might, however, be tempted to try something from the large collection of French and New World classics – dozens of exceptional wines at fair prices spanning a wide range of vintages. SAMPLE DISHES: home-potted shrimps with toast £6.75; roast duck breast with cider and apple sauce £14; chocolate pavé with coffee bean sauce £5.

Licensee D.A. Dalzell-Piper (freehouse)
Open 11 to 2.30, 6 to 11, Sun 12 to 2.30; bar food Mon to Sat 12 to 2, Tue to Sat 7 to 9; restaurant Tue to Sat 7 to 9
Details Children welcome in bar eating area Car park Patio No smoking in restaurant No music
No dogs Delta, MasterCard, Switch, Visa Accommodation: 5 rooms, B&B £70 to £85

KIRK DEIGHTON   West Yorkshire   map 8

Bay Horse ✿   NEW ENTRY
Main Street, Kirk Deighton LS22 4DZ   TEL: (01937) 580058

Kirk Deighton is a tiny, pretty village just minutes from the A1 and Wetherby town centre. The exterior of the Bay Horse does not give any clues that this is a special pub, looks almost prosaic, but, once inside, readers are captivated by its classy appeal. Karl Mainey used to be the chef/patron at the Spice Box in Boston Spa, and one former regular was delighted to see him back on the West Yorkshire dining scene. Although this is now a dining pub, drinkers are not discouraged, with John Smith's Bitter, Tetley Bitter and a guest on handpump in the flagstoned bar area. The hand-written menu, served throughout, is a classic example of good pub food without a trace of flimflam. The kitchen knows how to make proper versions of old warhorses, such as steak and kidney pie, fish pie, and calf's liver with bacon, mash and onions, but it can also move into the realms of tempura prawns with a Thai dipping sauce, and black pudding made in-house with dried fruits and oranges and baked with wild mushrooms, shallots and pancetta. Sunday lunch brings thick slices of tender, perfectly cooked roast beef with well-risen Yorkshire pudding and 'proper gravy'. Whitby crab and rare-beef sandwiches are available at lunchtime, and the home-made bread deserves a special mention. Some 20 house wines are available by the glass. SAMPLE DISHES: queenie scallops with risotto £5.50; belly pork with Chinese spices, ginger and limes £11; apple tart with vanilla ice cream £4.50.

Licensee Karl Mainey
Open Tue to Sun 12 to 3, all week 5 to 11; bar food Tue to Sun 12 to 2, Tue to Sat 6 to 9.30
Details Children welcome Car park Wheelchair access (not WC) No smoking in eating area Occasional background music No dogs Delta, MasterCard, Switch, Visa

KIRKHAM PRIORY   North Yorkshire   map 9

Stone Trough Inn ▮ ✿
Kirkham Priory YO60 7JS   TEL: (01653) 618713
WEBSITE: www.stonetroughinn.co.uk
S of A64, between Scarborough and York, 4m from Castle Howard

This enterprising establishment, on a hillside above the remains of Kirkham Priory, works as a classic local as well as an adventurous dining pub. A regional influence is seen in the patriotic line-up of first-class Yorkshire beers, including Timothy Taylor

Landlord, Black Sheep Best Bitter, Theakston Old Peculier and Malton Golden Chance. A series of snug alcoves huddled around a pair of large fireplaces in the low-beamed bar gives the place a rich Dickensian feel, while the separate candlelit restaurant has a similarly warm and welcoming atmosphere. The bar menu strikes an ambitious pose: starters might include crab, spring onion and Gruyère risotto with lemon oil, or a salad of slow-cooked chicken, bacon and toasted pine nuts with a lemon and tarragon dressing, while main courses run from relatively prosaic Cumberland sausages on caramelised onion mash with real ale gravy to a positively posh risotto of slow-roast tomatoes, asparagus, rocket and smoked cheese. Dessert options might take in winter berry crumble with creamed custard sauce, and lunchtime options include a range of classy sandwiches. Restaurant meals are more impressive still, perhaps featuring pan-sealed black bream on crushed new potatoes with a sorrel and black pepper hollandaise, or roast breast and confit leg of pheasant with a red onion tart and damson sauce. Nine house wines from £9.95 to £10.95 a bottle touch all points of the flavour compass and are also sold by the glass. The main list is strongest in the middle ground, with good producers like Enate from Spain and Saint Clair, the latest New Zealand star. SAMPLE DISHES: warm salad of crispy chilli beef with a honey and sesame seed dressing £5; braised oxtail with creamed mustard mash, roast root vegetable and rich red wine gravy £10.50; lemon and passion-fruit tart with raspberry coulis £4.

Licensees Adam and Sarah Richardson (freehouse)
Open Tue to Sat and bank hol Mon 12 to 2.30, 6 to 11, Sun 11.45 to 10.30; bar food Tue to Sun and bank hol Mon 12 to 2, 6.30 to 8.30, restaurant Tue to Sat and bank hol Mon 6.45 to 9.30, Sun 12 to 2.15; closed 25 Dec
Details Children welcome   Car park   Garden and patio   No-smoking area in bar, no smoking in restaurant   Background music   No dogs   Delta, MasterCard, Switch, Visa

KNIGHTWICK   Worcestershire

map 5

▲ Talbot 🍺

Knightwick WR6 5PH   TEL: (01886) 821235

BREW PUB

WEBSITE: www.the-talbot.co.uk
8m W of Worcester, just before crossing River Teme, turn N off A44 on to B4197 signposted Martley; pub at bottom of hill

For two decades Annie and Wiz Clift have been running this seriously rustic, white-painted inn overlooking the River Teme as part local pub, part restaurant-with-rooms and have turned it into the focal point of a considerable local economy: they make everything from pickles to salami, grow their own produce and buy all their raw materials (except fish) from suppliers in the area. The food served in the open-plan bar is substantial stuff with a few touches of invention: curried parsnip and bean soup or seafood pasta with saffron to start, then belly pork with red cabbage, crab cakes with red pepper, or – in heartier vein – shepherd's pie with chips. The restaurant offers a set-price menu that tips its hat to big-name chefs with, perhaps, braised ducks' hearts and salsa verde, then poached scallops with black pudding, orange, rosemary and chilli butter, followed by tarte Tatin. Added to this, the pub is also home to the Teme Valley Brewery, whose output includes This, That and Wot Ever Next throughout the year; you can also sample seasonal Green Hop Ales, Teme Valley Cider, and perry and apple juice from Yearsett Court Farm. The list of around 40 wines is bolstered by two local names, and there is plenty of decent drinking by the glass. SAMPLE DISHES: goats' cheese fritters with chilli pickle £5.50; venison and orange casserole £12; chocolate truffle cake £5.

Licensee Annie Clift (freehouse)
Open *8am to 11pm, Sun 12 to 10.30; bar food and restaurant 12 to 2, 6.30 to 9.30, Sun 12 to 2, 7 to 9; closed evening 25 Dec*
Details *Children welcome Car park Garden and patio No smoking in restaurant Jukebox in back bar Dogs by arrangement Amex, MasterCard, Switch, Visa Accommodation: 11 rooms, B&B £40 to £75*

KNOSSINGTON Leicestershire map 5

Fox & Hounds 🌼 NEW ENTRY

6 Somerby Road, Knossington LE15 8LY TEL: (01664) 454676

In the centre of a hamlet surrounded by farming and hunting country, this creeper-covered hostelry pulls in regular crowds from the surrounding towns and villages. This is thanks to Brian Baker, who took over in June 2003 and has rapidly transformed the Fox & Hounds into a popular rendezvous. It's still basically a pub with unpretentious furnishings and décor, but food is now the name of the game and standards are high. You enter straight into the low-beamed bar, with fireplaces at either end and small windows carved out of walls 'that are at least two feet thick'; the room also serves as a dining area, with an auxiliary dining space off this with two large tables suitable for groups. Although having just a pint – one of a constantly changing list that may include Marston's Pedigree, Adnams Bitter and Abbot Ale or Timothy Taylor Landlord – is a possibility in the bar, most people come here to eat. Pub classics, such as fish 'n' chips, have their place, but there's also pasta with Mediterranean vegetables and pan-fried fillet of Dover sole with a caper and shallot dressing. The set two-course lunch at £9.95 is excellent value. There's a compact list of 21 wines with two available by the glass. SAMPLE DISHES: field mushrooms with goats' cheese on toast with tarragon mayonnaise £4.75; roast rump of lamb with pea purée and mint dressing £13.50; hot chocolate and almond pudding with crème fraîche £4.75.

Licensee Brian Baker (Enterprise Inns)
Open *11 to 11, Sun 12 to 10.30; bar food Wed to Sun 12 to 2.30 (4 Sun), Tue to Sat 7 to 9.30*
Details *Children welcome Car park Garden No smoking in eating area No music Dogs welcome exc in eating area Delta, Diners, MasterCard, Switch, Visa*

KNOWL HILL Berkshire map 3

▲ Bird in Hand 🍇

Bath Road, Knowl Hill RG10 9UP TEL: (01628) 826622
WEBSITE: www.birdinhand.co.uk
on A4, 3m NE of Twyford

This substantial old coaching inn is now a modern hotel complex, though its origins stretch all the way back to the fourteenth century. The main lounge bar is all wood panelling, leather chairs and round tables; beyond this are the buffet bar and the small no-smoking eating area, decorated with a profusion of locomotive prints and photographs. Here you can enjoy a pint of Brakspear Bitter, Marston's Pedigree or Fuller's London Pride, and eat from a bar menu that lists starters of tomato and mozzarella bruschetta, simple snacks such as croque-monsieur, main dishes ranging from salmon fishcakes with spinach and white wine sauce to grilled T-bone steak, and various cold platters, sandwiches and baguettes. There is also a smart separate restaurant with its own ambitious menu: maybe haddock and saffron risotto to start, followed by chargrilled lamb steak with Mediterranean vegetable stew and a thyme and beetroot jus. An innovative wine list balances fresh modern flavours with some serious bottles in good vintages, and features some delightful sparkling wines and impressive dessert wines. Twelve tasty options come by the glass, and there are nine half-bottles. SAMPLE DISHES: hot crab ramekin £7; pan-fried sea bream marinated in Chinese spices £9.75; thin apple tart with cinnamon ice cream and cream £4.

Licensee Caroline Shone (freehouse)
Open 11 to 3, 6 to 11, Sun 12 to 4, 7 to 10.30 (summer Sat and Sun 11 to 11); bar food 12 to 2.30, 6.30 to 10; restaurant 7 to 9.30
Details Children welcome in bar no-smoking area Car park Wheelchair access (also WC) Garden and patio No-smoking area in bar, no smoking in restaurant No music Dogs welcome Amex, Delta, Diners, MasterCard, Switch, Visa Accommodation: 15 rooms, B&B £60 to £120

KNOWSTONE Devon

map 1

Masons Arms Inn

Knowstone EX36 4RY   TEL: (01398) 341231
1½m N of A361, midway between South Molton and Tiverton

New owners took over this thatched, thirteenth-century longhouse at the end of 2003, but thankfully little has changed. The main bar remains 'a real classic': heavy black beams, old settles and benches, flagstone floors, and a roaring log fire in a vast inglenook, with Exmoor Ale or Cotleigh Tawny Bitter tapped straight from the barrel. A few steps lead down to the lounge-cum-dining area, where a mix of polished wooden tables and an open fire create a cosy atmosphere. Food and wine remain the main preoccupation of the place, and it is on the menu that changes are more noticeable – less choice, and an emphasis on simplicity and good-quality local produce – with bar menus listing platters of cheese, cold meats, or fish alongside boeuf bourguignonne with tagliatelle, or pheasant pie. The rear restaurant (a modern extension looking on to a terrace and fine views over Exmoor) is where the real food action takes place. The evening menu is compact and appealing: say, home-made foie gras with fig chutney, then tuna steak with béarnaise sauce and confit onions, with walnut tart with hot chocolate sauce to finish. French country wines feature on a short list, with two offered by the glass. The village is on the Two Moors Way, so the bar and garden are popular with walkers. SAMPLE DISHES: wild mushroom soup £6; duck breast with honey sauce £14; pear and almond tart £4.

Licensee Edward van Vliet (freehouse)
Open Mon 6 to 11, Tue to Sat 12 to 3, 6 to 11, Sun 12 to 3; bar food and restaurant Tue to Sun 12 to 2, Mon to Sat 7 to 9
Details Children welcome in eating areas Car park Wheelchair access (not WC) Garden No smoking in restaurant Background music Dogs welcome Amex, Delta, Diners, MasterCard, Switch, Visa

🏵 🏵 *indicates a pub serving food on a par with 'seriously good' restaurants, where the cooking achieves consistent high quality.*

Use the maps at the back of the book to plan your trip.

▲ Charles Bathurst Inn

Langthwaite DL11 6EN   TEL: (01748) 884567
WEBSITE: www.cbinn.co.uk
Langthwaite signposted off B6270 at Reeth, 10m W of Richmond

A local lead magnate, Charles Bathurst, gave his name to this huge old inn set in a
sprawling rural village in breathtaking Arkengarthdale. The long, narrow bar has been
given a thoroughly modern look, with soothing pale green walls and expanses of new
pine, including floorboards and furniture. At one end of the room is a small fireplace
and above that a vast gilt-framed mirror, on which is written the day's menu. The
scope of the cooking is wide enough to take in simple lunchtime snacks of hot sausage
baguettes alongside more ambitious things such as duck noodle salad with cashew
nuts and a Thai vinaigrette, or guinea fowl, boned and stuffed with a lime and ham
duxelle. Despite the evidently high level of ambition, the place has an unpretentious
and informal feel – walkers are not only welcome but can be provided with packed
lunches and Thermos flasks as well as advice on routes. On the drinks side of things,
there are fine real ales including Black Sheep's Riggwelter, Theakstons, and John
Smith's Cask Ale, and a list of around two dozen modestly priced wines. All three
house wines are sold by the glass. SAMPLE DISHES: spiced tomato and lentil soup £4;
Chinese fillet of beef strips with noodles and a black bean sauce £10.50; Italian chocolate and almond cake with apricot coulis £3.75.

Licensee Charles Cody (freehouse)
Open *11 (3 Mon to Thur 3 Nov to Jan) to 11, Sun 12 to 10.30; bar food and restaurant 12 to 2, 6.30 to 9*
Details *Children welcome   Car park   Wheelchair access (not WC)   Patio   No smoking in restaurant*
Background music   Dogs welcome at quiet periods   Delta, MasterCard, Switch, Visa   Accommodation: 18 rooms,
B&B £65 to £90 (double room)

Hare

Langton Green TN3 0JA   TEL: (01892) 862419
WEBSITE: www.brunningandprice.co.uk
on A264, 2½m W of Tunbridge Wells

The Hare, on a busy main road, is a solid mock-Tudor building that looks out from
the back over the large village green where cricket is played in summer. High ceilings,
a number of windows, bare floorboards and walls covered with prints, maps and
charts, a collection of chamber pots, and much more besides, all help create a smart
look, and the open nature of the various dining rooms and bar result in an un-clut-
tered space. Available all day, good old-fashioned pub grub, such as garlic mushrooms
and ham, egg and chips, is mixed in with some more interesting ideas like John Dory
with orange, beetroot and herb salad, or roast pork loin with white-bean broth, potato
and apple mash and cidered Savoy cabbage. Portions are substantial, but if you've
room you might finish with citrus tart, or treacle sponge pudding with custard. Real
ales on tap include Greene King Abbot Ale and IPA as well as guests such as Ruddles
Best Bitter, Wells Bombardier Premium Bitter, and Everards Tiger Best. On top of
those, some 18 wines are sold by the glass from a list that gives roughly equal weight
to Europe and the New World. SAMPLE DISHES: prawn and cucumber gâteau with

cucumber salad £5; chicken breast on sage polenta with balsamic-roasted plum tomatoes £10; apple and fruits of the forest crumble with custard £4.25.

Licensees Oliver Slade and Christopher Little (Brunning and Price Ltd)
Open 11 to 11, Sun 12 to 10.30; bar food 12 to 9.30 (9 Sun); closed evenings 25 and 31 Dec
Details *Children welcome in eating areas   Car park   Wheelchair access (not WC)   Patio   Occasional live or
background music   Dogs welcome in bar   Delta, MasterCard, Switch, Visa*

LAPWORTH   Warwickshire   map 5

Boot

Old Warwick Road, Lapworth B94 6JU   TEL: (01564) 782464
WEBSITE: www.thebootatlapworth.co.uk
off A3400 3½m SE of M42, junction 4

The village of Lapworth is set in the Warwickshire countryside not far from
Packwood House (NT) and close to the Stratford upon Avon Canal, but it's also in
the angle of the M40 and M42, between Birmingham, Warwick, Redditch and
Coventry. On the one hand the red-bricked Boot feels rather like a big-city
pub/brasserie, with noise and price levels to match; on the other it looks rustic in a
designer kind of way, with its natural colours, rough plaster walls, wooden floors and
tables. Preserving jars of lemons and garlic heads decorate the window sills and chim-
neypieces, and the kitchen takes its cue from well-chosen raw materials. Deli-style
'first plates' like onion tart with shaved Parmesan and rocket, various salads (perhaps
crispy duck or smoked chicken) and pasta open the show, while main courses could
range from pork cutlet with baked apples, champ and mustard sauce to fillet steak
with smoked roast garlic, spinach and Mascarpone mash. Old Speckled Hen and
Wadworth 6X are on draught, along with John Smith's, and a well-balanced list of 40
wines includes ten by the glass (from £1.95). SAMPLE DISHES: lamb kofta with chilli
jam and raita £6; escalope of salmon with asparagus and hollandaise £10.25; pannacotta with passion fruit £5.

Licensee James Elliot (Enterprise Inns)
Open 11 to 11 (10.30 Sun); bar food and restaurant 12 to 2.30, 7 to 10 (9.30 Sun)
Details *Children welcome   Car park   Wheelchair access (not WC)   Garden and patio   Background music
Dogs welcome exc in dining room   Amex, Delta, MasterCard, Switch, Visa*

LAVENHAM   Suffolk   map 6

▲ Angel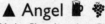

Market Place, Lavenham CO10 9QZ   TEL: (01787) 247388
WEBSITE: www.lavenham.co.uk/angel

Lavenham is an impressively old and atmospheric town, and the Angel dominates a
corner of the exceptionally fine medieval market square, just opposite the magnificent
Guildhall. The oldest part of the pub was first licensed in 1420, and evidence of its
antiquity is discernible in a wealth of ancient beams and timbers. The interior,
candlelit in the evening, with its solid oak furniture and upholstered seating, has a
comfortable, well-run feel, and a U-shaped central bar counter accommodates
drinkers. Among the highlights here are the beers and wines: the former come from
distinguished local brewers Adnams, Greene King and Nethergate (they only buy
from Norfolk and Suffolk breweries); and the wines – 50 or so good-quality bottles

plus eight house basics by the glass or bottle – are gathered up from around the world. Prices are very reasonable and everything barring one or two French classics is under £20. The printed menu changes daily but typically offers starters of marinated sweet cured herrings with honey, mustard and dill, while main course choices have included grilled fillets of turbot with crayfish, lemon and herb butter, or steak and ale pie. Finish perhaps with pear and hazelnut meringue. Guest accommodation is comfortable and attractively furnished. SAMPLE DISHES: curried pumpkin soup £3.75; lamb, apricot and redcurrant casserole £9; lemon roulade £3.75.

Licensees Roy Whitworth and John Barry (freehouse)
Open 11 to 11, Sun 12 to 10.30; bar food and restaurant 12 to 2.15, 6.45 to 9.15; closed 25 and 26 Dec
Details Children welcome   Car park   Wheelchair access (not WC)   Garden and patio   No-smoking area in bar, no smoking in restaurant   No music   Dogs welcome in bar   Amex, Delta, MasterCard, Switch, Visa
Accommodation: 8 rooms, B&B £50 to £75

LAXFIELD   Suffolk   map 6

Kings Head
Gorams Mill Lane, Laxfield IP13 8DW   TEL: (01986) 798395

For years this quintessential thatched Tudor inn has been a favourite with film and TV crews wanting to capture the spirit of rural England past. Known famously as 'the Low House', it is secreted down a narrow lane at the bottom of the village, behind the ancient church. The garden looks truly delightful, and inside there's a tiny parlour dominated by a massive three-sided, high-backed settle facing an open fire. This is a pub with no bar: Adnams beers and guest ales are tapped direct from casks and dispensed through a cubbyhole. Another room is set up principally for diners, with bell pulls to summon a serving 'wench' or the landlord. The printed menus tend to focus on unfussy, homespun dishes such as home-made soup, cottage pie, grilled kipper, and home-cooked ham with coarse-grain mustard sauce, although specials promise a few more modern ideas along the lines of grilled chicken livers wrapped in bacon with raspberry vinaigrette, or poached fillet of cod with a grape and white wine sauce. Salads, baguettes and ploughman's are also on offer, and puddings are listed on a separate board. Seven wines are served by the glass. SAMPLE DISHES: pan-fried garlic mushrooms £3.50; steak and ale pie £7.50; lemon and lime syllabub £3.50.

Licensees W.G. and M. Coleman (Adnams)
Open 12 to 3, 6 to 11, Sun 12 to 3, 7 to 10.30; bar food and restaurant all week 12 to 2, Tue to Sat 7 to 9; closed evening 25 Dec
Details Children welcome in specified areas and restaurant   Car park   Garden and patio   No music
Dogs welcome exc in restaurant   No cards

LEDSHAM   West Yorkshire   map 9

Chequers Inn
Claypit Lane, Ledsham LS25 5LP   TEL: (01977) 683135
WEBSITE: www.thechequersinn.f9.co.uk
1m W of A1 at junction with A63

First the bad news: for 170 years this rambling, creeper-clad village pub has shut on Sundays, by landowner's fiat. All else is good news. There's an extensive outdoor eating area complete with picnic benches and a chequerboard for fair-weather visitors, while inside are four low-beamed rooms with log fires, wooden furniture and settles; old photographs of the area hang on the walls, and a miner's lamp hangs from the ceiling. Upstairs there's a traditional, red-themed restaurant. The snack menu features anything from Yorkshire-style steak sandwiches, or baguette filled with boiled ham and mustard, to smoked salmon with scrambled eggs, although the most promising stuff is on the list of daily specials. The smarter menu shows that the kitchen takes its job seriously: a tian of smoked fish comes with 'ribboned' cucumber pickle, while duck breast studded with rosemary is served with two fruit purées (one white peach, the other apricot). Five of the fifteen or so wines are available by the glass, and the handpumps provide Brown Cow beers from nearby Barlow, along with Theakston and Timothy Taylor Landlord. SAMPLE DISHES: smoked chicken breast with potato and garlic salad £6; tuna loin with braised celery and asparagus £14; chocolate and orange mousse £4.50.

Licensee Chris Wraith (freehouse)
Open *Mon to Sat 11 to 3, 5 to 11; bar food and restaurant 12 to 2.15, 6 to 9*
Details *Car park   Wheelchair access (not WC)   Garden   No music   No dogs   Amex, Delta, MasterCard, Switch, Visa*

LEVINGTON   Suffolk   map 6

Ship

Levington IP10 0LQ   TEL: (01473) 659573

Imagine the lovely setting in a pretty village next to an unusual church and overlooking the River Orwell, add a thatched roof, outside tables, stoves within, and walls covered with ships in all sorts of guises – models, pictured on plates, tiles and mugs – and other nautical paraphernalia, and it is easy to see why the Ship is so popular. Dishes change regularly and are listed on individual boards hung up on a rack, so that they can be replaced as often as necessary. Starters can range from mussels baked with garlic, tomatoes and chorizo to a tian of seafood and avocado. Among main courses, expect a wide choice of meat and fish options, taking in traditional liver, bacon and French black pudding with bubble and squeak cake as well as modern dishes along the lines of seared monkfish with Parmesan risotto and a mussel and white wine sauce. Sunday lunch brings roast forerib of beef or roast Suffolk pork, and desserts are in the apple crumble tradition. Beers from Adnams and Greene King are on draught, and around ten house wines are available by the glass. SAMPLE DISHES: pheasant and wild mushroom terrine £5; Suffolk beef and ale pie £9; Eton mess £4.25.

Licensees Mark and Stella Johnson (Pubmaster)
Open *11.30 to 2.30, 6 to 11, Sun 12 to 3; bar food 12 to 2, 6.30 to 9.30, Sun 12 to 3; closed 25 and 26 Dec, 1 Jan*
Details *Children over 14 welcome in bar only   Car park   Wheelchair access (not WC)   Garden and patio No-smoking areas   No music   No dogs   MasterCard, Switch, Visa*

LEYBURN   North Yorkshire   map 9

▲ Sandpiper Inn

Market Place, Leyburn DL8 5AT   TEL: (01969) 622206

Standing proud on Leyburn's marketplace, this restored seventeenth-century stone inn comprises two well-maintained buildings with a stylish pub sign and a small patio garden to the front. The bar has a homely, cosy feel, especially when the fire is lit, and there's a separate restaurant with attractive olive-green walls, oak floorboards, candles on the tables and wall lights. 'Wonderfully chatty and very friendly staff' add to the cheery mood of the place. Sandwiches and a selection of light dishes such as devilled kidneys with bacon and mushrooms, omelette Arnold Bennett, or grilled gammon and eggs can be had at lunchtime. The dinner menu, served in both the bar and restaurant, focuses on a selection of modern-sounding dishes that would not be out of place in a big-city venue: fillet of beef with five onions and Shiraz sauce, breast of chicken on lentils and smoked bacon, plus seasonal ideas like grilled sea bass on garlic and celeriac purée with forest mushrooms, or pheasant with roasted pumpkin and pancetta. A special starter of apple-smoked black pudding with creamy leek sauce bowled over one reporter, as did a main course consisting of a tranche of lightly cooked Whitby cod with prawns and roasted fennel. Desserts could range from 'terrific' sticky toffee pudding with caramel sauce to a three-chocolate terrine with cappuccino sauce. Black Sheep Best Bitter and Special Ale are regularly on handpump alongside guests from, say, Archers or Daleside, while those who fancy a dram have 100 malts to choose from. Eight wines come by the glass from a balanced and good-value list. Bookings are recommended for a table in the restaurant; otherwise be prepared to arrive early. SAMPLE DISHES: crab and salmon cake with red pepper mayonnaise £5.50; crispy duck leg with plum and orange sauce £10.50; blackcurrant vacherin £4.25.

Licensees the Harrison family (freehouse)

Open *Tue to Sat 11.30 to 3, 6.30 to 11, Sun 12 to 3, 7 to 10.30; bar food 12 to 2.30 (2 Sun), restaurant Tue to Sat 6.30 to 9 (9.30 Fri and Sat), Sun 12 to 2, 6.30 to 9*

Details *Children welcome in bar eating area and restaurant exc after 8pm weekends   Car park   Wheelchair access (not WC)   Patio   No smoking in restaurant   Background music   Dogs welcome in snug area of bar only Delta, MasterCard, Switch, Visa   Accommodation: 2 rooms, B&B £50 to £85*

LICHFIELD   Staffordshire   map 5

Boat   NEW ENTRY

Walsall Road, Summerhill, Lichfield WS14 0BU   TEL: (01543) 361692
on A461, 4m SW of Lichfield near Muckley Corner

Smack bang beside a dual carriageway and just yards from the M6 toll road, neither the location nor the modern, unassuming, whitewashed exterior of the Boat inspire you to stop. Yet it's a 'nice place inside – spacious, airy and extended', reported one surprised traveller, delighted to have stumbled on a 'decent food pub' in this location. The open-to-view kitchen reveals chefs slaving away, there's a pleasant conservatory extension with blue and red café-style furnishings, comfortable leather easy chairs, and a pine-filled dining area. Blackboards offer an eclectic range of dishes: start perhaps with pigeon breast with bubble and squeak, crayfish terrine with lemon dressing, or fillet of beef stir-fry, and then go on to pork fillet with sweet potato mash and crispy Parma ham, calf's liver and bacon, steak, or red snapper fillet with roasted vegetables and lime dressing. There could be good old bread-and-butter pudding or warm chocolate tart to finish. Ever-changing real ales might include Tetley Bitter, Courage Directors or something from nearby Beowulf Brewery. Around half a dozen wines are offered by the glass. SAMPLE DISHES: Cajun chicken salad £6.50; slow-roast shoulder of lamb with redcurrant and mint £9; toffee and banana crumble £4.

Licensee Ann Holden (freehouse)
Open *12 to 2.30, 6 to 12 (summer Fri and Sat 12 to 12.30), Sun 12 to 10.30; bar food 12 to 2.30, 6 to 9.30, Sun 12 to 8.30; closed 25 and 26 Dec*
Details *Children welcome   Car park   Wheelchair access (also WC)   Garden   No-smoking area   Occasional live or background music   Dogs welcome   Delta, MasterCard, Switch, Visa*

LICKFOLD   West Sussex   map 3

Lickfold Inn 🎯 🍺

Lickfold GU28 9EY   TEL: (01798) 861285
off A272 Midhurst to Petworth road, signposted Lodsworth, 4m NE of Midhurst

Oozing character, the Lickfold Inn is built of herringbone-pattern red brick panels in a timber frame and its big, heavy old wooden door makes an impressive entrance. The bar is an ample, beamed space, warm and full of charm, with a huge fireplace and ochre-washed and panelled walls, plus candles and the odd farming implement dotted about. The room alongside is similarly informal in style, with white linen napkins on the tables, while upstairs a more formal room has linen-clad tables and good views from the windows. The menu is the same throughout. Lunchtimes bring on sandwiches, light bites like wild mushroom risotto, or more substantial dishes such as wild boar and apple sausages with mash and mustard sauce. The evening carte might feature goats' cheese on focaccia with red onion marmalade, followed by venison fillet with braised red cabbage and celeriac purée. Real ales are a good selection, with Ballard's Best Bitter and Young's Bitter as regulars, plus guests that often include Hop Back Crop Circle, and six wines come by the glass. Tables in the back garden have good views over open countryside. SAMPLE DISHES: smoked trout mousse with bruschetta £5; pan-seared salmon with sautéed potatoes and saffron and crayfish sauce £13; mango crème brûlée £4.75.

Licensees Tim Ashworth and Luke Stockley (freehouse)
Open *11 to 3, 5.30 (Sat 6) to 11, Sun 12 to 3, 7 to 10.30; bar food 12 to 2.30, 7 to 9.30*
Details *Children welcome in bar eating area   Car park   Wheelchair access (also WC)   Garden   Dogs welcome   Amex, Delta, MasterCard, Switch, Visa*

LIDGATE   Suffolk   map 6

Star Inn 🍇

The Street, Lidgate CB8 9PP   TEL: (01638) 500275
on B1063, 7m SE of Newmarket

You feel very much at ease when you walk into this pink-washed, traditional pub that looks out over open country. The three interconnecting rooms (two bars and a non-smoking dining room) are generally filled with a lively mix of appreciative locals, and there are interesting objects and pictures on the walls. The main room has an inglenook fireplace, a board floor and a miscellany of prints, including one of the Last Supper. On handpump is a range of Greene King beers – IPA, Abbot Ale and Old Speckled Hen – and the bottled beers include Estrella Dorada, while four Spanish brandies lurk among the spirits. Wines pick up the Spanish theme (although by no means exclusively) on a tempting and well-priced list that includes five by the glass. Catalan landlady Maria Teresa Axon is the key to this Anglo-Iberian counterpoint, which appears even more strongly on the menu, where sirloin steak in Stilton sauce is juxtaposed with hake à la vasca. A classic Spanish dish of lambs' kidneys in sherry, paella Valenciana from the Mediterranean coast, and salmon à la gallega from the Atlantic line up alongside wild boar in cranberry sauce, or home-made lasagne, although puddings are more uniformly Anglo-Saxon. Aside from the carte, there are two-course lunches for £10.50 (three courses for £14.50 on Sundays). SAMPLE DISHES: prawns in garlic £4.50; roast chicken aux herbes £11.50; baklava £4.

Licensees Maria Teresa and Anthony Axon (Greene King)
Open 11 to 3, 5 (6 Sat) to 11, Sun 12 to 3, 7 to 11; bar food Mon to Sat 12 to 2, 7 to 10, Sun 12 to 2
Details Children welcome   Car park   Garden   No smoking in dining room   Occasional live or background music   Dogs welcome   Amex, Delta, Diners, MasterCard, Switch, Visa

LIFTON   Devon   map 1

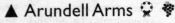

▲ Arundell Arms 🏆 🍇

Lifton PL16 0AA   TEL: (01566) 784666
WEBSITE: www.arundellarms.com
just off A30, 4m E of Launceston

Angling, shooting, riding and other country pursuits bring enthusiasts to this fine old coaching inn in a valley close to the uplands of Dartmoor. It is first and foremost a sporting hotel, with 20 miles of fishing rights on the Tamar and its tributaries; the owners sell tackle and give advice to novices. The Arundell Bar is a comfortable place in which to linger, with sporting prints on pale walls, elegant curtains and an open fire all helping to create a welcoming impression. Food is ordered at the bar and delivered to the tables by smartly uniformed staff. The menu kicks off with starters like organic smoked salmon with cucumber pickle, and smooth chicken liver pâté with walnut and apricot chutney, before main courses like fillets of plaice and Cornish cod in beer batter with chips and green herb mayonnaise, or grilled ribeye of Devon beef with Stilton butter and a celery flower fritter. Sandwiches and salads flesh out the picture, and you can round things off with, say, seasonal cranberry bavarois, or warm treacle tart with crème anglaise and clotted cream. More elaborate fixed-price menus are served in the formal restaurant. No draught beers are served in the hotel, but you can always have a pint of the real stuff with the locals in the Court House Bar, which is housed in a separate building. The Arundell Arms boasts a smart wine list, which opens with nine good-quality house wines available by the glass for £2.75 to £4.50. France is the main focus, with serious bottles from Bordeaux and Burgundy commanding serious prices. Look further afield – to Italy, Spain or the New World – for tasty bottles under £20, or choose from the large selection of half-bottles. SAMPLE DISHES: butternut squash soup with olive oil and Parmesan £4.25; pan-fried medallions of pork tenderloin with wood mushroom risotto, onion rings and peppercorn gravy £13; iced white chocolate parfait with coffee sauce £4.75.

Licensee Anne Voss-Bark (freehouse)
Open 11.30 (12 Sun) to 3, 5.30 to 11; bar food 12 to 2.30, 6 to 10, restaurant 12.30 to 2, 7.30 to 9.30; closed 3 evenings Christmas
Details Children welcome   Car park   Wheelchair access (also WC)   Garden   No smoking in restaurant   Background music   Dogs welcome exc in restaurant   Amex, Delta, Diners, MasterCard, Switch, Visa
Accommodation: 27 rooms, B&B £52 to £136

LINCOLN   Lincolnshire   map 9

Wig & Mitre ♀ ✿

30–32 Steep Hill, Lincoln LN2 1TL   TEL: (01522) 535190
WEBSITE: www.wigandmitre.com

Since 1977 the Hope family have been pleasing the crowds in their fourteenth-century building between the castle and the cathedral. Their flexible attitude to eating out is infectiously refreshing, and informality is one of the keys to their success. There have been some changes of personnel in the kitchen in recent months, but the well-tried formula remains. Drop in for breakfast or a sandwich, try out the set daytime menu (served from noon to 6pm), or simply call in for a drink: Ruddles Best Bitter, Marston's Pedigree and Black Sheep Best Bitter are on draught. The wine list meanwhile works its way downwards from smart French classics to everyday gluggers via some very interesting bottles for those with £20 or so to spend – with plentiful choices by the glass at all levels. Otherwise, take your pick from the main menu and specials board, which are available at all times: you might begin with sautéed scallops on coriander, peanut and garlic risotto before moving on to roast tournedos of belly pork with a fricassee of spinach and Puy lentils and roasted root vegetables, or saddle of venison served rare with fondant potatoes, confit of cabbage and a red wine and chocolate sauce. If the assiette of ice creams and sorbets doesn't tempt as a finale, you could plump for panettone bread-and-butter pudding with vanilla and Cointreau sauce. Alternatively, push the boat out with a portion of caviar and a glass of champagne. SAMPLE DISHES: roast cherry tomato soup £6; braised blade fillet of beef with foie gras, onion mash and gravy £14; lemon mousse with raspberry compote £5.

Licensees Toby and Valérie Hope (freehouse)
Open 8am to midnight, Sun 12 to 11.30; bar food 8am to midnight, Sun 12 to 11.30
Details Children welcome   Wheelchair access (not WC)   No smoking in restaurant   No music   Dogs welcome exc in restaurant   Amex, Delta, Diners, MasterCard, Switch, Visa

LINGFIELD   Surrey   map 3

Hare & Hounds   NEW ENTRY

Common Road, Lingfield RH7 6BZ   TEL: (01342) 832351
from A22 follow signs for Lingfield Racecourse into Common Road

A large statue of a hound stands guard outside the entrance to this cream-painted pub with a small paved garden and a huge car park. Inside, there are stools clustered around the bar, banquettes and sofas under the windows, and two other areas laid up with tables and chairs. The main menu, on a blackboard over the fireplace, is a mixture of pub and restaurant-style dishes ranging from haddock fishcakes, or Cumberland sausage with Cheddar mash and onion gravy, to tagliatelle with Thai curry, coconut crab bisque and mixed seafood, or roast mustard-crumbed pork fillet with sautéed potatoes, pak choi and a well-made creamy mustard sauce. There's also a short carte with a few more ambitious dishes like seared scallops with chorizo, fried gnocchi, tapenade and caper vinaigrette, or chargrilled sirloin steak with smashed new potatoes, wilted cos, crispy Parma ham and green peppercorn sauce. Finish with, say, sticky date pudding with crème fraîche and caramel sauce, or pistachio pannacotta with blueberry compote and pancakes. Real ales are familiar brews like Greene King IPA, Flowers Original and Old Speckled Hen, and the list of around 20 wines is an eminently affordable choice from around the globe. House French is £9.95, and six wines are sold by the glass from £3.35. SAMPLE DISHES: red lentil, tomato and coriander soup £4; guinea fowl with chickpea tagine £8; Amaretto and chocolate tart with blackberries £5.25.

Licensee Fergus Greer (Punch Taverns)
Open 11.30 to 11, Sun 12 to 8; bar food and restaurant all week 12 to 2.30, Mon to Sat 7 to 9.30
Details Children welcome   Car park   Wheelchair access (not WC)   Garden and patio   No-smoking area in bar   Occasional live music   Dogs welcome   Delta, Diners, MasterCard, Switch, Visa

LITTLE HAMPDEN   Buckinghamshire   map 3

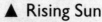

▲ Rising Sun

Little Hampden HP16 9PS   TEL: (01494) 488393
WEBSITE: www.rising-sun.demon.co.uk
from A413 take A4128 into Great Missenden then turn into Rignall Road, signposted Butler's Cross; after 2m take turn marked Little Hampden Only; by small village green take right fork

'Yep: the last bit of the journey is certainly a single track with passing places, up a hill,' one visitor remarked wryly – getting to Little Hampden can be a bit of an adventure. Finding the 250-year-old Rising Sun presents problems too, as the building hardly looks like a pub from the outside, but 'more like a house right next door to an identical house', with the pub sign fairly small and plain 'pinned beneath a window'. Inside, there's a comfortable, laid-back feel in each of the three interconnecting rooms and an uncluttered décor with polished wooden tables and a red-patterned carpet. Blackboards, above an enormous fireplace in one room, offer starters along the lines of warm smoked chicken and bacon salad with walnuts, and main courses of dressed crab with a creamy cheese and mustard sauce, or crisp-skinned roast Deben duck with red wine and black cherry sauce, as well as things like game, steak, or scampi with chips and salad, and enjoyable desserts such as bittersweet flummery with raspberries in syrup and cream, or apple and berry crumble with custard. Sunday roasts are popular, and fish is a strength. Adnams Bitter is generally on handpump alongside a guest such as Brakspear Bitter or Old Speckled Hen, and two wines are available by the glass. The Prime Minister's country residence, Chequers, is little more than a mile up the road. SAMPLE DISHES: sweet cured herring fillets with dill mayonnaise £4.75; roast shoulder of lamb with rosemary and honey sauce £9; chocolate truffle torte with cream £3.25.

Licensee Rory Dawson (freehouse)
Open Tue to Sat 11 to 3, Wed to Sat 6.30 to 10, Sun 12 to 3, 7 to 9; bar food Tue to Sun 12 to 2, Wed to Sat 6 to 9
Details Children welcome   Car park   Wheelchair access (not WC)   Garden   No smoking   Occasional background music   Guide dogs only   Delta, MasterCard, Switch, Visa   Accommodation: 6 rooms, B&B £45 to £70

LITTLE LANGDALE   Cumbria   map 8

▲ Three Shires Inn

Little Langdale LA22 9NZ   TEL: (015394) 37215
WEBSITE: www.threeshiresinn.co.uk
on unnumbered road to Wrynose Pass from A593 just W of Skelwith Bridge

'Clientele are serious walking folk,' noted a reporter of this remote Victorian stone-built pub; 'even children are in anoraks and boots.' With stunning views over

Tilberthwaite Fells, this long-established hostelry makes the perfect pit stop for those taking one of the many circular walks in the Langdale and Skelwith areas. For those driving, however, the twisty road from Skelwith Bridge warns that extreme caution is needed in poor driving conditions. The main bar is 'quite spartan', with stone floors, low beams, and a log fire, and it is here that hearty lunchtime snacks range from baguettes and ploughman's to local Cumberland sausage and chips, or home-made pies such as chicken and mushroom of a size to satisfy a hungry fell walker. A fuller menu is available in the evening: say, a starter fishcake with lime and cucumber crème fraîche, followed by local venison steak with a port and Stilton sauce. Move to the restaurant for a four-course set-price deal that could take in smoked breast of Cartmel Valley wood pigeon with pickled wild mushroom salad, then cream of vegetable soup, roast leg of Lakeland lamb with a confit of garlic and mint, with English Lakes ice creams to finish. Jennings Best Bitter and Cumberland Ale, Hawkshead Best Bitter, and the Coniston Brewery's Old Man Ale are the beers on offer. Five house wines from a New Worldy list of over 40 bottles are served by the small and large glass; prices start at £9.95. SAMPLE DISHES: chicken, walnut and apple terrine £5; beef in ale pie £8.25; chocolate nut pâté £4.

Licensee Ian Stephenson (freehouse)
Open Mon to Thur 11 to 10.30, Fri and Sat 11 to 11, Sun 12 to 10.30; 11 to 3, 7.45 to 10.30 Dec and Jan; 11 to 11 27 Dec and 1 Jan; bar food 12 to 2, 6 to 8.45, restaurant 7 to 8; limited food evenings Dec and Jan; closed 25 Dec
Details Children welcome   Car park   Wheelchair access (not WC)   Garden   No-smoking area in bar, no smoking in restaurant   No music   Dogs welcome in bar only   Delta, MasterCard, Switch, Visa
Accommodation: 10 rooms, B&B £35 to £94

LIVERPOOL   Merseyside   map 7

Baltic Fleet 🍺

33A Wapping, Liverpool L1 8DQ   TEL: (0151) 709 3116

Opposite the Albert Dock – home of the Tate Gallery and Beatles Museum – with views from certain vantage points of that famous skyline made up of the Liver, Cunard and Port of Liverpool buildings, this extremely popular wedge-shaped pub may be a little awkward to get to without a car. The interior is casually low key, understated, and uniquely shaped (being pretty much triangular), with old fixtures merging with a new lick of paint, while a small inglenook adds character and warmth. The blackboard menus at the bar counter roll out some refreshingly modern ideas, such as black pudding with caramelised apples, fish soup, or home-made gravad lax with dill mustard sauce to start, followed by breast of chicken with wild mushroom sauce, or fillet of salmon and tiger prawns en papilotte with basil butter sauce. Portions tend to be generous, so finish with something light like pink grapefruit sorbet. The pub brews its own ales on the premises, including Wapping Bitter, Baltic Extra and Summer Ale, and there are also Cains Traditional Bitter and Dark Mild, plus a guest. Eight wines are served by the glass. SAMPLE DISHES: creamy peppered mushrooms in a puff pastry case £4; venison sausages with mash and onion gravy £8; chocolate ganache cake £3.75.

Licensee Simon Holt (freehouse)
Open 11.30 to 11, Sun 12 to 10.30; bar food all week 12 to 2.30 (4 Sun), Wed to Sat 6 to 8.30 (9.30 Fri and Sat)
Details Children welcome in eating area   No smoking in 1 room   Background music   No dogs   Delta, MasterCard, Switch, Visa

The Monro NEW ENTRY

92–94 Duke Street, Liverpool L1 5AG TEL: (0151) 707 9933
WEBSITE: www.themonro.com

The Monro is smack bang in the middle of Duke Street in an area of the city that has undergone massive regeneration over the last couple of years. A plaque on the wall outside explains the pub's name: the *James Monro*, a ship belonging to the American-owned Black Ball Line, made the first scheduled crossing between Liverpool and New York in 1818. Inside, mood lighting and a tasteful décor of classic wooden features and velvet curtains suggest an eatery rather than a pub, although the fruit machine in the hallway harks back to the days when The Monro was a real spit and sawdust pub. Starters of crab and coriander tian with a sweet pimento coulis, or parcels of lime- and salt-cured salmon mousse with applemint and stem ginger syrup demonstrate how times have changed here. Among generous main courses ('neither of us could finish them – and that is truly saying something'), slow-roast rump of Welsh lamb comes with a casserole of braised vegetables and rosemary gravy, while Bangkok Thai hot curry is chicken cooked with garlic, ginger, onion, coconut milk and coriander. 'Lite bites' and sandwiches are served between noon and 6pm. Burtonwood Top Hat and Adnams Broadside are on handpump, and two wines are served by the glass. SAMPLE DISHES: bacon and cheese tortilla £4.25; Texas coarse-cut chilli £9; mixed fruit crumble with crème anglaise £4.25.

Licensee Stuart Sculthorpe (Burtonwood)
Open *12 to 12.20am, Sun 12 to 10.20; bar food and restaurant 12 to 2.30, 6 to 9.30, Sun 12 to 9.30*
Details *Children welcome   Wheelchair access (also WC)   No smoking in restaurant   Background music No dogs   Amex, Delta, MasterCard, Switch, Visa*

Philharmonic 🍺

36 Hope Street, Liverpool L1 9BX TEL: (0151) 707 2837
follow signs for cathedrals; pub is between them

Commissioned by Robert Cain (of Cains Brewery fame) in the 1840s, 'The Phil' is an architecturally stunning monument to high-Victorian design, with stained glass, lofty ceilings and ornate plasterwork entitled 'the Murmur of the Sea' depicting Apollo and two female companions – not to mention mosaics and a gold-painted frieze. In its early days the restaurant was used by people enjoying a pre-concert meal (the Philharmonic Hall is virtually opposite) while their coachmen waited for them upstairs; two rooms called Brahms and Liszt are a reminder that musical evenings were also held here. A bonus is the men's lavatories, which have become world famous for their original marble washbasins, copper taps and glazed urinals (ladies can ask for a tour!). Despite the opulence of the place and its enduring popularity, a friendly, informal atmosphere prevails. Local Cains Bitter is – appropriately – the house brew, but at least five real ales are on tap, including perhaps Orkney Dark Island, Old Speckled Hen and Fuller's London Pride. The modest wine list features six by the glass (from £2.25). On the food front, expect no-nonsense, filling grub like hot sandwiches on giant toasted white baps, steak pie, fish 'n' chips with mushy peas, and a few vegetarian options such as leek and Gruyère parcels, followed by chocolate puddle pudding. SAMPLE DISHES: Cajun-spiced chicken fillets £3.50; sausage and mash with onion gravy £5.50; treacle sponge with custard £2.50.

Licensee Marie-Louise Wong (Mitchell & Butler)
Open *12 to 11, Sun 12 to 10.30; bar food Mon to Sat 12 to 6, Sun 12 to 3*
Details *No children   Wheelchair access (not WC)   No smoking in 1 room   Background music   No dogs*
Delta, MasterCard, Switch, Visa

LLANFAIR WATERDINE   Shropshire   map 5

▲ Waterdine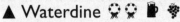

Llanfair Waterdine LD7 1TU   TEL: (01547) 528214
WEBSITE: www.the-waterdine.co.uk
4m NW of Knighton, off B4355 Knighton to Newton road, over Teme bridge at Lloyney

The Welshness of the name can be explained by the fact that only the River Teme separates Llanfair Waterdine from the principality. At the end of a lane through the village is this sixteenth-century drovers' inn, which looks Olde English to a T, with its rough-stone and half-timbered façade. Inside is a neatly spruced-up warren of tiny rooms, with a heavily beamed ceiling, a wood-burning stove in the giant hearth, and floors that are part flagstone, part shiny bare boards. The bar menu is on a blackboard, and the strength of the cooking lies in its astute handling of fine regional ingredients: roast rack of Shropshire lamb is served with a spinach and mushroom fricassee, and chef/landlord Ken Adams is also keen on meat from rare breeds (producing pork terrine with damson dressing, for example). Elsewhere, more familiar pub offerings range from ploughman's and baguettes to pork sausages with home-baked bread and chutney. Finish with exemplary farmhouse cheeses or a dessert such as wild blackberry bread-and-butter pudding with sweet basil sauce. The separate restaurant menu (also available in the bar) moves into more ambitious territory but stays true to its principles: fillet of local longhorn beef on rösti with roast shallots and wild mushrooms, for instance. Top-notch beers are from Wood of Wistanstow (including seasonal brews). An impressive spread of wines keeps pace with all the cooking styles on offer, with notable French and Californian bottles leading the field. House is £10.50 and 17 half-bottles add to the options. No bar food is served on Sunday lunchtime if the restaurant is busy. SAMPLE DISHES: cream of courgette and leek soup £4.25; beef and red wine pie £9.50; crisp lemon curd tart £5.25.

Licensee Ken Adams (freehouse)
Open *Tue to Sat 12 to 3, 7 to 11, Sun 12 to 3; bar food Tue to Sun 12.15 to 2, restaurant Tue to Sun 12.15 to 1.30, Tue to Sat 7 to 9; closed 1 week spring, 1 week autumn*
Details *Children welcome lunchtimes only   Car park   Wheelchair access (not WC)   Garden and patio No-smoking area in bar, no smoking in restaurant   No music   No dogs   MasterCard, Switch, Visa Accommodation: 3 rooms, B&B £55 to £120*

LODERS   Dorset   map 2

▲ Loders Arms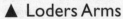

Loders DT6 3SA   TEL: (01308) 422431

In a hilly part of Dorset, and in a village revelling in splendid rural isolation, stands this tiny village pub. It has a small bar and eating area, and its décor is plain, with paintings for sale everywhere and high shelves of decorative plates. The menu, listed on blackboards, ranges from familiar pub staples along the lines of steak pie, spaghetti bolognese, and liver and bacon casserole to more upmarket options: perhaps a warm salad of pigeon breast, or black pudding with apricot and ginger chutney, followed by venison steak pan-fried with gin and juniper berries, or whole trout stuffed with dill and lemon. The Loders is a Palmers pub, serving Bridport Bitter, IPA and 200 – the brewery itself is in Bridport and holds the distinction of being Britain's only thatched brewery. Ten house wines, nine at £9.25 a bottle, are sold by the glass at £2.40 and £3.30. SAMPLE DISHES: crab and coriander parcel £4.50; rack of lamb with garlic and red wine sauce £12; whisky, orange and ginger cheesecake £4.

Licensees Jane and Clive Legg (J.C. and R.H. Palmer)
Open 11 to 3, 6 to 11, Sun 12 to 10.30; bar food and restaurant 12 to 2, 7 to 9
Details Children welcome in eating areas   Car park   Garden   No smoking in restaurant   Background music
Dogs welcome   Amex, Delta, Diners, MasterCard, Switch, Visa   Accommodation: 2 rooms, B&B £30 to £50

LONGSTOCK   Hampshire   map 2

Peat Spade ♡ 🍺
Longstock SO20 6DR   TEL: (01264) 810612
off A3057, 1m N of Stockbridge

Slap-bang in the centre of the village, the Peat Spade Inn is an easy-to-spot gabled red brick building with striking white leaded windows – parking may be more difficult. A motley collection of prints, colourful flower paintings, seaside postcards and a huge assortment of tightly packed toby jugs give the décor an individualistic feel, and the atmosphere remains calm and civilised even when the place is packed. Although a dining pub, the Peat Spade stocks Hop Back GFB and locally brewed Ringwood Fortyniner as well as guests from Hampshire Brewery and Thatcher's cider. Vegetables are organic, as meat is both organic and free-range; the pub's declared aim is 'to support the use of seasonal local food and sustainable farming'. This policy, combined with fine cooking skills, translates into such dishes as spiced organic vegetable soup, followed by free-range sage and onion bangers and mash. Other options on the short, interesting menu range from proscuitto stuffed with saffron organic egg, to main courses of venison and port casserole, or organic lamb rogan gosht and basmati rice. An organic wine from Argentina kicks off the short but carefully selected and fairly priced wine list, with ten sold by the glass. SAMPLE DISHES: herring fillets in dill marinade £5.75; baked cod with Parmesan crust £12; fresh lemon tart £4.50.

Licensees Sarah Hinman and Bernard Startup (freehouse)
Open Tue to Sun 11.30 to 3.30, Tue to Sat 6.30 to 11; bar food Tue to Sun 12 to 2, Tue to Sat 7 to 9; closed 25 Dec
Details Children welcome   Car park   Wheelchair access (also WC)   Garden and patio   No-smoking area in bar   Occasional background music   Dogs welcome   No cards

LOSTWITHIEL   Cornwall   map 1

▲ Royal Oak 🍺
Duke Street, Lostwithiel PL22 0AG   TEL: (01208) 872552

Lostwithiel, ancient capital of Cornwall, is a town full of history, embodied by the ruins of thirteenth-century Restormel Castle standing high on its western slopes. The Royal Oak, a neatly whitewashed inn with blue paintwork, dates from the same period and a tunnel from its cellar reputedly leads to the castle dungeons. Its main flagstoned bar is full of period charm, while the second bar has a low ceiling, old prints on the walls and circular tables and chairs; off this is a large dining area. The regular menu features steaks, salads, seafood dishes and simple lunchtime snacks, while blackboard specials might include barbary duck in orange and ginger sauce, whole plaice with French fries, and Mrs Hine's curry. Try to save room for something from the wide choice of tempting puds – chocolate fudge trifle, perhaps, or raspberry melba. An impressive line-up of real ales includes Fuller's London Pride, Marston's Pedigree, Bass and Sharp's Own, and 55 varied and reasonably priced wines are listed, of which nine are available by the glass. SAMPLE DISHES: prawn cocktail £4.25; lamb shank with mint sauce £11; passion-fruit pavlova £3.

Licensees Malcolm and Eileen Hine (freehouse)
Open *11 to 11, Sun 12 to 10.30; bar food 12 to 2, 6.30 to 9.15*
Details *Children welcome in family room   Car park   Garden and patio   Jukebox   Dogs welcome in public bar   Amex, Delta, Diners, MasterCard, Switch, Visa   Accommodation: 7 rooms, B&B £40 to £70*

LOWER ASHTON   Devon   map 1

Manor Inn
Lower Ashton EX6 7QL   TEL: (01647) 252304
off B3193 running N from Kingsteignton, 7m SW of M5 junction 31

At the heart of the picturesque Teign Valley in a village of whitewashed longhouses, this comfy, old-fashioned pub is a big hit with real ale enthusiasts. On offer is a superb choice of regional beers – RCH Pitchfork, Princetown Jail Ale and Teignworthy Reel Ale, plus guest ales, all served in tip-top condition. Local ciders, quality lagers and a decent, straightforward selection of wines by the glass complete the range of drinks, and simple, honest home-cooked food served in hearty portions is another draw. There's a regular menu of sandwiches, jacket potatoes, ploughman's and so on, while dishes on the daily specials board typically range from hot and spicy beef and mixed bean chilli to roast duck breast with morello cherry sauce, and fish dishes such as salmon and prawn au gratin. The attractive enclosed garden has views of surrounding countryside, and the area offers great walking, with local attractions including Canonteign Falls. SAMPLE DISHES: lamb and mint sausages with mint sauce £6.75; pork steak with cider, onion and apple sauce £7.95; treacle tart £3.50.

Licensees Geoff and Clare Mann (freehouse)
Open *Tue to Sun 12 to 2 (2.30 Sat and Sun), 6.30 to 11, 7 to 10 Sun; bar food Tue to Sun 12 to 1.30, 7 to 9.30 (9 Sun); closed Mon (exc bank hols)*
Details *No children   Car park   Garden   No music   Dogs welcome on a lead   Delta, MasterCard, Switch, Visa*

LOWER ODDINGTON   Gloucestershire   map 5

▲ Fox Inn ✿
Lower Oddington GL56 0UR   TEL: (01451) 870555

Not far from the market town of Stow-on-the-Wold, the villages of Upper and Lower Oddington are really one long, straggly village, although Lower Oddington distinguishes itself with a small and ancient church, at the end of a rural no-through road, and its charming, creeper-covered local, the Fox. There's always a buzz in the bar, where the pub's name is (dis)embodied in a series of snarling foxes' heads mounted over the blackened stone hearth. Beyond the simple main bar is a smarter dining room, but you can eat from the same menu anywhere. The long menu is mostly conservative in nature, though the cooking is consistently impressive and raw materials are of a high quality. Start perhaps with wild mushroom risotto, then go on to whole lemon sole baked with capers and lemon butter, or pork sausages with parsnip and potato purée and Dijon mustard cream sauce. To finish, there may be apricot and almond tart, or raspberry and white chocolate tart. Three regular real ales include Hook Norton Best Bitter and Greene King Abbot Ale, and there's a regularly changing guest. The wine list runs to nearly 50 wide-ranging bins, of which half a dozen are available by the glass. SAMPLE DISHES: Baxter's potted shrimps £6.50; slow-cooked lamb shank with whole garlic and rosemary £10.25; chocolate nemesis with clotted cream £4.50.

Licensees Ian Mackenzie and Graham Williams (freehouse)
Open 11 to 11, Sun 12 to 10.30; bar food 12 to 2.30, 6.30 to 10 (9.30 Sun); closed 25 Dec
Details Children welcome　Car park　Wheelchair access (not WC)　Garden and patio　No music　No dogs
MasterCard, Switch, Visa　Accommodation: 3 rooms, B&B £58 to £85 (double room)

LOWICK　Northamptonshire　　　　　　　　　map 6

Snooty Fox 😕　NEW ENTRY
16 Main Street, Lowick NN14 3BH　TEL: (01832) 733434

It's hard to miss the Snooty Fox, as the sixteenth-century longhouse is the only pub in this one-road village. It's now in the hands of Clive Dixon, who moved here from the Pheasant at Keyston (see entry) in January 2004, and refurbishment has brought out the best in this handsome building, with stone floors, exposed-stone walls, panelling, and elegantly beamed ceilings prominent among many period features. The civilised bar is a generous room with an impressive panelled bar and a couple of large fire-places; a public bar complete with winking gaming machines is partially divided at the far end, and there is a more formal restaurant on the other side of a wide, stone-flagged hallway. Blackboard bar snacks generally include a handful of starters from the restaurant carte (also available in the bar): say, deep-fried Brie de Meaux with roast onion jam, or coarse-cut country pâté with home-made chutney, as well as cottage pie, ploughman's, bangers and mash, chip butties, or steak sandwich, with Cornish pasty, chips and salad a typical special. After starters like Serrano ham with Spanish wood-roast peppers, the carte is divided into fish from Cornwall (grilled lemon sole, for instance), meats from the open-to-view rôtisserie in the restaurant (rack of Cornish lamb, say), and various weights of steaks, cut to order, from the grill. Strawberry and rhubarb trifle, or iced honey, nut and candied fruit parfait are a couple of enterprising desserts. Real ales are a broad slate, taking in brews from Greene King, Fuller's, Morland, Jennings, Oakham and Nethergate. From a wide-ranging list of 30-plus bottles, half a dozen wines are available by the glass. SAMPLE DISHES: celery and watercress soup £4; corn-fed rôtisserie chicken with dauphinois potatoes £9.50; soft hazelnut meringue with a compote of cherries and Kirsch £5.

Licensees Robert Clive Dixon and David Hennigan (freehouse)
Open 12 to 3, 6.30 to 11; bar food 12 to 2, 6.30 to 9.30, restaurant Wed to Sun 12 to 2, Tue to Sat 6.30 to 9.30; closed evenings 25 and 26 Dec and 1 Jan
Details Children welcome　Car park　Wheelchair access (not WC)　Garden　No smoking in restaurant
Live or background music　Dogs welcome in bar only　Delta, Diners, MasterCard, Switch, Visa

LOW NEWTON-BY-THE-SEA   **Northumberland**   map 10

Ship Inn
The Square, Low Newton-by-the-Sea NE66 3EL   TEL: (01665) 576262
off B1340, 2m N of Embleton

The Ship is an attractive village pub set on one of the most unspoilt coastlines in England, and the view from the National Trust-owned Newton Point over the bay to Dunstanburgh Castle is magnificent. Plainly furnished inside, with board floors and bare wooden furniture, the small bar offers a good range of handpumped ales, including Harveys Sussex Best Bitter and Pale Ale and seasonal beers. The simple, crowd-pleasing lunchtime menu offers snacks along the lines of crab sandwiches, free-range ham ploughman's, and ciabatta with goats' cheese, while evenings see more elaborate things such as venison steaks, Northumberland sausages in red wine sauce, and fish dishes like crab with chilli and lime pasta, sea bass or monkfish. Four wines are available by the glass from a list of around 14 bottles. Nearby is Newton Ponds Nature Reserve, where rare birds can sometimes be seen. In summer both beach and pub can be packed, while winter finds quieter times with walkers, locals and the hardy. SAMPLE DISHES: Craster kippers £4; roasted vegetables with couscous £6.50; sticky toffee pudding £3.75.

Licensee Christine Forsyth (freehouse)
Open *11 to 11, Sun 12 to 10.30 in high season; otherwise open every lunchtime but evenings may vary: customers are advised to phone ahead; bar food 12 to 2.30, 6 to 8 (times may vary)*
Details *Children welcome   Wheelchair access (not WC)   No smoking evenings while others eat   Occasional live music   Dogs welcome   No cards*

LUND   **East Riding of Yorkshire**   map 9

Wellington Inn 🍴 🌸
19 The Green, Lund YO25 9TE   TEL: (01377) 217294
on B1248 between Beverley and Malton

Lund is one of the lesser-known villages of the Yorkshire Wolds, and this high-ranking local pub is hard by the green facing the war memorial. Inside, it still looks and feels like a genuine hostelry, with traditional touches such as flagstone floors, open log fires in winter, and real beams. However, the blackboard bar menus deal in the sorts of upmarket dishes you might be surprised to find in a country inn, with devilled kidney and mushroom hotpot in a filo basket or citrus salad with fried halloumi and raspberry vinaigrette among starters, and main courses such as fillet of salmon on spicy noodles with stir-fried vegetables or braised lamb shank on sun-dried tomato and basil mash with a Mediterranean-style tomato sauce and a side dish of broccoli. To finish, the kitchen turns its hand to iced prune and Armagnac parfait as well as vanilla rice pudding with mulled berry compote. Some of these dishes show up on the separate dinner menu in the restaurant, although there are also more ambitious things like warm Roquefort cheesecake with a poached pear and honey and balsamic syrup, and fillet of halibut with smoked mussel and smoked salmon kedgeree and lightly curried mayonnaise. Timothy Taylor Landlord and Dark Mild, Black Sheep Best Bitter and John Smith's Bitter are on handpump, but the wine list far outstrips this selection. Six come by the glass, and drinkers on a budget will find enough to please the palate at under £15, but prices cruise up gently towards first-class bottles at around £40. South Africa is good at all price levels, and if you want to splash out perhaps go for the Vergelegen (£39.95). European wines include Bordeaux cleverly chosen from less-well-known estates and outstanding red Burgundy from Robert Arnoux. A dozen or so also come in half-bottles. SAMPLE DISHES: trio of pâtés with toasted brioche £5; king prawn and asparagus risotto with shaved Parmesan £12; rum and raisin crème caramel £4.25.

Licensees Russell and Sarah Jeffery (freehouse)
Open *Tue to Sun 12 to 3, all week 6.30 to 11 (7 to 10.30 Sun); bar food Tue to Sun 12 to 2, Tue to Sat 6.30 to 9, restaurant Tue to Sat 7 to 9*
Details *Children welcome in eating areas   Car park   Wheelchair access (also WC)   Patio   No-smoking area in bar   Background music   No dogs   Delta, MasterCard, Switch, Visa*

LUSTLEIGH   Devon   map 1

The Cleave

Lustleigh TQ13 9TJ   TEL: (01647) 277223
WEBSITE: www.thecleave.co.uk

This 'charming little gem' enjoys an idyllic setting in a quintessentially old English village of thatched cottages on the edge of Dartmoor. Thatched and painted white, the pub dates from the fifteenth century and has a sheltered south-facing cottage garden where meals may be served on fine days. A flagstoned entrance hall leads to the small, bright and comfortable lounge bar with inglenook and log-burning stove, and to the larger Victorian bar at the rear, panelled in dark wood with decorative plates lining the walls. Regular printed menus are supplemented by blackboard specials that range from simple options, such as steaks and pan-fried lemon sole, to ambitious sounding creations like pan-fried Pernod-marinated tuna steak with tomato and basil salsa. Cooking is careful and portions generous. Wadworth 6X, Bass and Otter Ale are the regular ales, and there is Addlestone's cider. All 14 wines are available by the bottle or glass. SAMPLE DISHES: deep-fried brie with sweet-and-sour sauce £5; poached salmon steak with lemon and tarragon sauce £11; rhubarb and raspberry crumble with clotted cream £4.

Licensee A. Perring (Heavitree)
Open *11 to 11, winter 11 to 3, 6.30 to 11; bar food 12 to 2, 7 to 9; closed Mon winter*
Details *Children welcome in family room   Car park   Wheelchair access (not WC)   Garden   No-smoking area in bar, no smoking in eating area   No music   Dogs welcome   Amex, Delta, MasterCard, Switch, Visa*

LUTON   Devon   map 1

Elizabethan Inn   NEW ENTRY

Fore Street, Luton TQ13 0BL   TEL: (01626) 775425

In a hamlet that's tucked down country roads, this 500-year-old cottage has at its heart a small bar with dining and drinking areas radiating off – the look and feel is 'classic English pub' (beams, log fires, pews, old dark wooden tables). Reporters see it as a 'smart dining pub' that is 'solid and popular and consistent'. Restaurant and bar food are served in the same dining areas, with jacket potatoes, sandwiches, and a warm salad of seared salmon with mixed leaves and fried potatoes, or breaded plaice and chips appearing on the lunchtime board. In the evening, there could be roast tomato and pepper soup, duck salad with balsamic dressing, or mixed seafood risotto to start, then Dover sole with capers, lemon and herb dressing, or Cumberland sausage with bacon and lamb's liver casserole in a red wine and rosemary sauce with baby onions, with puddings of 'cool and creamy' pannacotta, or a mixed berry and meringue iced parfait. Local brews on handpump include Teignworthy Reel Ale and Blackdown Best Bitter, with Fuller's London Pride, Timothy Taylor Landlord, and Wells Bombardier Premium Bitter from further afield. Six wines are served by the glass. SAMPLE DISHES: mushrooms sautéed in garlic and herb butter £4.75; seared Barbary duck breast with Cassis and blackcurrant sauce £13.25; chocolate, orange and mascarpone cheesecake £4.

Licensees Nick Powell and Anne Gibbs (freehouse)
Open 11 to 3, 6 to 11, Sun 12 to 3, 7 to 10.30; bar food 12 to 2, 6.30 to 9.30; closed 26 Dec, 1 and 2 Jan
Details Children welcome in bar eating area   Car park   Garden and patio   No smoking in eating area
Background music   Dogs welcome in bar area only   Delta, MasterCard, Switch, Visa

LUXBOROUGH   Somerset   map 1

▲ Royal Oak Inn of Luxborough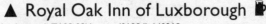

Luxborough TA23 0SH   TEL: (01984) 640319
WEBSITE: www.theroyaloakinnluxborough.co.uk
off A396, 4m S of Dunster; drive through Luxborough eastwards to Kingsbridge

You need to go through the long, straggling village of Luxborough to find the Royal Oak a mile further east, tucked into a narrow cleft of a valley at the bottom of a very steep hill. The ancient, rough, reddish-brown stone building contains a rambling series of rooms with flagged or cobbled floors, low beams and, in the main bar, a large open fireplace. One of the dining rooms has custard-coloured walls, another is in strong emerald green, and a third is done out in tomato red. The seasonally changing printed menus – supplemented by a blackboard, which is mainly fish based – are tempting, and some of the dishes sound an exotic note. You might begin with Loch Fyne mussels with tomato, orange and cardamom, and go on to knuckle of ham braised in red cider and served with mash and rich mustard sauce, or a roast fillet of cod glazed with crab Thermidor with mizuna leaves and chives. As an alternative to pudding try some of the good Somerset cheeses. An interesting and commendable selection of draught beers includes Exmoor Gold, Cotleigh Tawny Bitter, and IPA and 200 from Palmer, and there's Rich's farmhouse cider too. Three or four wines come by the glass from a list of around 20 bottles, with prices starting at £10.50. SAMPLE DISHES: smoked haddock and leek terrine with mustard mayonnaise £6.75; loin of venison and game risotto baked in puff pastry £14.25; Bakewell tart £4.25.

Licensee James Waller (freehouse)
Open 12 to 2.30, 6 to 11, Sun 12 to 2.30, 7 to 10.30; bar food and restaurant 12 to 2, 7 to 9
Details Children welcome   Car park   Garden and patio   No smoking in restaurant   Occasional live music
Dogs welcome   Amex, Delta, MasterCard, Switch, Visa   Accommodation: 12 rooms, B&B £55 to £85

LYDDINGTON   Rutland   map 5

▲ Old White Hart

51 Main Street, Lyddington LE15 9LR   TEL: (01572) 821703

Lyddington, a village of local red sandstone cottages overlooking the shallow Welland Valley, makes a great base for exploration, with Rockingham Castle and Rutland Water nearby, and Burghley House at Stamford less then ten miles away. The combination of sandstone and Georgian architecture give this pub a look of understated, foursquare elegance that the attractive garden at the back enhances. Inside, it feels like a friendly, comfortable local, with the dark seventeenth-century beams and studs lightened by the open fire and the warmer red tones of the comfortable seating and carpets and exposed stone walls. In the half-panelled main bar Greene King IPA and Abbot Ale are on draught, along with Timothy Taylor Landlord, and wines on offer include six by the glass. Food is set out on printed menus supplemented by black-board specials of fresh fish and vegetarian dishes. Among starters might be pan-fried duck fillets, oyster mushrooms, rocket and balsamic dressing, followed by slow-roasted shoulder of lamb in garlic and rosemary. Then, if you can't manage rich chocolate and raspberry torte with a white chocolate sorbet, how about coconut and pineapple crème brûlée? SAMPLE DISHES: warm salad of wood pigeon, black pudding and chard £6; pork fillet, wild mushroom and Stilton Wellington £11; caramelised rice pudding mousse with compote of autumn fruits £5.

Licensee Stuart East (freehouse)

Open 12 to 3, 6.30 to 11, Sun 12 to 3, 7 to 10.30; bar food and restaurant Mon to Sat 12 to 2, 6.30 to 9, Sun 12 to 2.30

Details Children welcome   Car park   Wheelchair access (not WC)   Garden and patio   No smoking in dining room   No music   No dogs   Delta, MasterCard, Switch, Visa   Accommodation: 5 rooms, B&B £50 to £80

LYDFORD   Devon   map I

Dartmoor Inn 🏵 🏵 🍇
Lydford EX20 4AY   TEL: (01822) 820221
on A386 Tavistock to Okehampton road

Philip Burgess is a crusading champion of West Country produce and has strong links with suppliers and producers throughout Devon and Cornwall. Not surprisingly, his country inn on a main road outside the village now operates more like a restaurant than a local watering hole. The décor might suggest something out of *Country Living*, with garlands of dried flowers among the ceiling beams, needlework samplers and naive prints on the walls, ceramic and wooden animals on the windowsills, and a colour scheme of greens, red and terracotta. A tiny bar dispenses Bass, St Austell Dartmoor Best Bitter and Fuller's London Pride, together with Luscombe organic cider, but most of the action takes place in a series of small rooms with smart, white-clothed tables. The lunchtime bar menu is a neat assortment of little dishes (a four-ounce chargrilled Ruby Red fillet steak with onions, chips and mustard butter, a ploughman's of Keen's cheddar with chutney, and smooth chicken liver pâté with toast) alongside trencherman stuff, including fillet of guinea fowl with pickled walnut relish, or farmhouse sausages with mustard mash and onions. Fixed-price lunches and suppers are great value, and the full evening carte (available in both bar and restaurant) promises such things as chargrilled scallops in their shells with ginger and green onion relish, thyme-roast rump of lamb with quince and rosemary jelly, steaks, and desserts such as prune fritters with cocoa sugar and a prune and Armagnac ice cream. The wine list favours quality over quantity, with star performers such as William Fèvre and Vincent Girardin prominent in the 25-strong main selection. For more down-to-earth drinking, nine flavoursome house wines come in under £15, and six of these are available by the glass. The pub is in a lovely spot, with a minuscule secluded patio at the back, and at the time of going to press there were plans to add three letting rooms. SAMPLE DISHES: omelette with creamed smoked haddock £7.75; slow-cooked lamb shank with mint and saffron sauce £13.75; vanilla crème brûlée with apple biscuits £4.75.

Licensee Philip Burgess (freehouse)
Open Tue to Sat 11.30 to 3, 6.30 to 11, Sun 12 to 3; bar food and restaurant Tue to Sun 12 to 2, 6.30 to 10, Sun 12 to 2; closed 2 days Christmas, bank hols
Details Children welcome exc under-5s Fri and Sat evenings Car park Wheelchair access (not WC) Patio No smoking Occasional live music Dogs welcome in certain areas Delta, MasterCard, Switch, Visa

LYDGATE Greater Manchester map 8

▲ White Hart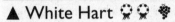
51 Stockport Road, Lydgate OL4 4JJ TEL: (01457) 872566
on A6050, 3m E of Oldham

Looking down on the city lights and urban sprawl of Oldham, the White Hart is a traditional Lancashire coaching inn tastefully re-invented for the twenty-first century, complete with a downstairs brasserie and a restaurant extension that also houses accommodation. There is still a bar area where those who wish to come for just a drink can enjoy a pint of Timothy Taylor Landlord or J.W. Lees Bitter from the Greengate Brewery in Manchester, although food and wine are the main preoccupations of the place. The brasserie menu features the products of the Saddleworth Sausage Company, which is based in the premises: choose a variety such as pork and leek or chicken and black pudding and match it with one of the flavoured mashes on offer: say, caramelised onion and sage. Otherwise, the style is emphatically modern and cosmopolitan, ranging from starters of lobster and salmon ravioli with smoked salmon and watercress to main courses along the lines of roast cutlets of venison with fondant potato, wilted greens and a Madeira and shallot jus, or roast globe artichoke with butternut squash and herb risotto. To finish, the array of British farmhouse cheeses will keep enthusiasts happy, while others might prefer white chocolate bavarois with raspberries, or sticky toffee pudding with butterscotch sauce. The wine cellar has been compiled with passion. The list splits into France and Rest of the World, with the former fielding some serious heavyweights. The opposition is lighter on its feet (barring smart Italians and Spain's most sought-after wine, Vega Sicilia) and there are plenty of choices by the glass and half-bottle. SAMPLE DISHES: omelette Arnold Bennett with crème fraîche £5.75; grilled fillet of plaice with shrimp and caper brown butter £14.75; strawberry crème brûlée £4.75.

Licensee Charles Brierley (freehouse)
Open 12 to 11 (10.30 Sun); bar food Mon to Sat 12 to 2.30, 6 to 9.30, Sun and bank hols 1 to 7.30, restaurant Tue to Sat 7 to 10, Sun 1 to 3; closed evenings 25 and 26 Dec
Details Children welcome Car park Wheelchair access (also WC) Garden No-smoking area in bar, no smoking in restaurant Occasional background music Guide dogs only Amex, MasterCard, Switch, Visa
Accommodation: 12 rooms, B&B £68.50 to £98.50

MADINGLEY Cambridgeshire map 6

Three Horseshoes
High Street, Madingley CB3 8AB TEL: (01954) 210221
WEBSITE: www.huntsbridge.co.uk
off A1303, 2m W of Cambridge, close to M11 junction 13

The setting is a demure-looking thatched pub a couple of miles from Cambridge with a pretty garden and tables to the rear. Go inside and you will find high stools at a light-oak bar counter, with furniture of the same wood, walls of olive green, stripped floor-boards and a log-effect gas fire; there's also a small dining area and a more formal conservatory at the back. It may feel like a village hostelry with a pleasantly unstuffy and informal atmosphere, but the daily-changing menu tells a different story. The cooking is highly individual and lively, working with good-quality ingredients and using plenty of bold, modern flavours in inventive – not to mention colourful – combinations with forthright Italian overtones. Although there's no requirement to keep to a three-course format, you could start with goose salami with cicoria, dandelion, rocket, figs, aged balsamic and extra-virgin olive oil, or a salad of mozzarella, olives, anchovies, capers, marjoram, mustard leaves and basil. Main courses make an equally strong impact, with the same eclectic influences brought into play: mallard breasts are marinated in Chianti, chargrilled and served with roast green and yellow zucchini, a potato, onion and ricotta cake, and dressed with hot olive oil and caper and anchovy oil, while a tranche of turbot might be roasted and presented with green olives, basil, cime di rape (turnip tops) and chickpeas cooked with vegetables, tomatoes and gremolata. Desserts are equally busy: for instance, warm baked pears with cinnamon, Marsala, vanilla, Muscovado and zabaglione ice cream. To cater for beer drinkers, the bar stocks Adnams Southwold plus guest ales like Timothy Taylor Landlord, but wine is where the excitement is. Over a dozen house wines come by the glass (£3 to £7.50), and there's an unusually good selection of sherries and sweet wines by the glass too. The 100 or so bottles on the full list are grouped by price and style, and chosen with flair wherever you look. The Three Horseshoes is part of the Huntsbridge Group (see the Pheasant, Keyston, the Old Bridge Hotel, Huntingdon, and the Falcon, Fotheringhay). SAMPLE DISHES: broad bean and beetroot soup with mint, parsley and Parmesan £6; roast partridge stuffed with mascarpone and sage £16.50; espresso and walnut cake with Jersey clotted cream £6.50.

Licensee Richard Stokes (freehouse)
Open 11.30 to 3, 6 to 11, Sun 12 to 2.30; bar food and restaurant 12 to 2, 6.30 to 9.30
Details Children welcome Car park Wheelchair access (not WC) Garden No smoking in restaurant No music No dogs Amex, Diners, MasterCard, Switch, Visa

MALPAS   Cornwall

map 1

Heron Inn

Malpas TR1 1SL   TEL: (01872) 272773
2m S of Truro on the River Fal

WATERSIDE

Great views are guaranteed at this updated pub overlooking the confluence of the Truro and Tresilian rivers; early birds in summer will not only get a space in the small car park but also claim one of the few outside tables. A nautical theme runs throughout the one long bar, which is a 'clean, efficient space'. There are dining areas at each end, an open fire in one of them, and walls have been colour-washed a shade of turquoise-blue; tables and chairs are all light wood, and old beams have been lightened in colour. The menu is more or less a cross-section of traditional pub fare: hot and spicy king prawns with sweet chilli dip, followed by beef lasagne, or cod, chips, peas and tartare sauce for lunch perhaps (unless you go for tortilla wraps or crostini), and for dinner maybe buttered calamari rings with dill mayonnaise, then chicken jalfrezi, or braised shank of lamb or boeuf bourguignon. Lighter lunch offerings include sandwiches of fresh crab, or local smoked salmon. St Austell's beers are on draught, and three house wines are served by the glass from an annotated list of 25 bottles. SAMPLE DISHES: Cornish smoked trout fillet £7; breast of duck with tangy orange sauce £9.75; caramel and apple pancake stack £4.

Licensee Calvin Kneebone (St Austell Brewery)
Open 11 to 3, 6 to 11 (10.30 winter), Sun 12 to 3, 7 to 10.30; bar food 12 to 2, 6.30 to 9
Details Children welcome Car park Garden No-smoking area in bar Occasional background music No dogs MasterCard, Switch, Visa

MANCHESTER   **Greater Manchester**   **map 8**

The Bridge   NEW ENTRY

58 Bridge Street, Manchester M3 3BW   TEL: (0161) 834 0242

Twenty years ago the Bridge was a fashionable wine bar, but over the years it became a tired-looking boozer. Revamped, it opened as a gastro-pub in January 2004. The long, narrow room, with wooden floors and large windows with heavy tied-back drapes, veers more towards owner Robert Owen Brown's vision of an informal restaurant than a pub for drinkers – customers are asked if they have a table reservation on entering, and there is a wine list on each table in the bar area. However, people do call in for a drink: perhaps a pint of Ruddles Best or Old Speckled Hen, or something from the range of specialist foreign bottled beers. The restaurant menu is served throughout, with a selection of sandwiches in the bar area described on a blackboard over the bar. The food is solid, hearty fare delivered with some style and due deference to local products, opening, perhaps, with well-flavoured slow-roast duck spring rolls with a dipping sauce of sweet-and-sour rhubarb, or a thick slab of rich, robust game terrine with a port glaze. Main courses include staples such as slowly braised lamb shank with root vegetables, rosemary and red wine, and pan-fried ribeye steak with chips fried in duck fat, field mushrooms and béarnaise sauce. Steamed ginger sponge pudding with custard and golden syrup is typical of desserts. SAMPLE DISHES: Bury black pudding potato cake with a poached egg and hollandaise £4.25; breast of chicken with wild garlic, wilted greens and smoked bacon broth £8; lemon tart £3.50.

Licensee Robert Owen Brown (Pub Estate Company)
Open 11 to 11, Sun 12 to 6; bar food and restaurant all week 12 to 3, 5.30 to 9.30, Sun 12 to 4
Details Children welcome in eating areas Wheelchair access (not WC) Background music No dogs Delta, MasterCard, Switch, Visa

Britons Protection Hotel   NEW ENTRY

50 Great Bridgewater Street, Manchester M1 5LE   TEL: (0161) 236 5895

You'll find this early nineteenth-century pub tucked into a corner spot behind the Bridgewater Hall. It may not look inviting at first as the glass is slightly tinted and it may seem closed until you get close up, but the interior is welcoming, with a warren of gleaming, spotless small rooms and the reassuring clutter of a pub replete with red-velour seats and patterned carpets. Traditional home cooking is what to expect: say, pork chop with mash and vegetables, or minced venison with vegetables, while broccoli soup might head a short list of starters. The food is simple, good value and 'on the whole very good', thought one, who thoroughly enjoyed a tasty turkey, pheasant, hare and pigeon pie with good thick pastry and accompanying carrots and shredded greens.

Real ale drinkers will be happy with the choice of Tetley Bitter, Robinsons, and Jennings Cumberland Ale, while those who prefer whisky are well served by a serious selection of over 250; only house wine is served by the glass. SAMPLE DISHES: royal game soup £2; battered haddock with chips £5; apple and blackcurrant crumble £2.

Licensee P.G. Barnett (Punch Taverns)
Open 11 to 11, Sun 12 to 10.30; bar food Mon to Fri 11 to 2.30; closed 25 Dec
Details No children   Wheelchair access (also WC)   Garden   No smoking in eating area   Occasional background music   No dogs   MasterCard, Switch, Visa

Kro 2 Bar

Oxford House, Oxford Road, Manchester M1 5AE   TEL: (0161) 236 1048
WEBSITE: www.kro.co.uk
between the BBC and the Students' Union

Expect a predominantly youthful crowd at this attractive, modern bar south of the city centre. High ceilings and glass walls allow plenty of daylight in and a lively hubbub reverberates about the place, especially in the evening, when a DJ provides entertainment. Brown leather sofas are ideal for relaxing in the bar, while the 'restaurant' area has modern wooden tables and chairs, and waiter service. There's also a large outdoor terrace with umbrellas and heaters to ward off the Manchester weather. A Danish theme runs through the menu, in the shape of marinated herrings, meatballs with potatoes and red cabbage, and so on, but there are also plenty of non-Danish sandwiches, pastas, salads and main courses such as pink peppered chicken, or duck breast with cloves and honey, as well as decidedly English breakfasts, served from opening time until 3pm (5pm at weekends). Regular real ales Jekyll's Gold (from Manchester's Hydes brewery) and Fuller's London Pride are supplemented with guest beers, and a list of 30 international wines includes six by the glass. SAMPLE DISHES: pariserbof (rare-cooked ground steak with capers, beetroot and onion topped with a fried egg) £5.25; braised lamb shank with garlic and mint on crushed new potatoes £10; white chocolate mousse £3.50.

Licensee Mark Ruby (freehouse)
Open Mon to Wed 8.30am to midnight, Thur to Fri 8.30am to 2am, Sat 10.30am to 2am, Sun 10.30am to midnight; bar food and restaurant 11.30 to 10; closed 25 Dec
Details Children welcome in eating areas   Wheelchair access (also WC)   Patio   No smoking in restaurant Background music   No dogs   Amex, Delta, Diners, MasterCard, Switch, Visa

Ox

71 Liverpool Road, Castlefield, Manchester M3 4NQ   TEL: (0161) 839 7740

The Ox may have set itself up as a dining pub with reservable tables, but it manages admirably to retain its function as a working pub (one that welcomes casual drinkers). The urban location allows for a small terrace with bench seating at wooden tables, while, within, the big bar is nicely broken up into sections by banquettes and brick pillars. The walls are painted a deep red or aubergine, the floor is black and strewn with rugs, and assorted wooden tables and a pick-and-mix range of seating (captain's chairs, church seats, maroon leatherette banquettes) create the look of a thoroughly modern gastro-pub. At lunchtime you can get sandwiches – not only pan-fried minute steak with melted blue cheese but also Thai-style marinated salmon with lime and coriander crème fraîche – and the pub also offers a lengthy menu with a distinctly global feel: say, flash-roasted garlic and chilli squid, or confit of duck leg with caramelised sugar-snap peas, baby braised onions and Madeira jus. There's a traditional streak, too, in dishes such as Boddingtons-jugged beef, and good old bread-and-butter pudding for dessert. Among the range of beers are Timothy Taylor Landlord, Marston's Pedigree, Old Speckled Hen, and Boddingtons Bitter, while the reasonably priced wine list offers around 15 by the glass. SAMPLE DISHES: sautéed chicken livers with wild mushrooms £5; rack of Welsh lamb £15; chocolate tart £5.50.

Licensee John Clarke (Rowanstar Pub Co)

Open *11 to 11; bar food Mon to Thur 12 to 2.45, 5.30 to 9.15, Fri and Sat 12.30 to 10.15, Sun 12.30 to 6.45, 7 to 9.15*

Details *Children welcome in family room   Wheelchair access (also WC)   Garden   No-smoking area Background music   No dogs   Delta, MasterCard, Switch, Visa   Accommodation: 9 rooms, room only £44.95 to £59.95 (double room)*

Sinclair's   `NEW ENTRY`

2 Cathedral Gates, Shambles Square, Manchester M3 1SW   TEL: (0161) 834 0430

Sinclair's is a Manchester institution. The half-timbered building dates from 1328, but it no longer stands on its original site. It was almost demolished in the early 1970s to make way for the Arndale Shopping Centre and was rebuilt and re-sited again after the IRA bomb. It is now right in the heart of a newly redeveloped sector of Manchester known as the Triangle shopping complex and the Printworks, and a conscious effort has been made to retain the pub much as it was in the past. The downstairs is a labyrinth of small snug-type rooms – two are set for eating, with a lunchtime hot servery – and upstairs is reached via narrow stairs. There's a strong traditional slant to the menu, with dishes such as beef and oyster pie, angels- and devils-on-horseback, carpetbagger steak stuffed with oysters (Sinclair's boasts that it has been specialising in oysters since 1848), as well as roast beef, and liver and sausage casserole in a giant Yorkshire pudding. But there's a modern streak, too, with light meals ranging from scrambled egg and smoked salmon, or mackerel and mustard mash with black pudding, to chicken Caesar salad and beef chilli nachos. Beer drinkers will find a complete range of Samuel Smith on draught, and three wines are served by the glass. SAMPLE DISHES: eggs Benedict £4.50; chicken suisse £7; apple and cinnamon pie £2.50.

Licensee Darren Coles

Open *11 to 11, Sun 12 to 10.30; bar food 12 to 8 (6 Sun)*

Details *No children   Wheelchair access   No-smoking area   Garden   Background music   No dogs   Delta, Diners, Mastercard, Switch, Visa*

MARKET OVERTON   Rutland   map 6

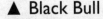 **Black Bull**

Market Overton LE15 7PW   TEL: (01572) 767677

On the corner of Main Street and Teigh Road, this stone-built, part-thatched old inn is a focal point in such an attractive village of stone-coloured buildings. A décor of pinkish walls, red-upholstered banquettes, dark beams, lamps on deep windowsills, a welcoming fire and friendly and hospitable staff all create a warm and cheery atmosphere of 'country hospitality at its best.' Food, listed on a blackboard, is ordered at the bar and brought to the table. Seafood is something of a speciality, running from 'Ye Olde Black Bull fish and chips' to fillet of salmon served with leak and creamed potatoes with whole grained mustard sauce, while meat eaters might opt for a 24oz T-bone steak. Five real ales are on draught – Hook Norton, Wells Bombardier Premium Bitter, Greene King IPA, Timothy Taylor Landlord and Adnams Bitter – and four wines are served by the glass. SAMPLE DISHES: oriental duck pancake £4.50; grilled sea bass £14; crunchy lemon meringue pie £3.75.

Licensees John and Val Owen (freehouse)
Open 12 to 2.30, 6 to 11, Sun 12 to 3, 7 to 10.30; bar food and restaurant 12 to 1.45, 6.30 to 9.45
Details Children welcome Car park No smoking in restaurant Background music Dogs welcome on a lead Delta, MasterCard, Switch, Visa Accommodation: 2 rooms, B&B £35 to £48

MARLDON   Devon   map 1

▲ Church House Inn
Village Road, Marldon TQ3 1SL   TEL: (01803) 558279
off A380, 2m NW of Paignton

This friendly and welcoming fourteenth-century inn stands next to the equally vener-able church in the centre of the village. It's a popular place with a lively atmosphere, drawing a mixed crowd, mainly locals, for both drinking and dining. The L-shaped main bar has a traditional look with dark beams, a stone fireplace and flagstone floors, while the dining area has a more contemporary minimalist style, its plain white walls adorned with mirrors and prints. Blackboard menus are the same in both areas, mostly relatively upmarket dishes such as smoked salmon and prawn roulade with asparagus vinaigrette, followed perhaps by chicken suprême with white wine, tarragon and cream sauce, or slow-roasted shoulder of lamb with thyme, rosemary and garlic sauce. Real ales are an above-average range, including Dartmoor Best, Shepherd Neame Spitfire and Fuller's London Pride, and eight wines plus some fizz are served by the glass from a flavour-packed list. Accommodation includes a one-bedroom flat and a three-bed self-catering holiday cottage. SAMPLE DISHES: warm spinach and goats' cheese flan with tomato and basil dressing £5.50; fillet steak topped with red Leicester cheese and a piquant sauce £16.50; Italian apple cake with sweet basil syrup £5.

Licensee Julian Cook (freehouse)
Open Mon to Fri 11.30 to 2.30, 5.30 to 11, Sat 11.30 to 11, Sun 12 to 10.30; bar food and restaurant 12 to 2 (2.30 Sun), 6.30 to 9.30; closed evenings 25 and 26 Dec
Details Children welcome in eating areas Car park Wheelchair access (not WC) Garden and patio No-smoking area in bar, no smoking in restaurant Occasional background music Dogs welcome in bar only Delta, MasterCard, Switch, Visa Accommodation: 1 room, B&B £40 to £50

MARSH BENHAM   Berkshire   map 2

Red House ❀
Marsh Benham RG20 8LY   TEL: (01635) 582017
off A4 between Newbury and Hungerford

This thatched, red-brick pub was transformed into a stylish gastro-pub a few years ago, although real ale drinkers can still enjoy Fuller's London Pride. It has a garden outside, and inside there's a bar-cum-bistro with red-painted walls, and, beyond it, a distinctly upmarket restaurant. The bistro menu offers two- or three-course set meals with three starters and three mains to choose from. Of the former, one might be a velouté of Jerusalem artichoke flavoured with chorizo, or perhaps salmon and prawn fishcake with sweet chilli dressing. Main courses range from leg of lamb steak with oriental couscous and mint reduction to gnocchi with wild mushrooms and asparagus, and puddings are the same as those on the restaurant à la carte menu – vanilla crème brûlée, maybe, or pear parfait with poached pear and dark chocolate sauce (or a selection of English and French cheeses). The French-led wine list opens with four house selections at £13.50, or £3.25 a glass, but while there's enough for drinkers on a budget, upmarket bottles dominate. SAMPLE DISHES: terrine of ham and shallots with apricot chutney; fillet of Scottish salmon filled with spinach mousseline with saffron potatoes and tomato beurre blanc; vanilla pannacotta with mandarin compote: 2 courses £13.95, 3 courses £16.95.

Licensee Bruno Gautier (freehouse)
Open 12 to 3.30, 6 to 11, bar food and restaurant 12 to 2.15, 7 to 10; closed 25 and 26 Dec, 1 Jan
Details Children welcome   Car park   Wheelchair access (also WC)   Garden and patio   No-smoking area in bar, no smoking in restaurant   Occasional background music   No dogs   Amex, Delta, MasterCard, Switch, Visa

MARSH GIBBON   Buckinghamshire   map 5

Greyhound Inn
West Edge, Marsh Gibbon OX27 0HA   TEL: (01869) 277365
off A41 Bicester to Aylesbury road, 4m E of Bicester

THAI

On the outskirts of the village, this stone-built country local fits in with its equally attractive neighbours, while, within, bare stone walls, a winter log fire, a stone floor and beamed ceilings give character. A single U-shaped bar leads round to a carpeted area, which is treated as the restaurant, with heavy-topped tables and dark padded chairs. In this apparently quintessential English setting you can expect an exclusively Thai menu (with a take-away option for those in a hurry), for that is where the owners hail from. The cooking proves to be impressive, replete with fresh herbs and spices, and everything is cooked to order. You might begin, familiarly enough, with spring roll, before proceeding to king prawn ruby curry. Choose from a variety of ice creams to finish. Greene King Abbot Ale and IPA and Fuller's London Pride are on handpump, and there are specialities such as Polish lager and (of course) bottled Thai beer. Six wines are served by the glass. SAMPLE DISHES: chicken satay £4.75; green chicken curry £7; piña colada ice cream £2.70.

Licensee Richard Kaim (freehouse)
Open Tue to Sun 12 to 3, 6 (7 Sun) to 11.30; bar food and restaurant Tue to Sun 12 to 2.30, 6 (7 Sun) to 9.30
Details Children welcome in eating areas   Car park   Wheelchair access (not WC)   Garden   No smoking in restaurant   No music   No dogs   Delta, MasterCard, Switch, Visa

MARSHSIDE   Kent   map 3

Gate Inn 🍺
Marshside CT3 4EB   TEL: (01227) 860498
between A28 and A299, 3m SE of Herne Bay

'A good example of a simple country pub,' thought a visitor to this well-worn cottage-style building on a narrow country road. Some prefer it in winter when the log fire is blazing away, fed by 'big fat logs', and there is a really cosy atmosphere; others have a soft spot for the garden in summer, when you can feed the ducks congregating on the stream that runs to one side. Whatever the season, this is clearly a village local, with notices about the cricket team or wine and wisdom evenings, but everyone is greeted warmly: children, adults, dogs (there's a jar of doggy treats on the bar). Food is homely, chalked up on a blackboard and expanded in a printed menu. Good-looking, generous, thick-cut bacon sandwiches, perhaps, or a spicy hotpot topped with a generous amount of home-cooked ham, as well as omelettes, mixed grills, jacket potatoes, and steaks and pasta, all reasonably priced and honestly cooked. Beers are from Shepherd Neame (Master Brew Bitter, Spitfire Premium Ale and Bishop's Finger, plus seasonal brews such as an autumnal Late Red, all tapped from the cask), and a short list of wines is available, with six served by the glass. SAMPLE DISHES: cheesy garlic bread £3.25; Mexican bean feast £6; Indian ice cream £2.75.

Licensee Christopher Smith (Shepherd Neame)
Open 11 to 2.30 (3 Sat), 6 to 11, Sun 12 to 4, 7 to 10.30; bar food 12 to 2, 6 to 9, Sun 12 to 2.15, 7 to 9
Details Children welcome in family room   Car park   Wheelchair access (also WC)   Garden   No-smoking area in bar (lunchtime only) and family room   No music   Dogs welcome   No cards

MARTON   North Yorkshire   map 9

Appletree ✿ ❦
Marton YO62 6RD   TEL: (01751) 431457
WEBSITE: www.appletreeinn.co.uk
Marton signposted on A170 between Kirkbymoorside and Pickering

Since taking over this village pub on the fringes of the North York Moors National Park, the Drews have gone from strength to strength. In addition to offering exemplary pub food, they now have a 'shop counter' selling all kinds of home-produced provisions. Bare stone walls, beamed ceilings and a large open fire define the bar, where you can sample John Smith's Bitter or one of the regularly changing guests from North Country breweries such as Malton or Hambleton. Candles are the main ornament in the red-walled, carpeted restaurant, but you can eat wherever you like. Start with something wacky like mustard ice cream with red cabbage and truffle oil, or something more mainstream like confit of duck with pink peppercorn sauce and parsley potatoes, and proceed to fillet of locally reared beef with rocket pesto and noisette potatoes, or roast rump of lamb with minted pea risotto and lamb jus. Fish also gets a good outing: salmon fillet poached in red wine with an oyster beignet, herbs and seafood tagliatelle, for example. A few lighter dishes such as black pudding with smoked bacon and scrambled egg top the simpler lunch menu, although desserts pull out all the creative stops for, say, chilled coconut, banana and cardamom black rice pudding, or marbled chocolate pyramid with Baileys chocolate mousse. Wine starts at under £10 a bottle on a well structured 70-strong list. Ten by the glass are mostly £2.60. SAMPLE DISHES: smoked chicken with caper berry salad and paprika oil £5.50; steamed halibut with braised fennel, mussels, clams and orange beurre blanc £16; Yorkshire treacle tart with lemon-curd ice cream £4.50.

Licensees Melanie and Trajan Drew (freehouse)
Open 12 to 2.30, 6.30 to 11, Sun 12 to 3, 7 to 10.30; bar food and restaurant 12 to 2, 6.30 to 9.30, Sun 12 to 3, 7 to 9; closed Mon lunchtimes, Tue, 3 weeks Jan
Details Children welcome in bar eating area   Car park   Patio   No smoking in restaurant   Background music   No dogs   Delta, MasterCard, Switch, Visa

MARTON   Shropshire   map 5

Sun Inn 🏵 🏵

Marton SY21 8JP   TEL: (01938) 561211
on B4386, 13m SW of Shrewsbury

The sombre grey/brown-stone building is of indeterminate age, with only a giant stone hearth in the bar area appearing visibly old. But the Sun is a convivial local boozer and a real family concern, with Ian MacCallum behind the bar, wife Rosie manning the restaurant, and son Steve in the kitchen delivering a strongly seasonal menu. The cooking concentrates on the separate no-smoking restaurant, where the menu offers a range of simple dishes in a modern European style: perhaps grilled calves' kidneys with rosemary and anchovy butter sauce to start, followed by herb-crusted saddle of lamb with mashed swede and carrot, potato gratin and rosemary sauce, or fillet of sea bass with mashed peas and potatoes, deep-fried prawns and mustard sauce. A pedigree kitchen background shows in well-honed and sound technical skills, spot-on timing, and a focus on first-class raw materials. The main menu is available at lunchtimes alongside a list of no more than half a dozen straightforward dishes of, say, gammon steak with egg and chips, beef stew with horseradish mash, and lamb's liver with bacon, onions and roast vegetables, but delivered in an accomplished manner. Equally excellent desserts may include steamed ginger pudding, or blackcurrant cheesecake. Given the quality of the cooking, set Sunday lunch is a bargain at £12.50 for three courses. A quartet of house wines at £11 a bottle, £2.75 a glass, opens the short but diverse wine list, and City of Cambridge Hobson's Choice is the real ale on offer. SAMPLE DISHES: cream of wild garlic soup £3.50; slow-roast crisp-skinned duck leg with braised green lentils £7; chocolate and walnut meringue £4.

Licensee Ian MacCallum (freehouse)
Open *Wed to Sun 12 to 2, all week 7 to 11 (10.30 Sun); bar food Wed to Sat 12 to 2, restaurant Wed to Sun 12 to 2, Tue to Sat 7 to 9*
Details *Children welcome   Car park   Wheelchair access (also WC)   Patio   No smoking in restaurant Background music   Dogs welcome exc in restaurant   Delta, MasterCard, Switch, Visa*

MELLOR   Greater Manchester   map 8

Oddfellows Arms

73 Moor End Road, Mellor SK6 5PT   TEL: (0161) 449 7826
at Marple Bridge, turn SE off A626, signed Mellor and New Mills

In a commanding position at the heart of a little hamlet of picturesque houses and cottages stands this substantial, three-storey gritstone inn. It is an imposing building with leaded windows, a small yard in front and its car park in an old quarry across the road. Behind the wooden porch is a spacious, flagged bar-room with carpeted sub-divisions off it (beware a head-banging beam near the counter!). Here well-kept beers are served by friendly staff in a relaxed atmosphere: Adnams Bitter, Marston's Bitter and Pedigree, plus guests such as Gale's Ragged Robin. An extensive and éclectic menu draws eaters from miles around. Fried black pudding with sweet chilli sauce, or crab au gratin make a good beginning. Then perhaps a glazed pork hock with fruit compote and red cabbage slow-braised with apple, or hot Thai chicken with lychees; steaks, or a roast of the day, offer alternatives, vegetarians are well catered for, and there are sandwiches and salads. Portions are generous, though, so you might have to ignore chocolate puddle pudding with milk chocolate sauce. Most of the 40 Old and New World wines are under £15 – some are under £10 – with a varying selection of eight or so by the glass. There's plenty of tasty everyday stuff with one or two grander offerings. SAMPLE DISHES: mussel chowder £5; yoghurt marinated garlic chicken £9; bread-and-butter pudding £4.

Licensee Robert Cloughley (freehouse)
Open *Tue to Sun 12 to 3, 5.30 to 11 (Sun 7 to 10.30); bar food Tue to Sat 12 to 2, 6.30 to 9.30, Sun 12 to 2; closed 25, 26 and 31 Dec, 1 Jan*
Details *Children welcome in eating areas   Car park   Wheelchair access (not WC)   Patio   No smoking in dining room   No music   Dogs welcome   Delta, MasterCard, Switch, Visa*

MELLOR BROOK   Lancashire   map 8

▲ Feilden's Arms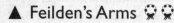

Whalley Road, Mellor Brook BB2 7PR   TEL: (01254) 812219
follow signposts for Mellor Brook from A59 between Whalley and Preston

The Feilden's Arms is an old pub that has been thoroughly and smartly modernised. The interior is divided into eating and drinking areas based around a long bar counter, although at busy times (such as Sunday lunch) the whole place is given over to diners. The bar menus stick to a familiar range of dishes like fish 'n' chips, pies (chicken, leek and tarragon, perhaps), and sausage and mash, and if you are after just a snack there is also a choice of sandwiches and hot baguettes. If restaurant formality is more your thing, there is the conservatory dining room, where a more ambitious menu offers modern British dishes along the lines of white-bean velouté with truffle oil, or game terrine with toasted brioche to start, followed by roast wild duck with sweet red cabbage, dauphinois potatoes and blackcurrant sauce, or baked cod with spaghetti of cucumber and caviar, and rum baba with apple compote to finish. Note that the restaurant menu is also available in the bar. Four red and four white wines are offered by the glass from a reasonably priced list. Beers are from Boddingtons. SAMPLE DISHES: shellfish bisque £2.25; fish pie £7; crème brûlée £3.

Licensees Nigel Smith and Fred Walker (freehouse)
Open *11.30 to 11 (10.30 Sun); bar food and restaurant 12 to 2.30, 6 to 9; closed 25 Dec*
Details *Children welcome   Car park   Wheelchair access (also WC)   Garden   No smoking in restaurant   Occasional background music   No dogs   Amex, Delta, Diners, MasterCard, Switch, Visa   Accommodation: 4 rooms, B&B £48 to £58*

MELLS   Somerset   map 2

▲ Talbot Inn

Selwood Street, Mells BA11 3PN   TEL: (01373) 812254
WEBSITE: www.talbotinn.com

The Talbot is easy to find once you've managed to locate the village, which is in a web of tiny country roads. The substantial tile-roofed building in the mellow local limestone has been a coaching inn since the fifteenth century. The large entrance arch, welcomingly cool and crepuscular on a bright day, leads through the building to a characterful courtyard behind, with tables, chairs and a pergola wrapped in rampant Russian vine. In the high-ceilinged public bar beyond – once a tithe barn – a horse-drawn single-furrow plough hangs above barrels of Butcombe Bitter, Fuller's London Pride and Smiles; the smaller bar has wood panelling, a flagstone floor and hunting prints. If you want to eat, booking ahead is essential. Food, fairly elaborate, favours dishes such as chargrilled sirloin steak with celeriac and wild mushrooms with red wine and port jus, and confit leg of Barbary duck with braised red cabbage and peppercorn sauce. Supplementing the menu's meat main dishes is a handwritten page of specials (mainly fish): steamed fillets of sea bass with parsley mash and a tomato, shallot and basil dressing, or pan-fried whole local trout with capers, prawns and nut-brown butter, for example. The wine list kicks off with three house selections, at £10.95, all in two sizes of glass (£2.95 and £3.95). SAMPLE DISHES: mussels in white wine, onions, garlic, parsley and cream £6; pot-roast shoulder of lamb with redcurrant sauce £15.50; mango crème brûlée £4.

Licensee Roger Elliott (freehouse)
Open 12 to 2.30, 6.30 to 11, Sun 12 to 3, 7 to 10.30; bar food and restaurant 12 to 2, 7 to 9.30; restaurant closed 25 and 26 Dec, 1 Jan
Details Children welcome in restaurant   Car park   Garden and patio   No smoking in restaurant Occasional music   Dogs welcome exc in restaurant   Delta, MasterCard, Switch, Visa   Accommodation: 8 rooms, B&B £55 to £75

MELMERBY   Cumbria

map 10

Shepherds Inn

Melmerby CA10 1HF   TEL: (01768) 881217
on A686 Penrith to Alston road, 8m NE of Penrith

Brown tourist signs point the way from Penrith to this red sandstone pub in a small village at the foot of Alston Ridge, part of the northern Pennines and justly designated an Area of Outstanding Natural Beauty. Décor in the large, high-ceilinged main bar is plain and simple but owners and staff give the place a warm and cheerful ambience. Good-value menus offer a generous choice of traditional dishes including steak and kidney pie, ploughman's (with a choice of three from a range of 14 English cheeses) or Cumberland sausages with egg and chips, as well as a few slightly more exotic and unusual options such as venison casserole with orange and juniper and a hazelnut and Roquefort dumpling. At lunchtime there is also a lighter snack menu, and tempting home-made desserts are shown off in a display cabinet. Real ales are Black Sheep Best, Boddingtons Cask and Jennings Cumberland Ale, and a short wine list offers good value, with several bottles under £10 and three wines by the glass. SAMPLE DISHES: deep-fried whitebait with curried mayonnaise £5; chicken escalope with green pepper sauce £9; lemon meringue pie £3.25.

Licensees Garry and Marcia Parkin (freehouse)
Open 10.30 to 3, 6 to 11, Sun 12 to 3, 7 to 10.30; bar food Mon to Sat 11.30 to 2.30, 6 to 9, Sun 12 to 2.30, 7 to 9; closed 25 Dec, lunchtime 26 Dec
Details Children welcome   Car park   Patio   No-smoking area   Live music; jukebox   Dogs welcome in 1 area of bar   Delta, MasterCard, Switch, Visa

MICKLEHAM   Surrey

map 3

King William IV

Byttom Hill, Mickleham RH5 6EL   TEL: (01372) 372590
going S on A24 about 2m S of Leatherhead, just after roundabout junction with A246 look for Frascati's restaurant on left; pub is up steep track to right of restaurant

On a hillside and reached via a steep and partially unmade track (best to park in the public car park before you make the turn), and up steep steps from the road, the King

William IV is a fine example of a country pub. The food is in keeping with the small, homely interior: alongside the usual lunchtime sandwiches, ploughman's and jacket potatoes, there could be calf's liver with smoked bacon, steak and kidney pie, and aubergine and vegetable lasagne, while desserts might take in apple tart or fruit crumble. On draught are Adnams Best Bitter, Badger Best Bitter and Hogs Back TEA and Advent Ale. Just three wines are sold by the glass. The pretty garden, on several levels, has plenty of seats and tables; barbecues are held here in summer. The surrounding area is interwoven with tracks and footpaths, making it ideal for walkers and cyclists. SAMPLE DISHES: spinach and corn pancakes £9; fillet steak en croûte £14.75; chocolate fudge cake £4.

Licensees Chris and Jenny Grist (freehouse)
Open 11 to 3, 6 to 11, Sun 12 to 10.30; bar food 12 to 2 (5 Sun), 7 to 9.30; closed 25 Dec, evening 31 Dec
Details No children under 12   Garden and patio   Occasional live or background music   No dogs
MasterCard, Switch, Visa

▲ Running Horses   NEW ENTRY

Old London Road, Mickleham RH5 6DU   TEL: (01372) 372279
WEBSITE: www.therunninghorses.co.uk
off main road through centre of village

Dark ceiling beams and a highwayman's hideout testify to the sixteenth-century origins of this simple old inn that was once a stagecoach stop. It is a popular place, and one reader advises that visitors should arrive early in the bar to bag one of the four tables with comfortable chairs. The alternative is an array of pews and stools, or the more formal and upmarket restaurant, where white tablecloths are the order of the day. The restaurant menu is available throughout, alongside an extensive bar menu, the latter delivering familiar pub fare along the lines of chunky sandwiches, mussels with fries, salmon and crab fishcakes, potato wedges, and farmhouse cheese platters. Look to the restaurant menu for interesting dishes such as duck liver and foie gras parfait, slow-roast shank of lamb with rosemary and Burgundy sauce with shallot mash, and 'fantastic' hot chocolate fondant with white chocolate ice cream, or an 'excellent' coconut and passion-fruit brûlée with an apple crisp. Fuller's London Pride as well ales from Adnams and Young's are on handpump, and eight wines are served by the glass. SAMPLE DISHES: lobster and salmon chowder £6.25; coriander-and-orange-crusted baked cod £17; espresso cream torte on hazelnut sponge £5.

Licensees Steve and Josie Slayford (Punch Taverns)
Open 11.30 to 11; bar food and restaurant 12 to 2.30 (3 Sat and Sun), 7 to 9.30
Details Children welcome in restaurant   Wheelchair access (also WC)   Patio   No music   Dogs welcome in
bar area only   Amex, Delta, Diners, MasterCard, Switch, Visa   Accommodation: 6 rooms, B&B £80 to £111

▲ *indicates where a pub offers accommodation. At the end of the entry information is given on the number of rooms available and a price range, indicating the cost of a single room or single occupancy to that for a room with two people sharing.*

MIDDLEHAM   North Yorkshire   map 8

▲ White Swan Hotel 🍺

Market Place, Middleham DL8 4PE   TEL: (01969) 622093
WEBSITE: www.whiteswanhotel.co.uk

Middleham has two Swans, a white one and a black one, and they stand facing each other across the market square. The White Swan is the smaller and has a low-key air of unpretension concealing solid worth. The serving counter divides the black-beamed bar: one side is flag-floored with bar stools and a big inglenook containing a wood-burner and a table alongside; the other is wooden-floored, with tables, chairs and floral wallpaper. Wherever you sit, you can sample Black Sheep's full range (Best Bitter, Special Ale and Riggwelter) and John Smith's cask brews, all in perfect condition; alternatively, a 20-bin wine list (with a dozen by the glass) starts at £9.50, and only a handful of French bottles breach £20. Food is listed on a menu card, with specials on a blackboard. Starters take in black pudding and bacon risotto, with main courses including chicken pie, or fish 'n' chips with mushy peas, alongside fricassee of lamb, and chargrilled lamb and chicken as well as steaks. It is worth noting that co-licensee Paul Klein is also the licensee of the Blue Lion two miles down the road at East Witton (see entry). SAMPLE DISHES: crispy duck and bacon salad with plum sauce £4; sausages with grain mustard mash and gravy £7; chocolate terrine with raspberry coulis £4.

Licensees Andrew Holmes and Paul Klein (freehouse)
Open 11 to 11, Sun 12 to 10.30; bar food and restaurant 12 to 2.15, 6.30 to 9.15
Details Children welcome in bar eating area   Wheelchair access (not WC)   Garden and patio   No smoking in restaurant   No music   Dogs welcome exc in food areas when food is being served   Delta, MasterCard, Switch, Visa   Accommodation: 12 rooms, B&B £47.50 to £79

MILLBANK   West Yorkshire   map 8

Millbank 🍴 🍇

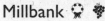

Millbank HX6 3DY   TEL: (01422) 825588
WEBSITE: www.themillbank.com
signposted on A58 between Sowerby Bridge and Ripponden

The interior of this old stone pub has a metropolitan edge, quite a contrast to the rural setting, which majors in lovely valley views from the decked terrace and beer garden. The much-modernised interior consists of stripped-down walls and floors, plus a few individual touches such as church chairs with their prayer-book boxes still attached, some abstract paintings, and a fireplace filled with stone heads and candles. A change in ownership towards the end of 2003 saw the chef, Glen Futter, form part of the new team in charge, so consistency has been maintained. Eating goes on to either side of the small main bar area, and hearty portions are the norm. Start perhaps with pork rillettes with plum chutney, or a salmon cake with orange hollandaise, and go on to venison loin with potato and mushroom purée, cabbage and bacon, or poached halibut fillet with home-made tagliatelle, lobster, chilli, ginger and spring onion. Vegetarians might like to try goats' cheese pie with roast pimento, courgette and tomato butter sauce. Finish with chocolate fondant cake with pistachio ice cream, or a selection of Yorkshire farmhouse cheeses. A fixed-price menu (£10.95 for two courses) is available Tuesday to Friday evenings and Tuesday to Saturday lunchtimes. A good range of bottled beers and English cider supplements the handpumped

Timothy Taylor Landlord and Tetley Bitter, as well as organic cider and gin. The wine list is packed with good-value options and takes the innovative step of pairing them with upmarket alternatives under the banner 'If you like this… You'll love this' – and with the quality on offer, there's no reason to doubt it. A dozen come by the glass. SAMPLE DISHES: parsnip and Parmesan soup £4.50; Goosnargh duck breast with potato and mushroom Anna and apricot and cardamom chutney £13; Crème de Cassis soufflé with pear sorbet £5.50.

Licensee Joe McNally (freehouse)
Open Tue to Sat 12 to 3, 5.30 to 11, Sun 12 to 10.30; bar food and restaurant Tue to Sat 12 to 2.30, 6 to 10, Sun 12.30 to 4.30; closed first week Jan, first 2 weeks Oct
Details Children welcome Wheelchair access (not WC) Garden and patio No smoking in restaurant Live or background music Dogs welcome in taproom only Delta, MasterCard, Switch, Visa

MITCHELL   Cornwall   map 1

▲ Plume of Feathers

Mitchell TR8 5AX   TEL: (01872) 510387
A30 from Bodmin take left towards Mitchell, ignore first left, drive past a bus shelter and round bend. Pub is 250yds on left.

This attractive granite-built pub in a small village inland from Newquay is a family-friendly venue, with a children's play area in its large garden. Though the open-plan interior has been considerably modernised, it still retains some of its old character in the shape of beams, an inglenook and other original features. Lunch menus list various sandwiches and ciabattas, and simple main dishes such as Cornish pasty with fries, or green Thai chicken with rice, while dinner tends towards more substantial things such as duck confit with mash and braised red cabbage, and blackboard specials ranging from lasagne to chargrilled swordfish steak with curried sweet potato. Children's options include meatballs on spaghetti and gnocchi with cheese, spinach and chives. A decent selection of four real ales changes regularly but always includes Sharp's Doom Bar Bitter. The short wine list focuses on value, prices starting at around £10, and six wines are available as small single-serving bottles. SAMPLE DISHES: moules marinière £6; pan-fried beef fillet with parsnip, chestnut mash and wild mushroom thyme ragoût £15; chocolate truffle tart £4.50.

Licensees M.F.J. Warner and J.E. Trotter (freehouse)
Open 10.30 to 11 (10.20 Sun); bar food and restaurant 12 to 6, 6 to 10; closed evening 25 Dec
Details Children welcome Car park Garden No smoking in restaurant Occasional live or background music; jukebox Dogs welcome exc in restaurant Delta, MasterCard, Switch, Visa Accommodation: 5 rooms, B&B £41.25 to £95

MONKS ELEIGH   Suffolk   map 6

Swan Inn ✿

The Street, Monks Eleigh IP7 7AU   TEL: (01449) 741391
on B1115 between Sudbury and Hadleigh

Monks Eleigh is near Lavenham and, like its famous neighbour, has a number of thatched and timber-framed medieval houses. Nigel and Carol Ramsbottom's Swan Inn is also a timber-framed building, parts dating from the fourteenth century, right in the heart of the village. There are views on to the main street from the south-facing windows in the bar, which is all light wood and bamboo, with carpeted floors and a modest bar counter. Food is taken seriously here, with dishes listed on blackboards displaying influences from far and wide. You might find roast red pepper filled with goats' cheese and pesto on garlic bruschetta, or French onion soup with Parmesan croûtons to start, with whole roast sea bass with ginger and coriander butter, or seared Scottish scallops teamed with minted tabbouleh, crispy smoked bacon and a tomato and red onion salad, among the very good fish options. Otherwise, look for a classic chargrilled fillet steak with whole-grain mustard sauce and hand-cut chips, or braised lamb knuckle with Puy lentil sauce, creamy mashed potato and buttered broad beans. To finish, apple and ginger pudding with sticky toffee sauce is a real winter warmer, but iced Amaretto spumoni is a lighter choice. East Anglian beers from Adnams and Woodforde's are on draught, and the pub has a creditable list of affordably priced, international wines; 14 are offered by two sizes of glass from £2.80, plus more from frequently changing blackboards. SAMPLE DISHES: grilled smoked haddock topped with Welsh rarebit on warm tomato salad £4.75; roast duck breast on a compote of aubergines, cherry tomatoes and basil with gratin dauphinois £12.75; fruit crème brûlée £3.75.

Licensees Carol and Nigel Ramsbottom (freehouse)
Open Wed to Sun 12 to 3, 7 to 11; bar food and restaurant 12 to 2, 7 to 9
Details Children welcome Car park Garden No smoking in restaurant No music No dogs Delta, MasterCard, Switch, Visa

MOULTON **North Yorkshire** map 9

Black Bull Inn ❦
Moulton DL10 6QJ TEL: (01325) 377289

'A food pub through and through,' noted a visitor to this long, low, whitewashed pub in the centre of Moulton. The dark-panelled main bar, divided up by dark wooden settles and filled with a mix of tables, has walls covered with old prints and caricatures of Victorian politicians, and a display case contains numerous awards. The drinking emphasis is on wine, as no real ales are served, although only three wines come by the glass. Whites are well represented – complementing the strong seafood slant of the food – with excellent selections from the Loire, Germany and above all Burgundy. Red Burgundy and claret also figure large, and prices are fair all round. Bar snacks (lunchtime only) include oysters, Craster smoked salmon, carpaccio with capers, lemon and Parmesan, and a crab and mayonnaise sandwich, with, among hot items, Welsh rarebit and bacon, or queenie scallops in garlic with a Wensleydale and thyme crumb topping, as well as sausage, mash and onion gravy, and a noteworthy feuilleté of smoked haddock with prawns, parsley sauce and mash. The restaurant – in the conservatory and in a striking converted Pullman carriage in the garden – offers many of the same dishes, plus variations of lobster and steak, as well as halibut, monkfish and scallops, with roast rack of lamb, or pan-fried duck breast with onion marmalade. If you have room, chocolate truffle terrine with orange and Grand Marnier cream could well turn up among puddings. SAMPLE DISHES: smoked salmon pâté £6.25; king prawn and squid laksa £18; baked lemon cheesecake £4.

Licensees A.M.C. and S.C. Pagendam (freehouse)
Open Mon to Sat 12 to 2.30, 6 to 11; bar food Mon to Sat 12 to 2, restaurant Mon to Sat 12 to 2, 6.30 to 10; closed 24 to 26 Dec
Details No children Car park Patio No music No dogs Amex, Delta, Diners, MasterCard, Switch, Visa

▲ Crown Hotel

Crown Road, Mundford IP26 5HQ   TEL: (01842) 878233
pub signposted from A1065 in village

This whitewashed inn, dating from 1650, is a popular local. Large coal and wood fires
burn in each of the two bars, one the beamed, basic Village Bar with a modern jukebox, dartboard and pool table, the other the Squires Bar, which is carpeted and filled
with circular polished tables. A spiral staircase leads up to a separate restaurant and
Club Room. Much of the menu (which applies throughout) is traditional: for example, local ham with egg, beans and chips, lasagne, or variations on burgers, steaks and
ploughman's. More modern dishes from the à la carte and specials list might include
smoked duck and pine-nut salad, and skate wing with crispy leeks and butter and
caper sauce, while desserts range from sticky caramel pudding to pecan and maple
tart. Among the beers might be Marston's Pedigree or local brews from Woodforde's
and Mundford's own Iceni Brewery. All 26 good-value wines are sold by the glass.
SAMPLE DISHES: salmon dijonnaise £4.50; lamb rogan josh £7; apricot bread-and-
butter pudding £3.50.

Licensee Barry Walker (freehouse)
Open 11 to 11, Sun 12 to 10.30; bar food and restaurant 12 to 3, 7 to 10
Details *Children welcome   Wheelchair access (also WC)   Garden and patio   No smoking in restaurant*
*Jukebox   Dogs welcome in bar only   Amex, Delta, Diners, MasterCard, Switch, Visa   Accommodation: 30
rooms, B&B £37.50 to £59.50*

▲ Mill Inn

Mungrisdale CA11 0XR   TEL: (017687) 79632
WEBSITE: www.the-millinn.co.uk
from A66 7m E of Keswick, turn N on unclassified road signposted Mungrisdale

WATERSIDE

This rather off-the-beaten-track whitewashed pub is a 'dependable place', set under
Blencathra at the edge of roadless mountain country amid glorious scenery. It stands
next to a gushing mill stream – outside tables allow fell walkers and tourists to take in
the vista – while the interior is bright and neatly decorated, with lots of highly polished
brass ornaments. The bar serves Jennings Bitter and Cumberland Ale, brewed in
Cockermouth, and the kindly priced wine list offers six by the glass. Food is honestly
cooked, the lunchtime menu offering a good choice of sandwiches and baguettes – say,
tasty roast beef with 'sufficient horseradish to give the requisite heat' – as well as a short
list of quite simple, homely dishes with a few modern touches: perhaps pan-fried Dales
lamb chops with minted gravy, 'good' chips and plainly steamed vegetables. Otherwise
there could be home-made soup, local Cumberland sausages, and steak and kidney pie
as well as a choice of steaks. SAMPLE DISHES: grilled black pudding on herb mash with
grain mustard and bacon sauce £4; lamb Henry £9.50; sticky toffee pudding £3.25.

Licensees Jim and Margaret Hodge (freehouse)
Open 12 to 11 (Sun 10.30); bar food and restaurant 12 to 2, 6 to 8.30 (summer 12 to 2.30, 5.30 to 9);
closed 25 and 26 Dec
Details *Children welcome   Car park   Garden and patio   No smoking in restaurant   Background music
Dogs welcome   Delta, MasterCard, Switch, Visa   Accommodation: 6 rooms, B&B £35 to £55*

MUNSLOW Shropshire   map 5

▲ Crown

Munslow SY7 9ET TEL: (01584) 841205
WEBSITE: www.thecrown.clara.net

This very tall, three-storey attractive building is set in Corve Dale an Area of Outstanding Natural Beauty. Within is a series of small rooms, all on slightly different levels, with fat ceiling beams hung with garlands of hops. The interesting menus feature plenty of local produce, from sliced homemade Gloucester Old Spot pork and apricot sausages, to roast rump of Sibdon lamb, or loin of Ludlow venison. Seafood, often griddled, is well represented too: fillet of Devon mackerel with horseradish potatoes and chive vinaigrette, perhaps, or loin steak of Devon Porbeagle shark with a tomato and basil risotto and pesto sauce. As an alternative to dessert, a separate menu lists an excellent selection of English cheeses (or make a fine lunch dish with chutney, pickles and home-made rolls), with perhaps warm spiced carrot cake with clotted cream and butterscotch sauce for dessert-eaters. Real ale is a strong suit, with a selection from Holden's range, plus Hobsons Town Crier and a guest, often from Wood Brewery. Selected wines are served by the glass: do ask what is available; prices on the full, French-dominated list start at around £11. SAMPLE DISHES: confit of Gressingham duck leg with a pineapple and mint salsa £5.25; breast of Shropshire farm chicken wrapped in pancetta with a wild mushroom and chive cream sauce £11; vanilla pannacotta with fruit compote and orange and almond tuille £4.

Licensees Mr and Mrs R. and J. Arnold (freehouse)
Open Tue to Sun 12 to 2.30, 7 to 11 (10.30 Sun); bar food 12 to 1.45 (2 Sun), 7 to 8.45; restaurant Fri and Sat 7 to 8.45, Sun 12 to 2
Details Children welcome in eating areas Car park Wheelchair access (not WC) Garden No smoking in restaurant Background music Dogs welcome Amex, Delta, MasterCard, Visa, Switch Accommodation: 3 rooms, B&B £40 to £70

MYLOR BRIDGE   Cornwall   map 1

Pandora Inn

Restronguet Creek, Mylor Bridge TR11 5ST TEL: (01326) 372678
*off A39 from Truro, take B3292 signposted Penryn, then Mylor Bridge road,
and follow steep road down to Restronguet*

The ancient, thatched pub is in a beautiful waterside setting with its own mooring for boats and a pontoon with tables that extends over the water. In the summer 'it is a very busy pub and you are lucky to get a table (or a parking space) if you arrive late'. There's much to attract in winter too: atmospheric rooms have low ceilings, flagstones, wall alcoves, a warming fire, and historical connections (the *Pandora* was the ship sent to retrieve the *Bounty*'s mutineers). Lunch brings snacks such as local crab sandwiches, home-cooked ham, or jacket potatoes, and the standard menu – pork fillet medallions with garlic and rosemary, and monkfish and scallops with Thai spices, sweet peppers and spring onion – is supplemented by daily specials listed on a blackboard in the bar. The pub is owned by the St Austell Brewery (licensee John Milan also runs the Rising Sun in St Mawes, see entry) and offers beers from its range, including Tinners Ale, HSD and Tribune, as well as Bass. Eight house wines are sold by the small or large glass, or for £11 a bottle. The tempting main list offers good drinking at fair prices throughout, with top-class wines in the upper reaches. SAMPLE DISHES: chicken liver pâté with Cumberland sauce £5; John Dory fillets with prawns and dill sauce £12.50; locally made ice cream £3.50.

Licensee R.J. Milan (St Austell)
Open 11 to 11, Sun 12 to 10.30; bar food and restaurant 12 to 3, 6.30 to 9.30
Details Children welcome   Car park   Wheelchair access (also WC)   Patio   No smoking in restaurant
Occasional live music   Dogs welcome   Delta, MasterCard, Switch, Visa

NAILSWORTH   Gloucestershire   map 2

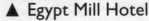 ## ▲ Egypt Mill Hotel
Nailsworth GL6 0AE   TEL: (01453) 833449

A hugely atmospheric building overlooking the River Frome, this former cloth mill and dye-house dates from the seventeenth century, though its unusual name most likely relates to a fourteenth-century corn mill that stood on the site. Old mill machinery is open to view in the cavernous split-level bar, ceilings are heavy with ancient beams, and exposed honey-coloured stone walls are lined with old food and drink advertising signs. A riverside terrace just adds to its charms. One menu serves throughout, aiming for a broad appeal with steak and kidney pudding, and haddock in crispy beer batter, alongside more fashionable ideas such as confit duck leg with black pudding mash and red wine jus. Lunch menus are a little simpler, featuring snack dishes like toasted English muffin with scrambled egg and smoked salmon. Real ales come from Gloucestershire's own Wickwar brewery, and there is a list of 27 wines, mostly under £15, with 12 available by the glass. SAMPLE DISHES: smoked chicken and celeriac remoulade with avocado and herb oil £6.75; pork tenderloin with mushrooms and Madeira cream £13; raspberry and lemongrass crème brûlée £4.50.

Licensee S.R. Webb (freehouse)
Open 11 to 11, Sun 12 to 10.30; bar food 12 to 2 (2.30 Sun), 6.45 to 9.30; closed evening 25 Dec
Details Children welcome   Car park   Garden and patio   No smoking in dining room   Occasional live or
background music   Guide dogs only   Amex, Delta, Diners, MasterCard, Switch, Visa   Accommodation: 17
rooms, B&B £54.50 to £95

NAYLAND   Suffolk   map 3

Anchor Inn ❀   [NEW ENTRY]
26 Court Street, Nayland CO6 4JL   TEL: (01206) 262313
WEBSITE: www.anchornayland.co.uk
just off A134 N of Colchester

The yellow-brick pub beside the bridge over the river Stour on the edge of Nayland is impossible to miss. Inside, it is roomy and modern in design but still retains a real pub feel, with a couple of fires in the main bar, original wooden flooring and a separate snug, while a small conservatory maximises the river views and is used primarily for dining. The Anchor has its own smokehouse tucked around the back, delivering such things as smoked salmon, haddock, mackerel and trout for a smoked fish platter, or smoked black treacle bacon for a lunchtime sandwich made up of white Suffolk huffer bread with Brie and cranberry and orange relish. Otherwise, there could be wild mushroom salad with lentils, croûtons and goats' cheese to start, then sweet-and-sour chicken with lemon-scented basmati rice, and rhubarb and custard trifle to finish. Greene King IPA and Adnams Bitter are on handpump, alongside guests such as Old Speckled Hen. Six wines are available by the glass, including a Sauvignon-style English organic from Carter's Vineyards. SAMPLE DISHES: pesto linguine with asparagus £4.25; smoked haddock rarebit with wilted spinach, saffron mash and a soft-boiled egg £10; cherry and almond tart £4.

Licensee Daniel Bunting (freehouse)
Open Mon to Fri 11 to 3, 5 to 11, Sat 11 to 11, Sun 12 to 10.30; bar food and restaurant Mon to Sat 12 to 2 (2.30 Sat), 6.30 to 9.30, Sun 12 to 3, 5.30 to 8.30
Details Children welcome in eating areas   Car park   Wheelchair access (also WC)   Garden and patio   No-smoking area   Occasional live or background music   No dogs   Delta, MasterCard, Switch, Visa

NETHER WALLOP   Hampshire   map 2

Five Bells   NEW ENTRY

Nether Wallop SO20 8HA   TEL: (01264) 781572

A stream meanders through Nether Wallop, a pretty thatched village with the Five Bells a dark-beamed country pub at its heart. A long, narrow bar, frequented mostly by locals, sports a fire and wood-burner, TV and fruit machine, while to the rear are two small dining rooms where a printed menu offers a range of modern British dishes. Ideas run from starters of game terrine with caramelised shallot dressing, or wild mushroom risotto with Parmesan and a poached egg, to main courses of pan-fried cod with candied tomatoes, olives and a tomato butter sauce, or sausage and mash with red onion gravy, with desserts of sticky toffee pudding with toffee sauce and caramel ice cream ('with nothing over-sweet for a change'), or vanilla parfait with praline. Wadworth 6X and Henry's Original IPA are on draught, and around eight wines are available by the glass. The Iron Age hillfort of Danebury and the Museum of Army Flying are both nearby. SAMPLE DISHES: scallops with creamed leeks and black pudding £7.50; seared salmon with crushed potatoes and sauce vierge £14.50; mocha chocolate mousse with a Baileys cream top £5.

Licensee Nicholas Geaney (freehouse)
Open 11 to 11; bar food Mon to Sat 12 to 9.30, Sun 12 to 3
Details Children welcome in bar eating area   Car park   Wheelchair access (also WC)   Garden and patio   No smoking in eating area   Background music   Dogs welcome in bar only   Delta, Diners, MasterCard, Switch, Visa

NEWTON LONGVILLE   Buckinghamshire   map 3

Crooked Billet 🏵 🍺 🍇

2 Westbrook End, Newton Longville MK17 0DF   TEL: (01908) 373936
WEBSITE: www.thebillet.co.uk
take left turn off B4146 from Leighton Buzzard towards Milton Keynes

The Crooked Billet occupies such a quiet corner of the village that one visitor sent precise directions: 'turn up a road that has a church to your left...and you find it about 300 yards up on the left'. The thatched old building still looks the traditional village pub, with lots of beams, polished wooden tables and pictures on the walls, although to the left as you enter you will notice two rooms set aside for eating, one tiled and one carpeted. This restaurant area is open only in the evenings and Sunday lunchtimes, when a full-dress menu (not available in the bar) of elaborately inventive cooking comes into play, offering perhaps salt- and pepper-roast duck breast with a plum and cucumber spring roll, egg fried rice and deep-fried Savoy cabbage, or roast cod with mussel and clam butter, mash, baby leeks and wilted spinach. The bar menu, available only at lunchtime, produces sandwiches, starters such as English white onion soup with a Stilton croûton and crispy shallots, or whitebait with tartare sauce, and main courses of beef and beer sausages with mash, wilted spinach and gravy, or pork loin stuffed with black pudding served with roast potatoes, spiced red cabbage and a chanterelle mushroom jus. John Gilchrist offers every one of the 300-odd wines by the glass. The quality is outstanding, with particularly fine selections from Burgundy and Bordeaux, but prices of these are not for the faint-hearted. Beer drinkers are not neglected, with Old Speckled Hen, Ruddles County and Wychwood Hobgoblin on handpump. SAMPLE DISHES: shellfish bisque £5; pan-fried sea bass fillet with champagne and caviar sauce £14; lemon and poppy seed pannacotta with pineapple carpaccio £5.50.

Licensees John and Emma Gilchrist (Greene King)
Open Mon 5.30 to 11, Tue to Sat 12 to 2.30, 5.30 to 11, Sun 12 to 4, 7 to 10.30; bar food Tue to Sat 12 to 2, Sun 12.30 to 2.30; restaurant Tue to Sat 7 to 10, Sun 12.30 to 3
Details Children welcome in restaurant Car park Garden No-smoking area in bar, no smoking in restaurant Occasional live music Dogs welcome exc in restaurant Amex, Delta, MasterCard, Switch, Visa

---

NEWTON-ON-THE-MOOR Northumberland map 10

▲ Cook and Barker Inn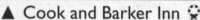

Newton-on-the-Moor NE65 9JY TEL: (01665) 575234
¼ m W of A1, in middle of village

In the 1800s the Cooks and the Barkers were joined in marriage in Newton and lent their names to this stone-built village inn (or so the story goes) that has views over fields to the North Sea. The beamed main bar area has an old-fashioned decorative style; leading off it are the snug bar, the informal dining area and the smart, spacious restaurant. If you are eating in the bar, you can expect traditional fare, with more ambitious dishes served in the restaurant. Start perhaps with woodland mushroom soup, or bacon and Camembert tart with asparagus, and follow it with steak and onion pudding with a rich red wine gravy, or lamb shank pot-roast with Asian spices served with minted couscous. The relaxed atmosphere and friendly and efficient service have been appreciated, as has a decent selection of real ales that includes Fuller's London Pride, Black Sheep Best Bitter, Theakston XB and Timothy Taylor Landlord. Half a dozen wines are sold by the glass from a well-presented list of around 35 bottles that covers a good range of flavours under £15 and is spiced up by some classy bottles with hefty price tags. SAMPLE DISHES: Northumbrian pheasant and venison pâté £4; roast tenderloin of Lincolnshire pork with apple and prune compote £7; crème brûlée £3.25.

Licensee Phil Farmer (freehouse)
Open 11 to 11, Sun 12 to 10.30; bar food and restaurant 12 to 2, 6 to 9
Details Children welcome Car park Wheelchair access (not WC) Garden No-smoking area in bar Live or background music No dogs Amex, Delta, MasterCard, Switch, Visa Accommodation: 19 rooms, B&B £37.50 to £95

NORTH CERNEY   Gloucestershire   map 2

▲ Bathurst Arms

North Cerney GL7 7BZ   TEL: (01285) 831281

In the midst of glorious Cotswold countryside, in a shady location on the banks of the River Churn, stands this rambling, creeper-covered pink-washed inn. Inside, the main bar area is just what you'd expect from its age and location, warm and welcoming with a flagstone and tiled floor, a hop-adorned beamed ceiling, panelled walls, a lot of pewter, brass and china, and two large stone fireplaces. The bar menu lists lunchtime sandwiches of bacon, lettuce and tomato, say, or Caesar salad with smoked chicken, alongside beef and mushroom pie with a horseradish suet crust, or haddock and chips, augmented by a blackboard of daily specials. In addition, the carte offers such dishes as chicken breast stuffed with basil and mozzarella, wrapped in smoked bacon and served with red pepper mash and a tomato and red wine compote, or roasted breast of duck with a vegetable spring roll, sautéed potatoes and a bramble and apple sauce. Hook Norton Best Bitter, Bathurst Brew and Cotswolds Way are on handpump. Care and effort have gone into the compilation of the wine list, which makes a discernible attempt to offer a variety of flavours at sensible prices. Six are priced at £2.50 for a small glass, with medium and large sizes also available. SAMPLE DISHES: baked North Cerney goats' cheese in roasted pepper with garlic croûton and mixed olives £5; slow-cooked lamb shank with fondant potatoes and bean and Old Spot sausage casserole £11.50; vanilla cheesecake with forest fruit coulis £4.

Licensee James Walker (freehouse)
Open 11 to 3, 6 to 11, Sun 12 to 3, 7 to 10.30; bar food and restaurant 12 to 2, 7 to 9 (9.30 Sat and Sun)
Details Children welcome   Car park   Wheelchair access (not WC)   Garden   Background music   Dogs welcome   Delta, Diners, MasterCard, Switch, Visa   Accommodation: 5 rooms, B&B £45 to £70

NORTH SHIELDS   Tyne & Wear   map 10

Magnesia Banks

Camden Street, North Shields NE30 1AH   TEL: (0191) 257 4831

The large and impressive Victorian building is not far from the fishing quay at North Shields, an area that has seen lots of gentrification in recent years. However, Magnesia Banks retains its traditional style, especially the old ceilings, ornamentation and mahogany bar, while dark walls are covered in advertisements announcing the pub's vibrant programme of attractions (music, quizzes, culinary theme nights, etc.) – this is a real community pub. Among the farther seating areas is one with a cosy log fire, while the recently added conservatory acts as a restaurant (and charges ten per cent more). While various snack menus crank up towards more substantial dishes like fish 'n' chips, or boeuf bourguignon, it's the blackboard of daily specials that offers the most interest, declaring lamb as the house speciality (the pub owns its own flock). Belsay Barn half-shoulder of lamb, marinated lamb steak, or lamb cutlets might feature, plus the likes of pan-fried tuna, and ribeye steak. On tap are Mordue Brewery's Workie Ticket and the Durham Brewery's Magus, plus up to five guest beers; or choose from 30-odd wines, with eight by the glass. SAMPLE DISHES: bresaola with Parmesan shavings £3.95; peppered venison steak £8.50; mixed berry pavlova £3.25.

Licensees Richard, Katherine and Dee Slade (freehouse)
Open Mon to Thur 11 to 11 (12 Fri and Sat), Sun 12 to 10.30; bar food and restaurant 12 to 10 (8.45 Sun)
Details Children welcome   Car park   Wheelchair access   No-smoking area in restaurant   Occasional live or background music   No dogs   Amex, Delta, Diners, MasterCard, Switch, Visa

NORTON   Shropshire   map 5

▲ Hundred House Hotel 🍺 ❦

Bridgnorth Road, Norton TF11 9EE   TEL: (01952) 730353
WEBSITE: www.hundredhouse.co.uk
on A442, 6m S of Telford

Outward appearances can sometimes be deceptive. Behind the unassuming symmetrical façade of this red-brick Georgian inn is a highly individual, beguilingly idiosyncratic hotel with red-brick, dark-panelled or red-painted walls, beamed ceilings,
boarded, tiled or carpeted floors, and – everywhere – bunches of dried flowers and
herbs adding a personal touch. The interior is a series of linked open-plan rooms,
with a separate no-smoking room at the back and a lovely flower-filled garden
outside. The Phillips family run it as a fine all-round operation founded on genuine
hospitality. Phillips Heritage Bitter (once brewed in-house and still brewed according
to a recipe owned by the family) tops the bill as regards real ale, but you can also
sample Highgate Saddlers Best Bitter, Old Tom and others. The menu is enhanced
by daily specials, and chef Stuart Phillips has some good ideas. Starters and light
snacks might include sweet potato soup with lemongrass and ginger or a duo of sushi
with lime-dressed salad as well as venison terrine. Main courses usher in everything
from roast sirloin of Shropshire beef to baked gurnard in a chilli and red pepper crust
with coriander beurre blanc. A separate à la carte menu moves up a gear for tea-
smoked duck breast with a warm pancake of confit duck salad in a sesame, orange and
ginger dressing, and roast breast of Bresse chicken with tarragon butter, potato gratin
and mushroom jus. Desserts take in the likes of raspberry crème brûlée and banana
and walnut pudding. Wines are the domain of David Phillips, who has earned his
spurs working in Australian vineyards. Four basic house wines are joined by a dozen
at £12.95 or £3.30 a glass and a list of around 30 bottles. SAMPLE DISHES: mussel risotto
with grilled langoustine £6; roast shoulder of pork with apple and lemon stuffing and
sage gravy £12; poached pear with pistachio ice cream and chocolate sauce £6.

Licensee Henry Phillips (freehouse)
Open 12 to 2.30, 6 to 11; bar food Mon to Sat 12 to 2.30, Sun to Fri 6 to 9.30, restaurant all week 12 to
2.30, 6 to 9.30; closed evening 26 Dec
Details Children welcome   Car park   Wheelchair access (also WC)   Garden and patio   No smoking in
restaurant   Occasional background music   Guide dogs only   Amex, Delta, Diners, MasterCard, Switch, Visa
Accommodation: 10 rooms, B&B £69 to £125

NORTON   Wiltshire   map 2

Vine Tree ♣ ♣

Foxley Road, Norton SN16 0JP   TEL: (01666) 837654
village signposted off A429 1½m N of M4 junction 17

This sixteenth-century former mill used to serve beverages through the front windows
to passing carriages; nowadays the action has moved inside to a series of small, linked
open-plan areas decorated with lots of quirky artefacts, prints on walls the colour of
tomato purée, and tables set with fat candles. On the food front, there is no blackboard
of daily specials for the simple reason that the main printed menu changes every day.
The style is direct and down to earth, and makes a far better impression than some of
the ostensibly fancier menus offered in other establishments. Starters have included

ham hock and vegetable terrine with grain mustard coulis, and confit of corn-fed chicken with shiitake and mango terrine and pear chutney, while typical among main courses are locally shot wood pigeon with thyme mash, provençale bourride with aïoli, and wild sea bass fillet with scallop, leek and herb risotto and a vanilla jus. Finish perhaps with Cointreau and orange soufflé with chocolate sauce. A regularly changing line-up of real ales might feature Fuller's London Pride, Donoghue Fiddler's Elbow, St Austell Tribute, Badger Best Bitter and Butcombe Bitter, while the wine list covers a good range of styles and prices and includes 20 or so wines by the glass. SAMPLE DISHES: seared rare tuna niçoise £6.25; braised shoulder of Welsh salt-marsh lamb with an Irish stew and herb dumplings £11; passion-fruit financier with strawberry clotted cream ice cream and mango sauce £4.75.

Licensees Charles Walker and Tiggi Wood (freehouse)
Open 12 to 3, 6 to 11, Sun 12 to 10.30; bar food Mon to Sat 12 to 2 (2.30 Sat), 6 to 9.30, Sun 12 to 9.45 (12 to 3, 6.30 to 9.30 winter); closed 25 Dec
Details Children welcome   Car park   Wheelchair access (also WC)   Garden and patio   No-smoking area Occasional live or background music   Dogs welcome   Amex, Delta, Diners, MasterCard, Switch, Visa

NORWICH   Norfolk   map 6

Wig and Pen 🍺 NEW ENTRY
6 St Martins Palace Plain, Norwich NR3 1RN   TEL: (01603) 625891

'A good all-round popular pub' was the verdict of one visitor, taken by the homely, friendly atmosphere of this seventeenth-century inn at the north side of Norwich cathedral (great cathedral views from window seats in the main bar). It finds favour with an assortment of young and old, locals and visitors, drawn by the range of well-cared-for ales and good pub food at fair prices, and it can get lively in the evenings. The bar menu sticks to pub standards – deep-fried Brie wedges, nachos, steaks, cod and chips, burgers and mixed grills – with regularly updated fish and game specials (from Howard's, the nearby fishmonger and game dealer) a feature of the blackboards. Otherwise, broccoli and Stilton soup, Moroccan lamb couscous, steak and mushroom pie, and goulash are typical choices. Finish with lemon mousse cake or chocolate lumpy bumpy. The line-up of draught beers is an impressive sight for enthusiasts: among them might be Adnams Southwold Bitter, Iceni Gold, Oulton Wet and Windy, and Fuller's London Pride. Around ten wines are sold by the glass. SAMPLE DISHES: filo-wrapped tiger prawns £4.75; crispy chilli chicken £7.25; hot chocolate fudge cake £3.

Licensee Craig McLaren (freehouse)
Open 11.30 to 11, Sun 12 to 5; bar food all week 12 to 2.30 (3 Sat and Sun), Mon to Sat 6 to 9.30
Details No children   Car park   Wheelchair access (not WC)   Patio   No smoking in eating area Background music   No dogs   Delta, MasterCard, Switch, Visa

NOSS MAYO   Devon   map 1

Ship Inn
Noss Mayo PL8 1EW   TEL: (01752) 872387   **WATERSIDE**
WEBSITE: www.nossmayo.com
from A379 E of Plymouth, turn S on B3186 and follow Noss Mayo signs

Linger too long at this waterside pub at the head of an inlet and you may find your car stranded in the car park, which is cut off from the road at high tide. It's easy to understand why you might want to hang around: the pub has been decorated with a stylish, contemporary nautical feel and has a friendly and relaxed vibe, ideal for sitting by the log fire with a newspaper and a leisurely pint of Summerskills Tamar, Princeton Dartmoor, Blackawton Westcountry Gold, or Thatcher's cider. Food, served in the bar or first-floor eating areas, spans smart sandwiches (mozzarella, tomato and basil, for example) and a list of traditional-style dishes such as fish pie, calf's liver with leek, bacon and onion mash, moules marinière (using mussels from the River Yealm), and a few more exotic options such as duck breast with noodles and pak choi. Most wines on the neat, varied and enthusiastically annotated list are priced from £15 to £20, and nine are available by the large or small glass. SAMPLE DISHES: Dartmouth smoked trout with smoked tomato salad £6; poached fillet of John Dory on spinach with spring onion croquettes and crayfish sauce £13; dark chocolate and raspberry torte £4.50.

Licensee Bruce Brunning (freehouse)
Open 11 to 11, Sun 12 to 10.30; bar food 12 to 9
Details Children welcome in non-bar areas before 7pm   Car park   Wheelchair access (also WC)   Patio   No smoking upstairs   No music   Dogs welcome downstairs   Delta, MasterCard, Switch, Visa

NOTTINGHAM   Nottinghamshire   map 5

Bell Inn   NEW ENTRY

18 Angel Row, Nottingham NG1 6HL   TEL: (0115) 947 5241
WEBSITE: www.thebell-inn.com

The Bell looks like an oversized doll's house, with its irregular windows, antique lantern, custard-yellow walls and black woodwork. Within, its great age is obvious (the building dates from 1437), with a long flagstone passage giving access to small bars on either side and opening into a hugely atmospheric part-panelled and beamed main bar. Food is available all day, served either in the bar or in the fully panelled Belfry restaurant upstairs. The cooking is down to earth and good value, and the menu doesn't venture far beyond garlic-breaded mushrooms, fried breadcrumbed plaice, burgers, steak and kidney pudding, and lasagne, but portions are generous and everything is freshly cooked; rolls, sandwiches and jacket potatoes, also available all day, provide lighter snacks. This is a Hardys and Hanson tenancy, so expect the brewery's Bitter, Mild, and Olde Trip as well as regularly changing guest ales. Some dozen reasonably priced wines are offered by the glass and bottle. SAMPLE DISHES: sweet-and-sour chicken balls £2.75; cod Mornay £6; banana bounty £3.75.

Licensee Brian John Rigby (Hardys and Hanson)
Open 10.30am to 11pm, Sun 12 to 10.30; bar food 10.30am to 8pm, Sun 12 to 6, restaurant 12 to 3
Details Children welcome in restaurant   Garden   Live or background music   Dogs welcome in bar only   Delta, MasterCard, Switch, Visa

Victoria Hotel 🍺

Dovecote Lane, Beeston, Nottingham NG9 1JG   TEL: (0115) 925 4049
3m SW of Nottingham city centre, off A6005 in Beeston; pub next to railway station

This former Victorian railway hotel in a suburb of Nottingham, just a few miles south-west of the city centre, has a friendly, lively clientele, a warming fire, racks of newspapers, and live jazz on Monday nights, and is something of a mecca for real ale fans. Choices in the ever-changing range are listed on a blackboard, typically including locally brewed Castle Rock Hemlock Best Bitter, Everards Tiger Best, Deuchars IPA, Bateman XB, Caledonian IPA and Bass, along with guests. The daily-changing menus are also chalked on a blackboard. They offer a tempting range of dishes in a modern Mediterranean-influenced style, with half of the repertoire made up of interesting vegetarian options: say, dolcelatte and rocket tartlet on garlic potatoes with salad, or red Thai vegetable curry. There might be cozido à Portuguese for meat eaters – a traditional Iberian casserole with pork, chorizo, black pudding, tomato, paprika and broad beans – or classic bar staples such as sausages and chilli con carne. Prices on the wine list open at £9 a bottle, £2.30 a glass; around 15 are served by the glass. SAMPLE DISHES: chicken liver pâté £4.75; chicken italienne £9.50; coffee liqueur cheesecake £3.50.

Licensees Neil Kelso and Graham Smith (freehouse)
Open 11 to 11, Sun 12 to 10.30; bar food and restaurant 12 to 8.45 (7.45 Sun)
Details No children after 8pm Car park Wheelchair access (also WC) Garden and patio No smoking in restaurant Live music Dogs welcome in bar only MasterCard, Switch, Visa

NUNNINGTON   North Yorkshire   map 9

Royal Oak

Church Street, Nunnington YO62 5US   TEL: (01439) 748271
off B1257, 2m N of Hovingham, adjacent to church

The Royal Oak is a useful staging post for tourists and travellers heading towards the North York Moors National Park, with Nunnington Hall (National Trust) worth visiting. It's a quaint old pub in a sprawling rural village of attractive stone houses. Inside are bare stone walls, beams and standing timbers, and a collection of horse brasses, old black iron keys, stone jugs and various oddments like ploughshares, iron pots and copper urns hanging from the beams. On handpump are Tetley Bitter as well as Theakston Best and Old Peculier, and seven wines are sold by the glass. The cooking is built around a mainstay of classic pub dishes, such as ploughman's, mushrooms stuffed with Stilton pâté, lasagne, chicken breast in cheese and mustard sauce, and steak pie, while on the lunchtime blackboard there are open rolls with a good choice of fillings, with further specials expanding the choice in the evening. SAMPLE DISHES: vegetable soup with lentils and bacon £4.25; crispy roast duckling with orange sauce £11.50; baked lemon cheesecake £4.50.

Licensee A.K. Simpson (freehouse)
Open Tue to Sat 12 to 2.30, 6.30 to 11, Sun 12 to 2.30, 7 to 10.30; bar food and restaurant 12 to 2, 6.30 (7 Sun) to 9
Details Children welcome in restaurant Car park Wheelchair access (also WC) Garden No smoking in restaurant No music No dogs MasterCard, Switch, Visa

OAKWOODHILL   Surrey   map 3

Punch Bowl Inn

Oakwoodhill RH5 5PU   TEL: (01306) 627249
off A29 Dorking to Horsham road, 5m NW of Horsham

'An example of a real old-fashioned, warm, comfortable pub', enthused one visitor to this attractive tile-hung Wealden-style pub that dates, in part, from the fourteenth century and stands at the edge of the hamlet. The cricket ground is opposite, and in summer you can sit at tables in the front garden and patio. The main, dark-beamed bar has bags of character, a cheerful mix of large log-burning inglenook fireplace, stone floor, pew-style benches, solid, scrubbed tables, horse brasses, horsy prints and old photographs of the pub. Adjoining dining areas, one with a pool table, are very well maintained. Blackboard menus stick mainly to pub staples, say steak, mushroom and Badger Ale pie, or braised lamb shank with mash and a 'good, tomatoey sauce', and curries or chilli, all served in hearty portions with lashings of fresh vegetables. Crispy duck salad with plum and soy dressing makes a more imaginative start, followed perhaps by fried red snapper fillet with mango lime and chilli salsa, and there could be banana crumble for dessert. Badger Dorset Best and Tanglefoot are on draught, and six wines are available by the glass, with the full list approaching 20 bottles. SAMPLE DISHES: warm chicken and bacon salad £6; Lincolnshire sausages, bubble and squeak and red onion jam £10; Eton Mess £4.

Licensees Phillip and Wendy Nisbet (Hall & Woodhouse)
Open 11 to 11, Sun 12 to 10.30; bar food Mon to Thur 12 to 2.15, 6.30 to 9.30, Fri and Sat 12 to 9.30, Sun 12 to 9
Details Children welcome in eating areas　Car park　Wheelchair access (not WC)　Garden and patio　No smoking in restaurant　Occasional live music; jukebox　Dogs welcome　Delta, MasterCard, Switch, Visa

OCKLEY　Surrey

map 3

Old School House

Stane Street, Ockley RH5 5TH　TEL: (01306) 627430
on A29 Bognor Regis road, 8m S of Dorking

SEAFOOD

At the southern end of the village, on the busy A29, this white-painted pub certainly looks as if it was once a school, and an old school bell hanging above the door provides confirmation of the fact. Dark beams and cream-painted walls set the tone in the modest bar, although the main business is eating rather than drinking. The printed menu majors on fish, ranging from chilli salt squid with spinach and citrus fruit salad to smoked haddock and leek risotto with a poached egg. More ambitious dishes are served in the more formal Bryce's Seafood Restaurant, where you can expect things like confit of Shetland salmon on braised Puy lentils with chorizo and cured ham, and roast fillet of Cornish cod on chickpea and chorizo cassoulet. Blackboard specials broaden the range, vegetarians will find a decent choice, and there could be Earl Grey-smoked duck on Waldorf salad, lasagne, or ribeye steak for meat eaters. A trio of real ales from Gale's brewery are a reminder that this is a pub, and wine drinkers should raise a smile at the sight of 15 house wines by the glass. The list continues with a well-chosen selection of 20 or so more serious bottles from around the world. SAMPLE DISHES: white fish soup with prawn dumplings £4.50; fishcakes with citrus mayonnaise £8; apple tarte Tatin £5.50.

Licensee Bill Bryce (freehouse)
Open 11 to 3, 6 to 11; bar food and restaurant 12 to 2.30, 6.30 to 9.30; closed Sun evening Nov, Jan and Feb
Details Children welcome　Car park　Wheelchair access (not WC)　Patio　No smoking in restaurant Occasional background music　Dogs welcome exc in restaurant　Delta, MasterCard, Switch, Visa

OLDBURY-ON-SEVERN　South Gloucestershire

map 2

Anchor Inn 🍺

Church Road, Oldbury-on-Severn BS35 1QA　TEL: (01454) 413331
off B4061, 2m NW of Thornbury

The Anchor is a sombre-looking building of rough old stone in a secluded position at the edge of a straggling village. Bright, colourful hanging baskets liven up the exterior, and posies on pine tables do the same in the tearoom-style dining area. This is in a modern extension while drinking takes place in the older part of the pub, which has exposed stone walls and a traditional pub atmosphere. One printed menu serves both areas – a longish list of mainly traditional dishes such as chicken and ham pie, roast beef with Yorkshire pudding and lasagne. Lighter options include pâté, home-baked ham, smoked salmon and a platter of Stilton and cheddar with pickles and wholemeal bread, and there is a range of salads. A superior line-up of real ales includes Butcombe Bitter, Wickwar BOB, Draught Bass and Theakston Old Peculier. Half of the 30 wines are available by the glass. SAMPLE DISHES: sautéed mushrooms in garlic butter with cheese and breadcrumb topping £4.25; chicken in red wine with bacon, thyme, onions and mushrooms £7.75; chocolate lumpy bumpy cheesecake £3.50.

Licensees Michael J. Dowdeswell and Alex de la Torre (freehouse)
Open Mon to Fri 11.30 to 2.30, 6.30 to 11, Sat 11.30 to 11, Sun 12 to 10.30; bar food and restaurant 11.30 to 2, 6.30 to 9.30, Sun 12 to 3.30, 6.30 to 9.30; closed evenings 25 and 26 Dec
Details Children welcome in restaurant   Car park   Wheelchair access (also WC)   Garden   No smoking in restaurant   No music   Dogs welcome exc in restaurant   Delta, MasterCard, Switch, Visa

OLD HEATHFIELD   East Sussex   map 3

Star Inn 🍇

Church Street, Old Heathfield TN21 9AH   TEL: (01435) 863570
WEBSITE: www.thebestpubsinsussex.co.uk
off B2203 or B2096, just S of Heathfield

The partly creeper-covered building began as a fifteenth-century hall house, but has been adapted over the years. It stands close to the church and has a large and very pretty garden. The inside seems more ancient than the outside: the bar has low ceilings, dark, worm-eaten beams and plain, warm-coloured décor; there's a wooden dado, wooden tables and wheelback chairs, and an open fire to warm winter visitors. This is very much an eating pub, and the lengthy menu (listed on blackboards) uses decent raw materials. Seafood chowder, or mussels with crusty bread make a good starter or lunchtime snack. Mains meanwhile run from gluten-free Cumberland sausages with mashed potatoes and a rich red-wine and onion gravy, via half a free-range duckling in honey and orange sauce, to fresh marlin wrapped in Cajun spices and served with mango and fresh pineapple salsa, green salad and new potatoes. For lubrication, there's Harveys Sussex Best Bitter, Shepherd Neame Spitfire and Hop Back Summer Lightning, plus six wines by the glass from a wine list offering over 40 bottles from £12.50 to £25, with plenty under £15. This is a sister establishment to the Horse & Groom a couple of miles away at Rushlake Green (see entry), with which it shares wine list, website and licensee Mike Chappell. SAMPLE DISHES: home-made chicken-liver and brandy pâté £5.50; Scottish sirloin with green peppercorn sauce £16; dark chocolate biscuit cake £5.

Licensees Mike Chappell and Fiona Airey (freehouse)
Open 11.30 to 3, 5.30 to 11, Sun 12 to 3, 7 to 10.30; bar food and restaurant 12 to 2.15 (2.30 Sat and Sun), 7 to 9.30 (9 Sun)
Details Children welcome   Car park   Wheelchair access   Garden   Background music   Dogs welcome in bar   Delta, MasterCard, Switch, Visa

OLD WARDEN Bedfordshire   map 6

Hare & Hounds NEW ENTRY

Old Warden SG18 9HQ   TEL: (01767) 627225

The Hare & Hounds makes a good first impression: from the outside it is a lovely old pub, in a prosperous, leafy village, with a garden that banks up towards woods. Much restoration has taken place inside, with coffee-coloured boxy leather sofas in front of a modern glass-fronted wood-burner in the tiny entrance bar, half-timbered walls shown off to great advantage with posh terracottas and sage greens; only loud pop music sounds an off-note. The printed menu is a well-chosen assortment of dishes, some staunchly old English, others tipping their hat to current trends. The kitchen places special emphasis on presentation and quality, and on any day you might find tomato and basil risotto, duck confit of 'gloriously rich flavours' served with lentils and young spinach leaves, 'absolutely delicious' calf's liver and bacon with caramelised onions and potato wedges, and a trio of local Shuttleworth pork (fillet, sausage and belly) with spring onion mash and apple sauce. Simpler dishes of Billingsgate haddock in beer batter with hand-cut chips and mushy peas, or char-grilled chicken breast with Caesar salad are to be found on the blackboard. Desserts are in the same mould: sticky toffee pudding with toffee sauce, or a duo of chocolate with mint anglaise. Wells Bombardier Premium Bitter is on handpump alongside Greene King IPA and Old Speckled Hen. The wine list is neat, modern and afford-able, with nine by the glass. SAMPLE DISHES: smoked duck breast pancake £7; lamb shank with roasted Mediterranean vegetables and a red wine and rosemary sauce £11; apple tart £5.

Licensees Jago Hurt and Jane Hasler (Chares Wells)
Open Tue to Sat and bank hol Mon 12 to 3, 6 to 11, Sun 12 to 10.30; bar food and restaurant Tue to Sat and bank hol Mon 12 to 2, 6.30 to 9.30, Sun 12 to 4; closed Sun evening winter
Details Children welcome in eating areas   Car park   Garden   No smoking in restaurant   Background music No dogs   Delta, MasterCard, Switch, Visa

OMBERSLEY Worcestershire   map 5

▲ Crown & Sandys

Ombersley WR9 0EW   TEL: (01905) 620252
off A449 Worcester to Kidderminster road, 4m W of Droitwich

There's no mistaking this 'very stark white and very pitch black' building, with its great curved Dutch gables and a pair of huge bay trees out front. Inside there are echoes of history in its centuries-old beams, but much of the action now takes place in a modern no-smoking 'bistro' with pale colours, exotic prints and 'tiny' square tables with faux marble tops. Flexible, easy-going staff keep things moving along smoothly. Fish is a big player on the menu – everything from cod and lemon sole to monkfish and tuna – 'cooked to your liking' with a choice of butters and sauces. Ingredients are impressively fresh, witness a warm salad of chicken, bacon and avocado with crisp leaves and a honey and Dijon mustard dressing. Elsewhere, expect dishes ranging from pork terrine, and chicken breast on a ragoût of leeks, bacon and prunes, to autumn vegetable risotto with spinach, feta cheese and tomato, plus puddings such as French apple tart. At lunchtime you can also get sandwiches and baguettes, plus robust main dishes like steak and kidney casserole. Beer drinkers should be pleased with real ales such as Banks's Bitter and Marston's Pedigree plus guests – perhaps Greene King IPA, Marston's Old Empire, or Quaffs and Shropshire Lad, both from the Wood Brewery – while wine buffs can dip into a substantial list that includes ten by the glass. SAMPLE DISHES: French onion soup with toasted croûtons £5; fried calf's liver on honey-roast parsnip mash with red wine and thyme jus £14; warm pecan pie with vanilla-scented crème fraîche £4.25.

Licensee Richard Everton (freehouse)
Open Mon to Fri 11.30 to 3.30, 5 to 11, Sat 11.30 to 11, Sun 12 to 10.30; bar food and restaurant Mon to Sat 11.30 to 2.30, 6 to 10, Sun 12 to 9
Details Children welcome Car park Wheelchair access (also WC) Garden and patio No smoking in restaurant Occasional background music No dogs Delta, MasterCard, Switch, Visa Accommodation: 3 rooms, B&B £55 to £65

OSMOTHERLEY North Yorkshire map 9

Golden Lion ☺
6 West End, Osmotherley DL6 3AA TEL: (01609) 883526

Hikers wishing to tackle the Lyke Wake Walk congregate in this pretty Yorkshire village before embarking on their trek. The stone-built White Lion, overlooking the green, was once solely a pub, although it now also does duty as a country restaurant. The main bar is smart but relaxed, with candles on the plain wooden tables, while upstairs is a slightly posher dining room with paper 'cloths' covering the tables. Menus cater for a wide range of tastes, with 20 or more choices per course. Soups, pasta, risottos and salads show up among the starters alongside, say, deep-fried soft-shell crab with lime mayonnaise, or roasted red pepper with fennel, tomato and mozzarella. Classic pub cooking is what to expect from main courses such as pan-fried cod with chips, lamb casserole with mash, or steak and kidney pie with a suet crust, although there are also a few bistro-style dishes like coq au vin, and pork with Parma ham, sage and Marsala sauce. Desserts are equally extensive, from 'very sherry' trifle to lemon and passion-fruit pavlova. Real ales are Timothy Taylor Landlord, Hambleton Bitter and John Smith's Bitter, and the list of around 30 wines opens with four house selections from £12 a bottle, also available by the glass. SAMPLE DISHES: avocado and king prawn salad £6.25; poussin chargrilled with rosemary and garlic £10; warm apple, prune and walnut cake with whipped cream £4.

Licensee C.F. Connelly (freehouse)
Open Mon to Fri 12 to 3.30 (4 summer), 6 to 11, Sat and Sun 12 to 11; bar food and restaurant 12 to 3.30, 6 to 11; closed 25 Dec
Details Children welcome Wheelchair access (not WC) Patio No-smoking area in bar, no smoking in restaurant Background music Dogs welcome Delta, MasterCard, Switch, Visa

OVINGTON Hampshire map 2

Bush Inn NEW ENTRY
Ovington SO24 0RE TEL: (01962) 732764

Hidden down meandering country lanes and set alongside the clear-running waters of the River Itchen, this gem of a seventeenth-century pub is 'almost a secret' one local reporter didn't want to divulge. The mood is relaxed: a series of dark and atmospheric small rooms around a central bar, lit by gas lamps, decorated with stuffed animals, fishing tackle and copper kettles, and warmed by a roaring winter log fire. If these features aren't enough of a draw, there is a short menu of appealing modern pub food offering, say, tempura shrimp, salad and jerk-seasoned fries, alongside simple classics such as beef and ale pie. Blackboard specials expand the choice with fresh fish and other seasonal choices. Stylish presentation of dishes adds to the enjoyment. Well-kept beers are from the Wadworth Brewery's range, including seasonal brews, and occasionally supplemented by guest ales. The short wine list throws up a couple of welcome surprises in William Fèvre's Chablis, and Water Wheel Shiraz from Australia, both of which are available by the glass (along with four others). SAMPLE DISHES: pan-fried mushrooms with garlic and green peppercorn butter £5.75; duck confit with frisée vinaigrette and sweet potato chips £11.75; mille-feuille white and dark chocolate mousse with strawberries £4.50.

Licensees Nick and Cath Young (Wadworth)
Open 11 to 3, 6 to 11, Sun 12 to 3, 7 to 10.30; bar food all week 12 to 2, Mon to Sat 7 to 9 (10 weekends summer)
Details Children welcome (but limited space for children)   Car park   Wheelchair access (also WC)   Garden   No smoking in 2 rooms   No music   Dogs welcome on a lead   Delta, MasterCard, Switch, Visa

OXSPRING   South Yorkshire   map 9

Waggon and Horses

Sheffield Road, Oxspring S36 8YQ   TEL: (01226) 763259
off A629, 1½m SE of Penistone

This former farmhouse became a pub some 150 years ago, originally serving navvies building the Penistone to Sheffield railway. Now a full-blown country pub with a cartwheel beside the front door and a log fire within, the Rafters bar is the one to aim for if you want a real old-fashioned pub atmosphere, a game of pool or darts, and a pint – fine Yorkshire ales Black Sheep Best Bitter and Timothy Taylor Landlord as well as Tetley Bitter are served. The main bar (dark pink carpet, cream-painted stone walls hung with ornamental brass trays and horse brasses) is more orientated towards eating, and a good-value menu of simple, traditional home cooking is offered throughout the day. Start perhaps with seafood gratin, or try black pudding with bacon, croûtons and a poached egg. Main courses typically include a range of steaks, fish 'n' chips with mushy peas, Yorkshire puddings with sausages and mashed potato, and a never-off-the-menu steak and vegetable pie, with lighter options of salads, such as cold roast beef, jacket potatoes, burgers and baguettes. All the wines on the short list come in under £12, and four are served by the glass. SAMPLE DISHES: smoked salmon cornets £5; tournedos Rossini £14; lime cheesecake £3.50.

Licensee Tony Brewis (freehouse)
Open 11 to 11, Sun 12 to 10.30; bar food and restaurant 11 to 9 (9.30 Fri and Sat), Sun 12 to 9
Details Children welcome   Car park   Wheelchair access (also WC)   Garden   No-smoking area in bar, no smoking in restaurant   Occasional live or background music   Guide dogs only   MasterCard, Switch, Visa

---

🏵 *indicates a pub serving better-than-average wine, including good choice by bottle and glass.*

A list of the top-rated pubs for food is at the front of the book.

PALEY STREET Berkshire map 3

Royal Oak NEW ENTRY

Paley Street SL6 3JN TEL: (01628) 620541
on B3024, off A330 just S of Maidenhead

'Unassuming pub from the outside, but with charm, character and appeal within' is how one reporter summed up this roadside pub. A tasteful revamp has brought stripped wall panelling and polished floorboards and has made the most of exposed brickwork, ceiling beams and timbers, while modern black leather chairs against polished tables, and a bistro-style dining area complete the look. Light walls provide a backdrop for an extensive array of TV chat show and cricketing mementos, leaving customers in no doubt that Michael Parkinson is Nick's dad. The food is straightforward, using decent raw materials and mixing a few modern ideas with the predominantly familiar: smoked haddock florentine, baked mushrooms with herb crumble and creamy pepper sauce, or grilled sirloin with mushrooms and tomatoes, for example, versus chorizo risotto, spicy Thai chicken cakes with coleslaw, and pan-fried duck on stir-fried noodles. Desserts tread a familiar line: say, Baileys crème brûlée, or chocolate bread-and-butter pudding. Fuller's London Pride is the only real ale on tap, and all six house wines are available by the glass. SAMPLE DISHES: warm crab, prawn and cheese tart with red pepper coulis £9; baked fillet of whiting with steamed courgettes and basil mayonnaise £13.90; chocolate bread-and-butter pudding with ice cream £6.50.

Licensee Nick Parkinson (freehouse)
Open all week 11 to 3, Mon to Sat 6 to 11; bar food 12 to 2, 6.30 to 10.30
Details Children welcome in restaurant   Car park   No wheelchair access   Courtyard   Non-smoking areas in restaurant   Background music   No dogs   Amex, Delta, Diners, MasterCard, Switch, Visa

PARRACOMBE Devon map 1

▲ Fox and Goose NEW ENTRY

Parracombe EX31 4PE TEL: (01598) 763239

The Fox and Goose may appear a rather stark village local – one reporter certainly felt that 'looks can be deceiving' – but those who venture in will be impressed by the food. The interior is adorned with plants, farm memorabilia, old village photographs, and general knick-knacks. Close inspection of the huge blackboards occupying one wall reveals a few surprises. Not only does fish dominate proceedings, but it is all landed locally along the north Devon coast: whole sea bass, for example, is caught off the Lundy Breaks, or there could be an intense, rich, thick fish soup, or turbot with saffron risotto. Moving along to the meat board, a few favourites catch the eye – steak, for example – or there's the more unusual steak and seaweed pie, plus Exmoor venison and freshly shot game in season. Small blackboards above the bar explain which farms (and farmers) produced the meat. Beers are a respectable selection tapped from the barrel and featuring Cotleigh Barn Owl Bitter and Exmoor Ale alongside Winkleigh cider, and ten wines are served by the glass. SAMPLE DISHES: smoked mackerel pâté £4.75; scallops and monkfish in sambuca and cream sauce £15; lemon pudding with lemon sauce £4.25.

Licensees P.J. Reed Evans and S.M. Dallyn (freehouse)
Open winter 12 to 2.30, 7 to 11 (10.30 Sun); summer 12 to 3, 5.30 to 11 (10.30 Sun); bar food and restaurant 12 to 2, 6 to 9; may be closed 25 Dec
Details Children welcome in bar eating area   Car park   Wheelchair access (not WC)   Patio   No smoking in restaurant   Jukebox   No dogs   MasterCard, Switch, Visa   Accommodation: 2 rooms, B&B £45

PARTRIDGE GREEN   West Sussex   map 3

Green Man   NEW ENTRY

Partridge Green RH13 8JT   TEL: (01403) 710250
WEBSITE: www.thegreenman.org

Partridge Green is a strung-out village with a green that's 'more common than green
with a few large houses dotted around', with the Green Man some distance away
alongside the road. It's a well-maintained building with a pleasant lawned garden,
water features and a patio. You can spot the intentions of the set-up as soon as you go
through the door. Much of the interior is given over to dining, with just one small bar
area dominated by a large table, with a cast-iron fireplace and large mirror adding
character; local ales Harveys Sussex Best Bitter and Horsham Best are on handpump.
The main dining room – L-shaped and open-plan, with another room off it – is decorated with bucolic prints and country bric-à-brac and has a 'quite upmarket' feel. A
printed menu offers a short list of light meals – perhaps honey-glazed chicken and
bacon salad – and main courses along the lines of lamb shank with orange mash and
root vegetable jus, or smoked haddock with bubble and squeak, spinach, a poached
egg and hollandaise, with a small selection of tapas (eel in garlic and olive oil, mussels
in chilli oil, boquerones, chorizo and so on) adding an extra dimension. A blackboard
extends the range with a sharp selection of modern dishes: say, grilled Mediterranean
vegetable stack with goats' cheese, pesto and sun-blush tomato dressing to start,
followed by crispy duck confit with sweet red cabbage and dauphinois potatoes, or
wild sea bass fillet in a herb crust with anchovy mash and courgettes provençale.
Desserts are in the same mould: rich dark chocolate and rum tart with coconut ice
cream, and pear, plum and apple soufflé pancake with cinnamon custard. Six wines
come by the glass from a reasonably priced list of 30-plus bottles. SAMPLE DISHES:
confit of guinea fowl on Puy lentils with a port reduction £6; steamed lemon sole fillet
with chive fish velouté £12; crème brûlée £4.75.

Licensee William Thornton (freehouse)
Open 11.30 to 3.30, 6.30 to 12, Sun 12 to 4.30; bar food and restaurant Mon to Sat 12 to 2, 7 to 9.30,
Sun 12 to 2.30; closed 26 Dec, 1 Jan
Details Children welcome in restaurant   Car park   Wheelchair access (not WC)   Garden and patio   No
smoking in restaurant   Background music   Dogs welcome in bar only   Amex, Delta, MasterCard, Switch, Visa

PAXFORD   Gloucestershire   map 5

▲ Churchill Arms ✿

Paxford GL55 6XH   TEL: (01386) 594000
WEBSITE: www.thechurchillarms.com
2m E of Chipping Campden

The tiny hamlet of old Cotswold stone and dry-stone walls has the Churchill Arms at
its centre, diagonally opposite the church. The L-shaped interior is open plan, with
bare floorboards and painted panelling: very much a pub, and used as such by the
locals. This is the setting for some sophisticated cooking, the dishes written on daily-
changing blackboards hung on a stone pillar. The nearest the style gets to traditional
pub fare are the chips, olive oil mash or boiled potatoes that can be served with main
courses, and sticky toffee pudding. Typical of starters are cauliflower soup with
poached quail's eggs and gremolata, or vanilla risotto with Gruyère, smoked haddock

and pancetta. Main courses could be pork belly with potato, chorizo and butternut broth and soy and balsamic sauce, monkfish with sweet-and-sour sauce and deep-fried okra, or lamb fillet with roasted fennel, ginger and sultanas. Hook Norton Best Bitter and two changing guest ales are on handpump, while the wine list offers around 25 bottles, with nine by the glass. Owned for many years by Leo and Sonya Brooke-Little, the pub was for sale as the Guide went to press. SAMPLE DISHES: chicken liver parfait with green tomato chutney £5.75; grilled flounder with sherry, rosemary and tomato £8.50; maple and mascarpone cheesecake with pineapple £5.

Licensee Leo Brooke-Little (freehouse)
Open 11.30 to 3, 6 to 11, Sun 12 to 3, 7 to 10.30; bar food 12 to 2, 7 to 9
Details Children welcome   Garden and patio   No music   No dogs   Delta, MasterCard, Switch, Visa
Accommodation: 4 rooms, B&B £40 to £70

PEMBRIDGE   Herefordshire   map 5

▲ New Inn

Market Square, Pembridge HR6 9DZ   TEL: (01544) 388427
on A44, between Kington and Leominster, 6m E of Kington

This New Inn is actually old, very old. The huge, ramshackle, black and white half-timbered building dates in part from the early fourteenth century and justifiably claims to be one of the oldest pubs in the country. The interior, 'all very homely and domestic', is divided into three separate areas – a convivial main bar, a no-smoking lounge and the restaurant – but the décor is uniform throughout: walls of exposed stone or painted terracotta, red patterned carpets, ancient pews, flowery watercolours, and subdued lighting from wall lamps and candles on the tables. Homespun cooking comes in gargantuan portions: seafood stew, mushrooms in garlic stuffed in a crois-sant, lamb fillet in redcurrant sauce, and beef and vegetable casserole with horseradish dumplings are all familiar points of reference. Kingdom Bitter comes all of six miles from the Dunn Plowman brewery in Kington, though the other beers are incomers: Fuller's London Pride, Black Sheep Bitter, and Timothy Taylor Landlord; there are also eight wines by the glass from £2. SAMPLE DISHES: smoked haddock and spring onion fishcakes £6; pork, apple and cider casserole with mustard dumplings £6.95; lemon chiffon pie £3.25.

Licensee Jane Melvin (freehouse)
Open 11 to 3 (2.30 winter), 6 to 11; bar food and restaurant 12 to 2, 6.30 to 9; closed first week Feb
Details Children welcome in eating areas   Car park   Patio   No smoking in restaurant   Occasional live music
No dogs   Delta, MasterCard, Switch, Visa   Accommodation: 6 rooms, B&B £20 to £40

PERRY WOOD   Kent   map 3

Rose & Crown

Perry Wood, nr Selling ME13 9RY   TEL: (01227) 752214
from A251 at Sheldwich, take road for Selling, continue through village and take right turn signposted Perry Wood

Garlands of dried hops and a vast collection of corn dollies create a genuinely rustic impression in the bar of this welcoming old pub hidden away in a maze of single-track roads. One menu is served throughout, and the food is good honest stuff, including home-made pies (chicken, ham and leek, for example), fishcakes with apple and rosemary sauce, or cheesy cottage pie, jazzed up with a few more exotic ideas that may run to Chinese crispy chilli beef, salmon Creole, and chicken balti. Baked potatoes, rolls and ploughman's are also on offer. To finish, take your pick from the array of desserts in the display cabinet. Real ale fans will be in their element here: four first-class beers are on offer at a time, all served in peak condition. Goacher's Mild, Harveys Sussex Best Bitter and Adnams Bitter are the regulars, joined by a guest ale, perhaps from the Cottage Brewery in Somerset. Wine drinkers are offered a handful by the glass from a modest, affordable list of 14 bins. On fine days you can eat and drink in the award-winning garden, which has a good children's play area and an aviary. A short walk through the woods leads to fine panoramic views of the surrounding countryside. SAMPLE DISHES: spaghetti bolognese £6; chicken breast in apple and cider £8.50; caramel and amaretti sponge cake £3.25.

Licensees Richard and Jocelyn Prebble (freehouse)
Open 11 to 3, 6.30 to 11, Sun 11.45 to 3, 7 to 10.30; bar food all week 12 to 2, Mon to Sat 7 to 9.30, restaurant Sat 7 to 9.30, Sun 12 to 2; closed evenings 25 and 26 Dec, 1 Jan
Details Children welcome   Car park   Garden and patio   No smoking in restaurant   Background music Dogs welcome on a lead   Delta, MasterCard, Switch, Visa

PETER TAVY   Devon   map 1

Peter Tavy Inn 🌑 🍺

Peter Tavy PL19 9NN   TEL: (01822) 810348
off A386, 2m NE of Tavistock

It may be only two miles from the A386, but this pretty village on the western flanks of Dartmoor feels remote, and its much-extended fifteenth-century pub is a great spot at which to start and finish a moorland walk. It sports a cracking old bar – black beams, a highly polished slate floor, rustic pine tables and high-backed settles – warmed by a wood-burner, with a newer extension blending well by incorporating old beams, sturdy furnishings and a log fire. Lunch delivers straightforward snacks such as Devon cheese ploughman's as well as filled baguettes and jacket potatoes, plus anything from chicken and bacon tartlet or roast beef with Yorkshire pudding to ham, egg and chips or game casserole. Evening blackboards bring more invention: say, crab and avocado tian, or goats' cheese and pancetta salad to start, then pan-fried red mullet with an olive and tomato salsa, or pan-fried pheasant suprême with pear and Stilton sauce. Finish with Turkish delight with white chocolate mousse, or sticky toffee pudding. The commendably local real ales on offer are Princetown Jail Ale, Summerskills Tamar, Sharp's Doom Bar Bitter, and Tavy Tipple from Blackawton. The concise wine list begins with French house wines at £8.75 (just two still wines cost over £20), and around eight come by the glass. SAMPLE DISHES: chunky vegetable soup £3.75; duck breast with plum sauce £13.50; apple and apricot crumble £3.75.

Licensees Graeme and Karen Sim (freehouse)
Open 12 to 2.30, 6 to 11, Sun 12 to 3, 6 to 10.30; bar food 12 to 2, 6.30 to 9; closed evening 24 Dec, 25 Dec, evenings 26 and 31 Dec
Details Children welcome in eating area   Car park   Garden and patio   No smoking in eating area Background music   Dogs welcome   Delta, MasterCard, Switch, Visa

A list of pubs serving exceptional draft beers is at the back of the book.

PHILLEIGH   Cornwall   map I

Roseland Inn

Philleigh TR2 5NB   TEL: (01872) 580254
take Philleigh turning off A3078 5m N of St Mawes

The Roseland Inn, a sixteenth-century cob-built pub on a narrow country lane close
to the parish church, certainly lives up to its name in summer, when the whitewashed
façade and sun-trap terrace are festooned with roses. The tranquil location draws visitors away from the coast in summer, and on winter Saturday evenings the place can be
a tad lively as it doubles as the clubhouse for the Roseland Rugby Club (hence the
corner dedicated to rugby trophies and mementoes). At all times, 'a super cottage-like
atmosphere is maintained' through beams, half-timbering, old-fashioned settles on
worn slate floors, and a roaring fire in winter. The focus is on food, with dishes ranging from traditional pub favourites like Cornish pasty, steak and mushroom pie, local
pork sausages with mash, sandwiches and soups, to more imaginative dishes highlighting local fish and game. Start with potted Cornish crab, or a locally smoked fish
platter with sushi, ginger and cracked pepper mayonnaise, perhaps, then go on to
herb-crusted halibut with roasted sweet pepper jus, or venison steak with red onion
marmalade, sweet potato mash and Stilton jus. Sharp's Doom Bar Bitter and Cornish
Coaster are on handpump, alongside Bass and Ringwood in summer, and there's
Callestick cider from Penhallow. Eight wines are served by the glass. SAMPLE DISHES:
warm goats' cheese salad with balsamic vinaigrette and sun-blush tomatoes £7; sea
bass fillets on celeriac mash with sesame seed dressing £14; double crème caramel
with sweet peach confit £5.

Licensees Colin and Jacquie Phillips (Pubmaster)
Open 11 to 3, 5.30 to 11 (11 to 11 summer); bar food and restaurant 12 to 2, 6 to 9
Details Children welcome   Car park   Wheelchair access (also WC)   Garden   No smoking in restaurant
Occasional live music   Dogs welcome   Delta, MasterCard, Switch, Visa

PICKERING   North Yorkshire   map 9

▲ White Swan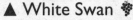

Market Place, Pickering YO18 7AA   TEL: (01751) 472288
WEBSITE: www.white-swan.co.uk

The unassuming exterior of this centrally located sixteenth-century coaching inn
belies its sophisticated and modern interior. A tiny bar (just three small tables) has
been styled in a 'smart, quite contemporary fashion' with taupe-coloured walls and
chocolate-brown leather banquettes and is warmed by a small winter fire; the slightly
larger lounge sports plum walls, winged armchairs and antique pine furniture. The
daily-changing printed menu, available throughout, 'reads very well indeed' with the
likes of chicken liver pâté with pear and date chutney, red chard and ricotta gnocchi
with warm tomato vinaigrette, and Yorkshire blue cheese and onion tart with watercress and mustard seed salad listed among the starters. Locally landed fish pie with a
free-range egg and parsley sauce, pan-fried Harome free-range duck breast with celeriac purée and Agen prunes, and grilled sea bass fillet with risotto nero and basil are
typical of main-course choices, and classic crème brûlée with rum-soaked raisins and
apple crisps may be hard to resist. Staff are 'excellent, smiling and friendly' and 'very
helpful', according to a reporter. To drink, there's Yorkshire-brewed ales such as Best

and Special from Black Sheep in Masham, and Goldfield from Hambleton of Thirsk, with about a dozen wines by the glass. The wine list is split into two parts: the first roams the world, finding plenty of good drinking around £20; the second is a specialist and more expensive range of clarets from St-Emilion that reflects the owner's passion for this region. SAMPLE DISHES: smoked venison with rocket and loganberries £7.25; braised shin beef with root vegetables and parsley creamed potatoes £12; peach melba fool with fruit and nut biscotti £5.

Licensee Victor Buchanan (freehouse)
Open 11 to 11, Sun 12 to 10.30; bar food and restaurant 12 to 2, 7 to 9
Details Children welcome exc in 1 bar Car park Wheelchair access (also WC) Garden and patio No smoking in 1 bar and restaurant No music Dogs welcome exc in restaurant Amex, Delta, MasterCard, Switch, Visa Accommodation: 12 rooms, B&B £70 to £150

PICKHILL   North Yorkshire   map 8

▲ Nag's Head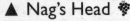

Pickhill YO7 4JG   TEL: (01845) 567391
WEBSITE: www.nagsheadpickhill.co.uk

Though nowadays much extended, the 200-year-old Nag's Head maintains the country inn tradition, providing food and accommodation for visitors exploring an area steeped in history or attending nearby race meetings. The tap room has Hambleton Bitter and Stallion from Thirsk, John Smith's and Black Sheep Best Bitter and Old Peculier on tap. Summer meals may be taken under a verandah at the front, otherwise eat in the smart library-themed dining room, or the dark-panelled bar, with its green velour bench seating and close-set tables. Dishes, chalked on boards, range from classics like cottage pie, hot chilli and rice, or a savoury seafood crumble 'with good fish content', to more contemporary avocado, walnut, celery and apple salad with a good dressing, followed, perhaps, by duck breast with lime, ginger and honey marinade and crispy roast leg, and cranberry crème brûlée to finish. Four wines of the month are all under £15 (from £3.50 for 175ml) and well above normal 'house wine' standards. The focus is on traditional regions and the main list should please enthusiasts with good names in mature vintages at reasonable prices. SAMPLE DISHES: smoked salmon with scrambled egg £7; apricot- and celeriac-stuffed pork tenderloin with spicy mango dressing £12.25; Yorkshire curd tart with raspberry coulis and crème fraîche £4.

Licensees Raymond and Edward Boynton (freehouse)
Open 11 to 11; bar food and restaurant 12 to 2, 6 to 9.30
Details Children welcome in eating area of bar Car park Wheelchair access (also WC) Garden and patio No smoking in restaurant Background music No dogs exc in accommodation MasterCard, Switch, Visa Accommodation: 16 rooms, B&B £40 to £90

PILLEY   Hampshire   map 2

Fleur de Lys

Pilley Street, Pilley SO41 5QB   TEL: (01590) 672158
off A337, 1m NW of Lymington

Parts of this thatched, whitewashed building date from 1096, making the Fleur de Lys a strong candidate for the title 'oldest pub in the New Forest', although the roll call of landlords on display in the entrance starts from 'only' 1498. The place consists of three interconnecting rooms, with a hotchpotch of bric-à-brac giving it true rustic style, but maintaining a public-bar atmosphere in one room and an unpretentious lounge-bar feel in the other two. The printed menu deals in the likes of crispy pork hock with apple and honey sauce, steak and kidney pie ('a real proper pie with a top and bottom'), and steaks, and there are a few options for vegetarians; look out for the appetisingly named 'smelly chips' served as a starter. Garlic bread with cheese and chilli, potato skins with cheese and bacon, and salads such as chicken Caesar make good snacks, and at lunchtime you can also get 'sarnies and stixs' with various fillings. Locally brewed Ringwood Best and Fortyniner are kept in good order. The pub also has a globetrotting list of 20 or so reasonably priced wines, with 12 house selections from £2.60 a glass, £10.35 a bottle. SAMPLE DISHES: hot game bangers and tomato chutney sarnie £3.75; ostrich rump with rich port gravy £16; bread-and-butter pudding (price not supplied).

Licensees Neil and Lolly Rogers (Enterprise Inns)
Open 11 to 3, 6 to 11, Sun 12 to 3, 7 to 10.30; bar food 12 to 2, 6.30 (7.30 Sun) to 9.30 (9 Sun); closed evenings 25 and 26 Dec
Details Children welcome in family room   Car park   Garden and patio   No-smoking area in bar
Occasional background music   Dogs welcome on a lead   Delta, MasterCard, Switch, Visa

---

PLUCKLEY   Kent   map 3

▲ Dering Arms

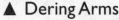

Station Road, Pluckley TN27 0RR   TEL: (01233) 840371
WEBSITE: www.deringarms.com
off B2077, close to Pluckley railway station

It may look impressively ancient, but the Dutch-gabled Dering Arms dates from the 1840s – built as a hunting lodge serving the Dering Estate. Unusually, it is an exact replica, on a smaller scale, of the long-gone manor house it once served. Enter the central entrance, itself recessed between two protruding wings, and the interior is as imposing as the exterior, although the bar areas are small and traditional: bare wood everywhere, old chairs with wonky leather seats, a haphazard collection of wall decorations, including a stuffed fish, and dim lighting. Starters of Sussex smokies (smoked mackerel) in a creamy cheese sauce, or game terrine with redcurrant vinaigrette, and main courses of confit of duck with bubble and squeak and wild mushroom sauce are what to expect on the bar menu. The same starters are served in the candlelit restaurant, where fish is the focus: main courses of perhaps monkfish in bacon, orange and cream sauce, or grilled red mullet with red pepper, tomato and basil olive oil. Pheasant casseroled with sherry and tarragon might be there for meat eaters, with something indulgent like chocolate fudge cake with a warm walnut sauce among desserts. Dering Ale is brewed exclusively for the pub by Goacher's of Maidstone, and an extensive wine list is supplemented by a blackboard selection of regularly changing house wines by the glass or bottle, starting at £10.95. It is worth noting that the pub is well over a mile from Pluckley village, next to the railway station. SAMPLE DISHES: crab Newburg £5; fillet of black bream with samphire and beurre blanc £15; lemon posset £5.

Licensee James Buss (freehouse)
Open 11.30 to 3.30, 6 to 11, Sun 12 to 3, 7 to 10.30; bar food and restaurant 12 to 2, 7 to 10; closed 26 to 28 Dec
Details Children welcome   Car park   Wheelchair access (not WC)   Garden   No music   Dogs welcome
Amex, Delta, Diners, MasterCard, Switch, Visa   Accommodation: 3 rooms, B&B £30 to £42.50

PLUSH Dorset   map 2

Brace of Pheasants NEW ENTRY

Plush DT2 7RQ   TEL: (01300) 348357
off B3143, 2m N of Piddletrenthide

The Pheasants is a 'charming and spruce' pub of white-painted rough stone with a
neat thatched roof. Inside, it has a decidedly traditional look, with a large brick fireplace, prints and copper kitchen utensils on the walls, beams lined with horse brasses
and the eponymous stuffed birds in a glass case. The separate dining room has similar
décor, but tables are laid with blue and yellow cloths and fresh flowers. The daily-
changing menu lists bistro-style dishes such as wild duck, pheasant and partridge
terrine with toasted brioche to start, and main courses of smoked haddock fillet on
butternut squash purée with a poached egg and butter sauce, or calf's liver and bacon
with black pudding, mash and rosemary gravy. A decent selection of real ales typically
includes Butcombe Bitter, Adnams and Fuller's London Pride, plus Stowford Press
cider, and a short but varied list of bottles, priced from £12.50 has ten wines available
by the glass. SAMPLE DISHES: grilled goats' cheese and balsamic onions on tasted focaccia £6.50; wild sea bass fillets with sautéed potatoes, chargrilled asparagus and herby
butter sauce £17; black grape brioche and butter pudding £5.

Licensees Toby and Suzi Albu (freehouse)
Open *Tue to Sun 12 to 2.30, 7 to 11 (10.30 Sun); bar food and restaurant 12.30 to 2.30, 7.30 to 9.30*
Details *Children welcome   Car park   Wheelchair access (not WC)   Garden   No smoking in 1 dining room*
Occasional live music   Dogs welcome exc in eating areas   Delta, MasterCard, Switch, Visa

PORTHLEVEN Cornwall   map 1

Ship Inn

Porthleven TR13 9JS   TEL: (01326) 564204
off B3304, 2m SW of Helston, on W side of harbour

WATERSIDE

Few pubs around the Cornish coast can boast the Ship's stunning location: set in the
cliffside and perched on the harbour wall, it enjoys views across the quaint working
harbour and out to sea from all windows. On wild winter days you may have to dodge
crashing waves and spray to reach the pub door, but in summer the view and setting
are best appreciated from the series of terraced lawns that rise up the cliff behind the
pub. There's an extensive choice of fairly conventional items such as jacket potatoes,
ploughman's and sandwiches; no-frills main courses take in steaks, chilli, gammon
steak with pineapple, and chicken tikka masala. A platter of locally smoked fish, crab
thermidor, Cornish fish pie, and mussels steamed in creamy white wine and garlic
sauce show a touch more ambition, and 'Kiddies' Meals' include locally made beef
burgers and sausages. Caramel apple pie and syrup sponge with chocolate sauce are
typical desserts. On draught are Courage Best Bitter, Greene King Abbot Ale, and
Sharp's Doom Bar Bitter. As for wine, there are a dozen to choose from, with a handful by the glass. SAMPLE DISHES: grilled goats' cheese on a pesto croûton with gooseberry sauce £5; crab and prawn Mornay £11.50; lemon meringue pie £4.

Licensee Colin Oakden (freehouse)
Open *11.30 to 11, Sun 12 to 10.30; bar food 12 to 2, 7 to 9; closed 25 Dec*
Details *Children welcome in family room   Garden   No smoking in family room   Background music   Dogs*
welcome   Amex, Delta, MasterCard, Switch, Visa

PORTSMOUTH   Hampshire   map 2

American Bar   NEW ENTRY

58 White Hart Road, Portsmouth PO1 2JA   TEL: (023) 9281 1585
WEBSITE: www.americanbar.co.uk
next to Isle of Wight ferry terminal

In summer there are zinc tables outside on the pavement, but the main action takes
place in the long, thin bar. A vaguely maritime theme prevails – a model of a sailing
boat, some photographs of fishermen, and odd bits of marine brass – for the building
is next to the Isle of Wight ferry terminal and opposite the fish market; proximity to
the latter greatly influences the menu. Immaculately fresh fish chalked up on the
daily-changing board might include sea bream with citrus butter, and whole plaice on
the bone with prawns and mushrooms. A printed menu of modern pub staples
expands the choice with starters such as duck liver pâté with orange marmalade,
followed by ham hock with honey and a grain mustard glaze, or sirloin steak with
herb butter and frites. Both menus are served in the bar and no-smoking conservatory
restaurant at lunch and in the evening, with 'Afternoon at the American', a simpler
menu offered from noon to 6pm, delivering good-value classics such as bangers 'n'
mash, fish 'n' chips, and baguettes. Courage Directors is on handpump alongside a
guest such as Gale's HSB. A short but serviceable global wine list has 15 by the glass.
SAMPLE DISHES: seared squid and chorizo with chilli-infused oil £4.50; skate wing in
garlic butter £10; chocolate nemesis £4.50.

Licensee Christopher Fisher (Enterprise Inns)
Open *11 to 11, Sun 12 to 10.30; bar food and restaurant 12 to 10.15 (11 Fri and Sat)*
Details *Children welcome   Garden and patio   No smoking in restaurant   Background music   Dogs welcome*
Amex, Delta, MasterCard, Switch, Visa

POULTON   Gloucestershire   map 2

Falcon Inn 🏵 🏵 🍇

London Road, Poulton GL7 5HN   TEL: (01285) 850844
on A417, between Cirencester and Fairford

A pair of stone falcons stand guard by the large fireplace in this dyed-in-the-wool
traditional village pub. The interior still has its quota of low ceilings, beams and a long
bar with stools for drinkers, but added to these are now three separate dining rooms
for those wanting to eat. The cooking is straight, true and consistent across the board;
dishes are uncluttered, and presentation makes the most of simply handled, top-class
raw materials (perhaps seafood from New Wave in Fairford and rare-breed meats
from Chesterton Farm in Cirencester). The monthly-changing menu, which charts a
modern European course, might open with smoked haddock, cheese and leek tart
with home-made pear chutney alongside ballotine of chicken stuffed with basil and
pine nuts, before confit of Barbary duck leg with a cassoulet of butter beans,
carbonade of venison, or roast fillet of cod with Vichy carrots and crispy bacon.
Skilfully crafted desserts span anything from apple, butterscotch and prune compote
to pistachio soufflé. At lunchtime, there's a shorter menu of similar dishes, plus sandwiches made with home-baked bread (including the Falcon chip butty). Hook
Norton Best Bitter is on draught along with a guest such as West Berkshire Good Old
Boy or Donnington SBA. A trim wine list concentrates on quality names from around

the world with eight by the glass from £2.85 to £3.95 covering the flavour spectrum. SAMPLE DISHES: pea and ham soup with truffle oil and Parmesan crisp £5.50; pan-fried fillet of salmon with basil sauce and rösti £13; orange parfait with almond praline and chocolate sauce £5.50.

Licensees Robin Couling and Jeremy Lockley (freehouse)
Open 11 to 3, 7 to 11, Sun 12 to 3, 7 to 10.30; bar food 12 to 2.30, 7 to 9.30
Details Children welcome in eating areas　Car park　Wheelchair access (also WC)　Patio　No smoking in 2 rooms　Background music　No dogs　Delta, MasterCard, Switch, Visa

PRESTBURY　Cheshire　　　　　　　　　　　　　　　　　　　　　map 8

▲ Legh Arms　NEW ENTRY

Bollin Grove, Prestbury SK10 4DG　TEL: (01625) 829130

Named after a local landowning family that still lives a couple of miles away at Adlington Hall, this ancient Grade II listed roadside pub displays its history with gabled dormer windows, half-timbering and heavy sandstone slates. Inside there are several heavily beamed areas including one with a stone fireplace and another sporting leather armchairs and a piano. Fish shows up well on the bar menu, whether it be spicy fishcakes with chilli sauce, 'very generous helpings' of seafood risotto packed with good things, or battered hake and chips. Alongside pork and leek sausages with spring onion mash, the global theme continues with, say, stir-fried beef and soba noodles, or spinach and asparagus tortillas; then there's home-made ice creams and apple pie to finish. A separate carte and a set menu are offered in the dimly lit restaurant, where the repertoire takes in warm venison carpaccio and grilled Dover sole with lemon, lime and rock salt, followed by desserts like crème brûlée. Robinson's Best Bitter and Hatters Mild are on handpump, and the 70-strong wine list, which is tilted towards restaurant customers and priced from £12 to £70, has six by the glass. SAMPLE DISHES: fish broth with pesto bruschetta £5; Thai chicken mild curry £7; chocolate torte £3.25.

Licensee Peter Myers (Robinson's)
Open 12 to 11; bar food and restaurant 12 to 2, 7 to 10 (Sun 12 to 10)
Details Children welcome in eating areas　Car park　Wheelchair access (also WC)　Garden　Background music　No dogs　Amex, Delta, MasterCard, Switch, Visa　Accommodation: 8 rooms (prices on application)

PRESTON BAGOT　Warwickshire　　　　　　　　　　　　　　　　map 5

Crabmill

Preston Bagot B95 5DR　TEL: (01926) 843342

The sympathetic restoration of this sprawling old cider mill has made much of original features, notably the ancient beams, and includes superb use of natural materials and colours, bringing a sharply observed stylishness to the interior. Food- and wine-themed cartoons are on the walls, plants in little metal buckets on the tables and assorted furnishings include 'luxurious' leather sofas for drinkers to relax on. The food has a stylish and modern slant, taking influences from everywhere and anywhere. Options on the printed menu include whole baked camembert with onion bread, and crispy duck salad, followed by main courses ranging from wild mushroom risotto to Chinese roast belly pork with spring onion and ginger mash. Desserts are typically along the lines of lemon and lime syrup cake with mascarpone. Four house wines at £11.95 a bottle (also available by the glass) open a short but varied list, and real ales include Wadworth 6X, Tetley's and Old Speckled Hen. SAMPLE DISHES: chicken livers and black pudding on horseradish rösti £6; chicken Kiev with olive oil and parsley mash £11; chocolate and pecan brownie with organic vanilla ice cream £5.

Licensee Sarah Robinson (freehouse)
Open 11 to 11; bar food and restaurant 12 to 2.30 (12.30 to 3.30 Sun), 6.30 to 9.30
Details Children welcome Car park Wheelchair access (not WC) Garden and patio No smoking in restaurant Background music Dogs welcome in bar Amex, MasterCard, Switch, Visa

PRESTWOOD   Buckinghamshire   map 3

Polecat Inn
170 Wycombe Road, Prestwood HP16 0HJ   TEL: (01494) 862253

The Polecat is a plain-looking early twentieth-century building on the main road through the village in that hinterland beyond High Wycombe – 'neither particularly rural nor particularly urban' but not far from some pleasant open countryside. One entrance leads into the Drovers Bar, another into the Old Bar, but the interior is more or less open-plan, with three linked areas (the third is the Galley Room) all with low beamed ceilings, glass case displays of stuffed and mounted animals (including the eponymous polecat), butterflies and other creatures, and fresh flowers everywhere. That the place is crammed full of tables indicates that this is principally a dining venue, and a popular one. Lunchtime snacks are a pretty traditional slate of sandwiches, jacket potatoes and ploughman's, and it is the printed menu and blackboard specials that deliver 'mildly ambitious' dishes of good, wholesome country cooking. You could start with smoked chicken and mozzarella croquettes with tomato and herb sauce, then go on to a generous plate of pork medallions with apple and pumpkin pancakes that got the thumbs up from one visitor. Sherry trifle shows up on a dessert list that also runs to meringues with cream and caramel. Lovers of real ales will be pleased to find Flowers IPA, Marston's Pedigree and Bass among those on offer, and there are some 16 wines by the glass. SAMPLE DISHES: kipper mousse with toasted lemon brioche £4.75; lamb, aubergine and tomato casserole £9; chocolate and orange biscuit cake £4.

Licensee John Gamble (freehouse)
Open 11.30 to 3, 6 to 11, Sun 12 to 3; bar food 12 to 2, 6.30 to 9; closed evening 24 Dec, all day 25 and 26 Dec, evening 31 Dec, all day 1 Jan
Details Children welcome in bar eating area Car park Wheelchair access (also WC) Garden No smoking in eating area Background music Dogs welcome No cards

RAMSBURY   Wiltshire   map 2

Bell
The Square, Ramsbury SN8 2PE   TEL: (01672) 520230
off A4192, 6m E of Marlborough

A new regime has settled in at this tall, imposing inn with its pillared porch and angular bay windows. The stylish interior comprises a classy lounge with sofas grouped around a fireplace, a bustling open-plan bar, and a spacious restaurant done out in earthy colours, with old oak floorboards and a closed-in fireplace complete with an original bread oven. An unchanging bar menu takes in old favourites like a 'house curry', lasagne, and hand-made sausages with mustard mash, while the concise Bistro Menu promises more upbeat ideas such as 'spankingly fresh' home-cured gravlax with sweet mustard dressing, or pan-fried wood pigeon with mango salad and sesame oil dressing, before, say, roast duck breast with red wine and hawthorn berry sauce, or fillet of halibut on black linguine with saffron sauce. Completing the picture are heart-warming desserts like orange bread-and-butter pudding. Real ales include Wadworth 6X and Henry's Original IPA as well as a guest brew. Six wines come by the glass from a decent list of 30 or so bottles. SAMPLE DISHES: roast king prawns with garlic butter £6.25; pork tenderloin with apple and Calvados sauce £13.25; chocolate fudge cheesecake £4.50.

Licensee Jeremy Wilkins (freehouse)

Open 12 to 3, 5.30 to 11; bar food and restaurant all week 12 to 2.30, Mon to Sat 6 to 9.30

Details Children welcome   Car park   Wheelchair access (also WC)   Garden   Background music   Dogs welcome   Delta, Diners, MasterCard, Switch, Visa   Accommodation: 5 rooms, B&B £50 to £75

RAMSDEN   Oxfordshire   map 5

▲ Royal Oak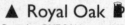

Ramsden OX7 3AU   TEL: (01993) 868213
take B4022 from Witney, turn right just before Hailey and follow road to village

This prosperous-looking old coaching inn of Cotswold stone stands at the centre of the village. Inside, the natural charms of the ancient building have been treated with respect: the open, linked rooms present a solid look with the natural colours of exposed-stone walls, floor tiles and the 'occasional, but enormous' ancient ceiling beam enhanced by terracotta plaster walls and soft lighting that extends to evening candles on plain wooden tables. Steak and mushroom suet pudding as well as char-grilled steaks, burgers, and lunchtime sandwiches and such dishes as sausage, mash and onion gravy are what to expect on the bar food front. On the separate, more ambitious restaurant menu (also served in the bar) might be brochette of monkfish with lemon butter sauce, roast English rack of lamb with Oxford sauce ('redcurrant, mint and mustard') and rösti, or loin of organic local pork with a Tuscan-style casserole of mixed beans, tomato and white wine, while desserts might run to sticky toffee pudding or lemon meringue pie. Hook Norton Old Hooky, West Berkshire Good Old Boy, Adnams Broadside and Butts Barbus Barbus lead a great range of real ales, conferring on the place a richly deserved reputation for good beer. There's also Dunkerton's cider, and a wine list that makes some canny selections in Western Europe and the southern hemisphere and offers around a dozen by the glass. SAMPLE DISHES: Royal Oak smokies £5; confit of duck with Puy lentils and a honey, cognac and redcurrant sauce £12; treacle and almond tart £4.

Licensee Jonathan Oldham (freehouse)

Open 11.30 to 3, 6.30 to 11, Sun 12 to 3, 7 to 10.30; bar food and restaurant 11.30 to 2, 7 to 10.30; closed 25 and 26 Dec

Details Children welcome in restaurant   Car park   Wheelchair access (also WC)   Garden and patio   No smoking in restaurant   No music   Dogs welcome   Delta, MasterCard, Switch, Visa   Accommodation: 4 rooms, B&B £35 to £60

A list of pubs with better-than-average wines, well chosen and decently priced, is at the back of the book.

REDE Suffolk   map 6

Plough
Rede IP29 4BE   TEL: (01284) 789208

This picturesque, partly thatched pub in a quiet village is traditional, unspoilt and comfortable. Inside, the separate bar and restaurant areas reveal their sixteenth-century origins with beams, one bearing the legend 'duck or grouse', floors of old red tiles or wood (as well as modern red carpet) and an open fireplace with a wood-burning stove. Greene King ales are on draught, and a reasonable selection of wines is kept behind the bar with small descriptive labels attached to their necks; all are served by the glass. The same menus, combining international dishes with the more traditional, are available wherever you choose to eat. Typical dishes include mustard veal with polenta and spinach purée, red mullet with red pesto and chargrilled vegetables, and braised partridge in a creamy Grand Marnier sauce. SAMPLE DISHES: fresh squid piri-piri £6; monkfish créole £13; coconut and cherry tart £4.

Licensees Brian and Joyce Desborough (Greene King)
Open 11 to 3, 6.30 to 11, Sun 12 to 3, 7 to 10.30; bar food and restaurant (exc Sun evenings) 12 to 2, 6.30 to 9
Details Children welcome   Car park   Wheelchair access (not WC)   Garden and patio   No smoking in restaurant   Background music   No dogs   Amex, Diners, MasterCard, Switch, Visa

REDMILE Leicestershire   map 5

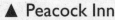 **Peacock Inn**
Church Corner, Main Street, Redmile NG13 0GA   TEL: (01949) 842554
S of A52, 6m W of Grantham

Belvoir Castle – the family seat of the Duke of Rutland – is just a couple of miles from this renovated and extended stone pub in a village beside the old Grantham Canal. Refurbishment has given the interior a new look, with wood fires, light beams and chairs around teak tables setting the tone; there's also a separate lounge area. In the two bars at the front of the pub you can have just a sandwich or burger, although the menu promises quite a few more interesting offerings, including 'moreish' baked avocado and bacon salad topped with melted Stilton, Italian-style meatballs, or chargrilled tuna steak with peppered rocket and anchovy and chilli butter, followed by desserts like treacle sponge with custard. Alternatively, eat in the smart dining room, where the menu moves into the realms of Caesar salad, confit of pheasant and roast chestnuts, or stuffed loin of lamb on celeriac mash doused in raspberry wine. Wells Bombardier Premium Bitter, Tetley Traditional Cask, and Burton Ale are the regular offerings for real ale drinkers, and the 50-strong wine list has a well-balanced selection from both the Old and New Worlds, with half a dozen by the glass. SAMPLE DISHES: chicken and vegetable terrine with onion marmalade £5; smoked haddock and wild mushroom linguine £9; chocolate cheesecake with white chocolate sauce £5.

Licensee Stephen Hughes (freehouse)
Open 11 to 11, Sun 12 to 10.30; bar food and restaurant 12 to 2 (3 Sun), 7 to 9
Details Children welcome   Car park   Wheelchair access (also WC)   Garden and patio   No smoking in restaurant   Occasional live or background music   Dogs welcome   Amex, Delta, Diners, MasterCard, Switch, Visa   Accommodation: 9 rooms, B&B £55 to £80

RIMINGTON   Lancashire   map 8

Black Bull   NEW ENTRY

Rimington BB7 4DS   TEL: (01200) 445220
village signposted off A682 Nelson to Gisburn road

The brick-built, gabled Victorian pub may look unprepossessing from the outside, but 'miss it at your peril', warns one reporter, for 'nothing can prepare you for the interior'. It's an 'absolute cornucopia' of transport-related artefacts, filling every conceivable space in one of the two main rooms, plus a passageway dripping with further memorabilia that leads to an extension housing the Platform 4 museum (which includes a working N-gauge model railway layout). It's a truly remarkable collection built up by the late landlord and continued by his wife, the current licensee. It may be an anorak's heaven, but other rooms, including a non-smoking dining room, are more conventionally styled in a comfortable and welcoming way. In reality, the Black Bull is a mix of transport shrine and first-class dining pub, yet it successfully caters for all-comers, including a hard core of village regulars who prop up the bar drinking Theakston Best Bitter, the only real ale on handpump. The bar menu lists such things as sandwiches, salads, a soup and a roast of the day, steaks, and richly flavoured game casserole, but the main action takes place on the blackboards. Starters might include scallops in garlic butter glazed with Emmental, and among main courses may be a home-made sausage filled with salmon, plaice, Dublin Bay prawn and potato in a light bouillabaisse sauce, or pan-fried medallions of venison with blackcurrants and Cassis and horseradish mousseline. There's a separate fish specials board with a couple of starters and five mains – say, grilled plaice with creamy dill sauce – and for those in a hurry there's the 'midweek express lunch' at £5.95. Three Australian house wines are available by the glass. SAMPLE DISHES: home-cured gravad lax with Dijon mustard sauce £6; grilled whole sea bass with garlic and lemon butter £13; pear and almond tart £4.25.

Licensee Barbara Blades (freehouse)
Open Tue to Sun 12 to 3, 7 to 11 (10.30 Sun); bar food and restaurant Tue to Sun 12 to 2.30, Tue to Sat 7 to 9.30
Details Children welcome   Car park   Wheelchair access (not WC)   Patio   No smoking in restaurant
Background music   No dogs   Delta, MasterCard, Switch, Visa

RIPPONDEN   West Yorkshire   map 8

Old Bridge Inn ▶ ❧

Priest Lane, Ripponden HX6 4DF   TEL: (01422) 822595

Once you have found Ripponden, the best advice is to walk over the old packhorse bridge that straddles the gushing waters of the River Ryburn to find this ancient, aptly named pub. There has been a hostelry of some kind here since the fourteenth century, and the place shows its history with an abundance of oak beams and low ceilings in three split-level rooms separated by a couple of steps. A 'fantastic' old range with a coal fire provides warmth in winter, and a cheery, chatty atmosphere prevails. Handpumped North Country ales include a range from Timothy Taylor, plus Black Sheep Best Bitter and Barnsley IPA; the owners also dispense Dutch pilsner and wheat beer and stock over 20 single malts. The kitchen deals in honest, flavoursome and plentiful pub food: 'we troughed out on wild boar sausages with mustard mash and red wine gravy, and meat and potato pie with mushy peas,' admitted one satisfied couple. There are also occasional forays further afield for, say, tuna and mozzarella fishcakes with spicy tomato and coriander salsa, or Brazilian beef casserole (with kidney beans and chilli sauce). Big helpings of blackberry crumble or chocolate and orange sponge round off proceedings. Bottles from the New World show up strongly on the eminently affordable list of around 25 wines, which has a decent choice by the glass. SAMPLE DISHES: smoked chicken pâté with sweet orange pickle £4.50; fisherman's pie £7; gooseberry crème brûlée £3.

Licensee Tim Eaton Walker (freehouse)
Open *Mon to Fri 12 to 3, 5.30 to 11, Sat 12 to 11, Sun 12 to 10.30; bar food all week 12 to 2, Mon to Fri 6 to 9.30*
Details *Children welcome in eating area   Car park   Wheelchair access (not WC)   Patio   No music   No dogs   Delta, MasterCard, Switch, Visa*

ROCKBEARE   Devon   map 1

Jack in the Green ✿

London Road, Rockbeare EX5 2EE   TEL: (01404) 822240
WEBSITE: www.jackinthegreen.uk.com
on old A30, 3m NE of Exeter

The small village of Rockbeare is these days bypassed by the main road down to Cornwall, but this large old inn is well worth the short diversion should you be in need of refreshment en route. It looks fairly plain from the outside, while the interior décor majors in old-fashioned pubby paraphernalia – horse brasses, copper pans and hunting prints – and mix-and-match furniture, including dark blue chesterfield-style sofas by the large red-brick hearth. Bar meals, listed on a blackboard, feature old favourites such as fish 'n' chips, steak and kidney pie, and ploughman's with a choice of ten different cheeses, as well as more fashionable fare, perhaps including lamb tagine with apricots, almonds and couscous. The restaurant menu (fixed price for two or three courses, also served in the bar) is more ambitious. Starters take in chicken terrine with aubergine, cream cheese and chives, or pan-fried pigeon breast with lardons and Madeira jus, and to follow there may be rump steak with port and Stilton sauce, or confit duck legs with butternut squash risotto and a red wine and cardamom jus. Real ale drinkers will be happy with the choice of Otter Ale, Branscombe Vale Bitter and Cotleigh Tawny, while those who prefer wine are well served by a serious list of over 100 bins. Plenty are under £15, including around a dozen house selections by the glass or bottle, but there are also several more expensive options. SAMPLE DISHES: chicken liver pâté £4.25; tagliatelle with crab and prawns and thermidor sauce £9.25; chocolate feuilleté with orange parfait £5.

Licensee Paul Parnell (freehouse)
Open *11 to 3, 5.30 to 11, Sun 12 to 10.30; bar food and restaurant Mon to Sat 12 to 2, 6 to 9.30, Sun 12 to 9.30; closed 25 Dec to 3 Jan*
Details *Children welcome in bar eating area   Car park   Wheelchair access (also WC)   Patio   No-smoking area in bar, no smoking in restaurant   Background music   No dogs   Delta, MasterCard, Switch, Visa*

See 'How to use the Guide' at the front of the book for an explanation of the symbols used at the tops of entries.

ROCKBOURNE   Hampshire   map 2

Rose & Thistle

Rockbourne SP6 3NL   TEL: (01725) 518236
WEBSITE: www.roseandthistle.co.uk
off B3078, 3m NW of Fordingbridge

Attractive, whitewashed and thatched, this one-time pair of sixteenth-century cottages makes an idyllic village pub with cooking that shows an admirable level of skill. Flagstones, beams, a welcoming fire and a buzzing atmosphere give the bar plenty of character. The menu in the separate restaurant, with its huge inglenook, tends towards classic ideas such as creamy garlic mushrooms, medallions of beef fillet with Stilton cheese and port sauce, with bread-and-butter pudding to finish. A blackboard lists fish specials, ranging from Cornish crab salad, to red mullet and fennel in a dry Vermouth liquor. The restaurant menu can also be ordered in the bar, which has its own menu of simpler, snacky dishes like chicken liver and wild mushroom pâté, locally made sausages, and rare roast beef ploughman's. Real ales include some prestigious names, such as Fuller's London Pride, Strong's Bitter and representatives from the nearby Hop Back Brewery. As well as the house wine, the 'Proprietor's Personal Selection' of 11 bottles, at £11.95, are also sold by the glass, and four are available in halves. SAMPLE DISHES: mussels in creamy cider liquor £6.25; grilled chicken breast topped with bacon and mozzarella £10.50; sticky toffee and date pudding £4.75.

Licensees Tim Norfolk and Jacqueline Oxford (freehouse)
Open *11 to 3, 6 to 11, Sun 12 to 8 (summer 10.30); bar food and restaurant (exc Sun evening winter) 12 to 2.30, 7 to 9.30*
Details *Children welcome   Car park   Wheelchair access (not WC)   Garden and patio   No smoking in restaurant   No music   Dogs welcome in bar   Delta, MasterCard, Switch, Visa*

ROMALDKIRK   Co Durham   map 10

▲ Rose and Crown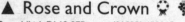

Romaldkirk DL12 9EB   TEL: (01833) 650213
WEBSITE: www.rose-and-crown.co.uk
on B6277, 6m NW of Barnard Castle

In the middle of a picturesque village, the Rose and Crown manages to be a restaurant and country hotel without forgetting that it is first and foremost a pub. Panelling, a grandfather clock, walls filled with gin-traps, brasses, and a range of photographs, and an enormous old stone fireplace make the point as you enter the bar, but further on there is the Crown Room, a well-appointed brasserie-style dining room, and a full-dress restaurant. Separate regularly changing menus are offered for lunch and dinner, with lunch including filled baps, but both offer a long list of dishes that range from starters of simple, well-made leek and potato soup to more enterprising smoked salmon soufflé with chive cream, or smoked trout mousse with new potato salad and lime and caper vinaigrette. Main courses might include smoked haddock kedgeree with prawns, quail's eggs and Parmesan, wild boar sausages with Puy lentils, smoked bacon and balsamic vinegar, and baked halibut with Cotherstone cheese and red onion marmalade, with apple and cinnamon crumble with custard to finish. The elegant restaurant, with its linen-clothed tables, operates a fixed-price four-course dinner menu and is also open for Sunday lunch. Beers come from Black Sheep and

Theakston. The ten wines available by the glass (£3 to £4.95) are listed on the back of the menu, and they make an excellent flavour-filled selection on their own. The separate wine list adds a further 50-odd bottles arranged by grape variety. SAMPLE DISHES: scallop, prawn and herb risotto £6.25; chargrilled calf's liver with black pudding mash and shallot gravy £11.75; hot walnut and syrup tart £3.50.

Licensees Christopher and Alison Davy (freehouse)
Open 11.30 to 3, 5.30 to 11, Sun 12 to 3, 7 to 10.30; bar food 12 to 1.30, 6.30 to 9.30; restaurant all week 7.30 to 9, Sun 12 to 1.30; closed 24 to 26 Dec
Details Children welcome   Car park   Wheelchair access (also WC)   Garden   No smoking in restaurant No music   Dogs welcome exc in eating areas   MasterCard, Switch, Visa   Accommodation: 12 rooms, B&B £75 to £124

ROMSEY   Hampshire   map 2

Three Tuns 🏵
58 Middlebridge Street, Romsey SO51 8HL   TEL: (01794) 512639

This remodelled, one-time old-world hostelry is now strutting its stuff in the competitive gastro-pub market, offering a contemporary look of clean, uncluttered lines offset by dark beams and timbers. Informal eating options set the pace (the restaurant has dark stained tongue-and-groove boarding with redwood-coloured panelled walls above, offering an informal stab at sophistication), but pubby roots have not been forgotten. The modern British brasserie-style menu reveals some classical influences in an 'excellent, smooth, rich' chicken liver and foie gras parfait with Sauternes jelly and also delivering straightforward flavours in a generous bowl of watercress soup with naturally smoked haddock. Beef cooked two ways with a bordelaise garnish, and pan-fried pheasant with foie gras, Puy lentils and bacon are the kind of things to expect as a main course, with sticky toffee pudding or chocolate tart with mascarpone typical desserts. A bar snack menu is available at lunch: say, Cumberland sausage with pomme purée and onion gravy, game pie, or baguettes filled with local Cheddar and spring onions, or hot beef, Stilton and watercress. The concise, global wine list (with a couple by the glass) befits the food, while handpumped ales are Ringwood Best and Gale's HSB. SAMPLE DISHES: butternut squash risotto with sage pancetta £6; roast breast of chicken with wild mushrooms and tarragon cream sauce £12.50; prune and Armagnac parfait £5.

Licensee David Tugwell (Enterprise Inns)
Open 12 to 11, Sun 12 to 10.30; bar food Mon to Sat 12 to 2.30, restaurant Mon to Sat 6.30 to 9.30 (10 Sat)
Details Children welcome   Car park   Wheelchair access (not WC)   Garden   No smoking in restaurant Background music   Dogs welcome in bar only   Delta, MasterCard, Switch, Visa

---

ROWDE   Wiltshire   map 2

George & Dragon 🏵 🍇

High Street, Rowde SN10 2PN   TEL: (01380) 723053

At first glance this seems like an unremarkable, custard-coloured pub with a walled back garden in the centre of a landlocked Wiltshire village. What makes Tim and Helen Withers' rustic hostelry special is daily supplies of fresh fish from Cornwall, which can be sampled in two bare-boarded rooms with lots of dark wood, shelves lined with tall jars of home-made preserves and a blackboard that tells its own story.

Here you might find red gurnard in beer batter with chilli soy sauce, roasted razor clams with garlic and olive oil or roast hake with peppers and aïoli. Those with vegetarian or carnivorous appetites could also choose from the short printed menu, which promises everything from mooli rice cakes with spiced lentil sauce to baked local ham with beetroot and piquant shallot sauce. Cheeses are sound West Country names like Wessex Purl and Harborne Blue, while desserts feature a fine selection of home-made ice creams and sorbets. To drink, there's Butcombe Bitter on draught plus a strong contingent of international bottled beers, including Thomas Hardy Ale, German Erdinger Hefe and Belgian Leffe Blond, but the real treasures are in the list of around 60 wines. This is sprinkled with welcome surprises like a 1998 Vouvray from Huët, mature vintage Pol Roger champagne and the South of France's top rosé, Domaine Tempier. Prices start at £10 for the five white and two red house wines (also sold by the small and large glass for £2.50/£3.35) and range all the way up to £60 with excellent quality at every level. SAMPLE DISHES: smoked chicken and pear salad £6; monkfish with green peppercorns, brandy and cream £16; chocolate roulade with fruit coulis £5.

Licensees Helen and Tim Withers (freehouse)
Open 12 to 3, 7 to 11 (10.30 Sun); bar food and restaurant Tue to Sat 12 to 2, 7 to 9; closed 25 Dec, 1 Jan
Details Children welcome in eating areas Car park Garden No smoking in restaurant No music Dogs welcome in bar Delta, MasterCard, Switch, Visa

ROYDHOUSE   West Yorkshire   map 8

▲ Three Acres Inn ✿

Roydhouse HD8 8LR   TEL: (01484) 602606
WEBSITE: www.3acres.com
off B6116 (from A629), 1m E of Kirkburton

It is all very cosy and intimate at this roadside inn, in three acres of grounds, set high on the moors between Barnsley and Huddersfield. In winter, when the surrounding terrain can resemble 'an Arctic tundra', the lovely Pennine views are best seen from a leather chair and open fire in the long, knocked-through bar. Whatever the time of year, the impossible-to-miss Emley Moor television mast acts as a homing beacon – it is a quarter of a mile from the inn. The big draw is an almost complete focus on food, with all tables 'draped and set beautifully', and the few bar stools usually taken by people waiting to eat; an oyster bar and adjoining deli emphasise the point. The lengthy menu notes the seasons with the likes of terrine of autumn game or dressed Cornish crab salad, but there are pub classics too: say, Yorkshire pudding and onion gravy updated with home-made black pudding and apple and Calvados compote, and a grain mustard shortcrust topping and home-pickled beetroot adding zest to a steak, kidney and mushroom pie. Global inspirations like 'very good' hot crispy Peking duck with egg noodles and Chinese greens expand choice. Real ale fans will find Timothy Taylor Landlord, Black Sheep Best Bitter, Adnams Bitter and Tetley Bitter on handpump, and some 80 wines – listed in price order from £11.95 – cover Old World and New; 12 come by the glass, and there's a decent showing of half-bottles. SAMPLE DISHES: crispy Japanese chicken with sweet chilli sauce and stir-fried greens £6; pot-roast wood pigeon with peas, pancetta and Puy lentils £13; orange and whisky jelly with Drambuie anglaise £5.50.

Licensees Neil Truelove and Brian Orme (freehouse)

Open *12 to 3, 6 to 11 (7 to 10.30 Sun); bar food and restaurant 12 to 1.45, 6.30 to 9.45; closed 25 and 31 Dec, 1 Jan*
Details *Children welcome in bar eating area   Car park   Wheelchair access (not WC)   Patio   Background music   No dogs   Amex, Delta, MasterCard, Switch, Visa   Accommodation: 20 rooms, B&B £55 to £80*

RUDGE   Somerset   map 2

▲ Full Moon

Rudge BA11 2QF   TEL: (01373) 830936
WEBSITE: www.thefullmoon.co.uk

The Westbury White Horse, a Stone Age hill carving, can be seen from the guest rooms at this rural seventeenth-century inn just ten miles from Bath. In front of the pub is a tiny lawn with picnic tables, and there's a larger garden to the rear, while inside are four small rooms with flagstone and tile floors or red patterned carpets, trestle tables and a rough-stone bar counter. Quirky decorative touches include an old cash till and riding boots on a mantelpiece. A regular printed menu lists 'old favourites' such as lasagne, or scampi and chips, as well as more interesting dishes like hoisin duck with Chinese pancakes, and roast guinea fowl on swede tart with port jus. Further choice is offered on a daily fish specials board. Butcombe Bitter, Abbeydale Moonshine and Wadworth 6X make up the real ale contingent, and there's Thatcher's Cheddar Valley dry cider too. Prices on the varied and interesting list of around 20 wines start at £8.95, and five are available by the glass. SAMPLE DISHES: Caesar salad £4.75; rabbit casserole £11.50; roasted plums in a brandy-snap basket £4.

Licensees *Pat and Christine Gifford (freehouse)*
Open *12 to 11 (10.30 Sun); bar food and restaurant 12 to 2.30 (2 sittings Sun lunchtime carvery, 12 and 2), 7 to 9.30 (9 winter)*
Details *Children welcome   Car park   Wheelchair access (also WC)   Garden and patio   No smoking in restaurant   Occasional background music   Dogs welcome exc in restaurant   Delta, MasterCard, Switch, Visa   Accommodation: 17 rooms, B&B £49.50 to £85*

RUSHLAKE GREEN   East Sussex   map 3

Horse and Groom

Rushlake Green TN21 9QE   TEL: (01435) 830320
off B2096, 4m SE of Heathfield

You can understand why the village is called Rushlake Green, with more green than houses. It is a vast expanse, which the pub overlooks; and its own well-tended garden, with shrubs, topiary, little arches with climbers, and trestle tables is a big draw in summer. Inside, the beams in both walls and ceilings seem blacker and thicker than most, the giant hearth is hung with a row of copper teapots, the carpet has the usual pubby red pattern, and stuffed deer heads and antlers hang on one wall. Green-tinted table mats depicting a vintage photograph of the pub show that the place is geared towards food, reinforced by the large number of blackboard menus. These offer some rewarding cookery of the likes of fresh mussels with garlic and white wine sauce to start, and main courses of duck breast with dauphinoise potatoes and black bean honey sauce. Traditionalists aren't neglected either, with home-cooked ham with a free-range egg and chips, for example. Harveys Sussex Best Bitter and Shepherd Neame Master Brew Bitter are on handpump, together with one seasonal guest beer, and six wines are available by the glass. The pub has a sister establishment: the Star

Inn at Old Heathfield. SAMPLE DISHES: chef's chicken liver pâté £5.50; home-cooked ham with a free-range egg and chips £7.50; bread-and-butter pudding £4.95.

Licensees Mike and Sue Chappell (freehouse)
Open 11.30 to 3, 5.30 (6 Sat) to 11, Sun 12 to 3, 7 to 10.30; bar food and restaurant 12 to 2.30, 7 to 9.30
Details Children welcome   Car park   Wheelchair access (also WC)   Garden   Occasional background music
Dogs welcome   Delta, MasterCard, Switch, Visa

ST BREWARD   Cornwall   map 1

Old Inn   NEW ENTRY

St Breward PL30 4PP   TEL: (01208) 850711
WEBSITE: www.theoldinnandrestaurant.co.uk

Constructed in the eleventh century to house monks building the adjacent church, the Old Inn is magnificently atmospheric with its stone walls and massive hearths, heavy beams and slate floors. It remains resolutely a village pub, with a darts team and quiz nights, but draws tourists in the summer for its fame as the highest inn in Cornwall, and for food – much of it sourced locally. A printed bar menu lists pub stalwarts such as pork sausages, sandwiches, ploughman's, mixed grills and steaks, while the daily specials on a blackboard are more ambitious, encompassing generous portions of braised lamb shank with red wine and rosemary gravy, and fish such as grilled plaice fillet. The restaurant menu, also served in the bar, could open with celery and Stilton soup, go on to a chicken breast wrapped in ham in a cheese and cream sauce, and finish with a hearty portion of banoffi pie. Sharp's Special, Doom Bar Bitter and Eden Ale are on draught along with Bass, and there's a useful list of some 16 wines, virtually all available by the glass. SAMPLE DISHES: salmon brochette £5.25; lamb's liver and bacon £8; apple and blackberry crumble £4.

Licensee Darren Wills (freehouse)
Open winter Mon to Thur 11 to 3, 6 to 11, Fri and Sat 11 to 11, Sun 12 to 10.30; summer Mon to Sat 11 to 11, Sun 12 to 10.30; bar food and restaurant 11 to 3, 6 to 9
Details Children welcome in family room and bar eating area   Car park   Wheelchair access (also WC)
Garden and patio   No-smoking area in bar, no smoking in restaurant   Live or background music   Dogs welcome in slate-floored areas only   Diners, MasterCard, Switch, Visa

ST MAWES   Cornwall   map 1

▲ Rising Sun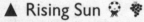

The Square, St Mawes TR2 5DJ   TEL: (01326) 270233
off A3078, S of Trewithian; or reached by ferry from Falmouth

This lively little inn is just across the road from the sea wall and overlooks the quaint anchorage of St Mawes harbour and its nineteenth-century quay. Although the place has been 'smartly done up', with a slight hotel feel to the lounges and restaurant, the bar is charmingly informal, which means that it remains at the heart of village life and positively bustles with visitors in season when drinkers spill out on to the front terrace. Chef Ann Long continues her search for the best local ingredients, and her blackboard bar menus show good use of fish: say, potted buttered crab, and grilled sea bass fillets. Lobster and crab bisque, and a main course of roast duck breast with risotto and plum sauce may be inspired by her more inventive set-price restaurant dinners, but tradition has its way with beer-battered cod and chips, cottage pie, and beef, mushroom and ale pie. There are lunchtime sandwiches, and perhaps raspberry oatmeal meringue, or chocolate tipsy cake for dessert. This St Austell pub regularly serves HSD and Tinners plus a guest ale. Eleven wines are on offer at £11 a bottle, £2.80 a glass, while thirty or so other wines complete a well-rounded list that gathers up some classy bottles from around the world without charging the earth for them (top of the range is Laroche's Chablis Premier Cru Vaudevay for £34.50). Licensee John Milan also runs the Pandora Inn at Mylor Bridge, see entry. SAMPLE DISHES: Roseland fish soup £5; scallop and bacon salad £12; apple crumble £4.25.

Licensee R.J. Milan (St Austell Brewery)
Open 11 to 11, Sun 12 to 10.30; bar food 12 to 2, 6.30 to 9 (all day July and Aug); restaurant Sun 12 to 2, all week 7 to 9
Details Children welcome Car park Wheelchair access (also WC) Patio No smoking in restaurant No music Dogs welcome Delta, MasterCard, Switch, Visa Accommodation: 8 rooms, B&B £50 to £130

ST MAWGAN Cornwall

map 1

Falcon Inn NEW ENTRY

St Mawgan TR8 4EP TEL: (01637) 860225
WEBSITE: www.falconinn.net

'You walk straight into a large and welcoming L-shaped bar with an open fire and lots of seating', and the dartboard 'is clearly well used', noted an enthusiastic reporter, who went on to sum up the Falcon as 'the kind of local most people dream of'. A mix of printed menu and blackboard specials is served throughout – the restaurant doubles as the residents' breakfast room – with many pub standards appearing on the repertoire: say, 'delicious' garlic mushrooms (served, unusually, as a gratin in a 'rich, creamy and very garlicky sauce'), Cornish smoked salmon and Greenland prawns with lemon and chive mayonnaise, sirloin steak, sausage and mash, pies and casseroles, plus a fair showing of seafood (simply grilled brill, or scallops in a creamy sauce with black pudding). Portions are generous, so not everyone will get as far as apple pie or locally made honeycomb and caramel swirl ice cream. This is a St Austell Brewery tenancy, so expect well-kept Tinners Ale, HSD and Tribute, with half a dozen wines by the glass from a list of over 20 bottles. There's a garden for fine weather, and St Mawgan is a pretty little village near a much-loved stretch of coast. SAMPLE DISHES: local goats' cheese salad £4.50; lime and chilli chicken with pasta in coconut sauce £8; tangy lemon tart £3.

Licensees Andy and Helen Banks (St Austell Brewery)
Open 11 to 3, 6 to 11, Sun 12 to 3, 7 to 10.30; bar food and restaurant 12 to 2, 6.30 to 9.30; closed evening 25 Dec
Details Children welcome in restaurant Car park Wheelchair access (not WC) Garden and patio No smoking in restaurant No music Dogs welcome Delta, Diners, MasterCard, Switch, Visa Accommodation: 3 rooms, B&B £25 to £45

ST PETER SOUTH ELMHAM Suffolk

map 6

St Peter's Hall and Brewery NEW ENTRY

St Peter South Elmham, near Bungay NR35 1NQ TEL: (01986) 782322
WEBSITE: www.stpetersbrewery.co.uk
from Bungay take A144, turn right on B1062 and follow signs to St Peter South Elmham

'The superlatives come out' when describing this place, exclaimed an inspector. Dating from 1280 and set in open countryside four miles south of Bungay, it began life as a moated manor house and later served as a monastery. Now it is home to the St Peter's Brewery and pub. Best Bitter and Strong Ale are always on draught in the little bar, along with a prodigious range of bottled brews, including porter, elderberry beer and organic ales. The excellent ales are by no means mandatory as the wine list, weighing in with seven house wines by the glass (£2.95 to £3.95) or bottle (£9.95 to £12.50), neatly covers the flavour spectrum and follows through with good value right on to dessert. At lunchtime you can order open sandwiches on local organic bread plus simple dishes ranging from salad niçoise with a poached egg and red pepper coulis to Gloucester Old Spot pork and leek sausages with parsley mash and braised onions. Evening meals are served in the grand surroundings of the lofty Great Hall, with its Brussels tapestries, bishop's chair and other antiques. But there's nothing archaic about the food: here you might feast on a warm tart of goats' cheese, leeks and thyme with baby spinach before full-flavoured baked turbot fillets with shellfish, spinach and crushed new potatoes, or duck breast with damson gin sauce, baked squash and rosemary potatoes. Farmhouse cheeses are kept in prime condition, and desserts range from quince crème brûlée to Italian ice creams. Service is friendly and smiling. Note the limited opening hours. SAMPLE DISHES: mushroom and roast chestnut soup £4; fillet steak with rosemary-roast root vegetables and garlic butter £15.50; lemon tart with mandarin sorbet £5.

Licensee John Murphy (St Peter's)
Open Fri and Sat 11 to 11, Sun 12 to 6; bar food and restaurant Fri and Sat 12 to 2.30, 7 to 9, Sun 12 to 2.30; also open Thur July and Aug 11 to 11, bank hols 12 to 6
Details Children welcome   Car park   Garden   No smoking in restaurant   Background music   No dogs   MasterCard, Switch, Visa

SALT Staffordshire

map 5

Holly Bush Inn

Salt ST18 0BX   TEL: (01889) 508234
WEBSITE: www.hollybushinn.co.uk
4m N of Stafford, off A51, A518 and B5066

Many claim this ancient thatched inn as the second-oldest licensed premises in the country, with origins going right back to 1190. In summer its white outside walls are festooned with flowers, and the bar certainly shows off its pedigree with heavy beams, timbers and stone pillars. No wonder the place hums with life. The regular menus offer simple, unpretentious and good-value food: slow-cooked lamb and barley stew, braised venison with chestnuts and celery and deep-fried cod are typical main courses. The kitchen also makes plentiful use of local produce: pork chops and other meats are supplied by a butcher in Eccleshall, hand-made cheeses come courtesy of John Knox of Leek (Staffordshire Blue is used as a glaze for stuffed pears, while Dream of the Abbey is pan-fried and served with redcurrant sauce). Desserts might include apricot and Drambuie bread pudding. Boddingtons Bitter, Marston's Pedigree and a guest beer are on draught, and there's is a short list of reasonably priced wines priced from £6.95. SAMPLE DISHES: warm watercress, potato and bacon salad £3.50; home-made steak and kidney pudding £8; steamed banana sponge with toffee sauce £3.25.

Licensee Geoff Holland (freehouse)
Open Mon to Fri 12 to 2.30, 6 to 11, Sat 12 to 11, Sun 12 to 10.30; bar food Mon to Fri 12 to 2, 6 to 9.30, Sat 12 to 9.30, Sun 12 to 9; open all day bank hols
Details Children welcome in bar eating area   Car park   Wheelchair access (also WC)   Garden and patio   No smoking in eating area   Occasional live music   No dogs   Amex, Delta, MasterCard, Switch, Visa

SANDY GATE   **Devon**   map 1

Blue Ball

Sandy Gate, nr Exeter EX2 7JL   TEL: (01392) 873401
off M5 junction 30 follow A3052 towards Clyst St Mary, go round roundabout and head back towards
M5, then turn left; pub is 300yds on right

This unpretentious thatched and cream-coloured roadside inn is just off the motorway on the outskirts of Exeter, and is under the same ownership as the Drewe Arms at
Drewsteignton (see entry). One of its two bars has a dark, rustic look, with flagstone
floor, settles and a warming log fire, while the second shows a lighter decorative
touch, with rugs on polished floorboards, scrubbed wood furniture and cream-
painted walls. The bar menu is a concise selection of simple and hearty dishes with a
traditional flavour, such as faggots with carrot and swede mash and red wine gravy, or
smoked haddock fillet topped with Stilton and a poached egg. There's also a separate
dining room with fashionably minimal décor and its own menu of relatively upmarket dishes such as grilled sea bass fillet with rösti, or seared local beef fillet on truffled
champ potatoes with beetroot and thyme salsa. This might be followed by a traditional bread-and-butter pudding served with raspberry coulis and home-made vanilla
ice cream. Beers are well-kept Bass and Gale's HSB, plus a guest such as Wyre
Piddle's Piddle in the Hole, and there's a New-World-accented list of 28 wines, all
available by the glass. SAMPLE DISHES: steak and Guinness pie £10; salmon and cod
fishcakes with caper dressing £10; hot chocolate fondant pudding with marinated
cherries and home-made chocolate ice cream £5.

Licensees Colin and Janice Sparks, and Andrew Payne (Enterprise Inns)
Open 11 to 3, 6 to 11, Sun 12 to 3, 7 to 10.30; bar food 12 to 2.30, 6 (7 Sun) to 9.30
Details *Children welcome in eating areas   Car park   Wheelchair access (also WC)   Garden and patio   No-*
smoking area in bar, no smoking in dining room   Background music   No dogs   Delta, MasterCard, Switch, Visa

SAPPERTON   **Gloucestershire**   map 2

Bell at Sapperton 😊 😊 🍺 🍇

Sapperton GL7 6LE   TEL: (01285) 760298
WEBSITE: www.foodatthebell.co.uk
follow signs from A419 midway between Cirencester and Stroud

The Bell is a large, prosperous-looking inn of Cotswold stone that fits perfectly in this
well-to-do village. It's been sympathetically converted with style, its chic, rural décor
incorporating bare wooden tables, exposed-stone or cream-painted walls, and lots of
log fires or wood-burners. As one of the rising stars of the Cotswolds dining scene,
changes in the kitchen could have been cause for alarm, but Ivan Reid from the
Churchill Arms, Paxford (see entry), has been appointed and early reports are enthusiastic. Not only has he continued the popular menu structure (local sourcing continues to mark the brasserie-tinged cooking), but he has also introduced a number of
new and more contemporary ideas. A cutlet of Gloucester Old Spot pork from
Chesterton Farm Butchers is served with a Parmesan and pimento crust and teamed
with sage risotto, while sweet potato mash accompanies local blade of beef 'braised in
its own goodness'. Pigeon faggot on a potato cake with white cabbage and mustard
dressing, and Portland crab layered with spiced tomato with an avocado and lime
relish figure among starters, with rich bitter chocolate mousse or tangy lemon tart

with raspberry sorbet for dessert. Some things remain unchanged: the choice of paired cheeses (Waterloo and Tornegus, for example) and the excellent bread from a Nailsworth baker, and the beers are as good as ever – evidence of the declared partiality for good-quality, locally brewed real ale is seen in the likes of Uley Old Spot Prize Ale, Hook Norton Best Bitter, Wickwar Cotswold Way, and Goff's Jouster. Prices look good for the quality on an extensive wine list that tours the world and throws in a collection of smart French bottles on top. House wines kick off at £12.25, with plenty of options by the glass. SAMPLE DISHES: potato and black pudding terrine with a fried free-range egg and crisp bacon £6; noisette of Shetland lamb with lamb and garlic ravioli and tomato sauce £15.50; strong vanilla bean ice cream with Pedro Ximénez sherry £5.25.

Licensees Paul Davidson and Pat Le Jeune (freehouse)
Open 11 to 2.30, 6.30 to 11, Sun 12 to 3, 7 to 10.30; bar food 12 to 2, 7 to 9.30 (9 Sun)
Details No children under 10 evenings   Car park   Wheelchair access (also WC)   Garden and patio
No-smoking area in bar   No music   Dogs welcome   Delta, MasterCard, Switch, Visa

SAWLEY   Lancashire   map 8

Spread Eagle ✿

Sawley BB7 4NH   TEL: (01200) 441202
WEBSITE: www.the-spreadeagle.co.uk
off A59, 4m NE of Clitheroe

WATERSIDE

Although a dining pub, the Spread Eagle maintains an inviting 'olde-worlde' look, with coal fires and a relaxing atmosphere in its spacious bar, with real ales like Moorhouses Pendle Witches Brew and Black Sheep Best Bitter on draught. Bar food is limited to rolls, soup and snacks such as chicken liver and foie gras parfait, but the star attraction here is the restaurant, which enjoys the benefit of picture windows overlooking the River Ribble. The menu aims to produce dishes of 'Lancastrian substance' in a European brasserie style, using good-quality local produce. Expect the likes of potted chicken and pork rillettes with home-pickled onions and spiced fruit chutney, followed by poached fillet of smoked haddock with crushed potatoes and a buttered broth of peas, smoked bacon, lettuce and mint, or braised medallion of beef with potato purée, cottage pie ravioli and a rich braising sauce. To finish, creamy Lancashire cheese with pickles and chutney is an alternative to blackcurrant délices. Note that restaurant food is not available in the bar and vice versa. Wine drinkers have plenty of choice, with a 50-bin list that offers excellent value throughout, prices starting at £10, with around ten by the glass. SAMPLE DISHES: tortellini of scallops and bacon £7; slow-cooked boneless shank of lamb with mash, stewed tomatoes and tarragon sauce £11.50; layered chocolate truffle cake £4.50.

Licensee Nigel Williams (freehouse)
Open Tue to Sat 12 to 4, 6 to 11, Sun 12 to 4; bar food Tue to Sat 12 to 2, restaurant Tue to Sun 12 to 2,
Tue to Sat 6 to 9
Details Children welcome in restaurant   Car park   Wheelchair access (also WC)   No smoking in restaurant
Background music   Guide dogs only   Amex, MasterCard, Switch, Visa

Which? Online subscribers will find The Which? Pub Guide *online, along with other* Which? *guides and magazines, at www.which.net. Check the website for how to become a subscriber.*

Sawley Arms

Sawley HG4 3EQ   TEL: (01765) 620642
off B6265 Pateley Bridge to Ripon road, 5m SW of Ripon

The typical English village setting – opposite the church and close to the green, with its old water pump – is a major plus for this old pub. It consists of a range of stone buildings (two cottage apartments are to let), and within is a series of rooms, with beams, alcoves stuffed with brass and copper jugs, upholstered benches and chairs, and countless plates and prints on the walls. But it is not a drinkers' pub; most people come here to eat, and the emphasis throughout is on food, with the bar no more than a wide hatch for ordering both food and drinks: John Smith's Bitter, ales from Theakston, and six wines by the glass. The short, enterprising menu is augmented by a daily-changing board of specials. Fish is a strength of the starters: salmon mousse, say, or a plate of smoked salmon and prawns with marie-rose sauce. Plaice Mornay with leeks and cheese-glazed creamed potatoes, or steak pie with a rich gravy and butter-crust pastry might be among main courses. Salads and sandwiches are also on offer. The World Heritage Site of Fountains Abbey is nearby. SAMPLE DISHES: Stilton, port and celery pâté £5.50; deep-fried scampi with tartare sauce £11.50; hot cherry pancake £4.50.

Licensee Mrs June Hawes (freehouse)
Open *11.30 to 3, 6.30 to 11; bar food and restaurant 11.30 to 2.30, 6.30 to 9; closed Sun and Mon evenings winter*
Details *No children   Car park   Wheelchair access (also WC)   Garden   No smoking   Background music No dogs   Delta, MasterCard, Switch, Visa*

▲ Olde Ship Hotel

9 Main Street, Seahouses NE68 7RD   TEL: (01665) 720200
WEBSITE: www.seahouses.co.uk
on B1430, 3m SE of Bamburgh

Seahouses has a working fishing harbour where boats take people to the Farne Islands (where Grace Darling made her name), National Trust-owned bird sanctuaries. The Olde Ship Hotel, in the centre of the village, has been a pub since 1812 (before that it was a farmhouse); its two front bars are festooned with nautical regalia and have pine floors made of old decking planks. The real ales on tap might include Black Sheep Best Bitter, Ruddles County, Old Speckled Hen, Bass and Theakston Best Bitter, plus guests, and some eight or so wines are offered by the glass, with most of the bottles on the short list coming in well under £15. On the food front, dinner is a fixed-price three courses and sorbet, while at lunch main dishes are all £6.50, and puddings are £3; the prices of starters vary. Among the last, soups, such as vegetable, and fish (Craster kippers) predominate, then there could be steak and Guinness pie, or smoked fish chowder, followed by plum upside-down pudding with custard. The bar menu could run to game pie, stuffed whiting, or sirloin steak. SAMPLE DISHES: crab soup £3.50; chicken Highlander £7.50; golden apricot crumble £4.

Licensees Alan and Jean Glen (freehouse)
Open *11 to 11, Sun 12 to 10.30; bar food and restaurant 12 to 2, 7 to 8.30*
Details *No children   Car park   Wheelchair access (not WC)   Garden and patio   No smoking in 1 room Occasional background music   Guide dogs only   MasterCard, Switch, Visa   Accommodation: 18 rooms, B&B £40 to £90*

▲ Seaview Hotel

High Street, Seaview PO34 5EX   TEL: (01983) 612711
WEBSITE: www.seaviewhotel.co.uk

A tall flagpole flies the Union and English flags on the deck-like terrace outside this handsome family-run hotel just up the street from the sea wall. The nautical, ship-board theme continues in the bars, one wardroom-like, its walls crowded with nautical pictures, the other with a tongue-and-groove deal counter and dado, boarded floor, and all manner of maritime memorabilia festooning the creamy walls and ceiling. In the drinks department, you can expect real ales including Goddard's Special Bitter (brewed in Ryde) and Adnams Bitter, a fine selection of malt whiskies, and a wine list that focuses strongly on claret (impressively listing nine under £20 alongside pricier famous names) and Burgundies; there are also a few half-bottles, but only two house wines are offered by the glass. Bar food (on a shortish menu supplemented by a black-board) emphasises local ingredients, particularly fish. Typical are sautéed herring roes on toasted brioche, crab mash with chilli sauce, and something more elaborate like grilled salmon with squid-ink pasta and a leek and Gruyère fondue. Elsewhere, shin of Isle of Wight beef is turned into a broth, and slow-braised lamb shank comes with rosemary-crushed potatoes, while vegetarians might settle for spiced aubergine imam bayaldi with tabbouleh. To finish, choose between steamed treacle pudding and chocolate roulade with marinated cherries. The restaurant menu is similar but more extensive. SAMPLE DISHES: duck parfait with roasted ciabatta and plum sauce £5.25; wild mushroom risotto with truffle oil and Parmesan £10; iced lemon brûlée £4.

Licensee N.W.T. Hayward (freehouse)
Open 10.30 to 2.30, 6 to 11, Sun 12 to 3, 7 to 10.30; bar food and restaurant 12 to 2, 7 to 9.30; closed 3 or 4 days Christmas
Details Children welcome   Car park   Wheelchair access (not WC)   Patio   No smoking in 1 dining room
Occasional background music   Dogs welcome exc in restaurant   Amex, Delta, Diners, MasterCard, Switch, Visa
Accommodation: 17 rooms, B&B £55 to £170

Lough Pool Inn ♥ ♥ 🍺 ❀

Sellack HR9 6LX   TEL: (01989) 730236
off A49, 4m NW of Ross-on-Wye

Sitting beside the meandering Wye, Sellack is nicely rural (though handy for Hereford), and the Lough Pool Inn is definitely worth the detour. There are picnic tables on the grass outside, a log fire in the bar and a heartening array of real ales – Wye Valley Butty Bach and John Smith's Cask Bitter, alongside guests from Brecon, Spinning Dog in Hereford and Freeminer from Gloucestershire. A range of bottled ciders and perries comes from small local producers, including Dunkertons and Broome Farm. Beyond the bar is a small dining room with pine floorboards and yellow walls. One menu is served throughout the pub, and, since licensee Stephen Bull is a chef of pedigree, this is a high-class act bringing together Spanish charcuterie, brochettes of Moroccan-spiced lamb with tabbouleh, and slow-braised blade of beef bourguignon with gratin dauphinois, as well as pub classics like carrot and coriander soup, or chargrilled Hereford rib eye steak with garlic tarragon butter and chips. Fish is given due attention, witness Brixham whiting in beer batter alongside full-fledged restaurant dishes like pan-fried red gurnard with orange and crayfish risotto and raw tomato sauce. Cakes and tarts prevail among puddings, or perhaps apple and Calvados parfait for contrast. The wine list is concise, good-value and full of interesting flavours; eight come by the glass, plus an excellent organically grown champagne. SAMPLE DISHES: Caesar salad with crispy bacon £6; honey and mustard ham hock with creamy mash and red wine jus £12; pecan tart £5.25.

Licensee Stephen Bull (freehouse)
Open 11.30 to 2.30, 6.30 to 11.30, Sun 12 to 2, 7 to 10.30; bar food and restaurant 12 to 2, 7 to 9.15; 1 Oct to 31 Mar closed Sun evening and Mon
Details Children welcome in eating areas   Car park   Wheelchair access (not WC)   Garden   No smoking in restaurant   No music   Dogs welcome   Delta, MasterCard, Switch, Visa

SHALFLEET   Isle of Wight   map 2

New Inn

Main Road, Shalfleet PO30 4NS   TEL: (01983) 531314
WEBSITE: www.thenew-inn.co.uk
on A3054 Newport to Yarmouth road

A nautical theme runs through this pleasant eighteenth-century pub, set hard on the road that eases one way at a time (thanks to the village traffic light system) through Shalfleet. Pictures of boats on walls, and charts and models on ledges and window sills fill the several different spaces inside. These include the main bar with flagged floor, large fireplace and a wood-topped brick counter; a carpeted saloon area with yellow walls and blue wood dado; and a tile-floored eating area. Four real ales always include local Ventnor Golden, plus maybe Goddards Fuggle-Dee-Dum, Green King IPA, Marston's Pedigree, or Bass. The printed menu and specials boards emphasise fish, especially locally caught crab, lobster, plaice and sea bass, in regularly changing dishes that may include hake fillets with lemon and tarragon, and seafood platters. Apart from old faithfuls like gammon ham, egg and chips, and various steaks, meat dishes may take in venison steak with garlic butter, or duck with orange sauce, and there are various ploughman's and filled baguettes, including a popular version with local crab. Eight wines come by the glass, and close to 60 by the bottle. SAMPLE DISHES: grilled sardines in herbs and garlic £4; Mediterranean haddock with basil, red onion and tomato £12; apple tarte Tatin £3.50.

Licensees Martin Bullock and Mark McDonald (Enterprise Inns)
Open 12 to 3, 6 to 11 (10.30 Sun); bar food 12 to 2.30, 6 to 9.30
Details Children welcome   Car park   Garden   No-smoking area in bar   No music   Dogs welcome   Amex, Delta, Diners, MasterCard, Switch, Visa

SHEPTON MONTAGUE   Somerset   map 2

▲ Montague Inn

Shepton Montague BA9 8JW   TEL: (01749) 813213

Rather like a 'genteel family home', said one report on this white-painted village-centre pub, where the atmosphere is relaxed and the service 'affable'. The interior comprises two dining areas, one with a giant exposed-stone inglenook and a collection of wall plates, off a central bar area, and the same menu is served throughout. Standard lunch offerings include such pub staples as sausages, mash and onion gravy, and steak and ale pie, though the new chef has more leeway with the evening carte: Gressingham duck with Marsala and nectarine jus, say, or whole plaice stuffed with a prawn mousse. These might be preceded by venison pâté, or devilled mushrooms, and followed by raspberry and almond tart. Greene King IPA is the regular beer, supplemented by guests such as Butcombe Gold and Brakspear Bitter, along with 30 wines from £10, including a board listing specials and five sold by the glass. SAMPLE DISHES: smoked salmon terrine with warm potato salad £7; marinated venison with red wine and raspberry vinegar reduction £13; bread-and-butter brioche pudding £4.

Licensees Julian and Linda Bear (freehouse)
Open Tue to Sat 11 to 2.30, 6 to 11, Sun 12 to 2.30; bar food and restaurant Tue to Sun 12 to 2, Tue to Sat 7 to 9
Details Children welcome in family room and restaurant   Car park   Garden and patio   No smoking in restaurant   Occasional live music   No music   No dogs   Delta, MasterCard, Switch, Visa   Accommodation: 3 rooms, B&B £55 to £70 (double room)

SHIPSTON ON STOUR   Warwickshire   map 5

▲ White Bear

4 High Street, Shipston on Stour CV36 4AJ   TEL: (01608) 661558
WEBSITE: www.whitebearhotel.co.uk
just off A429 Ettington to Moreton-in-Marsh road

Dating from the sixteenth century, but 'modernised' in Georgian times, this red-brick inn is easy to spot on Shipston's main street. Some exposed-stone walls and ceiling beams are reminders of its origins, and the interior comprises a popular bar, a quieter lounge bedecked with prints, and a restaurant at the back with a restrained, calming décor of neutral shades and white-clothed tables. One menu is served throughout. From a choice of around eight starters, you might begin with pork and pheasant terrine with red onion marmalade, or mussels with coriander and shallots. Main courses include their quota of pub staples, such as pork, cider and apple hotpot, although the range is extended by the likes of grilled halibut on vanilla risotto with chive butter sauce, guinea fowl with carrot and 'nips' mash and malt whisky sauce, or – for vegetarians – aubergine and cauliflower red Thai curry. Adnams Bitter and Broadside, plus Bass and a guest beer, are on draught, and 13 reasonably priced wines are served by the glass from a short international list. SAMPLE DISHES: tomato and mozzarella salad with garlic mushrooms £4.75; steak, Guinness and onion pie £8.25; ginger and lemon cheesecake £4.

Licensees George Kruszynskyj and Lou Snoxall (Punch Group)
Open 11 to 11, Sun 12 to 10.30; bar food and restaurant 12 to 2 (2.30 Sat and Sun), 6.30 to 9.30 (10 Fri and Sat); no food Sun evening
Details Children welcome   Car park   Garden   Occasional live music; jukebox in bar   Dogs welcome   MasterCard, Switch, Visa   Accommodation: 10 rooms, B&B £30 to £50

SHOCKLACH   Cheshire   map 7

Bull Inn

Shocklach SY14 7BL   TEL: (01829) 250239
off A534 Wrexham to Nantwich road; turn right after crossing River Dee, then 3m to village

This solid-looking old pub in an isolated hamlet is a thriving rural local catering for the local farming and commuting community. The atmospheric oldest parts of the interior are heavily beamed, though the dining area is in one of the more modern sections. Food options are spread across numerous menus (including one for children), extended further by specials on a blackboard plus another board listing curries. Bar lunches range from hearty sandwiches through filled jacket potatoes, all-day breakfasts, mixed grills, and steaks. From the carte you might choose roast duckling with sherry and redcurrant sauce, or fishcakes with tartare sauce. Start with something like chicken and bacon salad tossed in garlic mayonnaise and finish with apple crumble. Bass, and Banks's Bitter and Mansfield Cask Ale are the ales on offer, and 18 or so wines include four house wines by the glass. SAMPLE DISHES: garlic mushrooms £4.75; lamb Henry with mint gravy £12; crêpe filled with fresh fruit and ice cream and served with warm Tia Maria, golden syrup and cream sauce £4.50.

Licensee John Williams (Pyramid Pub Co)

Open *Tue to Sat 11.30 to 3, 6.30 to 11, Sun 11.30 to 3, 7 to 10.30; bar food and restaurant Tue to Sun (exc Tue lunchtime) 12 to 2.30, 6.30 to 9.30*

Details *Children welcome Car park No smoking in restaurant Background music Guide dogs only MasterCard, Switch, Visa*

SHUTFORD   Oxfordshire   map 5

George & Dragon   NEW ENTRY

Church Lane, Shutford OX15 6PG   TEL: (01295) 780320
WEBSITE: www.georgeanddragon.co.uk
village signposted off A422 about 4m W of Banbury

Shutford is a tiny hamlet close to the National Trust's Upton House, with the fourteenth-century George & Dragon at its heart, in a cul-de-sac opposite the church. Exposed stone and oak floorboards in both the bar and non-smoking restaurant are the backbones of a plain, understated look, one that's been updated by new owners Andrew and Allison Davis – he cooks, she is front-of-house. They run a good operation, offering a menu that is neither too long nor over-ambitious, with food that is simple, straightforward and reliant on first-class, seasonal raw materials. Blackboards mirror the printed menu, and there are fish specials: say, pan-seared pieces of monkfish with garlic and lemon on a bed of brown rice, or fillet of salmon with spring onion mash and oyster mushroom sauce. Starters include 'very good soups', honey- and ginger-glazed duck salad, or a 'nicely executed' Caesar salad with chilli chicken, with mains strong on pub classics such as braised shoulder of lamb with creamy mash and red onion jus, steak, mushroom and Guinness pie, and bangers and mash in onion gravy. From some half a dozen pudding choices there could be treacle tart and chocolate and orange tart. There are lunchtime sandwiches and snacks, and a set Sunday lunch at £11 for two courses includes a choice of roasts, or perhaps a puff pastry box filled with chicken in green peppercorn sauce. Hook Norton Best Bitter and a couple of guests are on handpump, and the wine list couldn't be simpler: just a dozen bottles, all under £20, with five by the glass. SAMPLE DISHES: potato and watercress soup £3.50; pan-fried ribeye steak with red wine sauce £11.50; bread-and-butter pudding £5.

Licensee Allison Davis (freehouse)

Open *Tue to Sat 12 to 2.30, 6 to 11, Sun 12 to 10.30; bar food and restaurant Tue to Sun 12 to 1.45, Tue to Sat 6 to 9*

Details *Children welcome in restaurant Wheelchair access (not WC) Garden No smoking in restaurant No music Dogs welcome in bar only Amex, Delta, MasterCard, Switch, Visa*

SINNINGTON   North Yorkshire   **map 9**

▲ Fox and Hounds

Sinnington YO62 6SQ   TEL: (01751) 431577
WEBSITE: www.thefoxandhoundsinn.co.uk
off A170 between Helmsley and Pickering

On the edge of the North York Moors National Park within easy reach of York and
the coast, this attractive sandstone pub makes a good base for exploring the area. The
front door leads into a cosy, low-ceilinged bar area, all neat and well looked after, with
lots of little ornamental bits and pieces about the place. The food is a major attraction
here, with separate lunch and dinner menus served throughout. Expect plenty of
cosmopolitan modern touches in, say, a strudel of roasted tomatoes, spinach and St
Maure ash goats' cheese with balsamic-glazed onions, or pan-seared halibut fillet with
a warm salad of roasted fennel, red onion, salmon, monkfish and basil, although the
kitchen is equally at home with more earthy cooking: slow-roast Goosnargh duck
comes with red plum and sour cherry chutney, while Charlie Hill's Old English
sausages are served on mash with red onion and coriander gravy. Desserts are equally
ambitious: perhaps tangerine cheesecake with raspberries topped with Chinese stem
ginger, crème fraîche and borage sorbet. Black Sheep Special Ale and Camerons
Bitter are provided for real ale drinkers, while wine buffs can dip into the concise and
fairly priced list, which opens with half a dozen house selections, all available by the
bottle (£11.50) and the glass (£3). SAMPLE DISHES: battered calamari with aïoli £5.25;
slow-roast belly pork with roast garlic and cracked chilli sauce £10.25; caramelised
bananas and iced pistachio parfait £4.75.

Licensees Andrew and Catherine Stephens (freehouse)
Open 12 to 2.30, 6 (6.30 winter exc Fri and Sat) to 11, Sun 12 to 2.30, 6.30 to 10.30; bar food and
restaurant 12 to 2, 6.30 (7 winter) to 9 (8.30 Sun)
Details Children welcome   Car park   Wheelchair access (also WC)   Garden and patio   No smoking in
restaurant   Background music   Dogs welcome exc in restaurant   Amex, MasterCard, Switch, Visa
Accommodation: 10 rooms, B&B £44 to £80

SLAIDBURN   Lancashire   **map 8**

▲ Hark to Bounty Inn

Slaidburn BB7 3EP   TEL: (01200) 446246
WEBSITE: www.hark-to-bounty.co.uk
on B6478, 8m N of Clitheroe

Hark to Bounty, with its thick stone walls and small windows dating from the thirteenth century, forms quite a significant part of the tiny village of Slaidburn. In the
cosy, oak-beamed bar, with its winter log fire, there's well-kept Theakston Best Bitter
and Old Peculier on draught, alongside guests such as Wadworth 6X and Shire Bitter,
with a number of malt whiskies and three wines by the glass. It's worth peeking into
the magnificently beamed function room, a courtroom until 1937, which still has jury
benches and the judge's box. Bar food includes salads, ploughman's, sandwiches and
jacket potatoes, plus starters like grilled sardines with lemon and parsley butter. Mains
include grilled fillet of haddock topped with Lancashire cheese rarebit, ribeye steak
with all the trimmings, and various pasta dishes. The restaurant offers Stilton and
blueberry cheesecake, then maybe medallions of pork fillet on mustard mash with

apple, mushroom and cream sauce. If room remains, there's chocolate and orange pudding to finish. SAMPLE DISHES: steamed Lancashire black pudding with grain mustard sauce £4; breast of chicken wrapped in bacon with a sauce of leeks, white wine and cream £9.25; nectarine pavlova £3.50.

Licensee Isobel Bristow (freehouse)
Open 11 to 11; bar food Mon to Sat 12 to 2, 6 to 9 (8 in winter), Sun 12 to 2.30, 6 to 8; restaurant Wed 6 to 9, Thur to Sat 12 to 2, 6 to 9, Sun 12 to 2
Details Children welcome Car park Wheelchair access (not WC) Garden No-smoking area in bar, no smoking in restaurant Background music Dogs welcome exc in eating areas Delta, MasterCard, Switch, Visa Accommodation: 9 rooms, B&B £29.50 to £69.50

SLAPTON   Devon   map 1

▲ Tower Inn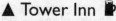
Church Road, Slapton TQ7 2PN   TEL: (01548) 580216
WEBSITE: www.thetowerinn.com

Narrow lanes weave through the charming village of Slapton, where cars seem like visitors from another planet. The inn was built in about 1347 to accommodate the men working on the Collegiate Chantry of St Mary, and then probably became the college's guesthouse to dispense alms and hospitality. The remains of the chantry tower stand alongside the pub and provide a real sense of atmosphere in the raised walled garden. Inside, it is all low ceilings, stone walls, pews and open fires, and in the evening candlelight creates a more formal atmosphere. Booking is advisable if you want to eat, particularly during high season. Separate menus operate at lunch and dinner. For the former, sandwiches include home-cooked smoked ham with apple and mustard, or crab (when available), while heartier appetites could go for beef, mushroom and ale pie, or smoked haddock on parsley mash with a spinach and lemon cream. The evening menus are a touch more elaborate, with starters like crab and prawn tower with basil oil, or baked goats' cheese with a baby pear, spinach and redcurrant salad. Main courses are equally fancy: baked chicken on a potato cake with cranberry and onion confit, or seared venison steak with creamed Savoy cabbage and a whisky, chocolate and orange sauce. Daily specials are chalked on a board, and to finish there might be apple and treacle crumble, local Salcombe ice creams, or a platter of West Country cheeses. The real ales are Dartmoor Best Bitter, Adnams Bitter and Tanglefoot from Badger, with guests in the summer. Weston's and Addlestone ciders are also available, as is a well-chosen wine list with seven by the glass. SAMPLE DISHES: pork, liver and herb terrine wrapped in vine leaves with spiced apricot and orange chutney £6; salmon fillet on wilted spinach with vanilla and saffron cream sauce £12.25; sticky toffee pudding with toffee sauce £4.25.

Licensees Andrew and Annette Hammett (freehouse)
Open 12 to 3, 6 to 11, Sun 12 to 3, 7 to 10.30; bar food 12 to 2, 7 to 9; closed 25 Dec
Details Children welcome in eating area Car park Garden No-smoking area Occasional live or background music Dogs welcome Amex, MasterCard, Switch, Visa Accommodation: 3 rooms, B&B £40 to £65

Directions have been included where deemed necessary, but if in doubt about a pub's location – especially if heading to a rural location – it is advisable to phone and check.

SMARDEN   Kent   map 3

▲ Chequers Inn

The Street, Smarden TN27 8QA   TEL: (01233) 770217
village off A274 Maidstone to Tenterden road, signposted just S of Headcorn

Smarden is a sprawling village, the heart of which consists of a cluster of houses on a narrow, twisting main street, with the white-weatherboarded Chequers on a corner. From the street you enter directly into a main bar made cosy by a low, beamed ceiling and furnished with a mixture of old church pews, simple chairs, a grandfather clock, and a diverse collection of prints and paintings. Bar food is straightforward: omelettes, gammon with eggs and chips, a range of baguettes, and variations on the ploughman's theme. The main menu, served in two dining rooms set with flowers and napkins, continues the theme of standards from the modern pub repertoire, with tempura prawns and sweet chilli sauce, and pâté with cranberry sauce to start, then steak and kidney pie, chicken and cider casserole, and veal T-bone steak with pink peppercorn sauce. Real ales are from the Harveys and Adnams Breweries, plus draught Bass and a guest, and a 25-bottle wine list starts in France and takes a brisk trot around the world. About ten wines are served by the glass. To the rear of the pub is a paved terrace with an attractive, well-maintained garden beyond, framed by mature trees and shrubs and overlooking a large pond and with views of the church – an idyllic setting on a sunny summer's day. SAMPLE DISHES: fishcakes with sweet chilli sauce £5; roast sea bass stuffed with mixed herbs £13.50; sticky toffee pudding £4.25.

Licensees Lisa and Charles Bullock (freehouse)
Open 11 to 11, Sun 12 to 10.30; bar food and restaurant 11.30 to 2.30 (3 Sun), 6 to 9.30 (10 Sat)
Details Children welcome Car park Garden No smoking in restaurant Occasional background music
Dogs welcome Amex, Delta, MasterCard, Switch, Visa Accommodation: 4 rooms, B&B £40 to £80

SMART'S HILL   Kent   map 3

Bottle House Inn

Smart's Hill, Penshurst TN11 8ET   TEL: (01892) 870306
W of B2188 1m S of Penshurst

Take care when negotiating the narrow country lanes that lead to this 'higgledy-piggledy' pub, although you are guaranteed a pretty drive in 'nice rolling countryside'. Within, an open fire, low beams, patterned carpet and dark wood tables create an 'olde worlde' look. The spacious bar has pleasant, chatty, welcoming staff who can offer you brews from Larkins, three miles off in Chiddingstone, or Harveys from Lewes, all of 20 miles away. There are also eight wines by the glass on a list that stays mostly under £15 and includes the local Penshurst Müller-Thurgau. Both bar and the restaurant alongside it have the same menu, a wide-ranging affair embracing everything from Swedish gravidlax and Harvey's Bristol Cream tomato soup to chicken Madras, and roast leg of pork with sausage and stuffing. An extensive dessert list makes choice difficult, but toffee and praline cheesecake, and chocolate espresso parfait with chocolate sauce are two that catch the eye. SAMPLE DISHES: salt cod pâté with olive oil £5; grilled duck breast with blueberry and cassis sauce £14; rhubarb and custard tart with clotted cream £4.25.

Licensees Gordon and Val Meer, and Paul Hammond (freehouse)
Open 11 to 11, Sun 12 to 10.30; bar food and restaurant Mon to Fri 12 to 10, Sun 12 to 9
Details Children welcome in eating areas Car park Garden and patio No smoking in dining room
Background music Dogs welcome exc in dining room Delta, MasterCard, Switch, Visa

Spotted Dog Inn ❀ NEW ENTRY

Smart's Hill TN11 8EE   TEL: (01892) 870253
W off B2188, 1m S of Penshurst

New licensee Kirsten Price has worked wonders since taking over this early sixteenth-century weatherboarded inn in prime walking country. The garden has been upgraded, and there's now an area of wooden tables on terraced flagstones; the views over the valley are as stunning as ever. Inside, all is warm and welcoming, with glowing fires to keep out the cold in winter plus notable features including a red-tiled floor, thick red curtains, and plenty of pine tables dotted around. A new kitchen team is delivering some 'visually stunning' food at 'extremely reasonable cost', with the emphasis on local and seasonal ingredients. Lunch and dinner menus change regularly, and there's always a back-up of specials (moules marinière and loin of venison with celeriac purée, for example). Reporters have praised pan-fried calf's liver with stir-fried vegetables, bubble and squeak and caramelised shallots ('a mixture of flavours and textures cooked to perfection') and roast pheasant breast with bread sauce, braised salsify, roast vegetables and château potatoes ('a plateful of autumnal colours'). Start perhaps with roast Italian vegetable and mozzarella tart or a small plate of pasta, and finish with pretty-looking vanilla cheesecake with lime curd. Larkins Traditional and Harveys Sussex Best are supplemented by a guest such as Old Speckled Hen and the wine list has some tempting bottles as well as six by the glass for £3 or so. Nearby Penshurst Place is well worth a visit. SAMPLE DISHES: grilled smoked mackerel fillet on spicy warm Thai salad £5.75; chicken breast, ham hock and tarragon pie with hand-fried crisps £9.25; warm apple sponge with cinnamon ice cream £4.75.

Licensee Kirsten Price (freehouse)
Open *Mon to Thur 11 to 3, 6 to 11, Fri and Sat 11 to 11, Sun 12 to 10.30; bar food Mon to Sat 12 to 2.30, 6 to 9.30, Sun 12 to 8*
Details *No children under 10 after 7pm   Car park   Patio   No-smoking area   Background music   Dogs welcome   Delta, MasterCard, Switch, Visa*

SNAPE   Suffolk

map 6

▲ Crown Inn

Bridge Road, Snape IP17 1SL   TEL: (01728) 688324
off A1094, on way to Snape Maltings

The Crown has a wealth of genuine beams and 'what they claim is probably the finest double Suffolk settle in existence', reports one visitor to this fifteenth-century pub a stone's throw from Snape Maltings. Brick floors, open fires and simple wooden furniture – some old and stripped, others modern varnished pine – set a relaxed, informal tone, but dining tables fill most of the open-plan space, giving the impression that this is more 'a restaurant with bar than a drinking pub'. The longish, crowd-pleasing blackboard menu rolls out the likes of lobster and crayfish tart, and seared scallops with crème fraîche and chilli jam to start, while mains could take in Thai red chicken curry, Turkish lamb sauté with thyme, mint, apricots and tomatoes on lemon couscous, or a straightforward steak and kidney pudding. Finish with a comforting dessert, such as pear and almond flan. The wines, approaching 40 bottles and majoring on France, are supplied by Adnams of Southwold, as are the ales.

SAMPLE DISHES: smoked chicken Caesar salad £5.50; smoked haddock, pea and mint fishcakes £9; sherry cheesecake £4.

Licensee Diane Maylott (Adnams)
Open 12 to 3, 6 to 11, Sun 12 to 3, 7 to 10.30; bar food and restaurant 12 to 2, 7 to 9; closed 25 Dec, evening 26 Dec
Details No children Car park Wheelchair access (also WC) Garden and patio No smoking in restaurant No music No dogs Delta, MasterCard, Switch, Visa Accommodation: 3 rooms, B&B £60 to £70

SNETTISHAM Norfolk   map 6

▲ Rose & Crown

Old Church Road, Snettisham PE31 7LX TEL: (01485) 541382
WEBSITE: www.roseandcrownsnettisham.co.uk

Appearances can be deceptive: this seemingly diminutive cottage of a pub (appropriately covered in roses in summer) has been heavily extended, and the cosy, warmly decorated front bar leads via a twisting narrow passage to a warren of bars and dining rooms. The bars (one non-smoking) serve Adnams brews, Bass and Greene King IPA – and of 30-odd wines (half European, half New World) over 20 can be had in 175ml or 250ml glasses. The biggest dining room, a family room, opens onto the walled garden at the back. Lunch and evening menus are supplemented by a blackboard of specials – wok-flashed chilli beef, pineapple, noodles and oyster sauce, for example – and there are always simple pub 'classics' such as home-made burger with chunky chips. Lunch menus include sandwiches, three-cheese and onion toastie, say, and light dishes such as shredded duck salad with beansprouts and sweet soy. Mains from the evening menu range from fillet of sea bass with cockle and leek cassolé, to whole stuffed partridge, crushed celeriac and rosemary and port jus. Finish with a caramelised white peach and stem ginger cheesecake. SAMPLE DISHES: fig and ewes' cheese salad with avocado oil £5.75; whole brill with Moroccan spiced potatoes and walnut sauce £11.75; honey and orange pannacotta £4.50.

Licensee Anthony Goodrich (freehouse)
Open 11 to 11, Sun 12 to 10.30; bar food and restaurant 12 to 2 (2.30 summer), 6.30 to 9 (9.30 summer)
Details Children welcome in family room and restaurant Car park Wheelchair access (not WC) Garden No-smoking area in bar, no smoking in dining room No music Dogs welcome Delta, MasterCard, Switch, Visa Accommodation: 11 rooms, B&B £55 to £100

SOUTHAMPTON Hampshire   map 2

White Star Tavern

28 Oxford Street, Southampton SO14 3DJ TEL: (02380) 821990
WEBSITE: www.whitestartavern.co.uk
corner of Latimer Street and Oxford Street, just N of Queen's Terrace (A33) in S of city

This was a hotel for sea travellers in days gone by, but its current incarnation has a contemporary/retro feel, with wood aplenty on walls, pillars and ceilings, large windows and several preserved fireplaces. Comfortable modern banquettes and armchairs, contemporary lighting and colours (plus some of the old chandeliers and a tiled floor) give the drinking area a bar-bistro atmosphere, and this continues into the large dining area behind. The lunch menu includes several starter-or-main dishes (like tuna Niçoise salad), plus the likes of ham and parsley terrine with home-made piccalilli, or classic club sandwich with home-cut chips. The longer dinner menu has up-to-the-minute ideas like crab and cucumber risotto, or maybe seared scallops, spinach and blue cheese cream to start, then confit of duck leg, spring onion and new potato salad with tarragon and mustard dressing. Among these might be more famil-iar starters such as leek and potato soup, and main courses of beef and mushroom casserole, while classic apple and plum crumble gets updated with an accompanying gin and tonic sorbet. Fuller's London Pride, Bass and Courage Best are on hand-pump, and eight wines are offered by the glass from a list of some 40 mainly French and New World bottles. SAMPLE DISHES: grilled crottin de Chavignol, roast Mediterranean vegetables and pesto dressing £5; sea bream with new potato fondant, cauliflower purée and red wine shallot jus £14.50; caramelised rice pudding with home-made strawberry and vanilla jam £6.

Licensees Mark Dodd and Lawrence Cescatti (freehouse)
Open *winter Tue to Sat 12 to 3, 5.30 to 11, Sun 12 to 10.30, summer Tue to Sat 12 to 11, Sun 12 to 10.30,; bar food and restaurant Tue to Sat 12 to 2.30, 6 to 9.30 (10 Fri and Sat), Sun 12 to 9; closed 25 and 26 Dec, 1 Jan*
Details *Children welcome Sat and Sun   Wheelchair access (also WC)   Patio   No-smoking area in restaurant Background music   No dogs   MasterCard, Switch, Visa*

SOUTH CROSLAND   West Yorkshire   map 8

King's Arms   NEW ENTRY

23–25 Midway, South Crosland HD4 7DA   TEL: (01484) 661669

Good food and a pleasant setting make this extensively refurbished dining pub a place where drinkers are made welcome and you can either eat cheaply or push the boat out. The small snug area has good views of Castle Hill at Almondbury, and the lounge has a modern feel, with comfortable leather sofas, a boldly coloured carpet and a wood-burning stove. The open-plan restaurant is more formal, with well-spaced tables covered in white cloths, high-backed leather dining chairs, and a pale wooden floor. Reporters have spoken highly of the food as well as service that is informative, approachable and generous. The menus are appealing, imaginative and varied: hot fish 'teacake' with mushy peas, or a sourdough roll with beef brisket, horseradish and onions from the lunchtime sandwich board, or poached smoked haddock with champ, a poached egg and grain mustard from the 'Lite-Bites' menu, while from the restaurant carte comes roast onion tart with goats' cheese and red pepper jam, then grilled red mullet with fennel, olives, tomato and basil, with tarte Tatin with cinna-mon and vanilla to finish. Hearty Sunday lunches are good value, whether you have the set-piece roast or grilled breast of chicken with Toulouse sausage cassoulet. Tetley Bitter and Black Sheep Best Bitter are on draught, and four wines are served by the glass. SAMPLE DISHES: steamed halibut and pea velouté £5.75; roast calf's liver with mash, bacon and onion £8; chocolate tart with griottines and caramel £4.50.

Licensee Tracy Lightowlers (Punch Taverns)
Open *Mon 4 to 11, Tue to Sat 12 to 11, Sun 12 to 10.30; bar food and restaurant Tue to Sat 12 to 2, 6 to 9 (9.30 Fri and Sat), Sun 12 to 4*
Details *Children welcome   Car park   Wheelchair access (also WC)   No smoking in restaurant   Background music   No dogs   Delta, Diners, MasterCard, Switch, Visa*

SOUTH LEIGH Oxfordshire map 2

▲ Mason Arms

South Leigh OX8 6XN TEL: (01993) 702485

'Traditional' is the word that springs to mind on first seeing this thatched, fifteenth-century inn, but the giant inn sign proclaiming 'Gerry Stonhill's "Individual" Mason Arms' should prepare you for the interior. The quirky décor, 'a cross between a gentleman's club, antique shop and wine cellar', is notably dark, even in the middle of the day: the only lighting is from candles, picking out the Turkish rugs on flagstone floors, the antique furniture, the stacks of leather-bound tomes and cigar boxes, rows of dust-covered old wine bottles and the 'politically incorrect' pictures. Though the printed menu changes little from year to year – Mr Baxter's potted shrimps (as supplied to the late Queen Mother) will always be found – there is a blackboard to ring the changes: stockpot soup or Jabugo ham among starters, with steak and kidney pie, fresh fish or seasonal game to follow. Though the style is simple, the cooking is based on top-quality ingredients. To finish there might be dark chocolate mousse, or good-quality cheeses. Burton Ale straight from the barrel is offered for beer drinkers, the wine list includes two by the glass, and connoisseurs of single malts and Armagnac are well served, as are fans of Cuban cigars. SAMPLE DISHES: fish soup £7; boeuf bourguignon £11; treacle tart £5.50.

Licensee Gerry Stonhill (freehouse)
Open Tue to Sun 12 to 3.30, Tue to Sat 6.30 to 11.30; bar food and restaurant 12 to 2.30 (3 Sun), 7.30 to 10.30; closed 1 week Christmas, 2 weeks August
Details No children Car park Wheelchair access (not WC) No music No dogs Amex Accommodation: 2 rooms, B&B £35 to £65

SOUTHWOLD Suffolk map 6

▲ Crown Hotel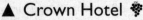

90 High Street, Southwold IP18 6DP TEL: (01502) 722275
WEBSITE: www.adnams.co.uk

The Crown is an upmarket pub, restaurant and hotel set on Southwold's main street, a handsome white-painted Georgian building. Several rooms provide different attractions: the back bar is where to head for a real pub atmosphere and fine beers from local brewery Adnams. The main bar also has a pubby look – stripped pine tables, cushioned settles, a coal-effect fire plus various paintings and a collection of clay pipes on the walls – but is mostly given over to eating. Lengthy menus feature lots of fashionable flavours in imaginative combinations, such as mussels with chickpeas and chorizo, or a salad of griddled scallop roes with duck confit and capers, but also make room for more conventional dishes such as pan-fried lemon sole with parsley and capers. A separate restaurant with its own menu is in the old parlour. A monthly selection of 20 wines by the glass or bottle complements the list of 200 bottles, which is full of sensible prices and interesting choices. SAMPLE DISHES: fish soup with rouille and croûtons £4; baked Suffolk chicken with braised sauerkraut and mashed potato £11; tarte Tatin with Jersey cream £5.

Licensee Michael Bartholomew (Adnams)
Open 10 to 11, Sun 12 to 10.30; bar food 12 to 2, 7 to 10; restaurant 12.30 to 1.30, 7.30 to 8.45
Details Children welcome in bar Car park Wheelchair access (also WC) No-smoking area in bar, no smoking in restaurant No music Dogs welcome in back bar Delta, MasterCard, Switch, Visa Accommodation: 14 rooms, B&B £75 to £150

SOWERBY   West Yorkshire   map 8

Travellers Rest ☺

Steep Lane, Sowerby HX6 1PE   TEL: (01422) 832124
off A646, 2m W of Sowerby Bridge

It may take some finding among Calderdale's steep and winding lanes, but this isolated pub up on the moors has spectacular views and promises a great deal once you get inside. A serious revamp has woven together the building's original features (including exposed-stone walls and flagstone floors) with contemporary gestures that are reminiscent of an upbeat wine bar. In this context, the bar menu has a decidedly homespun ring to it: corned beef hash with pickled red cabbage, cheese and onion pie with spiced beans in tomato with a pot of HP sauce, and hot roast beef sandwich with pickled onion, for example. The restaurant menu (available throughout the pub) tells a different story: goats' cheese and pine-nut spring rolls are accompanied by onion marmalade and wilted spinach, while main courses could range from rack of lamb on bubble and squeak with a cranberry and redcurrant jus to a fish special such as whole sea bass steamed with soy and ginger served on wilted Chinese greens. As a finale, two people could explore the delights of dark chocolate and nougat fondue with marsh-mallows, seasonal fruit and biscuits. Timothy Taylor Landlord and Golden Best are on draught, and the list of 20 global wines includes four by the glass. SAMPLE DISHES: moules marinière £7; pan-fried wild duck breast with orange, grapefruit and pickled beetroot £15; rhubarb crumble £4.50.

Licensee Caroline Lumley (freehouse)
Open Tue to Fri 5 to 12, Sat and Sun 12 to 12; bar food and restaurant Sat and Sun 12 to 2.30, Tue to Sun 6 to 9.30 (10 Sat, 8.30 Sun); open all day bank hols
Details No children   Car park   Wheelchair access (not WC)   Garden and patio   No smoking in restaurant Background music   Dogs welcome   Delta, MasterCard, Switch, Visa

SPARSHOLT   Hampshire   map 2

Plough Inn

Sparsholt SO21 2NW   TEL: (01962) 776353
off B3049 1½m W of Winchester

Crowds continue to flock to this much extended 200-year-old cottage a short drive from affluent Winchester and Farley Mount Country Park, so it's advisable to book if you're planning to come for dinner. Inside, all has been smartly refurbished in the rambling, open-plan bar area and neat, original front rooms. Large pine tables, plenty of attractive prints and farm tools brighten up the walls. The atmosphere is both buzzy and rustic. One blackboard menu advertises lunchtime sandwiches and bar meals, another focuses on slightly more elaborate and ambitious restaurant-style dishes such as smoked chicken with orange and walnuts followed by, say, good-quality cod fillet with olives, crushed potatoes and a drizzle of subtly flavoured herb oil or – for vegetarians – chilli and chickpea cakes with avocado salsa. Puddings could range from glazed lemon tart to chocolate cheesecake. This is a Wadworth pub, with 6X, Henry's Original IPA, JCB and Old Timer generally on draught. At least 12 wines (plus Champagne) are served by the glass from a well-balanced list. The expansive flower-filled garden, complete with children's playhouses, a wooden chalet and open country views is a great family attraction in summer. SAMPLE DISHES: spinach and

Brie soup £4; salmon and smoked haddock lasagne £9; bread-and-butter pudding £4.50.

Licensees Richard and Kathryn Crawford (Wadworth)
Open 11 to 3, 6 to 11, Sun 12 to 3, 6 to 10.30; bar food 12 to 2, 6 to 9 (9.30 Fri and Sat); closed 25 Dec
Details Children welcome in eating areas   Car park   Wheelchair access (also WC)   Garden   No-smoking area in bar, no smoking in eating areas   No music   Dogs welcome   Delta, MasterCard, Switch, Visa

STANFORD DINGLEY   Berkshire   map 2

Old Boot Inn
Stanford Dingley RG7 6LT   TEL: (0118) 974 4292
from M4 junction 12 take A340 N towards Pangbourne, then follow signs to Bradfield, then to Stanford Dingley

From the outside the white-painted Old Boot wears its age well; it is only when you step inside that you realise the building dates from the eighteenth century. It is all open-plan, with two big fires and yellow walls denoting the bar area, changing to pink for the more formal restaurant (tablecloths and posies of flowers), which extends into a light conservatory, but the blackboard menus are available throughout. The old boot theme is everywhere, from picture and brass versions to Old Boot Ale on handpump (alongside West Berkshire Brewery's Good Old Boy and a guest like Young's Special, as well as Stowford Press cider). The menu has its share of pub favourites, such as breaded Brie, lasagne, various pies, and fishcakes, but there are some more interesting things too: a parsley-flecked terrine of ham, Thai-style sea bass with yellow and red peppers, onion and courgette, or duck breast with Savoy cabbage, mushrooms and blueberries. Treacle tart with custard might be found on the list of homely puddings. Around ten wines are sold by the glass from a list of 30-odd bottles. With a garden extending to over half an acre, this is a pleasant spot in summer. SAMPLE DISHES: bacon-wrapped pigeon breast with a honey and thyme dressing £5.75; calf's liver and bacon with red wine jus £13; lemon soufflé £4.50.

Licensee John Haley (freehouse)
Open 11 to 3, 6 to 11; bar food and restaurant 12 to 2.15, 7 to 9.30
Details Children welcome   Car park   Wheelchair access (not WC)   Garden and patio   No smoking in conservatory   No music   Dogs welcome exc in restaurant   Delta, MasterCard, Switch, Visa

STANNERSBURN   Northumberland   map 10

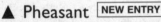 ▲ Pheasant   NEW ENTRY
Stannersburn NE48 1DD   TEL: (01434) 240382
WEBSITE: www.thepheasantinn.com
from B6320 at Bellingham, take minor road to Lanehead and Kielder Water

This charming creeper-covered pub is about a mile east of Kielder Water Reservoir in an isolated part of Northumberland. In winter 'the winds can be extremely biting', and one visitor much appreciated the roaring coal fire on arrival. There are two spick and span bars, with everything gleaming – the wooden tables have a mirror-like finish, even the beams overhead have a polished look – but a rustic element is provided by stone walls hung with a few pheasant pictures and old farming implements. A blackboard alongside the bar lists simple dishes such as leek and potato soup, or caramelised red onion and goats' cheese tartlet to start, followed by salmon with dill butter sauce, cider-baked gammon with Cumberland sauce, steak and kidney pie, and salmon fish-cakes with tartare sauce. Roast Northumberland lamb with a rosemary and redcurrant jus is one of the most popular items on the menu, and this proved to be two 'quite thick', tender and well-flavoured slices of leg served with a good selection of vegetables. Real ale fans will find Black Sheep Best Bitter, Timothy Taylor Landlord, Marston's Pedigree, Old Speckled Hen or Wylam Hedonist on handpump. There's a list of some 20 or so malt whiskies and around the same number of globetrotting wines, with most under £15. SAMPLE DISHES: sweet marinade of herring £4.25; fillet steak with green peppercorn sauce £14; sticky toffee pudding £3.50.

Licensee W.R.C. Kershaw (freehouse)
Open *winter Wed to Sat 12 to 2, 7 to 11, Sun 12 to 2.30, 7 to 10.30, summer Mon to Sat 11.30 to 3, 6 to 11, Sun 12 to 2.30, 7 to 10.30; bar food and restaurant 12 to 2.30 (2 Sun), 7 to 9; closed Nov to Mar, 25 and 26 Dec*
Details *Children welcome   Car park   Wheelchair access (also WC)   Garden   No-smoking area in bar, no smoking in restaurant   Background music   No dogs   Delta, MasterCard, Switch, Visa   Accommodation: 8 rooms, B&B £35 to £75*

STANTON WICK   Bath & N.E. Somerset   map 2

▲ Carpenters Arms

Stanton Wick BS39 4BX   TEL: (01761) 490202
WEBSITE: www.the-carpenters-arms.co.uk
off A368, ½m W of junction with A37 Bristol to Shepton Mallet road

The homeliness of this former row of miners' cottages gives way inside to a stylishly slick enterprise that takes in a formal restaurant, an informal Cooper's Parlour dining area, and a dozen bedrooms. Yet it has the feel of friendly local too, with Butcombe, Bass and Wadworth 6X on handpump, supplemented by Natch cider. Cream and primrose colours set off the bare stone walls, low beams and wooden panelling. The Cooper's Parlour menu (supplemented by blackboards) offers salads, sandwiches, a children's menu, and some of the restaurant dishes – say, roast cod on lemon-crushed potato with prawn and saffron sauce, or open lasagne of wild mushrooms and asparagus with truffle cream sauce – as well as steak and mushroom pie, and smoked salmon with fettucine and dill cream. Ten wines come by the glass, from £3.40 to £5, and the short list of bottles includes some more upmarket offerings. SAMPLE DISHES: Caesar salad £5; roast pork chop on black pudding and sage mash with cider cream sauce £12; rosemary crème brûlée £4.25.

Licensees Simon Pledge, A.M. Jones and T.S.C. Ruthven (freehouse)
Open *11 to 11, Sun 12 to 10.30; bar food and restaurant 12 to 2, 7 to 10; closed evenings 25 and 26 Dec*
Details *Children welcome in eating areas   Car park   Patio   No smoking in 1 eating area   Occasional live music   Dogs welcome in bar only   Amex, Delta, MasterCard, Switch, Visa   Accommodation: 12 rooms, B&B £64.50 to £89.50*

STATHERN   Leicestershire   map 5

Red Lion

2 Red Lion Street, Stathern LE14 4HS   TEL: (01949) 860868

The Red Lion may give its name to the street on which it stands, but it's tucked away and you need to look out for the sign by the village stores. Its rather ordinary exterior conceals quite a gem, fitting for the stablemate of the Olive Branch at Clipsham (see entry), 20 miles away. Hence, it is unambiguously a foodie pub, but still pleasingly a pub. The stone-flagged, beamed bar draws real ale fans for Brewster's VPA (from a few yards away in Penn Lane), Grainstore's Olive Oil (from faraway Oakham), or more distant guests like Brains SA from Cardiff. Local sourcing also marks the brasserie-tinged modern British cuisine. Roast Belvoir partridge is teamed with fondant potato and red wine sauce, Lincolnshire sausages (served with sage mash and onion gravy) are made by the local butcher, the pub smokes its own duck and cures its own gravad lax, and there's also roast fillet of brill with rösti and Japanese artichokes, or Thai-style salmon fishcake with soya-flavoured vegetables. Desserts run to lemon meringue pie, bread-and-butter pudding, and a selection of cheese that includes Quickes mature Cheddar and Cropwell Bishop Stilton. A concise list cherry-picks the wine world's highways and byways for interesting bottles from £9.95 to £38.50, with plenty under £15 and around half a dozen by the glass. SAMPLE DISHES: roast pumpkin soup £4; loin of venison with port and peppercorn sauce £14.75; banoffi pudding with banana ice cream £5.

Licensee Ben Jones (Rutland Inn Company Ltd)
Open *Mon to Thur 12 to 3, 6 to 11, Fri and Sat 12 to 11, Sun 12 to 5.30; bar food Mon to Sat 12 to 2, 7 to 9.30, Sun 12 to 3; closed 26 Dec, lunch 31 Dec, 1 Jan*
Details *Children welcome   Car park   Wheelchair access (not WC)   Garden and patio   No smoking in dining room   Background music   Dogs welcome in bar only   Delta, MasterCard, Switch, Visa*

STAVERTON   Devon   map 1

▲ Sea Trout Inn

Staverton TQ9 6PA   TEL: (01803) 762274
WEBSITE: www.seatroutinn.com
off A384, 2m N of Totnes

Dating from the fifteenth century, the Sea Trout is an attractive white-painted inn in a small village just a couple of miles from Totnes. To the rear is a landscaped garden with a pond and fountain, while inside is a rambling open-plan lounge bar with old beams, open fires and stuffed fish in display cases; adjacent to the lounge is a more formal dining room. There is also a separate public bar with a lively atmosphere. The bar menu features a range of simple, mostly traditional dishes, such as deep-fried whitebait, chargrilled gammon steak with pineapple, or lamb's liver with potato purée and sage and onion gravy. The menu in the separate conservatory restaurant, which overlooks the patio, is more adventurous and offers two or three courses for a set price during the winter. Starters might include pan-fried pigeon breast with warm onion jam and toasted almond salad, followed by a main course such as tournedos of beef topped with duck liver parfait, baked garlic croûton and a wild mushroom jus. Real ales come from Bridport brewery Palmers, and there's a list of around 40 wines from £9.75 a bottle, of which 12 are available by the glass. SAMPLE DISHES: potted salmon and prawn terrine £5.50; steak and Guinness pie £8.75; treacle tart with vanilla ice cream £4.

Licensees Nick and Nicky Brookland (Palmers)
Open *11 to 3, 6 to 11, Sun 12 to 3, 7 to 10.30; bar food and restaurant 12 to 2, 7 to 9; closed 25 Dec*
Details *Children welcome in restaurant   Car park   Wheelchair access (also WC)   Garden and patio No smoking in eating areas   Dogs welcome   Amex, Delta, MasterCard, Switch, Visa   Accommodation: 10 rooms, B&B £45 to £80*

STEDHAM   West Sussex   map 3

Hamilton Arms

School Lane, Stedham GU29 0NZ   TEL: (01730) 812555
WEBSITE: www.thehamiltonarms.co.uk

THAI

A walk through the woods is one way of finding your way to this pub in the Sussex countryside not far from Midhurst. From the outside it looks traditional English to a T, with its white walls, tiled roof and small flowery terrace for alfresco dining, but inside West yields to East in the guise of carved elephants, wood panelling, intricately fashioned low tables displays of Thai handicrafts and even a 'shop' in one corner selling oriental foodstuffs. You can still order pints of Ballard's Best, Fuller's London Pride and seasonal guest beers at the bar, along with a handful of traditional dishes like fish 'n' chips, or chicken Kiev, but the place is best known for its genuine Thai food. The pictorial bar menu advertises a range of 19 dishes, based mostly around curries and plates of rice and noodles along with a few salads and Chinese-inspired ideas like honey-roast pork with soy and cucumber. The full menu offered in the Nava Thai restaurant runs to some 80 dishes spanning most aspects of the cuisine: gaeng ped yang (roast duck in curried coconut milk) is reportedly 'simply excellent'. Twenty-eight wines show up on the eclectic list (six by the glass), and prices are kept well in check. SAMPLE DISHES: Thai egg salad with peanut dressing £4; red chicken curry £6; fried thick noodles with soy sauce and vegetables £5.50.

Licensee Suhail Hussein (freehouse)
Open Tue to Sat and bank hol Mon 11 to 3, 6 to 11, Sun 12 to 4; bar food and restaurant Tue to Sat 12 to 2.30, 6 to 10.30, Sun 12 to 2.30, 7 to 9.30
Details Children welcome in eating areas and games room   Car park   Wheelchair access (also WC)
Garden and patio   No smoking in restaurant   Occasional music   Dogs welcome on leads in bar area only
Delta, MasterCard, Switch, Visa

STILTON   Cambridgeshire   map 6

▲ Bell Inn

Great North Road, Stilton PE7 3RA   TEL: (01733) 241066
WEBSITE: www.thebellstilton.co.uk

Dominated by a large bell sign hung from a honey-coloured gable, this imposing old coaching inn is impossible to miss in Stilton's broad main street that was once the Great North Road. The birthplace of the famous blue cheese is now a smart hotel with a fairly formal restaurant, but the beamed Village Bar has a flagstone floor, open fire and a pleasant, pubby feel, or there's an open-air courtyard for summer drinking. The menu takes in shellfish bisque risotto, and deep-fried whitebait with thick pesto dip, as well as seared calf's liver and sweetbreads with mashed potato, spring cabbage and red wine jus, and cod marinated in soy, cuttlefish ink and sesame oil accompanied by baby corn and pak choi salad. And, needless to say, that cheese pops up – in soups, sauces, dumplings and cheesecake as well as on the cheese board. The beers on offer are JHB (from the local Oakham Brewery), Greene King's Abbot Ale and IPA, and Adnams Bitter, and ten wines are available by the glass. SAMPLE DISHES: black pudding and mushroom soup with truffle oil £4.50; steak and Guinness stew with Stilton dumplings £11; chocolate marquise with crème fraîche and raspberry coulis £4.

Licensees M.J. and L.A. McGivern (freehouse)

Open *12 to 2.30 (3 Sat), 6 to 11, Sun 12 to 3, 7 to 10.30; bar food and restaurant 12 to 2, 6.30 to 9.30, Sun 12 to 2.30, 7 to 9; closed 25 Dec*
Details *Car park   Garden and patio   No-smoking area in bar, no smoking in restaurant   Background music   No dogs   Amex, Delta, Diners, MasterCard, Switch, Visa   Accommodation: 19 rooms, B&B £72.50 to £109.50*

STOCKBRIDGE   Hampshire   map 2

Greyhound 😊 😊

31 High Street, Stockbridge SO20 6EY   TEL: (01264) 810833

It's all change at this sympathetically converted old inn that blends rustic charm with a degree of sophistication. Former chef Darren Bunn is now chef-patron, and the emphasis on modern, simply prepared dishes has been strengthened. Half the lounge is now turned over to dining, and drinking space is limited to just enough room for a few people standing at the bar in front of the fire, with one table not laid for food. But the appealing, compact modern menu reads well, with starters ranging from terrine of ham hock, potato and foie gras with spiced pineapple chutney, or a fishcake with a poached egg and chive beurre blanc, to main courses of fillet of black bream with roasted salsify, fennel and artichoke with herb crème fraîche, or breast of Gressingham duck with beetroot boulangère and beetroot bouillon. Finish with something like vanilla rice pudding with poached Bramley apple. Light lunch choices take in a plate of smoked salmon, Jerusalem artichoke soup with truffle oil, and Stilton and Cheddar platter with pear and saffron chutney. The wine list covers a good range, with some six or so available by the glass, and two real ales on handpump – Butcombe Bitter the regular, plus guests such as Brakspear Bitter, Hobgoblin or Ashers Best. SAMPLE DISHES: haricot blanc soup with truffle oil £6; fillet of Scotch beef with seared foie gras and port and lentil jus £21.50; coffee pannacotta with rum- and raisin-poached pineapple £6.

Licensee T.C. Fiducia (Innspired Pubs & Taverns)
Open *all week 12 to 3, Mon to Sat 7 to 11; bar food 12 to 2.30, 7 to 10; closed 25 Dec, 1 Jan*
Details *Children welcome   Car park   Wheelchair access (not WC)   Garden   No smoking in 1 eating area   No music   Dogs welcome   MasterCard, Switch, Visa*

STOCKLAND   Devon   map 2

▲ Kings Arms Inn 🍇

Stockland EX14 9BS   TEL: (01404) 881361
WEBSITE: www.kingsarms.net
signposted from A30 Chard to Honiton road, or from A35 take Shute garage exit W of Axminster

Signposts to the village have been described as unhelpful, but those who get lost can at least enjoy a drive through some charming countryside. Perseverance, however, will soon lead you to this thatch-roofed custard-coloured inn. If the outside doesn't look especially antique, the inside is a treat for fans of old pubs: ancient timbers, low ceilings with giant beams, wooden settles and a lot of exposed stone. It all looks very smart and well cared for, and posies on the tables add to the classy feel. One menu serves both bar and separate dining room, a lengthy list offering as many as two dozen starters and 30 main courses, taking in everything from lamb cutlets with roasted garlic to lemon sole meunière, via king prawn Madras, venison pie and pasta provençale. Alongside regular Exmoor Ale and Otter Ale are ever-changing guest beers, and there's a long list of malt whiskies. A substantial and eclectic wine list opens with 21 house wines at £10 a bottle, also available by the glass, and there are plenty of exciting options from £12.50 up to £50. SAMPLE DISHES: Brie in filo £5; monkfish marseillaise £13.50; blueberry and raspberry cheesecake £5.

Licensees Heinz Kiefer, Paul Diviani and John O'Leary (freehouse)
Open 12 to 3, 6.30 to 11 (Sun 10.30); bar food and restaurant 12 to 1.45, 6.30 to 9; closed 25 Dec
Details Children welcome in bar eating area and dining room Car park Wheelchair access (not WC)
Garden and patio No smoking in dining room Live music in bar weekends; background music in dining room
Dogs welcome exc in dining room Delta, MasterCard, Switch, Visa Accommodation: 3 rooms, B&B £40 to
£60

STODMARSH   Kent   map 3

▲ Red Lion
The Street, Stodmarsh CT3 4BA   TEL: (01227) 721339
follow Stodmarsh signpost from A257 about 2m E of Canterbury

A charming and traditional village inn run enthusiastically by a traditional village innkeeper, the Red Lion dates from the fifteenth century and oozes character from every brick and gnarled old beam. Hop wreaths and all sorts of stuffed animals, musical instruments and other knick-knacks abound throughout the warren of linked areas set around a central island bar, each with its own decorative theme. Food, listed on a huge blackboard, is straightforward country cooking using good-quality local meat and fish and served in hearty portions: perhaps seafood chowder or pan-fried pigeon breast with mustard sauce to start, followed by oxtail stew with herb dumplings or lobster topped with cheese, king prawns and smoked salmon. The choice of wines includes four by the glass, while real ales drawn directly from the cask include Greene King IPA and Old Speckled Hen. In winter mulled Biddenden cider is served, and one unusual option is fresh figs in vodka and bullshot. SAMPLE DISHES: hot dressed Hythe crab mingled with avocado and mozzarella cheese £6; wild rabbit casserole with oak-smoked ham and claret £13; pineapple and Malibu crumble £3.25.

Licensee Robert Whigham (freehouse)
Open all week 10.30 to 10.30; bar food all week 12 to 2.30 (3.30 Sun), Mon to Sat 7 to 9.30
Details Children welcome in eating areas Car park Garden and patio Background music Dogs welcome
Delta, MasterCard, Switch, Visa Accommodation: 3 rooms, B&B £30 to £50

STOKE-BY-NAYLAND   Suffolk   map 6

▲ Angel Inn
Polstead Street, Stoke-by-Nayland CO6 4SA   TEL: (01206) 263245

Visitors exploring the glorious country of the Stour valley or following the Constable trail should find that this spotlessly maintained pub makes a perfect pit stop. Right on the crossroads in the village centre, it's impossible to miss – although latecomers may find parking spaces more elusive. Inside, the atmosphere is upmarket rustic (rough red-brick walls, brick and tiled floors, polished oak tables), and this clearly appeals, because the bars can get crowded (booking ahead is sensible). With a glass of Adnams Best Bitter (or Greene King Abbot Ale or IPA) in hand, one can consider the menu: tempting starters might include smoked duck roulade, crostini of goats' cheese, or smoked trout with apple and beetroot relish, with main courses of steamed steak and kidney pudding with onion gravy, roast rump of lamb, or roast fillet of cod with sunblush tomato risotto. An interesting and eclectic wine list has around 40 bins and ten by the glass ranging from £2.65 to £4.20. SAMPLE DISHES: cream of broccoli soup £3.25; game pie £7.50; chocolate and pecan tart £4.25.

Licensee Clive Richardson (Horizon Inns)
Open 11 to 2.30, 6 to 11, Sun 12 to 10.30; bar food and restaurant 12 to 2, 6.30 to 9, Sun 12 to 5, 5.30 to 9.30; closed 26 Dec, 1 Jan
Details Children welcome   Car park   Wheelchair access (not WC)   Patio   No smoking in eating areas   No music   Dogs welcome on patio only   Amex, Delta, MasterCard, Switch, Visa   Accommodation: 6 rooms, B&B £54.50 to £69.50

STOKE HOLY CROSS   **Norfolk**   map 6

Wildebeest Arms ❦ ❦

82–86 Norwich Road, Stoke Holy Cross NR14 8QJ   TEL: (01508) 492497
off A140 4½m S of Norwich

In a quiet one-shop-cum-post office village a few miles south of Norwich, the Wildebeest Arms is unassuming from the outside, but inside it shows off its true colours with a cool, contemporary décor of natural wood and pale yellow walls dotted with African masks and ethnographica. A central bar counter divides drinkers and eaters. The menus have a strong Anglo-Mediterranean accent, and you can choose between the fixed-price menu du jour (not available Saturday evening or Sunday lunchtime) and the list of daily specials. Starters might embrace anything from seared rare beef with shaved Parmesan and truffle oil salad to pan-fried calamari with tomato and caper salad and red pepper vinaigrette. Main courses could include, say, chargrilled ribeye steak in a Gruyère and parsley crust with 'house' chips, or grilled fillet of sea bass with fondant potato, sautéed wild mushrooms and sauce vierge. To finish, there are desserts like chilled caramelised vanilla rice pudding, and tiramisù with vanilla syrup. Adnams Bitter and a guest are on handpump and the clear wine list is packed with good bottles at very reasonable prices, including some specials alongside the dozen house selections by the glass. SAMPLE DISHES: chargrilled smoked salmon with guacamole and aged balsamic £6.50; pot-roast duck breast with lardons and redcurrant jus £17; glazed lemon tart with mango sorbet and lime syrup £5.25.

Licensees Henry Watt and Sarah Boyd (freehouse)
Open 12 to 3, 6 to 11, Sun 12 to 4, 7 to 11; bar food and restaurant 12 to 2, 7 to 10, Sun 12 to 2.30, 7 to 9.30
Details Children welcome   Car park   Wheelchair access (not WC)   Garden   No smoking in restaurant   Background music   No dogs   Delta, MasterCard, Switch, Visa

---

STOKE MANDEVILLE   **Buckinghamshire**   map 3

Woolpack   NEW ENTRY

21 Risborough Road, Stoke Mandeville HP22 5UP   TEL: (01296) 615970
take A4010 from Aylesbury, pass railway station and at roundabout turn into Risborough Road; pub a short distance on left

---

A serious makeover has transformed this old watering hole not far from Aylesbury into a thoroughly modern place with a neat look and a contemporary feel. Inside, it's open-plan and airy, with a couple of alcoves complete with tables and armchairs to the front, a central bar, and a big new dining extension at the back with tiled floors, ornate columns, and lots of pale wood. The menu is trendy Italian and it sets its stall out with headings such as 'little dishes' (squid with coriander, chilli and salsa), 'leaves' (crispy duck with watercress, bean sprouts and plum sauce) and 'starches/greens'. Centrepieces depend on the output of the stone-fired ovens for a range of pizzas (a 'giardiniera' version with mushrooms, olives, red peppers, leeks and petits pois has been 'first-rate'), as well as the grill and rôtisserie for dishes such as rack of lamb with peas, onions, chorizo and new potatoes, or salmon escalope with vine tomatoes and pesto. Desserts range from lemon polenta cake to pannacotta with gratinated berries. Fuller's London Pride and Bass are among the beers on draught, and there's also a 'fairly jazzy' little wine list of over 20 bins from around the world; around half a dozen are offered by the glass. SAMPLE DISHES: onion and balsamic tart £5; swordfish with Tuscan bean cassoulet and chorizo £13; tiramisù £6.

Licensee Abby Selby (Mitchell & Butler)
Open 12 to 11; bar food and restaurant Mon to Sat 12 to 2.30, 6 to 9.30, Sun 12 to 4.30; closed 25 Dec, 1 Jan
Details Children welcome in bar eating area Car park Wheelchair access (also WC) Garden No-smoking area in restaurant Background music No dogs Amex, Delta, Diners, MasterCard, Switch, Visa

STOKENHAM   Devon

map 1

Tradesman's Arms
Stokenham TQ7 2SZ   TEL: (01548) 580313
off A379 Kingsbridge to Torcross road, 5m E of Kingsbridge

The name of this quaint, simply furnished, part-thatched pub close to Slapton Sands and the wildlife-rich freshwater lagoon, Slapton Ley, is taken from the traders who transported their wares by donkey from Dartmouth to Kingsbridge via the coastal bridle path, stopping at the inn on the way. Within, there are heavy beams, a wood-burning stove and lovely views of the parish church. Nicholas Abbott used to be at the Bull and Butcher at Turville in Buckinghamshire (see entry), but bought the Tradesman's Arms in the summer of 2003. He has some interesting plans to make the interior more open and welcoming – currently the dining room is cut off from the bar and lacks atmosphere – but in the meantime is working on building up the pub's lunchtime business (the previous owners opened only in the evening). His compact modern British menu features fresh ingredients and dishes are well presented, as witnessed by a starter of pan-fried scallops with smoked bacon and red onions. Main courses run to rack of Devon lamb with a rosemary and redcurrant jus, or pan-fried duck breast with a ginger and cranberry sauce, with blackboard specials offering the likes of smoked prawns with wasabi mayonnaise and lunchtime sandwiches and ploughman's. Adnams Bitter, Brakspear Bitter and Tetley Imperial might be the three real ales on handpump and eight wines are available by the glass from a well-chosen and excellent-value short list. SAMPLE DISHES: grilled goats' cheese with red onion marmalade £5; chargrilled pork steak stuffed with apricots with glazed pears and cider sauce £9; raspberry frangipane £4.25.

Licensee Nicholas A. Abbott (freehouse)
Open Mon to Fri 11 to 3, 6 to 11, Sat 11 to 3, 6.30 to 11 (11 to 11 summer), Sun 12 to 5, 7 to 10.30 (12 to 10.30 summer); bar food 12 to 2.30 (4 Sun summer), 6.30 to 9.30; open 12 to 2 25 Dec (no food)
Details Children welcome Car park Wheelchair access (not WC) Garden and patio No smoking in eating area Occasional live music Dogs welcome Delta, MasterCard, Switch, Visa

Crooked Billet

Newlands Lane, Stoke Row RG9 5PU   TEL: (01491) 681048
WEBSITE: www.thecrookedbillet.co.uk
off B481 Reading to Nettlebed road, 5m W of Henley-on-Thames

'You would never stumble on this place accidentally unless you were out walking or, conceivably, hunting', yet the Crooked Billet is a pub with a high profile and an impressive CV of appearances on film and TV. Inside, it is full of idiosyncratic touches: all around are end-on displays of bottles, big woven baskets full of corks and candles and even mineral water caps. A huge fire often blazes, and the dark red or terracotta walls are festooned with vintage black and white photographs. There's no bar: pints of Brakspear Bitter are dispensed direct from casks in the cellar; also look out for bottles of Frogmarsh Mill cider, which is cellar-fermented with champagne yeast. The wine list offers good quality at a price with ten or so by the glass from £3.65 to £6.50. The menu reads well, inspiration is global and the kitchen is fully committed to using local ingredients ('if you have any home-grown produce – we'll buy it,' claims owner Paul Clerehugh), though fish may be from further afield. You might begin with baby squid pan-fried with garlic, chilli, chorizo and spinach, or pan-fried partridge breasts with haggis hash and Shiraz jus. Main courses could be as straightforward as steak with herb butter and chips or as complex as grilled halibut escalope with a warm salad of aubergine, lemon mushrooms, chickpeas and baby spinach with a minted yoghurt dressing. Cheeses are from Oxfordshire, and desserts span everything from sherry trifle to grilled pineapple with caramel sauce and home-made vanilla ice cream. The pub is also renowned for its eclectic live music evenings, which normally attract a cover charge. SAMPLE DISHES: Portuguese potato and chorizo soup with spring greens £4.50; warm salad of pan-fried pheasant breasts with watercress, potatoes and a sherry vinegar and walnut oil dressing £10; Bakewell tart with custard £4.

Licensee Paul Clerehugh (freehouse)
Open *Mon to Fri 12 to 3, 6.30 to 11, Sat and Sun 12 to 11; bar food and restaurant Mon to Fri 12 to 2.30, 7 to 10.30, Sat and Sun 12 to 10.30*
Details *Children welcome in eating areas   Car park   Garden   Occasional live music   No dogs   MasterCard, Visa*

Hare Arms

Stow Bardolph PE34 3HT   TEL: (01366) 382229
WEBSITE: www.theharearms.co.uk

The Hare Arms is a distinctive building, dating from the Napoleonic wars, set high up overlooking a crossroads and the village. The front, with its old-fashioned porch, still resembles the private house it once was, but today's visitors enter through the modern conservatory (a no-smoking dining room) and on into the L-shaped bar. Here, 'loads of pub jugs, Guinness memorabilia and framed…cartoon adverts' cover the walls. It's a popular place, with quite a diverse group of customers drawn by an extensive choice on various menus. In the bar there's nothing too fancy, just the usual range of pub staples: say, steak and Guinness pie, deep-fried haddock and chips, or steaks, as well as the usual sandwiches and jacket potatoes. Vegetarians are well catered for, and Sunday lunch sticks with tradition, offering roast beef and Yorkshire pudding in adult and child-friendly portions. Desserts such as mile-high toffee pie range over three blackboards. The restaurant offers set and à la carte menus that cover the likes of baby Thai fishcakes or chicken liver pâté, then duck breast with orange sauce or chicken breast stuffed with mushrooms, plus desserts from the trolley. The beers are Greene King's (Abbot, IPA and Old Speckled Hen), plus such guests as Hook Norton's Old Hooky, and there's Much Marcle Millennium Cider as well. The 30 or so wines are mostly under £20, and six come by the glass. SAMPLE DISHES: smoked mozzarella tartlet £5.50; tournedos with Stilton pâté £16; lemon lush pie £3.50.

Licensees David and Trish McManus (Greene King)
Open 11 to 2.30, 6 to 11, Sun 12 to 2.30, 7 to 10.30; bar food 12 to 2, 7 to 10, restaurant Mon to Sat 7 to 9.30; closed 25 and 26 Dec
Details Children welcome in family room and conservatory   Car park   Wheelchair access (not WC)   Garden and patio   No-smoking area in bar, no smoking in conservatory or restaurant   No music   No dogs
MasterCard, Switch, Visa

STOW MARIES   Essex   map 3

Prince of Wales 🍺 [NEW ENTRY]
Stow Maries CM3 6SA   TEL: (01621) 828971
just off B1012, E of South Woodham Ferrers

This white-clapboard pub is well known throughout Essex as it is on the trail of beer drinkers from near and far. The first-class selection of real ales includes Ridleys IPA and Witchfinder Porter, Teignworthy Beachcomber and Scrum Down (brewed for the World Cup), and Hop Back Summer Lightning, and Weston's scrumpy is on draught. Food matches the drinking admirably; dishes are listed on individual mini blackboards, with specials mixed in with regular favourites. Good things like sirloin steak, Italian meatballs with noodles, and spicy garlic chicken are as popular as pub staples such as sausage, egg and chips, giant jacket potatoes with various fillings, and thick-cut sandwiches. There's an all-day Sunday barbecue in summer. Service is informal and quick. The real pub atmosphere is maintained within each of the three bars, through tiled ceramic flooring, red-brick walls, standing timbers and austere tables and chairs, with lots of pub memorabilia on the walls. SAMPLE DISHES: deep-fried whitebait £5.25; chargrilled chicken with cheese and bacon £6.25; jam roly-poly £3.50.

Licensee Rob Walster (freehouse)
Open 11 to 11, Sun 12 to 10.30; bar food 12 to 2.30, 7 to 9.30 (all day Sun summer)
Details Children welcome in family room and eating areas   Car park   Garden   No smoking in dining room
Occasional live music   Dogs welcome   No cards

STOW-ON-THE-WOLD   Gloucestershire   map 5

▲ Eagle and Child
Digbeth Street, Stow-on-the-Wold GL54 1BN   TEL: (01451) 830670
WEBSITE: www.theroyalisthotel.co.uk

With a fawn-painted plastered façade, the Eagle and Child – one of the oldest inns in England – clearly distinguishes itself from the Cotswold stone of its parent, the Royalist Hotel. The pub and adjacent hotel changed hands in 2004, and early reports suggest it is being run along similar lines. The pub consists of three linked areas:

a tiny bar and main eating area, which both reveal their age with low ceilings, great dark beams and ancient flagstones, and a modern no-smoking conservatory dining room that leads on to a small courtyard-cum-patio. Good raw materials are part and parcel of a printed menu that has wide appeal, with a style that is bright and inventive, mixing pub classics, such as beer-battered cod with chips and crushed peas, with the more contemporary: say, sea bass with ginger, honey, soy, pak choi and pilaff rice. Daily specials might include roast breast of chicken stuffed with Stilton and served with 'intensely flavoured' sweet potato mash and green beans, and desserts extend to banana parfait with caramelised bananas and chocolate sauce. Local Hook Norton Best Bitter and Archers Best Bitter are on tap, and a short and simple wine list includes some dozen by the glass from £2.50. SAMPLE DISHES: warm Thai chicken salad with prawn crackers and sweet chilli £6; grilled liver with bacon £11; warm chocolate fudge cake with red fruits and vanilla ice cream £4.75.

Licensees Peter and Amanda Rowan (freehouse)
Open 11 (12 Sun) to 11; bar food 12 to 2.30 (3 Sun), 6 to 9.30 (9 Sun), restaurant Tue to Sat 12 to 2.30, 7 to 9.30
Details Children welcome   Car park   Garden and patio   No smoking in restaurant   Background music   No dogs in dining areas   Delta, MasterCard, Switch, Visa   Accommodation: 8 rooms, B&B £90 to £140

▲ Kings Arms ✿

The Square, Stow-on-the-Wold GL54 IAF   TEL: (01451) 830364
WEBSITE: www.kingsarms-stowonthewold.co.uk

Stow-on-the-Wold is home to this lofty, grey-stone pub that was originally a pit stop for coach travellers. Inside is an interesting mix of ancient and modern, with eating and drinking spread over two floors. Huge ancient floorboards, exposed-stone walls and giant black ceiling beams set the tone, although seating includes Charles Rennie Mackintosh chairs. Nightlights, fat candles and ceiling spots illuminate the place. The daily menu, chalked on a blackboard, is based around carefully sourced ingredients: fish from Cornwall, free-range poultry, and local meat and seasonal vegetables. By contrast, the kitchen looks to Italy for much of its inspiration, offering antipasti and scallops with prosciutto and lemon relish as starters, followed by main courses ranging from Tuscan hare casserole with pappardelle to saffron and mozzarella risotto. There are also a few Middle Eastern touches, as in grilled halloumi with pea, cucumber and asparagus salad. Desserts pick up on the Italian theme with pannacotta with almond caramel or torta Caprese, although cheeses hail from this side of the Channel. There is no wine list; instead, bottles are displayed on shelves upstairs, with price tags (from £11) around their necks; ten are available by the glass. Beer drinkers head for the ground-floor bar, where Greene King IPA and a guest such as Archers Golden Bitter are on draught. SAMPLE DISHES: chicken livers with hummus, pine nuts and coriander £5; roast rack of lamb with spiced lentils and salsa verde £14; lemon tart with raspberries £4.50.

Licensees Peter and Louise Robinson (Greene King)
Open 11 to 11, Sun 12 to 10.30; bar food and restaurant 12 to 2.30, 6 to 9.30 (10 Sat), Sun 12 to 2.30, 7 to 9; closed 1 week mid-May, 1 week mid-Oct
Details Children welcome   Car park   Background music   Dogs welcome in bar only   Delta, MasterCard, Switch, Visa   Accommodation: 9 rooms, B&B £70 to £100 (double room)

STOWTING   Kent   **map 3**

▲ Tiger NEW ENTRY

Stowting TN25 6BA   TEL: (01303) 862130
off B2068, about 5m N of Hythe

Stowting is somewhat off the beaten track and not all that easy to find – it's one of those sprawling villages where you pass the sign to say you've arrived and then continue for another mile before you reach any houses. But once in the village you can't miss the Tiger, a big mid-nineteenth-century building, painted pale primrose, behind a patio partly covered by a pergola. You enter directly into the main bar with a fireplace at either end, and the look is simple and unadorned, with bare wooden floors and walls painted in dark indigo. To the rear is an extensive dining area, which has orange rag-rolled walls, tapestry wall hangings, sturdy pine tables and solid wooden school chairs. The menu, served throughout, is listed on a huge blackboard above one of the fireplaces. It offers a good variety, with lots of traditional stuff (steak and kidney pie, sausages and mash) as well as a few modern dishes (goats' cheese crostini with raspberry coulis, duck breast with parsnip mash and Cumberland sauce). 'A proper old-fashioned Sunday roast' with a generous helping of thickly sliced beef, 'nicely cooked so it was still pink in the middle', with 'excellent' roast potatoes and good crisp Yorkshire pudding was the highlight of the weekend for one reporter. Five real ales on draught may include several from Shepherd Neame – say, Master Brew Bitter, Spitfire Premium Ale and the seasonal Late Red Autumn Hop Ale – Fuller's ESB and London Pride, and a guest such as Everards Tiger Best. SAMPLE DISHES: goats' cheese and pear tart with chilli and lime syrup £5; grilled salmon fillet with tomato and basil sauce £11; bread-and-butter pudding £4.

Licensee H.T.Willett (freehouse)
Open *Tue to Sun 12 to 2.30, 6.30 to 11; bar food 12 to 2.30, 6.30 to 9*
Details *Car park   Wheelchair access (WC)   No dogs   MasterCard, Visa   Accommodation: 2 rooms, B&B £15 to £30*

STRATFORD-UPON-AVON   Warwickshire   **map 5**

One Elm NEW ENTRY

1 Guild Street, Stratford-upon-Avon CV37 6QZ   TEL: (01789) 404919
WEBSITE: www.peachpubs.com

On a busy corner on the edge of the town centre, the One Elm looks smart and neat. It's a huge place, the bar thronged with people who've just popped in for a drink, yet offering a menu and ambience that are much more brasserie than pub. It is all down to the winning, flexible formula of the Peach Pub Company: food is served all day, there is very little that isn't available both at lunchtime and in the evening, and lots of dishes come in two sizes. Cheese, charcuterie and antipasti are available as starters, nibbles or to share, then there could be goats' cheese, tomato and red onion tart, or moules marinière as either a starter or a main course, with more substantial mains ranging from roast monkfish with stir-fried pak choi and carrots with red pepper relish, or confit pork belly with horseradish cabbage, to the lamb shank braised with tomatoes, coriander and lime that impressed at inspection. Apple and Calvados 'strüssel', or Thai sticky rice with mango are typical desserts. Old Speckled Hen and Fuller's London Pride are on handpump, and seven wines are offered by the glass from a short globe-trotting list. The spacious, uncluttered décor mirrors the contemporary cooking with walls of custard-coloured brick or tomato-red plaster, lots of bare wood, ceiling spot-lights and fat candles. SAMPLE DISHES: confit chicken spring roll £4.50; tuna loin with sweet potato and lime, honey and sesame butter £13.50; spicy chocolate trio £4.50.

Licensee Lee Cash (freehouse)
Open *11 to 11, Sun 11 to 10.30; bar food and restaurant 12 to 2.30 (3 Sun), 6.30 to 10*
Details *Children welcome   Car park   Garden   Background music   Dogs welcome   Delta, Diners, MasterCard, Switch, Visa*

STRETE   Devon   map 1

Kings Arms ✿   NEW ENTRY
Dartmouth Road, Strete TQ6 0RW   TEL: (01803) 770377
on A379 between Dartmouth and Torcross

Much of this white-painted pub has been turned over to restaurant dining, but with Otter Ale, Adnams Best and Old Speckled Hen on handpump, as well as local Heron Valley cider, and a lively, modern bar menu, the Kings Arms has all the necessary allure to attract those looking for a straightforward, friendly pub. Helford River native oysters are available in season, or there could be pan-fried soft herring roes on green peppercorn toasts, potted shrimps, or grilled sardines among starters, with main courses of roast cod in an oven-dried tomato, Parmesan, olive and basil crust. Although fish dominates the menu, meaty options include antipasti of cured meats, Luscombe's of Totnes pork sausages with mustard mash, and a range of tapas running from chorizo sausage to black pudding with chickpeas, sultanas, garlic and parsley. The bar is separated from the restaurant by a few steps. Here, splendid views over Start Bay come with a menu of locally caught fish cooked simply, with a few Asian or Spanish touches. Around ten wines are sold by the glass from a list of 35 round-the-world bottles. SAMPLE DISHES: seared scallops with braised Puy lentils £7.50; fish pie £9.50; double chocolate torte with vanilla-roasted plums £4.75.

Licensee R.W. Dawson (Heavitree)
Open *winter 11.30 to 2.30, 6 to 11, Sun 12 to 3, 7 to 10.30; summer 10.30 (9 July and Aug) to 11, Sun 12 to 10.30; bar food 12 to 2, 7 to 9, restaurant Wed to Sun 7 to 9; restaurant closed last 2 weeks Feb, last 2 weeks Oct*
Details *Children welcome   Car park   Wheelchair access (also WC)   Garden and patio   No smoking in restaurant   Occasional background music   Dogs welcome exc in restaurant   Amex, Delta, MasterCard, Switch, Visa*

STRETTON   Rutland   map 6

Jackson Stops Inn
Rookery Road, Stretton LE15 7RA   TEL: (01780) 410237

How times change: the unusual name reputedly dates from a time when the property was on the market for so long that it became known by the name on the estate agent's for- sale board. The long, low, stone-built and partly thatched pub dates from 1721, and its convivial atmosphere is aided by a traditional look of stone fireplaces, exposed stone, quarry-tiled or carpeted floors, pine tables and copper warming pans and farm implements. The seasonally aware, modish menu might open with ham hock and foie gras terrine with apple and sultana chutney, while roast Gressingham duck could be teamed with onion compote, fondant potatoes, Savoy cabbage and redcurrant jus as a main course. An unusual lemon brioche-and-butter pudding with old English custard could head up desserts. Oakham Ales' JHB and seasonal Adnams Broadside or Bitter are on handpump, while the globetrotting wine list offers ten by the glass from £2.95. SAMPLE DISHES: asparagus risotto with shaved Parmesan £5; naturally smoked haddock with lyonnaise potatoes, greens and a poached egg £9; hot chocolate fondant with pistachio ice cream £5.

Licensee James Trevor (freehouse)
Open 12 to 2.30, 6.30 to 11, Sun 12 to 2.30; bar food and restaurant 12 to 2, 7 to 10, Sun 12 to 2; closed 31 Dec, 1 Jan
Details Children welcome   Car park   Garden   No smoking in 1 room   Background music   Dogs welcome
Delta, MasterCard, Switch, Visa

SULGRAVE   Northamptonshire   map 5

Star   NEW ENTRY

Manor Road, Sulgrave OX17 2SA   TEL: (01295) 760389
from M40 junction 11 take A422 towards Brackley and follow signs to Sulgrave Manor

This attractive 300-year-old stone and creeper-covered inn stands in pleasant countryside on the edge of Sulgrave, just two minutes' walk from the home of George Washington's ancestors. Inside, low ceilings, heavy beams, standing timbers, terracotta-washed walls, and stone floors make up the two compact, traditional bars, and in a later extension is a spacious no-smoking dining room that is similar in style. Old farming tools, rural knick-knacks, old prints, and newspaper front pages headlining historical events are everywhere. Regulars aplenty come for fresh, honest cooking, choosing from the printed menu, or blackboard specials, starters such as rich, hearty Tuscan bean soup, or three 'big fat' grilled sardines on toast with a 'good' salsa verde. Main courses are equally up to date: corn-fed chicken with provençale sauce, mash and fine beans, cumin-crusted cod with coconut lentils, onion bhajia and poppadoms, or rib of beef (for two) with béarnaise, mixed-leaf salad and chips. Puddings, if you get that far, might be caramelised apple tart or two-chocolate cheesecake. Hook Norton Old Hooky and Best Bitter are the beers, with guests such as Shepherd Neame Spitfire Premium Ale and Wadworth 6X. A short wine list offers five by the glass. SAMPLE DISHES: smoked duck, leek and mint risotto £5.50; salmon, bacon and leek fishcakes with tartare sauce £9; chocolate brownie with vanilla ice cream and chocolate sauce £4.

Licensees Jamie and Charlotte King (freehouse)
Open Mon to Sat 11 to 2.30, 6 to 11, Sun 12 to 5; bar food and restaurant Tue to Sat 12.30 to 2, 6.30 to 9, Sun and bank hols 12 to 3; closed 26 and 27 Dec
Details Children welcome in restaurant   Car park   Wheelchair access (not WC)   Garden and patio
No smoking in restaurant   Live or background music   Dogs welcome by arrangement   MasterCard, Switch,
Visa   Accommodation: 3 rooms, B&B £35 to £70

SUTTON GAULT   Cambridgeshire   map 6

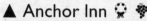 Anchor Inn

Sutton Gault CB6 2BD   TEL: (01353) 778537
WEBSITE: www.anchor-inn-restaurant.co.uk
off B1381 Sutton to Earith road, 6m W of Ely

Remotely situated in wide-open country by the New Bedford River (a straight canal also known as the Hundred Foot Drain), this seventeenth-century inn was built to provide lodging and sustenance for the labourers who were draining the Fens. Inside are pine tables on uneven floors, antique prints, wall-mounted working gas lamps, and log fires. Given the pub's out-of-the-way location, the modern and imaginative menu, with a blackboard of daily specials, might come as a bit of a surprise. Grilled dates wrapped in bacon with mustard cream sauce is a perennial favourite; otherwise the repertoire changes with the seasons: December might bring game and pistachio terrine with spiced pear and chilli compote before pheasant braised in cider and cream served with celeriac mash and Savoy cabbage, chargrilled haunch of venison with a red wine jus spiked with Valrhona chocolate, or – for fish lovers – roast tail of monk-fish with tagliatelle, Parmesan, mâche and salsa verde. Desserts might include custard tart with rhubarb compote and home-made ice cream and sorbet, and the line-up of British cheeses is worth exploring. Boathouse Bitter and Hobson's Choice from the City of Cambridge Brewery are on draught, along with Thatcher's scrumpy in summer. Worthwhile alternatives to mainstream names feature on a well-rounded if slightly pricy wine list and some decent options are offered by the glass. SAMPLE DISHES: Jerusalem artichoke soup with morels £5; roast cod with grain mustard and parsley mash, sprouting broccoli, brown shrimp butter £14; pear jelly with rich chocolate mousse and vanilla ice cream £6.50.

Licensee Robin Moore (freehouse)
Open *12 to 3, 7 (6.30 Sat) to 11 (10.30 Sun); bar food 12 to 2, 7 to 9 (6.30 to 9.30 Sat)*
Details *Children welcome   Car park   Wheelchair access (also WC)   Patio   No smoking in 3 rooms   No music Guide dogs only   Amex, Delta, MasterCard, Switch, Visa   Accommodation: 2 rooms, B&B £50 to £110*

SUTTON LANE ENDS   Cheshire   map 8

▲ Sutton Hall Hotel
Bullocks Lane, Sutton Lane Ends SK11 0HE   TEL: (01260) 253211
1½m S of Macclesfield turn E off A523, signposted Langley; after ½m turn left at Bullocks Lane crossroads

At the heart of extensive landscaped parkland, this venerable early sixteenth-century manor houses a convivial pub. Peacocks strut on the lawns and amid shrubberies, and views extend across the hilly landscape to the nearby edge of the Peak District National Park. The interior is a treat: the bar has gleaming copper measures lining a huge old fireplace, dark wood panelling, and a suit of armour, while the bar menu is not so old-fashioned, although it doesn't seek to be cutting edge either. It offers starters like French onion soup, or chicken and leek pancake with cheese sauce, with main dishes ranging from steak and kidney pie topped with smoked oysters to roast chicken chasseur. The menu in the separate restaurant might take you from warm smoked duck cooked in marmalade through roast rack of lamb with red wine and rosemary glaze to caramel and pecan cheesecake. Marston's Best, Bass, and Greene King IPA are on draught, plus guests like Timothy Taylor Landlord and Morland Original, and four wines are served by the glass from an extensive list. SAMPLE DISHES: Welsh rarebit £4.75; deep-fried crispy cod in batter with mushy peas £8.75; queen of puddings £3.50.

Licensee Robert Bradshaw (freehouse)
Open *11 to 11, Sun 12 to 10.30; bar food and restaurant 12 to 2.30, 7 to 10*
Details *Children welcome in restaurant   Car park   Garden   Background music   Guide dogs only   Amex, Delta, Diners, MasterCard, Switch, Visa   Accommodation: 10 rooms, B&B £79.95 to £94.95*

SUTTON UPON DERWENT   East Riding of Yorkshire   map 9

St Vincent Arms 🍺

Sutton upon Derwent YO41 5BN   TEL: (01904) 608349
on B1228, SE of York

Set in a village just a short drive from York, this is a hugely popular place – and deservedly so. A friendly, pubby atmosphere prevails throughout, emphasising the fact that the St Vincent is very much the traditional village local. And though three of the four rooms are given over to eating, it is a pub where food and beer are both taken seriously. There's a first-range of real ales, including Fuller's London Pride and Chiswick Bitter, Timothy Taylor Landlord, Wells Bombardier and Yorkshire Terrier from the York Brewery. On the food front, a regular menu lists pub staples along the lines of steaks, lasagne, and battered haddock and chips. More interesting is the list of daily specials: lemon sole with orange and Grand Marnier sauce, perhaps, or braised rabbit leg on spicy couscous, and banana parfait with flapjack and bitter chocolate sorbet to finish. Nine of the two-dozen wines are available by the glass. Note that booking is recommended if you intend to eat, especially at weekends. SAMPLE DISHES: moules marinière £5.25; grilled veal cutlet with spinach and provençale herb gratin £10.50; apple pie £3.50.

Licensees Philip, Simon and Adrian Hopwood (freehouse)
Open *11.30 to 3, 6 to 11; bar food and restaurant 12 to 2, 7 to 9.30*
Details *Children welcome   Car park   Wheelchair access (not WC)   Garden   No smoking in restaurant No music   Delta, MasterCard, Switch, Visa*

SWALLOWFIELD   Berkshire   map 2

George & Dragon ✿

Church Road, Swallowfield RG7 1TJ   TEL: (0118) 988 4432
Swallowfield signposted on B3349 S of Reading; proceed through village towards Farley Hill

Once you pass through Swallowfield and head out along Church Road, it seems ages before you come to anything – this old cottagey inn is definitely in the middle of nowhere. Smart but informal, it offers a welcome to drinkers (with Fuller's London Pride, Wadworth 6X and a guest like Adnams Bitter making an appearance on handpump), but is very much a dining pub nowadays, and booking – although it may seem surprising given the location – is essential. A series of rooms, including a conservatory, is decked out with polished-wood tables set for food. Walls are painted a distinctive warm pink, there are low ceilings and beams, a big fireplace, and chatty, friendly and youthful staff. The bar snacks menu is available only at lunchtimes, while the printed carte is backed up by blackboard specials. Dishes are well constructed, well presented and balanced, with sea bass teamed with creamed spinach and aubergine ragoût and lemon and caper butter, while poussin is topped with Gruyère mash and served with mushrooms, pancetta lardons, shallots and red wine sauce. Desserts err on the side of familiarity. Six wines of the week, chalked on a blackboard, are available by the glass. SAMPLE DISHES: fruits de mer risotto £7; seared calf's liver on bubble and squeak with Madeira jus £15; sticky toffee pudding with butterscotch sauce £6.

Licensee Paul Daley (freehouse)
Open *12 to 11; bar food and restaurant 12 to 2.30, 7 to 10*
Details *Children welcome   Car park   Wheelchair access (not WC)   Garden   Background music   Dogs welcome in bar only   Delta, MasterCard, Switch, Visa*

SWAN BOTTOM Buckinghamshire map 3

Old Swan
Swan Bottom HP16 9NU   TEL: (01494) 837239
off A413, between Great Missenden and Wendover, just N of The Lee

The Old Swan stands on a narrow lane that rises sharply out of the hamlet of Swan Bottom, a place so tiny it is not marked on most maps – 'just head towards The Lee from the A413 and you should find it easily enough'. Watch out for the low ceiling beams when you enter the main bar, and the dark orange walls may take some adjusting to, but there's a dining area to one side filled with rustic pine in various shapes and sizes; combined with chintz curtains and dried flower arrangements, this has a pretty cottagey look. The blackboard menu offers old-style country cooking along the lines of starters of home-made soup, chicken liver pâté, and prawn and bacon salad, with main courses running to bangers and mash, home-baked ham with eggs and chips, lasagne, gnocchi with tomato sauce, and sirloin steak. Fish is something of a speciality, so there could be roast Icelandic cod with creamed-potato and spinach, or smoked haddock pie. Lemon sorbet and crème brûlée are typical desserts. Adnams Bitter, Brakspear Bitter and Bateman XB are on draught, and Stowford Press cider is kept too. Around eight wines are sold by the glass. SAMPLE DISHES: goats' cheese on a bed of beetroot £5.75; Thai meatballs with coriander, lime, chilli and garlic £6.75; rhubarb and elderflower crumble £4.

Licensee Sean Michaelson-Yeates (freehouse)
Open Mon 7 to 11, Tue to Fri 12 to 3, 6 to 11, Sat 12 to 11, Sun 12 to 10.30; bar food and restaurant (exc Sun evening) 12.30 to 2, 6.30 to 9
Details Children welcome in eating areas   Car park   Wheelchair access (also WC)   Garden   No smoking in restaurant   No music   Dogs welcome in bar only   MasterCard, Switch, Visa

SWANTON MORLEY Norfolk map 6

Darby's 🍺
1–2 Elsing Road, Swanton Morley NR20 4NY   TEL: (01362) 637647

Darby's started life as a large country house in the eighteenth century and was divided into two cottages in the nineteenth, remaining unaltered until conversion into a pub in 1987. A narrow corridor leads into a spacious bar, which has a rustic feel created by beams, brick walls and an inglenook with a log fire. Plenty of fish and seafood appear on the menu in a variety of styles: prawns stir-fried in oyster sauce with pak choi, baked whole sea bass with lemongrass and ginger, and a starter of shrimp and salmon salad, for example. There are also a number of meaty offerings, ranging from Parma ham with rocket to start, followed by chargrilled lamb with a sherry, mushroom and chive sauce, and various chargrilled steaks and burgers. Baguettes, vegetarian options and a children's menu are also possibilities. Beers are a fine selection comprising regulars from Adnams, Badger, Woodforde's and Greene King as well as three guest ales. A short list of wines is reasonably priced, and there are four by the glass. In the garden is a children's adventure play area. SAMPLE DISHES: Thai fishcakes with chilli dipping sauce £5.50; pan-fried duck breast with a mushroom, ham and tarragon sauce £11.75; vanilla pannacotta in a pool of bitter chocolate sauce £3.50.

Licensees John Carrick and Louise Battle (freehouse)
Open Mon to Fri 11.30 to 3, 6 to 11, Sat 11.30 to 11, Sun 12 to 10.30; bar food and restaurant Mon to Fri 12 to 2.15, 6.30 to 9.45, Sat 12 to 9.45, Sun 12 to 9.15

Details *Children welcome   Car park   Wheelchair access (also WC)   Garden   No smoking in family room and restaurant   Occasional live music   Dogs welcome in bar and family room only   Delta, MasterCard, Switch, Visa*

SWERFORD   Oxfordshire   map 5

Masons Arms
Swerford OX7 4AP   TEL: (01608) 683212
on A361 just outside village

What was once a foursquare old Cotswold watering hole has been transformed into a stylish modern venue for eating as well as drinking. Pass through the door into the main area and you cannot help but notice the perfect white paint on the woodwork, roughcast walls, recessed lighting and pictures evoking the Mediterranean. It is all rather chic and urbane. A laminated lunchtime menu advertises sandwiches, 'light bites' such as herb risotto with crème fraîche and Parmesan, and more substantial dishes like grilled hake with 'home fries' or Thai green chicken curry. The real interest, however, is in the regularly changing list of specials, which highlights the kitchen's true cosmopolitan intentions. Here you might find starters like duck and liver terrine with piccalilli, or asparagus and pecorino ravioli with white wine and chive sauce, before main courses ranging from braised flank of beef with juniper, thyme and red wine served with steamed Savoy cabbage and mustard mash, or fillet of sea bass with ratatouille, new potatoes and gazpacho sauce. To conclude, take your pick from desserts like 'startlingly good' raspberry and hazelnut meringue, or chocolate terrine. There's also a concise restaurant menu dealing in similar dishes. The 25-strong wine list favours the New World, with four offered by the glass, while, for beer lovers, there's a choice between Hook Norton Best Bitter and a guest such as Marston's Pedigree. SAMPLE DISHES: smoked chicken, mango and couscous salad £5.50; venison pie £8.50; raspberry, Drambuie and honey brûlée £4.

Licensees *Bill and Charmaine Leadbeater, and Tom Aldous (freehouse)*
Open *10 to 3, 7 (6 summer) to 11, Sun 12 to 3.30, 7 to 10.30; bar food and restaurant 12 to 2.30, 7 to 9.30; closed 25 Dec*
Details *Children welcome   Car park   Wheelchair access (also WC)   Garden and patio   No smoking in restaurant   Background music   Dogs welcome exc in restaurant   Delta, MasterCard, Switch, Visa*

SWILLAND   Suffolk   map 6

Moon & Mushroom Inn 🍺
High Road, Swilland IP6 9LR   TEL: (01473) 785320

'A vintage English, slightly eccentric public house' is one reporter's view of this notable village pub in rural Suffolk. There's a small terrace at the front with a couple of tables and a larger garden at the back. Inside, the long, beamed main bar has comfortably cushioned benches, and a separate food bar off it. Topping the bill is a line-up of impeccably kept beers from independent East Anglian breweries: Norfolk is represented by Buffy's Hopleaf and Norwich Terrier, Woodforde's Wherry and Norfolk Nog, while Suffolk contributes Nethergate Umbel Ale, and there's even a brew from Essex in the shape of Brewers Gold from the Crouch Vale brewery. To go with the beer is a modest menu of simple, satisfying home-cooked food: various salads and ploughman's ranging from Cheddar to smoked duck pâté, plus a selection of dishes served from a hotplate at the bar. Typical offerings might include beef in porter with dumplings, braised local venison and mushrooms in red wine, or haddock fillet Mornay; help yourself to an assortment of vegetables. Desserts are old favourites like fruit crumble or bread-and-butter pudding. Ten wines are available by the glass from a fairly priced list of 20. SAMPLE DISHES: smoked mackerel salad £5; pork loin in creamy Stilton sauce £9; toffee and ginger pudding with butterscotch sauce £3.75.

Licensees Clive and Adrienne Goodall (freehouse)
Open Tue to Sat 11 to 2.30, Mon to Sat 6 to 11, Sun 12 to 2.30, 7 to 10.30; bar food Tue to Sat 12 to 2, 6.30 to 8.15
Details No children   Car park   Wheelchair access (not WC)   Garden and patio   No smoking in restaurant   No music   Dogs welcome in bar only   MasterCard, Switch, Visa

TADPOLE BRIDGE   Oxfordshire   map 2

▲ Trout at Tadpole Bridge

Tadpole Bridge, Buckland Marsh SN7 8RF   TEL: (01367) 870382
WEBSITE: www.trout-inn.co.uk
approx 1½m N of A420 Faringdon to Oxford road; follow signs to Buckland Marsh;
continue a further ½m beyond Buckland Marsh to river

'A real pub with decent food' is how one reporter summed up the Trout, a detached stone building in a remote location fronting the Thames. However, it gets very busy, with business people at lunchtime using laptops as well as eating. Stuffed or artificial fish in glass cases and fishing paraphernalia reinforce the pub's name in the yellow-walled interior, with its old timber uprights. Although there's a separate restaurant, you can order from its menu in the bar. Starter of pan-fried scallops with red onion marmalade and chicken liver mousse or chilli infused beetroot with crispy pancetta and Lancashire cheese served with a honey dressing show what the kitchen's imagination is capable of producing. Main courses rise to roast whole partridge on wet polenta with wild mushroom jus or pan-fried breast of duck with sweet potato rösti, béarnaise sauce, bacon and shallots. Less substantial dishes like tomato and black olive risotto with roasted vegetables and Parmesan are also possibilities. Two first-class regular real ales – Young's Bitter and Brakspears – are joined by one or two guest ales such as West Berkshire Full Circle. The wine list is very drinker-friendly, with 11 by the glass and all bottles under £25 offered on a 'pay for what you drink' basis. The list opens with a selection of sherries and includes a couple of pages of Bordeaux in a range of vintages, but there's also plenty of fruity modern drinking, and prices are reasonable throughout. Other drinking options include home-made sloe gin, cherry plum vodka and elderflower cordial. SAMPLE DISHES: trout tartare with trout gravad lax and seared fillet of trout £6; roast loin of venison with fig tart and sautéed cabbage £16; lemon posset with fresh raspberries £5.

Licensee Christopher J. Green (freehouse)
Open 10.30 to 3, 6 to 11, Sun 12 to 3.30; bar food and restaurant all week 12 to 2, Mon to Sat 7 to 9; closed Sun evenings exc July and Aug, 25, 26 and 31 Dec, 1 Jan
Details Children welcome   Car park   Wheelchair access (also WC)   Garden   No smoking in restaurant   Background music   Dogs welcome   Delta, MasterCard, Switch, Visa   Accommodation: 5 rooms, 1 suite, B&B £55 to £110

TETBURY   Gloucestershire   map 2

Trouble House ✿

Cirencester Road, Tetbury GL8 8SG   TEL: (01666) 502206
WEBSITE: www.troublehouse.co.uk
on A433, 1½m outside Tetbury towards Cirencester

The main Tetbury to Cirencester road runs past this unusually named low, cream-washed stone building, in former days known as the Wagon & Horses. It was redubbed the Trouble House perhaps as a result of some bother during the Civil War, or the misfortunes of two of its landlords in the nineteenth century, or the reputed presence of a ghostly 'Lady in Blue' – or more likely the local riots during the Luddite rebellion. The main entrance opens into a proper pub bar, with big black beams in the low ceiling, butter-yellow walls with terracotta-coloured panelling, log fires at each end of the room, and country-cottage artefacts. The eating area has a fire too, and a lounge has polished tables, easy chairs and an attractive stone fireplace and chimney. The same short menu is served throughout. Start with crab thermidor, or roasted hand-dived scallops with curried shellfish soup and salsify beignet, before going on to braised pig's trotter stuffed with foie gras mousse with creamy mash and shallot gravy. Game may be represented by roast partridge with lentil and potato broth and foie gras toast, and fish by roast monkfish with cassoulet beans and Toulouse sausage. Finish with white chocolate and vanilla milk pudding, or a selection of mainly English farmhouse cheeses. As the pub is tied to Wadworth, it stocks the range of the brewery's ales. A dozen or so wines are sold by the glass from an international list of around 40 bottles, with prices starting at £11.25. SAMPLE DISHES: cream of pumpkin and cinnamon soup with pumpkin fritters £4; pot-roast rump of veal with wild mushroom and potato casserole £13.50; citrus cream pie £5.

Licensees Michael and Sarah Bedford (Wadworth)
Open *Tue to Sat 11 to 3, 6.30 (7 winter) to 11, Sun 12 to 3, 7 to 10.30; bar food Tue to Sun 12 to 2, Tue to Sat 7 to 9.30; closed 1 week Sept, 25 Dec, 1 Jan, 2 weeks Jan*
Details *Children welcome in eating area   Car park   Wheelchair access (also WC)   Garden   No smoking in eating area   Background music   Dogs welcome   Amex, Delta, MasterCard, Switch, Visa*

THELBRIDGE   Devon   map 1

▲ Thelbridge Cross Inn

Thelbridge EX17 4SQ   TEL: (01884) 860316
WEBSITE: www.thelbridgexinn.co.uk
off B3137 from Tiverton, before Witheridge, take left fork on to B3042 for 2m

Set amidst gently rolling hills with wide views over both Exmoor and Dartmoor, this smartly painted roadside inn may appear isolated, but the church and other buildings are within half a mile. The building dates from the eighteenth century, and although the interior has been opened up it still manages to remain comfortable and cosy, with a roaring log fire, deep sofas and armchairs in the main bar area. Decoration is provided by lots of old prints, bank notes, toby jugs and framed 45rpm discs – a reminder that the landlord was the bass player in the former pop group Love Affair. Food is a major attraction, with visitors well fed from a carte that covers just about everything in the traditional pub repertoire: avocado and prawns, garlic mushrooms, roasts, curries and plenty of steaks. The separate restaurant is in a converted barn, although you can choose to eat in the bar. In addition, sandwiches, ploughman's, and main courses of ham, egg and chips are alternative choices on the bar menu, and daily specials always include vegetarian dishes, perhaps a leek, stilton and chestnut bake. Badger Best Bitter, Castle Eden Ale and Bass are on draught, along with Stowford Press cider. Half a dozen wines are sold by the glass, while the full list runs to around 29 bottles. SAMPLE DISHES: king prawn and mussel medley £6; slow-roasted lamb shank in red wine and rosemary sauce £11; lemon and ginger flan £3.25.

Licensees W.G. and R.E. Ball (freehouse)
Open 11.30 to 3, 6.30 to 11, Sun 12 to 3, 7 to 10.30; bar food and restaurant 12 to 2.30, 7 to 9.30 (9 winter)
Details Children welcome in eating areas   Car park   Garden   No smoking in restaurant   Background music
No dogs   Amex, Delta, Diners, MasterCard, Switch, Visa   Accommodation: 7 rooms, B&B £30 to £70

THIRLSPOT   Cumbria   map 10

▲ King's Head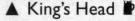

Thirlspot CA12 4TN   TEL: (017687) 72393
website: www.lakedistrictinns.co.uk
on A591, Keswick to Grasmere road, 6m N of Grasmere

It would be hard to find anywhere to fit the popular idea of Lakeland better than the surroundings of this seventeenth-century coaching inn: Helvellyn rises majestically in the background, and there are superb views down the valley towards Skiddaw and Blencathra. It is under the same ownership as the Travellers Rest in nearby Grasmere (see entry), and offers a similar package, comprising well-appointed accommodation, a smart restaurant and a relaxed, traditional bar. Though the emphasis is on dining, real ales are an excellent selection including Theakston Best and Old Peculier, Jennings Bitter and two guest beers, such as local Coniston Bluebird. Menus show some emphasis on local produce, though the cooking style is fairly cosmopolitan – taking in grilled Cumbrian air-dried ham with Swaledale cheese on ciabatta, calf's liver and bacon with a rich stout sauce, and stuffed Norfolk duck breast with sage sausagemeat stuffing and redcurrant sauce. Toffee and hazelnut gâteau is a typically sweet and sticky way to finish, or there's Lakeland cheeses. The list of 32 wines represents fair value and good choice, and nine are available by the glass. SAMPLE DISHES: grilled polenta with wild mushrooms £4.95; braised minted lamb with creamed potatoes and rosemary jus £10; sticky toffee pudding £4.

Licensees Derek Sweeney and Graeme Renwick (freehouse)
Open 11 to 11, Sun 12 to 10.30; bar food winter 12 to 3, 5 to 9.30, summer (Easter to Oct) 12 to 9.30; restaurant 7 to 9
Details Children welcome   Car park   Wheelchair access (not WC)   Garden and patio   No smoking in dining room   Background music   Dogs welcome exc in restaurant   Delta, MasterCard, Switch, Visa
Accommodation: 17 rooms B&B £35 to £110

THORNHAM   Norfolk   map 6

▲ Lifeboat Inn 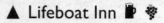

Ship Lane, Thornham PE36 6LT   TEL: (01485) 512236
WEBSITE: www.lifeboatinn.co.uk
follow A149 from Hunstanton; in Thornham turn left into Straithe Road, then right into Ship Lane

Well signposted from the A149, this large, white-painted sixteenth-century inn looks out over salt marshes, with the sea 'but a distant thin blue line'; a tidal path running past the pub leads down to the shore. The Smugglers' Bar aims to re-create as far as possible the original feel of the place, when it really was a haunt of smugglers. A blackboard of specials supplements the printed bar menu, with fish featuring prominently – mussels are the house speciality, cooked in white wine, garlic, cream and parsley. Other options run from cod and chips to roast monkfish tail with seafood bisque, couscous and pak choi, with steaks, beefburgers and hickory pork ribs as reliable meaty options backed up by lunchtime baguettes and ploughman's. The fixed-price restaurant menu has a modern feel, as in crispy duck and spring onion parcels with hoisin sauce, followed by roast cannon of pork with peppery noodles, date and prune cream and roasted bell peppers. A respectable selection of real ales includes Adnams Bitter, Greene King IPA and Abbot Ale, and local Woodforde's Wherry Best Bitter plus a regularly changing guest. Around a dozen wines come by the glass, representing a fair selection from the list of 40-odd bottles, which takes in everything from budget vins de pays to a prestigious Super-Tuscan. Dessert wines include an unusual sweet Pinot Noir from Austrian winemaker Helmut Lang (£19 for a half-bottle). SAMPLE DISHES: parsnip, carrot and mustard soup £4; pan-fried lamb's liver with smoked bacon and rosemary and red wine jus £8.75; raspberry pannacotta in a brandy-snap basket £4.

Licensee Charles Coker (freehouse)
Open 11 to 11, Sun 12 to 10.30; bar food 12 to 2.30, 6.30 to 9.30; restaurant 7 to 9.30
Details Children welcome   Car park   Wheelchair access (also WC)   Garden and patio   No smoking in restaurant   No music   Dogs welcome exc in restaurant   Delta, MasterCard, Switch, Visa   Accommodation: 14 rooms, B&B £56 to £100

THORNTON   West Yorkshire   map 8

Ring O' Bells 🍷 🍇

212 Hill Top Road, Thornton BD13 3QL   TEL: (01274) 832296
WEBSITE: www.theringobells.com

High above the village of Thornton in a wide expanse of moorland overlooking Halifax, this three-storey, honey-coloured-stone pub succeeds in pulling in the punters throughout the week. A traditional bar still dominates one of the rooms, but most of the open-plan space (including a conservatory) is taken up with rows of tables set for dining. Framed paintings (for sale), flower prints and pottery jugs add to the warm, congenial atmosphere. The menu is an eclectic mix of British stand-bys such as a daily curry, various pies, Yorkshire puddings filled with steak and kidney, and 'huge' deep-fried haddock in batter with crisp chips, mushy peas and tartare sauce ('the real McCoy'), plus some ideas from further afield: chicken Louisville melt, for instance (chicken breast with pineapple, bacon and mozzarella). Daily soups and other specials are listed on blackboards. This is also a promising venue for vegetarians, with lots of options including Roquefort and spring onion cheesecake surrounded by slices of pear doused in balsamic vinegar, or vegetable ragoût with cheese and polenta topping. Desserts are listed on a blackboard, and the kitchen also makes a feature of ice cream sundaes. Black Sheep Best Bitter and Special Ale and John Smith's Directors are on draught, and there's also plenty for wine buffs to explore. The list may look a bit fussy and old-fashioned, but it's extensive and reasonably priced with lots of up-to-date flavours alongside the classics. Work your way through the 100 or so bins and you will find a goodly number under £15, as well as a dozen halves and the same number by the glass. SAMPLE DISHES: Somerset Brie fritters with cranberry sauce

£4; pork escalope with white wine and green peppercorn sauce £9.75; raspberry ripple and marshmallow sundae £3.50.

Licensee Ann L. Preston (freehouse)
Open 11.30 to 4, 5.30 to 11 (Sun 6.30 to 10.30); bar food and restaurant 12.30 to 2, 5.30 (6.15 Sat and Sun) to 9.30 (9.45 Sat, 8.45 Sun); closed 25 Dec
Details Children welcome Car park Wheelchair access (also WC) Patio No smoking in conservatory and restaurant Background music No dogs Amex, Delta, MasterCard, Switch, Visa

THORNTON WATLASS   North Yorkshire   map 9

▲ Buck Inn

Thornton Watlass HG4 4AH   TEL: (01677) 422461
off B6268 midway between Masham and Bedale

The avidly supported local cricket team plays on the village green outside this genuine old pub in a picturesque village at the entrance to Wensleydale. Cricketing photographs and rugby shirts in a glass case emphasise the sporting theme in the bar, which also has its full quota of copper kettles and old bottles plus a proper fire. At the back is a contrasting dining area done out with lime-green walls, maroon curtains and a glass mirror. At lunchtime you can expect pub staples like steak and kidney pie with good 'crumbly' pastry, home-cooked ham and chips, omelettes, and 'beef and beer curry', as well as a 'cricketer's platter' comprising melon, ham, pâté, salad and French bread. In the evening the kitchen moves up a gear for tandoori king prawns, spicy roast duck breast in a honey and soy sauce, and fruity Caribbean chicken with rice. There are also desserts aplenty, ranging from strawberry and kiwi cheesecake to classic apple pie with a piece of Wensleydale cheese. Sunday lunch brings on a traditional roast with Yorkshire pudding. A better-than-average line-up of five Yorkshire ales includes Black Sheep Best Bitter, Theakston Best Bitter and John Smith's plus two guests usually from local microbreweries such as Hambleton. The modestly priced list of around 20 wines includes three house selections and a further collection of more expensive, mostly French bottles; added to this is a range of more than 40 malt whiskies, including many more unusual brands. SAMPLE DISHES: goats' cheese and tomato tartlet £4.50; stir-fried chicken with black-bean sauce £9.50; lime and lemon cheesecake £4.25.

Licensees Michael and Margaret Fox (freehouse)
Open 11 to 11, Sun 12 to 10.30; bar food and restaurant Mon to Sat 12 to 2, 6.15 to 9.30, Sun 12 to 9.30; closed evening 25 Dec
Details Children welcome Car park Wheelchair access (not WC) Garden No smoking in restaurant
Live or background music No dogs exc in bedrooms Amex, Delta, Diners, MasterCard, Switch, Visa
Accommodation: 7 rooms, B&B £45 to £70

THORPE LANGTON   Leicestershire   map 5

Bakers Arms

Main Street, Thorpe Langton LE16 7TS   TEL: (01858) 545201

The yellow-painted and thatched pub, in a row of terraced brick cottages in Thorpe Langton's Main Street, is easy to spot. It appears small, as the frontage is quite narrow, but the building's depth makes it roomy enough inside, and there's a garden behind as well. The bar (which has a little non-smoking snug off it) is quintessential traditional country pub: wooden chairs and tables, a stripped-pine dresser, dark beams, red carpet, warm fires and country prints and wall lights on burgundy-coloured walls. Draught beers include one on handpump (Tetley Bitter), and wines include six by the glass. Except at weekends, honest, reliable and imaginative food is served only in the evenings, and advance booking could be wise. The daily-changing blackboard menu may begin with cauliflower and Cheddar soup, or goats' cheese wrapped in Parma ham with maple syrup dressing, before continuing with whole baked sea bass with spinach, mushrooms and prawn jus, say, or confit of duck leg and breast with parsnips and apple compote, with a vegetarian dish of stuffed peppers with aubergine, tomato and goats' cheese. SAMPLE DISHES: pan-fried scallops with butter-bean and spinach mash and honey, mustard and lemon dressing £8; chump of lamb with a parsley and Cheddar crust and spiced butternut squash £14.50; vanilla brûlée with raspberries in a tuile basket £4.

Licensee Kate Hubbard (freehouse)
Open *Sat and Sun 12 to 2.30, Tue to Sat 6.30 to 11; bar food and restaurant Sat and Sun 12 to 2.30, Tue to Sat 6.30 to 9.30*
Details *No children under 12   Car park   Wheelchair access (not WC)   Garden   No-smoking area in bar No music   No dogs   Delta, MasterCard, Switch, Visa*

THORVERTON   Devon   map 1

▲ Thorverton Arms

Thorverton EX5 5NS   TEL: (01392) 860205

The long, low inn in the centre of the village is a blaze of light at night, with coach lamps everywhere and the windows lit by lamps on the sills. Inside is one long space, with bar seating to one side of the bar counter and the restaurant to the other. Red is the main colour, with a carpet in the bar replaced by a Turkey rug on bare floorboards in the restaurant, where a large gilt-framed mirror hangs over the fireplace. The bar menu includes substantial dishes along the lines of lamb and vegetable hotpot with boulangère potatoes, bolstered by lunchtime open sandwiches or ploughman's. The main menu is divided into the usual starters and main courses – mixed smoked fish salad with spiced salmon caviar, for instance, followed by grilled breasts of pigeon with Parma ham, roasted garlic, pesto mash and raspberry sauce – while a blackboard lists the daily specials: perhaps tuna steak pan-fried with sun-blush tomatoes and garlic served on pesto mash. Greene King Abbot Ale, Flowers IPA and Bass are on draught, and five wines are available by the glass. SAMPLE DISHES: scallops in chilli and lime butter with deep-fried parsnips and Parma ham £5.75; chargrilled medallions of beef filled with Somerset goats' cheese, topped with Plymouth scallops and served with fondant potato and a red wine jus £12.25; sticky toffee pudding and butterscotch sauce £4.

Licensees D. Ough and C. Lipscompe (Enterprise Inns)
Open *11.30 to 3, 6.30 to 11, Sun 12 to 3, 7 to 10.30; bar food and restaurant 12 to 2, 6.30 to 9*
Details *Children welcome in eating areas   Car park   Wheelchair access (also WC)   Garden and patio No-smoking area in bar, no smoking in restaurant   Occasional live or background music   No dogs   Delta, MasterCard, Switch, Visa   Accommodation: 4 rooms, B&B £35 to £45*

The Guide is totally independent, accepts no free hospitality, carries no advertising and makes no charge for inclusion.

TIRRIL   Cumbria   map 10

▲ Queens Head

Tirril CA10 2JF   TEL: (01768) 863219
WEBSITE: www.queensheadinn.co.uk
on B5320, 2m S of Penrith

The Queens Head is unmissable in the village centre, a long, low building with whitewashed walls. Within there's a spacious stone-floored public bar, a warren of small, dark, cosy rooms, open fires, low, dark beams and uprights everywhere, and plenty of nooks and crannies, some formed by high-backed settles. 'All in all,' noted a reporter, 'a very characterful place – just a pity there are so many people.' Indeed, proximity to Ullswater, Penrith, the M6, the River Earmont, and the Eden Valley (favoured by fishermen) means good business all year round, and food service can be slow as a result. The printed lunchtime bar menu ranges from various baguettes and pitta breads to familiar pub staples along the lines of jacket potatoes, steaks of beef, gammon and salmon, lasagne and Cumberland sausage, plus desserts such as syrup sponge pudding. A few blackboard specials fill in the gaps with the likes of home-made pie of the day and 'pasta à la mode'. Further blackboards also expand the menu in the restaurant, where you might start with garlic mushrooms, go on to pan-fried Barbary duck breast with blackcurrant and port gravy, and finish with sticky toffee pudding. As this is the home of the Tirril Brewery, you will find the brewery's John Bewsher's Best Bitter (Bewsher leased the pub from Wordsworth's nephew in 1827), Thomas Slee's Academy Ale, and Charles Gough's Old Faithful (named after a dog that remained for months by his dead master's side on the fells), and local guest ales. The 30-odd wines on the well-spread list are under £20, and nine of them, including a pudding wine, can be had by the glass. SAMPLE DISHES: Cumberland rarebit £3.75; shoulder of lamb with redcurrant gravy £11; baked apple Tirrilean £3.50.

Licensee Chris Tomlinson (freehouse)
Open 12 to 11, Sun 12 to 10.30; bar food and restaurant 12 to 2, 6 to 9.30
Details Children welcome   Car park   Wheelchair access (also WC)   Garden and patio   No smoking in 1 room and restaurant   No music   Dogs welcome exc in restaurant   MasterCard, Switch, Visa   Accommodation: 7 rooms, B&B £35 to £70

TITLEY   Herefordshire   map 5

▲ Stagg Inn

Titley HR5 3RL   TEL: (01544) 230221
WEBSITE: www.thestagg.co.uk
on B4355, NE of Kington

Chef and co-owner Steve Reynolds learned his trade with the Roux brothers, but since 1998 he has been pleasing the crowds at this village pub in the Herefordshire countryside. Drinkers and diners rub shoulders quite happily here. The bar still retains its traditional atmosphere, with natural colour schemes, a wood-burning stove, half-timbered walls and closely set ceiling beams thickly hung with mugs, while the restaurant is neat and unpretentious. Keenly sourced local produce is used to telling effect for a repertoire of sophisticated but appealing dishes. Tartare of organic trout might appear as a starter alongside pigeon breast on braised pearl barley; lamb from the Welsh Marches and Herefordshire beef are regular features, and you might also find stuffed free-range pork tenderloin with slow-roast belly pork and braised chicory, or – in season – mallard duck breast with wild rice, port and roast root vegetables. Seafood plays a supporting role with, say, seared scallops on curried celeriac purée with celeriac fondant, or sea bass fillet with duxelles, herb oil and dauphinois potatoes. The bar has a blackboard of lighter meals, such as crispy duck leg with cider sauce, locally smoked salmon salad, or steak sandwich with chips and garlic mushrooms. Finish with a selection of unpasteurised English and Welsh cheeses, or opt for a dessert like chocolate tart with crème fraîche ice cream, or passion-fruit jelly with Cointreau sauce. Real ale is also taken seriously, and there's a bias towards local brews including Hobsons Best Bitter, Town Crier and Old Henry, plus guests from the Spinning Dog Brewery; added to these are bottled ciders and perry from Dunkerton's and others, as well as home-made damson and sloe gins. Eight house wines at around £2.20 a glass kick off a reasonably priced list of around 70 bottles, bolstered by around a dozen halves. Classic styles and modern favourites are all well represented, and dark and rich Pedro Ximénez Viejo Napoleon sherry from Hidalgo is a rare pudding treat not to be missed. SAMPLE DISHES: blue cheese, pear and walnut tart £5.50; Gressingham duck breast with ginger, mustard and Sauternes sauce £14; mango parfait with caramelised rum banana £5.

Licensees Nicola and Steve Reynolds (freehouse)

Open *Tue to Sat and May Day bank hol 12 to 3, 6.30 to 11, Sun 12 to 3; bar food (exc Fri and Sat evenings and Sun) 12 to 2, 6.30 to 10; restaurant Tue to Sat 12 to 2, 6.30 to 10; closed first 2 weeks Nov, 25 and 26 Dec, 1 Jan, 1 week spring*

Details *Children welcome   Car park   Garden and patio   No smoking in restaurant   No music   Dogs welcome in bar only   Delta, MasterCard, Switch, Visa   Accommodation: 2 rooms, B&B £50 to £90*

TORCROSS   Devon   map 1

Start Bay Inn

Torcross TQ7 2TQ   TEL: (01548) 580553
WEBSITE: www.startbayinn.co.uk
on A379 Dartmouth to Kingsbridge coast road

SEAFOOD

'A thriving fish-and-chip shop in a pub' sums up the appeal of this fourteenth-century thatched inn. It stands right on the beach in one of the most beautiful parts of Devon, with views across the magnificent sweep of Slapton Sands: with these factors in its favour, no wonder it gets busy, especially in summer. Inside, the bar and dining areas are modestly decorated, with traditional furnishings, a brick fireplace and black beams. There is a simple laminated bar menu, but the main draw is the fresh fish brought in daily by local fishermen – these are listed on a board and change according to the catch, though crisp, lightly battered cod, haddock, plaice and lemon sole with excellent plump chips are a fixture. Non-fish dishes run to the likes of steaks, burgers and cold ham platters. Bass, Flowers Original, and Otter Ale are on draught, along with ciders from Addlestone's and Heron Valley, and the serviceable wine list approaches 20 international bottles, with nine by the glass. SAMPLE DISHES: smoked mackerel with salad £4; deep-fried cod and chips £6.50; spotted dick £3.25.

Licensee Paul Stubbs (Heavitree)

Open *11.30 to 11 (11.30 to 2.30, 6 to 11 winter), Sun 12 to 2.30, 6 to 10.30; bar food 11.30 to 2, 6 to 9.30 (10 summer)*

Details *Children welcome in family room   Car park   Patio   No-smoking area in bar, no smoking in eating area   Background music   Dogs welcome   MasterCard, Switch, Visa*

TREBARWITH   Cornwall   map 1

▲ Mill House Inn   NEW ENTRY

Trebarwith PL34 0ED   TEL: (01840) 770200
WEBSITE: www.themillhouseinn.co.uk
from A39, follow signs to Tintagel then signs to Trebarwith

The drive down through the wooded valley towards Trebarwith Strand evokes images
of ancient times, and it is no surprise that a certain King Arthur, if you choose to
believe the legend, built his castle nearby. A sharp turn down to the pub needs careful
negotiation. The inn, at the bottom of the valley beside a stream (as is the wont of
mills), is a rambling granite building. The owners since 2001 have refurbished the pub
with care and attention to detail, resulting in smart bedrooms, an atmospheric bar and
a charming restaurant. The bar is dark and full of character – slate floors, large dark
wooden tables, sofas, fires and only one small window. Sharp's Doom Bar Bitter,
Sharp's Own and Serpentine Ale (from the Organic Brewhouse) are on the pumps,
and the wine list, although short, manages to cover the globe. Snacks in the bar come
in the form of tapas listed on a blackboard – boquerones, patatas bravas, grilled
sardines, hummus, and lamb meatballs among them. The bar leads into the restaurant,
which has a different feel, and with its large windows, wooden floor, part-boarded
walls, and light colour scheme is more boathouse than country inn. Food can be eaten
in both bar and restaurant. Flavours are big and bold, as found in a rabbit, chorizo and
spinach risotto, and butternut squash, spinach and goats' cheese lasagne. Starters might
include beetroot and cumin soup with Greek yoghurt, or sautéed chicken livers on
sourdough bruschetta with borlotti beans and balsamic vinegar; desserts are as
cosmopolitan as pannacotta with roasted plums, and West Country farmhouse cheeses
come with pear and rocket. SAMPLE DISHES: tiger prawns with chilli, coriander and
lime £7; roast hake with bacon, mash and gravy £11; lemon tart £5.

Licensees John Beach and Nigel Peters (freehouse)
Open *12 to 11; bar food and restaurant Tue to Sun 12 to 2.30, Mon to Sat 7 to 9.30*
Details *Children welcome   Car park   Wheelchair access (not WC)   Garden and patio   Live or background
music   Dogs welcome exc in restaurant   Delta, MasterCard, Switch, Visa   Accommodation: 9 rooms, B&B £40
to £90*

TREBURLEY   Cornwall   map 1

Springer Spaniel   NEW ENTRY

Treburley PL9 7NS   TEL: (01579) 370424
on A388 between Launceston and Callington

Judging by outward appearances, this is a typically unassuming roadside pub with a
small garden for summer drinking. Inside, the simple décor maintains the low-key
feel, with a neat parquet floor, a wood-burning stove in the large fireplace, comfortable
wall benches, rustic tables, and numerous prints on cream-painted walls, although a
crowd of chatty locals provide a friendly atmosphere. The separate dining area is likewise simply furnished and has a relaxed and convivial mood. Extensive menus offer
the full range of classic pub dishes as well as some more imaginative ideas, such as
smoked duck and melon salad with raspberry dressing, and Thai-spiced salmon fillet
with spinach, while the daily specials board might feature braised pork loin steak with
provençale sauce, or venison and mushroom casserole. The strength of the cooking

lies in the use of first-rate Cornish produce and the fact that everything is made on the premises. Real ales come from Cornish brewery Sharp's, and there's also Cornish cider. Seven house wines are available by the glass from £2.60 and by the bottle from £9.95; the full list runs to around 30 interesting bottles. SAMPLE DISHES: wild boar terrine £5; beef in creamy Stilton sauce £12; minted white chocolate cheesecake £4.50.

Licensees Craig Woolley and Richard Beaman (Wagtail Inns)
Open 12 to 3, 6 to 11; bar food and restaurant 12 to 2, 6 to 9; no food 25 Dec and evening 26 Dec; open all day some days in summer
Details Children welcome in eating areas   Car park   Wheelchair access (not WC)   Garden   No smoking in restaurant   Occasional live music   Dogs welcome   Delta, MasterCard, Switch, Visa

TREEN   Cornwall   map 1

▲ Gurnard's Head Hotel

Treen, Zennor, nr St Ives TR26 3DE   TEL: (01736) 796928
WEBSITE: www.ccinns.com
on B3306, 6m SW of St Ives

New owners took over the Gurnard's Head in December 2003, but the transition appears to be seamless with the chef from the previous regime continuing in the kitchen. No changes to the setting, of course, overlooking the rocky promontory of Gurnard's Head and surrounded by rugged moorland; the South West Coast Path is close by, so the place is a much-used and welcome stop for walkers. There's free live music on Wednesday and Friday nights (no Muzak or fruit machines, though) to enhance the food and beer (Courage Directors and Best, and locally brewed Skinner's Cornish Knocker Ale). The same menus are available in the large bar, where there's a fire, and in the restaurant off it. Specials might include grilled goats' cheese with leaves, or grilled sea bream with garlic, thyme and pickled lemon, while the regular printed menu offers Cornish seafood broth, followed by suprême of chicken Normandy style, or chargrilled Aberdeen Angus sirloin steak with green peppercorn butter. Chocolate truffle cake with Tia Maria and coffee bean syrup, or bread-and-butter pudding made with double cream, sultanas soaked in brandy and clotted cream might need an afternoon to walk off, or there are Cornish and other British cheeses with biscuits. Some 16 wines are available by the glass. More reports please. SAMPLE DISHES: pork rillettes £5; confit of duck with Puy lentil purée and rich Madeira sauce £13; baked rice pudding with jam and clotted cream £4.

Licensee V. Bolton (Coast & Country Inns)
Open 12 to 3, 6 to 11, Sun 12 to 4, 7 to 10.30; bar food and restaurant 12 to 2.15, 6.30 (7 Sun) to 9.15
Details Children welcome   Car park   Wheelchair access (also women's WC)   Garden and patio
No smoking in restaurant and family room   Live music   Dogs welcome exc in restaurant   Delta, MasterCard, Switch, Visa   Accommodation: 7 rooms, B&B £32.50 to £70

TRISCOMBE   Somerset   map 2

Blue Ball Inn 🍇

Triscombe TA4 3HE   TEL: (01984) 618242
signposted off A358 between Taunton and Minehead

This impressive place consists of three huge converted fifteenth-century barns with an original thatched pub tucked behind. The stylish and atmospheric interior is on three different levels, with a high-pitched roof and a log fire in each area; it has been lavishly kitted out, with 'tons of wood', smart carpets, and upmarket furnishings and fabrics helping to create a smart, contemporary feel. There is no separate restaurant (although tables are laid with napkins and proper crockery in the evening), but the menus read well and they are based largely on local ingredients (including daily supplies of fish). The lunch menu has crusty rustic rolls with various fillings and ploughman's for the walking brigade, as well as a decent slate of dishes ranging from hot steak roll with salad and chips to coconut and chilli chicken with sweet potato crisps and pilau rice, or Quantock venison casserole with buttered mash and honeyed cranberries. Some of these dishes also feature on the daily-changing dinner menu, along with other options such as pressed terrine of confit of duck and pigeon, roast cod with a confit of fennel, and pan-fried duck breast with onion marmalade and orange butter sauce. Desserts might range from chocolate and mascarpone tart to sticky toffee pudding. Several locally brewed real ales are on handpump: Cotleigh Tawny is always available, along with, say, Sharp's Doom Bar Bitter, and Exmoor Gold and Stag. The 100-strong wine list has plenty of good drinking at fair prices, from a spot-on New Zealand selection to some affordable Burgundy. Eight are also available by the glass. Outside is a lovely garden and a decked area with views across the Vale of Taunton. SAMPLE DISHES: warm salad of goats' cheese glazed with honey and herbs £5.75; fillet steak with whole-grain mustard mash and Madeira sauce £17; Italian lemon tart £4.50.

Licensees Peter Alcroft and Sharon Murdoch (freehouse)
Open 12 to 2.30, 7 to 11, Sun 12 to 3, 7 to 10.30; bar food 12 to 1.45, 7 to 9.30
Details Children welcome   Car park   Wheelchair access (also WC)   Garden and patio   No smoking in eating areas   Background music   Dogs welcome   Delta, MasterCard, Switch, Visa

TROTTON   West Sussex   map 3

Keeper's Arms   NEW ENTRY

Trotton GU31 5ER   TEL: (01730) 813724
on A272 between Midhurst and Petersfield

One reporter thought this 'the kind of place you would take American visitors to show them a typical English pub'. Pretty countryside surrounds the atmospheric old building (good walking country), while within, the two large beamed rooms, both smoky from log fires, have a relaxed air: 'no need to ask if they accept dogs, along with muddy wellies.' Homely, too, are the photographs on the walls and eclectic furnishings, including leather armchairs by the fire. The daily menu is chalked on two blackboards, one for specials. A regular is gamekeeper's pie – pheasant, partridge, venison and wild duck cooked in red wine and topped with suet pastry – or there's hungry man's hock, a whole bacon hock simmered for five hours and accompanied by mash in a serving that's 'more than enough for two'. Specials include mussels with lemongrass, and home-cooked ham appears in items like simple ham, egg and chips. Light, well-made tempura vegetables with teriyaki sauce bring a more global view, and spotted dog and lemon cream crunch head up a list of desserts. Beers on handpump include Ballard's Best and Cheriton Pots Ale, and a couple of wines are served by the glass. SAMPLE DISHES: ham and lentil soup with sunflower bread £5; Thai-style fishcakes £8.50; cheese and ham platter £6.50; lemon cream crunch £3.50.

Licensee Stephen Oxley (freehouse)
Open Tue to Sun 12 to 2.30, Tue to Sat 6.30 to 11; bar food Tue to Sun 12 to 2, Tue to Sat 6.30 to 9
Details Children welcome   Car park   Wheelchair access (also WC)   Terrace   No smoking in restaurant, no-smoking area in bar   Occasional background music   Dogs in bar only   Delta, MasterCard, Switch, Visa

TROUBECK   Cumbria   map 8

▲ Queens Head Hotel ❦ 🍺

Townhead, Troutbeck LA23 1PW   TEL: (015394) 32174
WEBSITE: www.queensheadhotel.com
at start of Kirkstone Pass, 2½m from junction of A591 and A592

Formerly a coaching stop on the main route between Windermere and Penrith, the Queen's Head is now passed only by those who prefer the more picturesque alternative to the M6 – and anyone seeking breathtaking views of spectacular landscapes would be wise to wend this way. The well-preserved seventeenth-century inn is an attraction in itself: the main bar has the frame of a four-poster bed as its counter, plus the more usual slate-tiled floors, low oak beams and log fires, and upstairs the characterful mayor's parlour is the setting for Troutbeck's mayor-making ceremony. The main menu, available throughout, offers plenty of interesting options, some traditional, such as steak, ale and mushroom cobbler, others with a more contemporary edge, such as red bream on sweet tomato compote with basil and garlic. Daily specials are listed on a blackboard, and there is also a good-value set-price menu, plus light lunch options ranging from pan-fried ox liver on black pudding mash to wild mushroom risotto. An outstanding choice of real ales includes Coniston Bluebird Bitter and Old Man Ale, Jennings Cumberland Ale and Cocker Hoop and Black Sheep Special. There are plenty of good-value wines among the 30-odd well-chosen bottles, and seven are available by the large or small glass. SAMPLE DISHES: smoked pork, apricot and walnut salad £5.50; pan-fried, honey-glazed Barbary duck breast on fondant potato with lemon and pink peppercorn jus £14; banana and honey parfait with toffee sauce and cream £3.75.

Licensees Mark Stewardson and Joanne Sherratt (freehouse)
Open 11 to 11, Sun 12 to 10.30; bar food and restaurant 12 to 2, 6.30 to 9; closed 25 Dec
Details Children welcome Car park Wheelchair access (also WC) Patio No-smoking area in bar
No music Dogs welcome in bar only Delta, MasterCard, Switch, Visa Accommodation: 14 rooms,
B&B £47.50 to £95

TRUMPET   Herefordshire   map 5

▲ Verzons Country Inn   NEW ENTRY

Trumpet HR8 2PZ   TEL: (01531) 670381
on A438, 2m W of Ledbury

The former Georgian farmhouse may be in a fairly isolated rural position, but it is a popular dining destination. Extended many years ago into a roadside country hotel, it does not look much like a pub from the outside. Inside, however, there is the Hop Bar, which looks the part with its exposed brick walls, beams and assorted pub-style accoutrements. You will also find decent real ales on tap – Hook Norton Best and Shepherd Neame Spitfire. Lunchtime bar meals range from hearty, rustic dishes of boiled and baked ham, fried egg and chips to Nasi Goreng (an Indonesian rice dish). Evening menus are considerably more elaborate. A starter of pressed guinea fowl, shallot, mushroom and bacon terrine with a kumquat chutney, for example, might be followed by locally reared Herefordshire beef fillet, braised shin and sweet onions, horseradish risotto and Spitfire juices. Around 70 bottles feature on the wine list, with ten served by two sizes of glass; house wines are £9.75 a bottle. SAMPLE DISHES:

parsnip and sherry soup with hazelnut pesto £4; roasted pork fillet with braised cabbage, bacon, apple and chestnuts £12; baked nutmeg rice pudding with damson and sloe gin jam £4.50.

Licensee David Roberts (freehouse)
Open 11 to 11, Sun 12 to 10.30; bar food and restaurant 12 to 2, 7 to 9; closed evenings 25 and 26 Dec
Details Children welcome   Car park   Wheelchair access (also WC)   Garden and patio   No smoking in dining room   No music   Guide dogs only   Amex, Delta, Diners, MasterCard, Switch, Visa   Accommodation: 8 rooms, B&B £45 to £88

TUCKENHAY   Devon   map 1

▲ Maltsters' Arms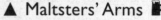

Bow Creek, Tuckenhay TQ9 7EQ   TEL: (01803) 732350
WEBSITE: www.tuckenhay.com
off A381, 2½m S of Totnes

WATERSIDE

In a remote spot accessible only by tiny lanes or boat, this eighteenth-century inn makes the most of its spectacular setting overlooking Bow Creek (a tidal tributary of the River Dart). It is a lively place with bags of character and a cheerful décor that brightens up the bar and dining areas. One wide-ranging menu is served throughout, and the emphasis is on local produce given uncomplicated modern treatment, as in mussels, cockles and clams in cream and vanilla, fillet of wild sea bass in olive oil with roasted cherry tomatoes, or plain and simple roast Devon chicken with herb stuffing and chipolatas. At least one organic dish is also available – perhaps farfalle in porcini mushroom pesto – while desserts could include tiramisù. Families should note that there is a menu of 'real food for children', where you will find pan-fried chicken breast and grilled plaice. Local Princetown IPA is always on draught alongside top-notch guest ales from Devon breweries such as Teignworthy, Otter and Blackawton, and you can sample local Ruddyturnstone cider too. Wines also show up well, with around 15 by the glass covering a good range of flavours, including the local Sharpham Estate white. Theme nights are a feature, while award-winning barbecues and live music are major attractions on summer evenings. Stylish accommodation is in the Old Winery, a stone building next to the pub. SAMPLE DISHES: minted pea and spinach soup £4; grilled fillet of salmon with seafood sauce £11; pineapple and nectarine crumble £4.25.

Licensees Denise and Quentin Thwaites (freehouse)
Open 11 to 11, Sun 12 to 10.30; bar food and restaurant Sun to Fri 12 to 3, 7 to 9.30 (all day July and Aug), Sat 12 to 9.30; open 12 to 2 25 Dec (no food)
Details Children welcome in family rooms   Car park   Wheelchair access (also WC)   Garden and patio   Occasional live music   Dogs welcome   MasterCard, Switch, Visa   Accommodation: 7 rooms, B&B £50 to £125

TUNBRIDGE WELLS   Kent   map 3

Sankeys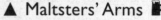

39 Mount Ephraim, Tunbridge Wells TN4 8AA   TEL: (01892) 511422
WEBSITE: www.sankeys.co.uk
on A26, virtually opposite Kent and Sussex Hospital

SEAFOOD

'Bars, brasserie and garden' is what you can expect at Guy Sankey's eating and drinking house in a row of shops just seconds from the common. The main bar is on the ground floor and the cellar is now more of a brasserie with oak paneling, leather sofas and church pews. The sunny, south-facing terrace garden is a boon in warm weather. Larkins Traditional Ale from Chiddingstone and Harveys Best are on draught, plus half a dozen more coming from Ireland, Bavaria and points between (not to mention an amazing array of bottled beers from around the world): 'we never stock a beer brewed under license', insists Mr Sankey. The wine list runs to around 50 bins, 15 of which are available by the glass, as are some rather appealing sherries; all are available to take home. Blackboards list lunchtime baguettes and daily specials, while the main menu focuses on fish and shellfish: perhaps Cuan Bay oysters, spider crab with chilli, Shetland cod in beer batter with chips, or even Atlantic halibut with a sauce made from Kriek cherry beer. Steaks, poultry and game add further variety, and to finish there are desserts such as hot chocolate and orange pudding. SAMPLE DISHES: grilled goats' cheese with pesto dressing and red onion marmalade £6.50; seafood paella £11.50; crème brûlée £4.25.

Licensee Guy Sankey (freehouse)
Open 10 to 11, Sun 12 to 10.30; bar food 12 to 10 (Sun 1 to 5); closed Christmas
Details No children Garden No-smoking area in bar Background music No Dogs MasterCard, Switch, Visa

---

TUNSTALL   **Lancashire**   map 8

Lunesdale Arms
Tunstall LA6 2QN   TEL: (015242) 74203
WEBSITE: www.thelunesdale.com
on A683, S of Kirkby Lonsdale

Set on the main road through a small, straggly village (that still boasts a post office), this modernised country hotel offers good value for fresh food prepared in a straight-forward style. The main bar is an open-plan L-shaped room with the bar counter at its centre. Primrose-yellow walls and a bare wooden floor are lifted by watercolours on the walls. Menus, listed on blackboards, make a show of pointing up the sources of supplies – home-baked bread, meat from local farms and organically grown vegetables and salads. Lunch offers light meals such as poached chicken, bacon and salad open sandwich, plus a few more substantial dishes like sausage with mash, red wine gravy and caramelised onions. The choice increases in the evening, adding starters of goats' cheese croûte with salad leaves, and main courses of roasted marinated monkfish with basmati rice and green beans, or ribeye steak. Finish perhaps with chocolate brownie and ice cream. Good cask ales come from the Black Sheep Brewery, and there's also a guest. Half a dozen wines are sold by the glass from a list of 30 bottles, prices starting around £10. SAMPLE DISHES: spicy roast pumpkin with feta and olive salad £4; lamb Shrewsbury with mash and green beans £8; cardamom, crème fraîche and honey cheesecake £4.

Licensees Emma Gillibrand and John Simmons (freehouse)
Open Tue to Sat 11 to 3, 6 to 11, Sun 12 to 3, 6 to 10.30; bar food Tue to Fri 12 to 2, 6 to 9, Sat and Sun 12 to 2.30, 6 to 9; closed 25 and 26 Dec
Details Children welcome Car park Wheelchair access (also WC) Patio Occasional live or background music Dogs welcome Delta, MasterCard, Switch, Visa

TURVILLE   **Buckinghamshire**   map 2

Bull and Butcher

Turville RG9 6QU   TEL: (01491) 638283
WEBSITE: www.bullandbutcher.com

Turville looks very much the archetypal English village, with a pretty old stone church and lots of ancient houses – it's hardly surprising that the place has been used in various TV and film productions, including *The Vicar of Dibley* and *Chitty Chitty Bang Bang*. The Bull and Butcher is one of the first buildings you encounter, a long, low, white-painted pub with a garden to one side and stables behind. Inside, the smoking and non-smoking bars are separated by a vast brick hearth with log fires lit on either side in cold weather, and there is an extension that incorporates an old, glass-topped well. The printed bar menu plays on the village's film and TV connections, with such dishes as Chitty Chitty bangers and mash, Midsomer burger, and Dibley pie (steak and ale), with blackboard specials adding Tuscan bean soup, fresh anchovy salad with capers and gherkins, ribeye steak with fries, and lamb rump with gravy and mint sauce. Puddings take in apple tart with caramel sauce, and lemon tart. Regular beers are from the Brakspear range, including the seasonal Hop Demon. Wine drinkers should applaud the policy of offering 16 wines by the 175 or 250ml glass from a short, well-balanced selection. SAMPLE DISHES: fresh Norwegian crayfish tail salad £8; champagne-poached salmon fillet with a light butter sauce £11; orange flower brûlée £4.50.

Licensees Hugo and Lydia Botha (Brakspear)
Open 11 to 11, Sun 12 to 10.30; bar food 12 to 2.30 (3 Sun), 7 to 9.45
Details Children welcome in eating area   Car park   Wheelchair access (also WC)   Garden and patio
No smoking in eating area   Background music   Dogs welcome on a lead   Delta, MasterCard, Switch, Visa

ULLINGSWICK   **Herefordshire**   map 5

Three Crowns Inn

Ullingswick HR1 3JQ   TEL: (01432) 820279
WEBSITE: www.threecrownsinn.com
off A465 between Hereford and Bromyard

Set in splendid isolation this small half-timbered and red brick country pub is set back from the single-track lane that leads from the tiny village of Ullingswick to Bleak Acre. The 'lovely old interior' of two interlinked dining rooms (complete with a couple of high-backed settles and tables with Singer sewing machine supports) sports a 'homely' look. Food is impressive, based on first-class raw materials, and the strength of the cooking lies in the fact that just about everything is freshly made from fine local and regional ingredients. The short, daily-changing menu could start with stir-fried mussels with spring onion and black beans (a dish with a 'complex yet clear flavour range'), followed by 'luscious' slow-roast noisette of Marches lamb with a tartlet of root vegetables, sautéed kidney and wild mushrooms, or whole grilled sole with marinated broccoli and boulangère potatoes. Finish with cinnamon crème brûlée with sable biscuit, or a plate of local cheeses. The presentation of dishes is attractive, and bread has come in for praise. Hobsons Best Bitter and Mild are kept, plus a guest from the local Wye Valley Brewery; Stowford Press cider is also available. Six fruity house wines are sold by the glass from a list of around 40 bottles, but these are the only options below £15 a bottle. Nonetheless there's fair value and good qual-ity here, complemented by a blackboard proffering tempting fine-wine options from France and Italy. SAMPLE DISHES: tempura courgette flower filled with goats' cheese £5.75; Bury Farm Berkshire pork chop with roast squash and chorizo casserole £13.75; ginger parkin with spiced cider syrup and rhubarb ripple ice cream £4.25.

Licensee Brent Castle (freehouse)
Open *Tue to Sat 12 to 3, 7 to 11, Sun 12 to 2.30, 7 to 10.30; bar food 12 to 2 (2.30 Sun), 7 to 9.30 (9 Sun); closed 2 weeks from 24 Dec*
Details *Children welcome   Car park   Wheelchair access (also WC)   Patio   No-smoking area in bar No music   No dogs   Delta, MasterCard, Switch, Visa*

ULVERSTON   Cumbria   map 8

▲ Bay Horse Hotel ♥ ❦

Canal Foot, Ulverston LA12 9EL   TEL: (01229) 583972
WEBSITE: www.thebayhorsehotel.co.uk
off A590, 8m NE of Barrow-in-Furness, take Canal Foot turn in Ulverston, then next signposted left turn following lane to pub

Formerly a staging post for the coaches crossing Morecambe Bay, this eighteenth-century inn is now appreciated more for its fine views, which take in the wide expanse of Cartmel Sands, the Leven Estuary and the peaks of the Lake District. The tradi-tional-looking beamed main bar has a warm, friendly and relaxed feel, though there is a separate restaurant for more formal occasions. Bar lunches offer simple snacks and light meals, hot and cold sandwiches, and more substantial main dishes such as grilled Waberthwaite sausage with date chutney, cranberry and apple sauce, or crab and salmon fishcakes on white wine, herb and cream sauce. Though the style is mostly straightforward, the odd exotic idea occasionally creeps in – perhaps South African bobotie – and vegetarians have a whole page of meat-free meals to choose from. The restaurant menu goes in for more ambitious fare such as roast rack of lamb with Dijon mustard and herb crust. Real ales are from reputable regional breweries, including Jennings, Thwaites and Hydes. The 100-strong wine list, focusing mainly on France, Australia and a very well chosen South African range, offers reasonable choice under £20 and temptingly indulgent bottles above. Eight wines are usually available by the glass. SAMPLE DISHES: smoked haddock and sweetcorn soup with hot garlic and paprika bread £6.75; pan-fried medallions of pork with leeks and Lancashire cheese on Madeira sauce £9.25; profiteroles with banana cream and hot chocolate sauce £4.50.

Licensee Robert Lyons (freehouse)
Open *11 to 11, Sun 12 to 10.30; bar food Tue to Sun 12 to 1.30; restaurant Tue to Sun 12 to 1.30, 7.30 for 8 (1 sitting)*
Details *Car park   Wheelchair access (also WC)   Garden   No smoking in dining room   Background music Dogs welcome   Amex, Delta, MasterCard, Switch, Visa   Accommodation: 9 rooms, D,B&B £77.50 to £185*

Farmers Arms

Market Place, Ulverston LA12 7BA   TEL: (01229) 584469
WEBSITE: www.farmersrestaurant-thelakes.co.uk

The Farmers Arms occupies a prominent position at the end of Ulverston's cobbled main street, with a small terrace in front for use of drinkers in fine weather. The large, open-plan bar is comfortably furnished in homely fashion with Lloyd loom chairs, carpeted throughout, and has a friendly atmosphere, with daily papers provided for customers to read. Menus are divided into 'traditional favourites' such as gammon with pineapple, dishes 'from around the world', including pasta carbonara, steaks and various salads, such as chicken with brie and cranberry, while daily specials, listed on a blackboard, might feature thyme and honey glazed rack of lamb. At lunchtime there is also a list of sandwiches and jacket potatoes, and breakfast is served every day except Sunday. Among draught beers are Timothy Taylor Landlord, Hawkshead Bitter and Hoegaarden, and a regularly changing selection of wines by the glass is listed on a blackboard. SAMPLE DISHES: hot garlic prawns on toast £4; seared salmon fillet with asparagus and prawn cream sauce £9; hot toffee crunch meringue and ice cream £3.25.

Licensee Roger Chattaway (freehouse)
Open 9.30 to 11, Sun 11 to 10.30; bar food and restaurant 11 to 2.30, 5.30 to 8.30
Details Children welcome in dining room   Wheelchair access (not WC)   Patio   No smoking in dining room   Occasional live or background music   No dogs   MasterCard, Switch, Visa

UPPER HAMBLETON   Rutland   map 6

▲ Finch's Arms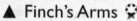

Oakham Road, Upper Hambleton LE15 8TL   TEL: (01572) 756575
WEBSITE: www.finchsarms.co.uk

Magnificent views from the rear dining room over gardens and lawns sweeping down to Rutland Water are one feature of this farmhouse-style pub in a peaceful village. Another is the delightful atmosphere of its two flag-floored rooms linked by a wood-panelled bar; each has beamed ceilings, ochre-coloured walls and, in deepest December, an open fire. The kitchen's eclectic approach produces crispy gammon hock with baked butter beans and new potatoes in Castelnaudary style, or beef, mushroom and Guinness suet pudding, as main courses in the bar, or steamed bream fillet and vegetables with aïoli in the Garden Room. Starters, equally varied, range from pan-fried scallops on egg noodles with fresh coriander and lemon butter, to roast quail with baked lentils and quail's egg on salad with a morels dressing. This might be followed by a liquorice sultana cream served in an eggshell, with a chocolate stick and chocolate sauce. To drink, there's Grainstore Cooking Bitter and guests such as Greene King Abbot Ale, alongside 20-odd wines from £11, with a dozen or so by the glass. SAMPLE DISHES: pan-fried foie gras, red chard, rocket with honey, walnut and balsamic £8.95; roast monkfish tail wrapped in Parma ham on chive mash £13.50; white chocolate mousse with a warm rum, banana and coconut coulis £4.

Licensee Colin Crawford (freehouse)
Open 11 to 11; bar food and restaurant 12 to 2.30, 6 to 9.30 (Sun: all day summer, till 7 winter)
Details Children welcome   Car park   Wheelchair access (also WC)   Garden and patio   No smoking in restaurant   Occasional live or background music   No dogs   Delta, MasterCard, Switch, Visa   Accommodation: 6 rooms, B&B £55 to £75

All details are as accurate as possible at the time of going to press, but pubs often change hands and it is wise to check beforehand by telephone anything that is particularly important to you.

UPPERMILL   **Greater Manchester**   map 8

Church Inn 🍺

Church Lane, Uppermill, Saddleworth OL3 6LW   TEL: (01457) 820902

With commanding views down a narrow side valley high above the craft shops and cafés of trendy Uppermill, this old gritstone pub clings to a hillside so steep that there are two storeys to the front but four to the rear. The Saddleworth Brewery is in the basement, producing tasty Hopsmacker and Robyn's Bitter and Shaftbender stout. These – plus guests like McEwan 80/- or Ruddles County – you can sup among ducks, geese and peacocks in the garden alongside, drinking in the view and watching llamas graze (there's a trekking centre nearby). The open-plan bar has stoves at each end for winter warmth, and decoration bespeaks a morris dancers' haunt: among the plates and brassery on the wall are a girning collar and photographs of the Longwood Thump rushcart festival (on August bank holidays). Food comes in gargantuan portions, and vegetarians are well catered for. The menu and blackboards offer pâté with Cumberland sauce or breaded king prawns, then perhaps chicken breast with mushrooms, garlic and tarragon sauce, cheese and onion pie, deep-fried jumbo cod, a daily roast dinner with Yorkshire pudding, or one of several suet puddings (try lamb and mint). Maybe only masochists would dare a dessert. Some 30 wines start at £6.75; two are sold by the glass, and there are around half a dozen single-serve bottles. SAMPLE DISHES: garlic mushrooms £3.25; steak and ale suet pudding £5.75; treacle roly-poly £2.25.

Licensee Julian Taylor (freehouse)
Open 12 to 11, Sun 12 to 10.30; bar food Mon to Fri 12 to 2.30, 5.30 to 9, Sat and Sun 12 to 9
Details Children welcome in eating areas   Car park   Wheelchair access (also WC)   Garden and patio   No-smoking area in bar   Background music   Dogs welcome on a lead   Amex, Delta, Diners, MasterCard, Switch, Visa

UPPER WOODFORD   **Wiltshire**   map 2

Bridge

Upper Woodford SP4 6NU   TEL: (01722) 782323
the Woodfords signposted from centre of Amesbury

An aptly named pub that stands right by a bridge where the road crosses the River Avon. However, this Bridge is roadside, looking over the car park with its garden on the other side of the road by the river. The open-plan space inside has three linked areas, all with mint-green walls: a poolroom with a fruit machine, and a bar and dining room both hung with botanical prints. The food, pretty much following a traditional path, is simple, unpretentious and honest. The printed menu, backed up by blackboard specials, might deliver roast tomato soup with pesto, followed by braised lamb shank with mashed potato and mint gravy, or fish in beer batter with chips and tartare sauce. Ice cream is home made, or there could be passion-fruit cheesecake to finish. The compact, global wine list (some 15 bins) has plenty under £20 and seven by glass, while on hand-pump there's Hop Back GFB and guest ales, perhaps Enterprise Brewery Best, Bridge and Grumpy Cow. SAMPLE DISHES: Bayonne ham with coleslaw and crispy bacon £5; grilled breast of chicken with mushrooms and tarragon £9; berry pavlova £4.25.

Licensee Andrew Sergeant (Enterprise Inns)
Open 12 to 3, 6 to 11; bar food and restaurant 12 to 2, 6 to 9 (8.30 Sun)
Details Children welcome   Car park   Wheelchair access (also WC)   Garden   Occasional live or background music   Dogs welcome in bar only   Delta, MasterCard, Switch, Visa

UPTON BISHOP Herefordshire map 5

Moody Cow at Upton Bishop

Upton Bishop HR9 7TT TEL: (01989) 780470
WEBSITE: www.moodycow.co.uk
at crossroads of B4224 and B4221, 4m NE of Ross-on-Wye

'Very consistently country' is how one reporter described the décor in this tall, rough-stone pub/restaurant with a pleasant patio for outdoor meals. Pictures and effigies of cows dominate the L-shaped interior, which consists of several linked areas on different levels; away from the bar is a restored stone barn that houses the no-smoking restaurant. The regular printed menu doesn't change a great deal, so expect plenty of old favourites, ranging from open sandwiches, Caesar salad and pastas to Moody Cow pie (steak and kidney with vegetables and potatoes under shortcrust pastry), chicken jalfrezi, and cod 'n' chips ('served in newspaper on request'). Alternatively, head for the blackboard, where there's a list of specials highlighting fish in the shape of, say, seared scallops with sweet chilli sauce, baked whole plaice in a Parmesan and rosemary crust, and pan-fried salmon with roasted garlic, red onion and rosemary, plus game in season. Everything, from bread and chutneys to ice cream, is made on the premises, and you might round things off with a dessert such as apple sorbet with Calvados jelly, or sticky toffee pudding. Wye Valley Bitter, Bass and Flowers IPA are on handpump alongside two guests, and seven wines are served by the glass from a list of around two dozen; house 'plonk' is £8.85. SAMPLE DISHES: warm red onion tartlet with Parmesan £5.25; cannon of lamb en croûte with rosemary jus £12; bread-and-butter pudding £4.75.

Licensee James Lloyd (freehouse)
Open *all week 12 to 2.30, Tue to Sat 6.30 to 11; bar food and restaurant 12 to 2, 6.30 to 9.30*
Details *Children welcome Car park Patio No smoking in restaurant Background music Dogs welcome in bar Amex, Delta, Diners, MasterCard, Switch, Visa*

UPTON SCUDAMORE Wiltshire map 2

▲ Angel Inn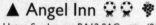

Upton Scudamore BA12 0AG TEL: (01985) 213225
Upton Scudamore signposted off A350 Warminster to Westbury road

From the outside, this Angel appears neatly garbed in white, with a paved patio, good-quality seating and plants in large tubs. The interior is equally spick and span: the lofty, light-filled bar area has a boarded floor, terracotta and beige check curtains over French windows and pine tables, while the spacious open-plan restaurant on different levels boasts well-spaced tables and a comfortable seating area with low sofas, books and magazines. Chef Paul Suter (ex-Angel Inn, Hindon, see entry) now holds sway in the kitchen and has quickly moved into top gear. Spot-on raw materials are skilfully deployed for a short dinner menu that is classy without being over-pretentious. Warm salad of beef strips with sweet chilli jam and bean sprouts has a touch of exoticism, while braised lamb shank with flageolet beans, chorizo and rosemary brings together all the components of an earthy peasant classic. Blackboard specials are dominated by fish, perhaps roast baby monkfish tails with basil mash and lentil cream sauce, or grilled red snapper with roasted butternut squash and herb butter sauce. Stunningly good bread and ice creams (a honey version served with apple and blackberry crumble, for example) are made on the premises. The lighter lunch menu includes dishes such as Cumberland ring with mash and an apple and pear salsa, or salmon and herb fishcakes with salad. A creditable choice of real ales includes Wadworth 6X, Butcombe Bitter and a guest brew. Modish modern wines like Wither Hills Sauvignon Blanc rub shoulders with old world counterparts like Vincent Pinard's Sancerre on an upbeat wine list arranged by style. Eight wines come by the glass (£3–£4 for 175ml) and 12 in half-bottles. SAMPLE DISHES: potted salmon and crab with grilled bread £6; pan-fried chicken breast with provençale vegetables and tarragon cream £13; sticky toffee pudding £4.25.

Licensees Anthony and Carol Coates (freehouse)
Open 11 to 3, 6 to 11 (10.30 Sun); bar food and restaurant 12 to 2, 7 to 9.30; closed 25 and 26 Dec, 1 Jan
Details Children welcome   Car park   Wheelchair access (not WC)   Garden and patio   No smoking in restaurant   Background music   Dogs welcome exc in restaurant   Delta, MasterCard, Switch, Visa
Accommodation: 10 rooms, B&B £60 to £75

WADHURST   East Sussex   map 3

▲ Best Beech Inn

Mayfield Lane, Wadhurst TN5 6JH   TEL: (01892) 782046
on B2100, 1m from Wadhurst towards Mark Cross

Parts of this roadside inn date from the seventeenth-century, but the character inside is largely Victorian. New owners have transformed the place in the last couple of years, and it is now divided into a traditional bar for drinking, and two separate eating areas that share the same menu. Evening diners encounter a carte of contemporary European cooking: squid ink risotto with a seared scallop and pancetta, or roast black pudding mousse topped with a quail's egg, are typical starters, while main courses might feature griddled beef fillet with wild mushrooms and shallots, or pan-fried pigeon breast with braised red cabbage, swede purée and juniper berry essence. Among desserts creamy rice pudding with a compote of fruits, or roast pink grapefruit French toast with an apricot sauce catch the eye. Simpler lunch dishes might include eggs Benedict, salmon fishcakes, or steak and kidney pudding, as well as sandwiches like ham and wholegrain mustard potato salad. Harvey's Sussex Best and Adnams are the regular real ales, while some 36 varied and reasonably priced wines start at £10, and six come by the glass. SAMPLE DISHES: crab ravioli with roast cherry tomatoes and basil foam £5; roast fillet of sea bass with rich potato mash, pancetta and fèves £15; crème caramel with summer berries and vanilla ice cream £5.

Licensees Roger and Jane Felstead (freehouse)
Open 11.30 to 3, 6 to 11, Sun 12 to 3, 7 to 10.30; bar food and restaurant 12 to 2, 7 to 9, Sun 12 to 2
Details Children over 12 welcome in bar eating area   Car park   Wheelchair access (not WC)   Patio
No smoking in dining room   Background music   Dogs welcome exc in restaurants   MasterCard, Switch, Visa
Accommodation: 7 rooms, B&B £39.90 to £109.90

WALBERSWICK   Suffolk   map 6

▲ Bell Inn

Ferry Road, Walberswick IP18 6TN   TEL: (01502) 723109
WEBSITE: www.blythweb.co.uk/bellinn

The 600-year-old core of this popular inn overlooking the village green is every inch a classic Suffolk coastal pub, with its low beams, flagstone floors, latticed windows, settles and prints. Wood fires burn in winter, and lighting is provided by ships' lanterns. Extensions have been tacked on over the years to cope with the influx of families and holidaymakers, and there's plenty of space in the garden at the back. The seasonal printed menu is bolstered by daily blackboard specials, with seafood showing up strongly in the shape of locally smoked sprats, deep-fried cod in beer batter, and grilled skate with a herb, lime and caper butter. Elsewhere, there's a global feel to dishes like hummus with chilli oil and pine nuts, Thai green chicken curry, and Tunisian lemon and almond cake. The full range of real ales from Adnams Brewery (across the Blyth Estuary in Southwold) are kept in good order; Adnams are also responsible for the carefully selected list of 40-plus wines, which features eight house selections by the glass (from £2.35). Prices are very reasonable throughout and a stretch to £20 or so will bag some quality reds. SAMPLE DISHES: salad of crayfish, mayonnaise and paprika £5.25; beef and root vegetable casserole with Stilton dumplings £7.25; blueberry tart £4.

Licensee Susan Ireland-Cutting (Adnams)
Open *summer 11 to 11, Sun 12 to 10.30, winter Mon to Fri 11 to 3, 6 to 11, Sat 11 to 11, Sun 12 to 10.30; bar food 12 to 2 (2.30 Sun and bank hols), 6 (7 winter) to 9, restaurant Fri and Sat 6 (7 winter) to 9*
Details *Children welcome in family room and eating areas   Car park   Wheelchair access (also WC)   Garden and patio   No smoking in restaurant   Occasional live or background music   Dogs welcome exc in restaurant   Delta, MasterCard, Switch, Visa   Accommodation: 6 rooms, B&B £60 to £90*

WARHAM ALL SAINTS   Norfolk   map 6

▲ Three Horseshoes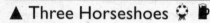

Bridge Street, Warham All Saints NR23 1NL   TEL: (01328) 710547

This unashamedly old-fashioned village pub turns its back on modern uniformity and in a quirky, quaint, unpretentious manner brings a feel of 'old England'. Two small, stone-floored rooms are lit by gaslight and filled with scrubbed wooden tables, there's a coal fire burning in a Victorian fireplace, and a grandfather clock marks time in the main bar. Curios such as an ancient one-armed bandit or a rare nineteenth-century village game of Norfolk twister are matched by old posters, clay pipes and such like. Blackboard menus list the daily specials: beef and onion soup, followed by braised lamb shank, or a pie generously filled with perhaps game cooked in wine and onions. Light lunches from the printed menu take in meaty locally made sausages and bacon in a warm crusty roll; filled jacket potatoes; variations of the ploughman's theme; and main courses such as cod in cheese sauce. Beers are another strength: regular Woodforde's Wherry Best Bitter, Greene King IPA, and regularly changing guest ales (four a week in summer) that might come from local microbreweries, all tapped by gravity direct from the barrel and served from a hole-in-the-wall bar. Some five wines come by the 250ml mini bottle, and the pub also boasts a choice of fruit wines. Bed and breakfast is available in the adjoining Old Post Office. SAMPLE DISHES: mushroom and Stilton tart £4; Norfolk beef pie £8; apple and sultana crumble £3.

Licensee Iain Salmon (freehouse)
Open *11.30 to 2.30, 6 to 11, Sun 12 to 3, 6 to 10.30; bar food 12 to 1.45, 6.30 to 8.30; no food 25 and 26 Dec*
Details *Children welcome in eating areas   Car park   Wheelchair access (also WC)   Garden and patio   No smoking in eating areas   No music   Dogs welcome   No cards   Accommodation: 4 rooms, B&B £24 to £52*

WARWICK   **Warwickshire**   **map 5**

▲ Rose and Crown

30 Market Place, Warwick CV34 4SH   TEL: (01926) 411117
WEBSITE: www.peachpubs.com

With a look from the contemporary school of pub design, the Peach Pub Company's
very first offering does not fit readily into any traditional notions of what a pub should
be, yet is more relaxed and informal than any restaurant. Two huge picture windows
flank the entrance, allowing plenty of light into the simply decorated L-shaped room.
Furniture is large wooden tables and chairs for diners, and leather sofas, bar stools and
coffee tables for drinkers. Unlike most pubs, this one opens for Continental breakfast, or a bacon and sausage sarnie, and lunchtime snacks are served until early
evening: these include interesting sandwiches (aubergine, ricotta and roasted tomato,
for example) and tapas-style 'deli plates' with pick-and-mix cheeses, cold meats and
assorted posh nibbles. This kind of flexibility is a hallmark of the style: several options
are offered as 'either-or' portions, such as Thai beef salad, and crab and chilli linguine.
Lunchtime main courses are simple, hearty dishes like faggots, mushy peas and onion
gravy, while the evening menu adds a few more choices, such as braised shank of
lamb with pea and mint risotto. To finish, there might be warm chocolate brownie
with vanilla ice cream. Fuller's London Pride, Old Speckled Hen, and Timothy
Taylor Landlord are among the real ales on offer, and around seven wines are available by the large or small glass from a list of some two dozen bottles, prices starting at
£10.50. SAMPLE DISHES: moules marinière £4.50; confit of duckling, creamed cabbage,
cinnamon and aniseed sauce £11.50; passion-fruit parfait with lime syrup £4.50.

Licensee Victoria Moon (Peach Pub Co)
Open 11 to 11, Sun 12 to 10.30; bar food 12.30 to 2.30 (Sun 12 to 3), 6.30 to 10; light meals available
2.30 to 6.30
Details Children welcome   Wheelchair access (also WC)   Patio   Background music   Dogs welcome   Amex,
Delta, MasterCard, Switch, Visa   Accommodation: 5 rooms, B&B £65 to £75

WATH-IN-NIDDERDALE   **North Yorkshire**   **map 8**

▲ Sportsman's Arms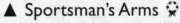

Wath-in-Nidderdale HG3 5PP   TEL: (01423) 711306
off B6265, 2m NW of Pateley Bridge

This lovely seventeenth-century stone inn is a treat to visit even if the approach over a
narrow stone bridge causes concern for the wing mirrors of your car. It is set in Upper
Nidderdale surrounded by moors famous for their grouse, has its own fishing on a
stretch of the Nidd, and Gouthwaite Reservoir, with its wild brown trout, is a short
walk away. The bar décor reflects this hunting and fishing theme, but the more
formal restaurant has white-clothed tables and gleaming silver and glass. Although
this is a hotel and restaurant, beer drinkers will find various ales on draught, including
Black Sheep Best Bitter. No wine list was supplied to the Guide, but we were
informed by the pub that there are 12 house wines ranging from £11 to £15, and 16
wines are served by the glass. The restaurant menu is also served in the bar, where a
blackboard lists daily specials. Fish and seafood are strengths and might turn up as a
starter of king scallops on seafood risotto with red pepper sauce, and as a main course
of fillet of Whitby cod on bacon mash with garlic butter. Otherwise expect whole

roast lamb with garlic, with summer pudding – the house speciality – among desserts. SAMPLE DIŚHES: herring roes with mustard sauce £6.50; grilled sea bass with rocket dressing £13.50; sago pudding £4.25.

Licensees Ray and Jane Carter (freehouse)
Open 12 to 2.30, 6.30 to 11.30; bar food and restaurant 12 to 2, 7 to 9.15 (Sun bar food only 7 to 8); closed 25 Dec
Details Children welcome in eating areas   Car park   Wheelchair access (not WC)   Garden   No smoking in restaurant   No music   Dogs welcome   MasterCard, Switch, Visa   Accommodation: 11 rooms, B&B £60 to £105

WATTON-AT-STONE   Hertfordshire   map 3

George & Dragon

High Street, Watton-at-Stone SG14 3TA   TEL: (01920) 830285
WEBSITE: www.georgeanddragon-watton.co.uk
on A602, 5m SE of Stevenage

Watton is a small village surrounded by lovely walking country, and at the sixteenth-century George & Dragon the countrified ambience is done very nicely: some flowery chintz here and there, old prints and brasses, dark oak furniture, and lots of beams 'outside and in'. The bar is the only smoking area, and there are a couple of designated dining rooms, but the food options, from both printed menus and blackboard specials, are the same wherever you choose to sit. Calf's liver parfait, poached cod on a bed of cabbage and bacon with a spicy mussel broth, and Irish stew rub shoulders with skate with black butter and caper sauce, Moroccan-style lamb shank, and char-grilled Aberdeen Angus sirloin steak, while puddings are old-school favourites like apple and blackberry crumble. A Sunday roast rib of beef 'with all the trimmings' and a turkey breast escalope grilled with garlic and chive butter have both been described as 'a pleasure', and those with lighter appetites will find salads, meatballs and a pasta of the day. Greene King IPA and Abbot Ale and a guest are on draught, while nearly 30 wines are sold by the bottle and ten by the glass and carafe. SAMPLE DISHES: smoked chicken timbale £5.75; roast breast of duck en croûte £13; lemon tart £3.75.

Licensees Jessica and Peter Tatlow (Greene King)
Open Mon to Fri 11 to 3, 6 (5.30 Fri) to 11, Sat 11 to 11, Sun 12 to 10.30; bar food and restaurant (exc Sun evening) 12 to 2, 7 to 10; no food 26 and 31 Dec
Details Children welcome in eating areas before 8.30pm   Car park   Wheelchair access (also WC)   Garden and patio   No smoking in dining rooms   No music   No dogs   Amex, Diners, MasterCard, Switch, Visa

WELTON HILL   Lincolnshire   map 9

Farmers Arms 🍇   NEW ENTRY

Welton Hill LN2 3RD   TEL: (01673) 885671
on A46, about 8m N of Lincoln

Welton Hill is no village as such, but is merely farmland and the odd house. Being somewhat isolated means that the Farmers Arms cannot rely on a regular flow of drinkers and over the years has transformed itself into a restaurant-cum-pub-cum-wine merchant. The original low-beamed bar is still in operation, dispensing the Tom Wood range of ales from the Highwood Brewery as well as Hop Back Summer Lightning, Timothy Taylor Landlord and beers from the Titanic and Nethergate

Breweries, but the emphasis is on simple, well-cooked, substantial fare. The printed lunchtime menu is a catalogue of popular dishes such as omelettes, jacket potatoes, gammon with pineapple, and battered haddock with chips and mushy peas, but the kitchen also delivers specials such as hearty roasts of beef served with vegetables, creamed potatoes, Yorkshire pudding and 'good roast gravy', omelette Arnold Bennett, and baked suprême of chicken topped with sage Derby on a roasted tomato and pepper sauce. Evening meals are more elaborate and may include a 'Chinese emperor's feast', pan-seared ostrich fillet, or Moroccan-style spiced vegetable tagine. Wine-and-food events are a regular feature here, showcasing a 'rapidly evolving' wine list that at last count ran to 90 bins, including 16 by the glass, plus fizz and dessert wines. The selection is engagingly individual and pricing very fair. SAMPLE DISHES: mussels steamed in Thai-spiced coconut cream £6.50; braised steak, ale and mushroom pasty with rich onion gravy £11; warm cinnamon and apple shortcake with a crumble topping £4.50.

Licensee Victoria Herring (freehouse)
Open Tue to Sun 12 to 2.30, 6.30 to 11.30 (10.30 Sun); bar food Tue to Sat 12 to 2, Tue to Sun 6.30 to 9
Details Children welcome   Car park   Wheelchair access (also WC)   Garden and patio   No smoking   Live or background music   No dogs   Delta, Diners, MasterCard, Switch, Visa

---

WEST BAGBOROUGH   Somerset   map 2

▲ Rising Sun   NEW ENTRY

West Bagborough TA4 3EF   TEL: (01823) 432575

Cob walls and a thatched roof would indicate a traditional pub interior, but if you have noted the rather trendy pub sign of a bright orange rising sun, then what's behind the huge, ancient wooden front door may not surprise you. The sixteenth-century building burned down in 2001, and the interior has been totally renovated. It is still heavily beamed throughout (80 tons of oak were used), but there is now a stylish slate-floored bar with spotlights, chunky furniture and heavy, tapestry-style curtains, and a tasteful, cosy rear snug. The downstairs dining area has more slate on the floor and an eclectic mix of furnishings, candles, modern art (for sale) and a baby grand in a corner; the upstairs dining room has antique tables, high-backed dining chairs, a high-pitched roof, and lovely views over the Vale of Taunton. Although very much a dining pub, walkers are welcome and the lunchtime menu and blackboard cater for them with upmarket sandwiches and light bites. Otherwise the short and varied menu holds out promises of good-quality cooking: dishes such as scallop salad with crispy bacon and balsamic dressing, and steamed game pudding with traditional suet pastry, or roast haddock with wilted spinach and Welsh rarebit. Inspiration is not merely local; you might arrive on a theme evening such as a Japanese supper offering miso soup, teriyaki beef and iced sashimi of fish. Real ales are from West Country breweries like Butcombe, Cotleigh and Exmoor, and around eight house wines are served by the glass. SAMPLE DISHES: pan-fried pigeon breast with grapes and a balsamic glaze £7; Cornish sea trout with black noodles and a chive and lemon sauce £15; Belgian mousse £4.25.

Licensee Elena Ellis (freehouse)
Open Tue to Sun 12 to 3, 7 to 11; bar food and restaurant Tue to Sun 12 to 3, 7 to 10
Details Children welcome in bar eating area   Wheelchair access (also WC)   Patio   No-smoking area in bar Live or background music   Dogs welcome   Delta, Diners, MasterCard, Switch, Visa   Accommodation: 2 rooms, B&B £85

WEST BAY   Dorset   **map 2**

▲ West Bay NEW ENTRY

Station Road, West Bay DT6 4EW   TEL: (01308) 422157
off A35, S of Bridport

The West Bay – a squat, two-storey building – stands right at the end of Station Road facing the beach: 'it looks as if it has been there for ever,' observed one reporter. The frontage is painted dark green and cream, while the interior is one big square space with a patterned carpet, faux timbered ceiling and a couple of traditional advertising signs on the walls. Blackboards advertise the food, and there's no shortage of choice. All kinds of starters open the show, from field mushrooms stuffed with pesto topped with Gruyère to warm pigeon breast and bacon salad. Steaks loom large among the carnivorous main courses, along with duck breast on stir-fried vegetables with hoisin sauce, and venison fillet with celeriac purée and a cranberry and redcurrant sauce. Daily supplies of fresh fish are a strong suit; depending on the catch, you might choose anything from whole lemon sole stuffed with crab butter to Cajun-style blackened monkfish tail on sweet potato mash with a lime yoghurt dressing. The weekly list of desserts is mostly in the rhubarb crumble and lemon meringue pie mould. At lunchtime you can also get 'snacks and light bites' – ploughman's, baguettes and salads – with a trio of traditional roasts putting in an appearance on Sundays. The West Bay is owned by Palmers of Bridport, and their IPA, 200 and Copper Ale are generally on handpump. Three dozen affordable wines include five house selections by the glass. SAMPLE DISHES: Thai crab cakes with plum sauce £5; honey-glazed shank of lamb on mustard mash £12; orange and lemon cheesecake £3.75.

Licensees John Ford and Karen Trimby (Palmers)
Open 11 to 3, 6 to 11.30, Sun 12 to 3, 7 to 10.30; bar food 12 to 2 (2.30 Sun), restaurant 12 to 2 (2.30 Sun), 6.30 (7 Sun) to 9.30; closed Sun evenings end Oct to Easter
Details Children welcome   Car park   Wheelchair access (also men's WC)   Garden   No smoking in restaurant   Background music   Dogs welcome in bar only   Delta, MasterCard, Switch, Visa   Accommodation: 4 rooms, B&B £50 to £70

WESTLETON   Suffolk   **map 6**

▲ Crown

Westleton IP17 3AD   TEL: (01728) 648777
WEBSITE: www.westletoncrown.com
on B1125, 8m N of Saxmundham

The Crown makes a handy base, being halfway between Southwold and Aldeburgh and close to Minsmere RSPB Reserve. The pub itself is warm and welcoming, with a log fire in the bar and walls covered in photographs of local scenes, old implements and so on. All four eating areas – conservatory, parlour, bar and brew room – are served by the same menu, which offers much of interest: locally smoked salmon with shrimp and green onion pancakes, or poached mackerel with tomato fondue in a cheese-crusted tart to start, and then pan-fried pheasant breast on roasted celeriac served with button sprouts roasted with vanilla, garlic and pancetta, with a Madeira, truffle and wine reduction, and treacle pudding with custard to finish. Lunchtimes bring out a good choice of sandwiches, ploughman's, and main courses along the lines of smoked mackerel fishcakes on stir-fried vegetable ribbons. Up to three guest ales join Adnams Bitter and Greene King IPA on handpump, and around half a dozen wines are served by the glass. SAMPLE DISHES: ravioli of soft herbs, spinach and cottage cheese £5.75; poached capon, salt-beef and ox tongue with mustard and parsley sauce £9; chocolate and doused apricot pudding with vanilla and crushed meringue ice cream £4.

Licensees Rosemary and Richard C. Price (freehouse)
Open 11 to 11, Sun 12 to 10.30; bar food and restaurant 12 to 2.15 (2.30 Sat and Sun), 7 to 9.30 Sun to Thurs, restaurant only Fri and Sat 7 to 9.30
Details Children welcome exc in bar   Car park   Wheelchair access (also WC)   Garden   No smoking in 2 rooms   Occasional background music   Dogs welcome in bar only   Amex, Delta, Diners, MasterCard, Switch, Visa   Accommodation: 19 rooms, B&B £62.50 to £139

WEST PECKHAM   Kent   map 3

Swan on the Green   NEW ENTRY

West Peckham ME18 5JW   TEL: (01622) 812271
WEBSITE: www.swan-on-the-green.co.uk
from A26 about 8m W of Maidstone, take B2016, then first left

For one reporter there is no doubt about it: the Swan is a 'first-class beer pub', with its own microbrewery delivering an ever-changing range of some eight beers (plus seasonal brews), among them Trumpeter Best, Green Hop Ale and Whooper Pale Ale. But this large and handsome Edwardian pub overlooking an open green offers a lot more besides – it is a strong all-rounder, catering equally for drinkers and eaters and attracting both groups in equal measure. The modish horseshoe-shaped open-plan bar area, with a seating area at either end, has a wooden floor, beamed ceiling, plain and sturdy polished pine furniture, and walls of pale lemon hung with arty modern black and white photographs. The daily-changing lunch menu is a neat and convincing balancing act between tried and tested favourites and dishes that have cosmopolitan overtones. Torn between pan-fried king scallops wrapped in Serrano ham with coriander dressing, and beef and Stilton burgers in ciabatta, one visitor was delighted with the latter: 'superb' and 'full of flavour'. A slightly more measured approach marks out the evening menu, where prawn, crab and spring onion tartlet with ginger and chive crème fraîche could open a meal that goes on to roast poussin with creamed celeriac and Savoy cabbage, fondant potato and a thyme reduction, and finishes with peach and apple tart. Five wines are served by the glass from a 20-bottle global list that starts at £11.50. SAMPLE DISHES: chunky tomato soup £5; pan-fried fillet of red mullet with sauce vierge £9.25; Baileys brûlée £4.25.

Licensee G. Milligan (freehouse)
Open 11 to 3, 6 to 11; bar food and restaurant all week 12 to 2.15 (3 Sun), Tue to Sat 7 to 9.15; closed Sun evenings winter, 25 Dec, 1 Jan
Details Children welcome   Car park   Garden and patio   Occasional live or background music   Dogs welcome Amex, Delta, Diners, MasterCard, Switch, Visa

WEST WYCOMBE   Buckinghamshire   map 3

▲ George & Dragon

High Street, West Wycombe HP14 3AB   TEL: (01494) 464414
WEBSITE: www.george-and-dragon.co.uk
on A40, 3m NW of centre of High Wycombe

This well-preserved former coaching inn stands on the main road through National Trust-owned West Wycombe. Its appeal lies in its bustling atmosphere, comfortable, homely décor, and good-value, carefully cooked food. The lunch menus offer a good variety of simple and traditional food, ranging from lasagne to lamb and spinach curry, as well as various filled ciabattas and tortilla wraps. The evening menus extend the repertoire to take in classics such as beef Wellington and dishes with a contemporary flavour such as roast chicken breast with black pudding in grain mustard sauce. The bar dispenses Adnams Broadside, Charles Wells Bombardier and Courage Best Bitter, plus Normandy farmhouse cider and a range of malt whiskies, while a wine shop on the premises (in the courtyard to the rear) provides 20-plus attractively priced French wines, eight of which are available by the glass. SAMPLE DISHES: hot crab pot £5.50; cassoulet £9.25; lemon meringue pie £3.75.

Licensee Philip Todd (Unique)
Open *11 to 2.30, 5.30 to 11, Sun 12 to 3, 7 to 10.30; bar food 12 to 2 (2.15 Sun), 6 to 9.30; closed 25 Dec*
Details *Children welcome in family room   Car park   Wheelchair access (not WC)   Garden   No-smoking area in bar   No music   Dogs welcome   Amex, Delta, Diners, MasterCard, Switch, Visa   Accommodation: 11 rooms, B&B £75 to £80; hotel closed 24 Dec to 3 Jan*

WHITCHURCH   Hampshire   map 2

Red House Inn ☺
21 London Street, Whitchurch RG28 7LH   TEL: (01256) 895558

Whitchurch is one of many commuter villages strung out along the Test Valley with this sixteenth-century white-painted pub (the doors and windows are painted red) at its centre, just a short stroll from the river and a still working silk mill. Separate doors from the street lead, one to a traditional public bar with real fire and fruit machines, the other to a beamy lounge bar filled with cottagey upholstered chairs, polished wood tables, and broken into two open-plan segments with bare floorboards defining the dining area. One locally brewed beer, Cheriton Pots Ale, is regularly on tap, together with a weekly changing guest from Cheriton or Hogs Back, and thoughtfully chosen wines include ten or so by the glass. Menu and specials list are kept to sensible lengths, and the contemporary repertoire shows ambition and style. Start perhaps with seared scallops with pea and mint purée and crispy Serrano ham, or teriyaki duck breast with a fresh cherry dressing. John Dory fillets served with crab and saffron risotto and Parmesan, or lamb fillet with spinach and roast pepper mousse and sweet potato fondant, are typical main-course choices, and there's a whole blackboard of steak variations; a berry meringue tower might follow. SAMPLE DISHES: salmon and chilli fishcakes, poached egg and chive beurre blanc £5.50; pan-fried chicken breast with a truffle and roast garlic stuffing £12; French lemon tart with vanilla ice cream £4.50.

Licensees Shannon and Caroline Wells (freehouse)
Open *11.30 to 3, 6 to 11, Sun 12 to 3, 7 to 10.30; bar food and restaurant 12 to 2, 6.30 to 9.30, Sun 12 to 3, 7 to 9.30*
Details *Car park   Garden and patio   No smoking in dining room   Occasional live music; jukebox   Dogs welcome in bar   MasterCard, Switch, Visa*

If you disagree with any assessment made in the Guide, do let us know – The Which? Pub Guide, *FREEPOST, 2 Marylebone Road, London NW1 4DF.*

WHITEWELL   Lancashire   map 8

▲ Inn at Whitewell 🌳

Whitewell, Forest of Bowland BB7 3AT   TEL: (01200) 448222
off B6243 Clitheroe to Longridge road, 6m NW of Clitheroe

'Sedate old-world charm with trimmings' is one view of this upmarket inn tucked
deep in the Trough of Bowland. Old stone, rambling plants and wonderful gardens
create a welcoming first impression, and inside it's the kind of place 'you might quite
like to get holed up in if it snowed'. There are log fires ablaze, newspapers to read, and
a maze of little anterooms to explore. In the bar you can choose from an extensive
menu (plus specials) that could open up with anything from toasted brioche with
creamed field mushrooms and glazed shallots to roast breasts of wood pigeon with
crushed potato, crispy bacon and red onion marmalade. Moving on, you might find
'a good example' of haddock in beer batter with chips and mushy peas, glazed
Barnsley chop with goats' cheese mash and courgette relish or – oddly enough –
grilled Norfolk kipper. Sandwiches and salads are served at lunchtimes, while desserts
could take in chocolate pot with a spiced orange biscuit, or passion-fruit crème
brûlée. The restaurant is a separate operation with its own menu taking in dishes such
as salad of peppered beef fillet, and breast of Goosnargh duckling with black pudding,
mash and a tomato and baked bean cassoulet. Well-kept Timothy Taylor Landlord is
on draught alongside Marston's Pedigree and Boddingtons Bitter. The wine list kicks
off with several pages of champagne, Bordeaux and Burgundy, but the short selections from the Rhône and Portugal are more impressive for quality and value, and the
Italian reds are all top-notch. Prices start at £9.90, and no fewer than 20 are offered by
the glass. Wines are also sold in the Vintners' Shop. SAMPLE DISHES: creamy potato
chowder with bacon and smoked haddock £5.25; grilled English pork chop with a
baked stuffed apple, caramelised onion and cider jus £10.50; yoghurt and cardamom
pot with fruit coulis £3.50.

Licensee Richard Bowman (freehouse)
Open 11 to 3, 6 (7 Sun) to 11; bar food 12 to 2, 7.30 to 9.30, restaurant 7.30 to 9.30
Details Children welcome   Car park   Garden   No music   Dogs welcome   Delta, MasterCard, Switch, Visa
Accommodation: 23 rooms, B&B £63 to £125

WHITLEY   Wiltshire   map 2

Pear Tree Inn 😊 🍺 🌳

Top Lane, Whitley SN12 8QX   TEL: (01225) 709131
from Bath take A365 at Box; just after Atworth take left turning signposted to Whitley

This very old rough-stone pub is set facing a neat lawned area and courtyard off the
aptly named Top Lane, which is the most northerly of the three roads running
through the village. Lots of natural materials and colours have been used in the dimly
lit interior, with decoration provided by an assemblage of white-painted gardening
implements on one wall and farm and kitchen utensils on others. Areas are set aside
for drinkers – on regularly changing draught could be Barnstormer and Gem Bitter
from Bath Ales, Oakhill Best Bitter, Heel Stone and Pigswill from Stonehenge Ales,
and an ale from Moles Brewery in nearby Melksham – but the modern and interesting menus, the same throughout the pub, pull in diners too. The approach is flexible
(starters can be served in main-course portions at lunchtime), and the style ranges

from Cornish crab spring rolls with sprouting beans, Chinese cabbage and chilli jam, to grilled sea bass fillets with red pesto, crushed potatoes, shaved fennel and rocket, or sautéed chicken breasts with haricot beans, pancetta, Savoy cabbage and Madeira cream. Traditionalists should be happy with pork and herb sausages with grain mustard mash, red wine gravy and crispy leeks. The home-baked bread has come in for praise, as have the roasted vegetables, and among puddings might be a classic-with-a-modern-twist steamed marmalade sponge with stem ginger ice cream. The wine list includes at least ten well-chosen offerings by the glass from £2.95 and, without shouting about it, an impressive line-up of Old and New World names, including Vincent Pinard's Sancerre and the fashionable Nepenthe wines from Australia. SAMPLE DISHES: pressed game terrine with sherry vinaigrette £5.50; roast monkfish loin wrapped in Parma ham with a Jerusalem artichoke and parsley risotto £16; baked vanilla cheesecake with rhubarb £5.25.

Licensees Martin and Debbie Still (freehouse)
Open 11 to11, Sun 12 to 10.30; bar food and restaurant 12 to 2, 6.30 to 9.30 (10 Fri and Sat), Sun 12 to 2 (2.30 restaurant), 7 to 9; closed 25 and 26 Dec, evening 31 Dec, 1 Jan
Details Children welcome in restaurant   Car park   Wheelchair access (also WC)   Garden   No smoking in restaurant   No music   Dogs welcome in bar only   Delta, MasterCard, Switch, Visa

WHITSTABLE   Kent

map 3

Sportsman 🏵 🏵

Faversham Road, Seasalter, Whitstable CT5 4BP   TEL: (01227) 273370
take Whitstable exit from A299, go through Whitstable and follow signs for Seasalter; pub at far end of village

WATERSIDE

Beyond the caravan park and beach dwellings you will come upon this white-painted pub surrounded by a glass-roofed verandah in a bleak and remote spot sheltered behind the sea wall. Inside, its three spacious rooms are clean, spare and well lit, with wooden floors, and a dado and original artwork (for sale) on the cream-painted walls. Tables, fashioned from huge chunks of pine, are simply laid with knives and forks wrapped in paper napkins; there are no flowers, no tablecloths – no nonsense. Likewise, the blackboard menu, which changes daily, offers the kind of dishes that give modern pub cooking a good name – and there's not a garnish or overblown gesture in sight. What it offers is a mixture of wholesome seasonal dishes ranging from Brussels sprout soup to roast pheasant with bread sauce and gravy, augmented by distinctive, up-to-the-minute inventions like smoked widgeon with Italian mustard 'fruits', and poached smoked haddock with curried carrot sauce. Rock oysters topped with slices of hot chorizo is a signature starter along with mixed antipasti, and you might wind up proceedings with, say, Indian tea junket with piña colada sorbet. This is a Shepherd Neame pub (the brewery is only a few miles away) serving their usual range of real ales, including seasonal brews. Six wines are usually available by the glass from a list of 30-plus bottles starting at £9.95. The Sportsman now has a sibling: The Granville, Street End, Lower Hardres, nr Canterbury; tel: (01227) 700402. SAMPLE DISHES: roast chicken and foie gras terrine £6; grilled red mullet with tapenade £11; rhubarb sorbet with burnt cream £5.

Licensees Stephen and Philip Harris (Shepherd Neame)
Open 12 to 3, 6 to 11, Sun 12 to 11; bar food Tue to Sat 12 to 1.45, 7 to 8.45, Sun 12 to 2.30; closed 25 Dec
Details Children welcome exc in main bar   Car park   Wheelchair access (not WC)   Garden and patio   No smoking in 1 room   Background music   Dogs welcome   Delta, MasterCard, Switch, Visa

WIDDOP   **West Yorkshire**   map 8

Pack Horse Inn   NEW ENTRY

Widdop HX7 7AT   TEL: (01422) 842803
from Hebden Bridge, take Heptonstall road and follow signs for Slack; fork right for Widdop at junction beside chapel

'No pretensions here; it's a genuine Yorkshire pub,' enthused a reporter of this remote moorland inn. Footpaths lead straight to the door, and the Pennine Way passes just behind (ramblers, 'of which there are legion', leave their boots in the porch). Once inside, you will find log fires, heavily beamed ceilings, large tables, a 'cornucopia of chairs and benches', and fascinating old photographs and maps, not to mention countless prints of ducks and game birds. The welcome is warm, and the service friendly. A printed menu offers a range of sandwiches, steaks and 'small meals' such as steak and kidney pie, or cottage hotpot, but the main action happens on the modest blackboard, where a dozen specials are listed. Starters include the likes of black pudding and bacon on mash, and Widdop beefy broth, while main courses take in thick Angus beef on horseradish mash, venison and rabbit pie with game sauce and a Yorkshire crust, and roast rack of lamb, all in 'simply huge helpings' with generous portions of vegetables. The separate restaurant is open only on Saturday evenings (booking is recommended), and it is worth noting that the pub is closed for lunch on weekdays in winter. Thwaites Bitter, Black Sheep Best Bitter, Old Speckled Hen and a summer guest are on handpump, and eight wines are available by the glass. SAMPLE DISHES: celery and Stilton soup £3; lamb's liver and bacon with mash and onion gravy £8; trifle £3.

Licensee Andrew Hollinrake (freehouse)
Open *Tue to Sun and bank hol Mon 12 to 3, 7 to 11; bar food 12 to 2, 7 to 9.30, restaurant Sat 7 to 9.30; closed weekday lunchtimes winter*
Details *No children after 8pm   Patio   No music   Dogs welcome   Delta, MasterCard, Switch, Visa*

WIDECOMBE IN THE MOOR   **Devon**   map 1

Old Inn

Widecombe in the Moor TQ13 7TA · TEL: (01364) 621207
from Bovey Tracey take B3387 through Haytor to Widecombe

Although this Dartmoor village may be a fair step from most places, tourists and visitors flock to Widecombe, and the pub gets its fair share of them – so book ahead, especially at weekends. There's a traditional atmosphere in the warren of small cosy rooms: roaring log fires in winter, flagged floors, wooden tables and chairs. Quick, efficient and friendly staff are good at coping with crowds, and children have their own menu and a family room with high chairs. Thirsts can be quenched with local Teignworthy ales, plus Gray's farmhouse cider. Almost all the wines are under £15, and five come by the glass. As for food – listed on a long menu and a blackboard – brace yourself for huge portions, although value is good. At busy times, starters – from home-made chicken liver pâté to haggis with neeps and tatties, or from prawn cocktail to moorland smokie – must be followed by main courses. Among these are sausages, steak and kidney pie, double gammon steak with a fried egg and pineapple, breaded plaice fillet, and a massive meat platter known as the Butcher's Delight. If you can manage dessert, expect the likes of Galia melon filled with lemon sorbet and fresh fruit, or zabaglione. SAMPLE DISHES: egg mayonnaise £3.75; cottage pie £6.50; chocolate nut sundae £3.25.

Licensees A. and S. Boult, D. Bowden and J. Houghton (freehouse)
Open 11 to 2.30, 7 (6.30 summer) to 11, Sun 12 to 3, 7 to 10.30; bar food 11 to 2 (12 to 2.30 Sun), 6.30 to 10
Details Children welcome exc in public bar   Car park   Wheelchair access (also WC)   Garden and patio
Occasional background music   Dogs welcome   Delta, MasterCard, Switch, Visa (credit card service charge 1%)

WILMINGTON   East Sussex   map 3

 ## Giants Rest
The Street, Wilmington BN26 5SQ   TEL: (01323) 870207
off A27, 2m W of Polegate

There is not much to Wilmington, so the detached Victorian pub with cream-painted upper and red-brick ground floor should be easy to spot just off the busy A27. The name the Giants Rest is a nice conceit, but the Long Man of Wilmington carved into the chalk Down above couldn't squeeze his 240-foot length into any of the beds here, doubles though they be. He couldn't even fit into the bar – two rooms that have been knocked together – with its comfortably worn wooden floors and wooden tables, benches and spindle-back chairs. A pleasant touch, consistent with the friendly and informal atmosphere: each table has a wooden puzzle or game to play while nursing a glass of Harveys Sussex Best Bitter, Timothy Taylor Landlord or Hop Back Summer Lightning. Food, written on blackboards and ordered at the bar, comes predominantly from local suppliers. Starters like bacon and garlic mushrooms, or avocado and prawns, lead to home-cooked ham with bubble and squeak, beef and beer pie, or grilled local whole plaice with herb butter. Desserts like apple and blackberry pie or sticky date pudding round things off. House wines on the short list are £12.50, and six or so are served by the glass. It's a popular dining pub, so wise visitors will book in advance. SAMPLE DISHES: garlic king prawns with lemon mayonnaise £5; wild rabbit and bacon pie £8; Victorian trifle £4.

Licensees Adrian and Rebecca Hillman (freehouse)
Open 11.30 to 3, 6 to 11, Sun 12 to 3, 6 to 10 (summer 11.30 to 11, Sun 12 to 10.30); bar food 12 to 2, 6.30 to 9
Details Car park   Wheelchair access (not WC)   Garden and patio   No-smoking area in bar   Background music   Dogs welcome on a lead   Delta, MasterCard, Switch, Visa   Accommodation: 2 rooms, B&B £40

WINCHCOMBE   Gloucestershire   map 5

 ## White Hart
High Street, Winchcombe GL54 5LJ   TEL: (01242) 602359
WEBSITE: www.the-white-hart-inn.com

Surrounded by open countryside and full of Cotswold charm, Winchcombe is a small town of old stone buildings with the smart, black and white half-timbered, White Hart at its centre. Décor shows a Swedish influence, the back room in particular with its sisal floor coverings, blue and white colour scheme, and lots of pale wood, though the taproom in a converted barn and the restaurant have a more traditionally English look. A Swedish theme also runs through menus in the shape of 'smorgasbord' platters and dishes such as Swedish meatballs with lingonberries, though non-Swedish bar snacks include Caesar salad and the 'ramblers' breakfast'. The separate restaurant menu offers more ambitious fare along the lines of poached monkfish with white wine, lobster and crab sauce, and the Stable Bar majors in pizzas. Real ales are Stanney Bitter, Greene King IPA and Wadworth 6X. The wine list is better than most and reasonably priced; four come by the glass. Sudeley Castle stands on the edge of the town. SAMPLE DISHES: toast skagen (dill marinated shrimps in mayonnaise with caviar, lemon and lime) £5.25; biff a'la Rydberg (pan-fried beef and potatoes with onions, topped with an egg yolk) £8.75; marängsuiss (bananas and cream filled meringue nests with chocolate sauce) £4.50. ·

Licensees Nicole and David Burr (Enterprise Inns)
Open 10 to 11, Sun 11 to 10.30; bar food 10 to 10; restaurant 6 to 10; closed 25 Dec
Details Children welcome Car park Patio No smoking in dining room Background and occasional live music Dogs welcome (£10 in accommodation) Delta, MasterCard, Switch, Visa Accommodation: 10 rooms, B&B £55 to £115

WINCHESTER   Hampshire   map 2

▲ Wykeham Arms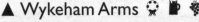

75 Kingsgate Street, Winchester SO23 9PE   TEL: (01962) 853834
S of Cathedral, near Winchester College

Named after the fourteenth-century bishop who founded the city's famous school, the Wykeham Arms is itself a venerable establishment, tucked away down the cobbled streets in the old part of town. Outer appearances are modest, but inside is a warren of rooms thick with atmosphere, with all manner of memorabilia lining the walls, including a huge collection of tankards. The Hamilton Bar is the spot for drinkers, while the no-smoking Watchmakers Bar is reckoned to be the pick of the eating areas. This is a popular venue, so booking is advisable if you want to eat. Lunch options tend to be simple things like a platter of smoked salmon, or steak ciabatta sandwich, and for heartier appetites confit duck leg on Parmesan-flavoured mash with leeks and bacon. Dinner menus are more elaborate: roast rack of lamb with dauphinois potatoes, braised red cabbage and a red wine and rosemary jus, for example, or perhaps roast duck breast on stir-fried noodles with pineapple and chilli chutney and hoisin and sesame dressing. With around 20 wines by the large or small glass and a number of half-bottles, the 90-bin wine list aims to please all-comers. It covers a full range of styles, with plenty under £20. Real ale drinkers are also well served, with five to choose from, including three from Hampshire brewery Gale's and a changing guest. SAMPLE DISHES: pork pâté with red wine mayonnaise £5.50; baked halibut steak with spicy prawn couscous £14; warm cherry and almond tart with Kirsch coulis £4.50.

Licensees Peter and Kate Miller (George Gale & Co.)
Open 11 to 11, Sun 12 to 10.30; bar food all week 12 to 2.30 (sandwiches only 2.30 to 3), Mon to Sat 6.30 to 8.45; closed 25 Dec
Details No children Car park Garden and patio No smoking in restaurant No music Dogs welcome in bar only Amex, Delta, Diners, MasterCard, Switch, Visa Accommodation: 14 rooms, B&B £50 to £120

A list of pubs serving exceptional draft beers is at the back of the book.

WINCLE   Cheshire   map 8

Ship Inn   NEW ENTRY

Wincle SK11 0QE   TEL: (01260) 227217
1m S of A54, between Congleton and Buxton, 5m SE of Macclesfield

The modest building of mellow red sandstone is in a remote location between hamlets 'lost along winding back lanes'; it may be difficult to find but is 'well worth the effort', and the scenery is superb. Considered one of Cheshire's oldest pubs, the Ship is one for all-comers and in all seasons, with four small, cosily old-fashioned rooms and a lawned garden with picnic sets and good views. It has been a popular walkers' haunt for decades, but is now sought out by those seeking good food. As well as standard pub offerings of sausages (albeit organic) with mash and onion gravy, Thai red coconut chicken curry, and steak and chips, reporters have been impressed with the kitchen's output of generous country dishes like game casserole with herb dumplings, fishcakes with tomato and rocket salad and lime aïoli, and well-timed trout, from the nearby trout farm, served with red cabbage and mashed parsnip. The crumble of the day with custard makes a fitting finish. Three real ales are usually on offer, with Ruddles County or Moorhouses Premier being supplemented by a couple of guests, plus a vintage organic cider from Weston's. Seven wines are available by the glass. SAMPLE DISHES: king prawns in Goan coconut sauce £7; fillet steak topped with Hartington Stilton and caramelised red onions with red wine jus £16; cheesecake with raspberry coulis £4.

Licensees Giles and Victoria Meadows (freehouse)
Open *Tue to Fri 12 to 3, 7 to 11, Sat 12 to 11, Sun 12 to 10.30; bar food Tue to Fri 12 to 2.30, 7 to 9, Sat 12 to 2.30, 6 to 9.30, Sun 12 to 2.30, 6 to 8*
Details *Children welcome in family room and eating area   Car park   Garden   No smoking in eating area Occasional live music   Dogs welcome   Delta, Diners, MasterCard, Switch, Visa*

WINSFORD   Somerset   map 1

▲ Royal Oak Inn

Winsford TA24 7JE   TEL: (01643) 851455
WEBSITE: www.royaloak-somerset.co.uk
off A396, 5m N of Dulverton

In a postcard-pretty village on the edge of Exmoor National Park, this thatched, yellow-painted inn dates from the twelfth century. It has evolved over the years into a smart, civilised inn-cum-hotel filled with lounges decorated in country-house style, with pastel colours, lamplight, relaxing sofas and easy chairs. Yet the spick-and-span bar areas remain traditional and pubby, with informal eating areas, cushioned pew seating, a wood-burning stove in a large stone fireplace, and plenty of tartan fabric. The bar menu ranges from good walkers' fare (soup, sandwiches, ploughman's, venison sausages and mash) to a full three-course meal, with braised lamb shank in red wine with rosemary and sweet potato mash as the centrepiece. Alternatively, dinner in the restaurant could open with local smoked trout pâté, go on to pan-seared duck breast with braised red cabbage and a rich port sauce, and finish with West Country cheeses. The restaurant wine list has around 25 bottles, mainly French, with a page of half-bottles, while the bar has its own list of nine fairly priced bottles, with three house wines sold by the glass from £2.80. Ales from Butcombe and Brakspear are on draught. SAMPLE DISHES: local smoked salmon with creamy dill dressing £5.75; suprême of chicken with spiced lemon cream sauce £9.25; summer pudding £3.25.

Licensee Charles Steven (freehouse)
Open 11 to 2.30, 6 to 11; bar food 12 to 2, 7 to 9, restaurant 7 to 9
Details Children welcome in bar eating area Car park Wheelchair access (also WC) Garden and patio
No-smoking area in bar Background music in restaurant Dogs welcome Amex, Diners, MasterCard, Visa
Accommodation: 14 rooms, B&B £89 to £145

WINTERBOURNE   Berkshire   map 2

Winterbourne Arms

Winterbourne RG20 8BB   TEL: (01635) 248200
WEBSITE: www.winterbournearms.tablesir.com
Winterbourne signposted off B4494 3½m NW of Newbury

The black-and-white timbered building 'with a Victorian feel' lies peacefully tucked away amongst cottages in the midst of this charming little village. Old photographs of the village and country prints line the walls of the three interconnecting bar areas, windows have curtains and there are warming fires at colder times of the year. Menus show a modern style, with starters of wild mushroom risotto, or chicken liver and green peppercorn terrine with plum chutney, and around ten main-course options taking in mélange of seafood with lemon-scented pasta and Chardonnay bisque, and fillet of pork filled with caramelised apples and served with leek mash and brandy cherry sauce. At lunchtimes there are a few simpler options, such as beer-battered cod fillet with chips, lamb and apricot pie, plus salads, filled baguettes and sandwiches. Desserts are things like warmed chocolate and nut brownies, or home-made meringues. The wine list of about 30 opens with house French white at £10.50, and 12 wines are served by the glass. Beers include Good Old Boy from the local West Berkshire Brewery, and guests can include Adnams and Old Speckled Hen. SAMPLE DISHES: seared scallops with vanilla fennel, tomato and bacon salsa £7.25; rack of lamb with sweet red pepper and aubergine couscous and balsamic and mint reduction £15; blueberry and orange Bakewell tart with mandarin ice cream £5.25.

Licensee Claire Owens (freehouse)
Open Tue to Sun 12 to 3, 6 to 11.30 (10.30 Sun); bar food and restaurant 12 to 2.30, 7 to 9.30; closed Sun evenings winter
Details Children welcome in restaurant · Car park Garden No smoking in restaurant Background music
Dogs welcome exc in restaurant Amex, MasterCard, Switch, Visa

WINTERTON   North Lincolnshire   map 9

George ✿

Market Street, Winterton DN15 9PT   TEL: (01724) 732270
off A1077, 6½m N of Scunthorpe

John O'Connor spent 11 years as restaurant manager at nearby Winteringham Fields, and for his first solo venture he found a pub (albeit in an out-of-the-way location) with an upstairs dining room. On the ground floor, the George is a decent, straightforward town local with a good log fire, dartboard, and Tetley Bitter plus a guest on handpump; upstairs, it's a modest restaurant serving some extraordinarily good food. The black-board details a short, tempting array of starters like pan-fried king scallops with black pudding and caramelised apple purée, or potted salmon confit and tartare of fresh salmon. Fish figure prominently among main courses too – say, grilled sea bass stuffed with fennel, shallots and Parmesan with a fennel sauce – but there's also jugged hare with fondant potatoes, or sirloin steak with shallot butter, grain mustard and mash. Desserts encompass sticky toffee pudding and cherry crème brûlée, and the short, kindly priced wine list has some six or so by the glass. SAMPLE DISHES: baked mushrooms stuffed with plum tomatoes and cheese £4.25; pan-fried tuna steak marinated with chilli and lime on a bed of noodles £14; lemon posset with seasonal fruits £4.

Licensee John O'Connor (Enterprise Inns)
Open Mon to Fri 3 to 11, Sat 11.30 to 11, Sun 12 to 5, 8 to 10.30; restaurant Wed to Sun 12 to 3, Wed to Sat 7 to 9.30
Details Children welcome in restaurant   Car park   Wheelchair access (not WC)   Patio   No smoking in restaurant   Background music; jukebox   No dogs   No cards

WINTERTON-ON-SEA   Norfolk   map 6

▲ Fishermans Return

The Lane, Winterton-on-Sea NR29 4BN   TEL: (01493) 393305
WEBSITE: www.fishermans-return.com

With only sand dunes protecting this 300-year-old red brick and flint inn from the encroaching sea, it may be a good idea to visit soon before it suffers the fate that has already befallen much of Norfolk's disappearing coastline. Not least among reasons to make the trip are the excellent beers and ciders, including Wherry Best Bitter and Norfolk Nog from Woodeforde's, and Broadside and Bitter from Adnams. There's a sun-trap patio in front of the pub, while inside, the homely lounge bar is comfortably furnished with traditional circular pub tables, and the larger main bar has varnished wood-strip-panelled walls and good-sized tables. Both have wood-burning stoves, and local prints and old photographs on the walls. Bar menus go in for straightforward pub food along the lines of burgers, omelettes, and toasted sandwiches, while ever-changing blackboard specials might feature skate with caper and mushroom sauce, or Dover sole meunière. Fourteen wines are available in three sizes of glass. SAMPLE DISHES: fish pie £5.75; boozy beef pie £8.25; strawberry cheesecake £3.50.

Licensees John and Kate Findlay (freehouse)
Open Mon to Fri 11 to 2.30, 6.30 to 11, Sat 11 to 11, Sun 12 to 10.30; bar food 12 to 2, 6.30 to 9
Details Children welcome in family room and eating area   Car park   Garden and patio   No smoking in family room and 1 eating area   Background music; jukebox   Dogs welcome   Amex, Delta, MasterCard, Switch, Visa   Accommodation: 3 rooms, B&B £45 to £70

WITNEY   Oxfordshire   map 2

▲ Fleece   NEW ENTRY

11 Church Green, Witney OX28 4AZ   TEL: (01993) 892270
WEBSITE: www.peachpubs.com

The Butter Cross is at one end of the long, narrow, tree-lined green, with a church at the other end and the Fleece in the middle, standing out because it is almost the only building that's plastered instead of being of rough old Cotswold stone. Part of the Peach Pubs group, which is building up a reputation for flexible menus, fair prices, and modern, stylish interiors, the Fleece keeps faith with the group's style through an uncluttered, open-plan interior set with clever lighting, bare oak and laminate flooring, dark leather wall seats, and tongue-and-groove tabletops on white legs. The trendy, crowd-pleasing menu, with Mediterranean influences, delivers stone-baked pizzas and antipasti as well as modern versions of traditional starters like sautéed garlic mushrooms with Parmesan cream sauce, and chicken liver pâté. Main courses range from stuffed chicken breast with Parma ham and creamed squash with tomato sauce to blackboard specials of leg of lamb on minted mash, while cranberry cheesecake and sticky toffee pudding are typical desserts. A modern, globetrotting wine list is in tune with the cooking and offers six by the glass, while Old Speckled Hen, Morland Original and IPA are on handpump. SAMPLE DISHES: tomato and feta tart with pesto £5.50; pan-fried calf's liver with pancetta and apple and chive mash £13; chocolate mousse cake £4.50.

Licensees Lee Cash and Natalie Langman (Peach Pub Company)
Open 8.30am to 11pm, Sun 8.30am to 10.30pm; bar food noon to 10
Details Children welcome   Car park   Wheelchair access (also WC)   Patio   No smoking in eating area
Background music   Dogs welcome   Delta, MasterCard, Switch, Visa   Accommodation: 10 rooms, B&B £65 to
£85

WIXFORD   **Warwickshire**   **map 5**

Three Horseshoes

Wixford B49 6DG   TEL: (01789) 490400
*from A46 at Alcester roundabout follow A435 towards Redditch; left on to A422, then left following signs
for Wixford*

This 'thoroughly creeper-covered' pub at the heart of a tucked-away, sprawling village, is very much a dining pub. The large and spacious interior is open-plan, with well-spaced tables – even the sizeable bar area has tables laid for eating – and is music- and smoke-free (just a very limited smoking area). Wine-red walls and black ceiling beams garlanded with hops contribute to the civilized atmosphere. The menu is entirely on blackboards and offers soup, steak, and vegetarian dishes as well as the likes of fresh dressed crab salad with crusty brown bread, braised lamb shank with minty mash and red wine sauce, and jam roly-poly to finish. A printed light lunch menu offers sandwiches, ploughman's lunches and filled jacket potatoes. Service is to the point and very efficient. Beers include Adnams, Marston's Pedigree and Tetley, as well as a guest (perhaps Wood's Shropshire Lad, or Pooh Beer from Church End Brewery), while one red and four white wines come by the glass from a mainly New World list of 20. SAMPLE DISHES: blue cheese and port pâté £4.25; half a roast guinea fowl with wild mushroom sauce £12; bread-and-butter pudding £4.25.

Licensee Simon Dearden (A.E. Poxon & Son Ltd)
Open 12 to 3, 6.30 to 11 (Sun 10.30); bar food 12 to 2 (2.30 Sun), 6.30 to 9.30; closed 25 Dec, 1 Jan
Details Children welcome   Car park   Wheelchair access (also WC)   Garden and patio   No-smoking areas
Occasional live or background music   No dogs   MasterCard, Switch, Visa

---

*See 'How to use the Guide' at the front of the book for an explanation of the symbols used
at the tops of entries.*

WOOBURN COMMON   Buckinghamshire   **map 3**

▲ Chequers Inn

Kiln Lane, Wooburn Common HP10 0JQ   TEL: (01628) 529575
WEBSITE: www.chequers-inn.com
from M40 junction 2, take A355 S, then first right on minor road; follow signs for Taplow, then Bourne End;
pub is on left of road

Despite its isolated rural setting in the Chiltern Hundreds, this sizeable seventeenth-century roadside inn is accessible enough for a lunchtime outing from London. It has a large, attractive garden, ideal for summer drinking, while the smallish bar has an open fire in winter as well as beams, brickwork and board floor. The blackboard bar menu is a long list of simple main dishes with only soup by way of a starter. Choices might be as old-fashioned as deep-fried cod with chips and tartare sauce, or sirloin steak with Café de Paris butter, but there are also more fashionable dishes such as black pudding, tomato and chorizo salad, and wild mushroom risotto. The separate restaurant aims for a more elegant style, with proper table linen, fresh flowers and candles, and its own ambitious menu: white asparagus and black truffle soup, for example, or halibut fillet *en papillote*. The wine list is peppered with expensive bottles, but a blackboard selection of 12 wines by the glass draws on the cheaper end and is occasionally supplemented by a range of bin-ends. Real ales are Green King IPA, Ruddles County, Abbot Ale and Morland Original. SAMPLE DISHES: goats' cheese salad with Dijon mustard and honey £9; breast of guinea fowl with potato purée and spinach £10.50; raspberry brûlée £4.

Licensee Peter J. Roehrig (freehouse)
Open 10am to 11pm, Sun 10am to 10.30pm; bar food and restaurant 12 to 2.30, 6.30 to 9.30
Details *Children welcome   Car park   Garden and patio   No-smoking area in bar   Background music*
Guide dogs only   Amex, Delta, MasterCard, Switch, Visa   Accommodation: 17 rooms, B&B £77.50 to £107.50

WOODHILL   Somerset   **map 2**

▲ Rose and Crown

Woodhill, Stoke St Gregory TA3 6EW   TEL: (01823) 490296
WEBSITE: www.browningpubs.com
between A361 and A378, 8m E of Taunton, via North Curry

This 300-year old inn is hard to find down country lanes deep in the Somerset Levels. It looks nothing too special outside, but inside there are low ceilings, alcoves, loose-box partitions and a 60-foot-deep well. The bar menu lists a wide range of pub fare, predominantly grills: lamb cutlets with mushrooms, gammon steak with pineapple, and lamb's liver with bacon, tomato and mushrooms, for example. Fish gets a good showing, from stuffed lemon sole with crab and seafood sauce, or grilled local rainbow trout, to skate wings meunière, or grilled Brixham plaice fillets, and vegetarians are offered a decent choice. Sandwiches, salads and snacks – local home-smoked ham with eggs and chips, for instance – are possibilities at lunchtime. The restaurant menu, which can also be ordered in the bar, is a set-price affair with a number of supplements. Expect hot peppered mackerel, followed by salmon fishcakes with garlic dressing, or duck breast in orange and brandy sauce. Exmoor Ale and Fox plus a guest are on draught along with Thatcher's cider. The wine list is an interesting compilation from around the world, with some good producers at reasonable prices;

two are sold by the glass. SAMPLE DISHES: warm duck breast and orange salad £6.50; chargrilled swordfish with lemon and garlic £13.50; raspberry pavlova £3.25.

Licensees R.F. and I.M. Browning (freehouse)
Open *12 to 3, 6.30 to 11, Sun 12 to 3, 7 to 10.30; bar food and restaurant 12 to 2, 7 to 9.30; closed evening 25 Dec, 1 Jan*
Details *Children welcome   Car park   Wheelchair access (not WC)   Garden and patio   No smoking in restaurant   Live or background music   Dogs welcome exc at peak times   Delta, MasterCard, Switch, Visa Accommodation: 6 rooms, B&B £36.50 to £78*

WOODLAND   Devon   map 1

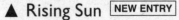

▲ Rising Sun   NEW ENTRY
Woodland TQ13 7JT   TEL: (01364) 652544
WEBSITE: www.risingsunwoodland.co.uk

This modernised, former drovers' inn stands isolated down country lanes, but one visitor recommends that it is 'well worth the two-mile detour' from the A38. The kitchen is keen to source local ingredients wherever possible and names producers on the menu, whether it's kiln-roast salmon from Dartmouth Smokehouse or a trio of pork sausages from C.M. McCabe in Totnes. Indeed, the varied menus have a something-for-everyone appeal, ranging from sandwiches, ploughman's with superb West Country cheeses, and decent pies (try venison with stout and juniper), to more imaginative fish (fillet of sole with pine-nut and basil butter, for example) and meat dishes (such as roast rack of Devon lamb in a lemon and pepper crust with thyme and rosemary jus). Pie nights are regular events, and there are occasional themed evenings such as Chinese, featuring perhaps Peking duck and egg-fried rice. Beer drinkers have some fine local ales to choose from, including the regular Princetown Jail Ale and guests such as Teignworthy Reel Ale and Sharp's Doom Bar Bitter, and there's also Luscombe organic cider. Ten wines are available by the glass. The open-plan bar sports two winter log fires, there's a family room with toys and games, and a south-facing garden with views over rolling countryside. SAMPLE DISHES: pan-fried pigeon breast with orange salad £5; roast belly of pork on spring onion mash with Luscombe cider cream sauce £10; rhubarb crumble £3.50.

Licensee Heather Humphreys (freehouse)
Open *Tue to Sat 11.45 to 3, 6 to 11, Sun 12 to 3, 7 to 10.30; bar food Tue to Sat 12 to 2.15, 6 to 9.15, Sun 12 to 3, 7 to 9.15; closed 25 Dec*
Details *Children welcome in family room and eating area   Car park   Wheelchair access (not WC)   Garden and patio   No smoking in eating area   No music   Dogs welcome   Amex, Delta, MasterCard, Switch, Visa Accommodation: 6 rooms, B&B £38 to £70*

WOOLSTHORPE   Lincolnshire   map 5

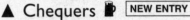

▲ Chequers 🍺   NEW ENTRY
Woolsthorpe NG32 1LU   TEL: (01476) 870701
WEBSITE: www.thechequers-inn.net
off A52 or A607, 6m W of Grantham

'It could be a setting from *The Pickwick Papers*,' mused one traveller after visiting this homely pub within striking distance of Belvoir Castle and the Grantham Canal. Country prints decorate the interior, log fires blaze when the weather closes in and there are black beams aplenty. This is a place that takes drinking seriously: Kimberley Best Bitter, Olde Trip and Belvoir Brewery Merrymaker are just some of the names that may crop up on the handpumps, while whisky fans have a choice of 50 to consider. Also worth noting are esoteric Continental bottled beers and French Grey Goose vodka. The wine list runs to around 45 well-spread bins, with a special collection from Italy and several by the glass. At lunchtime you can take your pick from sandwiches, omelettes and salads, or go for the great-value set menu. In the evening, put on your glad rags, sit in the smart restaurant and get in the mood with a glass of champagne. The carte promises modern-sounding dishes like duck and foie gras terrine with toasted brioche, then pan-seared marinated salmon fillet with seafood velouté, followed by passion-fruit and lemon tart. Don't confuse Woolsthorpe with its nearby namesake, Woolsthorpe near Colsterworth, which is to the south just off the A1. SAMPLE DISHES: pan-fried chilli tiger prawns with herb salad £5.75; roast rack of lamb with fondant potatoes and cumin jus £13.50; chocolate torte £4.75.

Licensee Justin Chad (freehouse)
Open 12 to 2, 7 to 11, Sun 12 to 10.30; bar food and restaurant all week 12 to 2.30 (3 Sun), Mon to Sat 7 to 9.30
Details Children welcome   Car park   Wheelchair access (not WC)   Garden and patio   No smoking in restaurant   Background music   Dogs welcome exc in restaurant   MasterCard, Switch, Visa   Accommodation: 4 rooms, B&B £40 to £50

WOOTTON RIVERS   Wiltshire   map 2

▲ Royal Oak

Wootton Rivers SN8 4NQ   TEL: (01672) 810322
WEBSITE: www.wiltshire-pubs.com

The sixteenth-century half-timbered and part-thatched building is traditional inside and out, with low ceilings and timbered walls supporting rooms unspoilt by modernity. Service is old-fashioned 'in the best possible sense', dispensing Fuller's London Pride, Wadworth 6X plus a guest ale, and an imaginative wine list that includes nine by the glass, alongside uncomplicated, basic pub food. Traditional dishes such as local ham with eggs and chips, sausages with mash and onion gravy, and steak, Guinness and redcurrant pie are mainstays of the menu, as is fresh fish: say, goujons of lemon sole with a sweet-and-sour sauce, or haddock in a pine-nut and pesto crust. Starters include an equally good showing of pub favourites along the lines of cream of tomato soup, and deep-fried Brie with a berry compote, as well as chicken liver and brandy pâté. Indulgent puddings include warm treacle tart, and chocolate brownies. SAMPLE DISHES: hot potted shrimps £5.25; beef and Burgundy casserole with parsley dumplings £11.50; sticky hot chocolate fudge cake £4.

Licensees Mr and Mrs John C. Jones (freehouse)
Open 10 to 3, 6 to 11; bar food and restaurant 12 to 2.30, 7 to 9.30; closed evening 25 Dec
Details Children welcome   Car park   Wheelchair access (also WC)   Patio   No smoking in restaurant   Jukebox in 1 bar   Dogs welcome   Amex, Delta, Diners, MasterCard, Switch, Visa   Accommodation: 6 rooms, B&B £30 to £50

All entries are indexed at the back of the book.

WORFIELD   **Shropshire**   map 5

Dog Inn

Main Street, Worfield WV15 5LF   TEL: (01746) 716020

Strictly speaking, this red-brick pub in the heart of the village is called the Dog Inn and Davenport Arms, but everyone knows it simply as The Dog. It's an unassuming kind of place, with a small garden at the back and a spruce restaurant housed in a small barn, with terracotta tiles on the floor, floral prints and deep-rose curtains 'involving yards and yards of fabric'. One menu is served at lunchtime and in the evening, and it takes full advantage of local produce for some quirky ideas such as black pudding thermidor (actually with mustard and tarragon sauce and Parmesan) and rack of lamb with aubergine caviar and rosemary sauce as well as beef in ale casserole with mustard croûtons or faggots with grey peas and bacon. Blackboards list daily specials, especially fish: wild smoked salmon from a nearby smokery, lobsters and other dishes ranging from spankingly fresh scallops with bacon and crispy sage to grilled whole plaice. At lunchtime, you can also get snacks, baguettes, ploughman's and the like, plus children's dishes (sausages, chicken nuggets, etc.), and among desserts might be chocolate roulade with orange and Cointreau. Beer drinkers can choose between Marston's Pedigree, Courage Best Bitter, Wells Bombardier Premium Bitter and Highgate Dark Mild. Three wines come by the glass from a short, wide-ranging list; prices start at £10.75. Dudmaston, a National Trust-owned house dating from the late seventeenth century, is not far away. SAMPLE DISHES: beef tomato with feta and green pimento dressing £4.50; chicken Laredo £9.50; ginger syllabub £3.50.

Licensee Vic Pocock (freehouse)
Open 12 to 2.30, 7 to 11, Sun 12 to 3, 7 to 10.30; bar food 12 to 2, restaurant 12 to 2, 7 to 9.30
Details Children welcome   Car park   Wheelchair access (also WC)   Patio   No smoking in restaurant
Occasional background music   Dogs by arrangement   Amex, Delta, MasterCard, Switch, Visa

WRIGHTINGTON   **Lancashire**   map 8

Mulberry Tree ✿

9 Wrightington Bar, Wrightington WN6 9SE   TEL: (01257) 451400
2m from M6 junction 27, on B5250

This modern-looking, open-plan pub has a clean and spacious feel with minimal décor – just a few copper pans and plain pictures on pale-coloured walls, and simple pine furniture. The separate bar and restaurant have distinct identities, the former suitably informal with a menu to match, and the latter with full table service. The cooking style is a refined, upmarket take on earthy country cooking, with starters of Tuscan white-bean soup or a warm terrine of black pudding, ham and cheese with piccalilli, followed perhaps by roast rump of lamb with hotpot potatoes, French beans and rosemary jus, or chicken suprême with pearl barley and winter vegetable broth. Simpler options are available at lunch, such as a club sandwich, ploughman's or Caesar salad. There is some crossover of dishes with the separate restaurant menu, which might also offer twice-baked Lancashire cheese soufflé, or Caribbean crab salad, followed by roast breast of Goosnargh duck with sage and onion mash, or slow-roast belly pork with white-bean ribollita and Parmesan crisp. The solitary real ale is Flowers IPA, and for wine drinkers there's a wide-ranging list of reasonably priced bottles from around the world, with eight by the glass. SAMPLE DISHES: deep-fried crottin with spiced pear, rocket and Parmesan £6.50; poached salmon fillet with sauce Choron £13.50; warm treacle tart with Drambuie anglaise and whisky ice cream £5.

Licensees Annie and Mark Prescott (freehouse)
Open *winter 12 to 3, 6 to 11 (10.30 Sun), summer 12 to 11 (10.30 Sun); bar food and restaurant 12 to 2 (6 Sun), 6 to 9.30*
Details *Children welcome Car park Wheelchair access (not WC) No smoking in restaurant Background music No dogs Delta, MasterCard, Switch, Visa*

WYTHAM   Oxfordshire   map 2

White Hart ✿
Wytham OX2 8QA   TEL: (01865) 244372
Wytham signposted on northbound carriageway of A34 (ring road) W of Oxford

The road to Wytham may be parallel to, and within yards of, the A34, but the village still has a rural feel and picture-postcard good looks. And it is well served by a pub that hits the spot for a stylish environment and good food. The interior is bright, open and full of colour, with a modern bar, warm paintwork, flagstone floors, a roaring fire and chunky light wooden furniture; and frequented by a relaxed-looking clientele (more jumpers and conversation than suits and business deals). The menu steps out in tune with the surroundings to deliver a modern British repertoire. Typical of starters are guinea fowl leg confit with beetroot and orange salad, and smoked haddock and spinach risotto with a soft-poached egg, while main courses might see pork fillet wrapped in crispy Italian bacon and sage pitched alongside chicken breast with sag aloo, mint yoghurt and mango salsa. Lunchtime sandwiches are also available. Hook Norton Best Bitter and Fuller's London Pride provide sustenance for beer drinkers, while a list of 40 or so wines offers 17 by the glass. SAMPLE DISHES: Stilton, black pudding and bacon salad with mustard dressing £5.50; boeuf bourguignon with chive mash £13; chocolate fondant with chocolate sauce £5.50.

Licensee David Peevers (Divine Dining Pub Co)
Open *winter 12 to 3, 6 to 11 (10.30 Sun), summer 12 to 11 (10.30 Sun); bar food and restaurant 12 to 3, 6.30 to 10*
Details *Children welcome Car park Wheelchair access (not WC) Garden No-smoking area in bar, no smoking in restaurant Background music No dogs Delta, Diners, MasterCard, Switch, Visa*

YANWATH   Cumbria   map 10

Yanwath Gate Inn   NEW ENTRY
Yanwath CA10 2LF   TEL: (01768) 862386
WEBSITE: www.yanwathgate.com
from A6 going south from Penrith turn right on to B5320 Pooley Bridge road to village

The Yanwath Gate Inn is the kind of place that gives English country pubs a good name. On the edge of the village in a dip in the land, it is a well-maintained building with lots of charm. The interior is attractive, with a light oak bar counter running most of one wall, stone walls, a huge inglenook, lots of solid scrubbed pine furniture, and a clean, bright décor. According to a reporter, most of the customers are 'there for the food', and plenty of seating accommodates everyone, with additional space in a room off the main bar as well as a pretty dining room. It's an all-blackboard affair here (including one for wine specials), and the menu is firmly in the realms of modern cooking. Home-baked bread is served with an olive oil dip, and on the bar lunch menu might be roast plum tomato soup with pesto, then Cumberland sausage with mustard mash, beef teriyaki stir-fry, or pan-fried sea bass ('perfectly cooked,' noted a visitor) with scallops and mango salsa; there's also a bargain set-price lunch menu for £6.50 for two courses. On the more extensive evening carte there might be chicken liver parfait followed by haddock and polenta fishcakes on grilled asparagus with mussel provençale. Guest ales change on a weekly basis – Theakston Black Bull Bitter plus keg beers – and a short, mainly New World wine list includes three by the glass. SAMPLE DISHES: Lebanese citrus and lentil soup £3.50; duck breast with ginger on a Thai potato cake with sweet soy sauce £11.50; Cointreau crème brûlée £4.50.

Licensee Dean El-Taher (freehouse)
Open *Tue to Sun 12 to 2.30, 6 to 10.30; bar food and restaurant 12 to 2, 6 to 9.30; closed Jan*
Details *Children welcome Car park Wheelchair access (not WC) Garden and patio No smoking Background music No dogs Amex, Delta, Diners, MasterCard, Switch, Visa*

YARMOUTH   Isle of Wight   map 2

King's Head
Quay Street, Yarmouth PO41 0PB   TEL: (01983) 760351
opposite harbour

There are two ways to get to the King's Head: park in the pay-and-display car park on the edge of this attractive seaside town and walk – it takes a few minutes – or, arrive by ferry from Lymington, and it's just a short stroll. It's one of the first buildings you come to as you head towards the heart of Yarmouth, opposite the entrance to the sixteenth-century fort. Inside is a series of open rooms and alcoves, with low ceilings, a few dark beams, half-panelled walls and, in the lounge area, a piano, seafaring prints and a large fireplace; towards the rear is a separate room with pine furniture, dark green walls and another fireplace. Menus are highly traditional, featuring lunchtime sandwiches and baguettes, as well as Italian stone-baked pizzas, steaks, and old favourites such as fish 'n' chips, chilli con carne, and steak and ale pie, followed, perhaps, by treacle sponge pudding or caramel parfait. On draught are Bass, Flowers Original, Boddingtons Bitter and Old Speckled Hen, and the short, well-selected wine list runs to around 20 bottles, with five offered by the glass. SAMPLE DISHES: crab au gratin £5; blackened Cajun rump steak £10; mint parfait £3.25.

Licensees Robert and Michelle Jackson (Enterprise Inns)
Open *11 to 11.30, Sun 12 to 10.30; bar food 12 to 2.30, 6 to 9.30*
Details *Children welcome in bar eating area Garden No smoking in eating area No music Dogs welcome exc in eating area Amex, Delta, Diners, MasterCard, Switch, Visa*

YATTENDON   Berkshire   map 2

▲ Royal Oak 😊
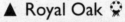
The Square, Yattendon RG18 0UG   TEL: (01635) 201325

The Royal Oak, right in the heart of Yattendon, is made up of a number of different linked buildings in old red brick partially covered in wisteria. But it is much more than a traditional village inn – this is more gastro-pub than boozer. True, there are real ales from West Berkshire and Worthington as well as Wadworth 6X on hand-pump, but the food is the focus, and you can eat it in bar, brasserie or restaurant (it's the same menu in all three). Start with a salad of smoked eel on truffle potatoes, caramelised shallots and horseradish cream, or maybe a soup of celeriac and fennel with a lemon and thyme cream. For a main course, try roast rack of English lamb on a flageolet bean purée with air-dried tomatoes, roasted salsify and balsamic jus, or poached boneless Cornish sole and seared scallops glazed with a light mustard and tarragon velouté. Note that vegetables cost extra. Puddings run the gamut from apple and rhubarb compote with cinnamon doughnuts and custard, to milk chocolate marquise with espresso-infused prunes and fromage blanc sorbet. Accompanying all this fine fare is a classy, mainly European wine list. Don't expect bargains – only three bottles come in under £15 and most are over £20. SAMPLE DISHES: warm salad of goats' cheese with kohlrabi and Seville orange dressing £6.75; poached halibut bouillabaisse with potato aïoli and new potato crisps £16.50; pistachio soufflé with prune and Armagnac ice cream and vanilla foam £5.75.

Licensee Corinne MacRae (freehouse)
Open 11 to 11, Sun 11 to 10.30; bar food and restaurant 12 to 2.30, 7 to 9.30
Details No children under 6 Car park Garden and patio No smoking in restaurant Background music
No dogs Amex, Delta, Diners, MasterCard, Switch, Visa Accommodation: 5 rooms, B&B £95 to £130

Scotland

▲ Applecross Inn
Shore Street, Applecross IV54 8LR   TEL: (01520) 744262
WEBSITE: www.applecross.uk.com
off A896, 18m W of Loch Carron

The drive over the single-track road of Bealach na Ba, Britain's highest mountain pass, is not for the faint-hearted, but, if the cloud has lifted, the view to Raasay and Skye is a wonderful experience. It may not be the easiest place to get to, but the white-painted inn, which stands hard by the shore, will make the journey worthwhile. To take in the atmosphere, head for the long, busy bar, where an elongated dining area stretching along the front of the building has views over the water. Fish and seafood, much of it landed locally, are the stars on the daily bar menu. Starters might take in crab bisque, squat lobster cocktail, or six local oysters, with main courses of pan-seared halibut in lemon and herbs, hand-dived scallops in garlic butter with crispy bacon, or Applecross Bay langoustines. Among meat options might be chicken broth, followed by local venison sausages with 'neeps 'n' squeak' and a rich onion gravy, or Diabeg pork chop with chive mash and apple and onion gravy. Finish perhaps with local berry cheesecake, or rich chocolate mousse. The Isle of Skye Brewery's Young Pretender, Blaven and Red Cuillin are on draught, with bottled Fraoch Heather Ale and Kelpie Seaweed Ale, plus a range of over 50 single malts and a couple of wines by the glass from a list of around 15 bottles. SAMPLE DISHES: local haggis with cream and oatcakes £5; venison casserole with mustard mash and organic green beans £11; cranachan £3.50.

Licensee Judith Fish (freehouse)
Open 11 to 11.30 (12 Fri, 11.45 Sat), Sun 12.30 to 11.30; bar food 12 to 9, restaurant 6 to 9; open 12 to 3 25 Dec (no food), closed 1 Jan
Details *Children welcome   Car park   Wheelchair access (also WC)   Garden and patio   No-smoking area in bar, no smoking in restaurant   Occasional live music; jukebox   Dogs welcome exc in restaurant   MasterCard, Switch, Visa   Accommodation: 7 rooms, B&B £25 to £70*

▲ Loch Melfort Hotel
Arduaine PA34 4XG   TEL: (01852) 200233
WEBSITE: www.lochmelfort.co.uk
on A816, 4m SW of Kilmelford

This family-run hotel is in one of the finest locations on Scotland's west coast. Its popular Skerry Bar/Bistro may be a sparsely furnished room (just nautical charts on the walls), but the large picture window looking on to the loch makes the most of a glorious view that sweeps over Asknish Bay to the island of Jura. As expected from such a setting, the kitchen makes full use of the best of local fresh produce, especially fish and shellfish (but meats and cheeses too). Langoustines from Luing (caught and landed in front of the hotel), Ardencaple oysters, lobster and Islay scallops all find their place. The standard menu is bolstered by daily blackboard specials: perhaps local shellfish bisque, escabèche of sea bass, or Irish stew with crusty bread. The printed menu runs from an array of sandwiches and baked potatoes to the likes of venison sausages with champ and onion gravy. In the restaurant things crank up a culinary gear with more elaborate offerings. Beers on tap include Theakston Best Bitter and McEwan 80/-, and bottled Scottish beers Heatherale, Froach and Fyne are also available, while from a wine list approaching 70 bottles just two come by the glass. If all this is not enough, the National Trust for Scotland's Arduaine Gardens are next door. SAMPLE DISHES: duo of smoked salmon and gravad lax with horseradish £4.75; braised lamb shank with mashed potatoes and vegetables £8.50; wild berry cheesecake £3.50.

Licensee Nigel Schofield (freehouse)
Open summer 10.30 to 11, winter 11 to 10.30 (11 Fri and Sat); bar food 12 to 2.30, 6 to 9 (8.30 Jan and Feb), restaurant 7 to 9
Details Children welcome Car park Wheelchair access (not WC) Garden No smoking in restaurant Background music Dogs welcome Amex, Delta, MasterCard, Switch, Visa Accommodation: 26 rooms, B&B £49 to £158

BRIG O' TURK   Stirling   map 11

Byre Inn
Brig o' Turk FK17 8HT   TEL: (01877) 376292
on A821 between Callander and Aberfoyle

It may seem 'somewhat cramped', but this tiny whitewashed stone pub boasts a spellbinding location just outside the Trossachs village of Brig o' Turk ('Bridge of the Wild Boar'), with its pretty stream, lakes and hills covered with bracken and twisty trunks of deciduous trees. Enjoy the view from the delightful garden or settle into the bar, with its motley collection of wooden chairs, stone floor and intriguing semi-ecclesiastical gargoyle corbels. Customers are well looked after by hard-working and diligent licensees. The kitchen makes commendable use of Scottish produce, including smoked Arbroath haddock (the basis of Cullen skink), Breadalbane haggis ('perfumed' with malt whisky and served with oatcakes), and Rannoch Moor venison (which might appear on the plate with a sweet red cabbage parcel and a port and juniper jus). Local Trossachs trout also finds its way on to the menu – perhaps fried and served with a pink peppercorn sauce and tiny scampi. There are plenty of so-called 'olde favourites', too, in the shape of steak and ale pie packed with meat from a local butcher, curry, pasta, and a trio of sausages with mash and onion gravy. Real ale fans should appreciate Heather Ale on draught, and there's a short, reasonably priced wine list with a couple of decent house selections by the glass. SAMPLE DISHES: chicken liver pâté with oatcakes and Cumberland sauce £3.75; baked fillet of Tayside salmon with hot sweet pepper dressing £9.75; clootie dumpling £4.

Licensee Anne Park (freehouse)
Open Mon to Thur 11 to 11, Fri and Sat 11 to 12, Sun 12.30 to 11; bar food and restaurant 11 (12.30 Sun) to 2.30, 6 to 8.30; closed Thur Nov to Mar
Details Children welcome Car park Wheelchair access (also WC) Garden No smoking in restaurant Background music No dogs MasterCard, Switch, Visa

CLACHAN-SEIL   **Argyll & Bute**   **map 11**

▲ Tigh-an-Truish

Clachan-Seil, Isle of Seil PA34 4QZ   TEL: (01852) 300242
on B844, 12m S of Oban

This eighteenth-century whitewashed stone pub stands beside the dramatically arched, single-span 'Atlantic Bridge' that links the island of Seil to the mainland. Its two bar areas are comfortable – one being a traditional snug that will suit those with children. Food varies with the seasons – a full menu is available from April to October, with only snack lunches in the winter – and the cooking is neat but not showy, focusing on local ingredients and producing satisfying dishes in substantial portions. Locally smoked salmon or chicken liver or mushroom pâté might precede steak and ale pie, home-made beef burger, or locally caught prawns; sticky toffee pudding or apple crumble will fill any remaining space. McEwan 80/- appears alongside regularly changing guest ales from Fyne Ales, among others, and a basic wine list includes four by the glass. This is a peaceful spot, noted for its excellent walks and scenery, and nearby is the island of Easdale, once a slate mining community and a fascinating 'living museum'. SAMPLE DISHES: moules marinière £5.50; smoked haddock Mornay £7; summer pudding £3.50.

Licensee Miranda Brunner (freehouse)
Open *winter Mon to Thur 11 to 2.30, 5 to 11, Fri to Sun 11 to 11, summer 11 (12 Sun) to 11; bar food 12 to 2, 6 to 8.30; food served all day in high season; closed 25 Dec, 1 Jan*
Details *Children welcome in family room   Car park   Wheelchair access (also WC)   Garden   No smoking in 1 room   Occasional live or background music   Dogs welcome exc in eating area   No cards   Accommodation: 2 rooms, room only £45*

CRINAN   **Argyll & Bute**   **map 11**

▲ Crinan Hotel

Crinan PA31 8SR   TEL: (01546) 830261
WEBSITE: www.crinanhotel.com
take B841 off A816 6m NW of Lochgilphead

Breathtaking views are to be had from this waterside hotel in a tiny fishing village at the northern end of the Crinan Canal, which links Loch Fyne to the Atlantic. There's a distinctive local feel in the bar, an elegant, wood-panelled room with pictures of marine wildlife and a pleasantly relaxed atmosphere. The food in here is not overly complicated, and a combination of fine raw materials and care in presentation elevate it out of the ordinary, with local seafood to the fore. What to expect are a warm tart of Loch Crinan scallops, smoked bacon and sun-dried tomatoes with goats' cheese cream to start, and main courses of grilled fillet of West Coast mackerel with parsley mash, brown shrimp butter and a caper and raisin dressing, or hand-made Barbreck lamb and rosemary sausages with a cassoulet of butter beans, bacon and sweet tomatoes, with Scottish Cheddar, oatcakes and quince jelly as an alternative to dessert. A list of carefully chosen wines offers only four by the glass, but there are a few half-bottles to consider. Only bottled beers are stocked. The hotel restaurant – the Westward – enjoys great views and a good reputation. SAMPLE DISHES: pappardelle with chestnut mushrooms, flat parsley and a Parmesan butter emulsion £5.50;

pan-fried Orkney crab cake with buttered greens, French fries and thermidor sauce
£12; a selection of Orkney ice creams £3.

Licensee Nicolas Ryan (freehouse)
Open 11 to 12; bar food 12 to 2 (2.30 Sat and Sun), 6.30 to 8.30 (9 summer), restaurant 7 to 8.30; closed
Christmas and New Year
Details Children welcome in bar eating area   Car park   Wheelchair access (also WC)   Patio   No-smoking
area in bar, no smoking in restaurant   No music   Dogs welcome exc in Westward Restaurant   Delta,
MasterCard, Switch, Visa   Accommodation: 20 rooms, D,B&B £130 to £300

DRYMEN   Stirling   map 11

Clachan Inn

2 Main Street, Drymen G63 0BP   TEL: (01360) 660824
off A811, 20m W of Stirling

Established in 1734 and – reputedly – Scotland's 'Oldest Registered Pub', this is a
'refreshingly untrendy' hostelry much loved by locals and foreign tourists looking for
good hospitality and decent malt whiskies. Inside, it is dark and old-fashioned, with
its tartan carpet, wooden tables and assorted bric-à-brac. The food is in keeping: reliable traditional soups like lentil or Scotch broth ('made with their own stock'),
lavishly assembled salads, and all manner of steaks procured from a sound local
butcher. Haggis might be served with oatcakes or used as a filling for jacket potatoes;
otherwise the kitchen goes walkabout with Malaysian lamb casserole, warm Cajun
chicken salad, and vegetable pakoras. Sausages and crisp, firm fried fillet of haddock
have both been heartily endorsed. Deuchars IPA, Belhaven Best and St Andrew's Ale
are on draught, and five workaday wines are available by the bottle, carafe or glass.
There are good walks in the nearby Queen Elizabeth Forest Park. SAMPLE DISHES:
prawn and mushroom pot £4.50; sirloin steak Diane £14; caramel apple pie £4.

Licensee Elizabeth Plank (freehouse)
Open 11 to 12, Sun 12.30 to 12; bar food and restaurant 12 to 4, 6 to 10; closed 25 Dec, 1 Jan
Details Children welcome   Wheelchair access (also WC)   Background music   Dogs welcome on a lead in
bar   MasterCard, Switch, Visa

DYSART   Fife   map 11

Old Rectory Inn

West Quality Street, Dysart KY1 2TE   TEL: (01592) 651211
off A955 Methil road, N of Kirkaldy

Dysart is an attractive village with 'a very pretty harbour', and the Old Rectory is a
popular venue: 'clearly a favourite,' noted a visitor who called in for lunch on a cold
November day and found the place nearly full. The draw is a tried and tested repertoire of good-value food served in both the bar and restaurant. The lengthy menu
might run to lunchtime options of cream of cauliflower soup or home-pickled rollmop herrings, then spaghetti with spicy chicken, red and green peppers and tomato
sauce, while the supper menu includes starters such as 'delicious' grilled sardines with
garlic and lemon, then main courses of boiled leg of ham with creamy apple and
onion sauce and sweetcorn relish, with desserts chosen from the trolley. Fish is listed
on a daily specials board, as are dishes of the day, and vegetarians are well catered for.
Monthly chef recommendations might include old favourites such as tournedos

Rossini and escalope of pork Holstein. Calders Cream Ale is on draught, there's a good selection of malt whiskies, and five wines come by the glass. SAMPLE DISHES: creamy smoked haddock soup £2.75; venison and mushroom casserole £5.75; chocolate brownie £2.

Licensees Mr and Mrs D. North (freehouse)
Open *Tue to Sun 12 to 3, Tue to Sat 7 to 12; bar food and restaurant Tue to Sat 12 to 2, 7 to 9.45, Sun 12.30 to 2.30; closed 1 week early Jan, 1 week early July, 2 weeks mid-Oct*
Details *Children welcome in eating areas   Car park   Wheelchair access (not WC)   Garden   No music Guide dogs only   Amex, Delta, MasterCard, Switch, Visa*

EDINBURGH   Edinburgh   map 11

Baillie

2–4 St Stephen Street, Edinburgh EH3 5AL   TEL: (0131) 225 4673

The Baillie is a traditional pub with a low-ceilinged basement bar, an open fire and a friendly, local feel. One of the attractions of the place is the range of real ales: among them might be Timothy Taylor Landlord, Courage Directors, Belhaven 70/-, Deuchars IPA, and McEwan 80/-. Food draws the crowds too, especially at lunchtime, with a good mixture of classic pub dishes: mussels steamed in white wine and cream, deep-fried beer-battered haddock, and ribeye steak with black peppercorn and brandy sauce. And food is now served in the evening, with deep-fried crispy battered haggis with a salsa dip flying the flag for Scotland alongside good-value comfort food such as lamb and mint sausages with mash and red onion gravy, home-made beef burger, and chicken, mushroom, pepper and baby spinach lasagne. Around ten wines by both glass and bottle complete the picture. SAMPLE DISHES: deep-fried Brie with redcurrant sauce £3.75; Mexican tortilla filled with Cajun chicken, roasted peppers, onion and mozzarella £6.25; sticky toffee pudding £2.75.

Licensee Richard Boakes (freehouse)
Open *11am to 1am, Sun 12.30pm to 1am; bar food lunch all week 11 (12.30 Sun) to 5, dinner 5 to 9.30; closed 25 Dec*
Details *Children welcome in eating area   Patio   Occasional live music   Dogs welcome exc during food service Delta, MasterCard, Switch, Visa*

Café Royal

19 West Register Street, Edinburgh EH2 2AA   TEL: (0131) 556 1884

Its spectacular décor is just one alluring feature of this classic Victorian city-centre bar just north of Princes Street. Inside you will see a splendid island counter and flamboyant fixtures and fittings, including an ornate ceiling, intriguing Doulton tiled panels featuring renowned inventors, a fine fireplace, and etched glass. There are marble floors, a revolving door, and elaborate screens to divide off the similarly ornate Oyster Bar restaurant. After you've feasted your eyes on the architectural extravagances, you might wish to check out a range of ales that includes Caledonian Deuchars IPA and 80/-, McEwan 80/- and a guest such as Boddingtons Bitter. There are also ten wines by the glass from a 60-strong list. The speciality here is seafood: oysters come five ways (from *au naturel* to grilled with tomato sauce and basil), and mussels receive similarly varied treatments. Alternatively, you might plump for seafood chowder, cured herring fillets, or goujons of lemon sole. Away from fish, the menu offers everything from sandwiches to sausage and mash with a back-up of specials like roast duck breast with honey and orange sauce. Finish with, say, sticky toffee pudding, or chocolate fudge cake. SAMPLE DISHES: crab and coriander cakes £5.50; Cajun chicken breast in tomato and tarragon sauce £5.75; glazed lemon tart £3.

Licensee David Allen (Scottish & Newcastle)
Open Mon to Wed 11 to 11, Thur 11 to 12, Fri and Sat 11 to 1, Sun 12.30 to 11; bar food Mon to Sat 11 to 10, Sun 12.30 to 10, restaurant 12 to 2 (2.30 Sun), 7 to 10
Details Children welcome in restaurant   Wheelchair access (not WC)   No-smoking area in restaurant   Background music   No dogs   Amex, Delta, Diners, MasterCard, Switch, Visa

Ship on the Shore
24–26 The Shore, Leith, Edinburgh EH6 6QN   TEL: (0131) 555 0409

The Ship looks like a traditional bar, with wooden floors, typical furniture, nautical paraphernalia, and an island bar, but it works hard at combining food and drink, welcoming those popping in for a casual drink as warmly as those in for a full-blown meal. Half the space is turned over to dining: candlelit tables, affable staff and a menu that tacks away from the more cliché pub food draws the crowds. The repertoire – strong on fish – befits the location, with the likes of steamed mussels marinière, salmon and coriander fishcake, and deep-fried calamares with garlic mayonnaise to start. Main courses could feature baked smoked haddock and prawns on mash with leek velouté, or pan-seared tuna with pineapple salsa. Pan-fried breast of chicken stuffed with haggis, or perhaps steak and ale pie provide sustenance for meat eaters. A decent range of beers includes Deuchars IPA, McEwan 70/- and Caledonian 80/-, and four wines are served by the glass. SAMPLE DISHES: seafood chowder £4.50; grilled fillets of sea bream with asparagus velouté £15; cheeseboard £5.50.

Licensee Roy West (freehouse)
Open 11 to 11; bar food 12 to 2.30, 6.30 to 9.30, Sun 11 to 2.30
Details No children under 5   Wheelchair access (also WC)   Background music   No dogs   Delta, MasterCard, Switch, Visa

GLASGOW   Glasgow   map 11

Babbity Bowster
16–18 Blackfriars Street, Glasgow G1 1PE   TEL: (0141) 552 5055

This discreetly restored Robert Adam house in the old Merchant City, named after an old Scottish country dance pipe tune, offers an equally warm welcome to locals and tourists. There's a cosmopolitan yet down-to-earth atmosphere to go with the menu of unpretentious, good-value food. Bolstered by blackboard specials, menus run the gamut of authentic Scottish fare, such as hearty soups, haggis, neeps and tatties, and clootie dumpling, as well as seafood like Loch Fyne smoked salmon, and mussels in creamy white wine sauce. The upstairs restaurant serves more ambitious meals along the lines of seared scallops in roasted garlic beurre blanc, roast poussin with a peppery sauce, or chicken chasseur. The garden is popular on fine days. Houston Peter's Well and guests like Durham Magus are on handpump, and ten wines are sold by the glass.

SAMPLE DISHES: vegetable crab cakes with sweet chilli dressing £5; duck breast with orange sauce £14.50; Arran ice cream £3.50.

Licensee John Fraser Laurie (freehouse)
Open 11 to 12, Sun 12.30 to 12; bar food 12 to 10, restaurant Tue to Sat 6.30 to 9.30
Details Children welcome   Car park   Wheelchair access (not WC)   Garden   Occasional live music   Dogs welcome   Amex, Delta, MasterCard, Switch, Visa

Brel

37–43 Ashton Lane, Glasgow G12 8SJ   TEL: (0141) 342 4966
WEBSITE: www.brelbarrestaurant.com

Named after the Belgian poet and songwriter Jacques Brel, this is a buzzy, good-value kind of place close to the university, much favoured by students and arty types attracted by the prospect of frequent live music plus food and drink at bargain prices. A former stable in a mews area flush with pub/restaurants, it keeps things simple with tiled floors and tables covered in brown-paper sheets and candles. There's a large bar and two dining areas, one a popular conservatory opening on to a grassy bank for sunny days. Given the Belgian connection, it's no surprise to find pots of mussels with frites topping the bill – perhaps jazzed up with sweet chilli or with lemon and spring onions. Merguez sausages are another speciality, and the menu also runs to braised meatballs in de Koninck beer, grilled tuna with roasted anchovies, and mixed-bean and potato ragoût. Bringing up the rear are desserts such as hot Belgian waffles with chocolate sauce and Grand Marnier. All manner of Belgian brews – both bottled and draught – dominate the drinks front, with everything from Belle Vue Kriek cherry beer and Duvel to Stella Artois; there's also a compact wine list with Chilean house selections opening the account at £9.50. SAMPLE DISHES: caponata on bruschetta £4; salmon fillet with red pesto and spinach £9.25; chocolate bread-and-butter pudding £3.75.

Licensee Laurie Keith (BB Grand)
Open 10 to 12; bar food 12 to 3, restaurant Mon to Thur 5 to 10, Fri and Sat 5 to 11, Sun 12 to 11
Details Children welcome in terrace conservatory   Wheelchair access (also WC)   Garden   Live or background music   Dogs welcome exc in restaurant   Amex, Delta, Diners, MasterCard, Switch, Visa

▲ Rab Ha's

83 Hutcheson Street, Glasgow G1 1SH   TEL: (0141) 572 0400

The Merchant City area of Glasgow is being attractively renovated, with some 'wonderful buildings being restored to their former glory'. In the midst of all this stands Rab Ha's (short for Robert Hall, the famed 'Glasgow Glutton'). Converted from a warehouse, the interior is conducive to eating and drinking, with its old-fashioned, unpretentious bar, large, separate restaurant, and friendly, efficient service. The all-day bar menu offers a straightforward trawl through familiar choices like burgers (made with hundred per cent organic beef), haggis with turnip and mashed potato, and mince and tatties, as well as nachos with sour cream, guacamole and salsa, and Thai red chicken with coconut rice. Evening meals move into the more ambitious realms of seared tuna loin with niçoise salad and a soy and sesame dressing to start, followed by pot-roast breasts and ballottine of poussin with sage and pancetta dumplings and baby vegetables in its own broth, with baked lemon tart with berry compote and raspberry coulis to finish. On draught are Belhaven Best and a selection of European beers, including Budvar and Furstenberg, and a handful of wines is served by the glass. SAMPLE DISHES: chicken tempura with soy and ginger £4; beef and Guinness pie £6; cheesecake £3.

Licensee Hamish McLean (freehouse)
Open 11 to 12, Sun 12.30 to 12; bar food 12 to 10, restaurant 12 to 3, 5.30 to 10
Details Children welcome No smoking in restaurant before 10pm Background music Dogs welcome exc in restaurant Amex, Delta, MasterCard, Switch, Visa Accommodation: 4 rooms, B&B £65 to £75

Ubiquitous Chip 🍸 🍇

12 Ashton Lane, Glasgow G12 8SJ TEL: (0141) 334 5007
WEBSITE: www.ubiquitouschip.co.uk

A popular fixture on the Glasgow eating and drinking scene, the Ubiquitous Chip comprises several distinct parts. The Wee Chip is the drinking arm of the establishment, serving a variety of wines, beers (real ales are Caledonian 80/- and Deuchars IPA) and whiskies, as well as a simple bar menu. An iron spiral staircase leads to Upstairs at the Chip, a bar/brasserie in a long room with basic décor, fires, plain wooden tables and a buzz provided by the arty, Bohemian bunch that frequent the place. This part overlooks the greenery-festooned courtyard and the restaurant (a *Good Food Guide* stalwart). Scottish produce abounds on the Upstairs menu, although much of it is given an exotic treatment: choices range from chicken breast with vegetarian haggis, stovies and turnip cream to Orkney salmon marinated in honey, tamari and ginger with creamed spinach sauce and mash, or roast quail stuffed with tartan purry served with roast paprika potatoes, spinach and red wine sauce. Upstairs offers its own selection of 18 wines by the glass from £2.50, all under £15 a bottle – and the huge range of bottles on the savvy main restaurant list is also available. SAMPLE DISHES: Loch Etive mussels marinière £5.75; pan-fried Scotch lamb's liver with Ayrshire bacon, mashed potatoes, and onions in Caledonian 80/- batter £7.25; bread pudding with fruit fattened in Rutherglen Muscat with double cream £4.25.

Licensee Ronald Clydesdale (freehouse)
Open 11 to 12, Sun 12.30 to 12; bar food and restaurant 12 (12.30 Sun) to 11; closed 25 Dec, 1 Jan
Details Children welcome in eating areas Wheelchair access (Wee Chip only; also WC) No music Dogs welcome Amex, Delta, Diners, MasterCard, Switch, Visa

INNERLEITHEN Borders map 11

▲ Traquair Arms 🍺

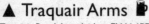

Traquair Road, Innerleithen EH44 6PD TEL: (01896) 830229

Quite close to Innerleithen's main street, this handsome Victorian stone building sits four-square on the road out to Traquair House (one of the oldest inhabited houses in Scotland). And its Victorian scale gives it 'a gracious feel', according to one visitor. The same menu is offered in both the comfortable restaurant and the pubby bar, with its log fire, medallion-patterned wallpaper and curtains and wooden-topped tables. It is a straightforward menu, based on such stalwarts as fried fillet of haddock, steak pie, grilled lamb chops, and roast pheasant – with omelettes, salads, baked potatoes, and Aberdeen Angus steaks extending the range – bolstered by daily specials. There's a selection of Scottish cheeses as well as a blackboard of daily-changing puddings. On handpump are rotating seasonal ales, say Bear Ale or Stuart Ale from the eighteenth-century brewery in Traquair House, plus a couple (maybe The Ghillie and Winter Fire) from the local Broughton Ales brewery. Out of about 20 bottles, three house wines are sold in two sizes of glass. SAMPLE DISHES: garlic mushrooms with garlic mayonnaise £3.75; cider and apple pork £7; steamed apple and cinnamon syrup sponge £3.25.

Licensee Dianne Johnson (freehouse)
Open 11 to midnight, Sun 12 to 12; bar food and restaurant 12 to 9
Details Children welcome   Car park   Wheelchair access (not WC)   Garden   No smoking in restaurant
Background music   Dogs welcome   Amex, MasterCard, Switch, Visa   Accommodation: 15 rooms, B&B £29 to £45

KILLIECRANKIE   Perthshire & Kinross   map 11

▲ Killiecrankie Hotel
Killiecrankie PH16 5LG   TEL: (01796) 473220
WEBSITE: www.killiecrankiehotel.co.uk
off A9, then B8079, 4m N of Pitlochry

In a beautiful valley amid trees and formal gardens, this mid-nineteenth-century dower house was converted into a posh country hotel in 1939. Despite the elegance and luxury, an informal atmosphere reigns throughout, not least in the mahogany-panelled bar and adjoining conservatory, where you can enjoy a traditional range of refreshments including a good selection of malt whiskies and the superb Red MacGregor ale from the Orkney Brewery, as well as decent bar meals. The extensive conservatory menu features local produce in abundance: smoked venison, lamb and beef (served with juniper chutney and salad), or sweet-cured Orkney herrings for starters, poached salmon with prawns, salad and a lemon and herb mayonnaise for a light supper, and main courses such as battered haddock with chips and peas, or locally made Cumberland sausages with spiced apple chutney. The separate restaurant, open for dinner only, has its own fixed-price menu. The wine list offers extensive choice from excellent producers around the world, with eight by the glass. There's plenty under £20, but this is a place where you can also splash out with confidence. SAMPLE DISHES: Stilton and walnut pâté with pear chutney £5; chargrilled chicken suprême with Thai sauce £8.75; banoffi pie £4.

Licensee Maillie Waters (freehouse)
Open 12 to 2.30, 6 to 11, Sun 12.30 to 2.30, 6.30 to 11; bar food 12.30 to 1.45, 6.30 to 7.45 (8.45 summer); restaurant 7 to 8.30; closed 3 Jan to 13 Feb
Details Children welcome   Car park   Wheelchair access (also WC)   Garden   No smoking   Occasional live and background music   Dogs welcome exc during mealtimes   Delta, MasterCard, Switch, Visa
Accommodation: 10 rooms, B&B £65 to £130

KILMAHOG   Stirling   map 11

Lade Inn   NEW ENTRY
Kilmahog, by Callander FK17 8HD   TEL: (01877) 330152
WEBSITE: www.theladeinn.com
on A281 at junction with A84, 1m NW of Callander

This low-ceilinged inn seems to have hit the jackpot with both locals and tourists, who home in on handpumps advertising WayLade, LadeBack and LadeOut – produced exclusively for the pub by the Trossachs Craft Brewery just opposite. But beer is not all: a bar menu flies the flag for Scottish produce and unpretentious home cooking, along the lines of Achiltibuie smoked Cheddar that finds its way into a tartlet with leeks; salmon that comes from the Marrbury smokehouse; and splendid local haggis that is served with a potato and chive croquette, champit carrots and turnip, and a whisky cream sauce. A neighbourhood butcher supplies the sausages (some of which are laced with Lade ales), and burgers are made from grass-fed beef. The specials board broadens the range with, say, grilled sardines or a duo of pheasant and pigeon breast 'with a little rich liver' and a light port sauce. Desserts are something of an after-thought, although tangy lemon tart has been enjoyed. A separate à la carte menu high-lights steaks and more flashy ideas like pork fillet with a compote of apples and brambles accompanied by a Dunsyre Blue cheese cream sauce. A pair of South African house wines heads the modest list of everyday tipples. SAMPLE DISHES: deep-fried goats' cheese with raspberry and red wine dressing £4.50; Creole-style fish with rice £8; lemon and ginger cheesecake £3.50.

Licensee Stephen Nixon (freehouse)
Open Mon to Fri 12 to 2.30, 5.30 to 11, Sat 12 to 12, Sun 12.30 to 10.30; bar food Mon to Fri 12 to 2.30, 5.30 to 9, Sat 12 to 9, Sun 12.30 to 9; closed 1 Jan
Details Children welcome in eating area   Car park   Wheelchair access (also WC)   Garden   No-smoking area   Occasional live or background music   Dogs welcome in bar only   Delta, Diners, MasterCard, Switch, Visa

---

KIPPEN   Stirling   map 11

▲ Cross Keys

Main Street, Kippen FK8 3DN   TEL: (01786) 870293
on B822, 10m W of Stirling

The former coaching inn dates from 1703, and its beer garden at the back has lovely views of hills. Inside there are three old-fashioned rooms to choose from, with 'a real coal fire in each', equestrian bric-à-brac, comfortable Windsor chairs, and a courte-ous, friendly atmosphere. The same daily-changing menu applies wherever you choose to sit, and although the repertoire doesn't stray far beyond pub standards, such as vegetable lasagne and grilled gammon steak with pineapple, the food is fresh, with excellent meat supplied by a local butcher and with fish also reliable. Start, perhaps, with sweet-cured herring fillet in a sherry marinade, or a good homely soup: say, cream of spinach. 'Proper home-made' lamb casserole could follow, or locally baked ham salad, or steak pie, and, for dessert, sticky toffee pudding, and toffee and apple meringue roulade both get the thumbs up. Belhaven St Andrew's Ale and the ominously named Bitter & Twisted from the Harviestoun Brewery are the real ales on offer. Three wines from a list of around 20 come by the glass, and there's a wide selection of malt whiskies. SAMPLE DISHES: Arbroath smokie mousse £4; grilled fillet of salmon with parsley butter £7.25; profiteroles £4.

Licensee Gordon Scott (freehouse)
Open Mon to Fri 12 to 2.30, 5.30 to 11, Sat 12 to 12, Sun 12.30 to 11; bar food Mon to Sat 12 to 2, 5.30 to 9, Sun 12.30 to 9; closed 25 Dec, 1 Jan
Details Children welcome   Car park   Wheelchair access (not WC)   Garden   No smoking in eating area   Occasional background music   Dogs welcome in bar only   MasterCard, Switch, Visa   Accommodation: 2 rooms, B&B £30 to £60

MELROSE   Borders   map 11

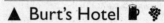

▲ Burt's Hotel 🍺 🍇

Market Square, Melrose TD6 9PL   TEL: (01896) 822285
WEBSITE: www.burtshotel.co.uk

On the market square of a small Borders town, this popular and comfortable eigh-teenth-century inn, originally the home of a local dignitary, has been run by the Henderson family for more than 30 years. Eating options include the restaurant and the less formal environment of the traditional bar. The menu in the latter is a varied list of simple but stylish dishes, such as pan-fried sea bream on seafood risotto with tomato oil, and braised rump of lamb with mash and thyme, along with old favourites like deep-fried haddock with tartare sauce. Dinner in the restaurant is somewhat more upmarket, with starters of pigeon breast in puff pastry with bramble coulis, followed perhaps by sea bass fillets on lobster risotto with curry oil. Real ales are a good selection, including Caledonian 80/-, Deuchars IPA and Fuller's London Pride, and there are around 80 single malt whiskies. The wine list opens with five tempting house selections from £12.25, also available by the glass, and runs to around 80 well-chosen, good-value bottles, including plenty under £15 and a page of fine wines. SAMPLE DISHES: ham hock terrine with potato salad and crispy leeks £4.50; chicken breast stuffed with bacon and mushroom mousse on tomato and basil coulis £9; sticky ginger pudding with vanilla ice cream and butterscotch sauce £4.50.

Licensee Graham Henderson (freehouse)
Open 11 to 2.30, 5 to 11, Sun 12 to 2.30, 6 to 11; bar food and restaurant 12 to 2, 6 to 9.30 (10 Fri and Sat); closed 24 to 26 Dec
Details Children welcome in eating areas   Car park · Wheelchair access (not WC)   Garden and patio
No-smoking area in bar, no smoking in restaurant   No music   Dogs welcome in bar   Amex, Delta,
MasterCard, Switch, Visa   Accommodation: 20 rooms, B&B £54 to £70

NETHERLEY   Aberdeenshire   map 11

Lairhillock Inn

Netherley AB39 3QS   TEL: (01569) 730001
on B979, 4m S of Peterculter

There are views over miles of open countryside from this 200-year-old inn in the hills between Stonehaven and Deeside. You can drink in the scenery from the popular conservatory or seek warmth and comfort around the fire that dominates the bar and lounge. Beer-drinkers will appreciate a line-up that includes Timothy Taylor Landlord, Courage Directors and ales from the Isle of Skye Brewing Company, while a collection of over 60 malt whiskies offer serious research opportunities for dram-fanciers. The bar menu provides plenty of choice, from Cullen skink and home-made wild boar sausages to 'Lairies gambas' (king prawns in lime, chilli, sweet pepper and coconut sauce) and steaks – Aberdeen Angus or ostrich. Baguettes and ciabatta steak sandwiches are also available at lunchtime, and Sunday lunch is a traditional buffet. The separate menu in the Crynoch Restaurant is based on local produce and combines classical cooking with modern ideas, along the lines of medallions of local venison on peppered potatoes with wild mushrooms or marinated duck suprême roasted and served with grilled polenta. The lengthy restaurant wine list is serious and Francocentric, that in the bar shorter and new-worldy; house wines are £16.50 a litre,

£2.30 a glass. SAMPLE DISHES: spicy spare ribs £5.50; haggis-stuffed chicken suprême with malt whisky sauce £9; banana and butterscotch sundae £4.

Licensee Roger Thorne (freehouse)
Open Mon to Fri 11.30 to 2.30, 5 to 11 (12 Fri), Sat 11 to 12, Sun 11.30 to 11; bar food 12 to 2, 6 to 9.30 (10 Fri and Sat), restaurant Sun 12 to 1.30, Wed to Mon 7 to 9.15; closed 25 and 26 Dec, 1 and 2 Jan
Details Children welcome in bar eating area and conservatory   Car park   Wheelchair access (also WC) Garden   No smoking in restaurant   Background music   Dogs welcome in pubic bar   Amex, Delta, Diners, MasterCard, Switch, Visa

---

PLOCKTON   Highland   map 11

▲ Plockton Hotel

41 Harbour Street, Plockton IV52 8TN   TEL: (01599) 544274
WEBSITE: www.plocktonhotel.co.uk

Billed as Plockton's only waterfront hotel, this is a bustling, urbane place, an impeccably run family concern noted for its warm, welcoming atmosphere. The bar is a good spot for a relaxed lunch, and the menu makes interesting reading. Plockton smokies is flaked smoked mackerel layered with cream, cheese and tomatoes, local prawns (landed daily) come either as a starter or a light main course, and there's haggis served with a tot of whisky. Fish from Gairloch and Kinlochbervie feature on the evening menu: perhaps sole or plaice on the bone simply grilled with butter and lemon juice, or herring in oatmeal traditionally fried in butter. Steaks, a casserole of Highland venison, or baked shank of lamb with red wine and rosemary sauce are typical of meat options, and finish with raspberry pavlova or white chocolate cheesecake. Real ales include Deuchars IPA and Hebridean Gold, there's a range of malt whiskies, and four wines come by the glass. SAMPLE DISHES: salad of sweet pickled herring and prawns £4; monkfish and smoked bacon brochette £11.75; malt whisky ice cream £3.75.

Licensees Mr and Mrs T. Pearson (freehouse)
Open 11 to 12, Sun 12.30 to 11; bar food and restaurant 12 to 2.15, 6 to 9.30
Details Children welcome   Wheelchair access (also WC)   Garden and patio   No smoking in restaurant Occasional live or background music   No dogs   Amex, Delta, MasterCard, Switch, Visa   Accommodation: 15 rooms, B&B £45 to £90

▲ Plockton Inn

Innes Street, Plockton IV52 8TW   TEL: (01599) 544222 ·
WEBSITE: www.plocktoninn.co.uk

This unpretentious and friendly pub, 100 yards from the harbour in a seaside village just a few miles from the main road to Skye, has a menu that pays tribute to the proximity of the sea with generous netfuls of fish and seafood in the restaurant and the bar. A platter of seafood smoked in the inn's own smokehouse, steamed Loch Leven mussels, and fish soup are all among starters, while main courses take in baked lemon sole with herb and lemon butter, skate wing with black butter, and cod fillet with tomatoes, olives and parsley. Meat eaters are not neglected, with choices ranging from venison with bramble and port sauce, or chicken breast wrapped in sage and bacon stuffed with cream cheese and baked with tomatoes, to Aberdeen Angus beef burger. Brown bread ice cream makes a good finish, and Scottish cheeses are something of a speciality. Select one of the 50 or so malt whiskies to sample in front of the log fire, or a pint of one of the real ales: Fuller's London Pride, Old Speckled Hen, or Greene King Abbot Ale. The wine list is a compilation of 20-plus bottles from around the world, with three house wines sold by the glass at £2.10. SAMPLE DISHES: gravad lax with dill sauce £5; Loch Carron scallops with bacon, garlic and cream £13; brown sugar meringues with fruit salad £3.50.

Licensee Kenneth J. Gollan (freehouse)
Open 11am to midnight, Sun 12.30 to 11; bar food and restaurant 12 to 2.30, 6 to 9.30
Details Children welcome   Car park   Wheelchair access (also WC)   Garden and patio   No smoking in restaurant   Live or background music   Dogs welcome   Delta, MasterCard, Switch, Visa   Accommodation: 14 rooms, B&B £35 to £80

ROSLIN   Midlothian 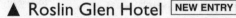 map 11

▲ Roslin Glen Hotel   NEW ENTRY
2 Penicuik Road, Roslin EH25 9LH   TEL: (0131) 440 2029

New owners have revived this 'huge Victorian pile' in a former mining village at the foot of the Pentland Hills. The revamping of the menu in the large restaurant and bar ('which can probably take around 70 people') and offering takeaway pizzas are just two of the changes. The food retains the traditional elements of soup of the day, beer-battered haddock and chips, steak and ale pie, Aberdeen Angus beef burgers, and Buccleuch steaks. These are coupled with more up-to-date favourites like nachos with all the trimmings, frittata with ham and Brie, fajitas of chicken, steak, salmon or vegetable, and toasted focaccia. Free-range garlic chicken breast, and herb-roast rack of lamb with haggis and redcurrant and rosemary gravy are also available, alongside Sunday roasts and puddings such as banoffi pie. What distinguishes the food here is the quality of ingredients and the care taken in the cooking. Drinks-wise, the only real ale served is Deuchars IPA, with just a pair of wines from a list of 10 bottles served by the glass. SAMPLE DISHES: steamed mussels with garlic bread £5; venison, port and Stilton pie £8.50; sticky toffee pudding £4.

Licensee Fiona Ingram (freehouse)
Open Mon to Thur 11 to 11, Fri to Sun 11 to 12; bar food and restaurant Mon to Fri 12 to 2.30, 5 to 9, Sat and Sun 12 to 9
Details Children welcome   Car park   Wheelchair access (also WC)   No-smoking area in bar, no smoking in restaurant   Background music   Dogs welcome in bar area only   Delta, MasterCard, Switch, Visa   Accommodation: 8 rooms, B&B £40 to £60

STRACHUR   Argyll & Bute   map 11

▲ Creggans Inn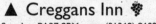
Strachur PA27 8BX   TEL: (01369) 860279
WEBSITE: www.creggans-inn.co.uk
on A185, to N of village

WATERSIDE

The view over Loch Fyne is superb (on a clear day) but, alas, if you choose to eat in the bar of this waterside inn, you cannot enjoy the best of it. You can however enjoy the fruits of the sea (and the loch): say, crab cakes with parsley butter, oysters and smoked salmon from the loch, and breadcrumbed haddock. Meat eaters are not neglected either, with such main courses as grilled lamb cutlets with red onion marmalade and dauphinois potatoes, and there are pasta dishes and sandwiches on offer too, as well as desserts like steamed carrot and ginger sponge. In the evening there's a daily-changing, fixed-price restaurant menu taking in, say, grilled fillets of West Coast sea bass scented with walnut oil, dill and red peppercorns and served with wilted baby spinach, Puy lentils and roast tomato salad, followed by banana and toffee pie. Apart from Maverick, you can also sample other Fyne Ales, such as Highlander and Piper's Gold, as well as Harviestoun Bitter and Twisted, Atlas Brewery's Latitude, and Kelburn's Goldihops, among others. The pub boasts a well-assembled wine list: the full slate runs to around 90 bins majoring on France and the rest of Europe, with a quick round-up from the rest of the world. Six good house wines start at £3.20 a glass or £12.50 a bottle, and there is a fair selection under £15 further up the ladder. Some rather good aperitif sherry is hidden away between the dessert wines and the port at the end of the list. SAMPLE DISHES: Cullen skink £4.50; venison sausages with mash and onion and thyme gravy £6.50; iced nougatine parfait £3.50.

Licensee Alex Robertson (freehouse)

Open 11 (12 Sun) to 11; bar food 12 to 3, 6 to 9, restaurant 7 to 9; closed 25 and 26 Dec

Details Children welcome   Car park   Wheelchair access (also women's WC)   Patio   No smoking in restaurant   Jukebox   Dogs welcome in bar only   Delta, MasterCard, Switch, Visa   Accommodation: 14 rooms, B&B £50 to £140

Wales

Nag's Head Inn 🍺

BREW PUB

Abercych SA37 0HJ TEL: (01239) 841200
2m W of Cenarth, where B4332 crosses River Cych

This pub on the banks of the River Cych has lots of character, from the orange-painted, partly creeper-covered exterior through to the atmospheric interior. There are flagstone floors, a wood-burning stove, an upright piano, large scrubbed-pine tables, beams and an array of international bottled beers on shelves lining the walls – 'a veritable museum for the specialist' – but the inn also brews its own beer (Old Emrys) and offers three weekly-changing guests, perhaps Tomos Watkin Canon's Choice and Fuller's London Pride. Locals drop in for a drink and a chat, while others are here for the generous pub food. There are no surprises, just big platefuls of duck with orange and Cointreau sauce, home-made moussaka, and chilli beef with nachos, with banoffi pie and chocolate junkyard for dessert. The long menu also includes a section for 'light eaters' for the less hungry, but these too can be 'quite a hefty portion'. The wine list is short and simple, consisting of about a dozen bottles, with three by the glass. SAMPLE DISHES: garlic mushrooms £4; sausage and mash with onion gravy £8; apple and caramel pie £3.25.

Licensee Steven Jamieson (freehouse)
Open *11.30 to 3, 6 to 11.30, Sun 11.30 to 11.30; bar food and restaurant 12 to 2, 6 to 9; closed Mon lunchtimes winter*
Details *Children welcome Car park Wheelchair access (not WC) Garden No smoking in restaurant Occasional background music Dogs welcome Delta, MasterCard, Switch, Visa*

▲ Penhelig Arms Hotel 🏆 🍇

Aberdovey LL35 0LT TEL: (01654) 767215
WEBSITE: www.penheligarms.com
on A493 Tywyn to Machynlleth road, opposite Penhelig station

Squeezed between the road and a steep rock, the Penhelig Arms is a smart three-storey terrace hotel, where owners Robert and Sally Hughes have created something special. The hotel looks over the estuary of the River Dovey, and stunning sunsets can be seen from the slate-floored terrace. Within, there's a small, smart, intimate lounge and dining room, and a bar located in a separate section accessed from the road or through the lounge. Known as the Fisherman's Bar, it is divided by an open fire and, by dint of not being modernised in any way, has retained its original character. The food here, mirroring that served in the restaurant, is smart and up to date, with starters such as salmon mousse with a cucumber salad, and wonderfully fresh crab with chicory and apple making quite an impression on an inspector. Tender baked pork loin with coarse-grain mustard and lemon sauce, and a 'prime-quality' whole lemon sole grilled with herb butter followed, with pannacotta with fresh fruit, and warm chocolate and hazelnut cake with vanilla ice cream to finish. Tetley Bitter is the main beer on draught, with Wadworth 6X, Greene King Abbot Ale, Hook Norton Old Hooky, Shepherd Neame Spitfire, or Brains Rev James Original Ale among regularly changing guests. The wine list runs to over 300 bins, and it is worth getting into a lather over: all the world's regions are covered in depth with plenty of famous names, new discoveries, old vintages and half-bottles, all at amazingly good prices whether you care to spend £13 or £40. Some 30 wines come by the glass. SAMPLE DISHES: roast pepper salad with mozzarella £5.50; chargrilled lamb cutlets with red onion chutney and rosemary gravy £10.75; treacle tart £4.

Licensee Robert T. Hughes (freehouse)
Open 11 to 3 (4 summer), 6 (5.30 summer) to 11, Sun 12 to 3 (4 summer) 6 (5.30 summer) to 10.30; bar food 12 to 2.30, 6 to 9.30, restaurant 12 to 2, 7 to 9.30; closed 25 and 26 Dec
Details Children welcome in bar eating area   Car park   Patio   Wheelchair access (also WC)   No-smoking area in bar, no smoking in restaurant   No music   Dogs welcome in bar only   Delta, MasterCard, Switch, Visa Accommodation: 14 rooms, B&B £39 to £98

AFON-WEN Flintshire						map 7

Pwll Gwyn

Denbigh Road, Afon-Wen CH7 5UB   TEL: (01352) 720227
off A541, 10m NW of Mold

Originally a dower house and later a coaching inn, this solid black-and-white-fronted building now functions as a friendly pit stop within handy reach of Offa's Dyke Path. Inside, collections of bric-à-brac, ceiling timbers, settles, and an inglenook in the bar area help to reinforce its pubby image and atmosphere. At lunchtime you can eat omelettes, baguettes, and baps in the bar, while the full menu offers starters like hot minted chicken with mint yoghurt dressing, or deep-fried Brie with port and cranberry dip. Steaks show up strongly among main courses alongside dishes like salmon steak with a basil and garlic breadcrumb topping, or pork Ffion (strips of fillet cooked in white wine, cream and apricot sauce). Finish with something like pancakes served with ice cream and a chocolate brandy sauce. There are also plenty of options for children and junior-sized portions. Tetley Cask, the regular ale, is joined by two guests, which might include Old Speckled Hen, Fuller's London Pride, or Everards Tiger. Six wines are sold by the glass from a modest list. SAMPLE DISHES: Stilton-baked mushrooms with bacon and garlic butter £4.50; lemon pepper cod fillet £8; syrup and pecan nut sponge £3.75.

Licensee Andrew Davies (freehouse)
Open Tue to Sat 12 to 3, 6.30 to 11, Sun 12 to 3, 6.30 to 10.30 (may close earlier in quiet months); bar food and restaurant Tue to Sun 12 to 2, 7 (6 Fri to Sun) to 9
Details Children welcome in eating areas   Car park   Wheelchair access (also WC)   Garden   No smoking in restaurant   Occasional live or background music   No dogs   MasterCard, Switch, Visa

BEAUMARIS   Isle of Anglesey   map 7

▲ Ye Olde Bulls Head Inn ✿

Castle Street, Beaumaris LL58 8AP   TEL: (01248) 810329

Beaumaris is famous for its castle, built by Edward I towards the end of the thirteenth century; it also boasts magnificent views of the Menai Strait and Snowdonia. Within walking distance of the castle is the splendidly historical Olde Bulls Head, where locals mingle convivially with tourists in the dark, cosy bar. Ancient beams, an array of antique weaponry, and an open fire add to the character of the place, and real ales to quaff include Bass, Worthington and Hancock's HB. Visitors wanting to eat should head for the thoroughly modern, conservatory-style brasserie, where there are blond-wood tables, a long zinc-topped bar, and windows and doors overlooking the court-yard. Bookings are not taken in the brasserie, and queues can form quickly at busy times. Order as much or as little as you like from a menu that spans everything from sandwiches and salads to up-beat offerings like genuinely authentic, rough-cut carpaccio with a poached baby pear and rocket, or braised pork with a balsamic glaze, parsnip mash and shiitake mushroom jus. The kitchen also handles fish deftly: witness 'tangy' mackerel escabèche with orange zest and red onions, or fillet of Cornish sea trout on braised leeks in a delicate laverbread sauce. Finish in true Welsh style with bara brith bread-and-butter pudding. The separate restaurant has its own set-price dinner menu. A modest selection of two dozen affordable wines can be found on the back of the brasserie menu, with ten by the glass; the full restaurant list (not available in the brasserie) runs to some 200 bins. SAMPLE DISHES: smoked haddock and fennel chowder £4.75; duck leg confit with ginger, lime and coconut curry £8; pecan pie with walnut ice cream £4.25.

Licensee David Robertson (freehouse)
Open 11 to 11, Sun 12 to 10.30; brasserie 12 to 2, 6 to 9, restaurant Mon to Sat 7 to 9.30; closed 25 and 26 Dec, 1 Jan
Details Children welcome   Car park   Wheelchair access (also WC)   No smoking in lounge and restaurant
Occasional background music   No dogs   Amex, Delta, MasterCard, Switch, Visa   Accommodation: 13 rooms,
B&B £92 to £140

BETWS-Y-COED   Conwy   map 7

▲ Tŷ Gwyn Hotel

Betws-y-coed LL24 0SG   TEL: (01690) 710383
WEBSITE: www.tygwynhotel.co.uk
on southern outskirts of village, at intersection of A5 and A470 by Waterloo Bridge

Built as a coaching inn on the main road from Holyhead to London, this pretty and welcoming pub by the River Conwy continues to serve travellers and locals well. The name means 'white house', which is appropriate, although the building is enshrouded in hanging baskets in summer. Antique furniture, old coffee pots hanging from the ceiling beams, and a plethora of horse brasses give both bars a rustic, traditional look, and the clientele is made up of everyone from walkers and anglers to passing motorists. Bar food, listed on a blackboard, takes in starters of moules marinière, or pheasant terrine with tomato and chive salsa, followed by best end of lamb with roast onion and peppercorn marmalade, Thai-style medallions of fillet steak, or grilled wild salmon with vermouth and basil velouté. There is usually also a decent choice of vegetarian options. Real ales include Tetley Bitter, Brains Rev James Original Ale and Wells Bombardier Premium Bitter, plus a rotating guest, and there's a short and straightforward list of European and New World wines with four by the glass. SAMPLE DISHES: garlic mushroom velouté £4; half a boneless duck char siu £13; chocolate orange truffle crème brûlée with fresh strawberries £3.50.

Licensee James Ratcliffe (freehouse)
Open 11 to 11; bar food and restaurant 11.45 to 2, 6.30 to 9 (9 Apr to Oct); closed Mon to Wed in Jan
Details Children welcome   Car park   Wheelchair access (also WC)   No smoking in restaurant   Background music   No dogs   MasterCard, Switch, Visa   Accommodation: 12 rooms, B&B £20 to £90

CAIO   Carmarthenshire   map 4

▲ Brunant Arms   NEW ENTRY

Caio SA19 8RD   TEL: (01558) 650483
take A482 from Llanwrda on A40; village signposted after about 8m

Caio was an important stopping-off point on the drovers' road to England, but it now seems quiet and 'undisturbed'; in fact, the Brunant Arms is the only surviving pub in this small picturesque village which once boasted five. The inn looks unassuming from the outside, yet it is charming within, with its log fire, old settles, beams and exposed-stone walls. There are three areas, one with a pool table and other games, the others mainly for eating, with a verandah with a Perspex roof at the back opening on to the garden. An extensive menu plays it safe with sandwiches, salads, jacket potatoes and ploughman's, as well as offering a lengthy list of main courses such as drover's pie (minced lamb topped with potato), cod in crispy batter, chilli con carne, and braised lamb shank. Blackboard specials are livelier: say, a hearty portion of white haddock and corn chowder, chicken casseroled with apricots and almonds, and boeuf bourguignonne, but the kitchen sticks with tradition when it comes to desserts, delivering the likes of spotted dick and treacle pudding. To drink, choose one of five varying real ales: Golden Valley from the Breconshire Brewery plus the likes of Wye Valley Supreme, Holden's Gornal Galloper, or guest ales from Woods, Salopian or the Cottage Brewery. The wine list consists of ten bottles, plus two house wines by two sizes of glass (£2.10 and £2.90; £6.95 a bottle) and eight mini-bottles. SAMPLE DISHES: smoked mackerel pâté £4; venison steak with Cumberland sauce £10.50; lemon sorbet cheesecake £3.25.

Licensee Justin Jacobi (freehouse)
Open Mon to Fri 12 to 3, 6 to 11, Sat 12 to 11, Sun 12 to 10.30; bar food 12 to 2, 6.30 to 9; closed Mon lunchtimes Nov to Easter
Details Children welcome   Car park   Garden   Jukebox   No dogs   Delta, MasterCard, Switch, Visa   Accommodation: 4 rooms, B&B £22.50 to £45

CAPEL CURIG   Conwy   map 7

▲ Bryn Tyrch Hotel

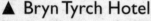

Capel Curig LL24 0EL   TEL: (01690) 720223
on A5, 5m W of Betwys-y-coed

The large bar at this old roadside inn has big sofas on plank flooring, a welcoming open fire, and stained glass over the bar counter that looks as if it was salvaged from a disused chapel, and the pews could have come from the same source. There's also a lounge area near the reception and a small dining area before the main bar, off which is a poolroom and another room for drinking and eating. The hotel takes great pride in its vegetarian and vegan cooking, including, perhaps, curried parsnip soup, followed by vegetable lasagne served with garlic bread and salad, or aduki bean and vegetable cottage pie. Otherwise the large chalkboard over the fire might offer smoked trout fillet with horseradish cream, pan-fried Welsh lamb's liver with lemon butter sauce, or pan-fried breast of pheasant with apple and cider sauce. Portions are hearty, but lovers of desserts could go for treacle tart (vegan) or sticky toffee pudding. Lunchtimes see a more snacky menu of ploughman's, burgers, salads, and Welsh rarebit. Bass, Castle Eden Ale and Flowers IPA lend pedigree to the drinking options, as does the well-chosen wine list of around 20 bottles, with 15 served by the glass. Large windows make the most of the views to Snowdonia, and there's plenty of room outside for al fresco eating and drinking. SAMPLE DISHES: vegetable samosa £4.50; lamb and leek sausages with port and redcurrant gravy £8.75; bread-and-butter pudding £4.25.

Licensee Rita Davis (freehouse)
Open 12 to 11.30; bar food and restaurant 12 to 9.30; closed Christmas; may close Mon to Thurs lunchtimes winter
Details Children welcome   Car park   Garden   No-smoking area in bar, no smoking in restaurant Occasional background music   No dogs   MasterCard, Switch, Visa   Accommodation: 16 rooms, B&B £39 to £41

CARDIFF   Cardiff   map 4

Y Mochyn Du   NEW ENTRY

Sophia Close, off Cathedral Road, Cardiff CF11 9HW   TEL: (029) 2037 1599

Originally the lodge at the entrance to Sophia Gardens and Bute Park – 'Cardiff's big central green lung' – the Mochyn Du (Black Pig) is a Victorian stone and half-timbered 'gingerbread house' set in woods with a conservatory-style extension and a large beer garden for warmer weather. The refurbished interior – wooden strip floor, upholstered benches and alcoves in the bar, carpet, partitions, dark wooden tables and chairs in the restaurant – has a corporate look that belies the individual menu backed up by blackboard specials and a Welsh atmosphere ('Welsh being the vernacular of many'). The kitchen is capable of producing some 'comforting, freshly made food', observed a couple who sampled cawl (a traditional lamb and vegetable broth), Celtic hotpot of chicken and dumplings, and fillet steak topped with local Y Fenni cheese sauce. Otherwise there could be burgers made from locally sourced beef, Felinfoel faggots with mushy peas, speciality pies, such as chicken and leek or steak, ale and mushroom, and lunchtime sandwiches and jacket potatoes. Real ales include Flowers Original, Bass, Brains Rev James Original Ale and Bitter, plus a seasonal guest, and six wines are available by the glass. SAMPLE DISHES: prawn platter £3.50; baked barbecue chicken £7; apple and blackcurrant crumble £3.50.

Licensee Gareth Hughes (freehouse)
Open 12 to 11; bar food and restaurant 12 to 3, 6 to 8.45, Sun 12 to 3; closed 26 Dec
Details Children welcome   Car park   Wheelchair access (also WC)   Garden   No-smoking areas in restaurant   Background and occasional live music   Guide dogs only   MasterCard, Switch, Visa

Waterguard NEW ENTRY

Harbour Drive, Cardiff Bay CF10 4PA   TEL: (029) 2049 9034
overlooking Cardiff Bay, beyond Pierhead Building towards Norwegian Church

An architectural curiosity ('like a mini castle or folly'), combining Victorian original with contemporary, the Waterguard is in a stunning location on the edge of Cardiff Bay. The former pilot's house was moved from its original site 'lock, stock and barrel' 100 or so yards towards the waterfront, and you enter through the 'small Tardis-like Victorian end' of dark brown walls, stained-glass window, and old prints on the walls. This opens into a bright space with a pale flagged floor, aluminium supports, windows looking on to the bay, modern leather club chairs, and high bar tables and stools to match. The menu also has an up-to-date feel, with things like Mediterranean garlic toast – focaccia with peppers, courgettes, mushrooms and melted mozzarella – and lamb with mint yoghurt and potato wedges. But more traditional dishes are also found, ranging from fish 'n' chips with mushy peas to sausage and mash. Moules marinière and Greek salad could turn up among starters, with banana split a typical dessert. There are beers from Samuel Smith, Ayingerbrau lagers, and a good range of specialist bottled beers. SAMPLE DISHES: nachos £2.95; pan-fried rainbow trout £7.50; chocolate dream £3.

Licensee John Clarke
Open *12 to 11, Sun 12 to 10.30; bar food 12 to 2.30, 6.30 to 9.30*
Details *No children   Wheelchair access (also WC)   Patio   No smoking in 1 room   Background music
Dogs welcome   Delta, MasterCard, Switch, Visa*

CAREW   Pembrokeshire   map 4

Carew Inn

Carew SA70 8SL   TEL: (01646) 651267

The imposing remains of Carew Castle and an eleventh-century Celtic cross stand immediately opposite this old stone pub, and a working tidal mill – the only one in Wales – is nearby. Inside the inn is a beamed public bar – with prints and a dartboard – where locals gather for a drink, although the rest of the place is given over to eating. The two cosy and old-fashioned dining areas on the ground floor have coal-effect gas fires, jugs on a high shelf and hunting prints, and there's a separate restaurant upstairs; the same menu applies throughout. The 'Favourites' section of the menu is just that: steak and kidney pie, scampi, and roast beef salad among them. The rest is a mixture of traditional, Continental and far-flung ideas, with starters as diverse as stuffed mushrooms, goats' cheese crostini, and nachos grande. Main courses continue the format, taking in seafood pancakes, chicken breast stuffed with sun-dried tomatoes and cream cheese wrapped in bacon, and Mexican spicy pork in a tortilla. Desserts range from jam roly-poly to rich chocolate pudding. Worthington Best Bitter and Brains Rev James are on draught, and three wines are available by the glass from a short list. SAMPLE DISHES: chicken liver and tarragon pâté £4; leg of lamb with rich minted gravy £11; sticky ginger pudding with ginger wine and brandy sauce £4.

Licensee Mandy Hinchliffe (freehouse)
Open *summer 11 to 11 (10.30 Sun), winter 11 to 2.30, 4.30 to 11 (10.30 Sun); bar food and restaurant summer 12 to 2.30, 5.30 to 9.30, winter 12 to 2, 6 to 9; closed 25 Dec*
Details *Children welcome in eating areas   Car park   Garden   No smoking in restaurant   Live or background music   Dogs welcome in public bar only   MasterCard, Switch, Visa*

CLYTHA   Monmouthshire   map 2

▲ Clytha Arms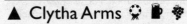

Clytha NP7 9BW   TEL: (01873) 840206
WEBSITE: www.clytha-arms.com
off old Abergavenny to Raglan road, S of A40, 6m E of Abergavenny

The rural aspect of this former dower house – in its own grounds on top of a wooded hill – is matched by the rural style of the décor within. The main bar has an old-fashioned wood-burning stove, pews of stripped wood, and old posters on the walls, while in the lively public bar locals play darts and other pub games and enjoy excellent beers. These include Felinfoel Double Dragon, Wychwood Hobgoblin, Boddingtons Bitter and draught Bass; and there's Old Rosie cider, and a good choice of malts, cognacs and Calvados. In the restaurant, blackboard specials, mostly fish, shellfish and game, supplement the à la carte and set-price menus, where you could find pork and mushroom faggots followed by duck breast with parsnip and orange brûlée. There are good things also on the bar menu, with its sandwiches and more substantial dishes such as cider-baked ham and warm potato salad, or bacon, laverbread and cockles, and liver, bacon and onions; note that customers in the bar can choose off the restaurant menu if they wish. The list of about 100 wines, plus a good number of half-bottles, travels the world and caters for all budgets at each destination. Trophy wines like Cloudy Bay and Tignanello top the range, but a lot of effort has gone into the under-£15 selection, which even includes two Welsh wines. It's just £2.20 for a glass of house wine (£11.95 for a bottle), and there are ten good ones to choose from. SAMPLE DISHES: mixed grilled shellfish £8.25; roast woodcock with wild mushrooms £16.25; chargrilled pineapple with coconut sorbet £5.

Licensee Andrew Canning (freehouse)
Open *Mon 6 to 11, Tue to Fri 12 to 3 (4 summer), 6 to 11, Sat 12 to 11, Sun 12 to 10.30; bar food and restaurant Tue to Sat (and restaurant Sun) 12.30 to 2.30, Tue to Sat 7 to 9; closed 25 Dec, open bank hol Mons*
Details *Children welcome   Car park   Wheelchair access (not WC)   Garden and patio   No smoking in 1 room and restaurant   Occasional live music   No dogs   Amex, Delta, Diners, MasterCard, Switch, Visa   Accommodation: 4 rooms, B&B £50 to £90*

CRICKHOWELL   Powys   map 4

▲ Bear Hotel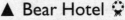

High Street, Crickhowell NP8 1BW   TEL: (01873) 810408
WEBSITE: www.bearhotel.com

Although dating from the fifteenth century, the Bear presents a cheerful Georgian front, its portico and arched entrance to an inner courtyard particularly attractive in summer when covered in flowers. Within, old furniture, country artefacts and ancient memorabilia abound. This is an immensely popular venue, either as a pub (it has three separate bars) for drinking and bar snacks, as a hotel (with rooms around the inner courtyard) and as a smart restaurant. Baguettes and sandwiches are a welcome proposition at lunchtime; otherwise the menus in the bar/bistro deal in comfort food and country cooking, running to, say, starters of leek and potato soup, or Welsh rarebit of Lancashire farmhouse and soft blue cheeses. Follow with cottage pie with bubble and squeak topping, or rump of beef braised with vegetables and potatoes in

Guinness, then try squeezing in bread-and-butter pudding made with rum and bananas, or rich sticky toffee pudding with butterscotch sauce. The restaurant moves up a gear, offering goujons of John Dory in tempura with a spicy lime and coriander dip, and pan-roast wild duck with fondant potato and spiced orange sauce. Bass, Old Speckled Hen, Brains Rev James Original Ale and Hancock's HB are on handpump. Good value is to be found on a wine list arranged by grape variety, with many available by the glass. SAMPLE DISHES: chicken livers pan-fried in wine with onions, garlic and sage £5.75; stuffed lambs' hearts braised with black pudding, vegetables and potatoes in red wine £9.50; poached pear and lemon délices £5.

Licensee J.L. Hindmarsh (freehouse)
Open 10 to 3, 6 to 11, Sun 11 to 3, 7 to 10.30; bar food 12 to 2, 7 to 9.30, restaurant Sun 12 to 2, Tue to Sat 7 to 9.30
Details Children welcome in bar eating area Car park Wheelchair access (also WC) Garden and patio No-smoking area in bar No music Dogs welcome exc in restaurant Amex, Delta, MasterCard, Switch, Visa Accommodation: 34 rooms, B&B £57 to £140

▲ Nantyffin Cider Mill Inn ✿ ❦

Brecon Road, Crickhowell NP8 1SG   TEL: (01873) 810775
WEBSITE: www.cidermill.co.uk
1½m W of Crickhowell at junction of A40 and A479

Sean Gerrard and Glyn Bridgeman are now in their thirteenth year of running Nantyffin Cider Mill, an atmospheric sixteenth-century country pub (at one time a drovers' inn) in some of the best walking country in South Wales. The kitchen remains as passionate about local flavours and good home cooking as ever, with the proprietors' own farm providing much of the organic, free-range meat. This policy may translate into a starter of home-reared confit duck with a cassoulet of haricot beans, tomatoes, garlic and pancetta, and main courses of roast suprême of Glanusk pheasant with confit leg and cranberry filling, or roast suprême of home-reared chicken with potato and cep broth. Fish and shellfish may appear among the daily specials: perhaps seared king scallops with a casserole of Puy lentils, coriander, tomatoes, cider and leeks, followed by seared sea bass with roast pepper and tomato compote, smoky chorizo dressing and rösti. The Drover Menu, a cheaper set-price deal from Monday to Thursday, could offer pasta ribbons with chorizo, followed by navarin of lamb with winter root vegetables and creamed mash, then poached winter fruits meringue. Welsh beers from Tomos Watkin, Brains, and Felinfoel continue to be popular, served alongside Wadworth 6X and Marston's Pedigree; Thatcher's Dry, Addlestone's, and Weston's Old Rosie ciders are also on draught. An excellent new wine list is full of interesting bottles and sets everything out with admirable clarity, although just four come by the glass. Prices quickly pass £15 but are fair for the quality. SAMPLE DISHES: warm black pudding salad with sautéed potatoes and bacon £5.50; confit of home-reared lamb with rosemary and garlic sauce £12; pears poached in red wine with orange mascarpone cream £5.

Licensees Sean Gerrard and Glyn Bridgeman (freehouse)
Open 12 to 2 (2.30 summer), 6.30 to 10.30 (6 to 11 summer); bar food and restaurant 12 to 2.30, 6.30 to 9.30; closed Sun evening winter, 1 week Jan
Details Children welcome Car park Wheelchair access (also WC) Garden No smoking in restaurant No music Dogs welcome in bar only Amex, Delta, MasterCard, Switch, Visa Accommodation: 23 rooms, B&B £45 to £100

CWMDU Powys
map 4

▲ Farmers Arms

Cwmdu NP8 1RU TEL: (01874) 730464
WEBSITE: www.thefarmersarms.com
on A479, 4m NW of Crickhowell

At first glance the white-painted pub on a corner in the centre of the village doesn't look that large, but it extends quite a way back to a steeply rising hillside, and the garden to the side is terraced. Most of the interior is given over to a large, rather formal and old-fashioned dining area, with red chesterfield-style wall seats and vintage family photographs, although there's also a bar with a wood-burning stove and an upright piano. The restaurant menu, also available in the bar, offers some ambitious dishes and makes resourceful use of local produce, although the repertoire is fairly limited and changes infrequently. Starters may include winter vegetable broth, or chicken, apple and asparagus strudel with a light tarragon cream. For main courses there might be fillet of sea bass baked in foil with lime and tarragon and served with courgette spaghetti and tomato and tarragon coulis, as well as various grilled steaks with a choice of traditional béarnaise sauce, or peppercorn, cream and brandy. Half a dozen desserts could include passion-fruit and mallow torte, or lemon cheesecake. Handpumped real ales might include Old Speckled Hen, Shepherd Neame Spitfire Premium Ale or Uley Pig's Ear, and the wine list – short and to the point, with four sold by the glass – majors in New World and Spanish bottles. SAMPLE DISHES: Glamorgan sausages with tomato sauce £5.25; poached escalope of wild salmon on laverbread mash with a red lentil and crab bisque £12; tower of meringue, banana and toffee £4.25.

Licensees Andrew and Susan Lawrence (freehouse)
Open *12 to 3 (4 Sat), 6.30 to 11, Sun 12 to 4, 7 to 10.30; bar food 12 to 2.15 (2.30 Sun), restaurant Tue to Sun 12 to 2.15 (2.30 Sun), 7 to 9.30; closed 2 weeks Oct to Nov, 2 weeks Jan to Feb; phone to check weekday lunchtime openings Oct to Feb*
Details *Children welcome Car park Garden No smoking in restaurant Background music Dogs welcome in bar area only Delta, MasterCard, Switch, Visa Accommodation: 2 rooms, B&B £20 to £45*

FELINFACH Powys
map 4

▲ Felin Fach Griffin ✿

Felinfach LD3 0UB TEL: (01874) 620111
WEBSITE: www.eatdrinksleep.ltd.uk
on A470, 4½m N of Brecon

This large, foursquare stone and brick building in splendid isolation in the middle of the Powys countryside is ideally placed for visitors wishing to explore the Brecon Beacons and Black Mountains. It has a relaxed and informal atmosphere throughout its various rooms, where natural bare materials are to the fore: rough old oak floors, solid beams, bare stone fireplaces, and smart photos and prints on the walls. There are some 'luxurious' leather sofas for sinking into with a pint of good Welsh ale from Tomos Watkin in Swansea, although the emphasis is firmly on the food, with a frequently changing menu somewhat removed from ploughman's and jacket potatoes. Expect expansive modern cooking, full of bright ideas like pan-fried scallops with asparagus and black pepper butter, or terrine of foie gras and gammon knuckle.

There is room for more traditional options among main courses, such as local venison with braised red cabbage and dauphinois potatoes, but you are just as likely to encounter rump of Welsh lamb with lentils, chorizo and colcannon. Wines number around 40, a large proportion being from the New World, with prices starting at £10.95 for the eight wines that are also served by the glass. SAMPLE DISHES: boudin noir with caramelised apple and balsamic reduction £5.50; plaice with roasted asparagus, ceps and parsley oil £14.50; rice pudding with caramelised pear £5.50.

Licensee Charles Inkin (freehouse)
Open 12 to 3, 6 to 11 (10.30 Sun); bar food and restaurant 12.30 to 2.30, 7 to 9.30 (9 Sun); closed Mon lunchtimes exc bank hols, Christmas, end Jan to first week Feb
Details Children welcome   Car park   Wheelchair access (also WC)   Garden   No smoking in restaurant
Occasional live or background music   Dogs welcome   Delta, MasterCard, Switch, Visa   Accommodation: 7 rooms, B&B £60 to £115

GLANWYDDEN   Conwy   map 7

Queen's Head 🏵

Glanwydden LL31 9JP   TEL: (01492) 546570
just off B5115 Colwyn Bay to Llandudno road

This plain, whitewashed pub is pristine both inside and out, the wooden bar counter, stained-glass panel, flagstone floor and deep lounge seating enhancing the atmosphere of a real village local. The pub is also the setting for some good food. The menu changes monthly and offers similar choice at lunch and dinner, although open sandwiches served at lunchtime are replaced in the evening by grills and steaks. Among hot and cold starters might be smoked goose breast with peach and apple chutney, or grilled goats' cheese and onion tart with roasted vine tomatoes and basil oil. The rest of the menu is divided into pastas and salads (mushroom ravioli with fresh tomato sauce, rocket and Parmesan shavings), and hearty mains of, say, Welsh lamb shank with Moroccan spices. Fish, listed separately, is something of a speciality: grilled fillet of sea bass with wilted spinach, Thai butter and new potatoes, or Manx queen scallops with Penbryn cheese. The list of home-made desserts runs to around half a dozen each of hot and cold options: cherry Bakewell tart among the former, baked chocolate pots among the latter. To drink, choose from Tetley Bitter and Burton Ales, or guests Greene King Abbot Ale, Old Speckled Hen and Marston's Pedigree, or go for one of the eight wines sold by the glass from a list of about 50 bottles. A self-catering cottage is available to let. SAMPLE DISHES: grilled goats' cheese and onion tart £5.75; baked fillet of crusty cod with crushed potatoes and pea mash £10.50; coffee and walnut fudge pie £4.

Licensee Robert Cureton (freehouse)
Open 11.30 to 3, 6 to 11 (10.30 Mon), Sun 11.30 to 11; bar food 11.45 to 2.15, 6 to 9, Sun 11.45 to 9; closed 25 Dec
Details No children under 7   Car park   Patio   No-smoking area   Background music   Guide dogs only
Delta, MasterCard, Switch, Visa

Report forms are at the back of the book; write a letter if you prefer; or email your pub report to whichpubguide@which.net.

GRESFORD   Wrexham   map 7

Pant-yr-Ochain 🍺

Old Wrexham Road, Gresford LL12 8TY   TEL: (01978) 853525
WEBSITE: www.brunningandprice.co.uk
take Gresford turning off A483 Wrexham bypass

Quietly set in its own grounds and 'not very well signed' – look for a worn gallows sign at the entrance to the long drive – this fine old Dutch-gabled house has made a successful conversion into a first-class dining pub. A veritable warren of rooms overflowing with nostalgic memorabilia creates an atmosphere of baronial splendour, but there is plenty of scope for simply popping in for a pint of real ale. And what a choice, with Flowers Original, Timothy Taylor Landlord and Drawwell Bitter from Hanby brewery in Shropshire joined by guests such as Phoenix Arizona and Weetwood Old Dog Bitter, and there are around 60 malt whiskies. But imaginative and serious pub food is what sets this place apart. The menu ranges far and wide, taking in leek and Shropshire Blue risotto with a red pepper dressing, followed by a 'seriously large' braised shoulder of lamb with mustard mash, roasted carrots and rich roast garlic and mint gravy, or fillet of red bream with creamed Savoy cabbage, fondant potato, and plum tomato and red pepper sauce. Lighter dishes run to open sandwiches of hot pork with tarragon mustard, or brie with celery, grape salad and walnut dressing. Puddings include sticky toffee roulade with butterscotch sauce, and white chocolate torte with dark chocolate sauce. The wine list, arranged by grape variety, has 15 by the glass, with bottle prices starting at about £10.50 for house wines. SAMPLE DISHES: terrine of slow roasted chicken and peppers with fruit chutney £4.75; braised boneless blade of pork with roast garlic and sage risotto, green beans and cider and mustard sauce £11.25; Morello cherry and frangipane tart with berry compote £4.25.

Licensee Lindsey Prole (freehouse)
Open *12 to 11 (10.30 Sun); bar food 12 to 9.30 (9 Sun)*
Details. *Children welcome before 6pm   Car park   Wheelchair access (also WC)   Garden and patio*
No smoking in 2 rooms   Occasional live music   No dogs   Amex, Delta, MasterCard, Switch, Visa

HAY-ON-WYE   Powys   map 4

▲ Old Black Lion

26 Lion Street, Hay-on-Wye HR3 5AD   TEL: (01497) 820841
WEBSITE: www.oldblacklion.co.uk

The Old Black Lion stands close to the site of the Lion Gate, one of the original entrances to the old walled town of Hay-on-Wye, and is an historical gem. The building dates from the fourteenth century, although it wasn't licensed until the seventeenth century, and is said to have housed Oliver Cromwell when the Roundheads besieged loyalist Hay Castle. Choose to eat in the 'totally traditional' oak-timbered bar or the restaurant, which overlooks the garden terrace. In the former you might enjoy beef and ale pie with cabbage mash, spicy venison meatballs in a rich tomato sauce with linguine, or whole grilled plaice with herb butter and chips. In the restaurant, a more extensive choice takes in starters such as goats' cheese and sun-blush tomato tart with red pepper dressing, or fillets of smoked eel in cream, spinach and garlic served on tomato toast, with main courses ranging from breast of mallard and confit leg with parsnip mash and cranberry and orange sauce to fillet of salmon in puff pastry with watercress and leeks and a chive butter sauce. Desserts might include Baileys bread-and-butter pudding, or citrus tart. The restaurant menu is available in the bar and vice versa. Dorothy Goodbody's Golden Ale and Old Black Lion Ale, from the Wye Valley Brewery, are the beers on offer, and the commendable wine list delves about in Europe and the New World to produce some tempting bottles. Six are available by the glass. Hay-on-Wye claims to be the largest second-hand book centre in the world and also hosts the famous annual literary festival. SAMPLE DISHES: celeriac, fennel and rosemary soup £4.25; pot-roast partridge in juniper and port sauce £14; warm walnut and treacle tart £4.25.

Licensee Vanessa King (Simply Inns Ltd)
Open 11 to 11, Sun 12 to 10.30; bar food and restaurant 12 to 2.30, 6.30 to 9.30; closed 25 and 26 Dec
Details Children over 5 welcome in eating areas   Car park   Patio   No smoking in restaurant   No music
No dogs   Delta, MasterCard, Switch, Visa   Accommodation: 10 rooms, B&B £42.50 to £110

HENDRERWYDD   Denbighshire   map 7

White Horse Inn 😊 NEW ENTRY

Hendrerwydd LL16 4LL   TEL: (01824) 790218
WEBSITE: www.white-horse-inn.co.uk
signposted off B5429 between Llandyrnog and Llanbedr, 5m SE of Denbigh

This whitewashed building with small-paned windows and flower-filled tubs on its forecourt is set amid the Arcadian splendour of the Vale of Clwyd, with the heather- and bilberry-clad hills of the Clwydian Range rising steeply in the distance. Built in the seventeenth century to serve drovers, it is now an upmarket dining-pub-cum-restaurant. The main dining area features displays of decorative plates, modern sculptures and textile renditions of classical frescoes. Tables in here and several smaller adjacent rooms are set for eating, except for a small area next to an open fireplace, but there is also the traditional Poacher's Bar, which is popular with walkers and has quarry-tiled floors, another open fire and walls hung with fishing paraphernalia. The bar snacks menu offers a fairly typical range of pub fare, while the separate main menu shows an awareness of culinary fashions with dishes such as Conwy mussels in a Thai-style sauce, platters of Spanish cured meats with rocket and Parmesan, roast Barbary duck breast on raspberry, vodka and balsamic sauce, or slow-cooked marinated shoulder of Welsh lamb with spicy harissa sauce. Two weekly-changing real ales are kept, along with approximately 50 malt whiskies and seven house wines by the glass from a varied global list of around 40 bottles. SAMPLE DISHES: duck liver mousse £7; garlic and thyme poussin £12; Eton mess £4.

Licensees Ruth and Vit Vintr (freehouse)
Open 11 to 11, Sun 12 to 10.30; bar food and restaurant 12 to 2.30, 6 to 9.15 (8.30 Sun)
Details Children welcome   Car park   Wheelchair access (also WC)   Patio   No smoking in restaurant
No music   Dogs welcome in snug bar only   Delta, MasterCard, Switch, Visa

LAMPHEY   Pembrokeshire   map 4

▲ Dial Inn

Ridgeway Road, Lamphey SA71 5NU   TEL: (01646) 672426
just off A4139 Tenby to Pembroke road

Now a cheerful, down-to-earth village pub without any fancy pretensions, the Dial Inn was at one time the dower house of Lamphey Court. It looks deceptively small and cottagey from the outside, but inside is a warren of linked rooms that feel surprisingly spacious. The main bar is to the front, while eating takes place in the large dining room to the rear, but in both areas the atmosphere is informal and friendly. Honest, straightforward cooking is served throughout in generous portions, and the kitchen places an admirable emphasis on local produce. Start perhaps with garlic mushrooms in puff pastry, or a duet of smoked duck and chicken, before moving on to prime Welsh fillet steak in whisky cream sauce, or cannon of Welsh lamb sautéed and flamed in port and served with cranberry and orange compote and parsley mash. A short bar menu offers further choice in the shape of simple fish and meat dishes, curries and pasta. Real ales include Worthington 1744 and draught Bass, and most of the wines on the short list are under £13, including house wines at £8.25. Six wines are served by the glass. SAMPLE DISHES: salmon and crab cakes with marie-rose dip £5.25; Gressingham duck breast with Cointreau and orange sauce £14; lemon sponge pudding £4.25.

Licensees Granville and Ruth Hill (freehouse)
Open 11 to 12, Sun 12 to 4, 7 to 11; bar food and restaurant 12 to 2.30, 6 to 9.30
Details Children welcome   Car park   Wheelchair access (also WC)   Patio   No smoking in restaurant   Background music   No dogs   Delta, Diners, MasterCard, Switch, Visa   Accommodation: 6 rooms, B&B £25 to £50

LITTLE HAVEN   **Pembrokeshire**   **map 4**

▲ Castle

1 Grove Place, Little Haven SA62 3UF   TEL: (01437) 781445
WEBSITE: www.castlelittlehaven.co.uk
off B4341, 6m W of Haverfordwest

Directly opposite the glorious beach of one of Pembrokeshire's most attractive (and smallest) resorts, the Castle is a lively and traditional family pub with an informal atmosphere. There are tables outside, while the interior is all flagged floors and exposed-stone walls hung with prints of maps, local shipwrecks and advertisements offering emigrants passage to America. Drinkers head for the two bars, where Worthington, Bass, Brains SA, and Tomos Watkin are on draught; there's also a pool-room and a restaurant that operates at night. The standard evening menu takes in old favourites like prawn cocktail, ribeye steak, and a pie of the day, but it pays dividends to consult the specials board. Here you will find plenty of fish in the shape of, say, baked cod with a savoury breadcrumb crust or grilled salmon fillet with champagne sauce alongside escalope of Welsh lamb filled with Caerphilly cheese and leeks. Desserts might be tiramisù or apple and blackberry crumble. Lunch is a simpler affair focusing on sandwiches, ploughman's, burgers, and scampi. The bargain hunter's wine list kicks off with house selections at £2.10 a glass, £8 a bottle. SAMPLE DISHES: smoked salmon pâté £4; chicken schnitzel with orange and sherry sauce £8.25; bread-and-butter pudding £3.25.

Licensees Mr and Mrs A.M. Whitewright (Celtic Inns)
Open 12 to 2.30, 6 to 11 (11 to 11 summer); bar food 12 to 2, 6.30 to 8.30, restaurant Thur to Sat (all week summer) 6.30 to 8.30
Details Children welcome in bar eating area until 9pm   Wheelchair access (also WC)   Patio   No smoking in restaurant   Jukebox   Dogs welcome on a lead   Delta, MasterCard, Switch, Visa   Accommodation: 2 rooms, B&B £60

Swan Inn `NEW ENTRY`

Point Road, Little Haven SA62 3UL   TEL: (01437) 781256

You can't get a better, or more picturesque, seaside location than this unspoilt little pub that's perched on a rocky vantage point overlooking a small beach. The front door leads straight into the bar, which has tiny rooms on either side, and there's a small, homely restaurant. Most of the interior walls are of rough grey stone hung with brass and copper trays, old photographs, watercolours, drawings and large maps, tables are well-worn dark wood, and the atmosphere is friendly and welcoming. The bar menu offers a decent choice of simple dishes, makes good use of seasonal raw materials and provides a distinctly local flavour with the likes of locally caught crab and other seafood, locally made cheese, and Pembrokeshire ham. Starters include 'absolutely top-notch' cawl, a traditional Welsh lamb and vegetable soup packed with tender meat and diced vegetables, or a generous portion of rich chicken liver pâté, while mains might include crab bake or chicken korma. In the restaurant, main courses range from grilled Dover sole to roast rack of Welsh lamb, or fillet of beef with a choice of sauces. Brains Rev James Original Ale, Worthington Best Bitter and guests such as Timothy Taylor Landlord, Hook Norton Old Hooky, Shepherd Neame Spitfire and Greene King Abbot Ale are on handpump, and three wines are served by the glass from a list of some 20 good-value Old and New World bottles. SAMPLE DISHES: smoked mackerel pâté £5; roast breast of duck with cherry and cinnamon sauce £14; Irish coffee-flavoured meringue £2.75.

Licensees Glyn and Beryl Davies (freehouse)
Open 11.30 to 3 (2.30 winter), 6 (7 winter) to 11, Sun 12 to 3, 7 to 10.30; bar food 12 to 1.45, restaurant Wed to Sat 7 to 9
Details No children   Garden   No smoking in restaurant   Background music   Dogs welcome on a lead No cards

LLANARMON DYFFRYN CEIRIOG   Wrexham   map 7

▲ West Arms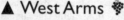

Llanarmon Dyffryn Ceiriog LL20 7LD   TEL: (01691) 600665
WEBSITE: www.thewestarms.co.uk
off A5 Llangollen to Oswestry road at Chirk, then follow B4500 for 11m

The pretty Ceiriog Valley is a remote spot, and the West Arms must appear as welcoming to today's walkers and tourists as it did to cattle drovers in the past. It dates from the late seventeenth century, its age evident in the low beams, slate floors, massive inglenooks and blackened beams that give the bar its character. The menus in here have some enterprising touches: Ceiriog fishcakes flavoured with a blend of spices and served with watercress mayonnaise, home-made lamb burgers containing sun-dried tomatoes, basil, pine nuts and Parmesan with a red wine sauce, and something like filo-wrapped feta and celeriac mousse with steamed vegetables among vegetarian options. A wide choice of sandwiches, toasted or plain, is also available, with a couple of children's main courses. The separate restaurant has its own two- or three-course set-price menu following a more upmarket route along the lines of grilled fillets of wild turbot and lemon sole with crabmeat and laverbread sauce, and steamed plum pudding with brandy butter to finish. Alongside Whitbread Trophy, Boddingtons Bitter and Flowers IPA is an extensive wine list that offers affordable examples of traditional classics like claret and Burgundy alongside innovative wines from Spain and Italy and a respectable showing from the New World. Only three or four are available by the glass. SAMPLE DISHES: terrine of smoked salmon £7; local Welsh black beef sirloin steak pan-fried in garlic with tomatoes and mushrooms £15; crème brûlée £4.25.

Licensee Geoff Leigh-Ford (freehouse)
Open 8am to 11pm; bar food 12 to 2, 7 to 9, restaurant all week 7 to 9, Sun 12 to 2
Details Children welcome   Car park   Wheelchair access (also WC)   Garden   No smoking in restaurant   Background music   Dogs welcome exc in restaurant   Delta, MasterCard, Switch, Visa   Accommodation: 15 rooms, B&B £52.50 to £174

LLANDENNY   Monmouthshire   map 2

Raglan Arms   [NEW ENTRY]

Llandenny NP15 1DL   TEL: (01291) 690800
off A449 between Usk and Raglan

Llandenny, deep in farming country, once sported three pubs, but the stone-built Raglan Arms is the sole survivor. Inside is a spacious lounge area 'not unlike a country-house drawing room', with settees around a huge open fireplace, plus stone pigs and even baskets of chestnuts in winter adding to the cosy feel of the place. Elsewhere there are country-style tables and a conservatory extension opening on to a decked patio. The menus change daily, and the focus is on blackboard specials. Fish is particularly well handled: an inspector thought mussels with leeks, black pepper and cream worthy of singling out, while a generous piscine mixed grill comes loaded with accurately cooked morsels. Away from the sea, you might find grilled goats' cheese with speck, wild boar with black pudding and mustard sauce, or vegetable tortelloni with tomato and olive salsa. Bringing up the rear are homely desserts like apple and oatflake crumble. Real ales such as Wye Valley Bitter and Felinfoel Double Dragon vary from week to week, and the workmanlike list of around 20 wines is a reasonably priced selection from around the globe. SAMPLE DISHES: duck rillettes with spiced apple chutney £4.50; whole sea bass with lemon butter £9.50; chocolate pot £4.50.

Licensees Ian and Carol Black (freehouse)
Open Tue to Sat 12 to 3, 7 to 11, Sun 12 to 3; bar food Tue to Sat 12 to 2, 7 to 9, Sun 12 to 2
Details Children welcome in eating area before 8pm   Car park   Garden and patio   No smoking in eating area   No music   Dogs welcome   Delta, Diners, MasterCard, Switch, Visa

LLANDWROG   Gwynedd   map 7

▲ Harp Inn 🍺

Ty'n Llan, Llandwrog LL54 5SY   TEL: (01286) 831071
WEBSITE: www.welcome.to/theharp
off A499, 5m SW of Caernarfon

In the middle of the village, opposite the church, this stone Georgian building looks every inch a 'down-to-earth village pub' and is undoubtedly an asset to the community. Locals and passers-by (among them energetic types attracted to the walks and climbs around Snowdonia and cyclists on the cycle path from Holyhead to London) mingle happily in the comfortable and cheerful bar or try their luck at shove-halfpenny or pool in the games room. A printed bar menu is supplemented by blackboard specials and takes in the likes of local bangers with onion potato cakes and gravy, beef and beer pie, curries, and battered cod with chips and peas. Up to nine real ales and ciders are kept in tip-top condition, with names from near and far including Bass, Plassey Bitter, Black Sheep and Wyre Piddle. Added to these are around 30 malt whiskies (including a contingent from Islay). Just eight wines are offered, all £10 per bottle and £2.50 or £3.50 by the glass. SAMPLE DISHES: salmon and dill fishcakes £5; lamb shank with redcurrant gravy £8; raspberry pavlova £3.50.

Licensee Colin Downie (freehouse)
Open Tue to Fri 12 to 2, 6 to 11, Sat 12 to 11, Sun 12 to 3; July and Aug Mon 6 to 11, Tue to Sun 12 to 11; bar food Tue to Sat 12 to 2, 6.30 to 8.30 (9 summer); also open bank hol Mon 12 to 11 and Sun July and Aug 6.30 to 9
Details Children welcome in eating areas and games room   Car park   Wheelchair access (also WC) Garden and patio   No smoking in restaurant   Background music   Dogs welcome on a lead in bar   Delta, MasterCard, Switch, Visa   Accommodation: 4 rooms, B&B £20 to £50

LLANFERRES   Denbighshire   map 7

▲ Druid Inn   NEW ENTRY

Ruthin Road, Llanferres CH7 5SN   TEL: (01352) 810225
WEBSITE: www.loggerheads.biz.co.uk
on A494 between Mold and Ruthin

Parts of the Druid date from the seventeenth century, and its farmhouse origins are clearly to be seen in the cavernous flagged hallway and the fine old ceiling beams and great stone fireplace in the lengthy, split-level bar. Horse brasses, watercolours and old pub memorabilia form the decoration, and there's a great pub atmosphere that comes through in a pleasant mix of local drinkers and longer-distance diners, with dogs and children clearly welcome. Food, chalked on one long blackboard in the bar ('those using the restaurant are directed by signs to study this and order at the bar'), is an exhaustive menu with a strong hand in the vegetarian and fish fields. Poached salmon and prawn salad, or wild mushroom and spinach lasagne topped with local goats' cheese, and, for meat lovers, eight weights of steak, or the likes of chicken breast stuffed with asparagus and Port Salut, just about set the style. For snacks, there's a selection of 20 or so baps and sandwiches, including a steak, onion and gravy bap, while starters range from pea and ham soup to cod and pancetta fishcake. As this is a Burtonwood tied house, the brewery's range of ales is on draught, and 11 wines come by the glass. SAMPLE DISHES: Stilton-stuffed mushrooms £4; Thai mixed seafood curry £11; lemon sponge and citrus sauce £3.

Licensee James Dolan (Burtonwood)
Open Mon to Fri 12 to 3, 5.30 to 11, Sat, Sun and bank hols 12 to 11; bar food and restaurant Mon to Fri 12 to 2.30, 6 to 9.30, Sat, Sun and bank hols 12 to 9.30
Details Children welcome exc in bar area   Car park   Patio   No smoking in restaurant   Background music Dogs welcome in bar area only   Delta, MasterCard, Switch, Visa   Accommodation: 6 rooms, B&B £28.50 to £60

The Guide is totally independent, accepts no free hospitality, carries no advertising and makes no charge for inclusion.

A list of pubs serving exceptional draft beers is at the back of the book.

LLANFRYNACH   Powys   map 4

White Swan

Llanfrynach LD3 7BZ   TEL: (01874) 665276
WEBSITE: www.the-white-swan.com
off A40/B4558, 3m SE of Brecon

The Brecon Beacons provide an awesome backdrop to this row of sympathetically converted rough-stone cottages opposite the ancient church of St Brynach. At the back is a garden and, under a massive pergola, a terrace divided into little 'rooms' by waist-high box hedges. Go inside, and you find stone walls (some painted, some exposed), a flagged floor, wooden furniture and bar counter, plus leather sofas, a log fire and some atmospheric lighting. Lunchtime bar snacks could take in bresaola with olive and roasted pepper bruschetta and confit of chicken terrine with red onion marmalade and honey-pickled vegetables as well as soup and ploughman's with Welsh cheeses. The full restaurant menu has similar dishes, plus more elaborate main courses like roast free-range duck breast with sweet potato and spinach mash, sweet-and-sour onions and coriander jus; there's also a separate list of fish specials such as chargrilled marlin with mango, ginger and lime salsa, or seared fillet of cod with garlic-sautéed seafood. Desserts range from a gingerbread biscuit with coconut and Malibu ice cream and pineapple to plum and cinnamon sponge pudding. Tomos Watkin OSB and Hancock's Bitter are on draught, and the global wine list kicks off with Chilean house selections at £11.95; at least six are generally available by the glass. SAMPLE DISHES: grilled sardines with chilli and garlic oil £5; marinated escalopes of pork with spiced aubergines, chorizo, and harissa £12; vanilla rice pudding with plums in red wine £4.

Licensee Stephen Way (freehouse)
Open *Wed to Sun 12 to 3, 7 to 11 (10.30 Sun); bar food and restaurant Wed to Sun 12 to 2 (2.30 Sun), 7 to 9 (8.30 Sun); closed 24 to 26 Dec*
Details *Children welcome   Car park   Wheelchair access (also WC)   Garden   No smoking in restaurant   Occasional background music   No dogs   MasterCard, Switch, Visa*

LLANGATTOCK   Powys   map 4

Vine Tree Inn

The Legar, Llangattock NP8 1HG   TEL: (01873) 810514
off A40, SW of Crickhowell

WATERSIDE

The Vine Tree takes up a terraced row of cottages, creating a long, narrow interior where exposed dark stone contrasts with sunny honey-coloured walls and there's many a snug little alcove in among the beams, horse brasses and plain wooden furniture. A large blackboard by the bar gives notice that the pub also has a very industrious kitchen and, despite the length of the menu, it delivers honest, straightforward dishes made from fresh ingredients. Food is ordered from the bar and then brought to your table, turning up perhaps black tiger prawns in tempura batter, or mushrooms in garlic and chilli to start, then rabbit in a wine and celery sauce, or lemon sole in a seafood sauce. Traditionalists will be happy with roast chicken, or the various steaks that come with a choice of sauces. Fuller's London Pride and a guest – perhaps Golden Valley from Breconshire Brewery – are on draught, and two house wines on a list of around 35 are served by the glass. The pub is right on the road and its car park is on the other side, right beside the River Usk, crossed here by an ancient bridge leading over to

Crickhowell. SAMPLE DISHES: haddock in a creamy cheese sauce £5; lamb chops in a garlic, rosemary and Marsala sauce £9.75; tiramisù £3.75.

Licensee Andrew S. Lennox (freehouse)
Open *12 to 3, 6 to 11, Sun 12 to 3, 6.30 to 10.30; bar food and restaurant 12 to 2.30, 6 to 10*
Details *Children welcome   Car park   Garden   No-smoking area in bar   No music   No dogs   Delta, MasterCard, Switch, Visa*

LLANGOLLEN   Denbighshire   map 7

Corn Mill   NEW ENTRY

Dee Lane, Llangollen LL20 8PN   TEL: (01978) 869555

WATERSIDE

WEBSITE: www.cornmill-llangollen@brunningandprice.co.uk

This inspired conversion of a slate and brick three-storey Georgian corn mill 'has given Llangollen a first-rate dining pub that also caters admirably for drinking visitors and locals', noted a reporter. It's right above the River Dee, at the much-photographed old weir and falls, and features a capacious decked outdoor drinking area that has been built across the millstream. Within, there are many levels, starting with the flag-floored bar, and a 'fresh pine and steel-wire staircase' winds up through the structure; all the pub's rooms are furnished with a mix of tables, from cosy two-seaters to refectory and farmhouse tables 'with room for a sports team', and offer vivid views. Eat wherever you choose to sit with dishes from a printed menu of modern brasserie staples ranging from salmon and chive fishcake with mushy peas and tartare sauce, or mussels cooked in white wine and cream, to a generous roast half-shoulder of lamb with 'excellent' roast potatoes, and pork and leek sausages with spring onion and Cheddar mash and rich onion gravy. Local Plassey Brewery ales feature strongly, especially their Border and Exhibition bitters, while guests might include Hook Norton Best Bitter or Boddingtons. From a short wine list that opens with house Italian at £9.95, ten are available by the glass. SAMPLE DISHES: cream of parsnip soup £3.50; braised beef with sherry, thyme and lemon-scented rice £9.25; chocolate and orange torte £4.25.

Licensee Andrew Barker (Brunning & Price)
Open *12 to 11; bar food 12 to 9.30 (9 Sun)*
Details *No children   Wheelchair access (also WC)   Patio   No smoking in eating area   No music   No dogs MasterCard, Switch, Visa*

MACHYNLLETH   Powys   map 4

▲ Wynnstay Hotel ✿

Maengwyn Street, Machynlleth SY20 8AE   TEL: (01654) 702941
WEBSITE: www.wynnstay-hotel.com

Built in 1780 as a private residence and subsequently a stopping-off point for stage coaches on the Aberystwyth to Shrewsbury route, this substantial white building still shows some reminders of the past, with its slate roof, dormer windows, and a high through-passage to its yard. Inside is a décor of clean, bold colours. A stable bar at the back has its own pool table; otherwise there is the prospect of sampling a regularly changing quartet of mostly Welsh brews such as Brains Bitter, in addition to Powys-brewed Ralph's cider. Bar food is served in a separate area with a low, beamed ceiling and a stone fireplace with a club fender. Gareth Johns's cooking is based on local ingredients (especially fish), so you can expect Conwy mussels, Borth crab, and plaice from Aberdyfi as well as Dyfi Valley steaks. Start with Ritchie's rarebit or pork and duck terrine before moving on to peppered duck with raspberry sauce or butterfly red mullet with capers, preserved lemons and olives. Welsh cheeses or a dessert like walnut and ginger cake with custard would round things off nicely. The fixed-price restaurant menu might run along the lines of smoked haddock and anchovy tartlet, entrecôte of beef with wild mushroom cream, then macerated pineapple with cracked pepper caramel. The list of 60-odd wines includes many that are specially imported by the owners; eight are available by the glass. SAMPLE DISHES: soused mackerel salad £5.50; suprême of chicken with a three-mustard sauce £8.50; lemon bavarois £4.25.

Licensees Phillip Copeland, Kathryn Vaughan and Charles Dark (freehouse)
Open 12 (11 summer) to 11, Sun 12 to 10.30; bar food 12 to 2, 6.30 to 9; restaurant all week 6.30 to 9, Sun 12 to 2
Details Children welcome Car park Wheelchair access (also WC) Patio No-smoking area in bar, no smoking in restaurant Occasional live music Dogs welcome Amex, Delta, Diners, MasterCard, Switch, Visa Accommodation: 23 rooms, B&B £50 to £95

NANT-Y-DERRY Monmouthshire map 2

Foxhunter 🏵 🏵

Nant-y-derry NP7 9DN TEL: (01873) 881101
between A4042 and A40, 6m S of Abergavenny

Keep your eyes peeled, because it's easy to drive right past this tall Grade II listed former stationmaster's house built of rough grey-brown stone. From the outside it may look unremarkable, but the open-plan main bar's plain wooden furniture, bare oak floor, white walls and occasional seafood-themed prints give the interior a fresh, uncluttered feel. A great chimneypiece – complete with a wood-burning stove – separates two rooms, and light is provided by ceiling spots. Top-class food is the main business here, although there's no obligation to eat and no pressure to order more than one course – although it would be a shame to miss out on what the kitchen can deliver. The menus are changed daily, and dishes are full-blooded, although there are plenty of classy unexpected twists along the way. Italy is a major inspiration – witness tagliolini with wild duck sauce and aged pecorino, zampone (stuffed pig's trotter) with herbed lentils and salsa verde, or crab and mascarpone risotto – but there are also oriental touches (bang-bang chicken salad, pan-fried scallops with soy, ginger, garlic and spring onions) as well as dressed-up pub favourites along the lines of mushroom and chervil soup with Parmesan cream, and even eight-ounce hamburgers. Vegetables are also given full rein: perhaps rainbow chard with rack of lamb or cavolo nero on the side with steak and kidney pie. Desserts are superbly crafted restaurant-style specialities like pannacotta with griottine cherries, while British cheeses are served with home-made fig 'salami' and walnut toast. Although the Foxhunter doesn't stock draught beers, there are a few creditable English and Italian bottled beers on offer. Wine is tackled with more gusto, although the four by the glass (£3.50) don't do justice to the considered Eurocentric range. SAMPLE DISHES: hake brandade with a poached egg and saffron hollandaise £7; roast pigeon with sautéed Savoy cabbage, leeks, garlic and thyme £15; chocolate pot with crème fraîche £7.

Licensee Lisa Tebbutt (freehouse)
Open Tue to Sat 12 to 2.30, 7 to 11.30; bar food and restaurant Tue to Sat 12 to 2.30, 7 to 9.30; closed Christmas, 2 weeks Feb
Details Children welcome Car park Wheelchair access (also WC) Patio No smoking in restaurant Background music Small dogs welcome MasterCard, Switch, Visa

▲ Old Kings Arms Hotel [NEW ENTRY]

13 Main Street, Pembroke SA71 4JS   TEL: (01646) 683611
WEBSITE: www.oldkingsarmshotel.co.uk

'A traditional inn of character' is how an enthusiastic reporter describes the Old Kings
Arms, a fifteenth-century inn that stands squarely in the centre of Pembroke. It is
certainly a local favourite and doesn't pander to fashion in any way or form – regulars
are here for Wychwood Hobgoblin, Bass, Worthington Bitter, and Shepherd Neame
Spitfire Premium Ale on draught and for the honest food. There are two bars (with the
lounge bar a pleasant room with bare stone walls and some panelling) and an atmospheric dining room at the back – a bare boards/partly slate floor, a large open fire, a
grandfather clock, a dresser, and dark beams – but food can be eaten in any room.
A printed menu lists the usual steak, ale and mushroom pie, steaks, pork sausages with
mash and onion gravy, and chicken curry, but there's also bacon, cockles and laverbread, and seared Welsh lamb fillet on wilted greens with a port and redcurrant sauce.
The cooking is generous and old-fashioned, and desserts are equally homely, along the
lines of sticky toffee pudding, apple pie, and home-made ice cream. About half of the
50-bin wine list is French; all three house wines are offered by the glass. SAMPLE
DISHES: smooth duck liver pâté £4.50; coq au vin £6.25; fruit pavlova £3.25.

Licensee Mrs S.E. Wheeler (freehouse)
Open 11 to 11; bar food and restaurant 12 to 2, 7 to 10; closed 25 Dec, 1 Jan
Details Children welcome   Car park   Wheelchair access (not WC)   Garden and patio   No smoking in
restaurant Mon to Sat lunchtimes   No music   No dogs   Amex, Delta, MasterCard, Switch, Visa
Accommodation: 18 rooms, B&B £35 to £55

Sloop Inn

Porthgain SA62 5BN   TEL: (01348) 831449
WEBSITE: www.sloop.co.uk   **WATERSIDE**
off A487, 4m W of Mathry

High cliffs, wheeling gulls and choughs swooping over the tiny harbour 'strewn with
lobster pots' – Porthgain must be one of the most picturesque fishing harbours in
Pembrokeshire. The long single-storey Sloop Inn is 'knocked through from a row of
ancient terraced houses' with rough-plastered walls and slate roofs. In the beamed
and slate-floored interior the bare brick walls are heavily decorated with a somewhat
'rough and ready' assemblage of maritime artefacts – 'if you fish, sail or drink you'll
feel at home here'. You can choose from light snacks – sandwiches, salads (fresh crab
perhaps, or Llangloffan cheese), moules marinière – or order full-blown main meals
like Welsh Black sirloin steaks, macaroni and seafood bake, or steak, kidney and
mushroom pie. Blackboard specials extend the choice, perhaps pan-fried monkfish
tail with a 'richly melded' red pepper and tomato fondue. Desserts (if you have room)
are such as bread-and-butter pudding, or sticky toffee and date pudding. Real ales
include Rev. James from Brains, Felinfoel Double Dragon Ale and Bass, and three
wines from the modest wine list are sold by the glass. SAMPLE DISHES: Porthgain
potted crab £4.25; shoulder of lamb, red cabbage and a rosemary and redcurrant sauce
£9.75; hot chocolate fudge cake £3.25.

Licensee Matthew Blakiston (freehouse)
Open 11 to 11, Sun 12 to 4.30, 6 to 10.30; bar food and restaurant 12 to 2.30, 6 to 9.30
Details Children welcome Car park Patio No-smoking area in restaurant Occasional live music; jukebox
No dogs MasterCard, Switch, Visa

RED WHARF BAY   Isle of Anglesey   map 7

Ship Inn

Red Wharf Bay LL75 8RJ   TEL: (01248) 852568

off A5025, 6m N of Menai Bridge

Red Wharf Bay has always been a safe anchorage, so the Ship's nautical ambience is no surprise, and its position overlooking the Bay's miles of beaches is glorious. The two beamed bars, partly carpeted, partly wooden-floored, have wheelback chairs and banquettes around the tables, prints and china in profusion on the walls, along with an old ship's wheel, and a 'roaring log fire'. This is a popular place, and one might wait for a table at busy times. A range of influences combine with local sourcing in a modern, eclectic menu: Welsh cawl of ham hock, root vegetables and barley, and tian of smoked salmon and crab with dill and lemon oil are typical starters. Main courses may be traditional – chargrilled Welsh ribeye steak with mustard and peppercorn cream sauce – or exotic – pan-fried pavé of salmon on egg noodles, marinated vegetables with chilli and soy vinaigrette, say – while desserts can be both: dark chocolate and mango mousse with almond shortbread, or bara brith bread-and-butter pudding with whisky and orange syrup. Ales are from Adnams and Greene King, along with Tetley's Imperial and Marston's Pedigree. Over 50 malt whiskies are stocked and half a dozen wines come by the glass. SAMPLE DISHES: duck and bacon fritter with bean-sprout salad and chilli jam £5.25; Welsh lamb shank braised in honey and rosemary with black pudding potato and green cabbage £9.25; raspberry and cassis crème brûlée £4.

Licensee Andrew L. Kenneally (freehouse)
Open summer 11 to 11, Sun 12 to 10.30, winter Mon to Fri 11 to 3, 6.30 to 11, Sat 11 to 11, Sun 12 to
10.30; bar food Mon to Sat 12 to 2.30, 6 to 9.30, Sun 12 to 9, restaurant Sat from Mar to Oct 6 to 9.30,
Sun winter 12 to 9; opening hours vary bank hols and high season
Details Children welcome in family room and restaurant Car park Wheelchair access (not WC) Garden
and patio No smoking in 2 rooms Occasional background music No dogs Delta, MasterCard, Switch, Visa

ST GEORGE   Conwy   map 7

Kinmel Arms

St George LL22 9BP   TEL: (01745) 832207

off A55, 2m SE of Abergele

St George is a small, attractive village in the foothills of the beautiful Elwy Valley, and the seventeenth-century Kinmel Arms serves the community well. Inside, it is buzzy and welcoming, with an impression of a light and lively area of space, with plenty of room for everyone: at a stool at the bar, near the fire, on a sofa, on cushioned wicker chairs in the conservatory, or in the eating area. The same menu is available throughout. Salads, baguettes and open sandwiches are lunchtime staples, but larger appetites might choose to start with mussels in white wine, cream and dill sauce, then go on to Welsh sausages with bacon and black pudding mash in a rich onion sauce, or battered cod with tartare sauce and chips. Indeed, fish is well represented with even more specials on a Friday. Beers are a familiar range, with three guest ales changing every six weeks or so, perhaps Archers Golden Bitter, Tetley Bitter, or Old Speckled Hen, and nine wines are sold by the glass. SAMPLE DISHES: blue cheese and bacon salad with hazelnuts and smoked hickory dressing £5; loin of pork stuffed with herbs, apples and dates with a cream sauce £8; crème brûlée with forest fruits £4.50.

Licensees Lynn Cunnah-Watson and Tim Watson (freehouse)
Open 12 to 3, 6.30 to 11, Sun 12 to 5.30; bar food 12 to 2, 7 to 9.30, Sun 12 to 4; closed 25 Dec
Details Children welcome in eating area   Car park   Wheelchair access (also WC)   Garden and patio
No-smoking area   Live or background music   Dogs welcome in bar only   Delta, MasterCard, Switch, Visa

ST HILARY   Vale of Glamorgan   map 4

Bush Inn

St Hilary CF71 7DP   TEL: (01446) 772745
WEBSITE: www.downourlocal.com/thebushinn
off A48 Cardiff to Bridgend road, 2m E of Cowbridge

Leave the M4 and take the old road from Cardiff to Bridgend to get a gentle rural view of southernmost Wales, where English and Welsh place names intermingle amid a peppering of castles. The Bush Inn fits the setting perfectly: a long, low building of sandy-coloured stone with a thatched roof, opposite a Norman church in a quiet village. The inside is as sixteenth-century as the outside, with exposed beams and stone walls, an inglenook and copper pans on the walls of the three bars and restaurant. Bar food (listed on menu plus specials board) involves well-executed old faithfuls, plus items like Welsh rarebit, or laverbread and bacon with oatmeal and provençale sauce. For mains there is fresh fish, grilled plaice perhaps, or deep-fried cod; baked ham and parsley sauce; or sausages with onion gravy. The restaurant menu adds some more up-market ideas liked stuffed fillets of lemon sole with a warm tomato vinaigrette, or pork medallions with puréed apple and redberry and juniper sauce. Beers are Bass, Old Speckled Hen, Hancock's HB and Worthington Bitter, with Fuller's London Pride as a regular guest, plus Old Rosey cider. Three house wines, at £9.45, open a varied list of 30 or so bottles, and two are available by the glass. SAMPLE DISHES: French onion soup £3; steak and ale pie £6.25; banoffi pie £3.50.

Licensee Sylvia Murphy (Punch Taverns)
Open 11.30 to 11, Sun 12 to 10.30; bar food and restaurant 12 to 2.15, 6.45 to 9.30 (6 to 9.45 Sat),
Sun 12 to 2.15, 6 to 8; closed evening 25 Dec
Details Children welcome in eating areas   Car park   Wheelchair access (not WC)   Garden and patio
No smoking in dining room   Background music   No dogs   Delta, MasterCard, Switch, Visa

SKENFRITH   Monmouthshire   map 5

▲ Bell at Skenfrith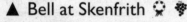

Skenfrith NP7 8UH   TEL: (01600) 750235
WEBSITE: www.skenfrith.co.uk
on B4521, between Abergavenny and Ross-on-Wye

Next to the hump-backed bridge spanning the River Monnow and close to one of the most atmospheric castles in the area (Skenfrith Castle), this seventeenth-century pub makes the most of its setting. Refurbishment has given the interior a modern, stylish look, the open-plan area decorated in natural shades, with some vintage photographs and well-spaced furniture. A new chef arrived in summer 2004. Lunchtime food has a degree of traditional pub appeal, albeit with a twist: a duo of sausages comes with champ mash and shallot jus, and deep-fried fish with home-cut chips, mushy peas and home-made tartare sauce. A starter might be local smoked salmon, caper, sherry and shallot dressing. In the evening, a meal might begin with Gower scallops with local black pudding and rouille, or carpaccio of venison with fig chutney and a rocket salad. Main courses show equal ambition: roast fillet of turbot with saffron mash, baby leeks and black olive tapenade, perhaps, or grilled fillet of Welsh beef with a wild mushroom and pancetta cream. Local cheeses are an alternative to white chocolate crème brûlée or sticky toffee pudding. Freeminer Bitter, Hook Norton Best Bitter, and Timothy Taylor Landlord are on draught, along with Broome Farm cider. The 100-strong wine list strides confidently from the ordinary world of easy-drinking wines for under £15 (where you'll find a dozen by the glass) to the rarefied heights of first-growth claret from the amazing 1989 and 1990 vintages. Prices are on the high side, but the selection is impressive. SAMPLE DISHES: beef faggot with crushed root vegetables and red wine sauce £7; duck breast with a port and grain mustard infusion £17; tarte au citron with blackcurrant sauce £4.50.

Licensees William and Janet Hutchings (freehouse)
Open 11 to 11, Sun 12 to 10.30; bar food 12 to 2.30, 7 to 9.30; closed Mon Nov to Mar, 2 weeks end Jan to early Feb
Details Children welcome   Car park   Wheelchair access (also WC)   Garden and patio   No smoking in eating area   Background music   Dogs welcome in bar only   Amex, Delta, MasterCard, Switch, Visa
Accommodation: 8 rooms, B&B £70 to £150

STACKPOLE   Pembrokeshire   **map 4**

Stackpole Inn
Stackpole SA71 5DF   TEL: (01646) 672324
off B4319, 3m S of Pembroke

In the heart of a tiny rural village, the former Armstrong Arms (the name change came with new owners in 2002) presents a low, squat front but opens up inside. Slate, flagstone and plank floors show its age – seventeenth century – with new beams and ceiling keeping things up to date. The menus offer a varied choice, with a mix of traditional and modern ideas. As well as bar snacks, more substantial meals may begin with starters such as marinated duck and pear with salad, or tiger prawns in garlic, white wine and cream. Main courses run to sirloin of organic Welsh black beef with sautéed potatoes, wild mushrooms and red wine jus, or pan-fried cod fillet with goats' cheese and basil mash and a white wine and shallot sauce. Beers include Welsh real ales Brains Rev James Original Ale and Felinfoel Best Bitter. There is also a short wine list, with a handful served by the glass; house wines are £9.90. The Stackpole Inn is on the National Trust-owned Stackpole Estate, close to the Pembrokeshire Coast Path. SAMPLE DISHES: smoked salmon with avocado salsa £6; rump of Welsh lamb with a garlic and herb crust £13; fresh lemon cheesecake £4.50.

Licensees Mr and Mrs R.H. and L.D. Dearling (freehouse)
Open Mon to Fri 11.30 (12 winter) to 3, 6 (6.30 winter) to 11, Sat 11.30 to 11, Sun 12 to 3, 7 to 10.30; bar food and restaurant 12 to 2.30, 6 (7 winter) to 9
Details Children welcome   Car park   Wheelchair access (also WC)   Garden   No smoking in restaurant Occasional background music   Dogs welcome in bar only   Delta, MasterCard, Switch, Visa

▲ Groes Inn

Tyn-y-Groes LL32 8TN   TEL: (01492) 650545
WEBSITE: www.groesinn.com
4m S of Conwy; from mini-roundabout at Conwy Castle take B5106 towards Trefriw for 2m

Summer bench seating offers a 'heartbreakingly beautiful' view eastwards across the
Conwy Valley and westwards towards the north Snowdonia range. Inside, the décor is
what might be expected from a pub dating from the sixteenth century, with low ceilings, beams and brasses, a wood-burning stove in a huge inglenook with a mantel
beam hung with pots, toby jugs, bookshelves behind the optics, and varied prints on
the walls. The bar menu is supplemented by a blackboard of specials, while a fixed-
price menu is offered in the more formal restaurant, with its old prints and portraits
and heavy swagged curtains. The choice in the bar is wide (and also available in the
separate restaurant), covering traditional and modern styles, and many of the first-rate
ingredients are local: for example, a trio of Welsh sausage with a warm potato salad
and honey mustard, or braised knuckle of Groes lamb in honey and rosemary. The
table d'hôte menu in the restaurant might include crispy black pudding, bacon and
red onion salad, and traditional braised beef and onion with herb dumplings.
Vegetables are said to be outstanding, and puddings maintain the momentum: mixed
berry champagne jelly with rose petal ice cream, for example, or Boodles orange fool.
Tetley Bitter and Burton Ale are provided for real beer drinkers, and four wines are
served by the glass. SAMPLE DISHES: seafood hors d'oeuvres £7.75; steak, ale and
mushroom pie £8.75; peach tarte Tatin £4.

Licensee Dawn Humphreys (freehouse)
Open *12 to 3, 6 to 11; bar food and restaurant 12 to 2.15, 6.30 to 9; closed 25 Dec*
Details *Children welcome   Car park   Wheelchair access (also WC)   Garden and patio   No-smoking area in
bar, no smoking in restaurant   Background music   Guide dogs only   Amex, Delta, Diners, MasterCard, Switch,
Visa   Accommodation: 14 rooms, B&B £79 to £146*

Round-ups

Pubs have all kinds of attractions, and people use them for all kinds of reasons. Those in the Round-up section are a mixed bag, but each has some special quality that makes it well worth visiting.

Some of the pubs listed here are superlative outlets for real ale; others have a fascinating history or architecture. There are hostelries close to public gardens, castles, rivers and canals; lively urban drinking pubs; and plenty of establishments that will appeal to walkers, bird-watchers, climbers and fishermen. Many places are also excellent family venues, and some may offer decent accommodation.

Most of these pubs serve food, although that is not the main reason for their inclusion in the Round-ups. Food is often incidental to the proceedings (especially in some town and city pubs), and a number of places provide only limited snacks, while a few serve no food at all.

Pubs in the Round-up sections are listed on the basis of readers' recommendations, backed up wherever possible – but not always – by inspectors' reports. Further feedback on these places is most welcome.

ENGLAND

ABBOTS BROMLEY

Staffordshire   map 5

Bagot Arms

Bagot Street, Abbots Bromley WS15 3DB
TEL: (01283) 840371

The Bagot Arms is an imposing white
building dispensing Marston's Pedigree
and Banks's Bitter and serving around
eight wines by the glass. Food extends
from sandwiches and baguettes to light
snacks such as mussels and main courses
along the lines of curries or lamb shank.
Open *Mon to Fri 12 to 2.30, 5.15 to 11, Sat 12 to
11, Sun 12 to 10.30*

ALDEBURGH

Suffolk   map 6

Ye Olde Cross Keys Inn

Crabbe Street, Aldeburgh IP15 5BN
TEL: (01728) 452637

Although most famous for its music
festival, Aldeburgh is also host to a poetry
festival (held in autumn), during which
poets congregate at this atmospheric old
place and read from their work. Adnams,
based in nearby Southwold, is responsible
for the wines (with around half a dozen by
the glass) as well as the draught beers.
Given the proximity of the sea, it will
come as no surprise to find that fish is the
focus of the menus, perhaps listing moules
marinière and fisherman's pie. Three
guest rooms are available.
Open *Mon to Fri 11 to 3, 5 to 11, Sat and Sun
11 to 11*

ALDERWASLEY

Derbyshire   map 5

Bear

Alderwasley, nr Wirksworth DE56 2RD
TEL: (01629) 822585

*Alderwasley signposted off B5035 W of A6
between Cromford and Belper; ignore second left-
hand turn signposted Alderwasley but continue
straight on; pub about ½m on left*

Outside the village, this solid stone-built
pub has so much character it's amazing it
all fits in: atmospheric nooks and crannies,
curtained doorways, a Scottish-themed
alcove with tartans and antlers, a tapestry
covering a wall in the dining room, old
dressers, gleaming coppers...and of course
bare dark beams and stone and wood
floors. Beers include Marston's Pedigree,
Old Speckled Hen and Black Sheep Best
Bitter, and there's an extensive all-day
menu. Accommodation includes four-
posters.
Open *12 to 11 (10.30 Sun)*

ALMONDSBURY

South Gloucestershire   map 2

Bowl Inn

16 Church Road, Lower Almondsbury
BS32 4DT
TEL: (01454) 612757

on A38, close to M4/M5 interchange

Licensed since the sixteenth century, this
whitewashed, red-roofed inn was built
originally as accommodation for the
monks constructing the twelfth-century
church next door. Its odd-sounding name
is a reference to its position on a slope
above the Severn, looking across the M4
bridge and Wales. Seasonally changing
beers from breweries like Bath Ales are on
draught, and around 40 wines are on the
list, while the bar food includes the likes
of a half-shoulder of lamb in red wine
sauce. There are 13 rooms.
Open *11.30 to 3, 5 (6 Sat) to 11, Sun 12 to 10.30*

ALREWAS

Staffordshire   map 5

Old Boat at Alrewas

Kings Bromley Road, Alrewas DE13 7DB
TEL: (01283) 791468

The Trent and Mersey Canal runs right
past the garden of this substantial cream-
painted pub, which once served as a
watering hole for canal builders and
bargemen. These days, a new chef/patron
is at the helm and his repertoire shows lots
of worldwide influences, from warm
salmon niçoise to spiced lamb kofta with
Moroccan couscous and tzatziki. A couple
of real ales are on draught and six wines
are available by the glass. Reports please.
Open *details not available as the Guide went to press*

ALSTONEFIELD

Staffordshire   map 5

George

Alstonefield DE6 2FX
TEL: (01335) 310205

village signposted on A515 6m N of Ashbourne

An ideal pit stop for walkers and cyclists
exploring the Manifold Valley, and
therefore popular at weekends, this old-
fashioned sixteenth-century inn is in a
peaceful village, with benches outside by
the green for summer sipping. A triangular
stone-built bar serves three beamed rooms
decorated with local photographs and
pictures. Burtonwood and a guest provide
refreshment, while tired legs can be fuelled
up from a traditional bar menu.

Open *Mon to Fri 11 to 3, 6 to 11, Sat and Sun
11 to 11*

ANICK

Northumberland   map 10

Rat Inn

Anick NE46 4LN
TEL: (01434) 602814

just N of A69, 1½m NE of Hexham

Pick a sunny day and soak up the views of
the Tyne valley from the well-maintained
hillside garden, with its dovecote. A genial
atmosphere prevails in the rat-themed
interior, where the bar lines up Ruddles
County, Old Speckled Hen and Mordue
Workie Ticket and you can dip into a good
supply of newspapers. Food on a hot
counter sets basics like chicken curry
against maybe tuna steak with garlic and
tomato sauce, and there's a range of hearty
puddings.

Open *11 to 3, 6 to 11, Sun 12 to 3*

APPLEBY

Cumbria   map 10

Tufton Arms

Market Square, Appleby CA16 6XA
TEL: (017683) 51593

Appleby, famous for its annual horse fair,
used to be the county town of what was
Westmorland, and at its heart lies the
Tufton Arms, a 21-room hotel that dates
from the seventeenth century but which
has been revamped in Victorian style. It
has a conservatory restaurant overlooking a
mews courtyard, and the Victorian Bar

serves Tufton Ale (now brewed by
Boddingtons). Food runs to local produce
in the form of, perhaps, roast rack of fell
lamb, or breast of organic chicken in red
wine sauce, and the long wine list offers
around 15 by the glass. Children welcome.

Open *11 to 11, Sun 12 to 3, 7 to 10.30*

APPLEY

Somerset   map 2

Globe Inn

Appley TA21 0HJ
TEL: (01823) 672327

*from M5 junction 26 take A38 for 3m; turn right
to Greenham, and after 1m turn right at
T-junction signposted Stawley; pub ½m on left*

In a hamlet hidden away down windy
lanes, the Globe is a popular stop with
walkers and cyclists as well as those out for
a meal. The large butter-coloured
building, half a millennium old, houses a
specific dining space and several bar areas
all serving food from the laminated menu
of unfussy pub stalwarts. A central
hatchway bar dispenses good Cotleigh
Tawny Bitter plus guests such as Palmer
IPA, and there's a well-chosen wine list
with five by the glass.

Open *Tue to Sat and bank hol Mon 11 to 3, 6.30 to
11, Sun 12 to 3, 7 to 10.30*

ASHBURNHAM

East Sussex   map 3

Ash Tree Inn

Brown Bread Street, Ashburnham TN33 9NX
TEL: (01424) 892104

just off B2204 (off A271), 4m W of Battle

Ashburnham Park and the historic town of
Battle are within striking distance of this
homely sixteenth-century local tucked
away down narrow country lanes. Three
inglenook fireplaces, old settles and
exposed brickwork define the décor in the
cosy beamed bars, and candlelight adds its
glow in the evening. Expect Harveys Best
and Old Speckled Hen on handpump, plus
a short printed menu of hearty country
dishes bolstered by weekend blackboard
specials. Children are welcome.

Open *12 to 3, 7 to 11*

ASHBY ST LEDGERS

Northamptonshire　　　　　　　　　map 5

Olde Coach House Inn

Ashby St Ledgers CV23 8UN
TEL: (01788) 890349

Children are welcome at this former
farmhouse, and in its extensive, rambling
interior are tables large enough to
accommodate families, as well as small,
intimate dining areas; there's also a
separate restaurant. Everards Original is
joined on the handpumps by a decent
choice of guest ales – perhaps something
from Hook Norton – and around eight
wines are served by the glass from a list of
over 30 bottles. In the garden is a
children's play area, and six guest rooms
are on offer. Dating from the nineteenth
century, the ivy-covered inn replaced an
older pub that was demolished.
Open *12 to 11, Sun 12 to 10.30*

ASHLEWORTH

Gloucestershire　　　　　　　　　map 5

Boat Inn

The Quay, Ashleworth GL19 4HZ
TEL: (01452) 700272

It's easy to see why this pub was built here:
it's on the west bank of the Severn, where
the old chain ferry used to cross the river,
and has been refreshing the boatmen and
their passengers since at least the late
eighteenth century. Five ales are on
draught at any one time: RCH Pitchfork,
Arkell's 3B and perhaps brews from Wye
Valley, Bath Ales or Cottage Brewing. In
summer a coffee shop serves drinks and
cakes; otherwise the food is limited to a
choice of filled baps.
Open *11.30 to 3 (11 to 3.30 Sat), 7 (6 summer) to
11, Sun 12 to 3, 7 to 10.30; closed Mon winter, 25 Dec*

Queens Arms

Ashleworth GL19 4HT
TEL: (01452) 700395

In a village that boasts a fine National
Trust tithe barn, this more modern red-
brick building is fronted by a neat lawn
and two mature yew trees woven through
with fairy lights. Original frosted-glass
panels divide the rooms, while displays of
flowery mugs and saucers give a domestic
feel. Dishes like tomato bredie (spiced
lamb stew) reflect the owners' South

African roots, as does the bias of the short
wine list. Expect hearty portions and
creamy, buttery sauces. Regularly changing
ales might include Shepherd Neame
Spitfire Premium Ale, Brains Rev James
Original Ale, and Archers Village Bitter.
Open *12 to 3, 7 to 11; closed 25 Dec*

ASWARBY

Lincolnshire　　　　　　　　　map 6

Tally Ho Inn

Aswarby NG34 8SA
TEL: (01529) 455205

*on A15 Peterborough to Lincoln road, 5m S of
Sleaford*

True to its name, this isolated (but
nevertheless popular) eighteenth-century
stone pub is bedecked with hunting prints
and plates. Beams abound in the main bar
area and a convivial atmosphere prevails.
Regular menus offer soups, baguettes and
snacks, while blackboards list dishes such
as spicy pork meatballs with rice and
Basque-style chicken, as well as occasional
piscine exotica like salmon fillet with
peanut and sweet chilli sauce, or red
snapper with pepper salsa. The decent
selection of draught beers generally
includes Bass and Greene King Abbot Ale,
plus a locally brewed guest such as
Batemans XB. Accommodation available.
Open *12 to 3, 6 to 11, Sun 12 to 3, 7 to 10.30*

BAKEWELL

Derbyshire　　　　　　　　　map 9

Peacock Hotel

Bridge Street, Bakewell DE45 1DS
TEL: (01629) 813635

A local favourite with all ages, this stone-
built pub on the market square will
happily refuel passing visitors with
something like deep-fried Brie followed by
steak and kidney pie – whether in the main
bar, one of the smaller rooms off it, or the
stone-flagged beer garden. The range of
guest ales might extend to Marston's
Pedigree, Black Sheep Best Bitter, or
Tetley Bitter.
Open *Mon 10.30 to 11, Tue to Sat 11.30 to 11,
Sun 12 to 10.30*

BARBON

Cumbria   map 8

Barbon Inn

Barbon LA6 2LJ
TEL: (01524) 276233

Those following outdoor pursuits like
walking (the boundary of the Yorkshire
Dales National Park is only a couple of
miles away) and fishing in the River Lune
can refresh themselves at this seventeenth-
century coaching inn in a peaceful village.
Beers include Theakston Best and a guest
such as Dent Aviator, three wines are sold
by the glass, food is served in the bar and,
in the evening, in the separate restaurant,
and there's a secluded beer garden to relax
in. Overnighters can choose from ten
rooms.
Open *12 to 3, 6 to 11.30*

BARHAM

Suffolk   map 6

Sorrel Horse

Barham IP6 0PG
TEL: (01473) 830327

The Sorrel Horse has been an inn since
about 1840 (although it was built in the
seventeenth century), and the interior,
despite updating, still sports a log fire and
oak beams. Boddingtons Bitter, Old
Speckled Hen and Adnams Bitter are on
draught, and, to eat, choose something
from the menu or from the blackboard
specials. To the back is a large garden with
a children's play area, and eight en suite
bedrooms are in a converted barn.
Open *Mon to Fri 11 to 3, 5 to 11, Sat 11 to 11,
Sun 11 to 10.30*

BARTHOMLEY

Cheshire   map 5

White Lion

Barthomley CW2 5PG
TEL: (01270) 882242

*off Alsager road, from M6 junction 16, 4m SE of
Crewe*

Users of the M6 can forget the stresses of
motorway driving at this quintessential
country pub just moments from junction
16. Dating from the seventeenth century,
the inn is thatched and timbered, with
diamond-paned windows, while the
interior has quarry-tiled floors, low, heavy

ceiling beams, wonky walls, scrubbed
tables and benches, and log fires. On offer
are Burtonwood Bitter and Top Hat, plus
a guest ale, and simple, good-value
lunchtime food.
Open *11.30 to 11 (Thur 5 to 11), Sun 12 to 10.30*

BATH

Bath & N.E. Somerset   map 2

Old Green Tree

12 Green Street, Bath BA1 2JZ

A quaint old street like Green Street, with
its traditional butcher's, fishmonger's and
sausage shop, deserves a pub like the Old
Green Tree, the sort of establishment
whose formula doesn't seem to have
changed for generations. Three tiny, dark,
wood-panelled rooms are the setting for a
fine range of ales kept in excellent
condition, with regulars RCH Pitchfork,
Old Green Tree and Wickwar Brand Oak
Bitter joined by guests. Beer-friendly food
like beef, ale and mushroom pie or
sausages and mash, served in portions fit
for giants, is good value. (The phone
number has not been printed in this entry
at the request of the pub.)
Open *Mon to Sat 11 to 11, Sun 12 to 10.30*

BECK HOLE

North Yorkshire   map 9

Birch Hall

Beck Hole YO22 5LE
TEL: (01947) 896245

off A169, 2m S of Grosmont

A tiny hamlet in a steep-sided valley in the
middle of the moors is just the place for a
pub that is as small and simple as they
come. Two bars with bench seating are
separated by the village shop, and a few
ramblers and locals soon add up to a full
house. Guest ales supplement the standard
beers from Theakston and Black Sheep,
while 'spicy, peppery' pork pies from the
local butcher, hearty sandwiches, scones
and beer cake are the extent of the food.
Open *winter 11 to 3, 7.30 to 11, Sun 12 to 3, 7.30
to 10.30, summer 11 to 11, Sun 12 to 10.30*

BECKLEY

Oxfordshire   map 2

Abingdon Arms

High Street, Beckley OX3 9UU
TEL: (01865) 351311

off B4027, 5m NE of Oxford

Just a few miles from Oxford's ring road,
this village pub has a traditional décor and
open fireplaces; look out for the old cider
flagon at the main entrance. Brakspear
Bitter and Special, plus seasonal ales, are
on draught, and as well as sausages and
mash and steaks the menu might run to
chicken curry and braised lamb shank.
New licensees are now in place: reports
please.

Open *11 to 3, 6 to 11, Sun 12 to 10.30*

BEELEY

Derbyshire   map 9

Devonshire Arms

Beeley DE4 2NR
TEL: (01629) 733259

Reputedly once a favourite haunt of
Charles Dickens, this eighteenth-century
inn is full of atmosphere: a warren of little
rooms have masses of dark beams and
timbers, thick stone walls and roaring log
fires. All-day bar meals take in devilled
whitebait, steak and ale pie, pasta, steaks,
and hot and cold filled baguettes, plus a
few blackboard specials. Book for
Victorian breakfast on Sunday mornings.
Cask ales are Black Sheep Best Bitter and
Special, as well as Theakston Old Peculier
and Marston's Pedigree. Four house wines
by the glass.

Open *11 to 11, Sun 12 to 10.30; closed 25 Dec*

BEMBRIDGE

Isle of Wight   map 2

Crab & Lobster

32 Forelands Field Road, Bembridge PO35 5TR
TEL: (01983) 872244

*from B3395 to Bembridge, turn right on to Lane
End Road, second right on to Egerton Road and
at junction follow brown signs*

Keep following the signs and don't lose
heart: the pub is at the end of a narrow
lane next to the coastguard station. The car
park has great views of the sea, and from
here steps run down to the beach, which
gives impressive views of cliffs. The large
main room of the cream-painted pub is
half-boarded and decorated with old
photographs and china, giving it the air of
a tea room, but the long bar at the back
pours more pints than cuppas, with
Goddards Fuggle-Dee-Dum, Flowers
Original and Greene King IPA on tap.
Crab and lobster aptly feature at
mealtimes, supported by a fish-biased
menu. Accommodation is available.

Open *Mon to Fri 11 to 3, 6 to 11, Sat 11 to 11,
Sun 12 to 10.30*

BERKSWELL

West Midlands   map 5

Bear Inn

Spencers Lane, Berkswell CV7 7BB
TEL: (01676) 533202

Once known as the Bear and Ragged Staff
– the name derived from the coat of arms
of the Earls of Warwick – the Bear is a
substantial sixteenth-century building.
Within, the beamed interior is the setting
for a varied menu: starters such as goats'
cheese and duck confit galette may be
followed by pork schnitzel and spinach
pappardelle, or by more traditional fare
such as steak and kidney pudding. Beers
on offer are Theakston Best Bitter and
Courage Directors, joined by guest ales
like Everards Equinox or Exmoor Gold.
All 21 bottles on the wine list are offered
by two sizes of glass.

Open *11 to 11, Sun 12 to 10.30*

BETCHWORTH

Surrey   map 3

Dolphin

The Street, Betchworth RH3 7DW
TEL: (01737) 842288

Seeing a working blacksmith's forge in the
Home Counties might come as a surprise,
but there's one opposite this substantial
early seventeenth-century pub in a village
near Dorking and the South Downs Way.
As the pub is tied to Young's, on draught
are the brewery's Bitter, Special and, from
October to March, Winter Warmer.
Around a dozen wines are served by the
glass, and the kitchen delivers traditional
pub food, from pâté to sausages and mash
or steak and mushroom pie.

Open *11 to 3.30, 5.30 to 11, Sat 11 to 11, Sun 12
to 10.30*

BEWDLEY

Worcestershire   map 5

Little Packhorse

31 High Street, Bewdley DY12 2DH
TEL: (01299) 403762

In an attractive town on the Severn, the Little Packhorse was a refreshment point for packmen and carriers when it was first built in the fifteenth century. Nowadays, it is an atmospheric and eccentric pub, its small interior adorned with bric-à-brac ranging from advertising signs to old clocks. Greene King IPA is on draught, along with a guest – perhaps Hook Norton Best Bitter – and traditional pub food is served in hearty portions.

Open *Mon to Fri 12 to 3, 6 to 11, Sat 12 to 11, Sun 12 to 10.30*

BILBROUGH

North Yorkshire   map 9

Three Hares

Main Street, Bilbrough YO23 3PH
TEL: (01937) 832128

off A64, between Tadcaster and York

A former coaching inn not far from York, the Three Hares is now an ambitious food pub, although it still retains much of its traditional atmosphere. Some modish ideas show up on the daily-changing bar menu (wild sea trout with a runner bean, maché and chorizo salad, for example) along with old favourites like beef and Guinness sausages with parsley mash, or braised steak, for die-hards. Guest beers from the York Brewery supplement regulars like Black Sheep Best Bitter and Timothy Taylor Landlord; ten wines are offered by the glass.

Open *Tue to Sat 12 to 3, 7 to 11, Sun 12 to 3*

BIRCHOVER

Derbyshire   map 5

Druid Inn

Main Street, Birchover
TEL: (01629) 650302

Set right on the edge of a small Dales village with Rowtor Rocks in the background, this stone built, creeper-clad inn dates from the mid-nineteenth century. Two charming, simply furnished bars contrast with a modern extension, which houses the more formal Garden Room and downstairs restaurant. A new licensee took over just before our deadline but it seems that the kitchen will continue to deliver an extensive global menu taking in dishes like green Thai beef fillet, shark provençale and lamb shank with couscous. Marston's Pedigree and Druids Ale (brewed for the pub by Leatherbritches) are on draught, and there are plans to extend the wine list. Reports please.

Open *Tues to Sat 12 to 3, 7 to 11; Sun 12 to 10.30; closed Mon*

BIRMINGHAM

West Midlands   map 5

Old Joint Stock

4 Temple Row West, Birmingham B2 5NY
TEL: (0121) 200 1892

A Grade II listed building near the city centre makes an impressive setting for this Fuller's Ale & Pie House. It stands on a pretty square opposite the cathedral, and the interior is a vast eye-catching space crowned by a big domed skylight. Everything is on a large scale, from huge windows and imposing chandeliers to the paintings on the walls. The full range of Fuller's beers is available alongside ales from Birmingham's Beowulf Brewery, and the pub stages a quarterly beer festival. Homemade pies are, of course, a feature of the menu, along with traditional dishes ranging from Welsh rarebit and poached egg to lamb's liver and bacon. No children.

Open *Mon to Sat 11 to 11; closed Sun*

Prince of Wales

84 Cambridge Street, Birmingham B1 2NP
TEL: (0121) 643 9460

The canal and Brindley Place, with its bars, restaurants and shops, are only a short walk from this Victorian pub. Inside are dark-panelled walls and banquettes, with old sepia photographs and even some Shakespearean quotes on the walls. A good line-up of real ales includes Adnams Broadside, Wells Bombardier Premium Bitter, Timothy Taylor Landlord, Greene King Abbot Ale and Ansells Bitter and Mild. A new licensee took over early in 2004: reports please.

Open *12 to 11, Sun 12 to 10.30*

Tap & Spile
10–15 Gas Street, Birmingham B1 2JT
TEL: (0121) 632 5602

Just at the edge of Brindley Place, the Tap & Spile represents the traditional end of the pub experience. Enter at ground level from Gas Street, or directly from the towpath below, into a series of rooms with stripped floors, exposed bricks, and pictures of the area's industrial heyday. Eight draught ales might include Greene King IPA and Old Speckled Hen, Adnams Best and Broadside, Fuller's London Pride, Wells Bombardier, and Marston's Pedigree. The long menu offers standard hearty pub food.
Open *all week 12 to 11 (2am Fri and Sat, 10.30 Sun)*

BLACKHAM

East Sussex   map 3

Sussex Oak
Blackham TN3 9UA
TEL: (01892) 740273

Set in a pretty part of the Weald, between the A264 and a country lane, this Kentish pub has the bonus of panoramic views. The interior is blessed with a lot of original features including etched glass windows and a wood-panelled bar draped with garlands of dried hops. Three Shepherd Neame real ales are on handpump and four wines are available by the glass. Separate menus operate in the bar and restaurant, and Sunday lunch is a traditional English affair.
Open *11 to 3, 6 to 11, Sun 12 to 4, 6.30 to 10.30*

BLACKMORE END

Essex   map 3

Bull
Blackmore End CM7 4DD
TEL: (01371) 851037

Allan and Carol Weir took over this attractive village pub in 2003 and are maintaining its traditional, relaxed atmosphere and reputation for 'good, honest' food. The interior is all beams and standing timbers, and the menu ranges from pub stalwarts like whitebait and chilli to specials along the lines of rack of lamb or sweet-and-sour chicken. Fuller's London Pride, Adnams and Greene King IPA are on draught and the list of 25 wines

includes six by the glass. Blackmore End is surrounded by impressive 'Constable countryside'. Reports please.
Open *Mon to Fri 12 to 3, 6 to 11, Sat 11 to 11, Sun 12 to 10.30*

BLAISDON

Gloucestershire   map 5

Red Hart Inn
Blaisdon GL17 0AH
TEL: (01452) 830477

In warm weather, people make good use of the large garden and the patio at this sixteenth-century inn in a village on the edge of the Forest of Dean. Another attraction is the good choice of real ales, with regulars Tetley Bitter and Hook Norton Best joined by three guests from local breweries. Expect traditional pub fare on the bar menu; there's also a separate restaurant.
Open *12 to 2.30, 6 to 11, Sun 12 to 3, 7 to 11*

BLEDLOW

Buckinghamshire   map 2

Lions of Bledlow
Church End, Bledlow HP27 9PE
TEL: (01844) 343345
off B4009, 2m SW of Princes Risborough; take West Lane, not Bledlow Ridge turning

A winding single-track lane leads to this long white building with a low red-tiled roof and a lawn at the front scattered with picnic tables for summer eating. Inside, several rooms have been knocked together to create an open-plan space, but each area retains a distinct identity, and a cosy pubby feel prevails in the snug and main bar. Local ales line up alongside Wadworth 6X, Bass or Marston's Pedigree on the five handpumps, and there's an economical wine list. A printed menu of 'properly home-made' pies, lasagne and so forth is complemented by blackboard specials.
Open *11.30 to 3, 6 to 11, Sun 12 to 4, 7 to 10.30*

BLETCHINGLEY

Surrey map 3

William IV

Little Common Lane, Bletchingley RH1 4QF
TEL: (01883) 743278

Converted from a couple of nineteenth-century cottages, this brick and tile village inn is near the junction of the M25 and M23, so makes a useful stopping-off point, especially as it has an attractive garden. Choose from Young's Bitter, Fuller's London Pride, Adnams Bitter or Harveys Sussex Best, or go for one of around six wines by the glass, and enjoy a steak, or, on Fridays, one of the fish specials.

Open *12 to 3, 6 to 11, Sun 12 to 10.30*

BLICKLING

Norfolk map 6

Buckinghamshire Arms

Blickling NR11 6NF
TEL: (01263) 732133

The gates of Jacobean Blickling Hall are next to this elegant pub, built in 1693 to house the servants and horses of Lord Buckingham's house guests. East Anglian breweries Adnams and Woodforde's provide the ales, and the blackboard lists unpretentious, well-cooked food; there's also a separate restaurant (evenings only). Accommodation is provided in three recently renovated en suite bedrooms.

Open *11 to 3, 6 to 11 (open 11 to 11 some days summer)*

BLISLAND

Cornwall map 1

Blisland Inn

Blisland PL30 4JF
TEL: (01208) 850739

village signposted off A30 NE of Bodmin

In a remote location down a maze of winding lanes, Blisland makes Bodmin seem a distant metropolis. The plain building overlooks the village green, and the welcoming landlord's passion for real ales and an all-day opening policy consolidate its position at the heart of the community. Up to eight ales, kept in perfect condition, should include Blisland Special or the stronger Blisland Bulldog, both brewed by Sharp's for the inn, accompanied by Cornish brews from the Doghouse brewery (a former rescue kennels), Wooden Hand, or more well-known ales such as Exmoor Gold. These are the liquid reward for a scenic drive across the flanks of Bodmin Moor. Also a short blackboard menu and 20 wines.

Open *11.30 to 11, Sun 12 to 10.30*

BODICOTE

Oxfordshire map 5

Plough

Bodicote OX15 4BZ
TEL: (01295) 262327

The Blencowe family have been running this friendly two-room pub since 1957 and have been brewing ales here since 1982. The range includes No. 9, Bitter and Life Sentence, plus more powerful winter ales like Triple X and Old English Porter. Food runs from sandwiches and baguettes to casseroles, roasts and steaks. Children welcome in eating area.

Open *Mon 12 to 3, Tue to Sat 11 to 3, 6 to 11, Sun 12 to 3, 7 to 10.30*

BOLLINGTON

Cheshire map 8

Poachers

Bollington SK10 5RE
TEL: (01625) 572086

take A523 N towards Stockport and turn right on B5091 to Bollington; in village turn left into Wellington Road, right into Palmerston Street, straight over; pub 200yds on right

On the way out of Macclesfield towards the wilds of the Peak District, this comfortably lived-in pub has resisted the gentrification of other establishments in the area and is a popular local haunt. Boddingtons Bitter and Timothy Taylor Landlord are joined by three regular changing guests from all over the country, and the wine list runs to two dozen bottles. The menu treads traditional ground, so expect the usual accompaniments with pork, lamb and beef steaks, with perhaps chargrilled sea bass with sun-dried tomato sauce among fish choices.

Open *Mon 5.30 to 11, Tue to Fri 12 to 2, 5.30 to 11, Sat 12 to 2, 7 to 11, Sun 12 to 2.30, 7 to 10.30*

BOTTOM-OF-THE-OVEN

Cheshire   map 8

Stanley Arms

Bottom-of-the-Oven, Macclesfield Forest
SK11 0AR
TEL: (01260) 252414

just S of A537, between Buxton and Macclesfield
Although near Macclesfield, the Stanley
Arms is in an isolated spot close to
Macclesfield Forest and miles of
moorland; it's also just inside the border of
the Peak District National Park. The
recently refurbished interior – small and
cosy, with open fires in winter – makes a
good spot for walkers to enjoy a reviving
pint of Marston's Bitter or Pedigree, while
the menu lists familiar-sounding dishes of
prawn cocktail or pâté followed by stuffed
roast chicken with gravy or duck à
l'orange. Children are welcome before
7pm in the lounge bar, and there's a
terrace and garden with great views. Seven
double en suite rooms are available.
Open *Mon to Fri 12 to 2.30, 5.30 to 11, Sat 12 to 11,
Sun 12 to 10.30*

BOWNESS-ON-WINDERMERE

Cumbria   map 8

Hole in't Wall

Lowside, Bowness-on-Windermere LA23 3DH
TEL: (01539) 443488

on A5074, on E shore of Lake Windermere
This unspoilt pub has character in spades,
from old beams, stone floors and artefacts
galore, and it positively oozes history; Will
Longmire (a champion wrestler) was
landlord in the nineteenth century, and
Charles Dickens has propped up the bar.
This century, you can expect something
from Robinson's (Best Bitter and Hartleys
XB) to go with the bar food chalked up on
a blackboard. It gets very busy in the
tourist season but remains friendly and
lively all year.
Open *11 to 11, Sun 12 to 10.30*

BRADFIELD

South Yorkshire   map 8

Strines Inn

Mortimer Road, Bradfield S6 6JE
TEL: (0114) 285 1247

2m off A57 (not in village), 6m NW of Sheffield
A stunning moorland location high up on
the edge of the High Peak National Park
overlooking Strines Reservoir makes this
historic stone pub a honeypot destination –
especially on warm summer's evenings.
People come to eat as well as drink in the
three traditional beamed bars: soup,
sandwiches, steaks and a 'pie of the day'
typify the standard menu, while the choice
of real ales could include Marston's
Pedigree, Banks's Riding Bitter and St
Austell Tribute; seven wines are available
by the glass. There's a play area in the
garden, complete with a mini-menagerie.
Accommodation includes three rooms
with four-posters, a family room and a
holiday cottage.
Open *winter 10.30 to 3, 5.30 to 11 (10.30 Sun);
summer 10.30 to 11 (10.30 Sun)*

BRANCASTER STAITHE

Norfolk   map 6

Jolly Sailors

Main Road, Brancaster Staithe PE31 8BJ
TEL: (01485) 210314

This traditional whitewashed north Norfolk
pub looks set to enhance its reputation for
fine ales with the introduction of a
microbrewery. The short menu
concentrates on local seafood such as
steamed Brancaster mussels or beer-battered
haddock 'n' chips alongside such pub
standards as steak and ale pie or sausages and
mash. Beyond the warming fires, there is
little distraction from the twin pleasures of
eating and drinking in the simple interior,
with its white walls and tiled floors.
Open *11 to 11, Sun 12 to 10.30; closed 25 Dec,
open 26 Dec 12 to 6*

BREDON

Worcestershire   map 5

Fox and Hounds

Church Street, Bredon GL20 7LA
TEL: (01684) 772377

Old Speckled Hen, Banks's and Marston's
Pedigree are on draught at this village inn,

together with eight wines sold by the glass. In the sizeable open-plan bar area you can expect to find fish specials and meat main courses along the lines of braised lamb shoulder with rosemary and mint gravy. Bredon Barn (National Trust), which dates from the fourteenth century, is in the village and is well worth a visit.

Open *11 to 3, 6.30 to 11, Sun 12 to 3, 6.30 to 10.30*

BRETFORTON

Worcestershire   map 5

Fleece Inn

The Cross, Bretforton WR11 5SE
TEL: (01386) 831173

Dating from the fourteenth century, this striking black and white building with a stone-tiled roof was a farmhouse until it became a pub in 1848, and was bequeathed to the National Trust in 1977. The interior, with its antiques and collections of pewter and Victorian measures, is divided into the Brewhouse, the Dugout (originally the pantry; the coffin-shaped table was used to prove dough) and the Pewter Room. A good line-up of real ales includes Ansells Best Bitter, Uley Pig's Ear Strong Beer, Hook Norton Best Bitter and two guests; local scrumpy is also on draught, and 20 wines are available by the glass. Regular folk nights are held, and there are occasional special events like an apple blossom weekend in April and an asparagus auction in early summer. Sandwiches and snacks are served, with the full menu running from, say, Thai fishcakes with chilli dip, through local faggots with mash, peas and onion gravy, to summer pudding.

Open *Mon to Fri 11 to 3, 6 to 11 (summer 11 to 11), Sat 11 to 11, Sun 12 to 10.30*

BRIGHTON

East Sussex   map 3

Evening Star

55–56 Surrey Street, Brighton BN1 3PB
TEL: (01273) 328931

The Dark Star Brewery, now based in the Sussex village of Ansty, started life at this pub close to the station, and the brewery's range of ales is on draught here, including Critical Mass, Hophead and Landlords Wit, plus guests such as Oakham JHB. Cold food is served at lunchtimes, with live music performances on Sundays.

Open *all week 12 (11.30 Sat) to 11, Sun 12 to 10.30*

BRISTOL

Bristol   map 2

Cornubia

142 Temple Street, Bristol BS1 6EN
TEL: (0117) 925 4415

'Circa 1775' declares a sign on the wall, and this old pub close to the station can't have changed much over the years – although it is now surrounded by large office blocks. The bow window is every inch the Old Curiosity Shop, and the interior is as small and basic as can be. The main business is ale, as the many beer mats stuck to the walls testify, with a regularly changing line up including, say, Butcombe Blonde, Otter Bitter and Oakham Old Tosspot plus a list of those coming soon to whet the appetite. Malt whiskies are listed on a blackboard and there's a short menu should food be required. No children.

Open *Mon to Fri 12 to 11, Sat 5 to midnight; closed Sun*

Hare on the Hill

41 Thomas Street North, Kingsdown, Bristol BS2 8LX
TEL: (0117) 908 1982

Forget the tower blocks opposite and enter a welcoming world of a real fire and warm lighting. Decked out in the Bath Ales livery of black wood, terracotta walls and bare floorboards, this popular local manages the trick of appealing to both traditional and modern tastes. The brewery's Gem, Spa and Barnstormer are joined by Belgian bottles, and the good-value menu offers fuelling dishes like sausage and mash, chilli, and beef and ale stew, while one visitor enjoyed flavoursome minted lamb casserole from among the blackboard specials.

Open *Mon to Thur 12 to 2.30, 5 to 11, Fri and Sat 12 to 11, Sun 12 to 10.30*

Old Fish Market

59–63 Baldwin Street, Bristol BS1 1QZ
TEL: (0117) 921 1515

Situated in Bristol's main shopping area, this fine example of a large urban tavern makes an ideal escape for those who have had their fill of retail therapy. The interior has a full checklist of Victoriana: large chandeliers, an impressive carved bar, walls covered in prints and oil paintings, even a handsome tiled lavatory. This is a

Fuller's Ale & Pie house offering their range of beers (along with Butcombe Bitter), plus more than a dozen wines by the glass and a new menu with Thai overtones. An undercover 'city garden' was in the pipeline as the Guide went to press.
Open *12 to 11, Sun 12 to 10.30*

Smiles Brewery Tap

610 Colston Street, Bristol BS1 5BD
TEL: (0117) 921 3668

The name says it all: Smiles Brewery can be glimpsed at the back of this small, well-maintained pub set back from a busy road opposite the children's hospital. It comprises two small rooms, the first with a black-and-white tiled floor and a tiny panelled bar, the second (a non-smoking version of a snug) with a wooden floor and mirrors on its blood-red walls. Four Smiles beers are regularly on show, including Best, Original, IPA and Heritage, plus monthly specials like April Fuel. Food consists of soup and ploughman's, fish 'n' chips, sausages and mash and various mixed platters. Children are welcome in the snug at lunchtime.
Open *11 to 11 Mon to Sat; closed Sun*

BROAD CAMPDEN

Gloucestershire map 5

Bakers Arms

Broad Campden GL55 6UR
TEL: (01386) 840515

Butcombe Bitter, Timothy Taylor Landlord, Wells Bombardier Premium Bitter, Hook Norton Best Bitter, and Stanway Stanney Bitter form the exemplary line-up of real ales at this creeper-covered pub in a quiet Cotswolds village. Walls of bare stone and an inglenook are features of the traditionally furnished interior, and there's now a separate restaurant: reports please.
Open *winter Mon to Fri 11.30 to 2.30, 4.45 to 11, Sat 11.30 to 11, Sun 12 to 10.30; summer 11.30 to 11, Sun 12 to 10.30; closed 25 and 26 Dec, evening 31 Dec*

BROADWAY

Worcestershire map 5

Crown and Trumpet

Church Street, Broadway WR12 7AE
TEL: (01386) 853202

off High Street (A44), on Snowshill road

The Crown and Trumpet is typical of the cottages and houses in this pretty village (which can get packed in high season), as it was built of Cotswold stone in the seventeenth century. Up to five real ales are on draught, among them perhaps Cotswold Gold, Old Speckled Hen and Hook Norton Old Hooky, joined in winter by Lords-a-Leaping (brewed by Stanway in Cheltenham). Five wines are sold by the glass, and the style of food served is what you would expect in a traditional English pub, with pies a speciality. Five letting rooms are available.
Open *Mon to Fri 11 to 3, 5 to 11 (summer 11 to 11 Fri), Sat 11 to 11, Sun 12 to 10.30*

BROCKLEY GREEN

Suffolk map 6

Plough Inn

Brockley Green CO10 8DT
TEL: (01440) 786789

off A143, 2m N of Haverhill, take right turn to Kedington, then 1m towards Hundon

In a quiet village, the Plough, on one of the relatively high points of the area, is in five acres of grounds. Seats on the patio have wonderful views of the Stour valley, and nearby is a terrace with a koi-stocked pond. Within is a roomy bar with oak beams and upright timbers, and a log fire in winter; the menu in here runs to steak and kidney pie and Cajun-spiced chargrilled chicken, with specials along the lines of smoked trout salad with crayfish tails. The restaurant has a separate menu. Greene King IPA, Woodforde's Wherry, Adnams Bitter and a guest are on draught, and ten wines are served by three sizes of glass. Children are welcome at lunchtimes and until 8.30pm. Accommodation and conference facilities.
Open *12 (11 summer) to 2.30, 6 to 11, Sun 12 to 3, 7 to 10.30; closed evenings 25 and 26 Dec*

BROOKLAND

Kent   map 3

Woolpack

Brookland TN29 9TJ
TEL: (01797) 344321

This atmospheric fifteenth-century pub is
open all day in August, when the large beer
garden comes into its own. The place is no
less popular with families in winter, with a
wood-burner in the recently refurbished
family room. On draught in the beamed
bar, with its large inglenook, is the
Shepherd Neame range of ales, with the
likes of steaks, pies and daily specials –
quiche and salad in summer, say – on the
menus.
Open *Mon to Fri 11 to 3, 6 to 11, Sat 11 to 11,
Sun 12 to 10.30*

BROOM

Bedfordshire   map 6

Cock

23 High Street, Broom SG18 9NA
TEL: (01767) 314411

on B658, 2m SW of Biggleswade

Log fires, low ceilings, and snug room are
what you might expect to find in a 300-
year-old pub. What you won't find here,
surprisingly, is a bar counter; instead, the
full range of Greene King ales is stored by
the steps leading to the cellar. House wines
are sold by the glass, and food follows a
traditional route of steak and mushroom
casserole and cottage pie.
Open *Mon to Fri 12 to 3, 6 to 11, Sat 12 to 4, 6 to
11, Sun 12 to 4, 7 to 10.30*

BUCKLERS HARD

Hampshire   map 2

Master Builder's House Hotel

Bucklers Hard SO42 7XB
TEL: (01590) 616253

off B3054, just S of Beaulieu

Ships were this Master Builder's forte,
with much of the Trafalgar fleet to his
credit. Now that the golden age of sail is
gone, the former shipyard is a peaceful
spot on the bank of the Beaulieu River and
part of Lord Montagu's Beaulieu Estate.
The eighteenth-century house has
polished up smartly, and the Yachtsman's
Bar plies a good trade with tourists as well
as the sailing fraternity. The bar menu is

limited, but there's a smart brasserie here
too, and 25 bedrooms.
Open *11 to 11, Sun 12 to 10.30*

BURNHAM MARKET

Norfolk   map 6

Lord Nelson

Creake Road, Burnham Market PE31 8EN
TEL: (01328) 738321

True to its name, Nelson memorabilia is
the main decorative theme at this solid all-
rounder, a typical flint building in
picturesque Burnham Market. A young
crowd fills the large main bar, while the
lounge and restaurant are set up for diners.
There's a blackboard bar menu of pub
standards, burgers and panini, and a full
restaurant carte (also served in the bar) that
might offer grilled goats' cheese and
roasted peppers followed by fillet steak
with Stilton mash and port sauce. Greene
King IPA, Courage Directors and Fuller's
London Pride are on handpump.
Accommodation is available.
Open *11 to 3, 6.30 (6 summer) to 11, Sun 12 to 3,
6.30 to 10.30*

BUTTERTON

Staffordshire   map 5

Black Lion Inn

Butterton ST13 7SP
TEL: (01538) 304232

Standing opposite the church in the
middle of a small, remote village, this
cottage-like old stone inn is a popular pit-
stop for Peak District walkers. Inside is a
maze of small rooms, decorated with
brewers' badges and with tankards hanging
from the ceiling beams. The regular menu
offers things like steak and ale pie, or cod
and prawn crumble, while blackboard
specials have featured sea bass steak and
red snapper with lemon caper sauce. A
good selection of real ales might include
Everards Tiger, and Theakston Mild and
Best.
Open *Tue to Sun 12 to 2.30 (3 Sat and Sun), all
week 7 to 11 (10.30 Sun)*

BYWORTH

West Sussex   map 3

Black Horse

Byworth GU28 0HL
TEL: (01798) 342424

The social hub of this attractive old village
is its sixteenth-century brick-built pub.
Tables outside offer pastoral views, while
inside two roaring fires, a pleasing jumble
of wooden furniture and a few historical
prints conjure up the kind of atmosphere
that cannot be faked (although the top-
floor restaurant feels rather detached from
the heart of things). Blackboards proffer
seared calf's liver with onion gravy, and
steamed beef and suet pudding, with some
pricey desserts to follow, and the bar
features an impressive line-up of local
ales.
Open *11 to 3, 5 to 11, Sun 12 to 3, 7 to 10.30*

Welldiggers Arms

Byworth GU28 0HG
TEL: (01798) 342287

From the 'if it ain't broke...' school of
country pubs, this engagingly rustic
venue on a lane running towards
Petworth has a loyal following. Trestle
tables jostle for space with standing
drinkers in the busy bar, where the day's
menu is chalked on a blackboard. Fish
and game are the specialities, and good
cuts of beef feature too. The food can be
quite pricey, but then proper attention is
paid to things like vegetable
accompaniments as well as the main dish.
Impressive views of the South Downs add
to the charm. Young's beers.
Open *Tue to Sat 11 to 3, Sun 12 to 3, Thur to Sat
6 to 11; closed 25 and 26 Dec*

CAMBRIDGE

Cambridgeshire   map 6

Clarendon Arms

35 Clarendon Street, Cambridge CB1 1JX
TEL: (01223) 313937

Not far from the city centre, this
unpretentious small pub has a reputation
as a relaxing refuge with friendly service.
In the eating area, blackboard menus offer
plenty of good-value and filling choices for
both carnivores and vegetarians; lunchtime
sandwiches are a good bet too. Beers are

from Greene King. Accommodation is
available.
Open *11 to 11, Sun 12 to 10.30*

Eagle

8 Bene't Street, Cambridge CB2 3QN
TEL: (01223) 505020

'One of the more interesting pubs in
Cambridge', this popular seventeenth-
century hostelry close to the city's historic
centre boasts a number of notable features
– especially the RAF Bar, whose ceiling is
covered with signatures from World War
II airmen. The place gets busy with
drinkers who come in to sample Greene
King ales and a weekly guest brew or take
their pick from the choice of 14 wines by
the glass. Food is good-value pub grub
ranging from baguettes and baked potatoes
to giant battered cod, wild boar and apple
sausages with mash, BBQ ribs and syrup
sponge.
Open *11 to 11, Sun 12 to 10.30*

Free Press

7 Prospect Row, Cambridge CB1 1DU
TEL: (01223) 368337

This small, atmospheric pub just five
minutes' walk from the city centre has its
own way of doing things. No music, no
smoking and no mobile phones
encourages a clientele of
conversationalists, games players and
newspaper readers (there's a free daily
supply of papers and old cuttings on the
walls along with all sorts of other
memorabilia). Greene King beers and an
impressive range of whiskies provide
lubrication, while the kitchen serves the
likes of soup, salads, chilli and a decent
range of vegetarian options.
Open *12 to 2 (2.30 Sat), 6 to 11, Sun 12 to 2.30,
7 to 10.30*

CAREY

Herefordshire   map 5

Cottage of Content

Carey HR2 6NG
TEL: (01432) 840242

This medieval pub is off the beaten track
in a small village near the River Wye. The
tiny, atmospheric bars have open fires, oak
beams, ancient settles and farmhouse
tables. Ales are from the Hook Norton and

Wye Valley Breweries, and the bar menu lists pub stalwarts like battered cod, ham, egg and chips, lamb casserole, and chicken curry.

Open *12 to 3, 7 (6 Sat) to 11, Sun 12 to 3, 7 to 10.30; closed lunchtime Mon, evening Sun winter*

CARTMEL FELL

Cumbria map 8

Masons Arms

Strawberry Bank, Cartmel Fell LA11 6NW
TEL: (015395) 68486

going N on A5074 turn left at sign for Bowland Bridge, then 1m up hill

You need a good map and plenty of patience to negotiate the tangle of lanes that leads to this remote and emphatically traditional Lakeland pub. Refreshment comes in the form of real ales such as Black Sheep, Timothy Taylor Landlord and local Hawkshead Bitter; there's also a remarkable collection of international bottled beers, plus around two dozen wines. New licensees were finding their feet as the Guide went to press, but their new menu is likely to feature dishes such as Greek-style slow-roast shoulder of lamb and 'smothered' chicken. Accommodation in self-catering apartments and cottages. Reports please.

Open *winter 11.30 to 3, 6 to 11, summer 11.30 to 11*

CASTLE HEDINGHAM

Essex map 3

Bell

10 St James Street, Castle Hedingham CO9 3EJ
TEL: (01787) 460350

Fish is a strong suit at the Bell, with mussels, calamari, sea bass, salmon, or swordfish showing up on the menu; the pub has a no-chips policy, and fish barbecues are a feature on Monday evenings. The inn was built in the sixteenth century, and in the series of small, linked rooms, which still have a feeling of age, some of the original wattle-and-daub walls have been uncovered. Regular ales Adnams Bitter and Greene King IPA are joined on the handpumps by two guests, perhaps Old Speckled Hen and something from the Mighty Oak Brewing Company. Live music is a regular event.

Open *Mon to Thur and Sat 11.30 to 3.30, 6 to 11, Fri 11.30 to 11, Sun 12 to 3.30, 7 to 10.30*

CAULDON

Staffordshire map 5

Yew Tree

Cauldon, nr Waterhouses ST10 3EJ
TEL: (01538) 308348

off A523 Leek to Ashbourne road at Waterhouses, 6m NE of Cheadle

A yew tree dutifully marks the spot, but it's what's inside that matters here. Mountains of Victoriana suggest that this could be a junk shop, auction room or museum, but beyond it all the unflappably cheerful landlord is pulling pints of Burton Bridge Bitter; the unique atmosphere draws the regulars and curious onlookers from miles around. Pies and sandwiches fill a hole, but this is not really an eating venue. 'You just have to see it to believe it!' concluded a reporter.

Open *10 to 2.30, 6 to 11, Sun 12 to 3, 7 to 10.30*

CHARLBURY

Oxfordshire map 5

Bull Inn

Sheep Street, Charlbury OX7 3RR
TEL: (01608) 810689

Dating from the sixteenth century, this Costwold stone inn has been tastefully renovated over the years. It's a rustically civilised place with hop-festooned beams, candlelight and exposed stone walls in the bar, plus a secluded seating area outdoors. The menu promises things like chargrilled chicken, bacon and avocado salad, chilli, and cod in batter. Draught beers are from Greene King and Hook Norton, while the wine list includes seven house selections by the glass. Accommodation available. New licensees took over in 2003: reports please.

Open *Mon 6 to 11, Tues to Fri 11.30 to 3, 6 to 11, Sat 11 to 11, Sun 12 to 4*

CHARLTON

Wiltshire map 2

Horse and Groom

The Street, Charlton SN16 9DL
TEL: (01666) 823904

on B4040 Malmesbury to Cricklade road, 2½m E of Malmesbury

Just a couple of miles from Malmesbury, said to be the oldest borough in England, the Horse and Groom was built in the

sixteenth century of honey-coloured sandstone. Three regular real ales are on the handpumps – perhaps Smiles Best, Archer's Village and Wadworth 6X – and ten wines are served by the glass. Beef, Stilton and Guinness pie might be among the main courses on the menu, with frozen orange soufflé among puddings. There are tables outside at the front, and the garden has picnic tables on the lawn and a wooded area with a giant climbing frame for children. Two bedrooms available.
Open *Mon to Fri 12 to 3, 7 to 11, Sat 12 to 11, Sun 12 to 10.30*

CHEDINGTON

Dorset   map 2

Winyard's Gap
Chedington DT8 3HY
TEL: (01935) 891244

off A356, between Crewkerne and Dorchester, at Winyard's Gap

Senior citizens' lunches are served here on weekdays, and among main courses might be boar sausages, ham and chips, steak and kidney pie, and lamb steak with redcurrant and mint sauce. Three real ales are on draught – perhaps Exmoor Ale, RCH Pitchfork and Harveys Sussex Best Bitter – with the same number of wines served by the glass. The inn, tucked under an ancient earthwork on a ridge above the source of the Axe, has a stunning view towards the Quantock Hills that inspired Thomas Hardy's poem 'At Winyard's Gap', a view that can be enjoyed from both bar and terrace. A new licensee took over early in 2004 – reports please.
Open *11 to 2.30, 6.30 to 11, Sun 12 to 2.30, 7 to 10.30*

CHERITON BISHOP

Devon   map 1

Old Thatch Inn
Cheriton Bishop EX6 6JH
TEL: (01647) 24204

New licensees took over this thatched sixteenth-century inn at the tail end of 2003; their declared aim is to maintain their Grade II listed pub, which has a beamed bar with a log fire, as a quality country inn. Menus range from lunchtime sandwiches and ploughman's to starters of

perhaps a warm pigeon breast salad with a strawberry and balsamic dressing and main courses of whole sea bass stuffed with chilli, ginger and spring onions. Around eight wines are served by the glass, and among the real ales on handpump are Branoc from Branscombe Vale and guests such as Adnams Broadside. Accommodation available. Reports please.
Open *11.30 to 3, 6 to 11 (summer 11.30 to 11), Sun 12 to 3, 7 to 10.30; closed 25 Dec*

CHESTER

Cheshire   map 7

Union Vaults
Egerton Street, Chester CH1 3ND
TEL: (01244) 400556

When the city-centre tourist trail becomes too much, take a ten-minute walk along the towpath to this authentic boozer for a warm welcome and a pint of Greenalls Bitter or a guest such as Timothy Taylor Landlord. What was the original pub, at the bottom of a steep terrace, has a rare corner door opening into the centre of local action, with TV sport and a bagatelle table. Adjoining it are what used to be cottages, now providing extra space for darts and a wallpapered 'best' room. No food.
Open *11 to 11, Sun 12 to 10.30*

CHIDDINGLY

East Sussex   map 3

Six Bells
Chiddingly BN8 6HE
TEL: (01825) 872227

The licensees are heading for a quarter-century's service and have the 'perfect English pub experience', as one reporter put it, down to a T. The red-and-black-brick exterior dates the pub to 1774; inside, it rambles from room to room, with brick floors, warming fires and cosy corners giving a rooted, rustic feel. A menu of pub staples at very good prices pulls in plenty of trade, and regular live music adds to the vibrant atmosphere of a well-loved local. The location makes it an ideal stop for walkers on the Vanguard and Weald Ways.
Open *Mon to Fri 11 to 3, 6 to 11 (12 Fri), Sat 11 to 12, Sun 12 to 10.30*

CHIDDINGSTONE

Kent   map 3

Castle Inn

Chiddingstone TN8 7AH
TEL: (01892) 870247

Chiddingstone-brewed Larkin's
Traditional is on draught at this old (it
became an inn in 1730) red-brick pub,
along with a guest such as Young's Bitter.
The menu in the restaurant might open
with crispy Peking duck with hoisin, go on
to roast partridge with smoked ham and
sage dauphinois potatoes and lentil sauce,
and end with white chocolate and orange
tart with coconut ice cream, while the bar
menu is a run-through of pub favourites.
Cream teas are served, and there's a
children's menu. The impressively long
wine list has just three by the glass. The
village is notable for its half-timbered
houses.

Open 11 to 11, Sun 12 to 10.30

CHILMARK

Wiltshire   map 2

Black Dog

Chilmark SP3 5AH
TEL: (01722) 716344

Opposite a church with a strikingly tall
spire, this fifteenth-century grey-stone and
red-brick pub bears the patina of centuries
in its low ceilings, great stone hearth, and a
floor of old black and red tiles in the
smoky main bar, where locals sup on Black
Dog and Puppy Club beers. A menu of
pub regulars is expanded on blackboards
and complemented by lunchtime
sandwiches and 'lite bites'. Enthusiasm for
wine is evident with 55 by the glass from a
110-strong list.

Open 11 to 11, Sun 12 to 10.30

CHURCHILL

N.W. Somerset   map 2

Crown Inn

The Batch, Churchill BS25 5PP
TEL: (01934) 852995

Built around 400 years ago as a coaching
inn, the Crown has also served as the
village grocer's and butcher's shops. It is
set beside a track at the base of the Mendip
Hills, and, inside, its two unspoilt bars
have flagstoned floors, stone walls, heavy
beams and open fires. Five handpumps
dispense regular brews (Palmers IPA, Hop
Back GFB, RCH Brewery's PG Steam,
Bath SPA, plus Bass), and three more
deliver guests – from Church End, for
example. Traditional pub fare at lunchtime
only, and a pleasant walled front terrace for
al fresco drinking.

Open 12 to 11, Sun 12 to 10.30

CHURCH KNOWLE

Dorset   map 2

New Inn

Church Knowle BH20 5NQ
TEL: (01929) 480357

The New Inn is an old, sixteenth-century
pub where the ambience is pleasantly
relaxed. It is near to Corfe Castle, with
views of the Purbeck Hills from the
garden. Three interconnecting rooms have
open fires and Turkish carpets, and the
long menu features haddock in beer batter,
game pie and a roast of the day. Real ales
kept are Flowers Original, Wadworth 6X
and Old Speckled Hen. Wine is taken
seriously, and a long list contains much of
interest (off-sales are available).

Open 11 to 3, 6.30 to 11, Sun 12 to 3, 6.30 to
10.30; closed Mon in Nov, Jan and Feb

CLIFTON HAMPDEN

Oxfordshire   map 2

Plough Inn

Abingdon Road, Clifton Hampden OX14 3EG
TEL: (01865) 407811

on A415 in Clifton Hampden between Abingdon
and Dorchester

Farm machinery in front marks out this
ancient thatched pub popular with the
Oxfordshire smart set. Inside, deep-red
walls reflect the warming glow of a log
fire, and low ceilings and red- and black-
tiled floors complete the picture. Eat in the
bar or more formal dining room from a
menu that promises updated standards:
perhaps gravad lax with fennel and shallot
compote, and lamb shank with rosemary
gravy. Beers come from Greene King, and
the wine list is seriously good. No
smoking throughout. Thirteen rooms
available. New landlord – reports on
progress, please.

Open 11am to midnight, Sun noon to 10.30

CONDER GREEN

Lancashire map 8

Stork Hotel

Conder Green LA2 0AN
TEL: (01524) 751234

When the tide is very high, the water comes right up to this large white-painted coaching inn by the banks of the Conder and the Lune estuary. Window boxes catch the eye in summer; otherwise focus your binoculars on the abundant birdlife inhabiting the mudlflats. Real ales include Boddingtons, Timothy Taylor Landlord and various guest beers, and the printed menu is supplemented by blackboard specials: mushroom stroganoff, deep-fried goujons of sole, and liver and onions, for example. Accommodation available.
Open *11 to 11, Sun 12 to 10.30*

CONINGSBY

Lincolnshire map 6

Inn at Lea Gate

Leagate Road, Coningsby LN4 4RS
TEL: (01526) 342370
on B1192 just S of Coningsby

Lincolnshire's oldest licensed premises is a substantial inn in a fenland location, with dark beams, open fires, and old settles sustaining the ancient feel in the dimly lit main bar. Well-kept Marston's Pedigree and Theakston XB are joined by a guest ale, and wines number 25. 'Good-quality' Lincolnshire sausages were the obvious choice for another visitor, but a huge range of snacks, grills and smarter dishes, such as honey-glazed breast of duck with Cumberland sauce, cater for all appetites. Accommodation is in a modern annexe.
Open *11.30 to 3, 6.30 (6 Sat) to 11 (10.30 Sun)*

CONISTON

Cumbria map 8

Black Bull

1 Yewdale Road, Coniston LA21 8DU
TEL: (015394) 41335 or 41668

In the shadow of the Old Man of Coniston (his big toe is a large piece of stone set in the wall of the residents' lounge), the Black Bull was built as a coaching inn about 400 years ago. Nowadays it functions as restaurant and 15-room hotel as well as a pub with its own Coniston Brewing Company. On draught

are Bluebird Bitter, Old Man Ale, Blacksmith's Ale and Opium, and there are a number of Continental beers too. Battered haddock with chips, or half a crispy duckling, plus steak, salads and vegetarian choices are what to expect on the bar menu, while the restaurant is a more upmarket affair, with scampi thermidor, and tournedos Rossini on the carte.
Open *11 to 11, Sun 12 to 10.30*

COOKHAM

Berkshire map 3

Bel and the Dragon

High Street, Cookham SL6 9SQ
TEL: (01628) 521263
on A4094, off A404 just N of Marlow

The Cookham Bel is part of a mini-empire of smart pubs – 'country pub and eating house' is their accurate description – extending as far as Reading, Windsor and Godalming. Drink Fuller's London Pride, something from Marston's, Courage or Brakspear, or choose from the decent wine list (about ten wines are available by the glass). Food takes centre stage, featuring lunchtime specials like creamy fish pie with cheese and spring onion crust served with market vegetables; from the main menu, slow roasted lamb shoulder with chive mash and redcurrant and mint jus is typical of the style. Reports please.
Open *11.30 to 11, Sun 12 to 10.30; closed eve 25 and 26 Dec, 1 Jan*

CORFE CASTLE

Dorset map 2

Fox Inn

West Street, Corfe Castle BH20 5HD
TEL: (01929) 480449

A thirteenth-century fireplace is a feature of the often busy lounge at this unspoilt village pub; alternatively, enjoy the setting of the snug little front bar. Among the good range of real ales might be Old Speckled Hen, Wadworth 6X, Everards Original and Timothy Taylor Landlord. The food served is straightforward pub fare. Children are not admitted, but in summer families can make the most of the mature sun-trap garden, which has views of the castle ruins.
Open *11 to 2.30 (3 summer), 6.30 to 11, Sun 12 to 2.30 (3 summer), 7 to 11*

Greyhound Inn
The Square, Corfe Castle BH20 5EZ
TEL: (01929) 480205

The garden behind this sixteenth-century coaching inn has fine views of the ruined castle and the Purbeck Hills, while the atmospheric interior is all low beams, oak panelling, cosy alcoves and sturdy furniture. Seven continually changing real ales are on the pumps, among them Fuller's London Pride, Timothy Taylor Landlord and Marston's Pedigree, with three scrumpies in summer. Scallops or lobster might turn up on the menu, and on Sunday there's a carvery. Children are welcome, and B&B is offered in three rooms.
Open *winter Mon to Fri 11 to 3, 6 to 11, Sat 11 to 11, Sun 12 to 10.30; summer 11 to 11, Sun 12 to 10.30*

CORFTON
Shropshire   map 5
Sun Inn
Corfton SY7 9DF
TEL: (01584) 861239
on B4368, 4½m NE of Craven Arms

Dating from the seventeenth century, this pub under Wenlock Edge has been much extended over the years. There's quite an emphasis on food here, with bar snacks running from baguettes to omelettes and beef and ale sausages from a local butcher. The restaurant menu may kick off with a seafood platter, followed by pies, steaks, or something like lamb rogan josh, or smoked haddock and prawns in a pasta bake. At the back of the pub landlord Norman Pearce brews his award-winning Corvedale ales, Norman's Pride and Secret Hop among them. There are also guest ales and 14 wines by the glass. The pub offers good facilities for the disabled and, for children, an obstacle course in the large garden. As the Guide went to press, plans were afoot to offer a B&B room.
Open *12 to 2.30, 6 to 11, Sun 12 to 3, 7 (6 summer) to 10.30; open all day bank hols*

COTTERED
Hertfordshire   map 3
Bull
Cottered SG9 9QP
TEL: (01763) 281243

This village hostelry is a Greene King pub and the draught ales are undoubtedly part of the draw, bringing in customers from Stevenage and beyond. Two fires in winter contribute to the warm atmosphere, and the food is another attraction: perhaps smoked haddock with prawn and cheese sauce, steak, Guiness and Stilton pie, and rump steak with red wine, horseradish and tomato sauce, plus fish on Tuesdays. Three wines are available by the glass.
Open *12 to 2.30, 6.30 to 11, Sun 12 to 3, 7 to 10.30*

COTTON
Suffolk   map 6
Trowel & Hammer
Mill Road, Cotton IP14 4QL
TEL: (01449) 781234

Allow time to search this place out in the many lanes that make up the village. The two large bars are decked out with traditional dark pub furnishings, but beers from Adnams, Greene King, Mauldons and Nethergate lift it above the country-pub norm, as does a good-value wine list. A regularly changing menu ranges from carrot and tarragon soup to prawns in filo with breaded lobster tails to start, with tandoori kingfish and a truffle and Brie omelette among main courses.
Open *Mon to Fri 12 to 3, 6 to 11, Sat 12 to 11, Sun 12 to 10.30*

CRASTER
Northumberland   map 10
Jolly Fisherman
Craster NE66 3TR
TEL: (01665) 576461

This white-painted harbourside pub makes seafood snacks a speciality: home-made crab soup, Craster kipper pâté, oak-smoked salmon, for example, though burgers and toasted Geordie stottie cake 'pizza' also make an appearance, as do sandwiches and toasties. Fresh, mainly local ingredients and good value lift the food above the norm. Beers include Tetley and Black Sheep Bitter.

Open *winter 11 to 3, 6 to 11, Sun 12 to 4,*
7 to 10.30; summer 11 to 11, Sun 12 to 10.30

CRAY

North Yorkshire   map 8

White Lion

Cray BD23 5JB
TEL: (01756) 760262
off B6160, 2m N of Buckden

This greystone former drovers' inn
nestling beneath Buckden Pike opposite a
stream commands some stunning scenery,
and is understandably popular with
walkers and people out for the day.
Moorhouses Premier Bitter and Pendle
Witches Brew and Timothy Taylor
Landlord are on draught, together with a
guest from Copper Dragon Brewery in
Skipton. Nine wines by the glass
complement the food: duck breast in red
wine and raspberry sauce, perhaps, or loin
of lamb with garlic and rosemary. Eight en
suite bedrooms, with more planned.
Open *11 to 11, Sun 12 to 10.30; closed 25 Dec*

CROSCOMBE

Somerset   map 2

Bull Terrier

Croscombe BA5 3QJ
TEL: (01749) 343658

Within this attractive stone pub, three
welcoming bars – the Snug, the Common
bar, and the Inglenook – are where
drinkers can enjoy Winchester's Buckland
Best Bitter and three guests such as
Adnams Bitter, Ruddles County and
Palmer IPA. A sense of history pervades:
the Bull Terrier was first licensed in 1612
and was originally a priory; at the rear the
elevated garden backs on to the church,
which has Jacobean beams. An interesting
walk leads across fields to the Bishop's
Palace at Wells. Overnight accommodation
in two rooms.
Open *12 to 2.30, 7 to 11 (10.30 Sun); closed Mon*
Oct to Mar

CUMNOR

Oxfordshire   map 2

Vine Inn

11 Abingdon Road, Cumnor OX2 9QN
TEL: (01865) 862567

A fire and comfortable sofas create a
relaxing and warm atmosphere at this
eighteenth-century vine-covered inn.
Hook Norton Best Bitter and Adnams
Bitter may be among the real ales on
draught, and four wines are sold by the
glass. The menu leans towards classic
dishes of Dover sole, fillet steak with
brandy sauce, and sea bass with butter
sauce. There are picnic tables and a
children's climbing frame in the garden.
Open *Mon to Fri 11 to 3, 6 to 11, Sat (and Fri*
summer) 11 to 11, Sun 12 to 10.30

DALWOOD

Devon   map 2

Tuckers Arms

Dalwood EX13 7EG
TEL: (01404) 881342

In its long history, this part-thatched,
flower-bedecked thirteenth-century inn
set at the heart of a pretty Axe Valley
village was formerly a farmhouse, hunting
lodge and a residency for stonemasons
working on the nearby church. Inside,
uneven stone floors, low-beamed ceilings
and open log fires provide the setting for
drinkers of Otter Bitter, O'Hanlon's Fire
Fly and Courage Directors. Fresh fish,
game dishes, steaks and vegetarian options
feature on menus, and about a dozen
wines come by the glass. Four en suite
bedrooms.
Open *12 to 3, 6.30 to 11, Sun 12 to 3, 6.30 to*
10.30; closed 26 Dec

DARTMOUTH

Devon   map 1

Cherub

13 Higher Street, Dartmouth TQ6 9RB
TEL: (01803) 832571

Dartmouth's oldest town house, this Grade
II listed building is a 'gloriously timbered
medieval edifice', resplendent with hanging
baskets in summer. The atmospheric bar has
a great fireplace, settles, low beams and a
quartet of fine real ales including Cherub
Best Bitter (brewed for the pub) and West

Country brews like Sharp's Doom Bar and Exmoor Gold. Plenty of 'quaffable' wines are offered by the glass, and menus are tilted towards fresh local seafood (check the blackboard). Bar food at lunchtime, restaurant meals in the evening.
Open *11 to 3, 5 to 11, Sun 12 to 3, 7 to 10.30*

DENT

Cumbria   map 8
Sun
Main Street, Dent LA10 5QL
TEL: (015396) 25208
in Dentdale, 4m SE of Sedburgh
The rough-stone, whitewashed Sun sits in the charming old wool town of Dent among fifteenth- and sixteenth-century cottages, cobbled streets and alleyways. It serves all the beers from the Dent brewery, which was opened in 1990 by the Sun's licensee in a converted stone barn at nearby Cowgill: there's Bitter, Aviator, Kamikazi and T'Owd Tup in cask, and three strong ales in both cask and bottle. The pub welcomes children and serves daily specials in addition to a range of snacks and bar meals. Three rooms available for B&B. Opening hours may vary in winter.
Open *winter Mon to Fri 11 to 2.30, 6 to 11, Sat 11 to 11, Sun 12 to 10.30; summer 11 to 11, Sun 12 to 10.30*

DOBCROSS

Greater Manchester   map 8
Swan Inn
The Square, Dobcross OL3 5AA
TEL: (01457) 873451
from M62 junction 22 take A6052, turn left just after Delph on to A62 and take first right; follow for 1m
Built in 1765 by the Wrigley family, later of chewing-gum fame, this local in a picturesque Pennine village preserves a stoutly traditional appearance with stone-flagged floors, panelled walls and welcoming winter fires. Food, however, is adventurous, with a range of curries alongside standards like fish 'n' chips and much for vegetarians. Jennings does the honours for beer. Evenings can be busy, so it's worth booking a table.
Open *Mon to Wed 12 to 3, 5.30 to 11, Thur to Sat 12 to 3, 5 to 11, Sun 12 to 4, 7 to 10.30 (no food Sun eve)*

DOLTON

Devon   map 1
Union Inn
Fore Street, Dolton EX19 8QH
TEL: (01805) 804633
from A377 Exeter to Barnstaple road going N, turn left on to A3124 towards Winkleigh; after about 5m turn sharply left on to B3217 signposted Dolton; inn on right just before village centre
Low beams, oak settles, an open fire and a chatty atmosphere set the right tone in this charmingly old-fashioned longhouse. It was once a hotel and still offers three rooms. Real ales on handpump might be Sharp's Doom Bar Bitter and St Austell Tribute, or brews from Country Life, Jollyboat, Teignworthy or Clearwater. Food has a good reputation, so we hope the new owners will keep the standards up – reports please.
Open *12 to 2.30, 6 to 11, Sun 12 to 10.30; closed Wed*

DORSTONE

Herefordshire   map 5
Pandy Inn
Dorstone HR3 6AN
TEL: (01981) 550273
off B4348 Hay-on-Wye to Hereford road, 5m E of Hay-on-Wye
The Pandy is a snug, white-painted inn that sits near the head of the Golden (Dore) Valley, between the gardens of Abbey Dore and the bookshops of Hay. Inside, low ceilings, exposed walls and a stone floor create a traditional English atmosphere, though the landlady's native South Africa influences the menu. Tomato bredie (casserole of lamb, tomatoes and potatoes) and bobotie co-exist peacefully alongside liver served with mash and onions or local rump steak, and there is good choice for vegetarians and fish eaters. For drinkers there's Butty Bach and Dorothy Goodbody ales from the Wye Valley brewery, along with Stowford Press cider and four wines by the glass.
Open *Mon 6 to 11, Tue to Fri 12 to 2.30, 6 to 11, Sat 12 to 11, Sun 12 to 3, 6 to 10.30; closed Mon nights from end-Jan to Mar*

DUNCTON

West Sussex　　　　　　　　　　　map 3
Cricketers
Duncton GU28 0LB
Tel (01798) 342473

Set in 'Sussex countryside at its best', with lawns sloping down to a green valley and stream, this white sixteenth-century pub retains an unspoilt, rustic atmosphere. Inside there's one big, beamed room with a log fire where drinkers can enjoy Youngs beers and guests such as Timothy Taylor Landlord and Shepherd Neame Spitfire, or pick something from the 30-strong wine list. There was a change of licensee in March 2004 and the new incumbent was planning to offer 'classic English bar food with a twist', plus fish specials in the evening. Reports please.

Open Mon to Sat 11 to 11, Sun 12 to 10.30

DUNTISBOURNE ABBOTS

Gloucestershire　　　　　　　　　map 2
Five Mile House
Duntisbourne Abbots GL7 7JR
TEL: (01285) 821432

First the Romans built a road (Ermine Street), then, some time in the seventeenth century, the Duntisbourne Estate put up this coaching inn on the street, now a lane parallel to the busy A417. The quirky old rabbit warren of a pub guards every ounce of original character, with the smoky hubbub of local gossip filling the tiny bars. A more formal dining room and a garden with terrific views are appealing alternatives. Donnington's BB, Young's Bitter and Timothy Taylor Landlord are regulars on the handpumps. Home-cooked food might run to breast of Barbary duck with a creamy brandy and pepper sauce, or shoulder of lamb with port and redcurrant jus.

Open 12 to 3, 6 to 11, Sun 12 to 3, 7 to 10.30

DURLEY

Hampshire　　　　　　　　　　　map 2
Robin Hood
Durley SO32 2AA
TEL: (01489) 860229
1¾m W of Bishop's Waltham off B2177

Rural Hampshire gets a makeover with this cosmopolitan bar/bistro decked out with all the requisite blond wood, pale leather sofas, modernist lighting and 'mood' prints on the walls. Bar food comes tapas-style, so order several dishes if you're after more than a snack. An informal, laid-back atmosphere extends into the separate dining area, where there's a full evening menu. Old Speckled Hen, Greene King IPA, Ruddles County and Caledonian 80/- keep beer drinkers happy, and wines by the glass are chalked on a blackboard above the bar.

Open 12 to 11, Sun 12 to 10.30

DUXFORD

Cambridgeshire　　　　　　　　　map 6
John Barleycorn
Moorfield Road, Duxford CB2 4PP
TEL: (01223) 832699

This old thatched former coaching inn was built in 1660 and derives its name from the old Scottish ballad. John Barleycorn is on the main road through the village, not far from Duxford Air Museum. A good line-up of real ales runs from regulars like Greene King and Ruddles, plus Old Speckled Hen, to specials like Bateman XXXB and Caledonian 80/-. The daytime snack menu with omelettes and jacket potatoes gives way to evening dishes such as chilli spiced beef, smoked haddock with poached eggs, or beef and Stilton pie. Four en suite rooms available.

Open 11 to 11, Sun 12 to 10.30

EARL SOHAM

Suffolk　　　　　　　　　　　　map 6
Victoria Inn
The Street, Earl Soham IP13 7RL
TEL: (01728) 685758
on A1120, 3m W of Framlingham

This neat white pub on the main village road ('The Street'), just by the green, offers beers from the Earl Soham brewery (which until recent years was out the back – now it's in larger premises down the road), including Victoria Bitter, Albert Ale, Gannet Mild and Sir Roger's Porter. There is also local apple juice, and five wines by the glass. Traditional pub food takes in ploughman's, casseroles, salads and fish specials. Children are welcome. Much of the village is designated as a conservation area, and The Street is built on top of an old Roman road with a 'kink' in the middle.

Open *11.30 to 3, 6 to 11, Sun 12 to 3, 7 to 10.30*

EAST BERGHOLT

Essex   map 3

Kings Head

Burnt Oak, East Bergholt CO7 6TL
TEL: (01206) 298190

off B1070, follow signs to Flatford Mill

Set in Constable country, the Kings Head draws in walkers as well as locals, who will find Adnams Bitter and Broadside, and Greene King IPA on draft, and dishes such as steak and kidney pudding and daily fish specials on offer, and a traditional roast at Sunday lunch. Three red and three white wines come by the glass. No food evenings Sunday and Monday. Lawned garden with picnic benches.

Open *12 to 3, 6.30 to 11, Sun 12 to 3, 7.30 to 10.30*

EAST LYNG

Somerset   map 2

Rose & Crown

East Lyng TA3 5AU
TEL: (01823) 698235

Low beams, stone floors, a grandfather clock and a large inglenook taking up one entire wall define the style inside this comfortable, well-kept village pub with an attractive garden behind. On draught are Butcombe Bitter and Gold and Palmer 200, while the menu keeps things simple: sandwiches, ploughman's, omelettes, mixed grill and steaks, though specialty ice creams lend a dash of interest for dessert lovers. Four wines by the glass. Accommodation in one room.

Open *11 to 2.30, 6.30 to 11, Sun 12 to 3, 7 to 10.30*

EAST RUSTON

Norfolk   map 6

Butcher's Arms

East Ruston NR12 9JG
TEL: (01692) 650237

The Butcher's Arms is aptly named: it's made up of a former butcher's shop and three cottages. Bass is on draught in the bar along with a guest such as Woodforde's Wherry Best Bitter, Nelson's Revenge or a brew from Adnams. Home-cooked food is served in the eating areas, and on weekdays there's a bargain £2.50 lunch. Children are welcome in the eating areas, and there's plenty of space outside.

Open *12 to 2.30, 7 to 11 (10.30 Sun)*

EGLINGHAM

Northumberland   map 10

Tankerville Arms

Eglingham NE66 2TX
TEL: (01665) 578444

In a typical Northumbrian village of grey-stone cottages, the Tankerville is an attractive pub with a welcoming log fire in winter. An engaging line-up of beers might include Mordue Workie Ticket, Black Sheep Best Bitter and Timothy Taylor Landlord, and over 25 wines are on offer. Blackboard specials complement an ambitious main menu: perhaps cream of leek and smoked salmon soup, then cannon of venison on a red onion tart with port sauce; there are also sandwiches and salads. No food Mon or Tue in Jan and Feb.

Open *12 to 2 (3 Fri to Sun summer), 6.30 (7 Sun to Thur winter, 6 Fri to Sun summer) to 11; closed 25 Dec*

ELSTEAD

Surrey   map 3

Woolpack

The Green, Elstead GU8 6HD
TEL: (01252) 703106

Solid and traditional, and popular, the Woolpack enjoys a classic position by the green in an attractive North Downs village. Old weaving equipment and the odd sheepskin gently theme the interior, where the best of the atmosphere is in the main bar, with its wooden counter and scrubbed-wood furniture. Well-kept beers come from Young's and Greene King, and ten wines are listed by the glass. A goodly number of traditional dishes is offered on the blackboard menus in the more polished dining area and served in generous portions. New ownership is anticipated as we go to press.

Open *Mon to Fri 11 to 3, 5.30 to 11, Sat 11 to 11, Sun 12 to 10.30; closed evening 26 Dec*

FALSTONE

Northumberland   map 10

Blackcock Inn

Falstone NE48 1AA
TEL: (01434) 240200

off B3620, 8m W of Bellingham

This old-time snug hostelry with its
traditional atmosphere draws in walkers
and visitors to Kielder reservoir and forest
as well as locals. One attraction is the
impressive line-up of real ales: John
Smith's Magnet, Theakston Cool Cask,
and guests such as Cains Dr Duncan's IPA
and others from Jennings, Wylam and
Brakspear. Food is traditional too, and two
wines are sold by the glass.
Accommodation in six rooms.

Open *winter Mon to Fri 7 to 11, Sat and Sun 12 to
2.30, 7 to 11 (10.30 Sun); summer also open
lunchtimes 12 to 3*

FEERING

Essex   map 3

Sun Inn

Feering CO5 9NH
TEL: (01376) 570442

Excellent real ales – for example, Crouch
Vale Brewers Gold, Young's Bitter, Mighty
Oak IPA and Icebreaker, Ridleys Old Bob
and Archers Black Jack Porter – around 35
single malt whiskies, and a friendly
atmosphere complete with log fires bring
in the visitors to this sixteenth-century
inn. Bar menus offer traditional favourites
such as liver braised with bacon, or 'B.O.G
pie' (beef, oyster and Guinness), but also
ostrich steak with cream mustard sauce, or
for vegetarians bean, cheese and pickle
loaf. Six wines by the glass. No credit/debit
cards. Pleasant courtyard and garden for
outside eating.
Open *12 to 3, 6 to 11 (10.30 Sun)*

FENNY BENTLEY

Derbyshire   map 5

Coach and Horses

Fenny Bentley DE6 1LB
TEL: (01335) 350246

Success has seen this roadside inn expand
from the original low-ceilinged and
beamed bar (now neatly spruced up) into
two additional dining areas, one
comfortably cottagey, the other more

formal. Open fires add to the welcoming
atmosphere, and fresh flowers give a touch
of refinement. Customers can drop in at
any time for food, and a 'rich, meaty' game
pie has met with approval. Marston's
Pedigree is the regular beer, with a guest
such as Timothy Taylor Landlord or
Bateman XB, and half a dozen wines come
by the glass.
Open *11 to 11, Sun 12 to 10.30*

FIR TREE

Co Durham   map 10

Duke of York

Fir Tree DL15 8DG
TEL: (01388) 762848

on A68, 4m S of Tow Law

The A1 may have long superseded the A68
as the highway to Scotland, but this former
coaching inn on the old road still makes a
smart choice as a stopover. Settle in to the
well-appointed lounge, or if the sun shines
you can admire views across pastures to
wooded hills from benched tables in the
garden. A traditional menu delivers sound
cooking and good ingredients. Black Sheep
ales satisfy beer drinkers, and the wine list
runs to around 40 bins. Five rooms are
available.
Open *11 to 2.30 (3 summer), 6.30 to 10.30 (11
summer); closed 25 Dec*

FLAUNDEN

Hertfordshire   map 3

Bricklayers Arms

Long Lane, Hogspit Bottom, Flaunden HP3 0PH
TEL: (01442) 833322

*3m SW of Hemel Hempstead; village signposted
off A41*

A new licensee took over this pretty,
Virginia-creeper-covered little pub since
last year's edition of the Guide, and has
refurbished the interior and extended
opening hours. Beers continue to be a
strong point: regulars now are Old
Speckled Hen, Fuller's London Pride and
Greene King IPA and Abbot Ale,
supplemented by guests from Archers.
Menus have become a little more
ambitious – starters might include red
pepper mussels, followed perhaps by
Banbury duck – though steak and kidney
pie and Sunday roasts are there to buoy up

tradition. Around a dozen wines by the glass. Reports please.

Open *Mon to Sat 11.30 to 11.30, Sun 12 to 11*

FORD

Gloucestershire   map 5

Plough Inn

Ford GL54 5RU
TEL: (01386) 584215

on B4077, 5m E of Winchcombe

At one time this sixteenth-century, slate-roofed, Cotswold-stone inn served as a courthouse, and within are the remains of some indoor stocks used to restrain prisoners, while the cellars acted as a jail. Today's customers, including local jockeys and stable hands, come in for Donnington SBA and BB, Addlestone cider and four wines by the glass, or for the simple, homely cooking: perhaps a main course of fish, steak or a pie. Three guest rooms available.

Open *11 to 11, Sun 12 to 10.30*

FORDCOMBE

Kent   map 3

Chafford Arms

Spring Hill, Fordcombe TN3 0SA
TEL: (01892) 740267

on B2188, off A264, 4m W of Tunbridge Wells

Barrie Leppard has been licensee for nearly four decades at this 1850s tile-hung and part-creeper-clad pub set in a garden which in summer brims with colour. Among ales on offer are Larkins and Marston's Pedigree, and eight wines come by the glass from a list of about 40. Children are welcome. Dishes such as beef stir-fry, prawn provençal, and gammon feature on menus. No food Monday evenings and some Sundays.

Open *11.45 to 11, Sat 11 to 11, Sun 12 to 10.30*

FORTY GREEN

Buckinghamshire   map 3

Royal Standard of England

Forty Green HP9 1XT
TEL: (01494) 673382

off B474 out of Beaconsfield at Knotty Green

Eleventh-century timbers and thirteenth-century plaster set the scene at this venerable hostelry, where Charles II sheltered en route for France after a defeat at Worcester – hence the pub's name. Even the beer is historic: Owd Roger, brewed here for three centuries, is now made by Marston's, but bottles are sold alongside Brakspear, Fiddler's Elbow and guests. On the food front you might find slow-cooked lamb marinated in mild ale and mead alongside devilled pork chops with roasted peppers and onion. Reports please.

Open *11 to 3, 5.30 to 11, Sun 12 to 3, 7 to 10.30*

FOWNHOPE

Herefordshire   map 5

Green Man Inn

Fownhope HR1 4PE
TEL: (01432) 860243

on B4424, 6m SE of Hereford

The Green Man dates from 1485 – and looks it, with its black and white half-timbering both inside and out. This is really more of a hotel than a pub, with its 22 bedrooms and leisure complex, but the two bars have a friendly atmosphere, and Marston's Pedigree, Old Speckled Hen and John Smith's Smooth are among the ales on draught, with an ample choice of wines by the glass. Salads, pasta, grills, steaks and fish specials are what to expect on the bar menus. Children welcome. The Wye, a magnet for fly-fishermen, is half a mile away. A new licensee took over in autumn 2003 – reports on progress please.

Open *11 to 11, Sun 12 to 10.30*

FRESHWATER

Isle of Wight   map 2

Red Lion

Church Place, Freshwater PO40 9BP
TEL: (01983) 754925

Not the easiest place to find: it's next to the church in the most villagey part of town. A large open-plan room with characterful worn sofas has the charm of a good local, and beers are a serious consideration, with Black Sheep Best Bitter, Fuller's London Pride, Flowers Original and local brew Goddards Special on the handpumps. Pheasant casserole and steak and mushroom pudding look set to match any appetite, and there's fish too. Comments on the pun-ridden menu or the ringing of a (banned) mobile phone bring revenue to the RNLI.

Open *Mon to Fri 11.30 to 3, 5.30 to 11, Sat 11 to 3, 6 to 11, Sun 12 to 3, 7 to 10.30*

FRILSHAM

Berkshire map 2

Pot Kiln

Frilsham RG18 0XX
TEL: (01635) 201366

*off B4009; from Yattendon go over motorway
bridge and straight on — do not turn right to
Frilsham*

Beer is a draw at this seventeenth-century
red-brick pub standing on a narrow
country lane. The West Berkshire Brewery
in Yattendon – once located right behind
the pub – still produces Brick Kiln Bitter
exclusively for the Pot Kiln, which serves
it alongside Arkell's BBB and Morland
Original Bitter plus a guest such as West
Berkshire's Dr Hexters Healer. Three
wines are served by the glass. Hungry
walkers are often in evidence, digging into
steak and kidney pudding perhaps, or liver
and bacon casserole.

Open *Wed to Sat and Mon 12 to 3, 6.30 to 11, Sun
12 to 3, 7 to 10.30*

FRITHAM

Hampshire map 2

Royal Oak

Fritham SO43 7HJ
TEL: (02380) 812606

village off A31 and B3078 from M27 junction 1

This tiny whitewashed and thatched
hostelry is everything one would hope for
of a pub on a working farm in the depths
of the New Forest. Unspoilt,
unpretentious and tucked away, the Royal
Oak offers a friendly welcome to all-
comers. Winter fires are a feature, as is the
fine range of ales drawn direct from casks
behind the bar, among them Cheriton
Pots Ale and Ringwood Fortyniner. The
series of small rooms is comfortably laid
out, with floorboards and solid wooden
furniture, while food (lunchtimes only)
matches the simple approach, with honest
ploughman's and home-made quiches,
pies and soups. There's a large garden to
the rear and fine surrounding walks.

Open *Mon to Fri 11 to 3, 6 to 11, Sat 11 to 11,
Sun 12 to 10.30*

FROXFIELD

Hampshire map 2

Trooper Inn

Alton Road, Froxfield GU32 1BD
TEL: (01730) 827293

*from Petersfield, follow signs to Steep and
continue climbing to Froxfield; pub on right*

Inside this substantial white-painted pub,
in the light, wood-floored bar, Ringwood
Best or Fortyniner might be among the
frequently changing guest beers. In the
two pine-furnished dining areas and
restaurant you might find on the menu a
puff pastry case of chicken, smoked bacon
and wild mushrooms in a creamy sauce,
followed by the house speciality of slow-
roast half-shoulder of lamb with honey
and mint gravy, or pan-fried salmon fillet
with scallops and champagne sauce. Deep
in the country, the pub is at Hampshire's
highest point. Eight bedrooms are
available.

Open *12 to 3.30, 6 to 12, Sun 12 to 2.30, 6 to 10.30*

GAWSWORTH

Cheshire map 8

Harrington Arms

Gawsworth SK11 9RR
TEL: (01260) 223325

*take A536 from Macclesfield towards Congleton
and take second left after Warren; pub is 200yds
down road*

Part of a working farm and staffed by the
resident family, the Harrington Arms
offers a unique insight into an earlier era of
rural pub history along with a warm
welcome and a good foaming pint of
Robinson's Best Bitter. The three-storey
red-brick house seems unchanged from a
1910 photograph, with a tiny main bar and
three small parlours inside, and custom
remains largely local. There's no written
menu; just ask the landlady what she has
in the kitchen – perhaps a soup, a cheese
sandwich and a pork pie. 'Our all-time
favourite country pub,' enthused one
visitor.

Open *12 to 3, 6 to 11, Sun 12 to 3, 7 to 10.30*

GLOOSTON

Leicestershire   map 5

Old Barn Inn

Andrews Lane, Glooston LE16 7ST
TEL: (01858) 545215

The Old Barn was built in the sixteenth
century, and its refurbished interior is still
appropriately beamed. Greene King IPA,
Bateman XB Bitter and a couple of guests
are on draught, and a full-dress menu
operates, with special seafood evenings
every six to eight weeks on a Thursday.
Two en suite letting rooms are available.
The Roman road from Leicester to
Colchester runs past the village.
Open *12 to 3, 7 to 11 (10.30 Sun); closed lunchtime
Mon*

GOSFIELD

Essex   map 3

Green Man

The Street, Gosfield CO9 1TP
TEL: (01787) 472746

On the main road through the village, this
old, low, pink building houses a jigsaw of
snug bars and a cosy dining room. The
lunchtime cold buffet, laid out on a huge
trestle table in the main bar, is a popular
draw and is complemented by blackboard
menus of traditional comfort food along
the lines of lasagne and steak and kidney
pudding. Greene King beers – both IPA
and Abbot Ale – are on the handpumps,
and there's a good range of wines by the
glass. New licensees have taken charge –
reports please.
Open *12 to 3, 6.30 to 11, Sun 12 to 3, 7 to 10.30*

GREAT EVERSDEN

Cambridgeshire   map 6

Hoops

2 High Street, Great Eversden CB3 7HN
TEL: (01223) 264008

With a light, clean, modern, cottagey
décor, this pub is the setting for good beers
from Nethergate and Adnams, and a
strictly Thai menu that offers dishes that
are 'freshly cooked and enjoyable',
according to a visitor well versed in Asian
cuisines. The mix of standing room and
dining areas in the open-plan interior
makes it a welcoming place for both
drinking and eating. Winter nights are
warmed by a log fire, while a grassed beer
garden comes into play in the summer.
Open *12 to 2 (3 Sun), 6 to 11 (10.30 Sun); closed
Mon lunchtime*

GREAT LANGDALE

Cumbria   map 8

Old Dungeon Ghyll Hotel

Great Langdale LA22 9JY
TEL: (015394) 37272

on B5343, 6m from Skelwith Bridge on A593

Real ales are a strong suit here, with the
bar dispensing Theakston XB and Old
Peculier, Jennings Cumberland, Black
Sheep Special Ale and Yates Bitter, plus
guests like Brains SA or Moorhouses
Pendle Witches Brew. For cider drinkers
there is Weston's Old Rosie, and the wine
list has three by the glass. Food is of the
filling and substantial sort (curry, chilli con
carne, Cumberland sausage), and the first
Wednesday of each month is folk music
night. The hotel is in a magnificent setting,
surrounded by fells, and has long been a
draw for serious walkers and climbers,
although others can just enjoy the views.
The hotel has 13 rooms.
Open *11 to 11, Sun 12 to 10.30*

GREAT OUSEBURN

North Yorkshire   map 9

Crown

Main Street, Great Ouseburn YO26 9RF
TEL: (01423) 330430

off B6265 5m S of Boroughbridge

Great Ouseburn, between the Ouse and
the Nidd, is quite close to the A1, so this
attractive eighteenth-century white pub,
with a red-pantiled roof, makes a
convenient stopping-off point. A new back
extension now houses a brasserie, but
otherwise the interior is nicely traditional.
The brasserie menu runs to dishes such as
sea bass with avocado and mango salsa, and
pork fillet with mustard mash. John
Smith's Bitter and Black Sheep Best are on
draught, and ten wines are served by the
glass. A beer terrace has recently been
completed.
Open *Mon to Fri 5 to 11, Sat 12 to 11, Sun 12 to
10.30*

GRITTLETON

Wiltshire   map 2

Neeld Arms Inn

The Street, Grittleton SN14 6AP
TEL: (01249) 782470

*from M4 junction 17 take A429 N and follow
signs to Grittleton*

Built in the seventeenth century of
Cotswold stone, the Neeld Arms is an
unpretentious pub, opposite Grittleton
House, its interior decorated in rustic
style. On the blackboard menu might be
miniature game pasties with Cumberland
sauce, followed by salmon and prawn
fishcakes with tartare sauce, or sweet-and-
sour beef curry with rice, and then lemon
tart with rhubarb sauce. Buckley's Best
Bitter, from Brains, and Wadworth 6X are
the regulars on handpump, with a couple
of guests that might include Hook Norton
Best Bitter. Four wines are sold by the
glass. All six guest bedrooms are en suite.
Open *Mon to Fri 12 to 3, 5.30 (5 Fri) to 11, Sat 12
to 3.30, 5.30 to 11, Sun 12 to 3.30, 7
(6 summer) to 10.30*

HAMBLEDON

Hampshire   map 2

Vine Inn

West Street, Hambledon PO7 4RW
TEL: (02392) 632419

At the edge of one of Hampshire's most
picturesque villages, deep in rolling
downland and close to the Meon Valley,
this homely village local serves unfussy
meals in the carpeted dining area, where
sea bass with parsley and lemon or ribeye
steak with pepper sauce set the standard.
A winning selection of real ales –
Ringwood Best, Butcombe Bitter, Gale's
Butser Bitter and more – might be best
enjoyed in the former public bar with its
piano, sofa and a shove-ha'penny board.
Open *11.30 to 3.30, 6 to 11, Sun 12 to 4, 7 to 10.30*

HAPPISBURGH

Norfolk   map 6

Hill House

Happisburgh NR12 0PW
TEL: (01692) 650004

Conan Doyle stayed at this inn, which
dates from the sixteenth century, in 1903
and wrote *The Dancing Men* here. As well
as Shepherd Neame Spitfire Premium Ale
on draught, plus four regularly changing
guests, Elementary Ale is brewed locally to
the pub's own recipe, and wines include a
dozen moderately priced bins. Food on the
printed menu leans towards the plain and
simple, while a board above the bar lists
the specials; a themed evening, such as
Italian or Greek, is held every other Friday.
Open *winter Mon to Wed 12 to 3, 7 to 11, Thur to
Sat 11 to 11, Sun 12 to 10.30; summer 12 to 11, Sun
12 to 10.30*

HARTFIELD

East Sussex   map 3

Anchor Inn

Church Street, Hartfield TN7 4AG
TEL: (01892) 770424

*village on junction of B2026 and B2110, 6m SE
of East Grinstead*

The small village of Hartfield makes a
good starting point, and refuelling stop, for
walkers in the Ashdown Forest and for
Pooh-sticks players (that bridge is close
by). On the menu here might be beef
satay, grilled gammon steak, salmon
fishcakes with spinach, or turkey with
Parma ham and goats' cheese, while on
draught are five real ales, including Fuller's
London Pride, Adnams Bitter and a brew
from Harveys. Children are welcome.
Two rooms are available for B&B.
Open *11 to 11, Sun 12 to 10.30*

HASCOMBE

Surrey   map 3

White Horse

Hascombe GU8 4JA
TEL: (01483) 208258

on B2130, 3m SE of Godalming

Flowers Original, Adnams Best and
Harveys Sussex Best are on draught at this
attractive-looking pub. The bar menu
might include Thai-style salmon and
prawn fishcakes, or beef in ale pie, and five
wines are served by the glass. The large
lawned garden and a family room inside
are a draw for families. Winkworth
Arboretum is nearby.
Open *Mon to Fri 11 to 3, 5.30 to 11, Sat 11 to 11,
Sun 12 to 10.30*

HAWRIDGE COMMON

Buckinghamshire   map 3

Full Moon

Hawridge Common, Cholesbury HP5 2UH
TEL: (01494) 758959

off A416 N out of Chesham, towards Cholesbury

High on the open reaches of the
common, this thriving one-time drovers'
inn is a popular pit-stop for Chiltern
walkers and others who are out and
about. The low-ceilinged interior now
has extensions for dining, but the
traditional atmosphere remains. Six well-
tended real ales are on tap (including
Adnams, Brakspear and Bass). Lunches
and bar food promise hearty stuff from
ploughman's to lamb and mint suet
pudding, while restaurant-style dishes
appear in the evening. Sit in the delightful
garden on a warm summer's evening or
relax on the covered terrace.

Open *Mon to Fri 12 to 3, 5.30 to 11, Sat 12 to 11,
Sun 12 to 10.30*

HEATH

West Yorkshire   map 9

Kings Arms

Heath Common, Heath WF1 5SL
TEL: (01924) 377527

*from A638 between Wakefield and Crofton take
A655, then turn left to Heath and Kirkthorpe*

Ales served at the part-panelled bar here,
with its old black range, are Tetley Bitter,
Clark's Classic Blonde, John Smith's
Bitter and Timothy Taylor Landlord, and
there's a short wine list. Food-wise, a
range of familiar pub staples is served,
with a board of specials extending choices,
and the restaurant has its own more
upmarket menu. Dating from the early
eighteenth century, the pub is in a
picturesque village overlooking Heath
Common, a 100-acre area of grassland
(ideal for walkers).

Open *winter Mon to Fri 11.30 to 3, 5.30 to 11,
Sat 11.30 to 11, Sun 12 to 10.30; summer 11 to 11,
Sun 12 to 10.30*

HELFORD

Cornwall   map 1

Shipwrights Arms

Helford TR12 6JX
TEL: (01326) 231235

on S side of Helford River, 7m E of Helston

With peaceful views of the Helford River
and the wooded creek on which the
village has grown up, this thatched pub's
terraced gardens, dropping down to the
water's edge, make a delightful spot on a
good day. Alternatively, take one of the
oak settles in the bar, with its open fire
and nautical memorabilia, and have a pint
of Castle Eden Ale or Sharp's Doom Bar
Bitter or one of the five wines sold by the
glass. The pub is known for its steaks,
and among other offerings might be
monkfish marinated in chilli, lime and
coriander, or Cajun pork chops. Children
are welcome.

Open *11 to 2.30, 6 to 10.30 (11 summer); closed
Sun eve winter*

HELSTON

Cornwall   map 1

Blue Anchor

50 Coinagehall Street, Helston TR13 8EL
TEL: (01326) 565765

The Blue Anchor is one of the oldest pubs
in the country: it was built in the early
fifteenth century as a rest home for monks
and became a tavern after Henry VIII's
Dissolution of the Monasteries. Own-
brew ales are Spingo Best, Spingo Middle
and Special, and Spingo also turns up in a
beef dish on a menu where hearty pies,
pan-fried duck, lamb and fishcakes also
feature. Four B&B bedrooms.

Open *11 to 11, Sun 12 to 10.30; closed eve 25 Dec*

HERMITAGE

West Sussex   map 2

Sussex Brewery

36 Main Road, Hermitage, Emsworth
PO10 8AU
TEL: (01243) 371533

on A259, just out of Emsworth towards Chichester

As its name suggests, this rustic
seventeenth-century pub once brewed its
own beer, but nowadays it's tied to
Young's and stocks the brewer's full range,

plus Smiles Heritage and Bristol IPA.
Expect few frills – just simple furnishings
– although over 40 kinds of sausages are an
attraction, among them pork, port and
Stilton; and chicken, orange and walnut.
Outside is a walled garden.
Open *11 to 11 (10.30 Sun)*

HESKET NEWMARKET

Cumbria   map 10

Old Crown
Hesket Newmarket CA7 8JG
TEL: (016974) 78288

Look for the sign or you'll miss the pub in
the midst of a modest Victorian terrace in
this remote Cumbrian village, and even
once inside you could be in someone's
living room but for the bar. Beers are
exclusively from the Hesket Newmarket
Brewery at the back of the pub (groups can
arrange a tour) with locally inspired names
like Helvellyn Gold, Blencathra and Cat
Bells Pale Ale. Food runs to eight curries,
traditional bangers and mash, and
vegetable lasagne.
Open *Mon and Tue 5.30 to 11, Wed to Sat 12 to 3,
5.30 to 11, Sun 12 to 3, 7 to 10.30; no food Mon and
Tue winter*

HILDERSHAM

Cambridgeshire   map 6

Pear Tree
Hildersham CB1 6BU
TEL: (01223) 891680

With its brick bar and wood-burning stove,
this is a quiet, unpretentious one-room
local. Nowadays, the tables have legs, but
they used to be suspended on chains, some
of which remain dangling from the ceiling.
Among the drinks available are Greene
King IPA, Abbot Ale and a changing guest
– perhaps Wadworth 6X – plus a modest
list of wines, with half a dozen by the glass.
Food is straightforward, along the lines of
steak and kidney pudding.
Open *11.45 to 2, 6.30 (6 Fri and Sat) to 11, Sun
12 to 2, 7 to 10.30*

HOLBETON

Devon   map 1

Mildmay Colours
Holbeton PL8 1NA
TEL: (01752) 830248
*off A379 Plymouth to Modbury road, 1m after
National Shire Horse Centre, signposted
Mothecombe and Holbeton*

Real ale is taken seriously at this white,
sixteenth-century pub, with regular beers
Colours Best and SP from Skinner's in
Truro joined by constantly changing
guests – perhaps something from
Blackawton or Sutton. The horse-racing
motif carries through from the pub sign to
the menu, where chicken liver pâté or a
half-pint of garlic prawns might be listed
under 'starter's orders' and Cheddar
ploughman's under 'nosebag nibbles';
otherwise, expect gammon topped with
melted cheese and a fried egg, or Mexican
chicken enchilada, with curry on
Wednesday, fish on Friday, and a carvery at
Sunday lunchtime. Children are welcome
in the large family room, and there are
seven en suite bedrooms.
Open *11 to 2.30 (3 summer), 6 to 11, Sun 12 to 3,
7 to 11*

HOLYWELL

Cambridgeshire   map 6

Old Ferry Boat Inn
Holywell PE27 4TG
TEL: (01480) 463227
off A1123, 3m SE of St Ives

Built as a ferry house beside the Ouse, this
low, whitewashed and thatched pub is said
to have sold alcohol since the year 560,
making it one of the oldest inns in England
(it's mentioned in the Domesday Book).
The ghost of Juliet, a suicidal victim of
unrequited love for a woodcutter,
reputedly walks at midnight on the
anniversary of her death on 17 March
1078, but the Greene King ales on draught
in the beamed, part-panelled bar are real
enough, as are dishes like bacon and
Speckled Hen pie, followed perhaps by
banoffi pie. The terrace gives good river
views, and B&B is provided in seven
rooms.
Open *11.30 to 11, Sun 12 to 10.30*

HOOK NORTON

Oxfordshire   map 5

Pear Tree Inn

Scotland End, Hook Norton OX15 5NU
TEL: (01608) 737482

Tied to the Hook Norton Brewery, just along the lane, the Pear Tree stocks the brewer's full range of ales. A log fire creates a warm and welcoming atmosphere in the wooden-floored bar, with its mixture of rustic furnishings. On the food front, expect straightforward pub fare along the lines of steaks and scampi, although the specials might be more enterprising at weekends. Around half a dozen wines are served by the glass, and there are also nine or so fruit wines. The pub has a children's licence until 9pm, and in the large garden is an outdoor chess set. B&B is available in three double rooms.

Open *Mon to Fri 11.30 to 2.30, 6 to 11, Sat 11.30 to 4, 6 to 11 (11 to 11 summer), Sun 12 to 4, 7 to 10.30*

HORSEBRIDGE

Hampshire   map 2

John o' Gaunt

Horsebridge SO20 6PU
TEL: (01794) 388394

1m off A3057, 8m W of Winchester

The Test Way long-distance path and the river are just 100 yards from this diminutive country pub. Walkers and cyclists mingle with locals in the totally traditional bar, where southern regional ales such as Ringwood Best and Fortyniner, Palmers IPA and Itchen Valley Godfathers are on draught. The kitchen delivers unfussy food in the shape of lamb curry, local sausages with onion gravy, and salmon and dill fishcakes. Accommodation should be up-and-running sometime in 2004.

Open *Mon to Fri 11 to 3,6 to 11, Sat 11 to 11, Sun 12 to 10.30*

HORSEY

Norfolk   map 6

Nelson Head

Beach Road, Horsey NR29 4AD
TEL: (01493) 393378

The bird sanctuaries of Hickling Broad and Winterton Dunes are near this brick-built pub, with the unspoilt beach and Horsey Mere even nearer. The interior is decorated with farming and nautical implements, and log fires burn in cooler weather. Children are welcome in the family room, and, appropriately, fish is something of a house speciality on the restaurant menu (also available in the bar). Woodforde's Wherry Best Bitter and Nelson's Revenge on draught are sometimes joined by a third ale from the same brewery, and a couple of wines are served by the glass from a choice of around a dozen bottles.

Open *11 to 3, 6 to 11 (10 Mon to Wed winter), Sun 12 to 3, 6 to 10.30; closed evenings 25 and 26 Dec*

HURLEY

Berkshire   map 2

Dew Drop

Batts Green, Hurley SL6 6RB
TEL: (01628) 824327

take Honey Lane off A423, just outside Hurley between Maidenhead and Henley-on-Thames, continue past council houses and through farm until wood; at T-junction take right turn on to smaller lane; inn is a few hundred yards on right

Dating from the seventeenth century, the Dew Drop is in a rural setting in woods just outside the village. A Brakspear tied house, it sells the brewery's range of ales, including seasonal ones. Both a printed menu and a board in the two bars (children allowed in one) announce what food is on offer, from sandwiches to home-made pies and fish specials, with occasional seasonal game dishes. Three wines are served by the glass. The large garden is ideal for summer eating and drinking.

Open *12 to 3, 6 to 11, Sun 12 to 3, 7 to 10.30*

HYDE

Gloucestershire   map 2

Ragged Cot Inn

Cirencester Road, Hyde GL6 8PE
TEL: (01453) 884643

take B4077 from Stow-on-the-Wold towards Toddington, turn left towards Temple Guiting and Hyde is about 1m down road; pub is on left

For all its middle-of-nowhere location, this seventeenth-century Cotswold-stone inn is a busy destination. A warren of rooms with bare walls provides a traditional pub ambience, while a substantial conservatory built of old materials adds extra no-smoking dining space and a view of the large, immaculately trimmed gardens. Choose from straightforward bar snacks or the likes of pheasant with bacon, onion and mushroom sauce from the restaurant menu. Cotswold Way, Smiles Best and Very Old Spot are on the handpumps, and eight wines come by the glass. Accommodation available.

Open *11 to 11, Sun 12 to 10.30*

INGLEBY

Derbyshire   map 5

John Thompson
Ingleby DE73 1HW
TEL: (01332) 862469

In a picturesque country setting, this traditionally furnished pub, dating from the fifteenth century, has a homely, friendly atmosphere. Own-brewed JTS ales – among them Summer Gold and Porter – are on draught, along with a guest, and three wines are served by the glass. Carvery-style meals are served at lunchtime, including perhaps roast beef with Yorkshire pudding (described by a reporter as 'beautiful'), when children are welcome throughout (there's a family room for use in the evening).

Open *Mon to Fri 11 to 2.30, 5 to 11, all day Sat and Sun; closed evening 25 Dec*

INGS

Cumbria   map 8

Watermill
Ings LA8 9PY
TEL: (01539) 821309
just off A591, 2m E of Windermere

Real ale fans can sample eight regular beers and the same number of guests at this 250-year-old former wood mill; among the former are Coniston Bluebird, Cotleigh Hawkshead Bitter and Moorhouses Black Cat, with Skinner's Betty Stogs Bitter and Timothy Taylor Landlord among the latter. Food is served throughout the pub, and around half a dozen wines are available by the glass. Those wishing to avoid the throngs of Windermere can take advantage of one

of the seven en suite bedrooms, and children – and dogs – are welcome. There are seats outside by the River Gowan.

Open *12 to 11, Sun 12 to 10.30*

INKBERROW

Worcestershire   map 5

Old Bull
Inkberrow WR7 4DZ
TEL: (01386) 792428

Close to the church in a quiet village, this half-timbered pub, dating from Tudor times, has a splendid beamed interior with a collar-beam-framed ceiling and memorabilia relating to *The Archers* – it was the model for the Bull in the radio series. Courage Directors, Flowers Original and Tetley cask are on draught, eight wines are sold by the glass, and traditional pub fare shows up on the menu and specials board, with fish 'n' chips the speciality on Fridays.

Open *12 to 11 (10.30 Sun)*

INKPEN

Berkshire   map 2

Crown and Garter
Great Common Road, Inkpen RG17 9QR
TEL: (01488) 668325

This out-of-the-way hostelry on the edge of Inkpen Common is reached via unclassified roads. The best room is the characterful bar that is all relaxed, rustic charm, with a huge oak settle, a log fire, dark wood-block flooring and beams. A good range of beers is chalked up on a board: West Berkshire Brewery's Mr Chubb's Lunchtime Bitter, Good Old Boy, Moonlight and a guest. The printed and blackboard menus take in fish dishes, steaks, traditional pies, a Thai selection and more. Accommodation available.

Open *Mon, Tues 6.30 to 11, Wed to Fri 12 to 3, 6.30 to 11, Sat 12 to 3, 6 to 11, Sun 12 to 3, 7 to 10.30 (12 to 10.30 Apr to Sept)*

Swan Inn
Lower Green, Inkpen RG17 9DX
TEL: (01488) 668326

Parts of this rambling whitewashed building date from the seventeenth century, and traditional country décor is the order of the day, with plenty of polished dark wood and a log fire in the bar. Organic beef from the owners' farm dominates the blackboard menu in the guise of burgers, curries, prize-winning sausages or simply plainly boiled and served with carrots. Beers (from Butts) and wines are organic too. The Cygnet Restaurant notches things up a gear. Accommodation available.

Open *Mon and Tue 12 to 2, 7 to 11, Wed to Sat 12 to 2.30, 5 to 11 (Sat 11 to 11 summer), Sun 12 to 2.30, 7 to 10.30 (12 to 10.30 summer); closed 25 and 26 Dec*

IPSWICH

Suffolk map 6

Fat Cat
288 Spring Road, Ipswich IP4 5NL
TEL: (01473) 726524
on E side of Ipswich, near main hospital

The sister establishment to the Norwich Fat Cat (see Round-up entry) stands in a red-brick terrace on the way out of town. Framed beer awards line the otherwise unassuming interior, with its dark wooden furniture, and old signs and beer memorabilia on the walls. At the rear, a solid conservatory extension opens on to a paved beer garden. Beer is the draw for locals and enthusiasts, with 17 real ales listed on a blackboard over the bar, backed up by Belgian brews, a handful of wines and a dozen fruit wines. Food is as basic as it comes – Scotch eggs, pasties, and sandwiches. Friendly service.

Open *12 (11 Sat) to 11, Sun 12 to 10.30*

KELD

North Yorkshire map 8

Tan Hill Inn
Keld DL11 6ED
TEL: (01833) 628246
off B6270 at Keld, then 4m N

As it's too remote to be on the national grid, a generator provides electricity for this inn on the Pennine Way – at around 1,700 feet above sea level, Britain's highest. Despite its isolated location, it's a popular place, particularly with walkers, who can thaw out in front of an open fire and seek revival from traditional pub food (with Yorkshire puddings to the fore); they can also stay the night in one of seven

bedrooms. Theakston Old Peculier, XB, and guest ales are on draught.

Open *11 to 11, Sun 12 to 10.30*

KINGSBRIDGE

Devon map 1

Crabshell Inn
Embankment Road, Kingsbridge TQ7 1JZ
TEL: (01548) 852345

This popular pub welcomes children – and dogs – especially in the well-equipped games room. The wide-ranging menu runs from sandwiches to a daily roast, fish, chips and peas, and platters of crab, lobster and mixed seafood. Bass, Crabshell Bitter and Flowers IPA are on draught, along with guests such as Fuller's London Pride, and a handful of wines are served by the glass. Outside, on the estuary, is a quay 125 feet long where boats moor; there are seats out here, although some of it is used as a car park.

Open *11 to 11, Sun 12 to 10.30*

KIRTLING

Cambridgeshire map 6

Red Lion
The Street, Kirtling CB8 9PD
TEL: (01638) 731976

Not far from Newmarket in countryside devoted to the racing industry, this long, low, cottagey building struck one visitor as 'the perfect pub to stumble across', with the 'authenticity and special atmosphere' that draws locals and tourists, diners and drinkers alike. Inside are a simple L-shaped bar and a couple of dining areas – one rustic, the other more formal – where a straightforward pub menu is served. Beers on draught include brews from Adnams and Nethergate. Hopefully, the new licensee will keep the magic alive – reports please.

Open *Tue to Sun 12 to 3, 7 to 11*

KNEBWORTH

Hertfordshire map 3

Lytton Arms
Park Lane, Old Knebworth SG3 6QB
TEL: (01438) 812312
from Knebworth on B197, take side road signposted Old Knebworth

Beer and wine drinkers are spoiled for choice at the Lytton Arms, with six real ales on handpump and a list of 50 wines, all sold by the glass. Food is a strong point too, with a menu taking in steak and ale pie, beef stew with dumplings, duck in plum sauce, and fish 'n' chips; vegetarian dishes are always available, and traditional roasts are served on Sundays.

Open *11 to 11, Sun 12 to 10.30; closed eve 25 Dec*

LACOCK

Wiltshire   map 2

Red Lion

1 High Street, Lacock SN15 2LQ
TEL: (01249) 730456

Lacock is famous for its abbey, established in the thirteenth century, and the museum commemorating Fox Talbot, pioneer photographer, and the village itself is a popular tourist spot, with its ancient stone and half-timbered buildings. The décor in the bar of this spacious eighteenth-century pub includes agricultural implements, bellows and a vast fireplace, while the menus offer traditional cooking in the form of beef and ale pie, and lamb and port casserole. Wadworth JCB and guest ales are kept, and around ten wines are served by the glass. Accommodation is available.

Open *11.30 to 2.30, 6 to 11 (summer Sat 11 to 11), Sun 12 to 3, 7 to 10.30 (summer 12 to 10.30)*

LANCASTER

Lancashire   map 8

John O' Gaunt

Market Square, Lancaster LA1 1JG
TEL: (01524) 65356

Slap in the middle of Lancaster, this long, narrow building is a popular haunt. Blackboards proffer various sorts of drinks and food, with much space devoted to the impressive range of draught beers: seven are served at any one time from breweries that include Tetley, Jennings and Bass. Around 40 wines are sold by the glass, and the traditional pub food includes the house speciality of Yorkshire pudding filled with chilli. 'I'd make it my local if I were nearer,' concluded one satisfied reporter.

Open *11 to 11, Sun 12 to 10.30*

LANGTON HERRING

Dorset   map 2

Elm Tree

Shop Lane, Langton Herring DT3 4HU
TEL: (01305) 871257

In summer, displays of flowers add splashes of colour to this cream-painted, slate-roofed pub in a rural setting near Chesil Beach. The interior has the atmosphere of an English country pub, with an open fire and high-backed settles, and the blackboard menu might feature something as traditional as steak and ale pie or local crab alongside pasta dishes. Marston's Pedigree is on draught alongside perhaps Bass, and all the wines on the list are served by the glass.

Open *12 to 3, 6 to 11, Sun 12 to 3, 7 (6.30 summer) to 10.30*

LAPWORTH

Warwickshire   map 5

Navigation Inn

Old Warwick Road, Lapworth BN4 6NA
TEL: (01564) 783337
on B4439, 1m SE of Hockley Heath

Stuffed fish decorate the bar of this friendly pub on the bank of the Grand Union Canal. At the rear of the building is a no-smoking dining room, where game might be on the menu. Bass and a constantly changing guest ale – perhaps Badger Tanglefoot or Everards Original – are on draught, and five wines are available by the glass. Children are welcome, and there is a canalside garden.

Open *Mon to Fri 11 to 3, 5.30 to 11, Sat 11 to 11, Sun 12 to 10.30*

LEEDS

West Yorkshire   map 9

Grove

Back Row, off Water Lane, Leeds LS11 5PL
TEL: (0113) 243 9254

Marooned among office buildings and new developments just south of the station, this old-fashioned pub – bare floorboards, a dartboard and well-worn paintwork – holds a broad appeal. Four rooms cater to a mixed clientele of regulars, real ale lovers, and club meetings, while music fans come for live folk and jazz. Well-kept beers include Banks's

Bitter, Deuchars IPA, Jennings Cumberland Ale, Wells Bombardier Premium Bitter and Adnams Broadside. One visitor enjoyed a pie 'full of large chunks of tender steak' from the menu of hearty, good-value home cooking (lunchtimes only).
Open *12 to 11, Sun 12 to 10.30*

Town Street Tavern
16 Town Street, Horsforth, Leeds LS18 4RJ
TEL: (0113) 281 9996

The suburb of Horsforth is well served by this multi-purpose tavern, a convenient lunchtime spot on the main shopping street. Downstairs is a large, popular bar with an excellent range of beers from breweries such as Black Sheep, Jennings, Timothy Taylor and Caledonian alongside European specials and a list of 30 or so wines. There are bar snacks too, but the upstairs brasserie is the place for serious eating: perhaps chicken livers in sherry and cream followed by lamb shank with mash. Friendly service throughout. This is the sister establishment of Bar T'at in Ilkley (see main entry).
Open *12 to 11, Sun 12 to 10.30*

Whitelocks
Turks Head Yard, Briggate, Leeds LS1 6HB
TEL: (0113) 245 3950

This long, narrow pub, in an alleyway off the main drag of Briggate, is a throwback to the Victorian era, with its mirrors, brass fittings, etched glass and black-painted woodwork. Real ales are from Wentworth, with guests from breweries like Caledonian, and around 15 wines are available by the glass. Sandwiches, steak pie, and Yorkshire pudding with onion gravy are the order of the day on the food front.
Open *11 to 11, Sun 12 to 10.30*

LEICESTER
Leicestershire   map 5

Globe
43 Silver Street, Leicester LE1 5EU
TEL: (0116) 262 9819

Local farmers once stopped here to hire labourers at harvest time. Now this red-brick Georgian building in the heart of Leicester's shopping lanes throngs with

suited workers intent on putting nothing more than an elbow to work. An impressive range of Everards ales is complemented by up to four guests. The narrow bar area packs out quickly, but there is room to relax in the beamed lounge or glass-roofed conservatory. Food is straightforward and filling at bargain prices.
Open *11 to 11, Sun 12 to 10.30*

LITTLE BARRINGTON
Oxfordshire   map 2

Inn For All Seasons
Little Barrington OX18 4TN
TEL: (01451) 844324

Creepers sprawl grandly over the walls of this large Cotswold-stone inn on a busy stretch of the A40. Flagstone floors and hop garlands give a snug, traditional feel in the bar, where Wadworth 6X and a guest such as Wychwood or Sharp's Doom Bar Bitter are on tap and 14 wines come by the glass (with over 100 on the full list). Burgundy-coloured carpets, cushions and curtains add a certain plushness to the dining room. The menu is particularly strong on fish, with daily deliveries from Brixham: perhaps pan-fried red mullet on a rosemary and tomato butter sauce.
Open *11 to 2.30, 6 to 11, Sun 12 to 2.30, 7 to 10.30*

LITTLE CHEVERELL
Wiltshire   map 2

Owl
Low Road, Little Cheverell SN10 4JS
TEL: (01380) 812263
on B3098 ¼ m W of A360

Decking outside the Owl overlooks the spit-level garden, with a brook running through it, and has views over farmland to Salisbury Plain. Inside, a wood-burning stove is called into use in winter; farming implements add decoration, and there's an assortment of wooden furniture. The menus run from ploughman's and sandwiches to seafood Mornay, followed by seared swordfish steak with caper hollandaise, or grilled Barbary duck breast with black cherry sauce, and over 20 wines are served by the glass. A good choice of real ales might encompass Wadworth 6X, Greene King IPA, Hook Norton Best

Bitter and Brakspear Bitter. The pub has two en suite bedrooms.

Open *winter 11 to 3, 6 to 11.30, Sun 12 to 4, 7 to 10.30; summer 11.30 to 11.30, Sun 12 to 4, 7 to 10.30*

LITTLE LONGSTONE

Derbyshire map 8

Packhorse Inn

Little Longstone DE45 1NN
TEL: (01629) 640471

off B6465, 2m NW of Bakewell

On the old packhorse route between Chesterfield and Monsal Head, this eighteenth-century inn is also in prime Peak District walking country. Converted from two cottages, it still has plenty of old-fashioned character, with log fires, local prints and photos on the walls. Two handpumps in the 'tap room' dispense Marston's Pedigree and a guest – perhaps Old Speckled Hen – and the daily menu deals in traditional home-made food (beef stew with Yorkshire pudding, for example). Children are welcome in the lounge and dining room, and the pub has a refurbished beer garden.

Open *noon to 11 all week*

LITTLE MISSENDEN

Buckinghamshire map 3

Crown

Little Missenden, nr Amersham HP7 0RD
TEL: (01494) 862571

'A really fascinating and genuinely traditional pub' that has been run by the same family for some 90 years. It's a spick-and-span place with simple furnishings in the Muzak- and machine-free bar and very likeable, chatty hosts. Well-kept draught beers from Adnams, Fuller's and others are supplemented by a guest from, say, Hop Back. Food is limited to decent sandwiches and a few snacks at lunchtime. There's an acre of land and a large beer garden at the back of the pub.

Open *Mon to Fri 11 to 2.30, 6 to 11, Sat 12 to 3, 6 to 11, Sun 12 to 3, 6 to 10.30*

LITTLE NESTON

Cheshire map 7

Harp Inn

19 Quayside, Little Neston, Wirral CH64 0TB
TEL: (0151) 336 6980

from Burton Road in Little Neston, turn W along Bull Hill at mini-roundabout and continue down Marshlands Road; at end go ahead on rough lane between houses and turn left along potholed track; pub 300yds ahead

This 'real haven – once found, never forgotten' is a modest, unpretentious white-painted pub that used to serve the coal miners who worked hereabouts, but now the locals are joined by ramblers and bird-watchers, who come to gaze on the Dee Marshes that begin literally at the door. A warming fire adds to the welcoming atmosphere in the unspoilt main bar, where photographs, documents and memorabilia recall the coal industry. Six real ales include regulars Timothy Taylor Landlord and Holt's Bitter, and the simple but satisfying food includes steak and kidney pie cooked from scratch. No children after 8pm.

Open *11 to 11, 12 to 10.30 Sun*

LITTLE SHELFORD

Cambridgeshire map 6

Navigator

63 High Street, Little Shelford CB2 5ES
TEL: (01223) 843901

from M11 junction 11 take A10 towards Royston; pub 2m S of Hauxton

An unpretentious and relaxed local hostelry this may be – it's one of a row of cottages on the main road through the village – but it pulls in custom from a fair distance for its genuine Thai food. Wash it down with Singha beer or a real ale such as Old Speckled Hen. The open bar area splits into smoking and no-smoking sides, and there's a small beer garden.

Open *Mon 6 to 11, Tue to Fri 12 to 2, 6 to 11, Sat 6 to 11, Sun 12 to 2, 7 to 10.30*

LITTLE STRETTON

Shropshire   map 5

Ragleth Inn

Little Stretton SY6 6RB
TEL: (01694) 722711

on B4370, off A49, just SW of Church Stretton

Its location in a wooded valley at the foot
of the Long Mynd means that this
handsome brick pub, dating from 1663, is
popular with walkers. Liquid refreshment
is provided in the shape of Hobson's Best
Bitter and an ale from the Eccleshall or
Wye Valley Breweries, plus three wines by
the glass from a list of around a dozen
bottles. As well as sandwiches,
ploughman's and jacket potatoes, expect
garlic mushrooms, peppered mackerel or
steak pie. In the garden is an unusual tulip
tree.

Open *Mon to Fri 12 to 2.30, 6 to 11, Sat 12 to 11,
Sun 12 to 10.30; closed evening 25 Dec*

LIVERPOOL

Merseyside   map 7

Brewery Tap

35 Stanhope Street, Liverpool L8 5XJ
TEL: (0151) 709 2129

Refurbishment is the name of the game
with Cains pubs, and this red-brick boozer
outside the brewery showcases their talents
with salvaged fixtures and fittings
returning it to something approaching its
former glory. It's out of the way, but worth
an evening visit combined with a brewery
tour. Alternatively, call in at lunch to fill
up on sausages, steaks and burgers –
washed down, naturally, with a range of
Cains ales.

Open *11 (12 Sat) to 11, Sun 12 to 10.30*

The Dispensary

87 Renshaw Street, Liverpool L1 2SP
TEL: (0151) 709 2160

The contents of an old chemist's shop
seem to have been transplanted in their
entirety to this friendly Victorian corner
pub. Cains is the outfit behind the
makeover, and their full range of ales is
offered. Home-made soups, steaks or
spaghetti bolognese are no doubt just what
the doctor ordered.

Open *11.30 to 11, Sun 12 to 10.30*

Doctor Duncan's

St John's Lane, Liverpool L1 1HF
TEL: (0151) 709 5100

An extravagantly Victorian interior, typical
of the Cains style, is regularly packed with
a sociable mix of locals, office workers and
students. Beers are the usual Cains range,
and straightforward dishes such as sausage
and mash or chicken tikka hit the spot. In
the odd peaceful moment it's a good refuge
from the bustle of Queen Square, with
minimal passing traffic and St George's
Hall gardens opposite.

Open *11.30 to 11, Sun 12 to 10.30*

Everyman Bistro

9–11 Hope Street, Liverpool L1 9BH
TEL: (0151) 708 9545

The Everyman Theatre is in an area
between the two cathedrals packed with
university buildings: hence, this basement
bistro buzzes with the conversation of
students and lecturers alongside the pre-
and post-performance theatre-goers for
whom the canteen-style décor appears to
have been designed. As well as an eclectic
and vegetarian-friendly menu from the
kitchen, two bars serve regularly changing
ales and a host of foreign beers.

Open *Mon to Wed 12 to 12, Thur to Sat 12 to 2am*

Globe

17 Cases Street, Liverpool L1 1HW
TEL: (0151) 707 0067

Opened in 1888, this small, friendly pub,
opposite Liverpool Central Railway
Station, dispenses with any airs and graces
in favour of a good old-fashioned drinkers'
haven. Split into two rooms and renowned
for its back-to-front sloping floor, the
Globe's huge front window is the perfect
place to watch the crowds of shoppers
heading in and out of Clayton Square
shopping centre while enjoying a pint of
Cains, Tetley Bitter or one of the guest
ales. Bar snacks such as cobs and salads are
available cheaply.

Open *11 to 11, Sun 12 to 10.30*

Ma Boyle's Oyster Bar

Tower Buildings, Water Street, Liverpool
L3 1AB
TEL: (0151) 236 1717

Turn off Water Street down an alley-like
side street between some of the finest
buildings in the city to find this
characterful subterranean den. Dim
lighting, large mirrors and wooden beams
set the old-fashioned scene, and office
workers provide a buzz at lunchtimes and
early evenings. Seafood comes in
traditional English or Chinese style, but
oddly enough oysters don't feature.
Sandwiches, toasties and other standards
make up the balance, and a decent range of
ales includes Hydes and Thwaites.
Open *Mon to Thur 11 to 8, Fri 12 to 12*

Old Post Office

Old Post Office Place, Liverpool L1 3DH
TEL: (0151) 707 8880

Handily secreted behind the main branch
of Littlewoods, close to the Neptune
Theatre and Bluecoat Chambers, this is a
useful little bolt-hole if you want to avoid
the city-centre throngs. It's also an ideal
place for decent steaks at knockdown
prices, although the limited menus also
run to roast chicken, ribs and mixed
platefuls loaded up with chips (or a jacket
potato) and side orders of mushrooms,
garlic bread and onion rings. Locally
brewed Cains real ales take their place
alongside all the usual keg suspects.
Open *11.30 to 11 (2am Fri and Sat), Sun 12 to
10.30*

Peter Kavanagh's

2–6 Egerton Street, Liverpool L8 7LY
TEL: (0151) 709 3443

This late-Victorian pub stands on the edge
of the city centre, but it is well worth
seeking out. Inside you'll find a veritable
Aladdin's cave of curios: bicycles and
radios, old photos and even a crocodile
skin hanging from the ceiling. A roaring
fire dominates a cosy room at the front,
though the majority of the seating and
trinkets can be found in the split-level
main room. Original fixtures and fittings
remain, and although some of the
furniture has seen better days, it all adds to
the character and charm. No food is
served, but there's a fine selection of real
ales, including Black Sheep, Cain's,
Abbott's Ale and Hobgoblin, plus guests.
Open *12 to 11 (10.30 Sun)*

Thomas Rigby's

23 Dale Street, Liverpool L2 2EZ
TEL: (0151) 236 3269

Real ale fans and office workers keep the
friendly staff busy all day long at this lively
city boozer. On the handpumps, four
Okells beers team up with four guests (the
likes of Black Sheep Best Bitter or Wood
Get Knotted), and bottled beers look
beyond the mainstream. The food, too, has
ambitions, with tempting sandwiches,
hearty dishes like Spanish pork and
blackeye-bean casserole and a daily
'Atkins-friendly' special; 'spicy, satisfying'
beef curry was a hit with one reporter.
Horatio Nelson was reputedly a regular,
and one of two seating areas off the large
main bar is named after him.
Open *11 to 11, Sun 12 to 10.30*

Vernon Arms

69 Dale Street, Liverpool L2 2HJ
TEL: (0151) 236 4525

A great selection of beers and excellent
service keep a mixed crowd happy both at
lunchtimes and in the evenings at this city-
centre boozer opposite the Municipal
Building. Gunpowder and Tetley are the
permanent fixtures, with six guest ales
changing regularly. Food, best enjoyed in
the diner-style booths at the back, is
unabashed pub grub (chilli con carne,
chicken and mushroom curry and so on),
with chips that get the nod from
aficionados.
Open *Mon to Sat 11.45 to 11*

White Star

2–4 Rainford Gardens, Liverpool L2 6PT
TEL: (0151) 231 6861

Set in the famous Cavern quarter of the
city, the White Star, which takes its name
from the famous shipping line, has
changed little in the hundred years since it
opened. Many of the original fixtures and
fittings remain intact, particularly in the
back room, or News Room as it is known,
while the walls are decorated with
company memorabilia, including a huge
picture of the *Titanic*. The bar area contains
blackboards listing the constantly changing

real ales, among them perhaps Wadworth 6X, Okells Castletown Bitter and a Cains brew. No hot food is served, but bar snacks are available.
Open *11 to 11, Sun 12 to 10.30*

LOW CATTON

East Riding of Yorkshire   map 9

Gold Cup Inn

Low Catton YO41 1EA
TEL: (01759) 371354

off A166, just S of Stamford Bridge
This whitewashed pub in a village at the foot of the Yorkshire Wolds is popular with walkers on the Wolds Way. Inside is a rambling three-roomed lounge, each with a log fire and bric-à-brac; to the back is a games room. Traditional pub fare is what to expect, along with an à la carte menu in the restaurant, with John Smith's and Tetley Bitter on draught. The spacious beer garden has access to the river Derwent.
Open *Mon to Fri (exc Mon lunchtime) 12 to 2.30, 6 to 11, Sat 12 to 11, Sun 12 to 10.30; closed evenings 25 and 26 Dec*

LUDGVAN

Cornwall   map 1

White Hart

Churchtown, Ludgvan TR20 8EY
TEL: (01736) 740574

from A30 N of Penzance at Crowlas, take turning signposted Ludgvan and continue for 1m
Panelled walls, beamed ceilings, a wood-burner and an inglenook come as no surprise in a village pub dating from the fourteenth century, which makes the White Hart 200 years older than the church next door. Food ranges from egg and chips or quiche to steaks or perhaps rabbit casserole. Beer drinkers can choose between Flowers IPA, Bass or something from Sharp's, while whisky lovers have a good selection to choose from. St Michael's Mount, a couple of miles away, is visible in the distance.
Open *11 to 2.30, 6 to 11, Sun 12 to 3, 7 to 10.30*

LUDLOW

Shropshire   map 5

Unicorn Inn

Lower Corve Street, Ludlow SY8 1DU
TEL: (01584) 873555
An ancient black and white building with the upper storey half-timbered, the Unicorn is every inch the traditional English pub. Food is the focus, and the blackboard menu splits into bar and restaurant versions, the restaurant being a peaceful no-smoking room down some steps from the bar: perhaps garlic mushrooms followed by lamb cutlets with onion and rosemary sauce. Hancock's HB, Fuller's London Pride and Greene King Abbot Ale might be on the handpumps, and eight wines come by the glass.
Open *12 to 3, 6 to 11, Sun 12 to 3.30, 6.30 to 10.30*

LUGWARDINE

Herefordshire   map 5

Crown & Anchor

Cotts Lane, Lugwardine HR1 4AB
TEL: (01432) 851303

off A438, 3½m E of Hereford
On draught at this unpretentiously old-fashioned inn are Marston's Pedigree, Butcombe Bitter, Timothy Taylor Landlord and Worthington Bitter; eight wines are served by the glass, and fish is something of a speciality on the menu. Interesting vintage photographs of Weston's Cider Company staff, farming implements, fishing rods, and hop garlands decorate the beamed bar. The paved patio and flowery garden are attractions in warm weather.
Open *12 to 11 (10.30 Sun)*

LYNMOUTH

Devon   map 1

Rising Sun Hotel

Harbourside, Lynmouth EX35 6EG
TEL: (01598) 753223
With a view of the postcard-pretty harbour, this whitewashed and thatched fourteenth-century smugglers' inn later drew literary visitors – R.D. Blackmore wrote part of *Lorna Doone* here, and Shelley reputedly came to honeymoon. Today it is showing stirrings of modernisation in small details such as the menu presentation. Exmoor

game and Lynmouth Bay lobster feature, and Exmoor Gold and Cotleigh Tawny Bitter are the regular ales, with guests from local microbreweries. Accommodation available in 16 rooms.

Open *11 to 11, Sun 12 to 11*

MANCHESTER

Greater Manchester   map 8

Dukes 92

Castle Street, Manchester M3 4LZ
TEL: (0161) 839 8642

turn right off A57 in to Chester Road; Castle Street is 500yds on left

Part of the ongoing recycling of Manchester's industrial heritage, this former mill by the Rochdale Canal makes a spacious and airy bar, brightened up by lots of greenery; it's also a good spot for outdoor drinking on fine days. A couple of beers are usually on offer, perhaps something from Moorhouses, and a handful of wines come by the glass. Over 30 cheeses are listed, along with a range of traditional pâtés, and the menu extends to platters of meze or oriental bites, toasties and open sandwiches. A restaurant is due to open as we go to press.

Open *11.30 to 11 (12 Fri and Sat), Sun 12 to 10.30*

Marble Arch

73 Rochdale Road, Manchester M4 4HY
TEL: (0161) 832 5914

There's little to attract visitors to this central part of town save to join the beer lovers making the pilgrimage to this lively brick-built pub. The appealing vaulted interior has old drinks adverts on the walls and a motley mix of furniture including some comfortable sofas and armchairs spread over the mosaic floor. Expect to find seven ales from the pub's own microbrewery, from light and dry Northern Quarter to sweet and malty Chocolate Heaven, plus three guests and a good range of bottles. Mop up the beer with beef stew and thick chunks of bread and butter, fish stew, or Thai red curry (food served Mon to Fri 12 to 2.30 and 4.30 to 8, Sat 12 to 2.30). Children are admitted only during food serving times. Excellent friendly service.

Open *Mon to Fri 11.30 to 11, Sat 12 to 11, Sun 12 to 10.30*

Rain Bar

80 Great Bridgewater Street, Manchester
M1 5JY
TEL: (0161) 235 6500

Another canalside conversion, this Victorian red-brick building has a spare, modern feel, with exposed brickwork tempered by the generous use of dark wood. Lunchtime sees an easy-going pace, but business picks up considerably in the evening. A good range of beers includes a seasonal special, and 30 wines come by the glass. Straightforward, good-value bar food runs to salads, sandwiches and hot dishes like sausage and mash or chilli; the upstairs restaurant has a separate menu.

Open *Mon to Thur 11 to 11, Fri and Sat 11 to 12, Sun 12 to 10.30*

Royal Oak

729 Wilmslow Road, Didsbury, Manchester
M20 6WF
TEL: (0161) 434 4788

The residents of Didsbury have largely shunned the traditional pub in favour of glossy bars and brasseries, but the Royal Oak is an object lesson in what they are missing. Journey back to an early twentieth-century scene, with papered walls hung with framed theatre programmes. Weekday lunchtimes see a spread of good-quality cheeses, hams, pâtés and bread laid out on the bar – just the job with a smooth pint of Marston's Pedigree or Banks's Original.

Open *11 to 11, Sun 12 to 10.30*

MARSHWOOD

Dorset   map 2

Bottle

Marshwood DT6 5QJ
TEL: (01297) 678254

on B3165 between Crewkerne and Lyme Regis, 4m SW of Broadwindsor

The idiosyncratic Bottle, a characterful thatched establishment, makes much of its annual nettle-eating extravaganza, with framed photographs of contestants lining the walls. On other days food is a gentler affair, with much that is organic, vegetarian or vegan. Organic wines also figure, and excellent beers include Old

Speckled Hen and Weymouth. Closed Mondays in winter.

Open *all week 12 to 3.30, Tue to Sun 6.30 to 11 (10.30 Sun)*

MARSWORTH

Buckinghamshire   map 3

Red Lion

90 Vicarage Road, Marsworth HP23 4LU
TEL: (01296) 668366

off B489, 2m N of Tring

Its location on the Grand Union Canal near the Ridgeway footpath means that the Red Lion is popular with narrowboat users and walkers, and the nearby Tring Reservoir is a haven for bird-watchers. The menu is a list of traditional pub staples ranging from ploughman's to ham, egg and chips, with perhaps apple pie or spotted dick among puddings. Fuller's London Pride, Vale Notley Ale and a guest are on draught, and four wines are served by the glass.

Open *11 to 3, 5 (6 Sat) to 11, Sun 12 to 3, 7 to 11*

MEDBOURNE

Leicestershire   map 5

Nevill Arms

Medbourne Green, Medbourne LE16 8EE
TEL: (01858) 565288

A popular meeting place for the local hunting fraternity, this end-of-terrace village pub stands appealingly by the side of Medbourne Brook. Inside, all is cosy and snug, with beams, an inglenook and the newspapers to read. A guest such as Batemans Rosey Nosey bolsters three regular real ales, including Fuller's London Pride, Adnams Bitter and Greene King Abbot Ale, and half a dozen wines are served by the glass. Pies, casseroles, curries and dishes like lamb in mint and redcurrant sauce dominate the two specials boards, otherwise there are run-of-the-mill bar snacks. Accommodation available.

Open *12 to 3, 6 to 11, Sun 12 to 3, 7 to 11*

MELLOR

Lancashire   map 8

Millstone Hotel

Church Lane, Mellor BB2 7JR
TEL: (01254) 813333

With 24 en suite bedrooms, this old coaching inn in a village overlooking the Ribble Valley has more of the feel of a country-house hotel than a pub, although Thwaites Lancaster Bomber and cask ale are on draught. Sandwiches are served at lunchtimes, while the full menu, also available in the evenings, lists pub stalwarts such as chicken Caesar salad, cod in beer batter, ribeye steak, and lamb shank braised with red wine and rosemary.

Open *11 to 11 (10.30 Sun)*

MEYSEY HAMPTON

Gloucestershire   map 2

Masons Arms

Meysey Hampton GL7 5JT
TEL: (01285) 850164

People wanting to take a break on the southern edge of the Cotswolds, near Cirencester, can choose from one of nine rooms at this seventeenth-century village inn. On the food front, expect main courses along the lines of chicken casseroled in creamy bacon and Stilton sauce; half a dozen wines are sold by the glass, and among real ales on draught are Hook Norton Best Bitter and Cotswold Way from Wickwar Brewery.

Open *11.30 to 2.30, 6 to 11, Sun 12 to 4, 7 to 10.30; closed Sun evening Nov to Mar; no food Sun evening all year*

MICHAELCHURCH ESCLEY

Herefordshire   map 5

Bridge Inn

Michaelchurch Escley HR2 0JW
TEL: (01981) 510646

Michaelchurch Escley signposted off B4348 about 6m SE of Hay-on-Wye

The Bridge is in the middle of nowhere, unless you happen to be camping at the site next door. And don't expect a pub sign to help you find it – just drop down the hill from the church, cross the brook and there you are. Mingle with locals in the popular bar or choose the smart low-ceilinged dining room with its fresh flowers. Beers are from the Wye Valley Brewery, plus a guest, and a broad choice of good-value wines comes by the glass. Good local ingredients, including the owners' pigs, are favoured on the main menu, and there are also straight-ahead bar meals.

Open *11 to 11, Sun 12 to 10.30*

MIDFORD

Bath & N.E. Somerset   map 2

Hope & Anchor Inn

Midford BA2 7DD
TEL: (01225) 832296
on B3110, 3m S of Bath

A 'secret', steeply terraced garden
approached via a zig-zag path is an
unexpected plus point in this village pub a
short drive from Bath. Inside, you can
expect a well-worn mix of heavy black
beams, rough-stone walls and flagstone
floors. Bar food runs along the lines of feta
cheese, tomato and avocado salad, and
home-made sausages and mash, while the
restaurant menu moves into the realms of
venison with sloe gin and blueberries.
Three real ales might include
representatives from Bath Ales and Otter
Brewery; there's also a modest wine list.
Open *11.30 to 2.30, 6 to 11 Mon to Sat; Sun 12 to
10.30; closed 25 and 26 Dec.*

MILTON STREET

East Sussex   map 3

Sussex Ox

Milton Street, Alfriston BN26 5RL
TEL: (01323) 870840
off A27, 1m NE of Alfriston

Down narrow lanes and benefiting from
excellent views across the South Downs,
this Ox is well placed for enjoying the
Sussex countryside. The large garden has a
wooden children's play area to entertain
those too young to indulge in Harveys
Sussex Best Bitter, the just-as-local Dark
Star Hophead, or Hop Back Summer
Lightening; there are weekly-changing
guests as well. Eat in the dining room or
the bar, and expect the likes of fresh
dressed crab, goats' cheese tart, or a Sussex
Ox burger.
Open *11 to 3, 6 to 11, Sun 12 to 10.30*

MORWENSTOW

Cornwall   ·   map 1

Bush Inn

Crosstown, Morwenstow EX23 9SR
TEL: (01288) 331242

The Bush has a long history: it was a
hermit's cell in the tenth century (a Celtic
piscina can be seen in a wall), and was
enlarged in the thirteenth century by
Cistercian monks – it was on a pilgrims'
route between Wales and Spain. The
unspoilt interior features ancient
flagstones, built-in settles, beams and a
stone fireplace. St Austell HSD and Duchy
are tapped from casks, and food along the
lines of pasties and ploughman's is served
at lunchtimes. Good clifftop walks are
nearby.
Open *12 to 2.30 (3 summer), 7 to 11, Sun 12 to 3,
7 to 10.30; closed Mon winter, closed eve 25 Dec*

MUCH WENLOCK

Shropshire   map 5

George & Dragon

2 High Street, Much Wenlock TF13 6AA
TEL: (01952) 727312

St George's adventures are celebrated in
the no-smoking dining room of this
traditional half-timbered pub with low
ceilings and beams hung with mugs and
jugs. Beers include Hobsons Town Crier
and Timothy Taylor Landlord, and food
comes in large portions from a printed
menu and a specials board. Feast on rack of
lamb or bacon-wrapped chicken, with a
worthwhile cheese plate to finish.
Accommodation available.
Open *winter Mon to Thur 12 to 3, 6 to 11,
Fri and Sat 12 to 11, Sun 12 to 10.30, summer 12 to
11 (10.30 Sun)*

NEWCASTLE UPON TYNE

Tyne & Wear   map 10

Crown Posada

31 The Side, Newcastle upon Tyne NE1 3JE
TEL: (0191) 232 1269

As the Quayside nightlife gets ever wilder,
the Crown Posada has become a glorious
misfit in its midst, cherished by lovers of
real pubs and real beer. This treasure-trove
of oak panelling, stained glass and old
lamps is long, narrow and easily filled.
Beer is superbly kept, with a standard line-
up of two Jennings ales, Bass and three
guests. Food means sandwiches and
snacks, and music won't intrude on your
conversation.
Open *Mon to Fri 11 to 11, Sat 12 to 11, Sun 7 to
10.30*

Free Trade Inn

St Lawrence Road, Newcastle upon Tyne
NE6 1AP
TEL: (0191) 265 5764

This engagingly ramshackle institution defiantly guards one of the best views in town – straight up the river to the Baltic arts centre and bridges new and old. Inside, the focus is on tip-top cask ales from Mordue and other local breweries, music from a renowned free jukebox, and banter. Devotees come from far and wide, especially for the Tuesday night quiz. Food runs to curries, steak and kidney pie, and lasagne, and accommodation is available.
Open *11 to 11, Sun 12 to 10.30*

NEW MILLS

Derbyshire   map 8

Pack Horse Inn

Mellor Road, New Mills SK22 4QQ
TEL: (01663) 742365
follow Market Street then Spring Bank Road N out of New Mills, turn left at White Hart pub and continue for about ½m

The twin attractions of fine ales (from Tetley and local microbreweries such as Ossett and Frankton Bagby) and sweeping views of the Peak District (best enjoyed from a table on the lawns or in the cobbled yard) ensure a steady stream of custom at this converted seventeenth-century stone farmhouse. A thorough conversion has created a bright and airy open-plan interior, with comfortable letting accommodation in an adjoining barn. Winter walkers stop in to warm their toes by the wood-burning stove and enjoy Thai-style prawns, garlic mushrooms, or more substantial curries or baked salmon.
Open *Mon to Fri 12 to 3, 5 to 11, Sat 12 to 11, Sun 12 to 10.30*

NEWTON

Cambridgeshire   map 6

Queens Head

Fowlmere Road, Newton CB2 5PG
TEL: (01223) 870436

In the centre of the village, this eighteenth-century inn attracts all-comers, from Cambridge dons to farm workers. Part of the appeal is the unpretentiously relaxed atmosphere in the bow-windowed bar, with its settle and benches; some come to play shove-ha'penny in the games room at the back. The range of Adnams ales is stocked, including seasonal brews, and a dozen wines are served by the glass, while food is of the no-nonsense, satisfying variety: mugs of hearty soup and good-value, made-to-order sandwiches.
Open *11.30 to 2.30, 6 to 11, Sun 12 to 2.30, 7 to 10.30; closed 25 Dec*

NEWTON UNDER ROSEBERRY

Redcar   map 10

King's Head

Newton under Roseberry TS9 6QR
TEL: (01642) 722318

Eight en suite bedrooms have been converted from a row of seventeenth-century cottages adjacent to this red-brick and stone inn. The main focus here is on the restaurant, where a number of menus range from a bargain set-price lunch to a full à la carte as well as a list of blackboard specials. Choose from lemon-crusted halibut fillet with a scallop and Muscadet cream, or fillet of beef glazed with Roquefort with a rosemary and red wine reduction; snacks and sandwiches are also possibilities. Theakston Best Bitter and John Smith's are on draught, and around 15 wines are served by the glass. The place gets busy at weekends, and is popular with walkers following the Cleveland Way.
Open *11.30 to 3, 5.30 (6.45 Sat) to 11, Sun 11.45 to 4, 7 to 10.30*

NORTHLEACH

Gloucestershire   map 5

Wheatsheaf Inn

Northleach GL54 3EZ
TEL: (01451) 860244

A pretty Cotswolds village is the setting of this sixteenth-century former coaching inn, its interior stylishly decorated. Food is taken seriously here, the kitchen producing such dishes as roast Gloucester Old Spot tenderloin with parsnip mash and sautéed cabbage, seared fillet of sea trout with sautéed potatoes and rocket, and warm chocolate fondant with home-made ice cream. The wine list extends to over 30 bottles, and on draught are Wadworth 6X and Hook Norton Best Bitter plus a guest:

perhaps Wychwood Hobgoblin or Redruth Cornish Rebellion. Eight guest bedrooms have recently been refurbished.
Open *12 to 11 (10.30 Sun)*

NORTH SHIELDS

Tyne & Wear   map 10
Tap and Spile
184 Tynemouth Road, North Shields NE30 1EG
TEL: (0191) 257 2523
opposite magistrates' court
Beers have long made the reputation of this traditional corner pub, with seven guests lining up beside Caledonian Deuchars IPA, Ruddles County and Boddingtons Bitter. Wines by the glass cover a good few grape varieties. For food (weekday lunchtimes and 12 to 7 weekends), bag a table early before the lawyers spill in from the courtrooms opposite. A new chef came on board in summer 2004; reports would be welcome.
Open *12 to 11, Sun 12 to 10.30*

Tynemouth Lodge Hotel
Tynemouth Road, North Shields NE30 4AA
TEL: (0191) 257 7565
This shrine to real ale draws worshippers from around Tyneside to join locals in the appreciation of draught Bass, Belhaven 80/-, Deuchars IPA and a guest such as Old Cornelius. There's no sign of any hotel, or much in the way of wine or food, and even the décor lets the beer do the talking with brewery names emblazoned on clocks, mirrors and pictures. Pleasant beer garden.
Open *11 to 11, Sun 12 to 10.30*

NORTH WOOTTON

Dorset   map 2
Three Elms
North Wootton DT9 5JW
TEL: (01935) 812881
Once a cider house, this greatly extended hostelry now conspicuously reflects its landlord's passions. It contains over 1,300 model cars and other vehicles from bygone days, among assorted memorabilia. Otter Bitter, Butcombe Bitter and Fuller's London Pride are on handpump, Burrow Hill cider is also available and there's a

choice of 15 wines by the glass. All manner of club sandwiches features on the menu, along with an extensive choice for carnivores and vegetarians alike. One double bedroom is available for overnight stays. The pub, which stands on the fringes of Blackmoor Vale, has a pleasant garden and great views towards Bulbarrow Hill (Dorset's highest point).
Open *11 to 2.30, 6.30 (6 Fri and Sat) to 11, Sun 11 to 2.30, 7 to 10.30*

NORTON ST PHILIP

Somerset   map 2
George
High Street, Norton St Philip BA3 6LH
TEL: (01373) 834224
on an A366 at junction with B3110, 6m S of Bath
The setting for many a costume drama, the George comprises a wondrous complex of tall half-timbered buildings dating back some 700 years. A cobbled passageway wide enough for carriages leads to a small inner courtyard. Step through a small bar area into a stunning dining room open to the roof timbers, where wrought-iron lamps and rich brocades set a baronial tone. Food is fittingly substantial, with beef Wellington and sea bass fillet joined by local trout or pheasant and a range of pies. Lunch brings lighter options. Beers come from Wadworth, and the wine list runs to more than 20 bins. Bedrooms include three four-posters.
Open *Mon to Fri 10.30 to 2.30, 5.30 to 11, Sat 10.30 to 11; Sun 12 to 2.30, 7 to 10.30*

NORWICH

Norfolk   map 6
Fat Cat
West End Street, Norwich NR2 4NA
TEL: (01603) 624364
from centre of Norwich follow A1074 out of city and turn right on to Nelson Street; pub on first corner
The fat black cat painted on the wall outside meows a siren song for ale buffs, who pack the place out at weekends. Enthusiastic and well-informed staff serve a monumental range of up to 30 real ales, plus bottles from Scotland, Ireland and Belgium. Wooden and glass screens create cosy booths for the supping thereof;

there's no food and just a few token wines, so you know what you're here for.

Open *12 (11 Sat) to 11, Sun 12 to 10.30*

NOTTINGHAM

Nottinghamshire   map 5

Lincolnshire Poacher

161 Mansfield Road, Nottingham NG1 3FR
TEL: (0115) 941 1584

on A60, just N of Victoria Shopping Centre

Beer lovers need look no further than this red-brick pub, decked out with traditional fittings. Three regular Bateman beers are joined by around seven guests, which might include Oakham JHB, Tom Wood Harvest, and Abbeydale Moonshine. A no-smoking area and child-friendly conservatory and garden broaden the appeal, and the short blackboard menu is a cut above basic pub grub, including a fair few vegetarian options.

Open *11 to 11, Sun 12 to 10.30*

Olde Trip To Jerusalem

1 Brewhouse Yard, Castle Road, Nottingham NG1 6AD
TEL: (0115) 947 3171

A strong contender for the 'oldest pub in England' tag (anyone care to outbid 1189?), this atmospheric inn at the foot of the castle rock burrows back into the original castle caves. And as if that weren't enough to give unique appeal, there's a 'cursed' model galleon with a morbid legend. Hardys & Hansons Old Kim, Kimberley Bitter and Best Mild are among the ales on handpump, ten wines come by the glass, and the menu offers satisfying straightforward pub food. It seems unlikely that a new licensee will rock the boat.

Open *11 to 11, Sun 12 to 10.30*

OAKHAM

Rutland   map 5

Grainstore

Station Approach, Oakham LE15 6RE
TEL: (01572) 770065

Handily placed right next to Oakham railway station, this converted three-storey grainstore is home to the eponymous brewery (tours can be arranged). The vats are visible through glass doors and the full range (including Rutland Panther, Cooking Bitter, Ten Fifty etc.) can be sampled in the open-plan bar with its bare boards and red metal pillars. Ten wines are offered by the glass. Food is currently limited to ploughman's, sandwiches, pies and so on, but there are plans to expand the range. Reports please.

Open *Mon to Sat 11 to 11, Sun 12 to 10.30*

OARE

Kent   map 3

Shipwrights Arms

Hollowshore, Oare ME13 7TU
TEL: (01795) 590088

from A2 just W of Faversham, take B2045 Western Link towards Oare, turn right into Bysing Wood Road, then left into Davington Hill, then right fork into Ham Road, which is signposted to pub

Through the windows of this old weatherboarded pub, you can see rows of masts in the neighbouring shipyard. Today, real ale fans seek the place out despite its isolated location for perfectly kept beers served straight from the cask: usually around five local brews from Goacher's and Hopdaemon. A framework of blackened timbers divides the interior into several small cosy areas, with a cottage dining room extension, while the large garden has trees for summer shade. Bar snacks and a blackboard of more substantial dishes steer a safe course. Wine drinkers are not forgotten, with eight by the glass.

Open *Tue to Sat 11 to 3 (4 Sat), 6 to 11, Sun 12 to 4, 6 to 10.30 (summer Mon to Fri 11 to 3, 6 to 11, Sat and Sun 11 to 11); closed 1 week Oct; may close earlier on quiet evenings in winter*

OMBERSLEY

Worcestershire   map 5

Kings Arms

Main Road, Ombersley WR9 0EW
TEL: (01905) 620142

A beguiling timeworn black and white timbered façade and secluded garden promise an unalloyed olde English experience, and the warren of tiny rooms obligingly delivers open fires, wonky ceilings, wooden beams and, in the oldest room (now a no-smoking dining area), a coat of arms with a fleur-de-lis and lions rampant. Starters take an unexpected Mediterranean turn but mains are true Brit, with a board of daily fish specials to boot. Two guest ales line up beside Marston's Pedigree and Banks's Bitter, and a decent wine list includes eight by the glass.

Open *11 to 3, 5.30 to 11, Sun 12 to 10.30; closed 25 Dec*

ONECOTE

Staffordshire   map 5

Jervis Arms

Onecote ST13 7RU
TEL: (01538) 304206

on B5053, 1m off A523 Leek to Ashbourne road, 4m E of Leek

Dating from the seventeenth century, this stone-built pub is on the bank of the River Hamps (the car park is reached via a small footbridge) on the edge of the Peak District National Park. Pub food along the lines of home-made pies is available, and Whim Arbor Light and guest ales – perhaps Worthington Bitter or Bass – are on handpump. Children are welcome in the family rooms, and there's a play area and picnic tables in the riverside garden, which is popular with families in summer.

Open *12 to 3, 7 (6 Sat) to 11, Sun 12 to 10.30*

OVING

West Sussex   map 3

Gribble Inn

Gribble Lane, Oving PO20 6BP
TEL: (01243) 786893

Beer is the thing at this thatched pub in a village near Chichester: the Gribble Brewery (owned by Hall & Woodhouse) is on the premises, and seven handpumps on the bar dispense the brewery's full range, from Pig's Ear to Reg's Tipple, plus seasonal ales like Plucking Pheasant and Wobbler. Doorstep sandwiches, sausage and mash, steak and kidney pudding, grills, and steaks are what to expect on the food front, and eight wines are served by the glass from a list of around 16. Children are welcome in the no-smoking family room, and there's a pleasant garden.

Open *winter 11 to 3, 5.30 to 11, Sun 12 to 4, 7 to 10.30, summer 11 to 11, Sun 12 to 10.30*

OXFORD

Oxfordshire   map 2

Kings Arms

40 Holywell Street, Oxford OX1 3SP
TEL: (01865) 242369

Opposite the Sheldonian Theatre, this busy early-seventeenth-century pub attracts a lively mix of locals, students and academics with its good-value food and drink. Inside there are lots of different areas including a no-smoking room and the Don's Bar. This is a Youngs pub, with usually three of the brewery's ales on draught alongside several guests such as Wadworth 6X. Non-beer drinkers will find that every wine on the list can be ordered by the glass, and tea and coffee with cakes are a handy bonus. The menu promises mugs of soup, 'all time favourite fillers' with chips, Caesar salad, cottage pie and the like.

Open *Mon to Sat 11 to 11, Sun 12 to 10.30*

Turf Tavern

7 Bath Place, off Holywell Street, Oxford OX1 3SU
TEL: (01865) 243235

between Holywell Street and New College Lane

Justly famous and notoriously difficult to find – unless you know your way around the alleys and lanes off the town's main drag – this animated low-ceilinged pub has an enviable reputation for its real ales: 11 are regularly on draught, including Turf Tavern Ale brewed for the pub by Titanic; there's also scrumpy and Weston's Old Rosie cider on draught. Seats can be at a premium, but there are three courtyards outside (one with its own bar). Food (served 12 to 7.30) is mostly familiar pub grub.

Open *11 to 11, Sun 12 to 10.30*

PAGLESHAM

Essex   map 3

Plough & Sail

East End, Paglesham SS4 2EQ
TEL: (01702) 258242

This 400-year-old weatherboarded pub with a large garden is in a quiet spot a short stroll from the River Roach. Mighty Oak, Ridleys and Greene King provide the draught ales, and, food-wise, go for one of the home-made pies (there's a pudding and pie evening on Thursdays in winter) or one of the fish dishes, and find one of the ten or so wines by the glass to complement it.

Open *12 to 3, 7 to 11, Sun 12 to 3.30, 7 to 10.30*

PELDON

Essex map 3

Peldon Rose

Mersea Road, Peldon CO5 7QJ
TEL: (01206) 735248

off B1025, 5m S of Colchester

In a peaceful and picturesque location just a mile from the Strood (the causeway to Mersea Island), this pale pink, fifteenth-century cottage has cosy and characterful timbered rooms plus a large, airy modern conservatory dining room. All is kept spick and span, and outdoor tables in a grassy garden with trees and a pond beckon in summer. Quality wines from Lay & Wheeler make a strong team with the range of Adnams beers. A straightforward menu with a few flourishes offers the likes of sea bass with prawn and dill risotto. Accommodation available.

Open *11 to 11, Sun 12 to 10.30*

PELYNT

Cornwall map 1

Jubilee Inn

Pelynt PL13 2JZ
TEL: (01503) 220312

Known as the Axe until 1887, when it took its current name from Queen Victoria's celebration of 50 years on the throne, this long, low, white-painted pub was built as a farmhouse in the sixteenth century. St Austell HSD and Tinners Ale are on draught, with usually two guests, four wines are sold by the glass, and the menu features fish in the form of perhaps lemon sole and trout along with steaks, lamb shank, and liver and bacon with onions. Outside is a sizeable garden, and 11 en suite rooms are available. New licensees took over late in 2003: reports please.

Open *Mon to Fri 12 to 3, 6 to 11, Sat 12 to 11, Sun 12 to 10.30*

PENELEWEY

Cornwall map 1

Punch Bowl & Ladle

Penelewey TR3 6QY
TEL: (01872) 862237

from A39 3m S of Truro, take B3289 towards King Harry Ferry

Inside this thatched and rose-covered pub is a rambling series of charming low-beamed rooms with fires, sofas and easy chairs. Tied to the St Austell Brewery, it stocks the brewery's ales along with Bass and three guests. Thirty bottles show up on the wine list, while the kitchen uses locally sourced ingredients like fish and seasonal game. The pub dates from the fifteenth century and in its time has seen service as a courtroom. Trelissick Gardens (NT) and the King Harry Ferry are nearby. New licensees took over early in 2004: reports please.

Open *Mon to Fri 11.30 to 3, 5.30 to 11, Sat 11.30 to 11, Sun 12 to 10.30; open all day June to mid-Sept*

PERRY GREEN

Hertfordshire map 3

Hoops Inn

Bourne Lane, Perry Green SG10 6EF
TEL: (01279) 843568

off B180, just before Much Hadham, 5m N of Ware

Situated in a quiet Hertfordshire hamlet, this seventeenth-century country inn is convenient for a visit to the Henry Moore Foundation sculpture park. Shepherd Neame Spitfire, Youngs Special and Greene King IPA are regularly on draught, and the kitchen specialises in sizzlers – maybe flame-grilled steak or a prawn stir-fry – along with poached salmon salad, steak and mushroom pie, and roasts on Sunday (when food is served all day). The large garden includes a secure paddock, and there's a new patio at the front of the pub.

Open *12 to 2.30, 6.30 to 11, Sun 12 to 10.30*

PIERCEBRIDGE

Co Durham map 10

George Hotel

Piercebridge DL2 3SW
TEL: (01325) 374576

This red-tiled, white-painted hotel, dating from the sixteenth century, is by the

bridge over the River Tees. Marston's Pedigree and Greene King Abbot Ale are on draught, and there's a list of around 30 wines. On the menu might be seasonal game, plus seafood dishes like Whitby crab or lemon sole, and chocolate and Grand Marnier mousse to finish. Children are welcome, and there are 35 en suite bedrooms.
Open *11 to 11, Sun 12 to 10.30*

PILLATON

Cornwall   map 1
Weary Friar
Pillaton PL12 6QS
TEL: (01579) 350238
In the Lynher valley above Saltash, the Weary Friar is next to the village church: hardly surprising, as it was erected in the twelfth century to accommodate the builders. Fish landed at St Ives might be among the daily specials – perhaps a trio of sole, monkfish and haddock with lemon and parsley butter – along with, say, pheasant breast, gammon with pineapple, or fillet steak with a mushroom and red wine sauce. Weary Ale plus guests like Sharp's Eden Ale are on draught, and four wines come by the glass. Children are welcome inside if eating, and there's a garden. Accommodation available in 12 rooms.
Open *11.30 to 3.30, 6.30 to 11, Sun 12 to 3, 7 to 10.30*

PITTON

Wiltshire   map 2
Silver Plough
White Hill, Pitton SP5 1DU
TEL: (01722) 712266
This attractive village pub has a pleasant garden and, at the back, a skittle alley. Food, served in both the bar and restaurant, takes in a parcel of smoked salmon (from the local smokehouse) stuffed with chives and cream cheese, followed by perhaps rabbit and pheasant casserole, then chocolate sponge with custard, and there's a decent choice of wines by the glass from a list approaching 30 bottles. Badger IPA, Best Bitter and Tanglefoot and Harveys Sussex Best are among the real ales on draught.
Open *11 to 3, 6 to 11, Sun 12 to 3, 6 to 10.30*

PLUMLEY

Cheshire   map 7
Smoker
Plumley WA16 0TY
TEL: (01565) 722338
Although it dates from Elizabethan times, this white-walled, thatched pub takes its name from the Prince Regent's favourite racehorse. Open fires and sofas make a comfortable setting in which to enjoy a pint of Robinson's Old Stockport Bitter or Best, one of the guest ales, such as Cwmbran's Double Hop, or one of ten wines by the glass from a list of around 20 bottles. Food runs from snacks to traditional pub favourites, and there's a children's menu too.
Open *11.30 to 3, 6 to 11, Sun 12 to 10.30*

POLKERRIS

Cornwall   map 1
Rashleigh Inn
Polkerris PL24 2TL
TEL: (01726) 813991
The Rashleigh is in an enviable position overlooking a cove beside an isolated beach and restored jetty; at one time it was a coastguard station. Rashleigh Bitter (brewed by Sharp's), Timothy Taylor Landlord and Sharp's Doom Bar Bitter are on draught, along with up to three guests, and eight wines are available by the glass. Bar food and the Monday-to-Saturday evening carte make full use of local fish and game.
Open *11 to 11, Sun 12 to 10.30; 25 and 26 Dec 12 to 2*

POLPERRO

Cornwall   map 1
Blue Peter
Quay Road, Polperro PL13 2QZ
TEL: (01503) 272743
It's worth coming to this charming, old-fashioned pub for its view alone: it's set in the cliff face overlooking the pretty fishing village and harbour of Polperro. As its location might suggest, fish is the focus of the kitchen, and another draw is the range of beers, with Sharp's Doom Bar Bitter joined by guests such as Cotleigh Golden Eagle, St Austell HSD and Sharp's Special; farm scrumpy is a possibility too.
Open *11 to 11, Sun 12 to 10.30*

POSTBRIDGE

Devon   map 1

Warren House Inn

Postbridge PL20 6TA
TEL: (01822) 880208
on B3212 1½m E of Postbridge towards
Moretonhampstead

One of the fires at this remote pub on
Dartmoor, with lovely views, is said to
have been lit when the place was built in
1845 (to replace a pub that stood opposite)
and has been burning ever since. As well as
the location, the choice of beers is an
attraction: Sharp's Doom Bar Bitter, Moor
Beer's Old Freddy Walker and Butcombe
Gold are the regulars, with perhaps Badger
Tanglefoot or Shepherd Neame Spitfire
Premium Ale among the guests. Rabbit or
game pie may turn up on the menus.
Open *winter Mon to Thur 11 to 3, 6 to 11, Fri and*
Sat 11 to 11, Sun 12 to 10.30; summer all week 11 to
11

POWERSTOCK

Dorset   map 2

Three Horseshoes

Powerstock DT6 3TF
TEL: (01308) 485328
Powerstock signposted off A3066 just N of
Bridport

The grey-stone hamlet of Powerstock lies
deep in the heart of west Dorset, with its
five-gabled pub near the top of the steep
hill just along from the church. Time
doesn't stand still inside, where bar and
dining room are both decked out in smart
dark tongue-and-groove panelling, and
dynamic young owners are attracting a
mixed clientele for beers from Palmers
(Palmers' Best Bitter IPA and Copper Ale)
and an ambitious menu served
throughout. Follow carpaccio of tuna with
tarragon-braised rabbit stuffed with
mushrooms and apricots, or steak topped
with a warm salad. The wine list runs to
some smart bottles. Three bedrooms are
available.
Open *11 to 3, 6.30 to 11, Sun 11 to 3.30, 6.30 to*
10.30

POYNINGS

West Sussex   map 3

Royal Oak Inn

The Street, Poynings BN45 7AQ
TEL: (01273) 857389
off A281, 4m NW of Hove

Devil's Dyke rises to the south of the
Royal Oak, a smart, custard-coloured pub
in a small village in the shadow of the
South Downs. The open-plan bar and
dining areas are light and bright, and from
the panelled bar well-drilled staff dispense
Harveys Best, Greene King Abbot Ale and
Old Speckled Hen. The menu runs from
light meals to the 'Best of British', and to
daily specials on a blackboard. The garden
– with a children's play area – is the setting
for popular barbecues on Sundays.
Open *11.30 to 11, Sun 12 to 10.30*

PRIORS DEAN

Hampshire   map 2

White Horse Inn

Priors Dean GU32 1DA
TEL: (01420) 588387
off A3 or A32, 3m N of Petersfield and ½m N of
Steep

Known as the Pub With No Name
because no inn sign hangs in the empty
iron frame outside, this is a warmly
atmospheric pub, with leather armchairs,
sofas, candles in bottles, and farming
implements for decoration. Six real ales,
which include the pub's own-label No
Name Best and Strong, and Ringwood
Fortyniner and Fuller's London Pride, are
joined by two guests on the handpumps.
There are also over 20 fruit wines by the
glass, and the kitchen makes full use of
local produce. The pub can be difficult to
find (OS ref. 726265).
Open *12 to 3, 6 to 11, Sun 12 to 3, 7 to 10.30*

RAMSGATE

Kent   map 3

Royal Harbour Brewhouse

98 Harbour Parade, Ramsgate CT11 8LP
TEL: (01843) 594758

The long, narrow, woodblock- and
concrete-floored room that is the
Brewhouse brings modern industrial
styling to Ramsgate's harbourside. On
sunny days the doors fold back and the

metal-framed chairs are pushed out café-
style on to the street. A simple blackboard
menu and a selection of pastries are
popular with diners and snackers, but beer
is the thing here, with 'delicious' in-house
Gadds brews (the vats are visible at the
back) and an impressive array of Belgian
specialities. 'Lovely, prompt and cheerful'
staff come in for special praise.
Open *Mon to Thur 10 to 12, Fri and Sat 10 to 1,*
Sun 12 (10 summer) to 12

RATTERY

Devon   map 1
Church House Inn
Rattery TQ10 9LD
Tel: (01364) 642220
Few pubs can claim an ancestry going back
to pre-Conquest times, but some parts of
this one date from 1028, when the
building accommodated craftsmen
working on the next-door parish church.
Beams, standing timbers and a massive oak
screen are reminders of the pub's
antiquity, and reporters find the ambience
comfortable and pleasant. St Austell
Dartmoor Best Bitter and Greene King
Abbot Ale are joined by occasional guest
beers like Hook Norton Old Hooky, and
game – perhaps guinea fowl – appears on
the menu in season. There are plenty of
seats outside, with wonderful views.
Open *Mon to Fri 11 to 3, 6 to 11, Sat 11 to 3, 6 to*
11 (11 to 11 summer), Sun 12 to 3, 6 to 10.30 (12 to
10.30 summer)

RATTLESDEN

Suffolk   map 6
Brewers Arms
Lower Road, Rattlesden IP30 0RJ
Tel: (01449) 736377
Although it's been smartly done up, the
Brewers Arms, in the centre of the small
village, still has exposed brickwork and
beams, with horse brasses contributing a
rural feeling. The food, served in both bar
and restaurant, is a combination of
traditional and more modern ideas,
running from moules marinière to
gammon steak with honey and mustard
sauce, or lamb burger on ciabatta. Ales are
from the local Greene King Brewery.
Open *11.30 to 2.30, 6 to 11, Sun 12 to 3, 7 to 10.30*

REEDHAM

Norfolk   map 6
Reedham Ferry Inn
Ferry Road, Reedham NR13 3HA
Tel: (01493) 700429
This seventeenth-century inn is in a lovely
spot on the River Yare next to the chain
ferry across the river (the only crossing for
cars between Norwich and Yarmouth);
behind is a leafy four-acre caravan and
camp site. The wide-ranging menu runs
from starters of prawn cocktail or a plate of
Italian salami to Chinese-style Barbary
duck stir-fried with plum sauce or pan-
fried medallions of local venison with
shiitake mushrooms in red wine sauce.
Woodforde's Wherry and Adnams Best
and Broadside are on handpump along
with a guest, and three wines are served by
the glass; Stowford Press cider is also
stocked, with sangria and mulled wine in
season.
Open *11 to 2.30 (3 summer), 7 (6.30 summer) to 11,*
Sun 12 to 10.30

RIBCHESTER

Lancashire   map 8
White Bull
Church Street, Ribchester PR3 3XP
Tel: (01254) 878303
Historical Ribchester lies on an old Roman
supply route to Hadrian's Wall and has a
Roman Museum as well as the remains of
some Roman baths just over the garden
wall from this substantial cream-stone
building, itself fronted by four striking
columns. The White Bull is a useful place
for a stopover, with a friendly atmosphere,
and there are pretty country views from
the banks of the River Ribble. A
traditionally furnished dining room serves
reasonably priced pub staples. Well-kept
Greene King Abbot Ale and Black Sheep
Best Bitter are joined by guest ales, and all
20 or so wines are also served by the glass.
Accommodation is available.
Open *11 to 11, Sun 12 to 10.30*

RIDGEWELL

Essex   map 6

White Horse

Mill Road, Ridgewell CO9 4SG
TEL: (01440) 785532

There's a large dining room at this welcoming pub on the main road through the village. You could start with a warm salad of calamari and tiger prawns and go on to pan-fried sea bass with hollandaise or chicken breast stuffed with Stilton and wrapped in bacon served on colcannon with a red wine jus. Two ales on handpump change twice a week, and there are 15 wines by the glass. Exposed beams and an unusual bar counter covered in pennies characterise the interior.

Open *Tue to Sat and bank hol Mon 11 to 3, 6 to 11, Sun 12 to 10.30*

RINGMER

East Sussex   map 3

Cock

Uckfield Road, Ringmer BN8 5RX
TEL: (01273) 812040

just off A26, 2m NE of Lewes

You might need to book if you want to eat at this sixteenth-century pub with views of the South Downs. Tiger prawns in garlic, or peppers stuffed with goats' cheese and sun-dried tomatoes might kick off the lengthy menu, and main courses range from ham, egg and chips to daily specials of sea bass fillet in a white wine and mushroom sauce, or lamb chops in a glaze of Worcester and redcurrant sauce. Harveys ales are stocked, and around half a dozen wines are served by the glass from a list of about 20 bottles. Children are welcome.

Open *11 to 3, 6 to 11, Sun 12 to 3, 7 to 11*

RINGSTEAD

Norfolk   map 6

Gin Trap Inn

High Street, Ringstead PE36 5JU
TEL: (01485) 525264

off A149, 2m E of Hunstanton

On the Peddars' Way long-distance footpath close to the north Norfolk coast, this well-maintained coaching inn is popular with both walkers and tourists. Ales from Woodforde's, including the pub's own Gin Trap Bitter, are on draught in the cosy, beamed bar, five wines come by the glass, and sustenance is provided in the shape of rabbit or venison and seafood: perhaps tuna carpaccio, tempura tiger prawns, or sea bass. Three en suite rooms are available.

Open *11.30 to 2.30, 6 to 11, Sun 11.45 to 2.30. 6.45 to 10.30; summer 10.30 to 11, Sun 12 to 10.30*

ROBIN HOOD'S BAY

North Yorkshire   map 9

Laurel Inn

New Road, Robin Hood's Bay YO22 4SE
TEL: (01947) 880400

Robin Hood's Bay is a pretty cliffside fishing village, popular in summer, of narrow streets and fishermen's cottages. The bar – beams, brasses and a fire – at this tiny pub is carved from solid rock. In here, Jennings Cumberland Ale, Adnams Broadside and Tetley ales are on draught, house wines are sold by the glass, and sandwiches are normally served at busy times. No smoking is permitted in the snug (where children are admitted) until after 9pm. A self-catering flat for two is available.

Open *12 to 11 (2 to 11 Nov to March), Sun 12 to 10.30 (2 to 10.30 Nov to March); closed evening 25 Dec*

ROKE

Oxfordshire   map 2

Home Sweet Home

Roke OX10 6JD
TEL: (01491) 838249

turn at signpost Home Sweet Home on B4009, between Benson and Watlington

The rural idyll of a thatched roof, a peaceful setting and an attractive walled garden overlooking fields of grazing sheep is fully realised here. Lodden Brewery's Hoppit Ale, Ferryman's Gold, Fuller's London Pride and a guest are on handpump, and the wine list runs to 30 bins with 14 by the glass. The menu extends the homeliness of beef and ale pie with ideas from the Mediterranean and beyond: perhaps rocket and cherry tomato salad with Parmesan shavings and balsamic dressing, followed by tuna and chilli fishcakes with a red Thai cream sauce. New owners took the helm early in 2004 – reports please.

Open *11 to 3, 6 to 11, Sun 12 to 3; closed evenings 25 and 26 Dec*

ROTHERFIELD PEPPARD

Oxfordshire   map 2

Greyhound

Gallowtree Road, Rotherfield Peppard
RG9 5HT
TEL: (0118) 972 2227

The askew tiled roof is an indication of the great age of this brick and timber building in a village not far from Reading. Real ales are provided by Fuller's, Brakspear and Lodden; an interesting bar menu pulls in the punters, with dishes such as chicken and sundried tomato salad; there's also a separate restaurant, with offerings such as breast of chicken stuffed with brie and spinach and wrapped in bacon.

Open *11 to 3.30, 6 to 11, Sun 12 to 6.30*

RYE

East Sussex   map 3

Mermaid Inn

Mermaid Street, Rye TN31 7EY
TEL: (01797) 223065

On a narrow cobbled street of equally aged buildings, the Mermaid dates from Elizabethan times: a corridor inside is hung with notables of that period, such as Sir Walter Raleigh and the Earl of Leicester, along with some Tudor examples, such as some of Henry VIII's wives. A huge inglenook takes up almost an entire wall in the bar, where there are pikes and swords and good-quality furniture and fabrics. The menu in here deals in baguettes, pasta dishes, moules marinière and a seafood platter, and on handpump are Old Speckled Hen and Courage Best. There are 31 guest bedrooms.

Open *11 to 11, Sun 12 to 10.30*

ST AGNES

Isles of Scilly   map 1

Turk's Head

St Agnes TR22 0PL
TEL: (01720) 422434

A 20-minute boat trip from St Mary's, the Turk's Head, a slate-roofed nineteenth-century cottage, overlooks the harbour and quay. Nautical memorabilia give character to the interior. On draught are Dartmoor Best and Turks Ale, although hot chocolate laced with St Agnes brandy is popular in winter, and local fish and home-made pies are likely to crop up on the menus. Children are welcome, and one bedroom is available for overnighters. St Agnes is a tiny island popular with wildlife watchers (look out for seals and an abundance of seabirds).

Open *11 to 11, Sun 12 to 10.30; closed some days winter*

ST ALBANS

Hertfordshire   map 3

Rose & Crown

St Michaels Street, St Albans AL3 4SG
TEL: (01727) 851903

In the little enclave of St Michaels, opposite the entrance to Verulanium Park and the Roman Museum, this pretty sixteenth-century pub comes complete with a secluded courtyard garden. Sporting memorabilia cover the uneven walls and there's a decent choice of beer on handpump, including Adnams, Fuller's and Courage Directors. Lunchtime food (not Sun) centres on American-style deli sandwiches (with potato salad, kettle crisps and pickled cucumber): 'Lauren Bacall' consists of coarse pâté, bacon, Swiss cheese, lettuce, onion and wholegrain mustard; a few additional blackboard specials ring the changes.

Open *11 to 11, Sun 12 to 10.30*

ST EWE

Cornwall   map 1

Crown Inn

St Ewe PL26 6EY
TEL: (01726) 843322

The Lost Gardens of Heligan are not far from this attractive, flower-bedecked sixteenth-century hostelry, set in a village named after the local saint. Inside, a slate floor and open fire add character to the bar, where drinkers can take advantage of plentiful St Austell beers, including Tinners, HSD, Duchy and Tribute. The bar menu is based on local produce, fresh fish and game, and the pub also has a separate no-smoking dining room. Outside is a sheltered garden with a heated marquee and there's accommodation in one double room with a four-poster.

Open *12 (11 summer) to 3, 5 to 11, Sun 12 to 3, 5 to 10.30*

ST IVES

Cornwall   map 1

Sloop Inn

The Wharf, St Ives TR26 1LP
TEL: (01736) 796584

With its fourteenth-century origins, this traditional slate-floored and dark-beamed pub harks back to St Ives's origins as a quiet fishing village. Glorious views of the harbour ensure its popularity in summer, but even in the depths of winter it buzzes with locals and artists (whose pictures are for sale on the walls). A strong line-up of beers includes Old Speckled Hen, John Smith's and Sharp's Doom Bar Bitter, and a handful of wines is served by the glass from a list of around two dozen bottles. The bar menu adds locally caught fish to the standard sandwiches and steaks, while the evening restaurant menu is a smarter affair featuring desserts with an appealing Cornish twist. Accommodation is available.
Open *9am to 11pm*

ST JUST

Cornwall   map 1

Star Inn

Fore Street, St Just TR19 7LL
TEL: (01736) 788767

Built of granite in the eighteenth century, the Star is part of a terrace on the narrow road through the village. Live accordion music nights are held occasionally (along with singing and joke-telling) in the atmospheric beamed bar. Real ales are from the St Austell brewery, and straightforward pub food is served at lunchtimes. Three B&B rooms are available.
Open *11 to 11, Sun 12 to 10.30; closed lunchtime 25 Dec*

SCALES

Cumbria   map 10

White Horse Inn

Scales CA12 4SY
TEL: (01768) 779241
just off A66 Keswick to Penrith road, 5m NE of Keswick

New licensees took over this long, low, beamed pub in summer 2003, but it remains a haven both for drivers using the A66 and for fell walkers tackling Saddleback. Liquid refreshment is from Jennings and local microbreweries, with a wine list running to around 30 bottles, and, food-wise, expect exemplary use of local produce – fell lamb, trout from Borrowdale – and daily-changing specials.
Open *12 to 3, 6.30 to 11 (10.30 Sun)*

SHAMLEY GREEN

Surrey   map 3

Red Lion Inn

Shamley Green GU5 0UB
TEL: (01483) 892202

Opposite the village green, this neat, white-painted pub is popular for its bar food; it's also open for breakfast and has a separate restaurant. Adnams Broadside, Marston's Pedigree and Young's Bitter are on handpump, and half a dozen wines are served by the glass from a list of around 30 bottles. Four rooms are available.
Open *Mon to Fri 7.30am to 11.30pm, Sat 8.30am to 11.30pm, Sun 8.30am to 10.30pm*

SHARDLOW

Derbyshire   map 5

Malt Shovel

The Wharf, Shardlow DE72 2HG
TEL: (01332) 799763

On the bank of the Trent and Mersey Canal, the Malt Shovel, as its name suggests, has been converted from an eighteenth-century maltings. Marston's Pedigree and Banks's Bitter are on draught along with a guest, and food is served at lunchtimes: expect steaks, casseroles, steak and Stilton pie, and fish in leek and white wine sauce. There are tables outside, and children are welcome.
Open *11 to 11, Sun 12 to 10.30; closed evening 25 Dec*

SHEEPSCOMBE

Gloucestershire   map 2

Butchers Arms

Sheepscombe GL6 7RH
TEL: (01452) 812113

You can soak up the lovely views of the Cotswolds from the sloping lawn at this seventeenth-century mellow-stone pub and in winter soak up the heat from the log fires in the characterful bars. Hook Norton Best Bitter and Wye Valley

Dorothy Goodbody are on draught, and the enterprising menu runs to chicken breast wrapped in bacon stuffed with garlic mushrooms, tuna steak with a caper and sun-dried tomato sauce, and broccoli and cream cheese bake.

Open *11.30 to 3, 6.30 (6 summer) to 11, Sun 12 to 4, 7 to 10.30*

SHEEPWASH

Devon   map 1

Half Moon Inn

Sheepwash EX21 5NE
TEL: (01409) 231376

off A3072, 4m W of Hatherleigh

A huge inglenook and a slate floor are features of the main bar at this long, white-painted village inn. Bar snacks are available, there's a good choice of malt whiskies, and ales on draught are from Ruddles, Courage, and Sharp's. Dinner is served in the restaurant, which has a wine list extending to 200 bins. The pub owns ten miles of fishing rights on the nearby River Torridge, so salmon and trout anglers are drawn here, and facilities extend to a rod room, tackle shop and personal tuition, with 14 bedrooms for those wanting to stay.

Open *11.30 to 2.30, 6 to 11, Sun 12 to 2.30, 7 to 10.30*

SHEFFIELD

South Yorkshire   map 8

Devonshire Cat

49 Wellington Street, Sheffield S1 4HG
TEL: (0114) 279 6700

A sister operation to the famed Fat Cat (see Round-up below), this is by contrast a modern pub – spacious, with lots of glass and pine – at the base of a new building housing student accommodation. It is also closer to the city centre. But like its sibling, the main attraction is the huge line-up of beers on handpump and in bottle. Main meals such as lamb and red wine casserole, jambalaya and cauliflower cheese come with a beer recommendation, as do sandwiches. A new licensee took over as we went to press, so reports please.

Open *11.30 to 11, Sun 12 to 10.30*

Fat Cat

23 Alma Street, Sheffield S3 8SA
TEL: (0114) 249 4801

Next to the Kelham Island Industrial Museum, this solid brick-built Victorian corner pub caters to more than just the workers of this rejuvenated industrial area. For this is real ale heaven, with ten handpumps on the bar (dominated by the renowned Kelham Island ales) and a range of imported bottles to enjoy uninterrupted by music or games machines. The main bar has a traditional front-parlour feel with a tiled fireplace, and there's also a separate no-smoking snug. A small blackboard menu offers basic, hearty fare.

Open *Mon to Thur 12 to 3, 5.30 to 11, Fri and Sat 12 to 11, Sun 12 to 3, 7 to 10.30*

SHINCLIFFE

Co Durham   map 10

Seven Stars Inn

High Street North, Shincliffe DH1 2NU
TEL: (0191) 384 8454

on A177 just S of Durham

At a junction in a village just outside Durham, this is a popular spot for both local businesspeople and tourists. The public bar is authentically pubby, while the pink-painted lounge focuses on food. The menus spread across three blackboards, cater to almost any taste, from chicken liver pâté with basil crostini to fish 'n' chips and pan-fried duck breast with Puy lentils and five-spice jus. Beers are Black Sheep Best Bitter, Marston's Pedigree, Castle Eden Ale and Theakston Best Bitter, and a dozen wines come by the glass from a decent list. New owners took over in early 2004 – reports please.

Open *11 to 11, Sun 12 to 10.30*

SHREWSBURY

Shropshire   map 5

Armoury

Victoria Quay, Welsh Bridge, Shrewsbury SY1 1HH
TEL: (01743) 340525

This wonderfully spacious pub looks out on the broad waters of the River Severn from 11 arched windows. It has served as both bakery and arsenal but in its current incarnation is lined with books and is

more reminiscent of a library. No chance of silence, though, as an impressive range of ales fuels the buzz of conversation, with six guests lining up alongside regulars Wadworth 6X and Shropshire Lad. An upbeat menu offers the likes of Chinese-style slow-roast belly pork, or parsnip and dolcelatte croquettes with niçoise salad.
Open *12 to 11 (10.30 Sun)*

Three Fishes
4 Fish Street, Shrewsbury SY1 1UR
TEL: (01743) 344793
An alehouse since 1780, this half-timbered fifteenth-century building stands on a steep cobbled street of similarly ancient structures. The interior is in keeping, with original beams in well-shined black against white plaster. A strict no-smoking policy comes as a surprise – and a welcome one, judging by the place's popularity. Beers are an impressive line-up of Deuchars IPA, Fuller's London Pride, Timothy Taylor Landlord, plus two or three guests, while the kitchen keeps things simple: expect sausages and mash, steak and ale pie and chicken curry. A new landlord took over in early 2004 – reports please.
Open *Mon to Thur 11.30 to 3, 5 to 11, Fri and Sat 11.30 to 11, Sun 12 to 4, 7 to 10.30*

SHUSTOKE
Warwickshire   map 5
Griffin
Shustoke B46 2LB
TEL: (01675) 481205
A formidable line-up of real ales at this oak-framed former coaching inn dating from the early seventeenth century includes Hook Norton Old Hooky, Marston's Pedigree, Theakston Old Peculier, and Banks's Original, and in summer there's scrumpy too. The short menu (available Monday to Saturday lunchtimes only) concentrates on snacks and traditional pub fare. Children are welcome in the conservatory.
Open *12 to 2.30, 7 to 11, Sun 12 to 2.30, 7 to 10.30*

SMARDEN
Kent   map 3
Bell Inn
Bell Lane, Smarden TN27 8PW
TEL: (01233) 770283
off A274, 7m SW of Charing; pub is ½m outside village (signposted from village)
Beams, ancient-looking red-brick walls and tiled floors in the series of small interlinked rooms are evidence of the great age of this half-tiled village pub. The wide choice of real ales on draught might include Flowers IPA, Shepherd Neame Spitfire Premium Ale, Bass and a guest, and menus are listed on blackboards: expect something like lamb shank with redcurrant and rosemary sauce, or grilled plaice with prawn and white wine sauce.
Open *11.30 to 3, 6 to 11, Sun 12 to 10.30; closed 25 Dec*

SNAPE
Suffolk   map 6
Golden Key
Priory Road, Snape IP17 1SG
TEL: (01728) 688510
The nearby Snape Maltings is the home of the annual Aldeburgh Festival, although concerts are held here all year, and the Golden Key makes a good place for a drink before or after a visit: Adnams provide the wines (with a good choice by the glass) as well as the beers. Seasonal fish and game make appearances on the menu, along with stalwarts like steak and Guinness pie and home-made puddings. One of the two dining rooms is no-smoking. Three en suite bedrooms are offered.
Open *11 to 3, 6 to 11, Sun 12 to 3, 7 (6 in summer) to 10.30*

SOUTHWOLD
Suffolk   map 6
Lord Nelson
42 East Street, Southwold IP18 6EJ
TEL: (01502) 722079
Affectionately known as 'The Nelly', this convivial pub stands a few yards from the venerable Sailor's Reading Room and you can smell the sea from its front door. A huge collection of Nelson and Victory memorabilia fills the interior and devotees reckon it's the best place in Southwold to

sample Adnams beer 'as it should be'.
Food provides refuelling sustenance
(BLTs, fish 'n' chips etc). There's a lovely
enclosed walled garden at the back – if the
bar gets too packed out.
Open *11 to 11, Sun 12 to 10.30*

SOUTH ZEAL

Devon   map 1

Oxenham Arms
South Zeal EX20 2JT
TEL: (01837) 840244

The standing stone in a wall in the
Oxenham Arms (named after a family who
subsequently owned the property) must
have been ancient when the pub was built
in the twelfth century. Other features are a
granite fireplace in the lounge and a
granite pillar in the dining room. On the
menu, Stilton and broccoli soup may be
followed by steak and kidney pie, or grilled
halibut fillet with lemon and parsley
butter, while on handpump are brews
from Dartmoor's Princetown Brewery and
Cornwall's Sharp's or St Austell Breweries.
People wishing to stay can choose from
eight bedrooms.
Open *11 to 2.30, 5 to 11, Sun 12 to 2.30, 7 to 10.30*

STANBRIDGE

Bedfordshire   map 6

Five Bells
Station Road, Stanbridge LU7 9JF
TEL: (01525) 210224

Refurbishment has changed the image of
this 400-year-old village pub: steel-grey
paintwork sets the tone on the windows
and doors, and the modern outlook is
carried through to the interior. A smart
restaurant in cool greys contrasts with
wooden bar furniture, while candles, cacti
and oriental rugs add some offbeat charm.
The food divides between 'light bites'
(warm chicken liver salad, spaghetti
bolognese) and restaurant dishes like duck
breast with wilted greens and chocolate
vinaigrette. Real ales could come from
Tetleys, Hook Norton, Marston's and
Black Sheep. Children have their own
menu and there's a play area in the
spacious garden.
Open *12 to 11, Sun 12 to 10.30*

STEEP

Hampshire   map 2

Harrow Inn
Steep GU32 2DA
TEL: (01730) 262685
off A3 just N of Petersfield

A truly classic country pub, a real step back
in time, the Harrow has been run by the
McCutcheon family for many years. The
compact bar is steeped in character, with
its huge inglenook, beams and rustic
furnishings, while the tiny bar counter is
festooned with hop garlands. A second
room, with a separate entrance, follows the
theme but offers more comfort in which
to enjoy hearty dishes like home-made
soups, shepherd's pie and treacle tart.
Local beers, such as Cheriton Pots Ale and
Ringwood Best, come straight from the
cask behind the bar.
Open *Mon to Fri 12 to 2.30, 6 to 11, Sat 11 to 3,
6 to 11, Sun 12 to 3, 7 to 10.30; closed Sun eve winter*

STOCKPORT

Greater Manchester   map 8

Arden Arms
23 Millgate, Stockport SK1 2LX
TEL: (0161) 480 2185

Slap in the centre of town, just yards from
the huge parish church and the cast-iron
market hall, this is a superb traditional
town pub – a commanding three-storey
Georgian building with fine etched
windows and a bright display of hanging
baskets. Modern town planning has
plopped a supermarket in front of it, but
the network of cobbled alleys leading to
the Robinson's brewery (source of the
pub's impeccable ales) lets nostalgia flow
unchecked. The interior, too, is full of
original features. Snacks, sandwiches,
ciabatta rolls and a few more substantial
dishes make up an appetising menu.
Open *12 to 11 (10.30 Sun)*

Queen's Head
26 Little Underbank, Stockport SK1 1JT
TEL: (0161) 480 0725

'A small but perfectly formed town pub'
with no frills, no gimmicks and no food.
Sometimes known as Turner's Vaults, it is
tucked away at the foot of the sandstone
cliffs in Stockport's medieval streets and

looks like something from a Dickensian Christmas card. Inside, it's full of Victorian and Edwardian decorative touches, from an imposing canopied skylight to old brass wine taps and – reputedly – the smallest gents' urinal in Britain (behind closed doors). Bargain-priced Samuel Smith's Old Brewery Bitter is kept in good order.

Open *11 to 11, Sun 12 to 3*

STOKE ABBOTT

Dorset   map 3

New Inn

Stoke Abbott DT8 3JW
TEL: (01308) 868333

signposted off B3163 SW of Beaminster

The domestic, cared-for atmosphere of the Webb family's pub is the added extra that lifts it above the traditional village inn norm. An extensive collection of decorative plates adds colour to a backdrop of flagstones and brick hearths in the imposing seventeenth-century grey-stone building. Beers come from Palmers, and the menu tours the world for inspiration, taking in plenty of vegetarian options.

Open *Mon to Thur 11.30 to 3, 6.30 to 11 (7 to 10.30 winter), Fri and Sat 11.30 to 3, 6.30 to 11, Sun 12 to 3, 6.30 to 10.30 (7 to 10.30 winter)*

STOKE FLEMING

Devon   map 1

Green Dragon

Church Road, Stoke Fleming TQ6 0PX
TEL: (01803) 770238

Opposite the church in the centre of the village, this large pub has a nautical theme, reflecting the landlord's background as a long-distance yachtsman. It's a busy place, with a jolly and relaxing atmosphere, with diners attracted by the Mess Deck's varied and reasonably priced bistro-style menu. Drinkers can go for one of eight wines by the glass or a pint of real ale: among four on draught might be Wadworth 6X and Flowers IPA.

Open *11 to 3, 5.30 to 11, Sun 12 to 3, 6.30 to 10.30*

STOUGHTON

West Sussex   map 3

Hare and Hounds

Stoughton PO18 9JQ
TEL: (023) 9263 1433

off B2147 at Walderton, 5m NW of Chichester

The Hare and Hounds, built about 300 years ago as two cottages, consists of three knocked-through rooms with log fires, flagstone floors and pine furniture. Separate menus operate at lunch and dinner, but in the evening you can expect steaks and fish such as trout and sea bass. Three regular ales – Timothy Taylor Landlord, Gale's HSB and Young's Bitter – are joined on the handpumps by three guests, among them perhaps Itchen Valley Wykehams Glory, and four wines are served by the glass. Hidden away in the South Downs, Stoughton is in good walking country; Kingley Vale Nature Reserve is nearby.

Open *11 to 3, 6 to 11, Sun 12 to 3, 7 to 10.30 (all day summer)*

STOURTON

Wiltshire   map 2

Spread Eagle Inn

Stourton BA12 6QE
TEL: (01747) 840587

from A303 about 6m NE of Wincanton, follow signs for village and Stourhead

A tour of the National Trust's Stourhead, a Palladian mansion built in the 1720s, and its estate can build a hunger and thirst, whether for lunch, afternoon tea or dinner. Ideally located in a courtyard at the entrance to the estate, the 200-year-old ivy-clad Spread Eagle will satisfy visitors' needs – even an overnight stay in one of the five rooms (including free admission to the house and gardens). Food-wise, pub standards are served all day, while dinner brings out game dishes such as wood pigeon suprême as well as fish and vegetarian options. Beers are from Courage plus a guest, perhaps from Butcombe; 25 wines.

Open *11 to 11, Sun 12 to 10.30*

STRATTON

Dorset   map 2

Saxon Arms

The Square, Stratton DT2 9WG
TEL: (01305) 260020

If you ever wondered how England's characterful old inns looked when the signs first went several hundred years ago, stop in at this impressive new construction in flint, thatch, brick and stone. The open-plan interior is equally well finished in natural materials but speaks to modern tastes for space. Dorset cheeses, ham and pâté feature in the ploughman's, and ice cream is locally made too. The main menu offers the likes of chicken, bacon and tarragon pie, scampi, and spicy bean burgers. Fuller's London Pride and Palmers IPA on handpump are joined by two guests.
Open *Mon to Fri 11 to 2.30, 5.30 to 11, Sat 11 to 2.30, 6 to 11, Sun 12 to 3, 6.30 to 10.30*

STRINESDALE

Greater Manchester   map 8

Roebuck Inn

Brighton Road, Strinesdale OL4 3RB
TEL: (0161) 624 7819
from Oldham take A62 Huddersfield road, then left on to A672 Ripponden road, then right after 1m on to Turf Pit Lane; follow for 1m

In a village in open country just outside Oldham, climbing towards the moors, the Roebuck is a cosy pub with exposed-stone walls and, in the dining room, comfortable banquettes (although food can also be eaten in the bar). Expect main courses of steaks, chilli, and perhaps veal or duck. Boddingtons Bitter and Bass are on draught, and around half a dozen wines are served by the glass.
Open *12 to 3, 5 to 11, Sun 12 to 10.30*

TEMPLE GRAFTON

Warwickshire   map 5

Blue Boar

Temple Grafton B49 6NR
TEL: (01789) 750010

Exposed stone, fires and window seats add character to the interior of this creeper-covered seventeenth-century pub, and outside is a patio for summer drinking: perhaps a pint of Theakston Best Bitter, XB or Old Speckled Hen, or one of around ten wines sold by the glass. Sandwiches, jacket potatoes and the likes of grilled gammon with egg and chips or chicken curry are the order of the day at lunchtimes; in the evening expect a touch more sophistication in the form of salmon and halibut gravad lax, followed by minted lamb cutlets on rösti with redcurrant gravy, then cranberry parfait with almond and chocolate sauce. Children are welcome, and accommodation is offered in 15 en suite rooms.
Open *11 to 11, Sun 11 to 11.15*

TESTCOMBE

Hampshire   map 2

Mayfly

Testcombe SO20 6AX
TEL: (01264) 860283
on A3057, between Stockbridge and Andover, by River Test

Next to the River Test, the Mayfly, an attractive building of honey-coloured brick with decorative gables, is particularly appealing in the summer when you can sit in the riverside garden and watch the ducks and swans. Within, fires burn in winter, and various drinking and eating areas are set with wooden tables and chairs; food is a semi-self-service hot and cold buffet. On draught are Marston's Pedigree, Wadworth 6X and a guest – perhaps Ringwood Best – and a decent number of wines are served by the glass.
Open *10 to 11, Sun 10 to 10.30*

THOMPSON

Norfolk   map 6

Chequers Inn

Griston Road, Thompson IP24 1PX
TEL: (01953) 483360

Dating from the sixteenth century, this attractive thatched pub is brightened up by colourful hanging baskets in summer. Ales are from Adnams, Fuller's and Greene King, and the lengthy menu lists mostly pub staples, from sandwiches and jacket potatoes to sirloin steak; a daily-changing blackboard extends the range, with perhaps game in season. Three B&B rooms.
Open *11.30 to 2.30, 6.30 to 11, Sun 12 to 3, 7 to 10.30 (12 to 10.30 summer)*

THREE LEGGED CROSS

East Sussex   map 3

Bull

Dunster Mill Lane, Three Legged Cross
TN5 7HH
TEL: (01580) 200586

*take Three Legged Cross road signposted in
centre of Ticehurst, off B2099*

This brick and tile-hung pub is in an
attractive, peaceful spot, with a sizeable
lawn at the front and excellent views to the
rear. Blackboards in the bar list the eating
options, and there's a separate snack menu;
the restaurant is open in the evening. Local
breweries Harveys and Rother Valley
supply the ales, and around half a dozen
wines are served by the glass. Outside are
an aviary and a children's play area.
Accommodation available.

Open *11 to 11, Sun 12 to 10.30*

THURGARTON

Nottinghamshire   map 5

Red Lion

Southwell Road, Thurgarton NG14 7GP
TEL: (01636) 830351

The Red Lion was built in the sixteenth
century as an alehouse for the monks of
Thurgarton Priory. In 1936 it was the
scene of a gruesome murder; framed
newspaper accounts are testament to this.
Straightforward pub food (served all day at
weekends) is what to expect, along with
Black Sheep Best Bitter, Banks's Mansfield
Cask and Hook Norton Best Bitter.
Children are welcome throughout.

Open *Mon to Fri 11.30 to 2.30, 6 to 11, Sat 11.30
to 11, Sun 12 to 10.30*

TICHBORNE

Hampshire   map 2

Tichborne Arms

Tichborne SO24 0NA
TEL: (01962) 733760

The tranquil hamlet of Tichborne in the
Itchen valley is, perhaps, best known for
the case of the Titchborne Claimant – a
renowned nineteenth-century incident
that is well documented by cuttings in one
of the bars of this thatched red-brick pub.
Ringwood Best and guest ales are served
direct from a stillage behind the bar, and
food spans everything from ploughman's

and jacket potatoes to specials such as
chicken, tarragon and mushroom pie and
lamb shank with minted gravy. The pub is
at its best in summer, when you can take
advantage of the splendid, flower-filled
rear garden. Excellent local walks.

Open *11.30 to 2.30, 6 to 11, Sun 12 to 3, 7 to 10.30;
closed 25, 26 Dec and eve 31 Dec*

TIVETSHALL ST MARY

Norfolk   map 6

Old Ram Coaching Inn

Ipswich Road, Tivetshall St Mary NR15 2DE
TEL: (01379) 676794

Brick floors, standing timbers, wood-
burners, pine furniture and old farming
implements all combine to bring character
to the spacious, well-maintained interior
of this sympathetically restored
seventeenth-century coaching inn. Food is
served all day, including breakfast from
7.30, from separate bar and restaurant
menus, with around 20 wines by the glass
and Adnams Bitter, Bass and a guest on
draught. Eleven en suite rooms are
available.

Open *11 to 11, Sun 12 to 10.30 (breakfast from
7.30); closed 25 and 26 Dec*

TOLLARD ROYAL

Wiltshire   map 2

King John Inn

Tollard Royal SP5 5PS
TEL: (01725) 516207

The King John was built in 1859 for the
workers at the village iron foundry; today
it satisfies tourists to the pretty village and
walkers in the nearby ancient forests as
well as locals. Butcombe Best, Marston's
Pedigree, Fuller's London Pride,
Wadworth 6X and Wells Bombardier
Premium Bitter are all on draught, a
handful of wines is served by the glass, and
food, from sandwiches and rolls to a full
three courses, is served in both the
restaurant and the bar. Children have their
own menu, and the pub has a no-smoking
family room. Three en suite rooms
available.

Open *11 to 3, 6 to 11, Sun 12 to 4, 7 to 10.30
(12 to 10.30 summer)*

TOPSHAM

Devon   map 1

Bridge

Topsham EX3 0QQ
TEL: (01392) 873862

The Bridge dates mainly from the
sixteenth century, although the original
building is 500 years older. Traditional pub
food is the order of the day – sandwiches,
ploughman's, pasties – and up to ten real
ales are drawn direct from barrels, among
them perhaps Branscombe Vale Bitter,
Exmoor Valley and Black Autumn. The
village museum is devoted to the ecology
of the Exe estuary and the history of
shipbuilding.

Open *12 to 2, 6 to 10.30 (11 Fri and Sat),
Sun 12 to 2, 7 to 10.30*

TRESCO

Isles of Scilly   map 1

New Inn

Tresco TR24 0QQ
TEL: (01720) 422844

This small, informal holiday base on
Tresco – a stone building overlooking Old
Grimsby harbour – houses an authentic
bar. The characterful panelled interior has
snug hideaway alcoves and is decked out
with marine artefacts and portraits of local
people. Today's locals, mostly a young
crowd, take time off here, giving it a
buzzy, friendly atmosphere. Beers are
from St Austell, Skinner's and Fuller's, and
printed and blackboard menus offer a wide
range, with 'really fresh' local seafood to
the fore. A conservatory and a beer garden
with palm trees make the best of fine
summer days. Accommodation is offered
in 16 rooms.

Open *winter 11 to 3, 6 to 11, Sun 12 to 3, 6 to
10.30; summer 11 to 11, Sun 12 to 10.30*

TRURO

Cornwall   map 1

Old Ale House

7 Quay Street, Truro TR1 2HD
TEL: (01872) 271122

Traditionalists and real ale aficionados
should find plenty to enjoy in this popular
beamed and wood-panelled pub. Eight
beers, dispensed under gravity, are
available at any one time including several

from local breweries – Skinner's
Kiddlywink and Sharp's Doom Bar, for
example. Sizzling dishes served in cast-
iron skittles with bread are the main
contenders on the menu, although the
choice of fairly straightforward food
extends to 'hands of bread', jacket potatoes
and blackboard specials along the lines of
liver and bacon or cashew nut paella,
followed by a selection of steamed
puddings and ice cream sundaes.

Open *11 to 11, Sun 12 to 10.30*

TUNBRIDGE WELLS

Kent   map 3

Beacon

Tea Garden Lane, Tunbridge Wells TN3 9JH
TEL: (01892) 524252

High above the town, this Edwardian
flight of fancy, adorned with turrets and
bay windows, has adopted a 'bar and
restaurant' tag and a smart modern livery
that speaks of a kitchen with ambitions.
The restaurant menu offers the likes of
crab, chilli, ginger and lemongrass samosas
followed by baked fillet of Enderby
haddock on Portuguese potatoes glazed
with Cashel Blue. There's also a more
straightforward bar menu and plenty of
space just for drinking both inside and out.
Beers are from Harveys and Timothy
Taylor, and a dozen wines come by the
glass.

Open *11 to 11, Sun 12 to 10.30*

UPPERMILL

Greater Manchester   map 8

Cross Keys Inn

Off Running Hill Gate, Uppermill OL3 6LW
TEL: (01457) 874626

Set high on the moorland fringe above
Uppermill, this weatherworn gritstone
300-year-old watering hole boasts
spectacular views of Saddleworth Moor
and the Tame Valley; it's also close to the
Oldham Way footpath. This is a place to
savour, with a grand fireplace in the main
bar and a vast lead-blackened range
dominating the splendid flagstone-floored
taproom. Home-cooked pies and savoury
suet puddings (minted lamb, for example)
are the pub's speciality, although the
choice of amazing-value food also includes
a full quota of old favourites ranging from

hot and cold sandwiches to plaice and chips, and vegetarian chilli. The full range of JW Lees' beers – including seasonal brews – are on draught.

Open *11 to 11, Sun 12 to 10.30*

VENTNOR

Isle of Wight map 2

Spyglass Inn
The Esplanade, Ventor PO38 1JX
TEL: (01983) 855338

A plum location right by the sea wall at the western end of the esplanade is a trump card for this ramshackle old pub. Extensions have been designed to make the most of the views and there is an outdoor terrace for use when the sun shines and crowds of holidaymakers descend on the place. A nautical theme prevails, inside and out. The regular printed menu offers standard pub food (baguettes, grilled gammon, steaks etc) or you can choose from the selection of more interesting blackboard specials. Badger Dorset Best and Tanglefoot are on handpump, alongside Golden from the nearby Ventnor brewery. Accommodation in three self-contained flats.

Open *10.30 to 11 (10.30 Sun)*

WAMBROOK

Somerset map 2

Cotley Inn
Wambrook TA20 3EN
TEL: (01460) 62348

The main bar and eating areas at this friendly, unpretentious inn have a look and feel that are more tea room than boozer, with fringed lampshades, china animals and works by local artists (for sale) on the walls, while a games room extension draws pool enthusiasts. Food comes in substantial portions, even from the 'small eats' list, and fish is a major feature. Otter Ale is on handpump. Events include occasional quiz nights and hedge-laying contests. Accommodation available in two rooms.

Open *11 to 3, 7 to 11; closed Sun eve Jan and Feb*

WARBLETON

East Sussex map 3

War-Bill-in-Tun
Warbleton TN21 9BD
TEL: (01435) 830636

The pub's name is probably a pun on the name of the village, although another story doing the rounds relates it to happenings in the civil war. Harveys Sussex Best Bitter is the linchpin ale, joined at the pumps by two guests, and the menu, served throughout, might run from stuffed mushrooms to poached salmon and lamb chops. Children welcome.

Open *11 to 3, 6.30 to 11, Sun 12 to 3, 7 to 10.30; closed eve 25 and 26 Dec, 1 Jan*

WARDLOW MIRES

Derbyshire map 8

Three Stags Heads
Wardlow Mires SK17 8RW
TEL: (01298) 872268
at junction of B6465 and A623, 2m E of Tideswell

You may think it's in the middle of nowhere, even though this fascinating little pub is actually beside a road that cuts through the Dales. Long-serving licensees run the Three Stags Heads in their own way – so don't expect fancy touches or standing on ceremony. Instead, soak up the good humour, warmth and hospitality and set your sights on the beers from regional breweries such as Abbeydale and Broadstone. Food is totally in keeping with the feel of the place and the menu focuses on hearty, rustic-sounding grub to suit the season: rabbit with mustard, pigeon breasts, steak and wine pie. Plenty of walks nearby. Note the restricted opening times.

Open *Fri 7 to 11, Sat and Sun 12 to 11; also open bank hols*

WARESIDE

Hertfordshire map 3

Chequers Inn
Wareside SG12 7QY
TEL: (01920) 467010
2m W from Ware on B1004

'In the middle of nowhere' is an understatement when it comes to tracking down this good-looking country pub. Once inside, however, you can relax in the

bar, which has its complement of requisite low beams and real wood fires, not to mention a couple of friendly resident dogs. Daily specials chalked up on a blackboard might be home-marinated olives, rabbit stew and fruit crumble, while the printed menu goes in for prawn cocktail, garlic mushrooms, steaks, and vegetarian harvest pie. Beers are from Adnams and Greene King and there's a short list of promising wines. Accommodation available.
Open *Mon to Fri 12 to 3, 6 to 11, Sat 12 to 11, Sun 12 to 10.30*

WASDALE HEAD

Cumbria   map 8

Wasdale Head Inn

Wasdale Head CA20 1EX
TEL: (019467) 26229

off A595, between Gosforth and Holmbrook; follow signs for 8m

Wasdale Head is a remote, unspoilt part of the Lakeland, dominated by towering Great Gable, and it's a Mecca for rock-climbers, ramblers and hikers. The aptly named Great Gable Brewing Company has its home in this pub, and you can now sample Great Gable and Wasd'ale in addition to Scawfell, Burnmore Pale Ale, Wrynose and Yewbarrow; also look for bottled Scottish Heather Ale and German wheat beers. The bar was named after the pub's first landlord, Will Ritson, who earned a reputation as the 'world's biggest liar'. Traditional staples like steak and ale pie, local lamb and game are the order of the day on the food front; alternatively, the restaurant offers a four-course set menu. Accommodation available.
Open *11 to 10 (11 summer), Sun 12 to 10*

WATLINGTON

Oxfordshire   map 2

Chequers

Love Lane, Watlington OX49 5RA
TEL: (01491) 612874

take B4009 from M40 junction 6 and turn right down Love Lane just before Watlington, signposted Icknield School

Watlington is on the Ridgeway footpath, so is popular with walkers in the Chilterns, and the Chequers, with its vine-decked conservatory and garden, makes a good break from the nearby motorway. On the

food front, expect sandwiches, jacket potatoes and main courses such as chicken balti. This is a Brakspear house.
Open *12 to 2.30, 6 to 11, Sun 12 to 3, 7 to 10.30; closed eve 25 and 26 Dec*

WEST HUNTSPILL

Somerset   map 2

Crossways Inn

Withy Road, West Huntspill TA9 3RA
TEL: (01278) 783756

Real ale fans make a beeline for this pub a couple of miles from the coast: three regular ales on draught – Fuller's London Pride, Bass and Flowers IPA – are joined by the same number of guests, among them perhaps Cotleigh Barn Owl Bitter and Church End Vicar's Ruin. The blackboard lists such things as ploughman's, pies and fish dishes, and half a dozen wines are served the glass. Three en suite rooms are available.
Open *11 to 3, 5.30 to 11, Sun 12 to 3, 7 to 10.30*

WEST TANFIELD

North Yorkshire   map 9

Bull Inn

Church Street, West Tanfield HG4 5JQ
TEL: (01677) 470678

On the bank of the River Ure, the Bull takes pride of place in a village located between the Yorkshire Dales and the North York Moors National Parks. The cosy, beamed interior splits into main bar and dining room. Blackboard specials – perhaps Thai fishcakes – supplement soup, pies and various steaks, although there's no lunchtime food from Monday to Wednesday. Yorkshire breweries supply the pumps with Black Sheep Best Bitter and Tetley Bitter, and around 15 wines all come in under £20. Accommodation available.
Open *Mon 11 to 3, Tue to Fri 11 to 3, 5 to 11, Sat 11 to 11, Sun 12 to 10.30*

WHALTON

Northumberland ·   map 10

Beresford Arms

Whalton NE61 3UZ
TEL: (01670) 775225

on B6524 from Morpeth

This attractive stone-built pub, which has a comfortable restaurant, dates from the nineteenth century, although most of the properties in the village are Georgian. No real ales are stocked, but most people come here for the food, attracted by a long and interesting menu: perhaps seared scallops with black-bean vinaigrette to start, followed by roast pheasant breast wrapped in bacon, or pan-fried sea bass with a prawn butter sauce. Accommodation is available.

Open *11 to 3, 5.30 to 11, Sun 12 to 3, 7 to 10.30; closed Sun eve winter*

WHITNEY

Herefordshire   map 5

Rhydspence Inn

Whitney HR3 6EU
TEL: (01497) 831262

off A438 Hereford to Brecon road, 4m E of Hay-on-Wye

This strikingly half-timbered pub was built in the fourteenth century on a drovers' route. Nowadays it still offers refreshments to travellers in the heavily beamed bar areas, with beers from Robinsons and Bass and bar food along the lines of grilled sardines with herb and garlic butter, followed by steak and kidney pie, or deep-fried cod. The separate restaurant, which has views of the Wye Valley, has its own menu.

Open *11 to 2.30, 7 to 11, Sun 12 to 2.30, 7 to 11; closed 25 Dec*

WHITSTABLE

Kent   map 3

Prince Albert

Sea Street, Whitstable CT5 1AN
TEL: (01227) 273400

The beach and the sea wall are just a pebble's throw from this tiny backstreet pub, which thrives on the virtues of liveliness and good drinking. First-class real ales are served in tip-top condition and drinkers take their pick from Greene King IPA, Fuller's London Pride or the current guest brew. To go with the beer, there's a short bar menu of decent home-cooked food ranging from fish and chips to steak and oyster pie, while the daily special might be something cosmopolitan like gnocchi with Gorgonzola. Note that food is served all day at weekends.

Open *11 to 11, Sun 12 to 10.30*

WINDSOR

Berkshire   map 3

Two Brewers

34 Park Street, Windsor SL4 1LB
TEL: (01753) 855426

Who said size matters? Well, the Two Brewers proves it most certainly doesn't. Handsomely located on a cobbled street right by Home Park gates, this pint-sized locals' hostelry, dark and atmospheric, comes bursting with quintessential English character and unpretentious charm. Wooden floors, beams, winter fires, wooden furniture and walls packed with all manner of fascinating regalia encircle a small central bar. Equally compact, the weekly-changing menu could deliver the likes of traditional bangers 'n' mash to a more adventurous special like red snapper with prawn pancake and chive sauce, and finish with homely treacle sponge or homemade crumble.

Open *11.30 to 11 Mon to Fri, 11 to 11 Sat, Sun 12 to 10.30 (food Mon to Thur L 12 to 2.30, D 6.30 to 10, Fri L 12 to 2.30; no food Sat or Sun)*

WING

Leicestershire   map 6

King's Arms

Top Street, Wing LE15 8SE
TEL: (01572) 737634

Wing is famous for its medieval grass maze, although this extended seventeenth-century stone inn also makes its mark in the local scheme of things. A new licensee took over just before our deadline, bringing in his son to head the kitchen. Food is likely to run along similar lines as before, with a lively modern repertoire and a blackboard of fish specials. Real ales include Grainstore Cooking Bitter and Ten Fifty, Marston's Pedigree and guests such as seasonal Yuletide; the short list of around two dozen wines has a handful of house selections. Accommodation available. Reports on the new regime please.

Open *12 to 3, 6.30 to 11 (to 10.30 Sun); 12 to 11 Sat summer, 12 to 10.30 Sun summer*

WINGFIELD

Suffolk   map 6

De La Pole Arms

Church Road, Wingfield IP21 5RA
TEL: (01379) 384545

Drinkers congregate in the Village Bar of
this restored sixteenth-century pub
opposite the church; others use the
College Bar and restaurant. The Arms has
a new chef/manager, but is still owned by
St Peter's Brewery in Bungay and serves
the full range of its distinctive draught
beers plus bottled brews; seven wines are
offered by the glass. Food is now from a
blackboard menu that promises dishes like
cod and Brie en croûte and roast shoulder
of lamb with shallots and garlic gravy.
Reports please.

Open *Tue to Sat (summer Mon to Sat) 11 to 3,
6.30 to 11, Sun 12 to 3*

WISBOROUGH GREEN

West Sussex   map 3

Cricketers Arms

Wisborough Green RH14 0DG
TEL: (01403) 700369

Tables are provided outside this old-
fashioned village pub so that customers
can watch the cricket on the green. If
there's no play, head inside and relax in
one of the nooks and crannies or warm
yourself by the stove that sits in the
double-sided fireplace. Sporting prints
decorate the walls, and alcoholic liquid
refreshment comes courtesy of Fuller's
London Pride, Greene King IPA and
Young's Bitter. Bar snacks and daily-
changing blackboards advertise dishes like
smoked haddock kedgeree, pies and local
fish. Live music every Thursday.

Open *Mon to Sat 11 to 11, Sun 12 to 10.30; closed
eve 25 Dec*

WISTANSTOW

Shropshire   map 5

Plough

Wistanstow SY7 8DG
TEL: (01588) 673251

Hilly south Shropshire forms the backdrop
to this unpretentious and popular inn, a
long, low, rough-stone building. Next
door is the acclaimed Wood Brewery,
which supplies the bars (separate public

and lounge) with Shropshire Lad, Parish
and Plough Inn Bitter (there's a guest too).
The large lounge is open to the roof, with
modern timbers, brick pillars and a log
fire. Menus on a giant blackboard draw on
a host of local suppliers, down to the crisps
and home-made chutney, and offer
traditional home cooking such as grilled
Marches pork chop with melted Y-fenni
cheese and leek topping.

Open *Tue to Sat 11.30 to 2.30, 6.30 to 11, Sun 12
to 2.30, 7 to 10.30; closed 25 Dec*

WISWELL

Lancashire   map 8

Freemasons Arms

8 Vicarage Fold, Wiswell BB7 9DF
TEL: (01254) 822218

Tucked away down a lane in the centre of
a tiny village at the foot of Pendle Hill, this
homely pub looks totally unpretentious
with its low ceilings, beams and horse
brasses. An extensive menu features pub
standards from chilli to steak and kidney
pie, with fish specials like Thai-style
prawns written on a board. Real ales are
from Jennings and Black Sheep, 80-plus
whiskies are available and ten wines are
offered by the glass.

Open *Wed to Sat 12 to 2, 6.30 to 11; Sun 12 to 2,
6 to 10.30*

WITHYHAM

East Sussex   map 3

Dorset Arms

Withyham TN7 4BD
TEL: (01892) 770278

Ceiling beams and wall studs point to this
inn's fifteenth-century origins as a
farmhouse. The main bar has an open fire,
and there's also a large dining room, and
on warm days a triangular lawn and pot-
plant-laden patio out front come into play.
Choose comfort food (think pies, roasts
and casseroles) from a blackboard in the
bar or a smarter brand of traditional
English fare on the set-price three-course
menu. Harveys beers and a fair range of
wines quench the thirst.

Open *11 to 3, 6 to 11, Sun 12 to 3, 7 to 10.30*

WOODBASTWICK

Norfolk map 6

Fur & Feather Inn

Slad Lane, Woodbastwick NR13 6HQ
TEL: (01603) 720003

1m N of B1140, 8m NE of Norwich

Woodforde's Brewery is right next door to this thatched pub in a Norfolk Broads backwater. Eight of its real ales are regularly on show (including Wherry Best and Nelson's Revenge); alternatively you can pick from the choice of nine wines by the glass. Food ranges from baguettes and jacket potatoes to smoked haddock, or spring onion fishcakes, to heavyweight home-steamed steak and kidney pudding.
Open *winter 11.30 to 3, 6 to 11, Sun 12 to 10.30; summer 11.30 to 11, Sun 12 to 10.30*

WOOLLEY MOOR

Derbyshire map 5

White Horse Inn

Badger Lane, Woolley Moor DE55 6FG
TEL: (01246) 590319

on W side of Ogston Reservoir, off B6014, between Matlock and Stretton

This rural pub benefits from wonderful countryside views, and the pretty garden is the ideal place to enjoy them. Children can entertain themselves in the play area (which has a wooden train) while adults peruse the menus, ranging from sandwiches and lighter bites – Thai fishcakes, perhaps, or a ploughman's lunch – to a full à la carte. Three real ales might include something from Black Sheep, Adnams or Jennings.
Open *winter 12 to 3, 6 to 11, Sun 12 to 10.30; summer 11.30 to 3, 6 to 11, Sun 12 to 10.30*

WYMONDHAM

Leicestershire map 5

Berkeley Arms

59 Main Street, Wymondham LE14 2AG
TEL: (01572) 787587

Colourful window boxes trumpet the presence of this quiet village's local. A menu of steaks, a bowl of tagliatelle with pesto, and beer-battered cod 'n' chips is served in both the rustic beamed bar and the more formal restaurant, with its Victorian fireplace, plus warm ciabatta sandwiches in the bar. Beers are Greene King IPA, Marston's Pedigree and a guest such as Adnams Broadside, and eight wines come by the glass. New owners took over at the end of 2003 – reports please.
Open *Wed to Fri 12 to 2.30, Mon to Fri 6 (5.30 Fri) to 11, Sat 12 to 3, 6 to 11, Sun 12 to 3, 7 to 10.30; bar food and restaurant Wed to Sun 12 to 2.30, Wed to Sat 6 to 8.30*

YEALAND CONYERS

Lancashire map 8

New Inn

40 Yealand Road, Yealand Conyers LA5 9SJ
TEL: (01524) 732938

The New Inn is an attractive ivy-clad building at the bottom of the hill at the end of Yealand Conyers: look for the collection of antique watering cans lined up on one side of the pub. In the low-beamed bar there's a different decorative theme – namely, wooden spoons. The food is geared to those who appreciate good value and hefty portions: among familiar starters might be chicken liver pâté and garlic mushrooms, while international main courses could run to Cumberland sausages, chilli bean tortilla, moussaka and a pie of the day. Robinson's Hartleys XB is the regular beer, supplemented by a seasonal ale – perhaps Old Tom in winter.
Open *11.30 to 11, Sun 12 to 10.30*

YORK

North Yorkshire map 9

Maltings

Tanners Moat, York YO1 6HU
TEL: (01904) 655387

In a quiet side-street just off Lendal Bridge, this is one of York's 'good proper pubs' where beer comes first, music second and food well down the list. The interior is from the 'patina of age' school of décor, with old tin adverts adding colour and a ceiling made of old doors sowing confusion among passing pub crawlers. Seven ales are sourced from Black Sheep, Roosters and a rota of guest breweries. Monday is live blues night and there's folk on Tuesdays. The 'Dragon's Pantry' serves up chips, sarnies and other solid sustenance at lunchtimes only.
Open *11 to 11, Sun 12 to 10.30*

SCOTLAND

ABOYNE

Aberdeenshire   map 11

Boat

Charlestown Road, Aboyne AB34 5EL
TEL: (01339) 886137

Built beside the River Dee, this pub once
served the now-defunct local ferry (hence
its name), but these days it's better known
as a pleasant country inn with a decent line
in food and drink. Lunch takes in soup,
mince and tatties, seafood platters and the
like, while steaks and a few more
ambitious dishes flesh out the evening
menu. Bass and various Scottish ales are
on draught, and four wines are served by
the glass from a lengthy list. Children are
welcome in the eating areas. One self-
catering flat is available.

Open *11 to 2.30, 5 to 11 (Fri 5 to midnight); Sat 11
to midnight, Sun 11 to 11; closed 25 and 26 Dec, 1 and
2 Jan*

ARDFERN

Argyll & Bute   map 11

Galley of Lorne

Ardfern PA31 8QN
TEL: (01852) 500284

on B8002, reached from A816 N of Lochgilphead

Originally a drovers' inn, this eighteenth-
century hostelry is now a welcoming
country retreat with fine views over the
waters of Loch Craignish. A new licensee
took the helm in 2003, but little seems to
have changed. Locals rub shoulders with
tourists in the friendly Galley Bar, where
log fires burn and the menu runs along the
lines of grilled black pudding with red
onion marmalade, mussels in garlic and
white wine, and steak and ale pie. Scottish
real ales such as Deuchars IPA and
Caledonian 80/- are on draught and the
pub stocks a wide range of malt whiskies.
Accommodation and watercolour courses
are available. Reports please.

Open *noon to 1am all year*

BADACHRO

Highland   map 11

Badachro Inn

Badachro IV21 2AA
TEL: (01445) 741255

Locals, walkers and yachts-people rub
shoulders in this atmospheric little pub,
which boasts a plum location on the jetty:
from the outside you can look past the
boats to two small islands way up on the
Scottish west coast. Apart from splendid
views, the big attraction here is the
prospect of sampling real ales from
independent Scottish breweries including
Houston, Isle of Skye and Black Isle.
Customers can also take their pick from
the decent selection of wines and whiskies,
while seafood is the big thing on the
menu.

Open *12 to 12; closed 25 Dec*

BROUGHTY FERRY

Dundee   map 11

Fisherman's Tavern

10–14 Fort Street, Broughty Ferry DD5 2AD
TEL: (01382) 775941

off A930 (shore road)

Once a fisherman's cottage, this listed
seventeenth-century house is a premier-
league destination for real ale fans north of
the border: McEwan 80/- is regularly on
draught, while guests might include
Belhaven St Andrew's Ale and IPA,
Inveralmond Ossian's Ale and Fraoch
Heather Ale, plus others from English
breweries. If wine is your tipple, there are
plenty to choose from, including 25 by the
glass. Straightforward bar lunches give
seafood top billing. Accommodation
available. The museum in nearby
Broughty Castle is worth a look.

Open *11am to midnight (1am Thurs to Sat)*

CAWDOR

Moray   map 11

Cawdor Tavern

Cawdor, Nairn IV12 5XP
TEL: (01667) 404777

on B9090 next to Cawdor Castle

Originally a joiners' workshop for the
adjacent Castle, this efficiently run
traditional pub belies its modern exterior.
Food is served throughout and the choice

ranges from splendid smoked haddock and sweet pea fishcakes to collops of venison with haggis and burnt honey jus. Drinkers are well served with two real ales from the Cairngorm Brewery in Aviemore, plus whiskies galore and a varied list of 90 wines. Children welcome until 8pm. Reports please.

Open *Nov to June: Mon to Thur 11 to 3, 5 to 11 (Fri to 12), Sat 11 to 12, Sun 12.30 to 11. June to Oct: Mon to Thur 11 to 11 (Fr and Sat to 12), Sun 12.30 to 11*

EDINBURGH

Edinburgh   map 11

Abbotsford

3 Rose Street, Edinburgh EH2 2PR
TEL: (0131) 225 5276

A polished island bar counter and wood panelling are traditional features of this typical Victorian pub, which is now a popular venue for devotees of real ale: five cask beers (perhaps including Belhaven 80/-) are always on draught. One menu is served in the bar and the upstairs restaurant: each day there's a soup, a roast, a pie and a curry, supplemented by other dishes that could include avocado and prawns with lemon and dill mayonnaise, mixed grill, and chicken breast stuffed with haggis with whisky cream sauce.

Open *Mon to Sat 11 to 11*

Caley Sample Room

58 Angle Park Terrace, Edinburgh EH11 2JR
TEL: (0131) 337 7204

The name says it all: sampling here refers to the wares of the nearby Caledonian Brewery, including Caley IPA, and the pub has a reputation for serving these and various guest beers in peak condition. The interior is decked out pretty sparely, with a long bar, a few benches and some wooden barrels to stand around. Food is equally utilitarian but filling and cheap.

Open *11 to 12 (1 Fri and Sat)*

Diggers

1–3 Angle Park Terrace, Edinburgh EH11 2JX
TEL: (0131) 337 3822

Formerly the Athletic Arms, a title that reflected its proximity to the Hearts football ground, this Edinburgh institution is now named in honour of some long-standing regulars – the grave diggers from the cemetery opposite. With high ceilings, a darts area and a genuinely cosy little snug, it retains the good old-fashioned feel of a classic Victorian local. Beer is the focus, and the pub has a city-wide reputation for the quality of its McEwan 80/-, which is joined by Deuchars and two guests.

Open *12 (11 Sat) to 12, Sun 12.30 to 6*

ELIE

Fife   map 11

Ship Inn

The Toft, Elie KY9 1DT
TEL: (01333) 330246
on A917, 5m SW of Anstruther

With welcoming winter fires and barbecues when the weather allows, this simply decorated pub overlooking the old harbour is a popular haunt. The beach in front doubles as a cricket pitch, and enthusiastic spectators line the sea wall to shout their support while supping beers from Belhaven and Caledonian. Food, served inside and out, is an eclectic mix ranging from local haggis with neeps and tatties to 'zapped chilli fusilli', and there's a good little wine list.

Open *11am to midnight (1am Fri and Sat), Sun 12.30 to midnight; closed 25 Dec*

FINDHORN

Moray   map 11

Kimberley Inn

Findhorn, Moray IV36 0YG
TEL: (01309) 690492
on B9011, N of Forres

'Just what you want from a beside-the-sea pub' noted one visitor from south of the border. This traditional old inn facing Findhorn Bay boasts a hearty fire for cold days, friendly staff and two regularly changing Scottish real ales (perhaps Orkney Dark Island and Black Isle Yellowhammer). Seafood specials such as local langoustines or mussels with white wine and garlic sit alongside pub stalwarts like burgers, chilli, haddock and chips, and the Kimberley's version of chicken tikka. Sit outside if you want to soak up the views.

Open *11 to 11, Sat 11 to 1.30am, Sun 12.30 to midnight*

GATEHEAD

East Ayrshire   map 11

Cochrane Inn

45 Main Road, Gatehead KA2 0AP
TEL: (01563) 570122

on A759 just SW of Kilmarnock

This roadside pub on a T-junction on the
Kilmarnock to Troon road provides an
interesting mix of good traditional food
(cullen skink or beefsteak pie) to the more
exotic (spicy lamb with tomatoes, ginger,
mango and chilli). Inside, flagged floors,
dark beams and dark wooden tables with
wrought-iron legs create the right
impression. On draught are John Smith's
Bitter and Beamish Red. Children
welcome in restaurant.

Open *11 to 3, 5 to 11 (12 Sat and Sun)*

GLASGOW

Glasgow   map 11

Lismore

206 Dumbarton Road, Glasgow G11 6UN
TEL: (0141) 576 0103

Fans of Scottish draught beers flock from
the university to the nearby Lismore for a
taste of the real stuff in the shape of brews
from Caledonian in Edinburgh, Houston
in Renfrewshire and Kelburn in Glasgow
itself. The pub holds a good stock of
whiskies and has even branched out into
selling wine. The décor is traditional
stained glass and dark wood, the
atmosphere convivial and there's live
music two or three times a week – but you
won't find any food served here.

Open *11 to 11 (12 Fri and Sat), Sun 12.30 to 11*

GLENCOE

Highland   map 11

Clachaig Inn

Glencoe PH49 4HX
TEL: (01855) 811252

just off A82, Crianlarich to Fort William road

Billed as 'the outdoor inn', the Clachaig
stands spectacularly in the shadow of some
of Scotland's highest peaks, and it does its
job by providing welcome sustenance for
the walkers and climbers that populate
these parts. There are three bars, where
you can choose from a printed menu that
leaps from Scottish favourites like haggis
with white onion and Drambuie sauce or

venison casserole to Tex-Mex specialities.
Unusually for this isolated area, you can
also sample a decent selection of Scottish
cask-conditioned brews, including Fraoch
Heather Ale and Isle of Skye beers.
Children are welcome in lounge bar, and
accommodation is available.

Open *11 to 11, Fri 10.30 to 12, Sat 10.30 to
11.30, Sun 12.30 to 12*

ISLE OF WHITHORN

Dumfries & Galloway   map 11

Steam Packet

Harbour Row, Isle of Whithorn DG8 8HZ
TEL: (01988) 500334

off A750, 12m S of Wigtown

A social focus for this quiet area, the Steam
Packet enjoys a plum harbour-side
location that draws in the summer crowds.
Eat in the dining room for views or in the
bar for more intimacy. Look to the specials
menu for ambitious dishes like grilled fillet
of haddock with prawn and chervil sauce,
while the printed menu offers sturdy back-
up with plenty of local seafood. Theakston
XB is the regular ale, plus a guest, and six
wines come by the glass from a
worthwhile list. Accommodation available.

Open *winter Mon to Thur 11 to 2.30, 6 to 11, Fri
and Sat 11 to 11, Sun 12 to 11, summer 11 to 11,
Sun 12 to 11; 25 Dec drinks only 11 to 3, 7 to 11*

KIRKTON OF GLENISLA

Angus   map 11

Glenisla Hotel

Kirkton of Glenisla PH11 8PH
TEL: (01575) 582223

*from Alyth head N on B954, turn left on to B951
and follow signs*

A patriotic line up of Scottish real ales is
the big draw at this updated seventeenth-
century 'inn on the glen': you might
encounter Ossian's Ale or Lia Fail from
the Inveralmond Brewery, or Peter's Well
from the Houston Brewing Company, for
example. Alternatively consider the
collection of 50 malt whiskies and the 40-
strong wine list. In the oak-beamed bar
you can plump for dishes like venison
burgers or fishcakes with lime and
coriander or dip into the full restaurant
menu, which makes admirable use of
Scottish produce including Orkney

herrings, hill-reared lamb, Aberdeen Angus beef and wild salmon. Children have their own menu. Well placed for country pursuits.

Open *Mon to Thur 11 to 11, Fri 11 to 12, Sat 11 to 1am, Sun 12 to 11; closed Mon to Fri afternoons Jan to Easter*

LINLITHGOW

West Lothian   map 11

Four Marys

65 High Street, Linlithgow EH49 7ED
TEL: (01506) 842171

The complex history of this lofty townhouse starts around 1500, and its name refers to four ladies-in-waiting of Mary Queen of Scots, whose life and death are commemorated in its fascinating décor. These days it's a bastion of Scottish brewing with Caledonian Deuchars IPA, Belhaven 70/- and St Andrews regularly on draught, and guests supplied by other well-respected north-of-the-border breweries like Harviestoun, Broughton and Orkney. Food is traditional pub grub, Scottish style, bolstered by a few international specials (perhaps chicken in pepper sauce).

Open *Mon to Wed 12 to 11, Thur to Sat 12 to 11.45, Sun 12.30 to 11*

RATHO

Edinburgh   map 11

Bridge Inn

27 Baird Road, Ratho EH28 8RA
TEL: (0131) 333 1320

off M8 and A8, 8m W of Edinburgh; follow signs for Edinburgh Canal Centre from Newbridge roundabout; pub is alongside canal

Part of the Edinburgh Canal Centre about 20 minutes' out of the city, the Bridge Inn boasts a warren of small rooms and eating areas. Snacks and bar meals are served all day in the Pop Inn Lounge, where the menu kicks off with nachos, filled wholemeal buns and jacket potatoes with all manner of toppings from coronation chicken to haggis. A more ambitious restaurant carte majors in steaks and dishes like Cajun salmon suprême. Belhaven 80/- is always on draught, with back up from guests including Deuchars IPA and

Orkney ales; three wines are served by the glass.

Open *Mon to Thur 12 to 11, Fri 12 to 12, Sat 11 to 12, Sun 12.30 to 11*

ROYBRIDGE

Highland   map 11

Stronlossit Inn

Roybridge PH31 4AG
TEL: (01397) 712253

on A86, 12m NE of Fort William

A neat low building with Highland views, this inn scores highly all round with one visitor. Real ales – a rarity in these parts – focus on independent Scottish breweries, with maybe Orkney Red MacGregor, Atlas Wayfarer and Cairngorm Stag making up the weekly selection. Local ingredients such as venison and Loch Lochy trout feature on the menu, and helpings are generous. Friendly service. Accommodation available in ten rooms.

Open *Mon to Wed 11 to 12, Thur to Sat 11 to 1am, Sun 12.30 to 11.45*

ST MARY'S LOCH

Borders   map 11

Tibbie Shiel's Inn

St Mary's Loch TD7 5LH
TEL: (01750) 42231

100yds off A708, 13m W of Selkirk

In 1823, the eponymous Isabella (Tibbie) Shiel moved into this idyllic stone cottage by the shores of St Mary's Loch. She turned the place into a hostelry, numbering well-known poets of the day among her guests, although today's clientele is more likely to comprise walkers, fishermen and windsurfers looking for sustenance. Greenmantle and Belhaven real ales fly the flag for Scotland, Stowford Press cider is on tap and the pub stocks over 50 single malts; three-dozen wines are also on offer. Hearty main dishes, snacks and traditional high teas reinforce the Scottish theme. Accommodation available. Walkers should note that the pub is on the Southern Upland Way.

Open *summer Mon to Thur 11 to 11, Fri and Sat 11am to midnight, Sun 12.30 to 11; winter Thur 11 to 11, Fri and Sat 11am to midnight, Sun 12.30 to 6*

STROMNESS

Orkney map 11

Ferry Inn

John Street, Stromness, Orkney
KW16 3AA
TEL: (01856) 850280

take the ferry from Aberdeen or Scrabster

Stromness is an attractive town of narrow winding streets with views over to Scapa Flow, a naval base in both world wars. As its name suggests, this tall, steep-roofed pub overlooks the bustling harbour where the ferries dock. In the bar, fitted out in mahogany to resemble the interior of a schooner, you can enjoy Orkney Brewery Dark Island and Red MacGregor real ales or dip into the short list of some 20 wines. One menu is served throughout and the repertoire is a daily choice of mostly traditional dishes, with local seafood showing up strongly. Children are welcome, and 20 bedrooms are available for B&B.

Open *Mon to Wed 9am to midnight, Thur to Sat 9am to 1am, Sun 9.30am to midnight*

WALES

ABERGORLECH

Carmarthenshire   map 4

Black Lion Inn
Abergorlech SA32 7SN
TEL: (01558) 685271

The River Cothi flows past the garden of
this unaffected village pub on the edge of
the Forest of Brechfa. A pleasing garden
close to the water is one of its attractions,
and inside it has successfully maintained
its sixteenth-century period charm –
a large oak table and a pair of high-backed
settles set the tone in the characterful bar.
Brains SA and Youngs Bitter are on
handpump, and guest brews are laid on
every few months. Eat traditional food in
the bar or restaurant.

Open *Tue to Fri 12 to 3.30, 7 to 11.30, Sat 12 to
11.30, Sun 12 to10; closed Mon exc bank hols*

BODFARI

Denbighshire   map 7

Dinorben Arms
Bodfari LL16 4DA
TEL: (01745) 710309

Spectacular terraced gardens are a glorious
feature of this heavily timbered inn up a
steep hill in the heart of the Vale of Clwyd.
The place has three bars and four dining
rooms: drinkers tend to make a beeline for
the Well and Armoury Bars, where they
can consider the extraordinary collection
of around 200 whiskies, not to mention
abundant treasures from the private wine
cellar and a choice of real ales including
Banks Mansfield Cask Ale, Marston's
Pedigree and a guest such as Caledonian
Deuchars IPA. Lunchtime food centres on
a daily self-service smorgasbord, while
evening meals are built around buffets and
a carvery. Children are welcome
throughout; dogs in the gardens only.

Open *Mon to Fri 12 to 3.30, 6 to 11, Sat 12 to 11,
Sun 12 to 10.30*

BWLCH-Y-CIBAU

Powys   map 7

Stumble Inn
Bwlch-y-Cibau SY22 5LL
TEL: (01691) 648860
on A490, 3m SE of Llanfyllin

If you stumble upon this refurbished pub,
you might see customers eating exotic
Eastern dishes like Peking duck with
noodles, Szechuan-style prawns, and
curries of varying strengths; the menu also
moves nearer to home with whole Dover
sole, and salmon in prawn and saffron
sauce. Expect real ales from Marston's,
Greene King, Hook Norton or Adnams on
handpump; otherwise there's a short wine
list with four available by the glass.
Children are welcome if eating. The pub is
in a small village in the Welsh Marches,
near the River Vyrnwy.

Open *winter Wed to Sat 6 to 11, Sun 12 to 2,
summer Wed to Fri 6 to 11, Sat 12 to 2, 6 to 11,
Sun 12 to 2, 6 to 10.30*

DRAETHEN

Caerphilly   map 4

Hollybush Inn
Draethen, Lower Machen NP10 8GB
TEL: (01633) 441326
*about 1m off A468 Newport to Caerphilly road;
pub signposted*

Abundant hanging baskets announce this
smartened-up country pub in a tiny,
upmarket hamlet. A well-tended terraced
garden gives fine views of hills and
woodland. The bar, with exposed-stone
walls, wooden beams and fires, makes a
quiet alternative to the busy restaurant
upstairs and draws its own share of diners
as well as drinkers. The bar menu sticks to
steaks, chicken curry and other pub fare
and does away with starters altogether.
Brains Bitter, Marston's Pedigree and
Fuller's London Pride are the regulars on
tap.

Open *Mon to Thur 11.30 to 3, 5 to 11, Fri and Sat
11 to 11, Sun 12 to 10.30*

EAST ABERTHAW

Vale of Glamorgan   map 4

Blue Anchor Inn
East Aberthaw CF62 3DD
TEL: (01446) 750329

off B4265, between St Athan and Barry

Jeremy Coleman has been at the helm of
this medieval thatched inn (and one-time
smugglers' haunt) for more than 25 years
and has turned it into a thriving pub that
draws trade from miles around. A fire
damaged the building early in 2004, but it
was due to re-open just before our
deadline: it is hoped that not much will
have changed in the warren of charming
rooms bristling with nooks and alcoves.
The good news is the pub will continue to
dispense real ales such as Buckleys Best,
Wadworth 6X and one regularly changing
guest beer, along with a selection of wines
(including three by the glass). As regards
food, expect wholesome pub dishes along
the lines of lamb and leek casserole and
Cumberland sausages.
Open *11 to 11, Sun 12 to 10.30*

LLANDDAROG

Carmarthenshire   map 4

Butchers Arms
Llanddarog SA32 8NS
TEL: (01267) 275330

off A48, 5m E of Carmarthen

Fans of all things horticultural should note
that this Victorian pub is not far from the
National Botanic Garden of Wales, while
travellers looking for liquid refreshment
will find Felinfoel Best Bitter and Double
Dragon Ale on handpump and a choice of
four wines by the glass. Fish is a big player
in the food department, with sea bass,
lemon sole and salmon often putting in an
appearance alongside dishes like halibut
fillet with prawn and lobster sauce;
carnivorous alternatives could include, say,
crispy stuffed duck with orange and Grand
Marnier sauce. Children are welcome in
the no-smoking restaurant, although the
same menus are available throughout.
Note that the pub is closed on Sundays.
Open *Mon to Fri 12 to 3, 6 to 11, Sat 11.30 to 3, 5
to 11; closed 25 and 26 Dec*

White Hart Inn
Llanddarog SA32 8NT
TEL: (01267) 275395

Home-brewed beers are the big attraction
here: Cwrwblafuf Ale is regularly on
handpump, with seasonal input from
Roasted Barley Stout and summertime
tipples produced from, say, nettles or
beetroot. If wine is your fancy, the
25-strong list includes five by the glass.
Lots of local produce shows up on the long
menus, including Welsh black beef and
fish, although it's equally possible just to
have a snack. The 600-year-old White Hart
is an attractive stone building with a
thatched roof, flower-filled hanging baskets
and tubs outside; you can sit at picnic tables
and admire the views over the countryside.
Open *11.30 to 3, 6.30 to 11, Sun 12 to 3, 7 to
10.30; closed 25 and 26 Dec*

LLANDINAM

Powys   map 4

Lion Hotel
Llandinam SY17 5BY
TEL: (01686) 688233

*on A470 in village centre, 8m SW of Newtown,
6m N of Llanidloes*

A lush setting in the beautiful Upper
Severn Valley brings travellers to this
welcoming riverside inn. The kitchen
makes hearty use of local produce
including Welsh beef, lamb, wild trout
and salmon, and there's plenty of choice
for vegetarians. Old Speckled Hen is
regularly on draught, alongside a guest
such as Wychwood Hobgoblin, and the
short wine list (from Tanners) has five by
the glass. In summer you can eat in the
garden, separated only by a meadow from
the water's edge. Children are 'very
welcome' and accommodation is available.
Open *12 to 3, 6.30 to 11, Sun 12 to 3, 7 to 10.30;
closed eve 25 Dec, Mon winter*

LLANGYBI

Monmouthshire   map 4

White Hart
Llangybi NP15 1NP
TEL: (01633) 450258

History and location are just two reasons
for knowing about this slate-roofed
twelfth-century village pub in the lovely

Vale of Usk. Traditional features including heavy beams, flagstones and open fires add character to the bar, where Bass is regularly on draught and there's usually a choice of three guests – perhaps Butty Bach or Tomos Watkin Old Style Bitter; three wines are also available by the glass. One menu applies to both the bar areas and the no-smoking restaurant, and the choice ranges from local game to fish and vegetarian dishes. A new licensee took over early in 2004.

Open *Mon to Fri 11.30 to 3, 6.30 to 11, Sat 11 to 11, Sun 12 to 4, 7 to 10.30*

LLANHENNOCK

Monmouthshire   map 2

Wheatsheaf

Llanhennock NP18 1LT
TEL: (01633) 420468

off B4236, 2m N of Caerleon

Set at the top of the hill running through the tiny hamlet of Llanhennock, this quaint L-shaped stone pub was once a farmhouse and still has a genuinely rustic feel. Food is only served at lunchtime, but it's wholesome down-to-earth stuff along the lines of fish chowder, a pie, faggots and peas or boiled ham with parsley sauce, bolstered by seafood specials. Bass and Worthington are regularly on draught, with guests from the Cwmbran Brewery. When the weather's kind, families can take advantage of the tables and chairs in the front garden, which also sports a Wendy house and slide.

Open *winter Mon and Wed 11 to 3, 5.30 to 11, Tue, Thur, Fri and Sat 11 to 11, Sun 12 to 3, 7 to 10.30, summer 11 to 11, Sun 12 to 3, 7 to 10.30*

LLANTHONY

Monmouthshire   map 4

Llanthony Priory

Llanthony NP7 7NN
TEL: (01873) 890487

off A465, 9m N of Abergavenny

The vaulted crypt of a twelfth-century Augustinian abbey provides a highly unusual setting for this remote pub. Approach through a wall straight into the open cloisters, and there you find the atmospheric old prior's house, which now functions as a hotel. Bass, Flowers Original

and Felinfoel ales are on draught in the tiny cellar bar and there's a blackboard menu of simple dishes based around local and seasonal produce including lamb and game. The ruins of the Priory, surrounded by beautiful trees and soaring mountains, are worth exploring in their own right.

Open *summer Mon 10 to 3, Tue to Fri 11 to 3, 6 to 11, Sat 11 to 11, Sun 12 to 10.30 (open 11 to 11 every day in July and Aug); winter Fri 6 to 11, Sat 11 to 11, Sun 12 to 4*

MOLD

Flintshire   map 7

Glasfryn

Raikes Lane, Sychdyn, Mold CH7 6LR
TEL: (01352) 750500

Views over rolling countryside at the back of this red-brick pub may remind you that it was once a farmhouse – even though it now stands opposite the civic centre and theatre. A cheerful buzz fills the honeycomb of distinctively decorated rooms, which are centred on a big, oak-panelled bar. Real ales are taken seriously here, with Flowers, Timothy Taylor Landlord and Plassey joined by three guests, and the wine list is an upbeat selection boasting 18 by the glass. The daily menu promises modern pub grub with a few twists – perhaps salmon and basil fishcakes on rocket leaves with red pepper and chilli relish followed by tiramisù with cappuccino ice cream.

Open *11.30 to 11, Sun 12 to 10.30*

MONKNASH

Vale of Glamorgan   map 4

Plough and Harrow

Monknash CF71 7QQ
TEL: (01656) 890209

off B4265 from Llantwit Major

The location far from major public transport and close to the Glamorgan coast path makes this idiosyncratic old pub a focus for walkers and cyclists. But fireside-loving beer fans, too, make the journey for the superb line-up of ales both on handpump and straight from the cask. Merlins Stout, Hereford Pale Ale, Smiles Heritage and Felinfoel Festive Ale were just a few of the offerings when an inspector visited. Fill up on wholesome

pub fare from the blackboard menu.
A new licensee seems intent on keeping
things as they are – reports please.
Open *12 to 11 (10.30 Sun)*

MONTGOMERY

Powys   map 4

Dragon Hotel

Montgomery SY15 6PA
TEL: (01686) 668359

There are still echoes of the past in this
black-and-white seventeenth-century
coaching inn on Montgomery's market
square: the ancient fireplace was once a
bread oven and a pane of glass is said to
have been signed by the local hangman.
Nowadays, everything is above board in
the bar, where beers might include
offerings from Wood's of Wistanstow,
house wines are served by the glass, and
the menu proffers baguettes, ploughman's,
paella and pork stroganoff. Dishes in the
restaurant are based on local produce
(noisettes of local lamb with garlic and
thyme jus, for example). Accommodation
available. Offa's Path is nearby.
Open *11 to 11, Sun 12 to 10.30*

NEVERN

Pembrokeshire   map 4

Trewern Arms

Nevern SA42 0NB
TEL: (01239) 820395

The setting – by the banks of the River
Nevern – is a bonus when visiting this
picturesque, creeper-clad seventeenth-
century inn. Sit outside, or take the weight
off your feet in the atmospheric bar, where
Wadworth 6X and Flowers Orginal are
among the rotating real ales on handpump,
and three wines are served by the glass. In
addition to bar snacks there's also a full
restaurant menu (Thursday to Saturday,
dinner only) offering such main courses as
beef stroganoff and salmon in dill sauce.
Ten en suite guest rooms are available.
Nevern's medieval church and ancient
bridge are worth a look.
Open *11 to 3, 6 to 11, Sun 12 to 3, 7 to 10.30; no
food 25 Dec*

OLD RADNOR

Powys   map 4

Harp Inn

Old Radnor LD8 2RH
TEL: (01544) 350655

off A44, between New Radnor and Kington

Set high on a hillside in the Welsh
Marches, not far from Offa's Dyke Path,
the sixteenth-century Harp is a welcoming
and peaceful retreat for holidaymakers,
walkers and locals alike. Handpumps
dispense a couple of regularly changing
real ales, including Six Bells from Bishop's
Castle, Timothy Taylor Landlord and
Shepherd Neame; three wines are served
by the glass. In the two dining rooms (one
no-smoking), you can choose from
blackboard menus that might feature
steaks, cod in beer batter, home-made
faggots, and pork and leek sausages.
Children have their own menu and the
pub has five letting rooms (one with a
four-poster).
Open *Closed Mons exc bank hols; Tue to Fri 7
(6 summer) to 11, Sat and Sun 12 to 3, 7 (6 summer)
to 11*

OVERTON BRIDGE

Wrexham   map 7

Cross Foxes

Overton Bridge LL13 0DR
TEL: (01978) 780380

*about 5m S of Wrexham, near junction of A528
and A539*

A grassed terrace outside this riverside
coaching inn makes the best of views over
the Dee and along a glorious wooded
stretch of the water. Hanging baskets
brighten the cream exterior, while inside
you'll find an inglenook and walls strewn
with framed prints, posters and maps, or,
in one of the four rooms, fishing
memorabilia. A large blackboard menu
(plus sandwiches and snacks) might offer
cauliflower soup, followed by 'very tender'
corn-fed chicken breast stuffed with
mushrooms and chestnuts. Banks's
Original and Camerons Strongarm are on
the changing roster of beers, and 32 wines
come by the glass.
Open *12 to 11, Sun 12 to 10.30*

PEMBROKE FERRY

Pembrokeshire   map 4

Ferry Inn

Pembroke Ferry SA72 6UD
TEL: (01646) 682947

off A477 N of Pembroke; turn left at roundabout at S end of Cleddau Bridge

These days an unromantic bridge whizzes motorists over the Cleddau, but once there was only a ferry and this pub is where you would wait for it. The waterside terrace gives a front-row view of the river and its traffic, and nautical artefacts decorate the interior. Worthington, Bass and Red Dragon are joined by guest beers, and the short, unpretentious menu, featuring fish and hearty meat dishes is complemented by blackboard specials. New licensees took charge at the end of 2003 – reports please.
Open *12 to 3, 6.30 to 11; closed 25 and 26 Dec*

REYNOLDSTON

Swansea   map 4

King Arthur

Higher Green, Reynoldston SA3 1AD
TEL: (01792) 390775

Legend has it that when the moon is full, the ghost of King Arthur emerges from the Cromlech and traverses the scenic landscape around this black-and-white pub at the base of Cefn Bryn. There are views of the countryside from the front and rear of the pub, and the interior is totally traditional with sporting memorabilia much in evidence. Bass, Worthington and Felinfoel Double Dragon are on draught. Children are welcome and accommodation includes a self-catering cottage.
Open *11 to 11*

RHYD-DDU

Gwynedd   map 7

Cwellyn Arms

Rhyd-Ddu LL54 6TL
TEL: (01766) 890321

on A4085, between Caernarfon and Beddgelert

The Welsh Highland Railway now operates to Rhyd-ddu and this stone-built pub at the foot of Mount Snowdon is fully geared up to receive its seasonal influx of tourists. Up to nine beers are dispensed in the bar, among them weekly guests such as Spinning Dog Chase Your Tail, Wye Valley Hereford Cathedral Bitter and Cottage Somerset & Dorset Ale. The wine list includes around 20 bins, while snacks, salads and steaks typify the food on offer. Summertime barbecues are held in the beer garden and the pub has a children's playground. All-purpose accommodation comprises three en suite bedrooms, a self-catering cottage, a campsite and two bunkhouses.
Open *11 to 11, Sun 12 to 10.30*

ROSEBUSH

Pembrokeshire   map 4

Tafarn Sinc

Rosebush SA66 7QT
TEL: (01437) 532214

village on B4313 just S of crossroads with B4329

A drive through ruggedly unspoilt countryside brings you to this red-painted, corrugated-zinc pub proudly flying the Welsh flag. It's beside a disused railway track, and a mock-up platform comes complete with life-sized model people and steam-engine sound effects. The interior is an exercise in nostalgia, with sawdust on the bare wooden floor, cosy fires, and walls loaded with assorted memorabilia. Outside is a well-maintained beer garden. There are no starters, just wholesome main courses like home-cooked faggots or Glamorgan sausage, with bread-and-butter pudding to finish. Worthington and a weekly guest are on handpump.
Open *12 to 11; closed Mon winter, 25 Dec*

RUDRY

Caerphilly   map 4

Maenllwyd Inn

Rudry CF83 3EB
TEL: (029) 2088 2372

from A468 Newport to Caerphilly road, follow signs to Draethen, then Rudry

Maenllwyd translates as 'grey stone', which was the building material used for this substantial 400-year-old farmhouse with impressive views of hills and woodland from two large terraces. Small, intimate rooms bristle with rural pedigree – bare stone, brick and beams, old plates and rustic furnishings, open fire ablaze. A long

menu sprawls across numerous blackboards, pulling in the crowds for hearty portions, with main courses running from steak and kidney pudding to grilled barramundi on sautéed red cabbage with apple. Drinkers can sup up Courage Best and Old Speckled Hen or choose from 20 decent wines by the glass.
Open *12 to 11, Sun 12 to 10.30*

RUTHIN

Denbighshire   map 7

Ye Olde Anchor Inn

2 Rhos Street, Ruthin LL15 1DY
TEL: (01824) 702813

at junction of A525 and A494

New licensees have settled in at this large, white, slate-roofed hotel in the centre of Ruthin (a medieval town on the Clwyd). Inside, the bar has olde-worlde trimmings aplenty, with prints and plates on the wall, low oak beams and inglenooks, plus a menu that shows some seasonal touches (braised rump of lamb in aged port and redcurrant sauce, and seared loin of pork with Calvados and apples, for example). Worthington 1744 and Greene King IPA are on draught, and wines are supplied by Tanners of Shrewsbury. Reports please.
Open *12 to 3, 5.30 to 11*

SOLVA

Pembrokeshire   map 4

Harbour Inn

31–33 Main Street, Solva SA62 6UT
TEL: (01437) 720013

The favoured pub of Solva locals and a tourist mecca in summer, the Harbour is a rambling old building with a cosy and cheerful atmosphere. A weekly line-up of five ales might mix mainstream names like Bass and Worthington with the likes of Felinfoel Double Dragon and Tomos Watkin Cwrw Haf. Solva is an important fishing village, and the landlord has his own boat so fresh supplies of mackerel, sea bass and crab in season bolster the traditional menu.
Open *11 to 11, Sun 12 to 10.30*

TALYBONT

Powys   map 4

Star Inn

Talybont LD3 7YX
TEL: (01874) 676635

½m off A40, 6m SE of Brecon

The Brecon Beacons provides an impressive backdrop to this eighteenth-century stone pub, which is also handily placed for a trip to Llangorse Lake, Talybont Reservoir, the Usk and the Monmouthshire and Brecon Canal. Outdoor types with a taste for real ale are drawn to the Star by its impressive line-up of six handpumps dispensing beers from Cardiff breweries Brains and Bullmastiff, plus perhaps Theakston Old Peculier, Felinfoel Double Dragon or Everards Original. The kitchen delivers familiar renditions of pub favourites using mostly local produce, including beef and lamb. Live music on Wednesday evening and two en suite guest rooms.
Open *Mon to Fri 11 to 3, 6.30 to 11, Sat 11 to 11, Sun 12 to 3, 6.30 to 10.30; 'all day, every day' in summer*

Beer and wine awards

Pubs serving exceptional draught beers

Most pubs in the Guide serve acceptable real ales. This list includes establishments which are making a special effort to provide excellent choice in terms of styles and strengths and demonstrate knowledgeable cellar work; and those which support independent local and regional breweries.

LONDON
Crown, E3
Duke of Cambridge, N1
White Horse, SW6

ENGLAND
Bath & N.E. Somerset
Hop Pole, Bath
Salamander, Bath

Berkshire
Bell Inn, Aldworth
Dundas Arms, Kintbury

Buckinghamshire
Crooked Billet, Newton Longville
Red Lion, Chenies
Stag & Huntsman Inn, Hambleden

Cambridgeshire
Cock, Hemingford Grey

Cheshire
Albion, Chester
Bhurtpore Inn, Aston
Dysart Arms, Bunbury
Grosvenor Arms, Aldford
Netherton Hall, Frodsham
Old Harkers Arms, Chester

Cornwall
Royal Oak, Lostwithiel
Trengilly Wartha Inn, Constantine

Cumbria
Britannia Inn, Elterwater
Drunken Duck Inn, Ambleside
King's Head, Thirlspot
Queens Head, Tirril
Queens Head Hotel, Troutbeck

Devon
Anchor Inn, Cockwood
Culm Valley Inn, Culmstock
Drewe Arms, Broadhembury
Duke of York, Iddesleigh
Maltsters' Arms, Tuckenhay
Manor Inn, Lower Ashton

Masons Arms, Branscombe
Nobody Inn, Doddiscombsleigh
Peter Tavy Inn, Peter Tavy
Tower Inn, Slapton

Dorset
Museum Inn, Farnham

East Riding of Yorkshire
St Vincent Arms, Sutton upon Derwent

East Sussex
Jolly Sportsman, East Chiltington
Queens Head, Icklesham

Essex
Bell Inn, Horndon on the Hill
Prince of Wales, Stow Maries

Gloucestershire
Bell at Sapperton, Sapperton
Kings Arms Inn, Didmarton

Greater Manchester
Church Inn, Uppermill

Hampshire
Flower Pots Inn, Cheriton
Hawkley Inn, Hawkley
Peat Spade, Longstock
Sun, Bentworth
Wykeham Arms, Winchester

Herefordshire
Lough Pool Inn, Sellack
Riverside Inn, Aymestrey
Stagg Inn, Titley

Kent
Gate Inn, Marshside
Hare, Langton Green
Rose & Crown, Perry Wood
Sankeys, Tunbridge Wells
Swan on the Green, West Peckham
Three Chimneys, Biddenden

Lancashire
Bay Horse Inn, Forton
Eagle & Child, Bispham Green

Leicestershire
Bell Inn, East Langton

Lincolnshire
Chequers, Woolsthorpe

Merseyside
Baltic Fleet, Liverpool
Philharmonic, Liverpool

Norfolk
Darby's, Swanton Morley
Fishermans Return, Winterton-on-Sea
Lifeboat Inn, Thornham
Lord Nelson, Burnham Thorpe
Recruiting Sergeant, Horstead
Three Horseshoes, Warham All Saints
Walpole Arms, Itteringham
Wig and Pen, Norwich

North Yorkshire
Buck Inn, Thornton Watlass
Malt Shovel, Brearton
Stone Trough Inn, Kirkham Priory
White Swan Hotel, Middleham

Northumberland
Dipton Mill, Hexham
Feathers Inn, Hedley on the Hill
General Havelock Inn, Haydon Bridge

Nottinghamshire
Martins Arms, Colston Bassett
Victoria Hotel, Nottingham

Oxfordshire
Tite Inn, Chadlington
Falkland Arms, Great Tew
Royal Oak, Ramsden

Rutland
Exeter Arms, Barrowden

Shropshire
Burlton Inn, Burlton
Crown, Munslow
Hundred House Hotel, Norton
Three Tuns, Bishop's Castle
Waterdine, Llanfair Waterdine

Somerset
Horse & Groom, East Woodlands
Royal Oak Inn of Luxborough,
  Luxborough

South Gloucestershire
Anchor Inn, Oldbury-on-Severn

Suffolk
Angel, Lavenham

Buxhall Crown, Buxhall
Crown, Westleton
Moon & Mushroom Inn, Swilland
St Peter's Hall and Brewery,
  St Peter South Elmham

Surrey
Plough Inn, Coldharbour

Warwickshire
Howard Arms, Ilmington

West Sussex
The Fox Goes Free, Charlton
Halfway Bridge Inn, Halfway Bridge
King's Arms, Fernhurst
Lickfold Inn, Lickfold
Three Horseshoes, Elsted

West Yorkshire
Bar t'at, Ilkley
Boat, Allerton Bywater
Old Bridge Inn, Ripponden

Wiltshire
Dove Inn, Corton
Horseshoe Inn, Ebbesbourne Wake
Pear Tree Inn, Whitley

Worcestershire
Talbot, Knightwick
Walter de Cantelupe Inn, Kempsey

SCOTLAND
Borders
Burt's Hotel, Melrose
Traquair Arms, Innerleithen

Edinburgh
Baillie, Edinburgh

Stirling
Lade Inn, Kilmahog

WALES
Gwynedd
Harp Inn, Llandwrog

Isle Of Anglesey
Ship Inn, Red Wharf Bay

Monmouthshire
Clytha Arms, Clytha

Pembrokeshire
Nag's Head Inn, Abercych

Wrexham
Pant-yr-Ochain, Gresford

Pubs serving better-than-average wine 🍇

This award goes to pubs where wines have been chosen with imagination and in keeping with the dishes on offer; where there is good global choice (from easy-drinking house wines to classics) at fair prices; where the lists themselves give useful information to aid choice; and where there is at least a good handful available by the glass.

LONDON
Anglesea Arms, W6
Atlas, SW6
Salusbury Pub and Dining Room, NW6
Victoria, SW14

ENGLAND
Bedfordshire
Knife & Cleaver, Houghton Conquest

Berkshire
Bird in Hand, Knowl Hill
Dundas Arms, Kintbury

Buckinghamshire
Chequers Inn, Wooburn Common
Crooked Billet, Newton Longville

Cambridgeshire
Anchor Inn, Sutton Gault
Old Bridge Hotel, Huntingdon
Pheasant Inn, Keyston
Three Horseshoes, Madingley

Cheshire
Bhurtpore Inn, Aston

Co Durham
Morritt Arms, Greta Bridge
Rose and Crown, Romaldkirk

Cornwall
Pandora Inn, Mylor Bridge
Rising Sun, St Mawes
Trengilly Wartha Inn, Constantine

Cumbria
Bay Horse Hotel, Ulverston
Drunken Duck Inn, Ambleside

Devon
Anchor Inn, Cockwood
Arundell Arms, Lifton
Culm Valley Inn, Culmstock
Dartmoor Inn, Lydford
Kings Arms Inn, Stockland
New Inn, Coleford

Nobody Inn, Doddiscombsleigh
Rock Inn, Haytor Vale

Dorset
Fox Inn, Corscombe
Museum Inn, Farnham

East Riding of Yorkshire
Wellington Inn, Lund

East Sussex
Griffin Inn, Fletching
Jolly Sportsman, East Chiltington
Star Inn, Old Heathfield

Essex
Bell Inn, Horndon on the Hill
Sun Inn, Dedham
White Hart, Great Yeldham

Gloucestershire
Bell at Sapperton, Sapperton
Falcon Inn, Poulton
White Horse, Frampton Mansell
Yew Tree, Clifford's Mesne

Greater Manchester
White Hart, Lydgate

Hampshire
Wykeham Arms, Winchester

Herefordshire
Lough Pool Inn, Sellack
Roebuck Inn, Brimfield
Stagg Inn, Titley
Three Crowns Inn, Ullingswick

Kent
Three Chimneys, Biddenden

Lancashire
Inn at Whitewell, Whitewell

Leicestershire
Red Lion, Stathern

Lincolnshire
Farmers Arms, Welton Hill
Wig & Mitre, Lincoln

Merseyside
Red Cat, Crank

Norfolk
Hoste Arms, Burnham Market
Lifeboat Inn, Thornham
Walpole Arms, Itteringham
White Horse, Brancaster Staithe
White Horse Hotel, Blakeney
Wildebeest Arms, Stoke Holy Cross

North Yorkshire
Abbey Inn, Byland Abbey
Angel Inn, Hetton
Appletree, Marton
Black Bull Inn, Moulton
Blue Lion, East Witton
Nag's Head, Pickhill
Red Lion, Burnsall
Star Inn, Harome
Stone Trough Inn, Kirkham Priory
White Swan, Pickering

Northamptonshire
Falcon Inn, Fotheringhay

Northumberland
Cook and Barker Inn,
    Newton-on-the-Moor

Nottinghamshire
Caunton Beck, Caunton

Oxfordshire
Boar's Head, Ardington
Lamb at Buckland, Buckland
Sir Charles Napier, Chinnor
Trout at Tadpole Bridge,
    Tadpole Bridge

Rutland
Olive Branch, Clipsham

Shropshire
Hundred House Hotel, Norton
Waterdine, Llanfair Waterdine

Somerset
Blue Ball Inn, Triscombe

Suffolk
Angel, Lavenham
Bell Inn, Walberswick

Cornwallis, Brome
Crown Hotel, Southwold
Star Inn, Lidgate

Warwickshire
Howard Arms, Ilmington
Inn at Farnborough, Farnborough

West Sussex
White Horse Inn, Chilgrove

West Yorkshire
Millbank, Millbank
Old Bridge Inn, Ripponden
Ring O' Bells, Thornton

Wiltshire
Angel Inn, Upton Scudamore
George & Dragon, Rowde
Pear Tree Inn, Whitley
Seven Stars, Bottlesford

SCOTLAND
Argyll & Bute
Creggans Inn, Strachur

Borders
Burt's Hotel, Melrose

Glasgow
Ubiquitous Chip, Glasgow

Perthshire & Kinross
Killiecrankie Hotel, Killiecrankie

WALES
Gwynedd
Penhelig Arms Hotel, Aberdovey

Monmouthshire
Bell at Skenfrith, Skenfrith
Clytha Arms, Clytha

Powys
Nantyffin Cider Mill Inn, Crickhowell

Wrexham
West Arms, Llanarmon Dyffryn Ceiriog

Index

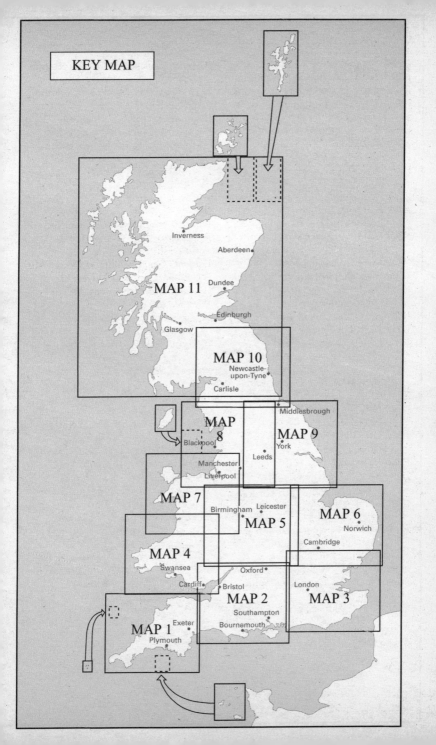

KEY MAP

MAP 1

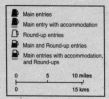

Main entries
Main entry with accommodation
Round-up entries
Main and Round-up entries
Main entries with accommodation, and Round-ups

0   5   10 miles
0   15 kms

Isles of Scilly
28 miles WSW of Land's End

St Martin's
Bryher
Tresco
St Mary's
St Agnes

B u
B

Port Isaac
Bay
Treba

St Breward

Padstow

Blisland

Bodmin

Watergate Bay
St. Mawgan

Newquay

C O R N W

Ligger Bay

Lostwithie

Mitchell

St Austell

Poli

St A
B

Truro
Malpas
St Ewe

St Ives
Bay
St Ives
Redruth

Penelewey
Philleigh

Treen

Mylor
Bridge

Veryan
Bay

St Just
Ludgvan
St Mawes

Penzance
Constantine
Falmouth

Helston
Falmouth
Bay

Porthleven
Helford

Land's
End

Mount's
Bay
Gunwalloe

Lizard Point

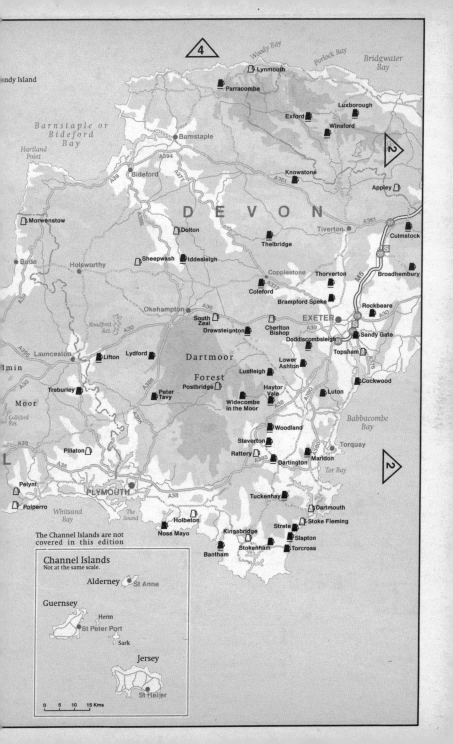

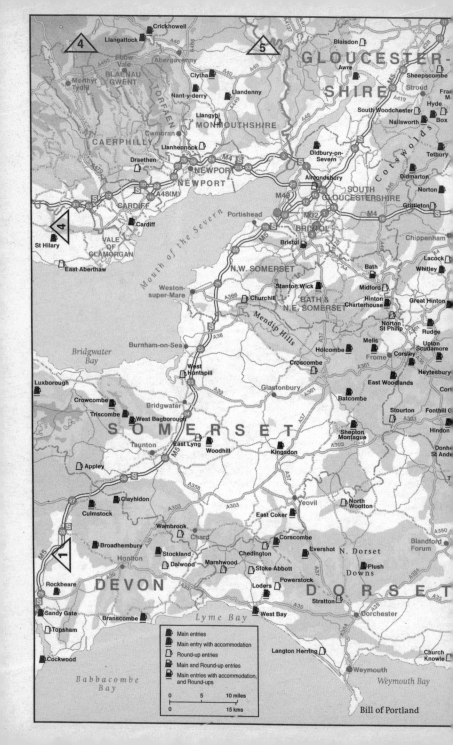

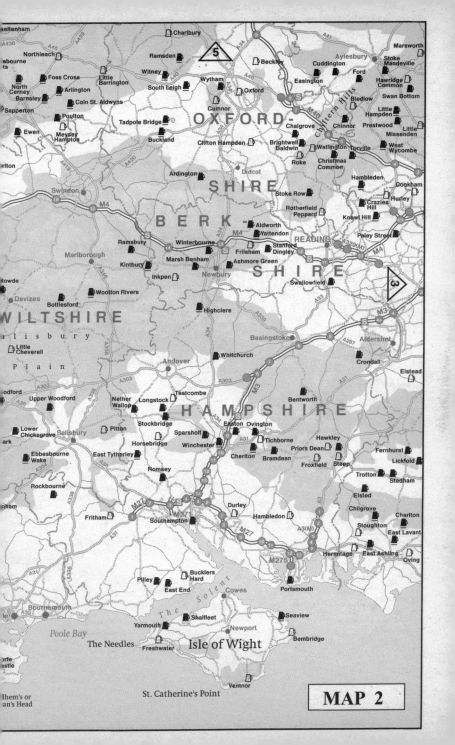

MAP 2

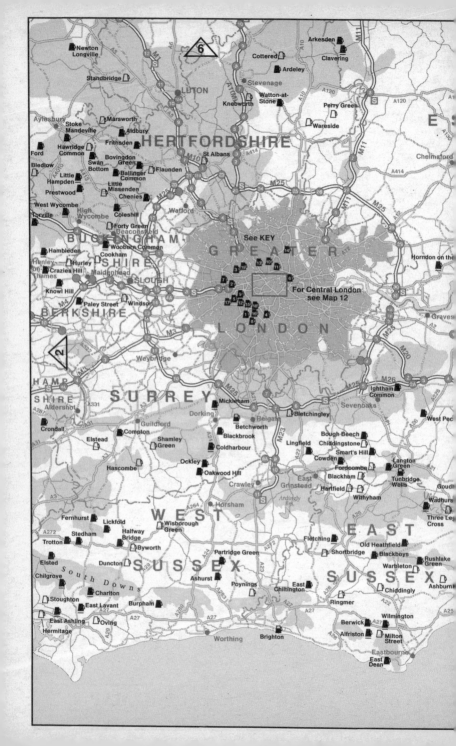

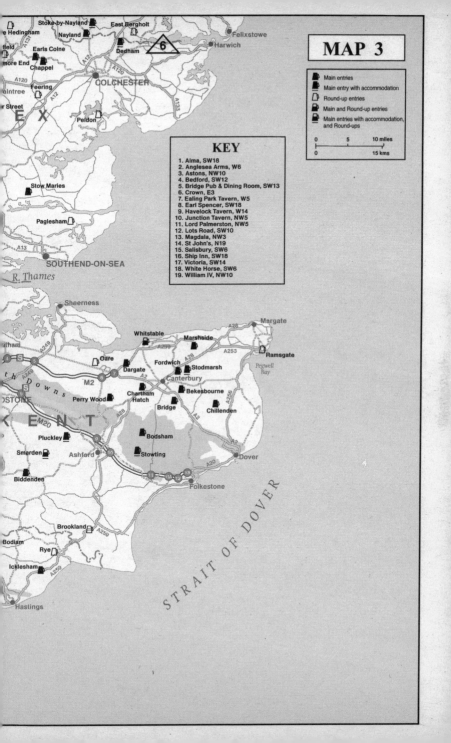

MAP 3

Main entries

Main entry with accommodation

Round-up entries

Main and Round-up entries

Main entries with accommodation, and Round-ups

0	5	10 miles
0		15 kms

KEY

1. Alma, SW18
2. Anglesea Arms, W6
3. Astons, NW10
4. Bedford, SW12
5. Bridge Pub & Dining Room, SW13
6. Crown, E3
7. Ealing Park Tavern, W5
8. Earl Spencer, SW18
9. Havelock Tavern, W14
10. Junction Tavern, NW5
11. Lord Palmerston, NW5
12. Lots Road, SW10
13. Magdala, NW3
14. St John's, N19
15. Salisbury, SW6
16. Ship Inn, SW18
17. Victoria, SW14
18. White Horse, SW6
19. William IV, NW10

MAP 4

- Main entries
- Main entry with accommodation
- Round-up entries
- Main and Round-up entries
- Main entries with accommodation, and Round-ups

0	5	10 miles
0		15 kms

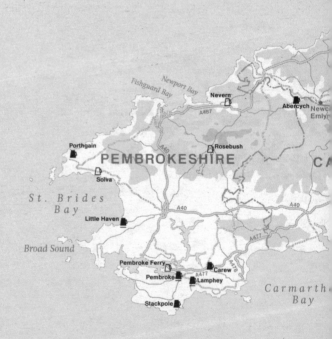

CARDI

BAY

Newport Bay

Fishguard Bay

Nevern

Abercych Newc
Emly

Porthgain

Rosebush

PEMBROKESHIRE

CA

Solva

St. Brides Bay

Little Haven

Broad Sound

Pembroke Ferry   Carew

Pembroke Lamphey

*Carmarth
Bay*

Stackpole

B R I S T O

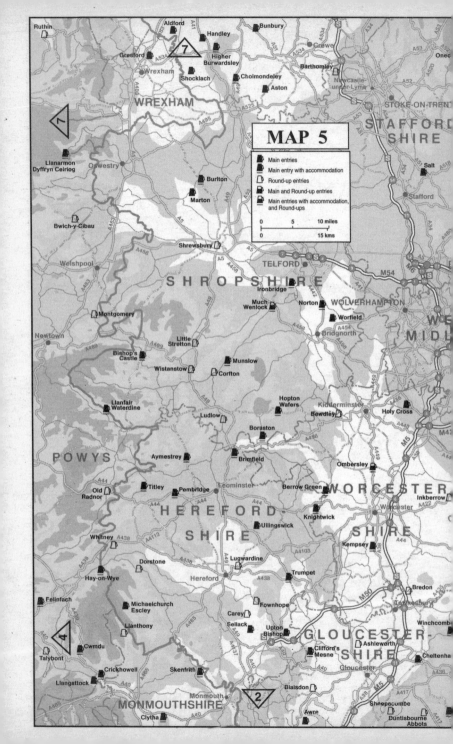

MAP 5

Main entries
Main entry with accommodation
Round-up entries
Main and Round-up entries
Main entries with accommodation, and Round-ups

| 0 | 5 | 10 miles |
| 0 | | 15 kms |

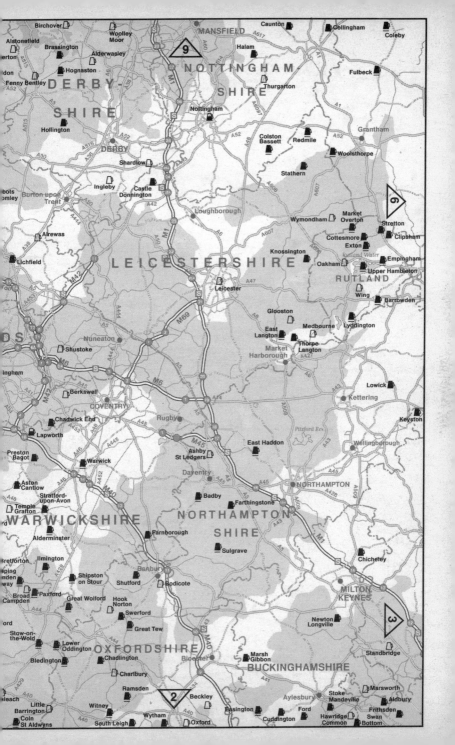

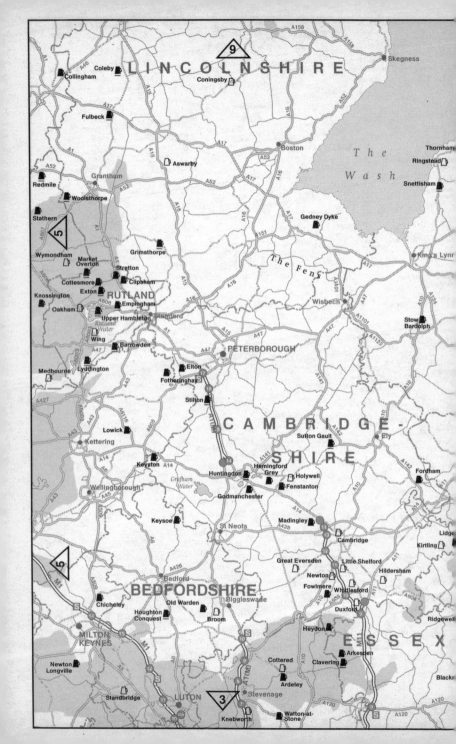

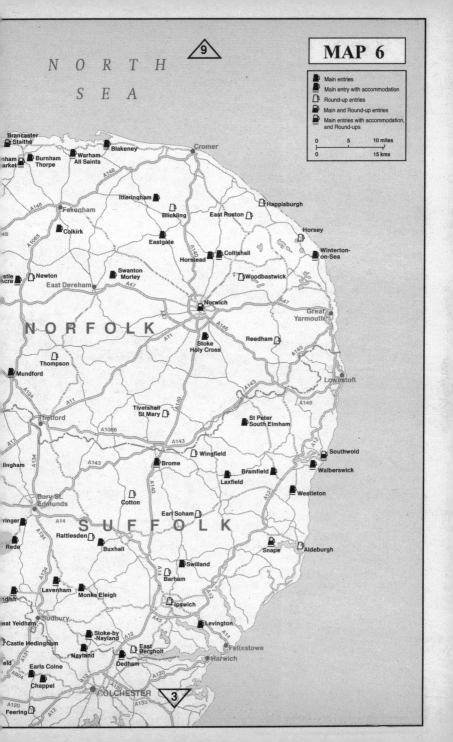

MAP 6

- Main entries
- Main entry with accommodation
- Round-up entries
- Main and Round-up entries
- Main entries with accommodation, and Round-ups

| 0 | 5 | 10 miles |
| 0 | 15 kms |

N O R T H

S E A

⑨

Brancaster
Staithe
Burnham
Thorpe
...ham
...rket
Warham
All Saints
Blakeney
Cromer

A146

A148

Fakenham
Itteringham
Colkirk
Blickling
East Ruston
Happisburgh
Horsey
Eastgate
Winterton-
on-Sea
A140
Horstead
Coltishall
...stle
Acre
Newton
Swanton
Morley
East Dereham
A47
Woodbastwick

A1065
A148

N O R F O L K
Norwich
Great
Yarmouth
A146
A11
A47
Stoke
Holy Cross
Reedham
A143
Thompson
Mundford
A134
Lowestoft
A11
Tivetshall
St Mary
A140
St Peter
South Elmham
A146
Thetford
A1066
A143
Wingfield
A11
A134
Brome
Southwold
...lingham
A143
A180
Bramfield
Walberswick
Laxfield
Cotton
Westleton
Bury St.
Edmunds
A140
S U F F O L K
Earl Soham
A14
...ringer
Rattlesden
Snape
Aldeburgh
Rede
Buxhall
A134
A130
Swilland
Barham
A14
Lavenham
Monks Eleigh
...dish
Sudbury
Ipswich
A45
Levington
A12
Stoke-by-
-Nayland
A14
Castle Hedingham
East
Bergholt
Felixstowe
A131
Nayland
Dedham
Harwich
A604
Earls Colne
A120
Chappel
A120
COLCHESTER
③
Feering
A12
A133

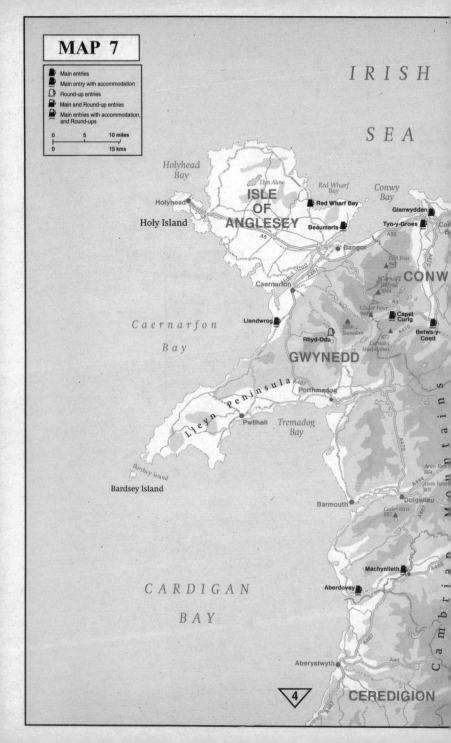

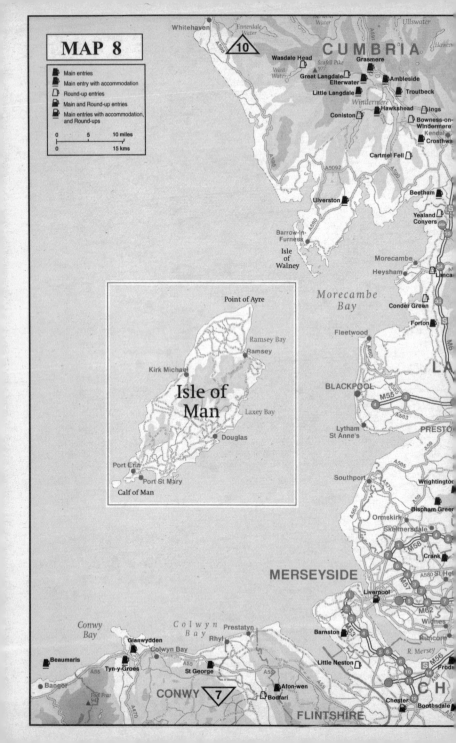

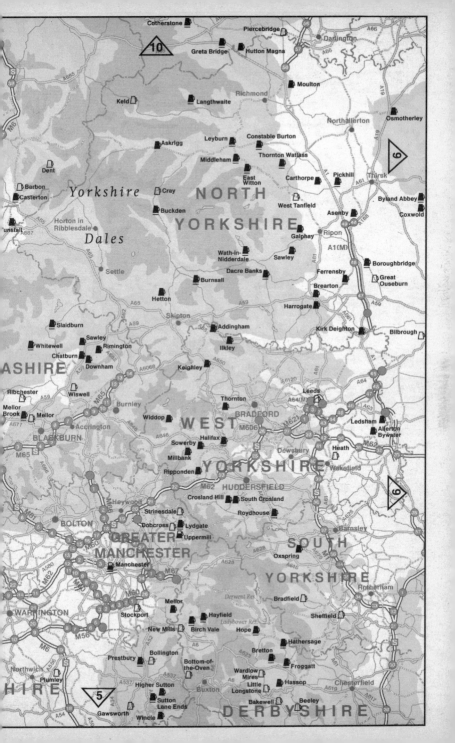

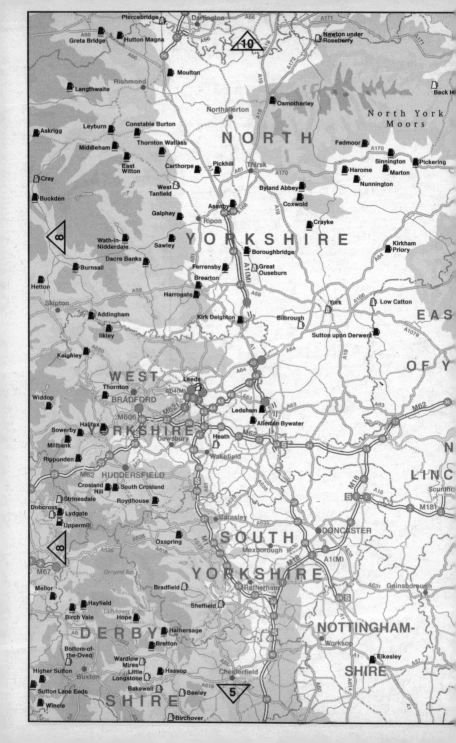

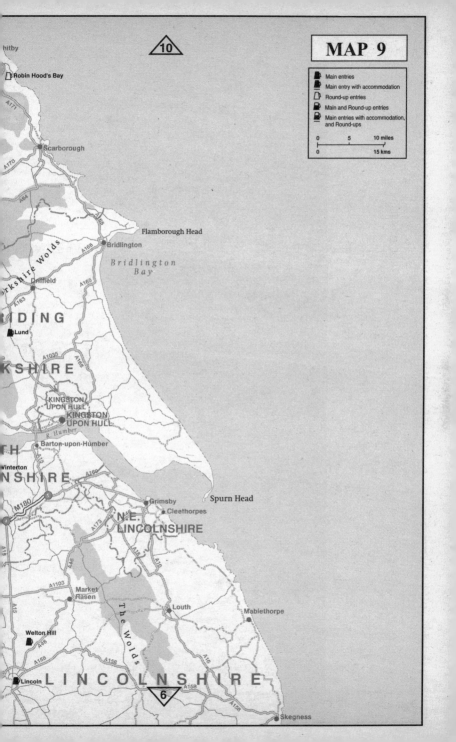

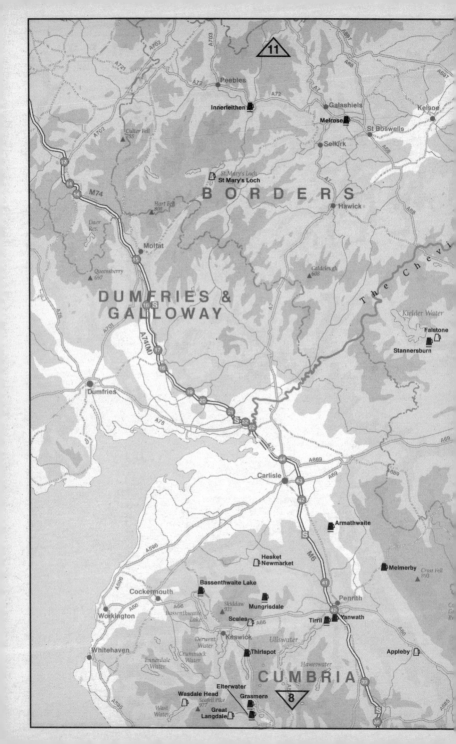

MAP 11

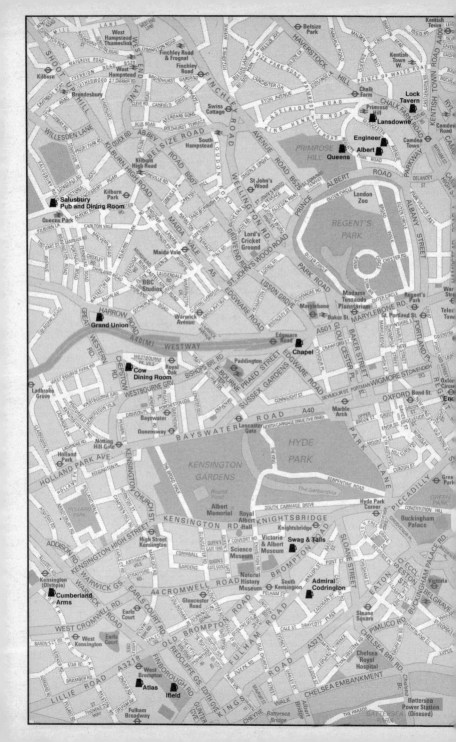

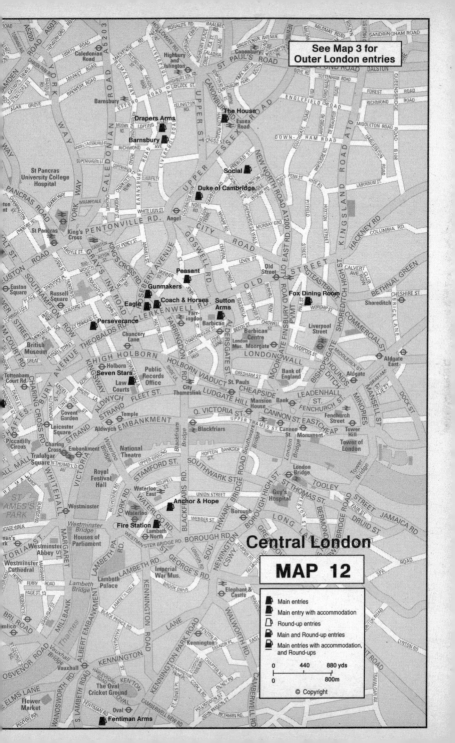

Report form

To *The Which? Pub Guide,*
FREEPOST, 2 Marylebone Road, London NW1 4DF

Or email your report to: *whichpubguide@which.net*

PUB NAME _____

Address _____

_____ Telephone _____

Date of visit _____

From my personal experience this establishment should be (please tick)

main entry ❏   Round-up entry ❏   excluded ❏

Please describe what you ate and drank (with prices, if known), and give
details of location, service, atmosphere etc.

Please turn over

My meal for ___ people cost £____ Value for money? yes ❑   no ❑

I am not connected in any way with the management or proprietors.

Name and address (BLOCK CAPITALS) _____

_____

_____

Signed

Report form   Pub 2005

To *The Which? Pub Guide,*
FREEPOST, 2 Marylebone Road, London NW1 4DF

Or email your report to: *whichpubguide@which.net*

PUB NAME _____

Address _____

_____ Telephone _____

Date of visit _____

From my personal experience this establishment should be (please tick)

main entry ❑   Round-up entry ❑   excluded ❑

Please describe what you ate and drank (with prices, if known), and give details of location, service, atmosphere etc.

Please turn over

My meal for ___ people cost £____ Value for money? yes ❏ no ❏

I am not connected in any way with the management or proprietors.

Name and address (BLOCK CAPITALS) _____

_____

_____

Signed

Report form

To *The Which? Pub Guide,*
FREEPOST, 2 Marylebone Road, London NW1 4DF

Or email your report to: *whichpubguide@which.net*

PUB NAME _____

Address _____

_____ Telephone _____

Date of visit _____

From my personal experience this establishment should be (please tick)

main entry ❑   Round-up entry ❑   excluded ❑

Please describe what you ate and drank (with prices, if known), and give
details of location, service, atmosphere etc.

My meal for ___ people cost £____ Value for money? yes ❑ no ❑

I am not connected in any way with the management or proprietors.

Name and address (BLOCK CAPITALS) _____

_____

_____

Signed

Report form

To *The Which? Pub Guide,*
FREEPOST, 2 Marylebone Road, London NW1 4DF

Or email your report to: *whichpubguide@which.net*

PUB NAME _____

Address _____

_____ Telephone _____

Date of visit _____

From my personal experience this establishment should be (please tick)

main entry ❑   Round-up entry ❑   excluded ❑

Please describe what you ate and drank (with prices, if known), and give
details of location, service, atmosphere etc.

My meal for ___ people cost £____ Value for money? yes ❏ no ❏

I am not connected in any way with the management or proprietors.

Name and address (BLOCK CAPITALS) _____

_____

_____

Signed

To *The Which? Pub Guide,*
FREEPOST, 2 Marylebone Road, London NW1 4DF

Or email your report to: *whichpubguide@which.net*

PUB NAME _____

Address _____

_____ Telephone _____

Date of visit _____

From my personal experience this establishment should be (please tick)

main entry ❑   Round-up entry ❑   excluded ❑

Please describe what you ate and drank (with prices, if known), and give
details of location, service, atmosphere etc.

Please turn over

My meal for ___ people cost £____ Value for money? yes ❏ no ❏

I am not connected in any way with the management or proprietors.

Name and address (BLOCK CAPITALS) _____

_____

_____

Signed